SECOND EDITION

Learning and Memory

Basic Principles, Processes, and Procedures

W. Scott Terry

University of North Carolina—Charlotte

Boston   New York   San Francisco
Mexico City   Montreal   Toronto   London   Madrid   Munich   Paris
Hong Kong   Singapore   Tokyo   Cape Town   Sydney

Executive Editor: *Carolyn Merrill*
Editorial Assistant: *Kate Edwards*
Marketing Manager: *Wendy Gordon*
Editorial-Production Administrator: *Anna Socrates*
Editorial-Production Service: *Omegatype Typography, Inc.*
Manufacturing Buyer: *JoAnne Sweeney*
Composition and Prepress Buyer: *Linda Cox*
Cover Administrator: *Kristina Mose-Libon*
Electronic Composition: *Omegatype Typography, Inc.*

For related titles and support materials, visit our online catalog at www.ablongman.com.

Library of Congress Cataloging-in-Publication Data

Terry, W. Scott.
    Learning and memory / W. Scott Terry. — 2nd ed.
      p. cm.
    Includes bibliographical references and index.
    ISBN 0-205-35462-9
    1. Learning, Psychology of. 2. Memory. I. Title.
  BF318 .T47 2003
  153.1—dc21   2002018549

Printed in the United States of America

10 9 8 7 6 5 4 3 2 1   07 06 05 04 03 02

To my wife, Lorraine Piersanti Terry,
and
In memory of my father, William Smith Terry

BRIEF CONTENTS

CONTENTS

4 **Instrumental Conditioning: Reward   89**

7   Human Memory: Conceptual Approaches   193

10   Storage and Retrieval   299

PREFACE

Learning and remembering what we have learned are fundamental psychological processes. The scientific study of learning and memory over the last one hundred years has produced a sizable body of principles, laws, and sometimes just heuristic rules. During this same hundred-year period, researchers who study learning have been asked to provide instruction in these principles. What do we know about learning, and how can this knowledge be usefully applied? My approach to writing a book on learning and memory is to present the basic methods and results of our research and to emphasize the relevance of our research to other disciplines.

I had several goals in mind in writing this book. The topical coverage is restricted to basic and central processes such as classical and instrumental conditioning or encoding and storage in long-term memory. Yet today these basic processes should also include implicit memory, spatial learning, and remembering in the world outside the laboratory. In addition to presenting some general rules for learning, it is just as important to specify the exceptions and limitations to those rules. When is spaced practice or immediate reinforcement better, and when might massed practice or delayed reward be better?

I have tried to write a book that will appeal to a broad audience of readers by including examples from a range of research literatures, from education, neuropsychology, psychiatry, nursing, advertising, and ecological (or everyday) memory. I value basic research on learning and memory. This includes laboratory studies, often of animals, using nonnaturalistic stimuli and procedures, as fundamental means of determining the principles by which learning occurs and memory persists. Yet, in my own teaching, I have found that the relevance of these basic principles needs to be made clear consistently. Lecturers often use everyday examples to maintain student interest. I believe that a more important purpose of such examples is to illustrate how basic principles can be translated into applications. It is simply not sufficient to be skilled and knowledgeable in the basics. Experts in animal conditioning are not necessarily good dog trainers (see Box 4.2, "How to Train a Dog," Chapter 4). We also need to consider the extent to which our laboratory results will generalize to other subject populations that differ in age, personality, learning style, or cultural background (Chapter 12).

Learning and memory can be illustrated by hypothetical examples from everyday life and by research done in a variety of disciplines. Most chapters cite research on learning by college students (and not simply as participants through subject pools), developmental comparisons with the very young or the elderly, and real-world applications; many chapters cite examples of gender or cross-cultural comparisons. These examples sometimes appear as boxed material, such as "Sleep Learning" (Chapter 9) or "Gender Differences in Spatial Cognition?" (Chapter 11). In other cases, extensive lists of citations are included, such as those on short-term memory deficits in medical and psychological disorders (Chapter 7), or memory for television commercials (Chapter 9). Chapters 2 through 11 conclude with an Applications section, covering topics such as habituation to warning signals (Chapter 2), or behavioral approaches to fear reduction (Chapters 2, 3, and 5). Applications are sometimes presented in parallel with the basic research: the buildup of proactive interference for word lists and for TV news stories (Chapter 7).

A book on learning should also include aids to facilitate learning. Each chapter begins with an outline and concludes with a detailed summary. Review and recapitulation paragraphs are interspersed throughout the chapters. Some topics and terms repeat across chapters. In addition, an instructor's manual is available that includes lecture outlines, suggested student activities, a video list, and test questions.

A number of people have influenced me, either directly or indirectly, in writing this book. I had the good fortune to have had mentors both in college and graduate school. At Fairfield University, the example set by W. Ronald Salafia determined my choice of a career as a teacher and researcher in the field of learning. At Yale, Allan Wagner, by his style in the classroom and in the laboratory, became a lasting role model. Both Ron and Allan, and their respective universities, offered exciting environments in which to learn. (A note to students: My guess is that many of your professors and instructors had similar relationships that led to their own decisions to become teachers. Ask them about it.) I would also like to thank my family, Lorraine, Christopher, and Jason, for their encouragement and especially their patience in living with an absent-minded professor.

In addition, a number of people were more directly involved. Becky Pascal has been my editor from the beginning and has been a constant source of encouragement. She worked to meld my interests with those of other instructors. Anne Rogers and the team at Omegatype Typography provided invaluable editing and production expertise. Several university and college professors commented on chapters and successive drafts of the first edition of this book, providing extensive commentary and their own insights into this field. For their efforts, I am both grateful and respectful. Any errors and mistakes that remain are mine, and the reviewers can safely reply, "I told you so." These reviewers include Charles L. Brewer, Furman University; Robert Crowder, Yale University; David J. Falcone, La-Salle University; Jeremiah M. Faries, Northwestern University; Valerie Farmer-Dougan, Illinois State University; Christopher M. Hakala, Lycoming College; Robert C. Haygood, Arizona State University; Catherine Wehlburg Hickman, Stephens College; Karen A. Jackson, Texas Woman's University; Kevin J. Kennelly, University of North Texas; John W. Kulig, Plymouth State College; Louis Manza, Lebanon Valley College; Richard E. Mayer, University of California, Santa Barbara; Kirsten Rewey, St. Vincent College; Geraldine Shaw, Georgetown College; Randolph A. Smith, Ouchita Baptist University; Kenneth M. Steele, Appalachian State University; Rick Stevens, University of Nevada, Las Vegas; Roger L. Thomas, Franklin College; and Mary C. Wetzel, University of Arizona. In addition, I want to thank the reviewers of the second edition: Douglas Cody Brooks, Denison University; and Laurence Miller, Western Washington University.

Finally, I would like to thank my students, both undergraduate and graduate, from the last too-many years for letting me try out ideas on them. I have found that if you present things in a good-natured manner, our students will respond similarly. They have been a valuable source of feedback.

Introduction

Students who take a course in the psychology of learning are usually pretty knowledgeable about learning by the time they have reached this point. Through instruction and on-the-job training, they have already picked up numerous everyday, commonsense principles about how to learn. Students can readily tell their instructors that it is better to spread studying over several days rather than to cram it all into one day (what psychologists call *the spaced versus massed practice effect*), and that temporary forgetting for otherwise well-known information occurs, especially on exam days (what we otherwise call *retrieval failure*). Students are aware of what psychologists call *context-dependent learning, that it is better to study in the place in which you will take the test*. These practical principles are accurate as broad generalities, but they are also only partially true. They are half-truths. This is a book full of half-truths.

Let me quickly explain what I mean. There are numerous facts, laws, and principles of learning that have been uncovered over the past 120 years that psychology has formally been in existence. However, these principles are more complex than the simple statements we popularly use to describe them (e.g., spaced practice is better than massed practice). Statements of these principles almost always require qualifiers; they are true under certain conditions. In this book, I will attempt to tell both halves, and thus in the end something closer to the truth as we know it now.

Take some well-known popular generalizations. Spaced practice produces better learning than does massed practice. Well, yes, usually. But much depends on what we are attempting to learn and how long we will have to retain it, just two of several possible qualifiers we might add here. Actually, one line of research on remembering people's names suggests that it is better to mass repetitions of a given name at first, and then gradually lengthen the interval between successive presentations (Landauer & Bjork, 1978).[1] Repeat the new name immediately; repeat it again after a little while; and keep increasing the interval to the next repetition. As a second example, we all know that forgetting occurs over time. The best you can hope for is that the memory stays stable. But under some conditions, more is remembered later than was recalled earlier. This is the phenomenon of reminiscence, or hypermnesia, and is the opposite of forgetting. Or another principle: Punishment is said to be ineffective in altering behavior because it only temporarily suppresses an unwanted behavior. In fact, punishment works very well, *if* applied according to certain parameters (such as the immediacy, intensity, and consistency with which it is administered), and it can often produce more lasting effects than does reward. The decision to use punishment is partly a moral or ethical decision and partly one of judging whether effective parameters are to be used (see Chapter 5). Finally, common sense seems to say that feedback is more effective when it is given immediately and consistently after each performance of a behavior. Yet, again, this is not always so. Skilled movements are sometimes learned faster with delayed or only occasional feedback (see Chapter 11).

Other forms of learning pose questions that have alternative correct answers. Do subliminal learning tapes, such as those that are supposed to induce self-control or weight loss, work? Both yes and no answers can be defended. Some data indicate they are effective, but more probably due to placebo or expectancy effects rather than to any effects on our subconscious. Does this mean that there is no such thing as subliminal learning? No, learning can occur at many levels of awareness or consciousness. Does sleep learning occur? Instead of buying the hard-copy version of this text, should you get the audio book version and play the tapes throughout the night? The answer depends on what you mean by *learning*. Research conducted in sleep labs indicates that factual information may not be acquired if we are truly asleep when the tapes are played, but possibly some other forms of learning (such as conditioning of the Pavlov variety) might occur.

The point of these examples is to give a sample of what real principles of learning look like. The goal of this book is to present a scientifically accurate and sophisticated view of the principles of learning. And this includes the qualifying statements: when a given principle holds and when exceptions occur. As Einstein said, "Everything should be made as simple as possible, but not simpler."

The Origins of the Study of Learning

The field of scientific research broadly described as learning has the same origins as psychology itself, beginning just over a hundred years ago. They are both outgrowths of philos-

---

[1]The standard format for noting sources in psychology is to cite the last names of the authors and the year of publication. Complete source information is provided in the References at the end of the book, where the citations are listed alphabetically and by year.

ophy and science. In particular, the philosophical movements of empiricism and rationalism in the seventeenth and eighteenth centuries, and the development of evolution theory within biology in the nineteenth century, fostered an interest in the scientific investigation of learning. These movements are still active influences in contemporary psychology.

Philosophy of Epistemology

The nature–nurture question, which asks how we are affected by biology on the one hand (i.e., nature) and by environment on the other (i.e., nurture), has long been a source of literary, political, and scientific speculation. If a child were raised in isolation from others, what would that child know? Would language develop, and, if so, what sort of language would it be? Would the child believe in God? Would the child grow to be morally pure, or cruel and beastlike? The French philosopher Rousseau thought that there existed a "noble savage" who would be discovered living beyond the reach of the degrading influences of civilization. However, the discovery of what were called feral children, living apart from other humans and supposedly reared by wild animals, revealed a sad plight (Candland, 1993). These children were not only intellectually deprived, but also emotionally devastated.

The nature–nurture issue crystallized in the area of philosophy known as *epistemology,* the study of how we come to have knowledge. This is the central question for the field of learning. The philosopher Descartes, while not denying that we learn, suggested that there were other sources of knowledge that did not depend on experience. Some knowledge is innately given, for example, our ideas of God, infinity, or perfection. This idea is known as *nativism.* Other knowledge is derived by a reasoning, logical, and intuiting mind, as illustrated by the derivation of geometric axioms and algebraic logic. This latter source of knowledge is known as *rationalism.* In each case, knowledge is present independent of particular experiences with the world (Descartes, 1641/1960).

By contrast, the British philosopher John Locke (1690/1956) suggested that the origin of all knowledge is in experience, as provided to the mind through the senses. This is the notion of *empiricism.* For instance, our notion of causation derives from our frequent experiences in which some event in the world (which we later label a *cause*) is typically followed by some other event (the *effect*).

An example of the empiricists' view of knowledge is their treatment of associations among ideas. What are the origins of our associations of STOP to GO or of TABLE to CHAIR? Locke, following Aristotle's writings, suggested these associations derive from our experience in which the two objects are contiguous: They are close together in time or space. Therefore, the mental representations of the objects, their ideas, are also contiguous in our minds. This associative principle of contiguity was supplemented by the principles of frequency (we associate ideas that are often contiguous), similarity (ideas that are similar), and contrast (ideas that are opposite). Locke, and the line of British empiricist philosophers that followed, allowed that new knowledge could be derived within the mind by *reflection,* or thinking and reasoning with previously learned ideas. This mental chemistry approach of combining existing knowledge to produce new ideas is similar to Descartes' rationalism, except that the source of the initial ideas differs in the two philosophies.

The two epistemological positions represented by Descartes and Locke were certainly known to the first generation of psychologists, who were well versed in philosophy. (The

Ph.D. is literally a doctor of philosophy degree, and for some early psychologists theirs were obtained for a dissertation in philosophy.) The influence from empiricism led researchers to investigate how we acquire knowledge through environmental experiences. A background in associationism made these first psychologists receptive to scientific methods of investigating association learning, such as Pavlov's and Thorndike's conditioning procedures and Ebbinghaus's method of verbal learning (Kendler, 1987). For example, how could a dog come to associate two stimuli? By using Pavlovian conditioning, an experimenter would present a tone followed with food several times, and then look for changes in the dog's reactions to the tone. Here we see the associative principles of contiguity and frequency.

Rationalism and nativism were also influential to the field of learning, usually addressing somewhat different questions. For instance, early psychologists were asking whether various perceptual capacities, such as depth perception, were innate or acquired.

Evolution

Nineteenth-century advances in the sciences would also influence the field of learning, particularly the ideas of using controlled laboratory experiments, quantifying or measuring outcomes, and reducing complex phenomena to simpler processes. A more specific influence from biology, coming nearer the beginnings of psychology itself as a discipline, was Darwin's *On the Origin of Species*, published in 1859. In it, Darwin presented his theory of *evolution* to describe how organisms change over generations in order to better adapt to the environment to which they are exposed. Darwin first noted that there were individual differences among members of a species; not all individuals were identical. Some of these differences could increase the likelihood of survival and reproduction. If these differences were inherited, then the evolution of adaptive specializations would occur across generations.

The capacity to learn evolved as an adaptive specialization. Whereas evolution theory at first stressed anatomical changes over time as a means of adapting to the environment, psychologists would emphasize learning as a means of adapting within the organism's lifetime. In addition, the belief that different species were related through a common evolutionary history suggested there was a continuity of mind across species. Thus, animals other than humans could be studied, with generalizations proceeding in either direction along the phylogenetic scale.

Contemporary Influences

This discussion of philosophy and biology may seem to be of historical interest at best, but each has had a continuous influence on the field of learning during the last hundred years. The contemporary influence of nativism is present in theories that suggest that there are innate predispositions for acquiring language, for developing phobias to only certain stimuli, or to comprehending the principles of number and cause and effect (Pinker, 1994; Speilke et al., 1992). In one modern example, the ideas of nativism, empiricism, and evolution are represented in a theory of *biological preparedness* for learning. The prime example of preparedness is the human capacity for language. Language is said to be a biologically prepared form of learning, something we learn quickly and readily due to our evolutionary history. This is shown by several aspects of human language: its universality; its common developmental progression in children across cultures; the fact that it is readily acquired even in language-poor environments; the possibility that there is a critical period for learning language; and that certain areas of the brain seem dedicated to language (Pinker, 1994). Environment is also obviously essential to language development, determining the particular language we learn and the specific rules of our native language. But the fact that we even learn a language, as complex as this is and as intellectually immature as we are as infants, suggests the existence of a biological predisposition.

Another example of nature–nurture interaction is the theory that evolution has produced several memory systems through which organisms can learn. There may be specialized learning systems, such as one for song learning in birds or phobia learning in humans (Seligman, 1972). Other systems might accommodate incremental learning of habitual behaviors, versus the memory for individual events that so characterizes human memory (Sherry & Schacter, 1987). Certainly, there is disagreement among learning theorists who advocate stronger versus weaker contributions of innate predispositions. The point I am making here is that contemporary theory reflects the nativism of Descartes, the empiricism of Locke, and the evolution theory of Darwin.

The Definition of Learning

Learning is the acquisition of knowledge. Just as the philosophers of epistemology are interested in the nature and origin of knowledge, so also are psychologists. However, psychologists have defined learning both broadly and in a manner amenable to scientific study. Knowledge must be broadly defined to include not just verbal knowledge, but also habits and skills, attitudes, and knowledge or behavior outside conscious awareness. The everyday meaning of the word *knowledge* implies a level of conscious awareness and verbalizable recall that is not present in many instances of learning. For instance, the learning displayed by nonhuman animals is sometimes better identified by terms such as conditioning rather than by knowledge. In some cases, I would not be comfortable in saying that a mouse "knows" what a stimulus means, although I am comfortable in saying the mouse has learned a conditioned reaction to the tone. The same reasoning applies to much of our knowledge. We may have acquired skills, attitudes, or habits that we do not consciously know, and, as we will suggest in this text, certainly not all of what we have learned is verbally recallable. So in addition to an intuitive definition of learning, scientific study requires a precise, operational definition of what can be observed as indicators that learning has occurred. Thus, the study of learning is guided formally by an objective definition, as well as informally by the actual practices and interests of the researchers (see Table 1.1).

Learning may be defined as a relatively permanent change in behavior, or behavioral repertoire, that occurs as a result of experience. This formal definition specifies what is included under the rubric of learning, and, just as important, what is to be excluded. This definition has several components.

First, learning involves an observed *change in behavior.* The point here is that the detection of learning requires some objective evidence. Psychology is a science because it is objective and quantifiable. Learning and memory themselves are not observed directly; they are processes that occur in the nervous system. As much as we may be interested in

(margin note, handwritten, vertical: "do we learn M.I./psychosis as well?")

TABLE 1.1 The Breadth of Learning

The everyday use of the term *learning* does not describe all of the diverse phenomena that psychologists study in the field of learning. Hillner (1978, pp. 1–2) presented a list of some of what is included by the term:

1. Learning encompasses both animal and human behavior. It is applicable to the behavior of intact or whole organisms, and even to the adaptive behavior of inanimate model systems such as computer simulations.
2. Learning involves events as diverse as the acquisition of an isolated muscle twitch, a prejudice, a symbolic concept, or a neurotic symptom.
3. Learning is not limited to the external responses of the organism, but also to internal physiological responses.
4. Learning is concerned with the original acquisition of a response or knowledge, with its later disappearance (extinction), its retention over time (memory), and its possible value in the acquisition of new responses (transfer of training).
5. Learning is related to such nonlearning phenomena as motivation, perception, development, personality, and social and cultural factors.
6. Learning has a physical reality (physiological, biochemical) as well as a strictly psychological (functional) reality.
7. Learning deals with the behavior of the average subject and with individual differences among subjects.
8. The study of learning is associated with a long academic and scholarly tradition, but also serves as a source of practical application and technology.
9. The learning process is continuous with, and a component of, the more general linguistic, cognitive, information-processing, and decision-making activities of the organism.

the inner workings of the brain (or mind), we need to observe the organism's behavior in order to validate our hypotheses about what is going on inside.

Certainly, researchers are coming closer to detecting the neural basis of learning. Changes in the synaptic processes of a sea snail, the *Aplysia,* have been found during conditioning (Kennedy, Hawkins, & Kandel, 1992); the circuit for eyeblink conditioning in the rabbit has been mapped (Thompson et al., 1987); and PET scans show which brain regions in humans are active when we retrieve word meanings (Raichle, 1994). But most learning and remembering involve nervous processes that are as yet undetectable. Learning and memory are therefore treated as intervening variables. They are hypothesized theoretical processes that intervene between the environment (which we can manipulate) and behavior (which we can measure).

What kinds of behaviors can we use to measure learning? Learning outcomes are multidimensional. This means that different types of measures can be used, each of which exhibits different aspects of what has been learned. The experiments described in the succeeding chapters of this book will present numerous examples. In addition to recording the overt behavior of organisms (e.g., maze running), we can also record physiological responses of the internal activity of the body (e.g., heart rate) and verbal reports (e.g., recollections of past experiences). Consider a learning experience you have had as child: a sibling jumping out of a darkened room or closet in order to scare you. The fear learned from such an episode could be expressed verbally in our recollections of the event years later; physiologically by increased heart rate in fearful anticipation of a repeat of the episode; and behaviorally by the avoidance of entering dark hallways or rooms in the house.

The range of behaviors that we can use is illustrated by considering applications to personnel training and consumer psychology. For instance, say a psychologist has conducted a training workshop in an employment setting. How do we know what the workshop participants learned? Kraiger, Ford, and Salas (1993) suggested using three types of assessments. One outcome of training is the factual knowledge that the participants can recall. Another outcome is skill learning, represented by some behavior that the participants can now do quicker, more accurately, and maybe even more automatically. Finally, affective (or emotional) measurement includes attitude changes. Do the participants now feel more competent, confident, or committed as a result of training?

Consumer behavior, at first, would seem to be best measured by the choices that consumers make, a behavioral measure. However, researchers are also interested in the physiological changes in the body that indicate mental processing or that precede shifts in overt behavior. We can measure the learning that results from an advertisement or product exposure by various physiological measures, such as EEG changes to a replay of the ad, muscle tension, or pupil dilation. Learning about an advertised product could provoke changes, indicating familiarity, interest, boredom, excitement, or other psychological reactions (Bagozzi, 1991).

Learning involves changes in *behavioral repertoire*, or the stock of behaviors that might be performed. Not all learning is immediately evidenced by overt behaviors. What you have just learned from this text is probably not affecting your behavior now. Thus, the definition also specifies that learning includes the potential for a change in behavior to be demonstrated when testing conditions prompt the display of this new knowledge.

The distinction between potential and actual changes in behavior is demonstrated nicely by a classic study of socially learned aggression. Albert Bandura and his students conducted a series of studies showing that children will imitate aggressive behaviors that they see adult models perform (e.g., Bandura, 1965). Children watched a videotape in which the models punch an inflated clown doll, or BoBo doll, by kicking it, throwing it, and so on. The children were later allowed to play with the BoBo doll. In one condition of the experiment, the model in the tape had been praised for playing aggressively, and the children later imitated many of the specific aggressive behaviors. In another condition, the model had been scolded for misbehaving, and the children who had seen this version of the tape now performed many fewer aggressive responses (see Figure 1.1). So far, we have a difference in performance between the two experimental conditions: Children imitated the praised model and less so the scolded model. Then the experimenter offered a reward for each aggressive response the child could produce. The incentives increased performance of the behaviors and eliminated the previous performance difference between the praise and scolding conditions. For the children who had seen the scolded model, the aggressive behaviors had entered the behavioral repertoire, even though these behaviors were not immediately displayed.

The Bandura study is also important for showing that the gender difference in aggressive behavior disappeared when incentives were offered to demonstrate what the

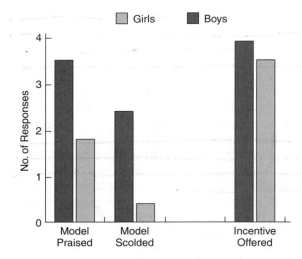

FIGURE 1.1   Mean number of different aggressive responses imitated by children during the first phase of testing as a function of the consequences to the model they had observed; and the number of responses imitated when an incentive was offered to perform.

Source: Bandura, 1965.

model had done. The girls remembered the aggressive behaviors they had observed, but they inhibited imitating these responses until it was acceptable to do so.

Learning occurs *as a result of experience.* This book attempts to describe what some of these learning-producing experiences are. They may be as varied as a conditioning experiment conducted in the lab, a lecture heard, a skill practiced, or an attitude developed due to some now unrecalled event. The definition of learning excludes those changes in behavior that are not due to experience. One such nonlearning source of behavioral change is maturation. Organisms show some behavioral changes because of the physical, neural, or cognitive maturation that takes place over time. For example, when sparrows reach a certain age and at a certain time of year, they begin to sing. In some species, singing is not dependent on particular learning experiences of having heard other birds sing. Singing, and even the particular song, is innate. In human infants and children, walking and talking are also dependent on maturation. Physical maturation in the muscles and the bones and cognitive maturation of coordination allow walking to occur. When we casually talk about children learning to walk or talk, we are wrong in thinking that they are dependent only on learning. As we will see in what follows, however, the line between biological maturation and learning is often blurred. The point of the *experience* phrase in the definition is to ask us to consider what is the source of a behavior change.

Although experience can produce permanent changes in behavior potential, not every experience can be readily described as a "learning" experience. The line between learning and other experientially induced changes is not always clear. For instance, mice reared in an enriched environment (i.e., with other rats and lots of playthings) develop more cells in an area of the brain that is important for learning, the hippocampus (a brain region that will be frequently mentioned in this text; Kemperman, Kuhn, & Gage, 1997). Rats whose mothers spent more time licking and grooming them as pups are less reactive to stress as adults (Liu et al., 1997). Would we then say that a more complex environment or better mothering produces "learned" changes? Contemporary learning psychologists are interested in environmental influences on behavior, whether any changes in behavior we observe can be ascribed specifically to learning or more generally to experience. The point of the *experience* phrase in the definition of learning is to ask us to consider what is the source of a behavior change.

Finally, learning is said to be *relatively permanent.* This may seem contrary to everyday experiences in which we all too frequently forget facts, names, appointments, and so on. But we may in fact remember more than we realize. Bahrick (1984a) has shown that substantial amounts of Spanish vocabulary first learned in high school are retained even 25 years later. After 40 years, people can still recognize 70 percent of their high school classmates' names and pictures, although at first, only 20 percent of their graduating class could be named (Bahrick, Bahrick, & Wittlinger, 1975). Similarly, even though college professors seemingly forgot their students' names within weeks of the semester's end, the professors did recognize former students' pictures and could match names and faces years later (Bahrick, 1984b). Thus, much more was learned than was apparent on tests of the ability to recall names.

The purpose of the "relatively permanent" phrase is to exclude transient changes in behavior, changes that are not due to learning. Responding could temporarily fluctuate due to increases or decreases in, as examples, arousal, fatigue, or motivation. In these cases, the change in responding is not learning-induced. For example, rats run faster in a maze if they are hungrier or if given caffeine. This does not mean they suddenly "know more" about the maze's route. They are simply more motivated or energized. Knowledge of the maze's layout will be present even after hunger or arousal has returned to normal levels. We have to be careful to separate the transient effects of variables such as arousal and motivation from their permanent effects on learning (Kimble, 1967).

Some Caveats

Although there is a well-specified definition of learning, the study of learning includes phenomena that do not fit precisely within the formal definition. There are gray areas. Two such areas are short-term memory and the distinction between maturation and learning.

The study of short-term retention, or remembering over intervals of seconds or minutes, violates the "relatively permanent" clause of the definition of learning. These short-term memories are based on experience (e.g., we could present a list of digits for you to remember, or a tone stimulus to a dolphin), and a behavioral change is measured (after a few seconds, can you repeat that list of numbers, or can the dolphin select the tone from among several others?). So how do we accommodate this discrepancy in our definition of learning? There are several possibilities. Maybe we need to broaden our definition to include the effects of experiences that occur over a range of intervals, from the very short to the very long. Alternatively, we could acknowledge that short-term memory contributes to the formation of longer-term memories (Atkinson & Shiffrin, 1968; Wagner, Rudy, & Whitlow, 1973). We know that certain variables affect short-term and long-term retention in the same manner. Thus, understanding the nature of short-term remembering will provide a fuller understanding of how learning occurs.

Another gray area with respect to our definition is the separation between learning and maturation. The problem here is that the two often coexist and interact with one another. How can we tell where one leaves off and the other begins?

At one extreme, there are some human behaviors that are substantially influenced by maturation. Infant development of sitting upright, standing, and eventually walking are primary examples. Gesell and Thompson (1929) conducted a classic experiment in which one infant twin of a pair received several weeks of practice at stair climbing. The other twin, denied this explicit practice, later took only a week to equal the proficiency the practiced sibling had achieved in four weeks. Similarly, Lenneberg (1967) describes a child who had been prevented from practicing language sounds for several months by a tracheal tube. When the tube was removed the child showed age-appropriate prelanguage development, progressing through the stages of cooing, babbling, and so on. In Gesell's case, early practice gave little benefit, and in Lenneberg's case, the absence of practice produced little decrement.

On the other hand, even maturationally influenced behaviors can be affected powerfully by the environment. While acknowledging the maturational contribution to the development of behaviors such as walking, McGraw also showed that a rearrangement of the environment could speed the appearance of skilled performance. One twin of a pair was given roller skates at age 12 months. Skating, although requiring balance, reduces the extent of leg movements required in walking. The child learned to skate before he learned to walk (Dalton & Bergenn, 1995).

Other behaviors clearly illustrate the interaction of experience and maturation. Marler's (1970) study of white-crowned sparrows is especially instructive here. These birds have a repertoire of about seven sounds, six of which are essentially uniform across geographic regions. However, the male song during breeding season shows variability, known as dialect variation. Marler raised some birds in isolation from others of their type. When singing began several months after hatching (the timing of which is maturationally determined), the birds sang a song that was, in outline, the appropriate song for the white-crowned sparrows. However, in detail, the song was significantly different or abnormal. Exposing the birds to a song of their own type during the period from 10 to 50 days after hatching leads to normal song development, which itself is manifested months later. Curiously, the local dialect needs to be heard to be acquired, but exposure to a different dialect will not cause it to be acquired. Thus, song is determined by the interaction of maturation (an innate predisposition) and learning (experience with specific songs). (See Ball & Hulse, 1998, for a recent review of research on the development of birdsong.)

An interesting case of song learning was noticed in New York's Central Park. Birders there were puzzled to hear a warbler singing weeks before this bird's usual migration back north. The mystery was solved by the observance of a white-throated sparrow that alternately sang the warbler's song and its own, thereby confusing the birders (NPR, 04/09/01).

The Learning/Performance Distinction

Earlier, we noted that learning itself is not directly observed. This process occurs in the mind or the brain, which is beyond direct observation. Instead, we infer that learning has occurred based on some behavior of the organism. However, these behavioral measures are sometimes imperfect and indirect. There is not always a one-to-one correspondence between what the organism knows and what the organism does.

Sometimes no behavioral change is observed even though (we realize later) learning has occurred. The classic example of this is Tolman and Honzik's (1930) study of *latent learning*. Rats were placed in a maze but were not given food or any other explicit reward in the goal box. Not surprisingly, the rats persisted in entering the blind alleys across several days of this training. (Other rats who were fed in the goal box learned to run directly to the goal box.) When food was suddenly offered in the goal box, there was an immediate improvement in performance. The animals now made few wrong turns on their way to the goal box. The rats had indeed learned the layout of the maze in those previous trials without food reward, but this knowledge remained *latent,* or hidden, until the subjects were motivated to complete the maze quickly. Similarly, your knowledge of this chapter may remain latent until an exam is given. This absence of performance has been aptly referred to as the "problem of behavioral silence" (Dickinson, 1980). If an experience does not produce a change from the previous behavior, we really do not know whether learning has not occurred or learning has occurred and is hidden.

Test anxiety may be one too familiar illustration of the learning–performance distinction. Students who truly know the material can perform poorly on the exam because of excessive anxiety. Performance does not accurately assess the underlying learning that is present. (To cite one extreme case, Capretta and Berkin [1962] noted that soldiers crossing an unstable rope bridge over a deep ravine performed worse on a digit span task than when tested under nonstress conditions.) Interestingly, Naveh-Benjamin (1991) has dissociated two sorts of anxious students. There are those who study but get anxious taking exams. These students benefit from training in anxiety management. And there are students who haven't learned the material and therefore have good reason to be anxious. These latter students benefit more from study-skills training. This example shows that there can be alternate interpretations for poor performance. It may sometimes indicate poor learning, but it may also indicate the presence of factors, such as anxiety, that inhibit expression of learning.

Another example of a performance deficit is shown in the comparison of introverts and extraverts in a simple memory task: recall of lists of 15 to 20 words that were briefly presented. The extraverts repeat back more of the words. Does this mean that extraverts have better memories than introverts? Actually, the difference seems to be that extraverts are more willing to guess and "recall" words they are not sure of, whereas the introverts are more cautious (Eysenck, 1983). The extravert will get more correct items by guessing when uncertain (and, incidentally, also misrecalls more words that were not on the list). The reluctance to report uncertain memories can be reduced by using an alternative test or measure. For example, we might give our subjects a multiple-choice test. The subjects may then recognize the correct word. In this case, the introverts and extraverts may perform equally.

We have presented several examples of performance deficits. But even if performance improves, it still may give a misleading picture of the underlying ability. The psychiatrist Cameron (1963) was interested in why his elderly nursing home residents seemed to have such poor memories. Drawing on observations and theory from animal experiments, he decided to try giving these residents RNA (ribonucleic acid, a protein involved in cellular activity), which had improved learning in laboratory animals. On both formal and informal assessments of memory (e.g., "Can you remember what you did yesterday?"), he found that the patients improved over the several weeks of testing. However, this enhanced performance may not have been due to the RNA, but rather to several other confounded factors: practice at the memory tests, increased motivation to please the experimenter, the extra attention the residents were now receiving, or the expectation that memory should improve (what we might call a placebo effect). We now realize that it is unlikely that the patients' underlying ability to remember improved. Performance can improve for reasons other than changes due to learning or memory.

Learning: A Recapitulation

Let's review the key ideas of the previous sections. Research on learning is guided by a formal definition that makes our study more objective: Learning is a relatively permanent change in behavior, or behavioral repertoire, that is due to experience. This definition excludes changes in behavior that are transient, and are thus likely to reflect behavioral changes due to fluctuations in attention, motivation, or arousal level. The study of learning intersects with studies of innate or maturationally determined behaviors. Although our formal definition emphasizes changed behavior as an indicant of learning, we also acknowledge that behavioral performance can be a misleading indicator of what has been learned.

The Relationship between the Terms
Learning and *Memory*

The words *learning* and *memory* in everyday language have related but distinct uses. The same holds for the technical meanings within psychology. The distinctions psychologists make are both ones of denotation (or exact meanings) and of connotation (suggested or implied meanings). Thus, in the past, learning was used to refer to conditioning and reinforcement tasks, to (nonhuman) animal subjects, or to skills requiring repeated trials for acquisition. Memory was used in reference to verbal recall tasks, to studies of human subjects, and to material presented for study just once. Historically, learning was associated with a behavioral tradition that emphasized the unconscious conditioning of specific behaviors, and memory with the cognitive approach that studied the conscious recollection of previous experiences (the behavioral and cognitive approaches are described later). All of the preceding represent the connotative meanings of learning and memory: what the terms have usually implied. There are numerous exceptions to each of these rules, especially in contemporary research, such that each distinction (e.g., animal versus human) does not perfectly correspond with a distinction between learning versus memory.

A more exact distinction is to say that learning refers to acquiring knowledge or behavior, whereas memory refers to retaining and recalling the knowledge or behavior. As a researcher or student, one could primarily be interested in the *acquisition,* or encoding, of new information: learning associations among stimuli, learning skills, or learning facts. Or, after these things have been learned, one could be interested in the *retention,* or retrieval, of the associations, skills, or facts. Essentially, we make a distinction between two phases and attempt to study each separately.

For instance, in studying learning, one might consider those factors that affect acquisition, such as the amount of reinforcement, the spacing of study trials, or the presence of individuals who model certain behaviors. We would measure the development or progression of

B O X **1.1**

The Learning Curve

The phrase *learning curve* has entered everyday language, often used as a metaphor in comparing individuals. One person is said to be farther along the learning curve than another, for instance. An advertisement for computer software claims it will put you farther ahead of your competitors on the learning curve. There is even an accounting-management textbook titled the *Learning Curve* (Riahi-Belkaoui, 1986). What exactly is the learning curve?

The phrase refers to a particular shape of the curve that develops over training trials, particularly as described by Clark Hull, a prominent Yale learning theorist of the 1940s (Hull, 1943). He said the basic learning curve is a negatively accelerated curve. This means that learning (or rather performance, which is what is actually measured) starts off with a period of very rapid growth, in which each trial produces large increments in performance. These increments get smaller and smaller on later trials, which is what negative acceleration means. There is a point of diminishing returns, such that continued practice has smaller benefits. Figure 1.2 shows the hypothetical increments across successive trials as Hull depicted them.

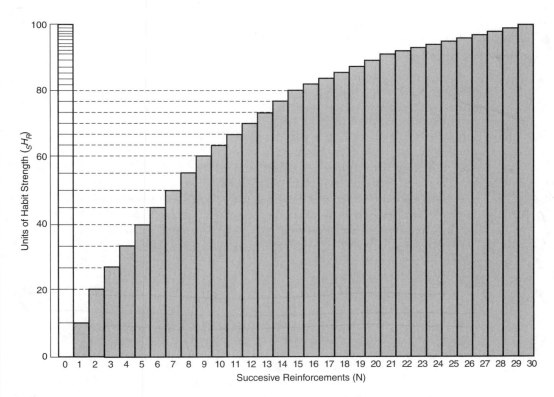

FIGURE 1.2 Hull's Theoretical Learning Curve. Notice that the increases in height in the curve are smaller and smaller across trials. This is a negatively accelerated learning curve.

Source: From *Principles of Behavior* (pp. 108, 116, 117), by C. L. Hull, 1943, New York: Appleton-Century-Crofts. Adapted with permission.

(continued)

Box 1.1   Continued

We could make an analogy to learning how to play tennis. At first, the improvements with each lesson may be fairly large. With yet more practice, improvements seem smaller. Performance may eventually reach an asymptote, or plateau, after which little or no further improvement is seen.

Learning curves are not always negatively accelerated. Sometimes performance improves only very slowly at first, and then the negatively accelerated process kicks in. This produces an S-shaped curve: small increments at the start of training, large increments in the middle, and a return to slow growth at the end. So, to say that you are farther along the learning curve may mean that you are in the phase of rapid acceleration or have passed through it, whereas someone else is still stuck in that early phase of slow growth.

This prototypical learning curve has been documented in many situations, and is incorporated in contemporary theories of learning (e.g., the Rescorla-Wagner; see Chapter 3). Although the learning curve may be an accurate description of what we do observe, its interpretation can be challenged. Possibly learning is not incremental as suggested by the curve, but is sudden and complete from one trial to the next. By averaging over subjects whose individual performances increase suddenly after different numbers of trials, we can produce a gradual curve that may not be an accurate representation of any one subject.

Other contemporary theorists suggest that the rate of growth is better described by a power curve rather than by a negatively accelerated curve (Newell & Rosenbloom, 1981). This means that the *trials* variable is expressed in log numbers rather than ordinal numbers, which compresses the larger numbers and produces a straight line rather than a curve.

---

learning, as illustrated by a *learning curve*. This would be a graphic plot of some measure of behavior on the *Y*, or vertical, axis (e.g., number or size of the correct responses) as a function of the number of trials given shown on the *X*, or horizontal, axis (see Box 1.1). Such a study might make minimal demands on memory by testing learning after short intervals of time. On the other hand, in studying memory, one might consider those factors that affect the retention or retrieval of the previously learned material, such as the length of the retention interval, or the presence of distracting activities during that interval. We could measure the course of memory by a *forgetting* curve. This would be a plot of the measure of behavior (again, the number or size of the correct responses) as a function of time or events since learning was completed. Sometimes minimal demands are made on the learning portion of the study by presenting easily acquired material that can be immediately remembered.

This learning–memory distinction can be illustrated by considering the role of the spacing of study trials. The well-known generalization is that spaced practice is better, but does spacing facilitate learning or does it aid retention after learning? A more complete answer to this question will be presented in a later chapter, but, for now, consider a study by Keppel (1964). His college student subjects (or *participants,* as we now call them) learned a list of paired items, such that the first item would be a cue to recall the second. For example, asking subjects to remember that TABLE is paired with SHOE. One group of subjects studied and attempted to recall the list eight times in a single session. This is the massed-practice group, because the study trials came one right after another. A second group received two study and test trials on each of four days. This is the spaced-practice condition. Keppel's results are shown in the left panel of Figure 1.3, which is a learning curve showing the number of correctly recalled associated words across practice trials. Acquisition seems to

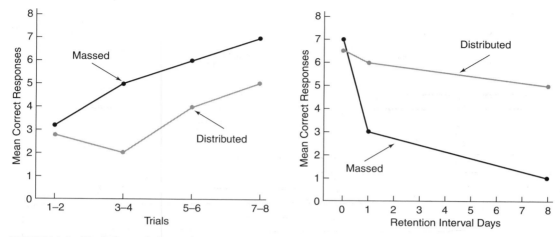

FIGURE 1.3 The left panel shows the acquisition of paired associates as a function of massed versus spaced practice. The eight trials were blocked in a single session, or spaced over 4 days. The right panel shows associates recalled when testing occurred immediately after learning, or 1 or 8 days later.

Source: From "Facilitation in Short- and Long-Term Retention of Paired Associates Following Distributed Practice in Learning," by G. Keppel, 1964, *Journal of Verbal Learning and Verbal Behavior, 3,* pp. 96 and 97. Copyright 1964 by Academic Press. Adapted with permission.

be better with massed practice than with spaced practice. The spaced-practice group took additional study trials to reach the level of correct recall attained with massed practice.

Once the lists are learned, which condition produces better memory? The right panel shows the retention for the massed and spaced groups when tested 1 day or 7 days after the last training trial. This is a forgetting curve. Here, the spaced-practice group seemed to remember more after a longer interval.

In this example, learning is studied in the first phase, involving the acquisition of the TABLE–SHOE associations. Memory is studied in the second phase, involving the retention of the associations. You might argue (validly) that the learning phase of the spaced group also tested memory by requiring recall from one day to the next. Logically, this argument could also be applied to the massed group, but on a shorter scale of minutes, because it also had to remember from one trial to the next. Indeed, some psychologists assert that any test of learning also involves a test of memory (e.g., Spear & Riccio, 1994). Therefore, maybe this study is not a good example of the distinction between learning and memory. But this is exactly the point. To label a study as being one of learning versus memory is often based on convention and consensus.

So how do we decide whether any variable is better or worse if different results are found in acquisition versus retention studies, as shown before in Keppel's experiment? Such discrepancies extend beyond individual experiments. Schmidt and Bjork (1992) have summarized the situation: "because learning and retention are thought to be different phenomena, they tend to be studied with separate methods, by different scientists, and even in different laboratories." They go further to make the important point that "Rather than viewing learning and posttraining retention as separable…we argue that the effectiveness of learning is revealed by…the level of retention shown" (p. 209). Their preference is to emphasize longer-term retention and transfer of learning to new situations.

Basic and Applied Research

One might expect a textbook on learning to include detailed information on how to learn the material in the book. Instead, the processes of learning are illustrated by preparations such as eyeblink conditioning or word-list memorizing, sometimes with participants other than humans. This discrepancy reflects the different purposes of research, these being an interest in basic or in applied content areas. Within each, we are asking sometimes different and sometimes related questions.

Basic research is an interest in understanding the fundamental processes of learning and memory. It seeks to demonstrate cause-and-effect relationships between key variables. To demonstrate the probable causality of one variable, we must control, eliminate, or hold constant other contaminating variables that could affect behavior. This often can be accomplished using a simple task, a simpler organism, and a highly controllable setting such as the laboratory. For instance, if you want to discover whether synaptic changes occur in learning, you want to study organisms that have few and large neurons, such as worms or snails. The questions asked by basic researchers do not always have obvious and immediate applicability to everyday learning outside of the lab.

However, it is incorrect to assert that basic research is conducted without any regard to practical application. The stereotyped portrayal of the Ivory Tower scientist, aloof from the concerns of everyday life, exaggerates the scientist's disinterest. Basic researchers believe in the potential usefulness of their research, even if they are not the ones who will apply the findings. Sometimes, the applications cannot be known until the research is conducted. As one physicist put it, basic research sometimes provides a solution in search of a problem (Lemonick, 1995.) Other times, basic researchers will themselves demonstrate the practical implications of their findings. For example, basic research on the learning of aversions to new tastes by rats has been applied to controlling sheep poaching by coyotes (Gustavson & Garcia, 1974), and to blocking the development of food aversions in people undergoing chemotherapy (Bernstein, 1991).

Applied research is relevant to, or will apply to, solving a specific practical problem. The distinction between basic and applied might be better thought of as a continuum rather than a dichotomy. (As with many of the terms encountered so far in this chapter, we first set out a dichotomy and then suggest the truth lies somewhere in between.) Any given piece of research falls somewhere along the basic applied continuum depending on the relevance of the study to a specific target population, task, and/or setting to which we wish to apply our results. Some examples may illustrate.

What is the effect of caffeine on memory? Caffeine is a known stimulant, often used by students to boost alertness, and would logically seem to facilitate learning. Research on maze learning by rats has shown varied results: Caffeine sometimes facilitates performance, but also can inhibit performance (Lashley, 1917; Terry & Anthony, 1980). These studies are obviously examples of basic research. In other experiments, college students are asked to remember word lists. These subjects and this task have greater relevance if we are trying to generalize to humans. Yet this study still retains aspects of basic research, in that the caffeine is given under controlled conditions in the lab, using blind-run and placebo conditions, and so on. The results of one such experiment were that caffeine impaired the immediate retention of the lists (Erikson et al., 1985). One final study to consider is possibly the most relevant to student learning: What is the relationship of caffeine intake to grade point average? Now we are getting to the important question. Gilliland and Andress (1981) surveyed University of Oklahoma students to determine the amount of caffeine consumed and correlated consumption with the students' GPAs. The results showed a negative correlation: Higher caffeine consumption was associated with lower overall grades, and, conversely, lower caffeine went along with higher grades. This example would seem to present the most applicable and the most ecologically valid of the caffeine findings presented so far. Yet one can imagine reasons other than caffeine for these results. Do procrastinating students drink lots of coffee while cramming for exams and papers? Does self-reported caffeine consumption accurately reflect actual consumption? By leaving the lab for the actual world, we lose control over certain variables in our attempt to simulate naturalistic conditions. There can be a trade-off between experimental rigor and ecological validity in research, as occurs in the study of everyday remembering (see Box 1.2).

The point is not that one type of research is better than the other. Basic and applied research are each appropriate for answering certain kinds of questions. The optimal solution is for basic and applied research to inform one another.

Our discussion of the roles of basic research raises some additional issues. First, aren't the effects of many of the studied variables just common sense? Second, what is the relevance of using animals in research?

Common Sense and Common Knowledge

As noted at the start of this chapter, many readers already possess sophisticated knowledge about how to learn. After all, students are professional learners. Is much of what psychologists teach about learning already common knowledge?

Indeed, Houston (1983) presented UCLA undergraduates brief descriptions of real-life situations in which a principle of learning applied. For example, if a child has been feeding pigeons at her window sill for several weeks, what happens if the feedings stop? Answering in a multiple-choice format, most students realized that the pigeons would stop coming (what we learning psychologists refer to as *experimental extinction*). The students also correctly predicted the outcome in 15 of 20 other situations. Houston then tested the same questions with people he found in a park on a Sunday afternoon. They were able to identify the expected outcomes corresponding to psychological phenomena, answering about 75 percent of the questions correctly. Does this show that we are teaching the obvious?

Although some beliefs about the nature of memory are shared by professionals and the general public, there are also some particularly discrepant conceptions. Klatzky (1984) refers to these as _memory myths_. These include distorted beliefs about amnesia, hypnosis, aging, and forgetting in general. For example, the common conception of amnesia is that it involves extensive forgetting of the past, particularly of personal identity, and that it occurs frequently (judging by its frequency in afternoon television dramas). In fact, amnesia typically does not

BOX 1.2

Studying Everyday Memory

In 1978, Ulric Neisser, recipient of an American Psychological Association award for distinguished scientific contributions, criticized experimental psychology for its failure to study memory and cognition as they are used in our lives. "If X is an interesting or socially significant aspect of memory, then psychologists have hardly ever studied X" (Neisser, 1978, p. 4). Neisser was criticizing psychologists for too much basic research conducted in the laboratory and too little research on how memory works outside the lab. Neisser's remarks came at a conference on applied memory research, possibly the first such conference, and were soon followed by a proliferation of research on memory as it occurs in the everyday world.

Ten years later, Banaji and Crowder (1989) chastised researchers whose newfound interest in everyday memory had failed to produce a body of new scientifically valid principles of memory. Their article was titled "The Bankruptcy of Everyday Memory," words equally provocative to Neisser's earlier remarks. Banaji and Crowder argued that the ecological realism obtained by studying memory in naturalistic settings does not automatically ensure that generalizable principles of memory will be found. These authors pointed to an analogy to chemistry. Chemists look for general principles of chemical interactions. No one criticizes chemists for doing controlled lab studies in order to isolate key variables, instead of studying everyday compounds in the kitchen or bathroom. Banaji and Crowder note that because certain variables are uncontrolled in the everyday world, a flawed research design cannot produce valid findings from which to generalize.

For example, Banaji and Crowder present one scenario in which eyewitnesses to a traffic accident are questioned. But who can say which witness is more accurate, or what conditions increase accuracy, when so many variables are uncontrolled? Witnesses may have observed from different perspectives or seen different things; the first story given to the police could contaminate that given the researcher later; and the delay until the researcher questions witnesses varies. How can valid results be obtained under such poor experimental conditions?

Somewhere between the two extremes of Neisser and of Banaji and Crowder probably lies the truth. Several commentators pointed out that the research setting, laboratory versus field, does itself determine the scientific validity of the results; that real-world research can produce generalizable effects; and that the study of everyday memory can provide a setting for testing the theories and principles derived in the laboratory. The study of everyday memory has since continued to develop, certainly with an increase in scientific rigor (see Cohen, 1996.) Like basic research, controlled experiments are frequently used to study ecological memory, in addition to methods of naturalistic observation and self-reports. Just as with basic research, ecological research generates new questions to ask, a criterion sometimes used to judge the usefulness of psychological theories. Importantly, the study of everyday memory may provide practical remedies for real problems, such as determining the veracity of eyewitness testimony, the validity of repressed memories, or the remediation of memory loss produced by injury, illness, or aging.

---

involve loss of personal identity; it goes back for only a short time period; and it is more likely to involve an inability to form new memories rather than a loss of old memories (see Chapter 7).

Another memory myth is that older folks forget the recent past while still remembering the distant past ("the old days"). This is opposite of the usual forgetting curve, in which older memories are most forgotten. It is true that memory does decline with age, although probably not as much as our stereotypes suggest. Studies of memory for current events, or what were current at one time, show that older and younger individuals both remember more contemporary events, and both age groups forget more the farther back in time the events occurred. Everyone, from age 40 to 80, recalls more from the most recent decade and less from earlier times.

One other too-common belief is that hypnosis can uncover hidden memories that are otherwise inaccessible. The older studies of hypnosis usually contrasted two groups: hypnotized and nonhypnotized subjects. What these simple studies failed to equate is the suggestibility of the subjects, their motivation to try to recall, and, importantly, the elaborate instructions to reexperience the remembered event given the hypnosis group. In fact, such instructions alone in nonhypnotized individuals can increase recall to that of hypnotized levels (see Chapter 10).

A final myth worth dispelling is the belief that forgetting is a weakness. Certainly, some of our memory failings are problematic, worrisome, embarrassing, even dangerous. Yet total recall could pose its own problems. If every event of the same type was remembered equally, how would you discriminate current from outdated information? Some mundane examples include remembering my current phone number and where I parked this morning, but not my last phone number or where I left the car yesterday. These examples become significant for the survival of an organism. An animal needs to remember where food has been found recently, but not a location that has since become depleted. Psychologists have suggested the radical idea that forgetting may have evolved as a positive characteristic of memory, not a flaw.

As for the other commonsense learning principles Houston (1983) studied, they may be generally true, but each can have important exceptions. For example, there are ways of patterning reward that will determine how quickly the pigeons will stop coming to the window sill. Using small amounts of food and/or infrequent feedings, rather than large and frequent feedings, may promote more persistence of the pigeons' visits.

Why Animals?

The reasons for using nonhuman animals in experiments on learning can be simply stated. First, the experiences of animal subjects often can be more highly controlled, obviously within the experiment itself, but also prior to the experiment in terms of the genetic and life history of the organism. Second, given our shared evolutionary history, there is a presumed similarity between animals and humans, and therefore an assumed generality in the basic principles of learning. Granted, there may be exceptions to these generalities.

A third, and controversial, reason for using animals is that procedures can be used on animals that cannot be applied ethically to humans. This justification is controversial because some would question why animals are not given similar protection from painful or dangerous procedures. How prevalent is dissatisfaction with animal use in psychological research? One survey of 1,200 psychology majors at 42 colleges found fairly strong support for the continued use of animals (Plous, 1996). About 70 percent supported the use of animals in psychological research and believed such research was necessary. Interestingly, a greater number (85 percent) believed that before a proposed study is approved, the investigators should be required to assess the degree of pain the animals will experience. This step is required in several European countries. (Incidentally, the survey found that fewer faculty in psychology departments are using animals than in previous years, and fewer psychology students take lab courses using animals.)

Neal Miller, in accepting the Distinguished Professional Contribution Award from the American Psychological Association, listed some contributions of behavioral research on animals (1985). These include the development of behavior therapies and biofeedback for psychological disorders; applications to behavioral medicine, such as in the control of cardiovascular and asthmatic responses; research on the effects of early experience on neural development; the psychoactive effects of drugs; and benefits to animals themselves, both for those under our care and for wildlife. Domjan (1987) adds to this list the modeling or simulation of human behavior disorders, such as helplessness, depression, or drug addictions; and the identification of the neurological bases of learning and remembering. The extent of the contribution of animal research in psychology is not always acknowledged. Some introductory psychology textbooks reference certain findings to studies of human participants, when in fact the phenomena first emerged from animal laboratories (Domjan and Purdy, 1995).[2]

Conceptual Approaches to the Study of Learning

When rats (who, along with college students, are psychologists' favorite research subjects) learn a maze, what exactly do they learn? Is it a list of specific turns, like a memorized set of directions? Do they acquire a sort of cognitive map of the layout of the maze? Or should we be describing the neural changes that underlie the learning of routes or maps? These questions illustrate three broad approaches to studying learning. A behavioral approach focuses on the acquisition of specific responses or behaviors. A cognitive approach emphasizes the learning of cognitions and expectancies. A neuropsychological approach studies the changes that learning produces in the brain. These approaches, along with others, have played a major role in our understanding of learning and memory. The several approaches are not mutually exclusive. Psychologists sometimes adopt one perspective or another in conducting their research, although now questions more commonly are being asked from a combination of perspectives.

The Behavioral Approach

The *behavioral approach* emphasizes the relationship among, first, observable behaviors, second, the antecedent stimuli that precede behavior, and, third, the consequences that follow behavior. What are the environmental stimuli and conditions that come to evoke behavior? What are the consequences or outcomes that affect the likelihood of behavior? And

---

[2]In this text, I will typically refer to the participant populations as human or animal, which only means a distinction between human animals and other animals (Dess & Chapman, 1998). Strictly speaking, from an evolutionary or biological perspective, humans are animals, too.

what are the behaviors themselves that are learned? The goal of behavioral psychology is to predict and control behavior on the basis of knowledge of the antecedents, the behavior, and its consequences.

Behaviorism takes as the basic material for its science observable stimuli and behaviors. One version of this approach, known historically as radical behaviorism, shuns theorizing about inferred or hypothetical (and therefore speculative) processes within the organism's mind. Instead, behaviorism attempts to describe the lawful relationships among stimuli, responses, and consequences. These are called "functional" relationships. An example of a functional statement is "the likelihood that a certain behavior will occur increases if the response has been followed by a reinforcing stimulus in the past." To give a specific application, if a child's aggressive behavior is rewarded, the likelihood of aggression in the future will increase. If these functional relationships correctly and accurately describe behavior, there is no need to postulate unobserved thought processes to explain the behavior (i.e., the child has a bullying personality, or aggression is cathartic).

Other behaviorists who have a predilection toward theorizing are willing to posit hypothetical processes or constructs that intervene between input and output. This has been called *methodological behaviorism*. Thus, the behavior that an individual exhibits is taken as an indication of the current level of a hypothesized factor, such as drive, habit strength, expectancy for reward, or learned helplessness. As a specific example, we can hypothesize an internal variable of "thirst drive." Thirst is affected by environmental manipulations, such as water deprivation or salt content in food; and thirst affects behavior, by energizing and guiding behaviors that lead to water. The environment and behavior are still objective and observable, but the hypothesized internal state of thirst is not.

Historically, behavioral psychology attempted to explain learning without recourse to mentalistic concepts such as mind or consciousness. Although initially developed to describe the results of animal learning experiments, this approach can be readily applied to learning by humans.

The Cognitive Approach

The *cognitive approach* derives from computer-influenced, information-processing approaches to the mind. Information, or knowledge, is encoded, transformed, stored, and retrieved. The influence from computer science is obvious: These are analogous to processes within a computer. The basic tenet of the cognitive approach is the postulation of an *internal representation*. That is, the organism is said to form an internal representation that is used as the basis for further processing or for guiding behavior (Pearce, 1997). (Cognitive researchers will often talk about this representation being in the mind, but this does not necessarily refer to a mental mind apart from the physical representation in the brain.) This internal representation, as well as the cognitive processes of storing it, transforming it, retrieving it, and so forth, are all inferred on the basis of behavior, much as in the approach of the methodological behaviorists.

Although cognitive psychology obviously applies to humans, the generality of the cognitive approach can be illustrated in research on animals. Here we have to depend on behavior and not verbal report in order to infer cognitive processes. How can a researcher determine whether a rat has acquired a cognitive map of a familiar maze? Can the rat select a shortcut to the goal box, using a different route from the one we originally trained? If the animal is confronted with a blocked alley, does the rat readily select an alternate route to the goal box? We use these sorts of tests to infer the presence of an internal representation of the maze. Does the animal act as if it has learned a map of the maze, or instead as if it has memorized a series of turns?

The Neuropsychological Approach

Rule
Out

The *neuropsychological approach* has existed in parallel with both the earlier behavioral and the newer cognitive perspectives. Taking various contemporary names that reflect different emphases, such as neurobiology, neurophysiology, or the broader neuroscience, this approach seeks to determine the underlying biological basis for learning and memory. What are the changes that occur in the nervous system during learning?

Neuropsychology is often combined with the other approaches. Beginning in the 1920s, the eminent psychologist Karl Lashley attempted to find the areas of the rat's brain necessary for learning and memory (e.g., Lashley, 1929). He did this by systematically removing various regions of the brain. Twenty years later, the neurosurgeon Wilder Penfield studied memory localization by stimulating the brain of his human patients with weak electric current (Penfield & Rasmussen, 1950). The patients, who were conscious during this portion of the operation, sometimes reported sights and sounds that felt like memories. A few years later, the Swedish biochemist Holger Hydén sought to find a biochemical change that occurred in the rat's brain when a new behavior was learned, a sort of memory molecule (e.g., Hydén & Egyhazi, 1963). Specifically, after training his rats to balance on a tightrope (don't ask!), he assessed RNA changes in the cerebellum, an area of the cortex that is involved in movement coordination. These classic experiments illustrate the strategy of combining approaches: behavioral (maze learning), cognitive (memory recall), and physiological (lesioning, brain stimulation, and assaying RNA).

Contemporary neuropsychology uses methods such as brain scans and case studies of brain-injured individuals. For example, the positron emission tomography (or PET) scan detects the utilization of glucose in the brain. You have probably seen photographs of scans in which the brain is color-coded to show which areas are most active. (My publisher is not about to spring for color illustrations.) We can ask an experimental subject to perform different memory activities, and then scan the brain. For instance, I could first ask you to remember a list of simple words, such as DOG, TABLE, GLASS, and so on. This is a memory *encoding* task: It involves putting a list of words into memory. Later I could ask you to recall that list. This test is a memory *retrieval* task: It involves recalling what is (maybe) in memory. The PET scans made during these two tasks are compared, and several brain regions will be active during both tasks. However, some areas are more active while encoding the list, and other areas are more active during retrieval of the list. Figure 1.4 shows drawings of the left and right halves of the brain, with markers showing points that were particularly active during encoding versus during retrieval (Nyberg, Cabeza, & Tulving, 1996). As can be seen, when learning the list, many more points in the left-front part of the brain are active; when recalling the list, there are more points active in the right-front part. Other research has shown differential activation while remembering faces rather than words.

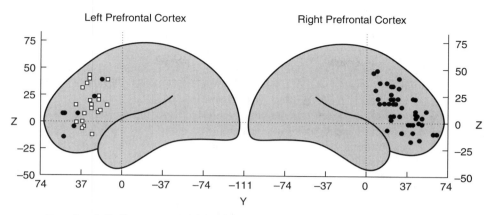

FIGURE 1.4 Peak activation areas in the left and right hemispheres of the brain during two memory tasks. The left half of the brain shows more encoding peaks, whereas the right half shows more retrieval peaks.

Source: From "PET Studies of Encoding and Retrieval: The HERA Model," by L. Nyberg, R. Cabeza, and E. Tulving, 1996, *Psychonomic Bulletin & Review, 3,* p. 143. Copyright © 1996 by the Psychonomic Society. Reprinted with permission.

Historically, there has been tension between the behavioral and cognitive approaches. In the example that began this section, we posed the question of whether maze learning could be best described in terms of learning a series of turns versus acquiring a cognitive map of the maze. Behavioral and cognitive approaches are often presented as opposite explanations. Maybe, instead, they should be considered as complementary. Possibly maps or routes are learned, depending on other circumstances. Curiously, research from a neural sciences approach may offer a reconciliation between behavioral and cognitive psychologies, by showing that there are both habit learning and cognitive learning systems in the brain (Petri & Mishkin, 1994). For example, learning that food is always found in one particular location in the maze, day after day, is habit learning, and this learning is impaired by damage to an area of the brain called the hippocampus. If the food location is varied from day to day, remembering where it is today is cognitive learning, and performance is impaired by damage to another part of the brain, the amygdala (McDonald & White, 1993).

Summary

The point of this book is to present a scientifically accurate and sophisticated view of the principles of learning. This includes adding qualifying statements to general principles: specifying when a given principle holds and when exceptions occur.

The Origins of the Study of Learning

The philosopher Descartes suggested that some knowledge was independent of experience. Some knowledge is innate, which is the idea of nativism. Other knowledge is derived by a reasoning, logical, and intuiting mind; this is rationalism. By contrast, the philosopher John Locke suggested that the origin of all knowledge is from experience, as provided to the mind through the senses. This is empiricism.

Darwin's theory of evolution suggested to psychologists that the ability to learn may have evolved as an adaptive specialization. Learning is a means of adapting to the environment within the organism's lifetime. That different species are related through a common evolutionary history suggests that learning by animals can offer insights into how humans learn.

The Definition of Learning *Read*

Learning is defined as a relatively permanent change in behavior, or behavioral repertoire, that occurs as a result of experience. Each phrase of the definition is significant. Because learning itself, in the mind or in the brain, is not directly observable, behavior change is necessary to provide objective evidence that learning has occurred. In general, measures of learning can be physiological, behavioral, or verbal.

The phrase *behavioral repertoire* acknowledges that not all learning is immediately evidenced in behavior. Learning includes the potential for a change in behavior, to be demonstrated when conditions prompt the display of this new knowledge. Learning is said to produce relatively permanent changes in behavior, which excludes transient changes in arousal, fatigue, or motivation.

Biologically determined maturation illustrates gray areas around the edge of our definition of learning.

The Learning/Performance Distinction

There is not always a one-to-one correspondence between what an organism knows (i.e., learning) and what an organism does (performance). Tolman and Honzik's study of latent learning showed that rats learned the layout of the maze without reward, but this knowledge remained hidden until the subjects were motivated with food to complete the maze quickly. In an exam situation, students who have truly learned the material can still perform poorly on the exam (maybe due to excessive anxiety, for instance).

The Relationship between Learning and Memory

Learning refers to the acquisition, or encoding, of knowledge or behavior. We could illustrate its development with a learning curve, a graphic plot of a measure of behavior on the vertical axis (e.g., number or size of the correct responses) as a function of the number of trials given, shown on the horizontal axis. Memory refers to the retention of knowledge or behavior that has been learned. We could illustrate the course of memory by a forgetting curve, plotting a measure of behavior on the vertical axis, as a function of time or events since learning was completed on the horizontal axis.

Basic and Applied Research   *Read & take notes*

Basic research is an interest in understanding the fundamental processes of learning and memory, by demonstrating cause-and-effect relationships between key variables. We must often use artificial situations or tasks in order to control, eliminate, or hold constant contaminating variables that could affect behavior. Applied research, the other end of the continuum, is designed to be relevant to, or will apply to, answering a specific practical problem. Each type of research is appropriate for answering certain kinds of questions.

Are most principles of learning already common knowledge? In fact, there are discrepancies between what professionals and laypeople believe about memory. These memory myths include distorted beliefs about amnesia, hypnosis, and forgetting in the aged.

Nonhuman animals are used in experiments on learning because their experiences can be highly controlled and because there is a presumed similarity in learning processes between animals and humans. Research on animals has made numerous contributions to the welfare of both animals and people.

Conceptual Approaches to the Study of Learning

There are several broad approaches to the study of learning. A behavioral approach focuses on the acquisition of specific responses or behaviors. It emphasizes the relationship between these observable behaviors to the stimuli that precede behavior, and to the consequences that follow behavior. A cognitive approach emphasizes internal (mental or neural) cognitions and expectancies. It derives from information-processing approaches to the mind, in which information is encoded, transformed, stored, and retrieved. A neuropsychological approach studies the changes that learning produces in the brain. It seeks to determine the underlying biological basis of learning and memory within the nervous system.

2 Habituation and Other Forms of Simple Stimulus Learning

Researchers often start with a simple model, system, or paradigm with which to derive some first principles, and progress to more complex phenomena and laws. Learning about single stimuli, uncomplicated by associations, contingencies, or rules relating them to other events, would seem to offer such a simple learning situation.

As a starting point, suppose an innocuous stimulus is presented some number of times. Your behavior at first indicates that you notice the stimulus, but since it has no apparent significance, your reaction to the repetitions of the stimulus decrease. This effect is called *habituation,* a simple form of learning. A noise in the house at night awakens you, but you realize it is just the house settling or the furnace humming, and so you come to ignore these house sounds. However, you can probably think of times when you became more reactive to a stimulus after a first exposure. A noise in the house awakens you; and as you worry about what it might be, the behavioral and physiological reactions increase each time the noise recurs. Rather than habituating, you are sensitized, or more responsive to the stimulus.

Exposure to a stimulus can affect our behavior in other ways also, even if we are not aware of the previous exposure. For instance, a stimulus could be flashed on a screen so briefly (only a fraction of a second) that it cannot be consciously recognized. Yet this *priming* presentation can affect reactions to a repetition of the stimulus later, such as increasing our liking of the previously seen stimulus. Repetition increases our preference for particular songs, for works of art, and for particular foods.

The starting point for this chapter is that stimulus repetitions reduce one form of responsiveness to a stimulus. However, we will see that stimulus exposure potentially can produce a number of other reactions: greater responsiveness, preference and liking, and speeded reactions. "The main lesson to be learned from the study of habituation—and this makes it an even more appropriate subject to start with—is that habituation is almost never as simple as it first seems" (Walker, 1987, p. 34).

The Orienting Response

The occurrence of a novel or an unexpected stimulus elicits an *orienting response* (OR, also called an orienting reflex or orienting reaction). Pavlov aptly described the OR as an investigatory reflex. The organism reacts to identify the nature and source of the stimulation, which may be important to the survival of the organism. The OR to unfamiliar or unexpected stimuli is actually not a single response, but is a composite of several physiological and behavioral reactions. First, a stimulus may evoke a startle response. This may involve whole body startle to extremely loud noises, or simply head movements or an eye blink to milder stimuli. In addition, the novel stimulus produces sense receptor orienting. We turn to look in the direction of a sight or sound; dogs perk up their ears to hear better; rabbits twitch their noses to increase olfactory sensitivity. There is also a readiness for a fight or flight response. Orienting reactions have an evolutionary basis as a preparation for danger, and so defensive behaviors are primed. Finally, there is increased arousal. This arousal could be described physiologically, as measured by heart rate or breathing changes, and also psychologically, as measured by degree of attention and alertness (Siddle, Kuiack, & Kroese, 1983).

Not all of these components occur to every new stimulus. A sudden and intense stimulus, such as a starter's pistol that goes off unexpectedly, can elicit a head-jerking startle, whereas a tone stimulus presented in a lab experiment may simply elicit an eye blink. An animal in the wild may react to a sound by preparing to fight or flee, whereas this is less likely to occur with our pets at home (and hopefully not with the human experimental participants we study in the lab). Thus, the particular components of the OR that occur depend on stimulus intensity, the situation, the potential for danger, and other factors.

The novelty of a stimulus is just one factor determining whether an orienting response is made, but it is not a necessary factor. A familiar but meaningful stimulus can also elicit an OR. Hearing one's name mentioned unexpectedly is a potent elicitor of an OR, although this is hardly a novel stimulus. A predatory animal will orient to the sound of its usual prey, a familiar stimulus.

Habituation

Habituation is the decrease in orienting (and other) reactions to a stimulus that is repeatedly presented. An often-used phrase describes habituation as "the waning of responsiveness" to repetitive stimulation. An initially new stimulus becomes less novel and more familiar with repeated presentations, and thus becomes less likely to elicit the various components of the OR. The word *habituation* is used in the research literature both to refer to the procedure (repetitive presentation of a stimulus) and to the effect or outcome (a decrease in responding).

Habituation is a simple form of learning in which the organism learns something about a single stimulus. Unlike most other indications or measures of learning that we will consider in later chapters, learning is shown by less responding over trials. This is just the opposite of the learning curve described earlier, which increases over trials.

If the stimulus turns out to have some significance to the organism, because it is followed by other events or consequences, orienting may be replaced by learned adaptive responses. For example, in Pavlov's experiment, the novel tone stimulus is followed by food. Orienting to the first several tone presentations is gradually replaced by conditioned responses, such as salivating to the tone, as the dog learns that the tone is followed by food. In most habituation experiments, only the to-be-habituated stimulus is presented so that the addition of other acquired responses does not complicate interpretation.

Habituation of the orienting reaction applies to neutral or innocuous stimuli. These stimuli are sometimes distinguished from intense and/or painful stimuli that in and of themselves are of more significance to the subject. The responses to noxious (or aversive) stimuli, called defensive responses or unconditioned responses, are often the same as the orienting reaction to innocuous stimuli, only usually larger in magnitude. These defensive reactions to noxious stimuli also habituate: Innate, reflex responses to potent stimuli may decrease across repeated presentations of the stimulus (Wetherington, 1982). Although some researchers differentiate orienting responses from defensive responses, other researchers treat both sorts of reactions as being on a continuum, with the strength or kind of response being more a function of stimulus intensity.

Habituation is ubiquitous: It is seemingly found everywhere. Habituation occurs across the phylogenetic scale, from snails to humans. It occurs in various segments of nervous systems, including isolated spinal neurons and at synapses. Conferences on habituation have brought together diverse groups of basic researchers, from those interested in the physiology of habituation, to those studying animal behavior, to those studying attention and memory in children (e.g., Tighe & Leaton, 1976). These investigators share a common terminology, have uncovered similar principles of learning, and sometimes even use the same theoretical explanations. Such cross-fertilization between different levels of research is desirable for the scientific advancement of learning, but is often difficult to accomplish.

Methods of Studying Habituation

A variety of tasks and measures may be used to investigate habituation. The whole-body startle reaction to loud tones can be studied using rats (e.g., Davis, 1974). Orienting produces increased blood flow to the brain as it prepares to process novel stimuli, and so vasoconstriction or vasodilation can be measured by electrodes placed on the forehead of human subjects. Blood flow can be similarly measured in rabbits through a photocell transducer mounted on the ear (the blood flow tends to overshoot the rabbit's head and so continues up the ear; Whitlow, 1975).

In humans, physiological responses such as the galvanic skin response, or GSR, are often used to monitor reactions to new stimuli. The GSR is probably familiar to you as a component of the lie detector test, in which electrodes are placed on the body (e.g., the hand or arm) to detect subtle changes in electrical conductivity in the skin that are associated with changes in arousal or emotionality. Illustrative data from a habituation experiment measuring GSR are shown in Figure 2.1. Siddle, Kuiack, and Kroese (1983) presented 15 brief tones, one every minute or so, to college student participants tested individually in a laboratory setting. Some students were presented with a high-pitched tone,

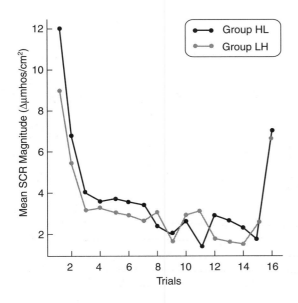

FIGURE 2.1   Habituation of the Galvanic Skin Response to a Simple Tone Stimulus. One group received high-pitch (H) tones; the other group received low-pitch (L) tones. After 15 presentations, the opposite tone was presented to each group.

Source: From "The Orienting Reflex," by D. A. T. Siddle, M. Kuiack, and B. S. Kroese, in *Physiological Correlates of Human Behavior* (p. 161), edited by A. Gale and J. A. Edwards, 1983, London: Academic Press. Copyright 1983 by Academic Press. Reprinted with permission.

and the others heard a low-pitched tone. As can be seen in the graph, the skin conductance response decreased across stimulus presentations for each group of subjects. After 15 stimulus presentations, the experimenters switched tones. The final tone in the series was the one habituated for the other group, so the high-pitched tone was replaced by a low-pitched tone, and vice versa. Orienting returned when the tones were changed.

Changes in heart rate, typically a brief deceleration, or eye blinks to various stimuli are also frequently measured in habituation experiments. Finally, brain wave changes (EEG and other measures of electrical activity) offer measures of neural sensitivity to stimulation, arousal, and attention.

One widely used measure of orienting is that of eye fixations to novel visual stimuli. We tend to visually explore new stimuli, and gradually shift our gaze away from these stimuli once they become familiar. Measuring the change in duration or number of eye fixations to a stimulus is a good indicator of habituation. In a sense, the eyes become the windows of the mind. Measuring eye movements is especially useful for studying learning by infants. A novel object or image is shown repeatedly, and habituation is shown by a decrease in fixations across trials. We could interpret this as an indication that the child comes to recognize the stimulus as familiar. Following habituation to one stimulus, a second experimental phase is sometimes given in which two stimuli are presented for a comparison, one old and one new stimulus. The child may then show more inspection of the new stimulus than of the old one (see Box 2.1).

Parametric Features of Habituation

Thompson and Spencer (1966) derived a list of parametric features of habituation. Parametric refers to taking one dimension of an independent variable and systematically vary-

BOX **2.1**

Dishabituation as a Measure of Infant Perception and Cognition

Habituation tasks have been used to study perception, learning, and even reasoning in infants. The cognitive capabilities of preverbal children are difficult to measure, where the problem of behavioral silence is particularly acute: The absence of a response does not mean an absence of knowledge. Measuring the frequency and duration of eye fixations to familiar stimuli, and changes in fixations to novel stimuli, provides a valuable method for investigating learning in infants. In this method, one stimulus is presented repeatedly producing habituation, that is, a decrease in the eye fixations to the stimulus. Then test stimuli can be presented to see whether dishabituation occurs, indicating the test stimulus is noticed as different from the familiar stimulus. This technique can be used to address several intriguing questions about what infants are capable of perceiving, remembering, or thinking.

Adults typically divide the light spectrum into several distinct primary colors. Intermediate hues can be reliably assigned to one or another of these categories. For example, between those colors labeled as blue or green are intermediate hues, what we might call greenish blue and bluish green, which adults consistently categorize (if forced to) as either blue or green. An explanation based on learning alone presumes that such labels develop from differential reinforcement, that is, from being rewarded for labeling one color "blue" and another "green." This empiricist viewpoint suggests that preverbal infants, who have not learned these divisions of the color spectrum yet, might not show the same categorizing as do adults. But, how can we tell how infants would classify intermediate hues? Bornstein, Kessen, and Weiskopf (1976) used the dishabituation procedure, first presenting 4-month-old infants with 15 repetitions of a 15-second light. Different groups of infants were shown lights of different colors, for example, greenish BLUE for one group and bluish GREEN for another group (the color in small capital letters is the adult category label). Fixation times declined from 8 to 9 seconds on the first presentations to 2 to 3 seconds over the last few. Thus, habituation occurred. The infants were then given test presentations of the habituated color, and one color on either side (see Table 2.1). In each case, less eye fixating occurred to the hue within the same adult color category, even though each tested hue was equidistant from the habituated color. For example, after habituating to bluish GREEN, the infants spent even less

TABLE 2.1   Design and Results of One Color Condition in a Study of Infant Dishabituation to Novel Colors

Color	Blue			Green
wavelength (nm)	450	480	510	540
Group 1 fixation time (sec)	Blue 5.8	*greenish Blue* 5.9	bluish Green 7.0	
Group 2 fixation time (sec)		greenish Blue 7.0	*bluish Green* 4.9	Green 4.0

Note: The colors that were first habituated are in italics. Group 1 was habituated to greenish Blue. These infants show less eye fixation to a blue light and increased looking to a greenish-colored light. Group 2 was habituated to bluish Green. These infants generalized habituation to Green and dishabituated to greenish Blue.

Source: Bornstein, Kessen, & Weiskopf, 1976.

(continued)

Box 2.1   Continued

time looking at GREEN, and spent more time fixating to greenish BLUE.

Similar results were shown with the other color boundaries (e.g., yellow–red). By 4 months of age, colors are seen categorically. Wide ranges of reds, yellows, greens, and blues are being perceived as equivalent, whereas there are sharper boundaries between these color categories.

This same technique is being used to study infants' perception of number (Wynn, 1992). If the infant is shown a fixed number of objects on several trials (e.g., one puppet or two puppets), will orienting occur when the number is changed? Wynn found an increase in eye fixations when a

puppet was added or subtracted on test trials. In another study, 6-month-old infants were shown a puppet that jumped either two times or three times (for different groups of children) on each habituation trial. A sudden change in the number of jumps on the test trial elicited dishabituation and increased looking (Wynn, 1995).

The starting point for research like this is, indirectly, the philosophical question of nativism versus empiricism: Do we innately perceive colors, do we learn the concept of number? Curiously, a technique used to study learning (habituation) can be used to show evidence for native perceptual abilities.

---

ing it to map out the changes in effect. For example, one can vary the spacing of stimulus presentations across a range of values and measure the amount of response at each spacing. Similarly, other features of the stimulus such as its intensity or duration could be varied. Thompson and Spencer had been studying habituation of multiple responses simultaneously, a behavioral response of leg flexion and a physiological measure of activity in the spinal neurons, to mild shocks presented to a cat's paw. The spinal reflex, which can be isolated from the brain, provides a simplified nervous system with which to model a learning phenomenon. The researchers noticed parallels between the effects of similar variables on the habituation of these two different sorts of responses. From their own observations and others in the literature, they derived the list of parametric features of habituation, which have become a sort of standard or benchmark for evaluating whether response changes that occur in other species, preparations, or response systems are really habituation. A number of the Thompson and Spencer parametric features are remarkably general. A consideration of several of these features illustrates the process of habituation.

Frequency.   Habituation is a function of the number of repetitions of a stimulus. The exact number of repetitions necessary to produce a substantial response decrement varies considerably. Sometimes EEG suppression in rats occurs after a single presentation of a tone stimulus (Leaton & Buck, 1971), whereas rat startle response to loud tones continues to decline across hundreds of presentations. As shown in Figure 2.1 earlier, human habituation occurs after a few presentations of a mild tone stimulus.

Spontaneous Recovery.   If the stimulus is withheld for a period of time, the response tends to recover. The next time the stimulus is presented, the response will be larger than before the delay interval. The response tends to *spontaneously recover* during an interval of time without stimulations. Indeed, if the delay interval is sufficiently long (e.g., overnight in an animal experiment), the reaction to the previously habituated stimulus may completely recover. (Spontaneous recovery is illustrated in Figure 2.3 [page 37] in experiments that will be described later.) Actually, for many years, this feature was used to argue that habituation was not an example of learning. If the habituation procedure produced only a temporary and passing change in responding, then habituation did not fit the *relatively permanent* clause in the definition of learning. Why would we later come to believe that habituation is learning? The answer is in the next feature.

Effects of Repeated Habituations.   If the stimulus is habituated a second time, and after another delay, a third time, a fourth, and so on, habituation occurs more quickly on each successive occasion than it did during the first session, and the amount of recovery (or loss of habituation) will be less after each delay. That is, there appears to be something like a savings effect: Fewer stimulations are required to rehabituate the stimulus, thus *saving* or reducing the number of stimulus presentations necessary to reduce the response, as compared to the initial course of habituation. With sufficient experience, habituation may become more enduring.

Spacing of Stimulations.   The shorter the interval between successive stimulus presentations, the more quickly responding declines. Basically, closely spaced stimulus repetitions produce more habituation than do widely spaced repetitions.

The massed-spaced effect is variable across studies and suggests there may be a more complicated relationship than Thompson and Spencer (1966) originally stated. As with Keppel's study of massed and spaced practice discussed in Chapter 1, the two conditions may produce differing results during habituation than when tested afterwards. This can be shown in a study by Gatchell (1975) in which college student participants received a series of tones, one tone presented every 20 seconds for one group or every 100 seconds for the second group. Across 15 tone presentations, there was a decrease in the response by both groups of students, which is simply the frequency effect mentioned before. By the last of the 15 tones, there were smaller responses to stimuli spaced 20 seconds apart than to stimuli 100 seconds apart, which is a massed-presentation effect.

The complication here goes back to our earlier distinctions between learning and memory. Are massed presentations producing better learning? How lasting are the differences between the massed and spaced conditions? The interesting test observation is to see whether massed and spaced stimulations differ in the amount of recovery after a delay. Gatchell (1975) gave his subjects a 15-minute rest interval and then presented the tones again. Both groups showed spontaneous recovery: a larger response after the delay than before. The massed group showed more recovery to the first tone presentations following the delay than did the spaced group. The massed group also responded more during the re-habituation trials than did the initially spaced group. Similar effects had been shown earlier by Davis (1970) using the rat-startle preparation.

The lesson here may be that to suppress responding immediately, use massed presentations. Spaced presentations may be less efficient in the short run, but more effective in producing durable habituation.

Dishabituation.   Another means of temporarily reducing habituation is through the procedure of dishabituation. Habituation to one stimulus can be temporarily blocked by presenting another novel stimulus. After one stimulus has been habituated, the presentation of a differ-ent novel stimulus increases orienting to the first stimulus when it is re-presented. This after-effect of the second stimulus is called *dishabituation.*

For example, in one study, college student participants received 15 presentations of the same 4-second tone. The size of the OR decreased, which is simply habituation. Then a new stimulus, say, a patch of red light was projected via a slide projector. The light itself should elicit an OR. When the tone is next presented, its sixteenth presentation, there is a larger response to it than to the previous (fifteenth) occurrence. The light stimulus was the dishabituator; the enhanced response to the sixteenth tone shows dishabituation. Dishabit-uation is a transient aftereffect of the dishabituating stimulus. Presenting the tone again (the seventeenth presentation) should lead to a reappearance of the smaller, habituated re-sponse (Siddle, 1985).

If the light were to be presented repeatedly and habituated, it would become less ef-fective as a dishabituator (Lehner, 1941). In this case, a third stimulus, say, for example, a buzzer, might be introduced to dishabituate the habituated dishabituator. (Sorry, just having some fun.)

Dishabituation is a sensible reaction to changed conditions of stimulation. The dis-habituator reinstates arousal, investigatory reflexes, sense receptor orienting, and so on, in preparation for potential changed environmental conditions.

Habituation to One Stimulus Generalizes to Other Stimuli.   The habituation to a specific tone or light, so that it no longer elicits the OR, may spread to other like stimuli. That is, after habituating one stimulus there can be generalization of habituation to other stimuli that are similar. The degree of generalization depends on the similarity of the test stimuli to the habituated stimulus. For example, in the Siddle, Kuiack, and Kroese (1983) study noted earlier in this chapter, habituation to a high- or low-pitched tone did not gener-alize to the opposite tone (see Figure 2.1). The different tone elicited a large OR. However, if a tone of medium pitch had been presented, likely a smaller or weaker OR would have occurred. Test stimuli that are similar to the originally habituated stimulus should elicit smaller responses; test stimuli that are different stimuli should elicit more orienting.

An example of the stimulus specificity of habituation can be seen in a study by Furedy and Scull (1971). College students were presented two stimuli for habituation, an air puff to the forehead and a mild shock to the forearm. The two stimuli were presented 65 times in an unpredictable sequence, with intervals between one stimulus and the next vary-ing from 5 to 40 seconds. The researchers were particularly interested in the size of the GSR response to the puff or shock when the just-previous stimulus had been the same (e.g., response to puff when the previous stimulus had been a puff also) or when the previ-ous stimulus had been different (response to puff when the previous stimulus had been shock). Overall, there was a smaller GSR to shocks than to puffs; the shock really was mild. More important, the reaction to an airpuff was smaller when the preceding stimulus had been an airpuff; and the reaction to a shock was smaller when the preceding stimulus had been a shock. There was a stimulus-specific decline in responding.

These results also make the important point that the organism habituates to the stim-ulus. We may casually talk of habituating a response, but what we have really done is ha-bituated the stimulus. The response should still be elicited by other stimuli.

Summary of the Parametric Features of Habituation.   The response to a novel stimulus decreases as a function of the number of repetitions of the stimulus. The habituated response spontaneously recovers over time without stimulus presentations and can dishabituate following the occurrence of some other novel stimulus. Habituation cumulates across repeated series of stimulus presentations. Habituation generalizes from the habituated stimulus to other similar stimuli. Although closely spaced presentations may suppress the orienting response quickly, there is evidence that more widely spaced presentations produce more long-term habituation.

Explanations of Habituation   *Leave Out!!!*

Why does responding decrease after a certain number of stimulus presentations? One explanation suggests that habituation is not a learning phenomenon at all and instead is due to changes in either the sense receptors or the muscle effectors. Theories that do assert that habituation is learning fall into two broad categories of explanation, cognitive and physiological.

Nonlearning Explanations

One nonlearning explanation suggests that habituation is due to sensory adaptation. Possibly, the sense receptors simply become less sensitive as a function of repeated stimulus presentations. An example of adaptation is when you detect a distinct odor or smell on entering a room, but, later, the smell is no longer noticed. Here, the olfactory receptors lose their sensitivity to detect a constant odor.

    A second nonlearning alternative is response or effector fatigue. The subject may be too tired to respond, or, more precisely, the response system is depleted. Either sensory adaptation or motor fatigue will build up over trials, and both will recover with rest, thus producing effects that look like habituation and spontaneous recovery.

    Neither of these alternatives seems likely when only 10 to 20 mild tones have been presented, but sensory adaptation or response fatigue becomes plausible with the large number of stimulations and more intense stimuli often used in animal studies. Control procedures are necessary to rule out, or at least assess the contribution of, each stimulus to any response decrement we observe. One such control procedure is to test for dishabituation. After habituating one stimulus, a different novel stimulus in the same sensory modality is presented, followed by a re-presentation of the initially habituated stimulus. If responding occurs to the dishabituator and to the previously habituated stimulus, then, obviously, the sense receptors detected the stimuli and the effectors are capable of responding. Other procedures include omitting an expected stimulus (see what follows) or changing the stimulus, as in the Siddle and colleagues' study shown earlier in Figure 2.1. Again, both reinstate orienting, showing that the sense receptors and the response systems were still functioning adequately.

Physiological Theories

Dual Process Theory.   As noted earlier, Thompson and his colleagues developed a spinal-reflex preparation with which to study habituation. They were able to study both overt behaviors (e.g., paw flexion to shock stimuli) and nervous system reactions (nerve potentials in the sensory and motor neurons). With both sets of measures, they documented the parametric features of habituation, some of which were noted earlier.

However, one complication that they found is that sometimes repetitive stimulation did not reduce responding. Instead, the size of the responses increased across repetitions, a phenomenon known as *sensitization.* Sensitization can be described as an increased responsiveness to repeated stimulation, in contrast to the decreased responsivity characteristic of habituation. That tingle you notice on your arm may habituate when you realize it is just your sleeve rubbing. If the tingle was caused by a spider walking on your arm, sensitization will occur, and you will then overreact to the next tingle.

The practical and theoretical challenge is to be able to anticipate whether habituation or sensitization will occur and when it will occur. Subsequent work by Thompson (e.g., Thompson & Glanzman, 1976) revealed that there appeared to be two types of spinal neurons involved in reacting to repetitive eliciting stimuli. Those neurons most directly involved in the reflex arc (sensory nerves carrying input to the spinal neurons, interneurons within the spinal cord, and motor neurons carrying output to the muscles) showed habituation. These were labeled Type H, for habituation, neurons. Other neurons apart from the stimulus–response arc were found to reflect the general level of arousal of the nervous system. These Type S, for sensitization, neurons were activated by the more intense shock stimuli and had the effect of enhancing the responsiveness of the motor neurons. The *dual-process theory* of habituation states that the overall behavioral response to repetitive stimulation depends on the balance between two factors: habituation and sensitization. Which factor predominates depends on the combination of several variables, but primarily on stimulus intensity.

This dual-process theory of habituation and sensitization has several implications (Groves & Thompson, 1970). It suggests that the two processes are independent, and there should be experimental variables that influence one or the other process. An elegant example of the manipulation of sensitization is shown in Davis's (1974) study of the effect of background noise level on the startle response. Two groups of rats received the same series of loud, startle-eliciting tones. The difference was that one group heard these against a background noise level of 60 decibels; the second group had a background level of 80 decibels. Those with the quieter background showed habituation (i.e., less and less startle) over 100 trials; those with the louder background showed sensitization (i.e., more and more startle) across trials. These results suggest that the loud background level activated the Type S neurons to a degree that counteracted the habituation that was occurring in the Type H neurons. In another experiment, Davis showed that exposure to the loud noise immediately before the session with the startle stimuli also produced sensitization, but not if a delay occurred between noise exposure and startle testing. The arousing aftereffects of the noise sensitized responding to immediately following startle stimuli, but with a delay before testing the arousal dissipated and so normal habituation occurred.

Sensitization thus seems to be a transient aftereffect of intense stimulation, and its effect on performance may be due to the increased level of arousal. Thus, sensitization seems to affect performance. Whether it is also an instance of learning is an unresolved issue.

Aplysia: A Model System.   A second example of the physiological approach, like Thompson's, also seeks to discover the underlying synaptic events involved in learning.

Eric Kandel, a physician who decided to go into basic research, studies habituation in a giant marine snail, *Aplysia californica.* This particular snail is used because it has a simple nervous system with few neurons. Many of these nerve cells are relatively large, and their functions are known. But what behaviors can *Aplysia* perform that we can study? *Aplysia* uses a siphon to take in sea water from which food is filtered, and that can be withdrawn back into the body cavity in times of danger. Stimulation of the siphon, either by touch or by a squirt from a water jet, elicits this withdrawal (see Figure 2.2). Siphon withdrawal, controlled by a few identifiable neurons, shows habituation and many of the features listed by Thompson and Spencer (1966).

Both dishabituation and spontaneous recovery of siphon withdrawal to a tactile stimulus are illustrated in Figure 2.3. After six touch stimulations, responding has nearly ceased. This indicates habituation. A light is then flashed as a dishabituator (indicated by *L* on the abscissa), which reinstates responding to the next presentation of the tactile stimulus. The light stimulus is repeated again later, but it has a smaller dishabituating influence when given after the ninth tactile stimulus presentation. A 60-minute rest interval leads to spontaneous recovery of response to the touch stimulus: Presentation of the tactile stimulus produces a large response, which then rehabituates. Once again, the light stimulus produces dishabituation to the tactile stimulus.

By measuring nerve potentials on the stimulus and the response sides of the siphon circuit, Kandel and his colleagues have isolated the change that occurs in habituation to a decrease in the sensitivity of the motor neuron to stimulation by the sensory neuron. Basically, habituation occurs at the synapse between two cells. The sensory neuron, which de-

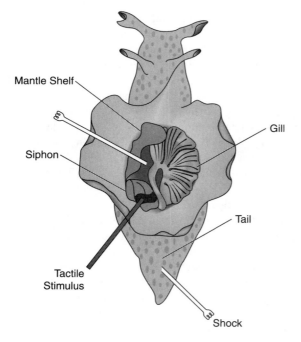

Mantle Shelf

Siphon

Tactile
Stimulus

Gill

Tail

Shock

FIGURE 2.2 *Aplysia,* **an Ocean-dwelling Slug Studied by Eric Kandel.** This view looks down at the *Aplysia* from above. The mantel and other structures are spread apart to show the gill and siphon. Touch by the tactile stimulus causes withdrawal of these parts; repeated tactile stimulation produces habituation; a shock stimulus produces sensitization.

Source: From "Relationships between Dishabituation, Sensitization, and Inhibition of the Gill- and Siphon-Withdrawal Reflex in *Aplysia californica:* Effects of Response Measure, Test Time, and Training Stimulus," by R. D. Hawkins, T. E. Cohen, W. Greene, and E. R. Kandel, 1998, *Behavioral Neuroscience, 112,* p. 25. Copyright © 1998 by the American Psychological Association. Reprinted with permission.

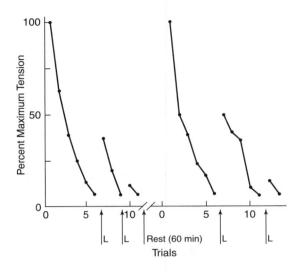

FIGURE 2.3 Habituation of Siphon Withdrawal of *Aplysia* to a Tactile Stimulus. The response measured is the tension of the siphon withdrawal to tactile stimulation. Dishabituation to the tactile stimulus occurs following presentation of a light stimulus.

Source: Lukowiak & Jacklet, 1972.

tects the touch, retains its sensitivity; the motor neuron controlling withdrawal retains its responsivity. Thus, we can rule out sensory adaptation and response fatigue as confounding explanations. The learned change is in the flow of synaptic chemicals between the two nerve cells, so that the sensory neuron does not activate the motor neuron.

Biological psychologists have long sought an *engram,* a word used to refer to the change that occurs in the nervous system to encode new learning. The work of Thompson and Kandel and their students illustrates how contemporary researchers are closing in on the engram. This is obviously basic research, not applied, and it has contributed substantially to our understanding of the neural basis of learning. In fact, Eric Kandel was awarded the Nobel Prize in Medicine or Phsyiology in 2000.

Cognitive Theories

There are several versions of the cognitive approach to habituation, each unique in some respects, but all sharing certain postulates. Orienting responses are said to be elicited by stimuli that are not recognized, that is, stimuli that do not have a representation stored in memory. Repeated presentations of a stimulus lead to the formation of a memory representation of the stimulus. Habituation of orienting indicates the acquisition of that memory.

The Russian psychologist Sokolov, who introduced many Western researchers to the study of orienting reflexes (e.g., Sokolov, 1963a), calls his memory representation the *neuronal model* of the stimulus. Sokolov's theory postulates a comparator mechanism, which compares the current sensory input to the neuronal model to determine whether the stimulus is familiar. An OR is made if the comparator does not find a matching representation in memory, whereas the OR is inhibited if the comparator finds a match. This idea of comparing a stimulus in the environment to one in memory is another characteristic of the cognitive theories.

The theories of Wagner (1976; Whitlow & Wagner, 1984) and Olson (1976), developed from experiments on animals and human infants, respectively, elaborate on the memory system. They state that a stimulus could be represented in short-term memory, long-term memory, or both. The more permanent, durable habituation seen across sessions or over long interstimulus intervals reflects the formation of a long-term representation of the stimulus. This is the learning we have been talking of when we say that the stimulus becomes known or familiar. However, a present stimulus may also be recognized if it has occurred very recently and is still represented in short-term memory. That is, the comparator can attempt to match a current stimulus in the environment with the neuronal model in long-term memory, or with stimuli represented in short-term memory (see Figure 2.4).

Short-term habituation is demonstrated by varying the interval between stimulus repetitions. A given stimulus should elicit a smaller response after a short interval of time since the last stimulus presentation than after a longer interval, even though the total number of repetitions up until that point has been the same. Short-term habituation is illustrated by Davis and Heninger's (1972) study of the magnitude of the eye blinks to a series of sudden white-noise bursts. The time between stimulations varied between 0.5 and 4 seconds, and these intervals were randomly intermixed. The reaction to the noise stimulus was smaller the closer in time that it had followed the previous stimulus. This may be because the repetition after 1 second is represented in short-term memory and is therefore recognized by the comparator. After 4 seconds, the stimulus may no longer be in short-term memory, and the comparator will not find a match there. Note that any short-term effects are in addition to long-term habituation. Even after 4 seconds, there is still an overall decrease in the size of the response across sessions. The comparator can find a match in long-term memory, but this contribution is presumed to be equivalent in the short- and long-interval conditions.

An emphasis on *stimulus* habituation suggests that once a stimulus is habituated, it will no longer evoke an OR. This is not an adequate description of what really happens in habituation. Learning is not simply recognizing that a stimulus is familiar, but also know-

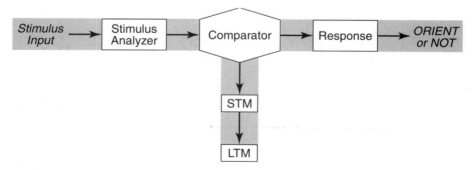

FIGURE 2.4   A Generalized Cognitive Model of Habituation. Stimulus input is compared to representations in short-term memory and in long-term memory. A match between input and what is stored in memory will lead to inhibition of responding. A mismatch will lead to an orienting response.

ing that the stimulus occurs in a particular setting or at a particular time. Cognitive theories incorporate the notion that the neuronal model of a stimulus forms an *expectancy,* or makes an active prediction, for what stimulus will occur, where it will occur, and when. You have probably habituated to the bell that rings in the school halls to signal class changes. If the bell now rings off schedule or if one rang in your home, it would no doubt elicit a startle reaction. This notion is incorporated in Sokolov's (1963a, 1963b) and Wagner's (1976) ideas that the surprising occurrence of a stimulus elicits orienting. An expected occurrence of that same stimulus does not elicit orienting, even though the stimulus is objectively the same in both cases.

The usefulness of a scientific theory is often determined by its power to suggest new research. This is what the cognitive theories have provided by their tests of the neuronal model. Sokolov (1963a) presented his subjects a fixed series of stimuli. For example, each trial might consist of two stimuli, a tone (T) and a light (L) presented in the recurring sequence, T–L. These T–L pairs are repeated until habituation is observed. Then on a test trial, the stimuli are presented in a different order, L–T. Orienting to these stimuli returned. What had been habituated was not simply the stimuli. The subjects also learned that the tone and light occurred in a specific sequence, and so orienting returned when the expected sequence did occur.

Another example of this same idea is known as the *missing stimulus effect* (e.g., Siddle, 1985; Siddle & Lipp, 1997). After exposure to a fixed sequence of stimuli, such as T–L, on test trials, the second stimulus is omitted, so just T–_ occurs. The absence of an expected light stimulus in this case provokes an OR, just after the time when the second stimulus should have occurred. What is really interesting is that an OR is triggered by—nothing. The absence of an expected something elicits orienting. Cognitive theory says that, based on our experiences, we form a memory for a particular pattern of stimulation and an expectancy for certain stimuli to occur at certain times. When environmental events conform to the predictions, less responding is seen. When events violate the expectancy, orienting occurs.

The missing stimulus effect occurs in daily life with the sudden realization that what was expected did not happen: The alarm clock didn't go off, or the phone did not ring when you had been expecting a call. The missing stimulus effect is vividly illustrated by my own experiences with opposite ends of the child-rearing spectrum: suddenly awakening at night because the baby *did not cry* for a late feeding; and 17 years later awakening because *I did not* hear him come home yet.

Explanations of Habituation: Summary.   A response may decrease because the stimulus is not detected (sensory adaptation) or because the response apparatus is temporarily inhibited (effector fatigue). These are two nonlearning explanations that are alternatives to learning-based habituation. Physiological theories of habituation, such as Thompson's, derived from the study of spinal neurons, and Kandel's, from the study of *Aplysia,* seek the physiological and biochemical basis for the changes that underlie habituation. Cognitive theories, those of Sokolov or Wagner, attribute habituation to the acquisition of a memory for the repeated stimulus. This memory eventually includes detailed information about the stimulus, such as its temporal patterning, and the relationship to other stimuli.

Other Effects of Stimulus Exposure *Leave Out*

Simple exposure to a stimulus produces learning that can be revealed by a variety of other behavioral outcomes. Habituation is just one outcome. Learning from exposure to a stimulus can be manifested in several other phenomena.

Preference for Familiar Stimuli

Exposure to a stimulus sometimes leads to an affective, or emotional, change in the preference for the stimulus. This is known as the *mere exposure effect* (Zajonc, 1968), so-called because the stimulus has merely been presented in the absence of rewards, problems, or other tasks that might actively evoke stimulus processing. Both animals and humans show this increased liking of familiar stimuli. Abraham Maslow (1937), later known for his contributions to humanistic psychology, conducted a study in which his experimental participants performed a number of tasks across several evenings in a laboratory setting. Some tasks were re-

---

BOX 2.2

Avoidance and Preference for New Food Tastes

Many animals are reluctant at first to consume new foods. This makes good evolutionary sense, to be cautious about new foods whose effects on the body are unknown. *Taste neophobia,* or fear of new tastes, is a robust phenomenon among certain animal species. Some phenomena we have considered in this chapter, habituation and mere exposure, suggest that taste neophobia could be overcome by simple exposure to the new food. Indeed, animal researchers often must incorporate this as a preliminary stage in a research study. We realize the animal subjects will need to adapt, or get used to, the various food reinforcers to be employed.

The reduction of neophobia via exposure has been experimentally demonstrated. Domjan (1976) gave rats 30 minutes daily access to a solution of saccharin in water, a new taste for the rats. Saccharin consumption increased across the 20 days of the study. In another experiment, longer periods of access each day also led to increased drinking of the saccharin solution.

Is the reduction of taste neophobia purely a habituation effect? Taste learning might involve

something more, specifically learning that the food is safe to eat. This is referred to as the *learned safety* hypothesis. Learning that a food is not poisonous is different from learning to ignore a stimulus that is without consequence, as a habituation explanation might suggest. Rats given a single exposure to a distinctive flavor later were retarded in learning an aversion to this taste when it did cause illness, what is called a latent inhibition effect (Siegel, 1974). Exposure to illness after a new taste can also increase neophobia in general, as the organism becomes cautious about any novel tastes.

Getting children to eat new foods is often a challenge. Can exposure to a new food increase liking? Most of us have heard the line "I tried it once; I didn't like it." The problem is, once is not enough. Studies of adults (Pliner, 1982) and children (Birch & Marlin, 1982) have shown that many exposures, 10 or more, may be necessary to induce acceptance of new cheeses or juices.

peated, for example, copying sentences or reading lists of foreign names. Other tasks were used as distractors to mask the true purpose of the study, for example, completing personality inventories. When subsequently asked to judge their preferences, subjects choose familiar tasks, the familiar lab, and even the familiar pictures that had been on the wall!

Animals also develop a preference for the familiar, especially places or foods (Hill, 1978). Rats are at first wary of a new food, taste, or odor. This *neophobia,* or literally "fear of the new," declines with continued (safe) exposure to the food. Rats exposed to a saccharine solution will at first drink very little, but eventually come to prefer it over other less familiar tastes (see Box 2.2 for a further discussion of food neophobia). Apparently, here familiarity breeds liking and not contempt.

In one demonstration of the mere-exposure effect, college-aged and elderly subjects were shown a list of Japanese ideograms (Wiggs, 1993). These are complex symbols representing words or ideas, and that are unfamiliar to U.S. subjects. Each stimulus was presented for 2 seconds. Later, these ideograms and some new ones were presented and the subjects were asked to rate their "liking" of each stimulus on a seven-point scale. The results, shown in Figure 2.5, show average liking of stimuli by the two age groups as a function of how often the stimuli had been presented during the mere exposure phase. Stimuli seen three times previously were more liked than stimuli seen once or never before. These liking effects were found with both age groups.

According to the cognitive theories of stimulus learning, exposure leads to the formation of a memory for the stimulus. It would thus seem obvious that this memory could be tested simply by asking subjects if they remember the stimulus (e.g., have them choose the familiar one from an array of distractors). But what if the subjects could not recognize the previously experienced stimulus—if they simply could not "remember" it? Would they still prefer it? The intriguing possibility is that the affect, expressed as a liking or preference, is

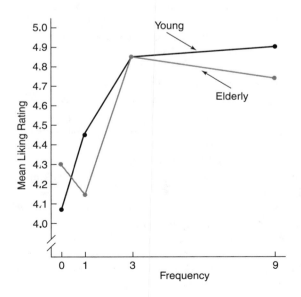

FIGURE 2.5   Liking for Japanese Ideogram Stimuli. Graph plots mean liking rating by elderly and young adult subjects who had previously seen each stimulus 1, 3, or 9 times, or had never seen it.

Source: From "Aging and Memory for Frequency of Occurrence of Novel, Visual Stimuli: Direct and Indirect Measures," by C. L. Wiggs, 1993, *Psychology and Aging, 8,* p. 406. Copyright © 1993 by the American Psychological Association. Reprinted with permission.

a separable judgment from conscious memory for the stimulus. Kunst-Wilson and Zajonc (1980) tested this hypothesis by flashing pictures of irregularly shaped nonsense objects at a speed faster than their subjects could consciously perceive them. Later, the subjects were shown pairs of shapes and were asked one of two questions: Which shapes had they seen before and which shapes did they like better? Performance on the memory test for the previously seen shapes was at chance levels: The subjects could not correctly distinguish between the old shapes and new ones presented for the first time during testing. This finding seems perfectly reasonable, because the images had initially been presented for such a short duration that they could not be consciously perceived, much less remembered. However, when asked which objects they liked, there was a consistent preference for the preexposed shape. The subjects seemed to prefer these objects even though they did not recognize the shapes as familiar.

Similarly, Wilson (1979) asked his participants to attend to a story presented to one ear through headphones while ignoring a tone pattern that was played to the other ear. On a subsequent test for the tone pattern, the participants were asked to identify the presented tonal pattern in comparison with other test patterns. The experimental participants could not correctly choose the correct from incorrect patterns. Yet when asked to rate their preferences, the participants liked the tonal patterns they had previously heard more than those played for the first time. Oddly, Wilson's paper has the incongruous subtitle "exposure effects without learning." Wilson was referring to learning in this case as conscious awareness and recall, and not to the unaware learning of the tone pattern exhibited through preference testing.

The interpretation of Zajonc's mere exposure effects with unattended stimuli has aroused controversy concerning the independence of emotional preferences from memory (Lazarus, 1982). For our purposes, the study by Kunst-Wilson and Zajonc (1980) is an important demonstration of the fact that experience can have a variety of effects, not all of which are subject to conscious recall. How general are such effects outside the lab? Littman and Manning (1954) found that smokers could not correctly select their brand of cigarette in a blind taste test from among several others. But when asked to pick which cigarette tasted better, they consistently (and unknowingly) chose their usual brand. Mere exposure may also play a role in the effectiveness of advertising. A preference is induced simply because the product has become more familiar.

We have emphasized learning about stimuli presented subliminally or in other ways to block conscious learning. But the effects of exposure on preference also readily occur with stimuli presented for longer durations. One review of the extensive literature of exposure and affect suggests that a few, brief, distributed exposures produce more positive affects than do the reverse conditions: many, long, massed exposures (Bornstein, 1989). Why does mere exposure make a stimulus more pleasing? One possibility is that organisms have preferred or optimal levels of arousal. Unknown stimuli may be too arousing, maybe even fear-evoking in animals, whereas very familiar stimuli are not arousing enough. A few exposures to a stimulus are sufficient to habituate some of its stimulating properties, but not so much as to make it boring (Berlyne, 1969). Alternatively, a perceptual fluency hypothesis states that we affectively prefer stimuli that are easily perceived. That is, images, sounds, tastes, and so on that are more readily perceived because of previous experience are more preferred. Several exposures to a difficult-to-read word should increase our perceptual fluency in reading that word. Fluency was demonstrated in a series of studies that did not include preexposures, but instead adjusted the stimulus conditions to make perception easier or more difficult (such as varying the contrast between figure and background). Conditions that facilitated visual perception also increased preference (Reber, Winkielmanm, & Schwartz, 1998).

Perceptual Learning

Exposure to a stimulus can affect later learning about the stimulus. It seems reasonable to suppose that we could more easily use a familiar stimulus for new learning than attempting new learning with an unfamiliar stimulus. For example, it should be easier to attach a familiar name to a new face than an unfamiliar name. One truism about learning is the more you know, the more you can learn. Once we have learned to perceive, recognize, or identify a stimulus, it is easier to learn other things about this stimulus, such as its name or its use. We call this *perceptual learning.*

In Gibson and Walk's (1956) classic perceptual learning experiment, young rats were continuously exposed in their home cages to cutouts of a triangle and a circle for 90 days. Subsequently, these same stimuli were used as cues in a discrimination experiment. One of the shapes would be used to identify the correct turn in a simple maze that led to the food-rewarded goal box. The other shape marked the incorrect choice that led to the nonrewarded goal. Gibson and Walk found that subjects given the preexposures learned the discrimination in the maze faster. This makes sense. The experimental subjects had already learned to distinguish between the two shapes, just as we had to do when we were children, and could proceed immediately to connecting one with reward and the other with nonreward. The control subjects without prior exposure to the shapes still had to master this discrimination between circle and triangle. *Perceptual Learning,* both the subject and the title of an award-winning book by Eleanor Gibson (1969), is a robust phenomenon in animals and humans. Simply stated, prior experience with a stimulus can facilitate later learning about the stimulus.

Researchers have studied perceptual learning using numerous classes of stimuli, from colors and faces to reading X-ray negatives. Simple exposure to different stimuli does not ensure learning to differentiate among them. When asked to select the picture of a penny from among eight versions shown, few people could identify the real one (Nickerson & Adams, 1979). (Does Lincoln face right or left?) Perceptual differentiation among stimuli seems to require attentional weighting: increasing our attention to features that distinguish among stimuli (Goldstone, 1998). In the penny example, we assign a higher weight to the color "copper," to differentiate a penny from a dime, than to which direction Lincoln is facing. (He is facing to our right.)

Perceptual learning occurs in learning to discriminate language sounds, such as "ba" and "da," or the *r/l* difference that is present in English (but not in Japanese). Adult English language users differentiate these sounds. However, the language Hindi has a pair of *t* sounds, which adult speakers of Hindi differentiate but which English-speaking adults do not. Do we learn to differentiate sounds in our language through exposure? Or is the capacity to discriminate there to begin with, and we lose those differences that are not present in the language we are hearing? Werker (1989) studies infant perceptual categorization, and finds that infants in English-speaking environments can discriminate the two Hindi *t*'s at 6 months of age, but lose this ability between ages 8 and 12 months. Experience may both promote new categories of knowledge and may also prevent the loss of existing categories.

A reverse effect also can be produced by preexposure. If habituation means that we learn to ignore a repetitive and meaningless stimulus, then we should have trouble learning something new about the habituated stimulus. Does familiarization with a stimulus make it easier or more difficult to learn to use the stimulus as a signal? One possible resolution seems to be whether the exposed stimulus is subsequently trained in the same place in which the preexposures occurred or in a different context (Hall & Channell, 1985; Hall & Schachtman, 1987). If the triangle is presented day after day without food in a laboratory apparatus and then food is suddenly introduced, the subject will have difficulty realizing that the triangle has anything to do with the food reward. After all, the appearance of the triangle did not correlate with food introduction. If the preexposures occur in one context, such as the home cage as in Gibson and Walk's experiments, and the reward learning occurs in a different context, as the maze being located in a different room, dishabituation may occur when the subject moves from one context to another. The familiar stimulus is now noticed, and so the triangle–food connection may develop quicker.

Priming Facilitation

One hypothesis for stimulus exposure effects presented earlier was the perceptual fluency idea. A sort of short-term facilitation of fluency can be produced by a single preexposure to a stimulus given just before the target stimulus occurrence. *Priming* occurs when one presentation of a stimulus facilitates the processing of a closely following repetition of the same or a related stimulus. For example, if a series of words are briefly flashed on a computer screen for you to read, one occurrence of the word TABLE will produce faster identification of, or reaction to, a repetition of the word TABLE. The to-be-identified stimulus has been primed, meaning that the processes necessary to perceive, identify, and emit this word have already been activated.

Priming was demonstrated in a study by Hamann, Squire, and Schacter (1995). A long series of words were first presented. The subjects, adults in this case, were simply asked to rate each word on a five-point scale of how pleasant they thought each word was. In the next phase of the experiment, some of these rated words and some new words were flashed on a screen for durations ranging from 33 to 83 milliseconds. The task here was to read off each word, if possible. The results are shown in Figure 2.6. As can be seen, very few words could be identified from 33-millisecond exposures, but most could be read with the longer exposures. The more relevant finding in the present discussion is that the primed words, those seen earlier in the session, were more likely to be identified from brief exposures. New words could not be perceived at these presentation durations. Priming facilitated word identification.

Test words can be presented in other ways so as to make identification difficult. For instance, the words could be presented auditorily but partially masked by white noise to reduce detectability, or presented as a fragment with missing letters (H__D for HERD). In each case, the primed word is more readily identified (heard, seen, or completed), even though other words are possible alternatives (e.g., BIRD, which sounds or looks like the primed word HERD). (Priming facilitation will be discussed in subsequent chapters.)

Priming is often studied in reaction-time tasks. If the subject is asked to respond to some stimulus, reactions are faster in the stimulus that has just occurred than if the same

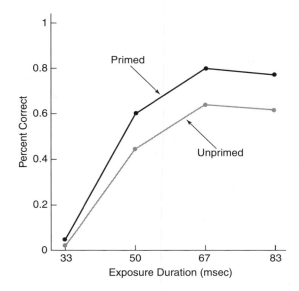

FIGURE 2.6　Effects of Priming on Perceptual Word Identification. Some words were rated for pleasantness earlier in the session. During testing, words are flashed on a screen for durations ranging from 33 to 83 milliseconds and the subjects attempted to identify the words. The "primed" words (i.e., those that had been seen earlier in the session) were identified more readily than were unprimed (new words).

Source: Hamann, Squire, & Schacter, 1995, p. 11.

stimulus had not occurred or if some unrelated stimulus was presented. The speeded reactions due to priming might seem to be at odds with the reduced attention to a repeated stimulus that defines habituation. Is processing of a repeated stimulus facilitated or inhibited? Again, the answer seems to be "both." One can react quickly to a stimulus while attending to it less. One recent study found that a priming presentation of a stimulus word indeed produced faster reaction to a repetition of the word; but the primed word was less likely to be recalled later when memory for the stimulus words was tested (Wagner, Maril, & Schacter, 2000).

Recapitulation: The Effects of Repeated Stimulus Presentation

Our consideration of the extensive research literature on the effects of exposure to a given stimulus event shows multiple, and frankly conflicting, results may be found. A repeated stimulus can be reacted to more quickly; that is, the first occurrence of a stimulus can prime reactions to a second occurrence. Seeing the word DOG will facilitate reading it again shortly afterwards. Familiarization can also lead to a liking or preference for the now-familiar stimulus, what we called the *mere exposure effect.* A lengthy series of repetitions of a meaningless stimulus can lead to *habituation,* or a decrease in orienting to the stimulus; or to *sensitization,* an increase in responding. Habituation could interfere with later learning that the stimulus is significant. How can one learn about a stimulus that is being ignored? On the other hand, familiarization with a stimulus can facilitate new learning, what Gibson called *perceptual learning.* This pattern of opposite effects from ostensibly the same manipulation, stimulus exposure, is disconcerting. However, there are some rules making the outcome of a particular manipulation somewhat more predictable.

Applications

Habituation certainly occurs outside the laboratory, often in some fairly mundane ways. That reminder you posted on the refrigerator, too far in advance, becomes unnoticed by the time you need to act on it. Filmmakers using animals have to habituate them to the sights and sounds of the set. You decide to study in a new place, thinking there will be less distraction, but in fact there is more distraction as you orient to this new environment.

The habituation of background office noises was explicitly investigated in a laboratory simulation (Banbury & Berry, 1997). The students attempted to study some prose while office noises, and sometimes also speech sounds, were played in the background. The noise initially disrupted learning, but after 20 minutes of exposure, the noise was less disruptive. As with other forms of habituation, a brief interval without stimulation restored the disruptive effect of the noise.

Other instances of habituation have considerably more significance.

Habituation to Warning Signals

Warning signals, signs, and notices are used to inform us and steer us away from potentially dangerous behaviors. However, the constant presence or repetition of a warning can lead to habituation: The warning is simply not noticed. What we know about habituation can be used to retard its development (e.g., Wogalter & Laughery, 1996). For example, altering the characteristics of the warning from time to time should slow habituation. The surgeon general's warnings on cigarette packages are varied in part because people habituate to a single repeated message.

Another approach is to force people to acknowledge the warning. My computer, for example, asks me if I am sure I want to delete something. I have to respond "yes" before deletion occurs. Unfortunately, many of us now automatically hit the "yes" button before thinking about the warning message, only to realize too late what the question was.

Exposure Therapy for Fears

An application of considerable importance is the use of stimulus exposures in treating anxiety and phobias. These methods, sometimes called *emotional flooding* or *implosion,* use controlled exposure to feared stimuli or situations. The idea is that repeated or prolonged exposure will reduce the fear provoked by the stimuli. If you have a fear of flying, your therapist might at some point prescribe a long plane flight. If you fear snakes, attendance at the Indiana Jones Film Festival may be suggested.

(Some therapies go a step further by pairing the phobic object with pleasant consequences such as relaxation. These counterconditioning therapies are discussed in the next chapter.)

Exposure therapy often starts off with presentation of a milder version of the phobic object and gradually increases its intensity or proximity across presentations. This gradually reduces the fear and the subject comes to tolerate the phobic object. An example from animal behavioral therapy is a report by Tuber, Hothersall, and Voith (1974). They treated a large dog named Goliath who was fearful during thunderstorms: The dog ran around the room, jumping on furniture, knocking over things, and generally causing mayhem. Treatment consisted of playing a thunderstorm sound effects recording, starting at a low volume that did not elicit fear. The volume was gradually increased as the dog came to tolerate the noise without adverse reaction, until the recording could be played at high volume. The researchers said the dog did not react to real thunder sounds afterwards.

Is gradual acclimation to the sound better than exposure to the full-intensity sound from the start? Some researchers find that a lower final level of response to an intense sound is achieved by using gradual increments from weak to strong stimuli (Davis & Wagner, 1969), whereas others find that there is more habituation by using the intense stimuli from the start (Thompson et al., 1973). If we recall the dual-process theory of sensitization and habituation, the discrepant findings of stimulus intensity may be attributed to the amount of sensitization elicited by the intense stimuli, which counteracts the habituation that occurs. Consideration of some further examples may offer more definitive advice for clinical use.

A therapist cannot always expose patients to the actual phobic stimulus. Wolpe (1969) used *imaginal flooding* procedures in which the subjects are asked to imagine their worst fears. For example, one client was a dentist who would not give anesthesia injections for fear of his patient dying. Wolpe had the dentist vividly imagine giving the injection, standing back, and seeing the patient slump forward dead. Not surprisingly, the dentist was upset by these images (i.e., "Dr. E. became profoundly disturbed, sweating, weeping and wringing his hands," p. 190). Wolpe had the dentist repeat the mental scene a few more times, and the fear and emotionality decreased each time. After this treatment, the dentist was able to give injections in his practice.

Do exposure therapies work? They have proved difficult to evaluate because of the many variations across clinical research studies: different versions of exposure therapy; combinations of exposure with medication, relaxation, or insight therapy; in vivo exposure to actual phobic stimuli or exposure in imagination as Wolpe used; students who volunteer as subjects versus clinic patients who seek therapy; and the criteria for evaluating success of the therapy. Linden's (1981) review generally found positive results (from 50 to 100 percent improvement) across these many variations in procedure, although complete remission was rare. Some patients (10 to 20 percent) required additional treatment. Wolpe (1969) reported some successes but also some failures with flooding alone, and recommended that exposure be combined with other therapy (specifically, systematic desensitization, discussed in the next chapter). Interestingly, his successful procedures use gradual introduction and incremental exposures to the feared event.

Summary

Habituation is a simple form of learning. Yet however simple, the fact is that exposures to a stimulus have complex effects on the organism's subsequent reactions to that stimulus.

The Orienting Response

A novel stimulus elicits an orienting response, a composite of physiological and behavioral reactions that includes startle, sense-receptor focusing, increased arousal, and a readiness for fight or flight. A familiar stimulus can also elicit orienting, especially if the stimulus is meaningful or unexpected.

Habituation

Habituation is the decrease in size or frequency of the orienting reaction to a stimulus that is repeatedly presented. Habituation is a simple form of learning. Habituation of orienting applies to neutral or innocuous stimuli, although defensive reactions to painful and noxious stimuli also show habituation.

Habituation is studied via responses such as startle, eye blink, changes in blood flow, or galvanic skin response. A widely used measure with infants is the change in duration or number of eye fixations to visual stimuli.

Thompson and Spencer described several parametric features of habituation. These features represent a standard set of criteria for evaluating habituation across different species, tasks, or responses. More frequent repetitions of a stimulus produce a greater decrement in the size or frequency of the response. If the stimulus is withheld for a period of time, the response tends to recover. Habituation is affected by the spacing between successive stimulus presentations. Massed stimulations produce more habituation in the short term; spaced repetitions sometimes produce more long-term habituation as assessed hours or days later. The presentation of a different stimulus will temporarily restore orienting to the first stimulus, a phenomenon called dishabituation. Habituation is stimulus-specific. Responding diminishes specifically to the repeated stimulus, not to all novel stimuli, although habituation may generalize to similar stimuli.

Explanations of Habituation

A response decrement could occur for reasons other than learning. Sensory adaptation or effector fatigue are two such possibilities.

One physiological theory, the dual-process theory, states that the response to repetitive stimulation reflects the combination of habituation and sensitization. Type H neurons show habituation, whereas Type S neurons react to intense levels of stimulation and increase responsiveness. For example, the startle response actually increases across stimulations if tested against a sensitizing loud background noise level.

Another biological approach is to study habituation in *Aplysia*. Siphon withdrawal, controlled by a few identifiable neurons, shows many of the parametric features of habituation. By measuring nerve potentials on the stimulus and the response sides of the siphon circuit, Kandel has found that habituation is a decrease in the sensitivity of the motor neuron to stimulation by the sensory neuron.

Cognitive theories hypothesize that a neuronal model of the stimulus is stored in memory. Sensory input is compared to this neuronal model. Habituation occurs when there is a match, and orienting occurs when a new stimulus deviates from the model. Modern theories postulate a stimulus can be stored in either short-term or long-term memory. Short-term habituation is demonstrated by varying the interval between stimulus repetitions. There is a smaller response after a short interval than after a longer interval. The neuronal model also accommodates dishabituation due to changes in the sequence of stimuli, and responding to the absence of an expected stimulus (the missing stimulus effect).

Other Effects of Stimulus Exposure

Exposure to a stimulus sometimes leads to a preference or liking of the stimulus. This is known as the mere exposure effect because the stimulus has merely been presented.

Kunst-Wilson and Zajonc presented pictures of nonsense drawings at a speed faster than could be consciously perceived. Later, performance on a memory test for the previously seen shapes was at chance levels: The participants could not correctly choose between old and new shapes. However, in a test of preferences, participants consistently preferred the preexposed shape. The participants liked these objects even though they did not recognize the shapes as familiar.

Perceptual learning refers to the ease of forming associations between familiar stimuli and other stimuli. Rats who were familiarized with shape cutouts in their home cages later readily learned to use these shapes as signals for reward. Habituation to various tone or light stimuli can retard later learning of connections between these stimuli and other stimuli, such as reward. The same nominal procedure, stimulus exposure, leads to opposite effects. One explanation for this discrepancy is that habituation occurs when exposure and training occur in the same context; switching contexts produces dishabituation, which facilitates learning.

Applications

Our knowledge of habituation can be used to reduce habituation to important stimuli, for instance, by sustaining attention to warning signals and labels. This may be done by varying the signals or requiring active acknowledgment from the subject.

Stimulus exposure is used in treating anxiety and phobias. This method, sometimes called emotional flooding or implosion therapy, uses controlled exposure to feared stimuli or situations. Exposure begins with a milder version of the phobic object and gradually increases in intensity or proximity across presentations. Exposure may be to the actual phobic object itself, or imaginal flooding can be used in which the subjects imagine their phobic objects or situations.

Do exposure therapies work? They have proved difficult to evaluate because of many variations in subject populations, procedures, and assessment criteria used across clinical research studies. Although Wolpe reports some success with his patients, he recommends combining exposure with other methods of therapy.

Classical Conditioning

Most students have some general familiarity with Pavlov's experiments. In a typical salivary conditioning experiment on dogs, the sound of the bell was followed a few seconds later by the presentation of some food. Several of these bell–food trials were administered and salivation to the bell was monitored. After several pairings, the dog began to salivate during the bell (Pavlov, 1927/1960, which is the standard reference to G. V. Anrep's translation). Classical conditioning, or Pavlovian conditioning as this procedure is also known, suffers from something of a multiple-personality problem. On the one hand, it historically has been considered to be a simple, almost reflexive form of learning that does not require sophisticated nervous system involvement. Conditioning simply transfers a response from one stimulus to another. Only a limited and rather inflexible set of behaviors can be conditioned. These beliefs underlie popular culture references to someone who responds like "Pavlov's dog," a caricature promoted by writers such as Aldous Huxley (in his *Brave New World*) to the Rolling Stones.

On the other hand, researchers have long known that conditioning is more complex than any popular stereotype suggests. Osgood, in the standard textbook of experimental psychology from the 1950s, wrote, "Naivete with regard to conditioning is due...more to the fond hope that the process would prove as simple as conventional diagrams imply. The phenomena of conditioning are actually very complicated" (1953, p. 316). Contemporary theories of conditioning have a distinctly cognitive flavor in describing this complexity. "Pavlovian conditioning is not a stupid process by which the organism willy-nilly forms associations between any two stimuli that happen to co-occur. Rather, the organism is better seen as an information seeker using logical and perceptual relations among events …to form a sophisticated representation of the world" (Rescorla, 1988, p. 154). By using the knowledge learned in conditioning, organisms can flexibly, not simply reflexively, respond in an adaptive fashion.

Research on classical conditioning has gone through cycles in its 100-year history. At first eagerly grasped by behaviorists as a tool to study associative learning, Pavlovian conditioning was replaced by operant conditioning with its emphasis on the modification of voluntary behavior by reinforcement. However, research into Pavlovian conditioning once again became popular (e.g., *Classical Conditioning: The New Hegemony,* Turkkan, 1989). What factors contributed to this renewed dominance of Pavlovian conditioning? Why have psychologists accorded classical conditioning such an important place in their research and theorizing on learning? Some researchers consider the role that learning through classical conditioning serves in ensuring survival, viewing conditioning from an ecological or evolutionary perspective (Hollis, 1997). Applications of conditioning to new areas such as drug tolerance, the immune system, and cardiovascular functioning have connected conditioning to the field of health psychology. And classical conditioning offers model systems for neuroscientists to study the biology and physiology of learning.

Possibly foremost among our reasons for studying classical conditioning is that it is a method used by basic researchers to study associative learning. *Associative learning* refers to the hypothesized connections that are formed between the internal representations of events, such as stimuli and responses, during learning. Via associations, one item comes to activate the representation of the another. A simple illustration is word associations, for example, the stimulus word TABLE often evokes CHAIR as a response. But when and how are associations formed? Classical conditioning is one tool we can use to study the conditions under which associative learning occurs.

The Definition of Classical Conditioning

Simply put, *classical conditioning* can be defined as the presentation of two (or more) events in an experimentally determined temporal relationship. A change in responding to one of those events is measured as an indication of whether an association has been learned between them. The learning that occurs in classical conditioning can be validly described on several levels: behaviorally, as the learning of a new response; cognitively, as the acquisition of knowledge about the relationship between stimuli; or neurally, as the pattern of synaptic changes that underlie conditioning.

Say we are to perform an experiment in which mild but aversive electric shocks are to be presented randomly in time. Because of our ethical discomfort with shocking animals or college students, let us suppose the participants are all faculty in the Economics Department. The shocks, delivered to the participants' forearm, are unavoidable, but our participants would desperately like to know when each is about to occur. We arrange for a tone to sound for a few seconds before each shock. What will the participants learn about the two stimuli? After several pairings of tone followed by shock, the tone will probably come to elicit a behavioral reaction of hand flexion; physiological reactions such as muscular tensing or bracing; and knowledge of the tone–shock relationship that can be verbalized. Any or all of these responses may possibly occur and could indicate that an association was acquired between the two stimuli.

Classical conditioning is a procedure that incorporates several features illustrated in the preceding example. First, two stimuli are presented. One stimulus is significant to the subject at the start of the experiment, such as food or shock. This is labeled the *unconditioned stimulus (or US)*. It elicits the *unconditioned response* (or UR), often reflexively without prior training. For example, in Pavlov's experiments, food served as the US to elicit salivation as the UR. The second stimulus, such as a tone, light, or bell, is called the *conditioned stimulus* (or CS). This stimulus is actually a to-be-conditioned stimulus at the onset of the experiment. The CS is a neutral stimulus, but neutral only in the sense that it does not now elicit the same response as does the US. For example, the tone at first does not evoke flexion or salivation. Certainly, if the tone is novel, it will evoke orienting reactions (as described in Chapter 2).

The CS and the US are presented in an experimentally specified order and temporal spacing, usually in the sequence of CS first followed by the US. In Pavlov's experiments, a tone might sound for a few seconds and then food powder would be pumped via a tube into the dog's mouth (see Figure 3.1). After a sufficient number of pairings, the CS may come to elicit some of the responses originally elicited by the US. Thus, salivation occurs to the tone. This response during the CS (tone) is called the *conditioned response* (or CR). The development of a conditioned response to the CS is taken as an indication that conditioning has occurred.

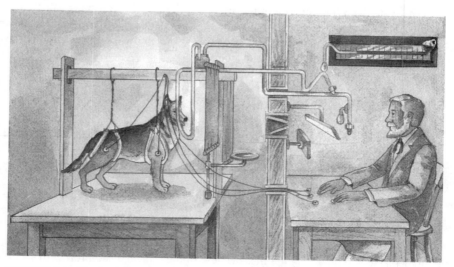

FIGURE 3.1   Pavlov's Salivary Conditioning Apparatus.

Source: From *Understanding Human Behavior* (p. 88), by C. R. Mynatt and M. E. Doherty, 1999, Boston: Allyn & Bacon. Copyright © 1999 by Allyn & Bacon. Reprinted by permission.

(More appropriate translations of Pavlov's terms would be unconditio*nal* and conditio*nal*. A response is unconditionally elicited by the US at the start of the experiment, but a response to the CS is conditional on the pairing operation. However, psychologists' habit of using the *-ed* ending is hard to break.)

Because the conditioned—and unconditioned—responses are both salivation, how do we determine which stimulus is eliciting the salivation? *Conditioned* responding usually occurs during the CS, before the onset of the US. That is, the dog salivates during the several seconds the tone is on before food is presented on that trial. Thus, a CR is sometimes referred to as an anticipatory response. We can also intersperse CS-alone test trials, omitting the US, among the conditioning trials. In this manner we can see responding to the CS in the absence of any response elicited by the US.

Methods of Studying Classical Conditioning

Pavlov's procedure of salivary conditioning is infrequently used today. The tendency is to use smaller animals or to use humans, both of which are more economical in time and money, or to use preparations that are relevant to a specific application. A few exemplar methods referred to often in this chapter are described below, but these examples do not exhaust the list of techniques (see Table 3.1).

Some Representative Procedures

Eyeblink Conditioning. One commonly used procedure is *eyeblink conditioning.* Here the US is a puff of air directed toward the eye, which elicits an eyeblink as the UR (and other responses as well, such as heart rate changes, but typically only one response is measured at a time). A CS, such as a tone, can be presented just before the airpuff US. The CR would be

TABLE 3.1 Examples of the Stimuli Used and Responses Measured in Sample Conditioning Tasks Described in This Chapter

TASK:	Salivary Conditioning	Eye-Blink Conditioning	Taste-Aversion Learning	Morphine Tolerance	Fear Learning (Watson & Raynor)
A CS → US:	tone → food	tone → airpuff	saccharin → poison	room → morphine	rat → loud noise
UR:	salivation	blink	illness	analgesia	fear[a]
B CS → :	tone →	tone →	saccharin →	room →	rat →
CR:	salivation	blink	aversion	pain increase	fear[a]

A: on CS–US conditioning trials; **B:** on CS-alone test trials after conditioning has occurred.

[a]"Fear" is a nonspecific term that refers to startle, crying, or attempts to escape the source of the fear.

an eyeblink that occurs to the CS. The eyeblink can be detected by monitoring electrical potentials generated by the eye muscles and recorded from surface electrodes on the skin around the eye. Alternatively, movement of the lid can be detected when the blink breaks a light beam reflected off the eye. In either case, a signal from the recording device is fed into a polygraph or computer. From this record, the size of the blink can be measured.

The eyeblink response has been used with dogs, cats, and even rats, although with some difficulties (Gormezano, 1966; Osgood, 1953). However, many animals, such as cats, are not that cooperative about having apparatus strapped to their heads. Rabbits and humans are more accommodating (well, maybe passive) and each therefore has been the source of much of our recent data. The rabbit preparation has been especially useful in mapping out the neural circuitry involved in eyeblink conditioning. Conditioning human participants is convenient in that participants are often available, and an experiment can usually be completed within a single session.

GSR.   Another measure of conditioning is the change in the amplitude of the galvanic skin response, or GSR. This measure of the electrical conductivity of the skin varies with subtle changes in the level of emotionality of the subject. As noted in Chapter 2, the GSR also varies as part of an orienting response. The GSR is measured via electrodes usually placed on the arm or palm. A US such as a loud noise or a mild shock will cause an increase in the GSR as the unconditioned response. On conditioning trials, a CS such as a soft tone or a light is followed afterwards with the US, and after several of these pairings, a conditioned GSR elevation may occur during the CS.

Eyeblink and GSR conditioning procedures fit the traditional definition of classical conditioning, one that closely follows Pavlov's original method by using well-defined stimuli and responses (Gormezano & Kehoe, 1975). In contemporary research, however, the label of "classical conditioning" is often applied to situations that deviate from the traditional in any of several ways. Some procedures do not have a reflex-eliciting US, the unconditioned response is not specifically recorded or measured, the CR is not the same as the UR, or conditioning is assessed indirectly by the effects that the conditioned stimulus has on other behaviors. Each of these characteristics is illustrated in one or another of the conditioning preparations described in what follows.

Conditioned Taste Aversion.   At one time or another, most of us have probably acquired a food aversion after becoming ill, even if the food itself did not cause the illness. One researcher referred to this as the "sauce Bernaise" effect (Seligman, 1972). Experimental studies of taste aversion typically employ rats as participants. To condition an aversion, a novel taste, saccharin-flavored water for instance, is presented as the CS, which is followed by an injection of an illness-inducing drug as the US. The UR is sometimes referred to as "gastrointestinal distress," although typically no direct measurements are made of the extent or magnitude of the rat's sickness. After the animal has recovered from its illness, the taste CS is represented to assess the degree of conditioning. Learning is indicated by a decrease in the amount of saccharin-flavored water consumed or by avoidance of the saccharin flavor, as compared to consumption prior to conditioning. Note that gastrointestinal distress to the taste CS is not directly measured as a CR. Instead, conditioning is indirectly assessed by the participant's tendency to avoid the taste, hence, the label "taste-aversion learning." Actually, a variety of behaviors, some species-specific, have been observed as indications of an acquired aversion to the conditioned food. Cats shake it off their paws, coyotes bury it, and rats will tip over the food cup (Gustavson, 1977).

Learning which foods are poisonous has obvious survival value. Unlike more traditional responses, such as salivation or the eyeblink, taste aversions are acquired after only a single taste–illness pairing, and are learned with wide temporal separation between the taste and the illness. For these reasons, taste aversions can be learned inadvertently. Chemotherapy used in treating cancer produces gastrointestinal distress as a side effect, and patients will sometimes develop an aversion to those foods consumed shortly prior to treatment (Bernstein & Webster, 1980; Carey & Burish, 1988).

Evaluative Conditioning.   In *evaluative conditioning,* an affectively neutral stimulus, one that is neither particularly liked or disliked, is presented along with another stimulus that already evokes an affective evaluation. We then see if the emotional tone of the neutral stimulus changes as a function of this conditioning experience. The stimuli, both neutral and affective, are often words, names, faces, or pictures. The *evaluative conditioning* procedure does not use reflex evoking USs, and depends on the participants' ratings (or evaluations) as measures of the CR and UR. Still, the procedure is frequently referred to in conditioning terms (Davey, 1994; Martin & Levey, 1987).

One recent example of evaluative conditioning used samples of both German and U.S. college students as participants (Hammerl, Bloch, & Silverthorne, 1997). The USs were scenic photographs of city, park, and public locations that were rated very high or very low on a scale of "liking." Other pictures, rated as being fairly neutral on this scale, were used as the CSs. Each neutral picture was then presented for 2 seconds, followed by a liked or disliked picture for 2 seconds. Five of these pairing trials were given. What the participants actually see is a long series of slides arranged in a particular sequence in which a neutral slide is immediately followed by one of the liked (or disliked) slides. A cover story is used to try to mask the true purpose of the experiment. The participants are later asked to rate the individual pictures for liking. The neutral pictures that had been paired with liked stimuli received more positive ratings than they had before; the neutral slides paired with disliked pictures now received more negative ratings.

Gorn (1982) used evaluative conditioning to demonstrate how advertising affects product preferences. He showed slide images of a product, a ball-point pen, during music that had been rated by other U.S. college students as pleasant (music from the film *Grease*) or unpleasant (classical Indian music). Evaluative conditioning was measured by allowing the students to choose from among pens of various colors. The pen chosen more often was of the color paired with the preferred music, and the pen chosen less often was of the color paired with the disliked music.

Evaluative conditioning illustrates how attitudes might be conditioned. Staats and Staats (1958) showed slides naming nationalities (Dutch, French, Swedish), and at the same time words were presented through headphones that had either a positive or negative evaluation (words such as GIFT and SACRED, or UGLY and FAILURE). Each nationality was paired with a series of positive or negative evaluative words. A cover story was given to try and mask the true purpose of the research. When the participants were later asked to rate the nationalities on a seven-point scale of liking, those paired with positive adjectives were rated more pleasant, and nationalities paired with negative adjectives were rated as less pleasant. A similar effect was shown in a parallel study of evaluative conditioning of men's first names, suggesting that our likes and dislikes of names may be based on the various associations that the names have acquired. Although offering a plausible account of attitude learning, evaluative conditioning effects are sometimes transient (e.g., Anderson & Clavadetscher, 1976).

Summary of the Methods of Conditioning. The traditional definition of classical conditioning is exemplified in salivary or eyeblink conditioning: Reflex-eliciting stimuli are used as USs, the food or the air puff, and the conditioned response is similar in form to the unconditioned response, salivation or an eyeblink. Broadening the domain of conditioning beyond strictly reflex-eliciting stimuli has demonstrated the laws and regularities of conditioning apply to a wide range of naturalistic behaviors. In addition to the taste aversions described here, conditioning has also been shown to play a role in aggressive, territorial, and mating behaviors in animals (Hollis, 1997). Advocates of the more restrictive traditional definition of conditioning argue that the term is being applied too broadly. Some methods represent mixtures of several forms of learning, including particularly reinforcement learning (presented in the next two chapters). For instance, developing an aversion to a taste could be attributed to classical conditioning. The subsequent avoidance of that taste (or food) is an instance of instrumental reinforcement learning (see avoidance learning in Chapter 5). Classical conditioning has also become a synonym for *associative learning,* when in fact it is just one of several methods for studying associative memory.

What Stimuli Can Serve as CSs?

The usual textbook examples of to-be-conditioned stimuli are discrete signals such as lights, tones, and bells. However, even in Pavlov's lab, many other stimuli were demonstrated to be effective CSs. Exteroceptive stimuli including touch, smells, and tastes have been successfully conditioned. Interoceptive stimuli, or stimulation of an internal organ or tissue, have been used as CSs. The treatment of enuresis, or bedwetting, attempts to transfer control from exteroceptive cues, such as a buzzer activated by wetting (the US), to the interoceptive cues of feeling a full bladder (the CS, e.g., Houts & Liebert, 1984).

The sudden *offset* of an already present stimulus can serve as an effective CS (e.g., Logan & Wagner, 1962). In a film, the forest suddenly becoming quiet is a sure signal that something dramatic is about to happen.

Diffuse stimuli of time or place can act as conditioned stimuli. *Contextual stimuli,* the place or environment in which training occurs, are prominent stimuli and are readily conditioned (e.g., Dweck & Wagner, 1970; Siegel, Hinson, Krank, Riley, & McCully, 1982). Thus, we may fear the dentist's office, just as our pets fear going to the veterinarian's. In *temporal conditioning,* there is not an explicit CS. Instead, the US (e.g., food) is simply presented at fixed, recurring intervals. The passage of time since the last US serves as the CS for the next US. Marquis (1941) tested newborn infants who had been maintained on a 3-hour feeding schedule during the first 8 days after birth. When feeding was delayed for the first time on the ninth day, an abrupt increase in activity was observed at the end of the 3-hour interval among these infants, in comparison to a control group that had been fed every 4 hours, suggesting the infants had been conditioned to 3-hour intervals. Finally, circadian, or time-of-day cues, can function as CSs. Dogs were trained to respond differently to the same stimulus presented at different times of the day. In the morning, a tone signaled food, but in the afternoon, the same tone in the same lab and in the same apparatus, signaled shock. The dog learned to salivate to the morning tone and flex its paw to the afternoon tone (Asrytan, cited by Wyrwicka, 1972).

What Stimuli Can Serve as USs?

Unconditioned stimuli are typically events that have some biological significance to the organism (Gunther, Miller, & Matute, 1997). Although the US may be innately significant to the organism, as food and shock are, the US can have acquired significance. The USs in the evaluative conditioning procedure described earlier, such as the classical Indian music or the songs from *Grease,* have acquired significance. In other human experiments, conditioning has been attempted by asking the participant to imagine a US rather than actually presenting an aversive US, that is, "imagine you have been shocked" (Dadds et al., 1997). For example, one could imagine becoming nauseous and ill while smoking a cigarette. The intention here is to condition an aversion to smoking. The use of mental imagery and imagination form the basis of some behavioral therapies such as systematic desensitization to reduce phobias or aversion therapy to reduce smoking or drinking (both described later in this chapter). The participant does not even have to be given the US, but only observe some other participant receiving it. In a taste-aversion procedure, rats who themselves were not made ill still developed an aversion when they saw another rat become ill after eating a certain food (the "poisoned partner" effect, Revusky, Coombes, & Pohl, 1982).

It is important to remember that USs are complex events. They have specific sensory components, for example, taste, touch, sound, as well as general emotional components, for example, pain and fear. USs elicit both specific reactions, such as limb flexion or heart rate change, and diffuse responses, such as general activity. Thus, we should expect conditioned responses to be multidimensional also.

Is an unconditioned stimulus necessary for conditioning? Could two neutral stimuli, such as a tone and a bell, become associated through pairing? The difficulty in answering this question is that in the absence of a biologically significant US, there is little motivation to respond to the neutral stimuli to show whether associative learning had occurred. Special methods, those of sensory preconditioning and second-order conditioning (described later) can be used to detect potential CS-to-CS associations.

Basic Phenomena of Conditioning

Acquisition

Acquisition refers to the development of a conditioned response as a result of CS–US trials. Some procedures, such as eyeblink conditioning, require several pairings to produce CRs and are ideal for plotting learning curves (see Beck's curves in Box 3.1). Other procedures produce such rapid conditioning that a single pairing is sufficient. Not surprisingly, taste-aversion learning is one of these. In some cases, multiple CS–US pairings are given, but

BOX **3.1**

Anxiety and Conditioning

Many experimental variables have been presented that influence classical conditioning. One variable not yet considered is that of individual differences: Do all people show conditioning more or less the same or are there differences due to a person's particular life history or physiology that affect conditioning? Pavlov described temperamental differences among his dogs that he believed affected ease of conditioning. Surely people differ from one another also.

One personality variable that has been well studied is that of anxiety. Do anxious people condition any differently from those who are less anxious? There are several reasons for picking this particular trait. The British psychologist Hans Eysenck (1981) believed that anxious individuals have a higher level of arousal in certain brain areas that should facilitate conditioning. This increased arousal is plausible, given that measures of autonomic nervous system activity are elevated in anxious people (e.g., heart rate or sweating). Anxious individuals experience higher levels of emotional responsiveness, which would add to the mild fear produced by an aversive US, such as an airpuff or shock.

A nice test of these predictions is the study by Sally Beck (1963), who conditioned eyeblinks using women students from an introductory psychology subject pool. Anxiety was assessed by the Taylor Manifest Anxiety Scale, a self-report measure of emotionality (Taylor, 1953). In addition, Beck varied the intensity of the tone CS (soft or loud) and the airpuff US (weak or strong). The results showed more conditioning with loud tones than with soft; and with strong puffs of air than with weak puffs. So far, no surprises. Within each of these conditions, the participants who scored higher on the anxiety scale showed more conditioning than did participants who scored lower on anxiety. Higher anxiety did not quite enhance responding as much as did an increasing the intensity of the airpuff (see Figure 3.2).

A cognitive explanation of the effects of anxiety assumes that anxious individuals are more likely to rehearse aversive experiences, such as the

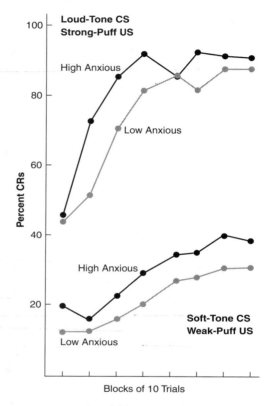

FIGURE 3.2   Acquisition curves for eye-blink conditioning as a function of CS intensity (tone loudness), US intensity (force of the airpuff), and anxiety level of the subjects.

Source: Adapted from Beck, 1963, p. 432.

receipt of a noxious US (Davey & Matchett, 1994). Following conditioning involving a loud-tone US, an explicit "rehearsal" stage was added in which the participants were encouraged to imagine, as vividly as possible, the tone US. Subsequent testing showed that the anxious individuals became more fearful of the CS. The conditioned response had increased without further direct experience with the conditioning stimuli, but through rumination about them.

This enhancing effect of anxiety may sound paradoxical at first. We usually assume that anxiety inhibits learning. However anxiety may retard performance in a more complex task. For example, in discrimination training a CS+ is paired with the US, but a CS– is not. High anxious participants respond more to CS+, but they also respond more to CS– than do low anxious. There is a smaller difference in responding between the two CSs than among the low anxious, or less discrimination (Hilgard, Jones, & Kaplan, 1951).

Eysenck has speculated on the implications of these findings. High anxious individuals, who are exposed to aversive life experiences just like the low anxious, unfortunately may acquire more conditioned fear reactions from those experiences. The high anxious may also discriminate less between stimuli that do or do not predict dangers, and thus they may generalize these fears to more stimuli. The result is more generalized anxiety, provoked by more stimuli in the world.

---

measurement of conditioning is made only once at the end of the sequence, as in the evaluative conditioning procedures mentioned earlier.

Control Procedures.   Although a conditioned response to the CS may indicate that conditioning has occurred, the response could occur for other reasons. Presentations of either the CS alone or the US alone can lead to the development of responses that could be mistakenly attributed to conditioning. A rat that has been given poison as the US may then shy away from all new foods and not only the conditioned taste. Eyeblinks and GSRs occur as orienting and startle responses to the novel stimuli used as the CSs. Therefore, control conditions are needed to demonstrate that any behavioral change we observe is due to conditioning and not to incidental aspects of the procedure. The amount of responding to the CS in a control condition can serve as a baseline with which to compare responding by the conditioning group.

In the *unpaired control* procedure, both the CS and the US are presented during the experimental sessions, but the two stimuli explicitly occur separately from one another. To phrase it differently, the CS and US are negatively correlated: One stimulus never occurs close in time to the other. Experimental participants receiving CS–US pairings and control participants receiving unpaired CSs and USs therefore are equated in their overall exposure to the various stimuli. This procedure has been suggested to be too conservative (Rescorla, 1967). A form of learning to the control CS may occur, what will be referred to as inhibitory conditioning later, in which the CS becomes associated with the absence of the US.

In the *truly random control* procedure (Rescorla, 1967) the CS and the US are each separately programmed to occur randomly in time during the experimental sessions. The idea is that the occurrences of the CS and US are not correlated; they have a zero correlation. Because the schedule is random, the CS and US may occasionally occur together "by chance," but most times each stimulus occurs separate from the other. The use of the random control has been challenged because occasional coincidental pairings are sometimes enough to produce conditioning between the CS and US, and so the random procedure may not be a fair control (Papini & Bitterman, 1990). However, over a sufficiently long period of exposure to a random schedule of CSs and USs, little conditioned responding is seen to the CS.

So what is the appropriate control condition to use? The answer may be to determine for each preparation (eyeblink, GSR, etc.) whether the different controls produce different baseline levels of responding. For instance, Schneiderman, Fuentes, and Gormezano (1962) studied eyeblink conditioning in the rabbit and included a number of control conditions. These included separate groups of participants that received presentations of the CS only, the US only, unpaired CSs and USs, and randomly scheduled CSs and USs. The results showed a substantial frequency of CRs only in the group that received paired CS–US presentations, the classical conditioning group. None of the controls showed many eyeblinks during the CS.

Extinction

Extinction is the presentation of an already conditioned CS alone, but without the US. The result is a decrease and maybe the eventual disappearance of the CR, which we call extinction of the response.

One might think that extinction is the opposite of acquisition: If pairing the CS and US leads to conditioning, then it seems logical that the process could be reversed to remove conditioning. However, extinction does not eliminate the CS–US association, but only suppresses it. We see this is when the supposedly extinguished response reappears after the CS has been withheld for a while. Then, re-presentation of the CS leads to a recurrence of the previously extinguished response. This *spontaneous recovery* shows that responding to the CS was only inhibited by extinction.

Spontaneous recovery is nicely illustrated by repeating extinction over several sessions. An example is shown in Figure 3.3 using data from salivary conditioning in dogs (Wagner, Siegel, Thomas, & Ellison, 1964). Within each session, the response to the CS alone extinguishes. From the end of one session to the start of the next, spontaneous recovery occurs. Extinction proceeds more rapidly day by day, and less spontaneous recovery occurs, so eventually the response could disappear.

The pattern just illustrated has a practical implication for what to expect if you attempt to extinguish an unwanted conditioned response. Repeated extinctions likely will be necessary to completely eliminate the behavior. For example, after a single session in which snake or spider phobias were eliminated by exposure to the feared stimuli, there was significant "relapse" when participants were retested after 4 weeks (Rachman & Lopatka, 1988). This could have been due to spontaneous recovery. Additional sessions of exposure would be needed to more permanently reduce the fear.

There are other manipulations that demonstrate the persistence of conditioned associations in spite of extinction. Reexposure to the unconditioned stimulus alone, in the absence of the CS, will reinstate responding the next time the CS occurs (Rescorla, 2001). Let's say you have finally gotten over that aversion to tomato sauce you picked up when you had a stomach virus a while back. Another bout of nausea (provoked through unrelated circumstances) could reinstate the aversion of tomato sauce, even if you haven't actually tasted any sauce since. This has led some researchers to assert that "Pavlovian associations are forever" (Baeyens, Eelen, & Crombez, 1995).

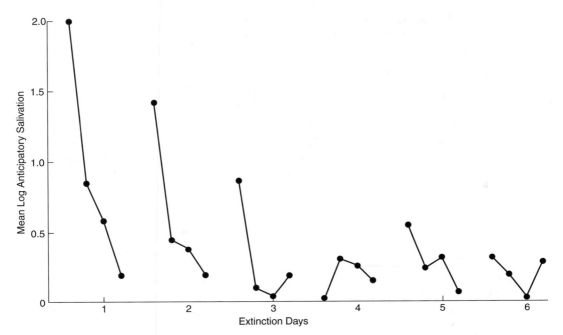

FIGURE 3.3   Reinforcement history and the extinction of a conditioned salivary response.

Source: Adapted from Wagner et al., 1964, p. 356.

Generalization

Other stimuli that are similar to the CS will also evoke a conditioned response. New tones similar in sound characteristics (e.g., pitch) to the tone CS will also elicit a CR, although maybe not as large as that evoked by the CS. This is known as *generalization:* conditioning to a trained CS generalizes to similar stimuli. Generalization is assessed by presenting the test CSs, without the US, to see whether or how large a CR occurs to them. Care needs to be taken in conducting a generalization test and in interpreting the results. Extinction or learning that the test stimuli are not paired with the US could counteract any generalization that occurs.

Generalization may occur along many different dimensions of similarity, for example, size, shape, color, and meaning. A story in the local newspaper described a crocodile that had become accustomed to eating marshmallows offered by residents in a golf course community. The crocodile soon took to eating golf balls, too. Some of my students who are also parents have told me that their infants, after receiving an injection in the doctor's office, then cried at the sight of anyone dressed in white.

Discrimination   *Read*

Not all of the stimuli in the environment are paired with unconditioned stimuli. So, we need to discriminate among stimuli that are, or are not, paired with significant other events. In the procedure for discrimination training, one CS (sometimes labeled the CS+) is followed by the US and another CS (labeled the CS–) is not. For example, a tone is paired with food, but a light occurs alone. CS + US trials and CS– trials are usually intermixed within conditioning sessions. The CS+ should come to evoke a conditioned response. During the early trials of discrimination training, some responding to the CS– is also likely due to generalization from the CS+. With continued training, responding to CS– should decrease, although it may not be completely eliminated. Thus, discrimination opposes the tendency to generalize and is a procedure that can be used to explicitly differentiate among CSs.

At one time, it was believed that if the CSs were so similar that they could not be discriminated, experimental neurosis would occur. In research done in Pavlov's lab, a dog was first trained to discriminate between a circle and an oval; then the oval was gradually made closer to the circle in shape. When the dog could no longer detect which CS was which, it began to bark and cry, resisted entering the experimental apparatus, and ceased salivating even to the food (Pavlov, 1927/1960; see Abramson & Seligman, 1977).

Note that this same procedure, of starting with clearly distinct stimuli and gradually increasing their similarity, can be an effective means of teaching difficult discriminations. This is known as *transfer along a continuum* (e.g., Haberlandt, 1971). Consider an analogy to learning our Crayola colors as children. We first learned to distinguish between red and blue, then added purple, and eventually we discriminated red violets and blue violets. The fact that transfer along a continuum does not produce the neurosis that Pavlov reported probably has to do with the gradualness of the training, and also ensuring that the final stimuli are detectably different.

The Role of Contiguity

We have repeatedly referred to CS–US pairings in classical conditioning, but so far without precisely defining what a *pairing* means. The idea is that the two events need to be *contiguous,* or close together, in time in order to become associated. The role of contiguity raises two important questions: Does the sequence of stimuli matter? How close is close enough?

When we talk of pairing the CS and US, we actually mean that the CS begins a short time before the US. In *forward conditioning,* the onset of the CS precedes the onset of the US, for example, tone and then food, or tone and then airpuff (see Figure 3.4). Our long history of research documents that forward pairings are effective in producing a CS that will elicit conditioned responses. Early experimenters searched for the optimal interval between CS onset and US onset for conditioning, hoping this number might then tell us some mathematical constant for the nervous system (Hull, 1943). However, the length of the interstimulus interval (or ISI) that is most effective depends on the response, species, and task being used. As examples, eyeblink conditioning in rabbits and humans occurs rapidly when tone precedes the airpuff by half a second. Salivary and GSR conditioning are obtained with ISIs of 5 to 10 seconds between onset of the CS and onset of the US. Fear conditioning in rats, measured indirectly by suppression of appetitive behavior, can be readily obtained with intervals ranging from 30 seconds to 3 minutes (see Gormezano & Moore, 1969, for a summary of the older literature). Taste-aversion learning occurs with intervals of a different order of magnitude, even if hours separate the taste from the illness, al-

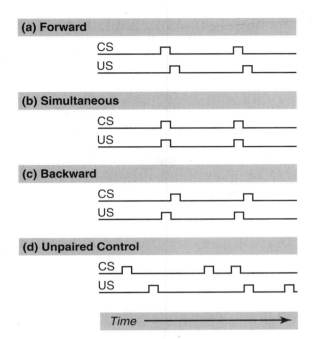

FIGURE 3.4 Sequential arrangements of CS and US in classical conditioning: forward, simultaneous, backward, and explicitly unpaired (control).

though, again, the shorter intervals are better. Although there are specific CS-to-US intervals that produce the fastest learning in a given preparation, conditioning can usually be obtained across a range intervals.

Does contiguity demand this forward sequence? Arranging the CS and US to be exactly coincidental would also seem to well define contiguity, and maybe should produce the most conditioning. In *simultaneous conditioning*, the CS and US have onset at the same time. With simultaneous CS and US pairings, CS-only test trials need to be given occasionally to assess any potential conditioned responding apart from the unconditioned response. The typical finding is that there is actually a low likelihood that the CS will evoke a conditioned response. In *backward conditioning*, the US has onset first and is followed by the CS. Backward pairings can produce conditioned responses under limited circumstances: when a small number of pairings are given (Heth, 1976), or when the sudden occurrence of the US is especially surprising (Wagner & Terry, 1975). However, conditioned responding in the backward procedure is not as strong or enduring as is forward conditioning.

Why is there such a difference between forward versus simultaneous and backward pairings? First, the fact that the forward sequence is so effective suggests that the purpose of conditioning is to produce an adaptive response. A CS that precedes and signals the US allows opportunity for a response to be made in anticipation of the US. Second, maybe simultaneous and backward pairings do produce some associative learning, but these arrangements are simply not conducive to producing conditioned responses. This is the learning–performance distinction. To phrase it casually, the organism may know the tone follows the shock, but it does no good to prepare for a shock that has already come and gone. Finally, learning that occurs with these other arrangements may be fundamentally different. In the case of backward pairings, the CS reliably signals the cessation of the US, what will be labeled conditioned inhibition later in the chapter. In fact, different response measures may detect either excitatory or inhibitory conditioning from the same procedure (McNish et al., 1997).

Summary of the Basic Phenomena.   Already we have seen how classical conditioning is sensitive to many procedural variables. Conditioning occurs rapidly in taste-aversion learning procedures, and more slowly in the eyeblink preparation. The strength of conditioning is affected by the sequence of the CS and US and the interval of separation between the two stimuli. Many events can serve as CSs or USs, both discrete stimuli (such as tone or food) and diffuse stimuli (such as place). Conditioning generalizes from the trained CS to similar stimuli, but a discrimination can be learned among stimuli that are or are not paired with the US.

Other Factors Affecting Conditioning

In the real world, a significant stimulus occurs in the presence of many stimuli, but not all available stimuli become conditioned. There is a process of *stimulus selection* by which only certain of the stimuli become associated with the US. For instance, suppose a person acquires a fear of the dark after childhood experiences of being locked in a dark closet. Why does darkness become conditioned to evoke fear, rather than the closet or other enclosed places, or vice versa? If you become ill after eating, why do you develop an aversion to one of the foods, but not to the plate and fork you used, the music that played in the background, or the other foods you ate? Each of these stimuli is contiguous with the US, but seemingly only certain stimuli become conditioned. Several factors determine which stimuli acquire conditioning: previous experience with the CSs, the presence of competing CSs, how predictive each CS is of the US, and the relevance of the CS to the US. Each of these factors are described in what follows.

Prior Exposure

One factor seems obvious in the preceding illness example: Previous experience in which a stimulus occurred without the US reduces the likelihood of the stimulus being conditioned when the US is present later. Eating off those plates in the past had no adverse consequences, nor did eating some of those foods previously. Either could, in fact, lead to illness. There are cases of lead-based pottery plates that were toxic, and a familiar food such as milk being contaminated with salmonella. In these cases, the plates and the milk were the last things thought to cause the illnesses because each is generally safe. Exposure to a CS by itself, before pairing it with the US, may inhibit new learning of an association between the CS and the US. Administering preconditioning exposures to the CS is called *latent inhibition* (Lubow, 1973). For instance, exposure to a particular food reduces the likelihood of a taste aversion developing when that food is later paired with illness. Although chemotherapy patients can develop taste aversions to new foods, pretherapy exposure that reduces the novelty of them sometimes inhibits the development of an aversion (Siddle & Remington, 1987).

Why does preconditioning exposure to a CS make it difficult to condition? Habituation and interference are two possible explanations. We could say that the stimulus habituates during preconditioning exposure, and so is no longer attended to. Alternatively, learning that the CS typically occurs alone would interfere with later learning that it is now accompanied by the US.

Compound CSs

When two or more conditioned stimuli occur together before the US, each may become conditioned but to varying degrees. This can be demonstrated experimentally in a *compound CS* procedure: Two CSs, a tone and a light, for example, are presented together and followed by the US. After the tone+light compound comes to elicit a conditioned response, conditioning to each stimulus is assessed by separately presenting the tone and the light. There is sometimes a weaker conditioned response to each stimulus alone than to the compound (see Figure 3.5). There would be less salivation, for example, to the tone or the light separately than to the tone+light compound.

The division of conditioning between the two elements (i.e., which CS acquires more conditioning and which less) can be dramatically altered in several ways, most of which make intuitive sense. One CS that is more salient than another, because it is louder, brighter, or otherwise more attention-getting, would *overshadow* the less-salient stimulus.

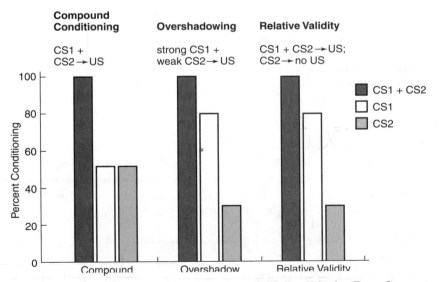

FIGURE 3.5   Conditioning to Three Compound CS Conditioning Procedures.
Hypothetical outcomes of amount of responding to the compound (CS1 + CS2 presented simultaneously) and to each element (CS1 or CS2) alone.

After conditioning to a compound made up of CSs of unequal intensities, the more salient stimulus will produce a greater reaction than the less salient one.

The amount of conditioning to each element of a compound could also vary if the two CSs begin at different times. Egger and Miller (1963) presented one element of the compound (a tone) starting 2 seconds before the food; the other element (a flashing light) began 1.5 seconds before. Control groups showed that either element alone produced perfectly fine conditioning with these temporal values. However, in compound, the first CS (the tone) picked up the most conditioning. Egger and Miller reasoned that the first CS was a more "informative" predictor of the food, whereas the second CS was redundant.

Subsequent research has shown a more complex picture, depending on the combination of the intervals between the CSs and the US. If the first CS comes on too far in advance of the food (say, 30 seconds), the second CS may convey more immediate information. This idea has been employed by Bernstein (1991) to minimize taste-aversion learning by pediatric cancer patients who were undergoing treatment. Between a meal and a chemotherapy session, she gave the children a novel taste, a new flavor of Lifesavers. Because the candy was closer to the subsequent illness, it became the "scapegoat" and protected the prior meal's food from becoming aversive. This study is a nice combination of a basic laboratory finding with a real-world application.

Conditioning is also affected by the *relative validity* of the several CSs (Wagner, Logan, Haberlandt, & Price, 1968). Given several CSs, more conditioning will accrue to the one that is a more reliable predictor of the US. If a potential CS occurs without the US (e.g., taste without illness), then this CS is not a valid predictor of the US. Take, for example, conditioning trials to a compound CS of tone+light followed by food. Interspersing additional presentations of the light alone would reduce its validity as a predictor of food and increase that of the tone.

Compound CSs: A Recapitulation.   When multiple CSs are available, conditioning may be divided, sometimes in grossly unequal portions, among them. This can be labeled stimulus selection. The distribution of conditioning among CSs is affected by overshadowing of one stimulus by another, the informativeness of the stimuli, and the relative validity of each as a predictor of the US.

Surprise   ~~Skip~~

At the start of this chapter, I said that interest in classical conditioning goes through cycles. Much of our renewed contemporary interest in conditioning was stimulated by an experimental finding known as the Blocking Effect (Kamin, 1969) and a theory that describes the course of conditioning, the Rescorla-Wagner model (1972; Wagner & Rescorla, 1972).

The Blocking Effect.   Leon Kamin (e.g., 1969) observed that under certain conditions, a CS paired with the US failed to condition. *Blocking* of conditioning to one CS occurs when the CS is presented in compound with another CS that has already been trained with the US. The already trained CS blocks conditioning to the new CS. *Blocking* is demonstrated by using a multiphase experiment. During the first phase of the experiment, one CS is conditioned. For example, a tone is paired with the food. In the second phase of the experiment, the tone and a new stimulus, a light, for example, are presented simultaneously and followed by food. This phase resembles the compound CS procedure. Our real interest is in the amount of conditioning to the added cue, the light. When it is tested alone, there is little if any conditioning it. The tone apparently blocked conditioning to the light. (A control condition would be used to demonstrate that conditioning to the light would occur if the first phase had been skipped.) Even though the light and food were contiguous, and frequent light–food pairings are given, conditioning to the light was severely inhibited.

Why was conditioning to the added stimulus blocked? The answer has been phrased in several ways. Kamin suggested that what normally occurs on a conditioning trial is that the sudden occurrence of the US is surprising, which causes the participant to "retrospectively review" in memory what recent events might have caused this US. (If you got a static electricity shock, you might think back: "What did I just do to cause that?") In the blocking procedure, the exact moment of occurrence of the US during the second phase was expected: It was signaled by the previously trained tone. Maybe expected USs do not provoke the kind of processing necessary for conditioning. Maybe a US has to be surprising to produce conditioning.

Rescorla-Wagner Model.   The idea that conditioning depends on the surprisingness of the US has been captured, both intuitively and mathematically, in a simple formula described by Robert Rescorla and Allan Wagner (Rescorla & Wagner, 1972; Wagner & Rescorla, 1972). The Rescorla-Wagner model (or the Wagner-Rescorla model, as it is known to those of us who are Wagner's students) provides a trial-by-trial description of the increments in conditioning that occurs to each CS that is present.

The starting point is the learning curve (first discussed in Chapter 1), which plots the amount of responding over successive trials. The increment in conditioning in any trial is a function of the difference between (a) the amount of conditioning possible with a given US and (b) the strength of conditioning already accrued to the CSs that are present in this trial. If the discrepancy between the maximal and existing conditioning is great, then we could say that the US is surprising and so additional conditioning to the CSs occurs.

The amount of conditioning that a given US will support, the end point of the learning curve, is represented by lambda (λ) in the Rescorla-Wagner model. In a given trial, one or more CSs may be present. The associative strength of the several CSs is summed and is represented by V. The increment in new conditioning in that trial is determined by the difference between lambda and V. If the difference is large, because the CSs have little strength to begin with, there will be large increases in conditioning to those CSs present. This would correspond to the large increases seen early in the learning curve. If the difference is small, because one or all of the CSs already have a great deal of strength, the increment will be small. This corresponds to the later sections of the learning curve, in which the increases per trial become smaller.

The full formula is

$$\Delta V = \partial \cdot \beta \cdot (\lambda - V)$$

In English, this reads as the change in V, delta V, equals alpha times beta times (lambda minus V). (Alpha and beta are parameters that represent the CS and US, respectively. For the most part, these are constants in the equation.)

An illustration of the course of conditioning with a tone–light compound is shown in Figure 3.6. In the left panel, in each trial, the amount of conditioning is set at 50 percent of the difference from the last trial to the maximal amount of conditioning. Thus, in the first trial when conditioning is assumed to be zero, the increment is 50 percent, or halfway to 100 percent. In the next trial, conditioning increases to 75 percent, half the distance between 50 and 100. What is important to notice is that conditioning is divided between the tone and the light equally in this example.

How does the Rescorla-Wagner model explain the blocking effect? As a result of the first phase, the tone has acquired some associative strength. The right panel of Figure 3.6 shows the hypothetical course of conditioning during the second phase, when both tone and light are presented. During the second phase, the difference between the amount of conditioning possible (lambda) and the amount present (summing tone and light, even though the latter has no strength to start with) is smaller. The result is that the trial-by-trial increments in conditioning are small (relative to the control condition shown in the upper panel), and what little there is is divided between the tone and light. The net result is little conditioning to the light.

The Rescorla-Wagner model, although only briefly presented here, has been successful in describing a variety of conditioning phenomena. The model has also generated a good deal of research to show its failings, but, of course, the strength of any good theory is its ability to stimulate new research (Miller, Barnet, & Grahame, 1995). The Rescorla-Wagner model has been applied to other phenomena outside of classical conditioning, including perceptual illusions and verbal learning (reviewed by Siegel & Allan, 1996). An extension of the formula to human learning of cause-and-effect relationships is the "delta

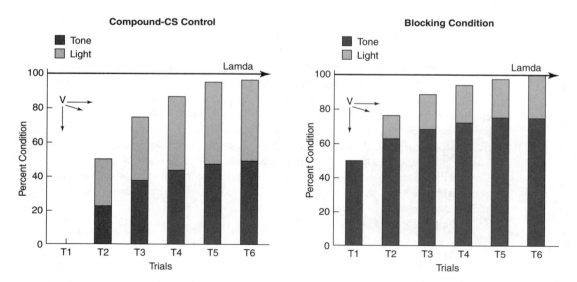

FIGURE 3.6   Hypothetical Growth of Conditioning to Each Element of a Compound CS and Their Summed Strengths (V), According to the Rescorla-Wagner Model. The left panel shows conditioning when V starts at zero. The right panel shows the blocking effect when V has a positive value because of preconditioning to the tone.

rule," used in connectionist models of learning and memory (a numerical example is presented in Chapter 7).

CS–US Relevance *Study*

Another factor that affects conditioning is the relevance of the CS to the US. Referring back to our taste-illness example, how likely is it that the illness was caused by the food versus by the plates? In learning about cause-and-effect relationships in the world, organisms may have a bias toward perceiving that something eaten is more likely to cause illness than something seen or heard. CS-to-US relevance has also been called *belongingness, the idea that certain CSs and USs seem to belong or go together, such as tastes and illnesses.* A symmetrical property of relevance asserts that sights or sounds in the environment are relevant signals for external stimuli such as shocks or airpuffs.

Although CS-to-US relevance makes sense, it is also possible that tastes readily condition simply because they are more salient or intense CSs. We need a research design that shows that interoceptive and exteroceptive cues are equally adequate, but they differ in their relevance depending on the type of US used. Garcia and Koelling (1966) demonstrated this in their now classic studies. (John Garcia was awarded the Distinguished Scientific Contribution Award by the APA in 1979.) Rats were presented with a compound CS consisting of a tone, a light, and a taste, all simultaneously. This was arranged by allowing the rats to lick saccharin-flavored water from a drinking tube. Each lick completed a circuit that turned on the tone and flashed the light. Garcia and Koelling referred to this as "bright-noisy-tasty water." This CS was paired with either of two USs: for one group of animals, electric shock was delivered through the floor of the conditioning chamber; for the second group of animals, an illness-inducing drug was injected. Following this conditioning treatment, the two groups were tested for fear of the exteroceptive stimuli (the tone and light) or aversion to the interoceptive stimulus (the saccharin taste). The results showed that rats that had been made ill after exposure to the compound CS refused to drink saccharin, but did not show fear to the tone and light. Conversely, rats shocked after the compound were fearful when the tone and light were turned on, but did not avoid the saccharin.

Each type of CS, exteroceptive and interoceptive, was conditionable. But conditioning was selective: taste selectively associated to illness, and tone and light selectively associated with shock. The Garcia and Koelling study also nicely illustrates the advantages of basic research in a laboratory setting. In this situation, the conditioned stimuli could be highly controlled, ensuring equal exposure and contiguity of each with the US.

What determines CS-to-US relevance? One explanation is that it is an example of *prepared learning.* Organisms are prepared to form associations between certain classes of stimuli because of experience with these sorts of stimuli during their evolutionary history (Rozin & Kalat, 1971; Seligman, 1970). Taste-aversion learning may be one of several instances of prepared learning, which also include the human capacity to learn language and biases toward acquiring certain types of phobias (discussed in the Applications section of this chapter).

An alternative explanation of relevance is that there is a learned bias toward associating certain classes of stimuli. It is learned during the lifetime of the organism (Davey, 1995). Selective associating occurs because an individual's prior experience with taste stimuli has shown them to be related to illness, and other types of cues were not. We could add that this associative bias would be strengthened by vicarious learning and social learning, or drawing on the experiences we observe in other members of our species.

We should note that conditioning does occur between nonrelevant CSs and USs, although maybe not as readily as with prepared CSs. Animals do condition to color, feeding containers, places, and other exteroceptive cues (see Mackintosh, 1983). For instance, Wilcoxon, Dragoin, and Kral (1971) found that bobwhite quail learned an aversion to both the taste and color of poisoned water, whereas rats learned only the taste aversion. The differences in learning between relevant and nonrelevant stimuli may be partially due to other parameters of conditioning, such as the timing and duration of stimuli (Krane & Wagner, 1975). Even among foods, not all foods are equally conditionable as a result of an illness experience (see Table 3.2).

Conditioned Inhibition

Our references to conditioning so far have actually been to excitatory conditioning. Simply put, in *excitatory conditioning,* one stimulus becomes associated with the occurrence of another, for example, CS and US. By contrast, in *inhibitory conditioning, a conditioned stimulus becomes associated with the absence of the US.* Using stimuli to anticipate food or danger, what we call excitatory conditioning, is important for an organism's survival. Knowing when food is not available or danger is not present, or inhibitory conditioning, may be just as important. Imagine a situation relevant to student life: predicting the dreaded pop quiz. Unfortunately, cues are rarely available to signal on what days the quiz (the US) will occur, hence the name "pop quiz." Inhibitory conditioning would occur if a cue reliably signals when the quiz *will not* occur. If the teacher arrives empty-handed, then a quiz is not imminent. Instead of remaining tense and anxious, the students can relax!

TABLE 3.2   Targets of Learned Food Aversions in Humans

Category	Percent of All Aversions
Meat; poultry; fish	21
Vegetables	14
Alcohol	14
Eggs or egg dishes	4
Bread, crackers, or flour products	3
Rice, potatoes	3

Note: Taste aversions develop when novel or distinctive foods are followed by illness. But are some foods more likely targets than others? Midkiff and Bernstein (1985) surveyed nearly 1,500 introductory psychology students concerning which food groups were more likely to produce food aversions. All told, over 1,000 aversions were reported, with 57 percent of the students reporting at least one aversion. The researchers found that foods in certain categories were more likely to become aversive, specifically proteins. A sample of their results is shown.

How is an inhibitor produced? Inhibitors must be actively trained by arranging what is essentially a negative correlation between the CS and a specific US. This means the US is more likely to occur without the CS than with it; and the CS is more likely to occur without the US. The procedure of discrimination training suggests one means of training an inhibitor: CS+ is paired with the US, and CS– is not followed by the US. The CS– may become an inhibitor. Another very effective method is to present the potential inhibitor, call it CS*x* (where *x* is the mystery stimulus), simultaneously with a conditioned excitor, but leave out the US. That is, the training sequence would alternate CS+US trials and CS+/CS*x*-no US trials. To describe this procedure casually, at those times when the US fails to appear after CS+, its absence is attributed to the CS*x*.

Inhibition may also result from backward, or US–CS, pairings. The backward CS occurs during a time interval in which the US is very unlikely to be presented, that is, immediately following a previous US occurrence. This corresponds with our pop-quiz analogy: The least likely time for a pop quiz to be given is in the next class session after a quiz. After all, what instructor tests two days in a row?

Conditioned inhibitors often do not evoke a measurable response: no eyeblinks, no salivation (an inhibitory response would be eye-opening instead of eye-blinking). So how can the presence of inhibition be detected? One method is based on the idea that inhibitory stimuli inhibit responding to excitatory stimuli. In the *summation test,* the suspected inhibitor (CS*x*) is presented at the same time as an excitatory CS, to see if it will reduce responding otherwise seen to the excitor (e.g., Neumann, Lipp, & Siddle, 1997). The rationale is like adding a negative number to a positive number: The net result will be less than the positive number was to begin with, for example, the sum of –3 and +5 is +2. So adding an inhibitor to an excitor reduces the size of the response to the excitor.

Another method of detecting inhibition is known as the retardation of conditioning test. If we try to convert the inhibitory CS into an excitor by pairing it with the US, the inhibition retards excitatory conditioning. Again, an analogy to negative numbers may be helpful: –5 is farther from +5 than is 0. Conditioning a neutral stimulus that starts at zero will reach +5 faster than conditioning an inhibitor that starts at –5.

What Is Learned in Classical Conditioning?

Classical conditioning is an example of associative learning. Given the presence of four elements in a traditional Pavlovian trial, the CS, the US, the UR, and eventually the CR, we can ask what is associated with what? There are several theories of what is learned in classical conditioning.

1. According to *stimulus–response* (S–R) theory, the CS becomes associated with the UR. That is, the CS comes to elicit the unconditioned response, or some portion of the UR. The presence of a US ensures that a UR will occur contiguous with the CS. This response-learning theory seemingly fits a simple description of what happens during Pavlovian conditioning: A tone now elicits an eyeblink, salivation, or leg flexion, and so on. It even applies to subtle aspects of the response. In one preparation, pigeons were conditioned to make a pecking response as the CR by using either food or water as the US. Interestingly, the pecks took the form of biting movements when the US was food (and eating is the UR),

but sucking movements when the US was water (and drinking is the UR). The pigeons were making the same response that had originally been elicited by the particular US used (Jenkins & Moore, 1973). The appeal of S–R theory is that it provides a simple and direct account of what is conditioned in classical conditioning.

Although S–R theory adequately describes some forms of the conditioned response, there are several problems with it. For one, the presence of an overt UR is not necessary for conditioning to occur. Atropine will dry up salivation and curare will block paw flexion. Yet participants conditioned while under the influence of these drugs will show appropriate CRs when the drugs wear off (Mackintosh, 1974; Solomon & Turner, 1962). Another difficulty is that sometimes the CR is not the same as the UR. In heart rate conditioning, a shock will often elicit acceleration as the UR, but the CR will sometimes be deceleration. (Actually, the relationship is more complex in cardiac conditioning, but this does illustrate a deviation from S–R theory.) If the drug morphine is used as a US, heart rate, general activity, and sensitivity to pain all decrease. The CR however, is the opposite in each case: Heart rate, pain sensitivity and activity all increase (Siegel, 1991; these studies are described further in what follows).

An alternative theory states that conditioning produces an association between the CS and the US. This is the *stimulus–stimulus* (S–S) theory. The modern version of the S-S theory is decidedly cognitive in orientation. The first step in learning is the formation of internal representations of the CS and the US. The participant is said to learn about these stimuli: their sensory modality, duration, location, and so on. Conditioning further involves the formation of an association between the two representations, just as you have acquired an association between the representations of TABLE and CHAIR.

An advantage, as well as a disadvantage, of the S–S theory is that it does not specify what the conditioned response will be or what form it will take. Instead, knowledge is said to be acquired, with some flexibility as to how that knowledge is applied. The CR is not a rigid, reflexive reaction that becomes attached to the CS.

The contrast between the S–R and S–S approaches is illustrated by the question of whether two CSs can become associated in the absence of a US. The methods of sensory preconditioning and second-order conditioning can be used to detect CS-to-CS associations. In *sensory preconditioning,* two CSs, say, a tone and a light, are paired in the first phase of the experiment (see Table 3.3). There is no unconditioned stimulus. Does any conditioning take place? In the absence of an obvious conditioned response after numerous pairings, S–R theory says no. In the second phase, the tone is paired with food, until conditioned responses are observed. In the final phase, the *light* is tested for CRs. A CR to the light indicates there is an association of the light to the tone, which S–S theory expects. It is as if the participant is chaining through associations: light to tone and tone to food. Sensory preconditioning experiments have not always produced evidence of conditioning, so, in fact, many early studies seemed to support the S–R theory. However, inherent in the first phase of a sensory preconditioning experiment is a habituation procedure that compromises conditioning in the second phase. Studies that controlled for this demonstrated that preconditioning indeed occurs (Pfautz, Donegan, & Wagner, 1978).

Second-order conditioning exchanges the sequence of the first two phases from sensory preconditioning. In *second-order conditioning,* a CS that has previously been conditioned is now used to condition another CS. For example, in the first phase, a tone is paired with food,

TABLE 3.3 Procedures for Second-Order Conditioning and Sensory Preconditioning

Second-Order Conditioning

	Phase I	*Phase II*	*Phase III*
Stimuli presented	CSI → US	CS2 → CS1	Test CS2
CRs made	CR to CS1	CR to CS1 None to CS2	CR to CS2?
Example	tone → food \ salivation	light → tone \ salivation	light \ salivation?

Sensory Preconditioning

	Phase I	*Phase II*	*Phase III*
Stimuli presented	CS2 → CS1	CS1 → US	Test CS2
CRs made	none	CR to CS1	CR to CS2?
Example	light → tone	tone → food \ salivation	light \ salivation?

Note: During Phases I and II, one CS is paired with the US and the two CSs are paired. Phase III is used to test the CS not previously paired with a US.

and then in the second phase, a light is paired with the tone. Test trials with the light alone are used to detect the transfer of conditioning to it. It may be possible to use the light to condition some third CS, which would be third-order conditioning. The more general label "higher-order conditioning" is used to encompass all orders of distance from the original US.

A paradox in second-order conditioning is that, because the US is not present on the CS1–CS2 trials, one could say that conditioning occurs when an extinction procedure is in effect. Actually, the second-order conditioning occurs rapidly over the first several pairings, and then grows weaker with continued pairings. So, the absence of the US does have a detrimental effect (Rescorla, 1980).

Additional support for the S–S theory comes from studies of US devaluation. If the US is altered after conditioning has occurred, will responding to the previously trained CS change to match the new value of the US? For example, a tone is first paired with a food US. Then, in a second phase, the food is paired with poison in a taste-aversion conditioning procedure. This manipulation should devalue the food US. Will the response to the tone CS after the food be reduced? This task could be described as a behavioral syllogism: If tone means food, and food means illness, then does tone mean illness? The results suggest that even animal participants act as if they have solved the syllogism, showing a weaker CR to the tone after as compared to before devaluation (Rescorla, 1987). According to the cognitive version of the S–S theory, a CR of a specific size and shape was not acquired. Rather, a response is available that can be flexibly altered depending on the current status of the organism's knowledge.

③   A third theory of what is learned states that a different form of conditioning, instrumental conditioning, controls the acquisition and performance of conditioned responses. This is a reinforcement theory (discussed further in Chapter 4). Conditioned responses are acquired, shaped, and reinforced, or more colloquially "rewarded," because they make the US more palatable or less aversive (Perkins, 1968). This *preparatory response* theory might be labeled an R-S theory, in that the CR prepares for receipt of the US. An eyeblink CR is reinforced if it leads to the airpuff US striking your eyelid rather than your eyeball. If the mouth is premoistened by a salivary CR, the dry food powder US is made more palatable. Preparatory response theory essentially says that CRs are shaped over trials to better anticipate and coincide with the onset of the US.

A preparatory response interpretation was offered for one interesting case of a failure of conditioning. Wagner, Thomas, and Norton (1967) attempted to condition a leg-flexion response in dogs to a tone CS. They used an unusual US: direct electrical stimulation of an area of the brain that caused a leg-flexion UR. Stimulation of the motor cortex does not produce any sensory consequences: no sound, touch, pain. Some dogs readily learned to make leg flexions to the tone, but some participants did not condition even after as many as 2,000 trials. Observation of the animals revealed that those who showed conditioning were freestanding during the experiment. These animals learned a CR of redistributing their weight when the tone came on to prevent falling over. The dogs who did not condition were suspended in a sort of hammock. These dogs would not fall when the leg raised and so did not need to respond to maintain their balance. As Wagner and colleagues described it, "the CR may be part of a preparatory adjustment which serves to minimize the abruptness, forcefulness, or otherwise noxious postural consequences of the elicitor UR" (1967, p. 191).

Unfortunately, behavior is not always as sensible as preparatory response theory predicts. In another pigeon study, the CS was a panel that illuminated at one end of the conditioning chamber, which was followed by the food tray opening for a few seconds (the US) at the other end (Hearst & Jenkins, 1974). The counterintuitive outcome in this "long box" was that the pigeon approached and pecked at the lighted panel at one end, but could not get back to the food tray in time before it closed! This behavior does not sound very reinforcing. Other studies that have also explicitly introduced an instrumental reinforcement arrangement have actually found it reduces conditioned responses (Coleman, 1975; Gormezano & Coleman, 1973).

So, What Is Learned in Pavlovian Conditioning?

The three theories of what is learned in Pavlovian conditioning are summarized in Table 3.4. Each emphasizes a different pair of elements: the S–R theory (a CS-to-UR association is learned); the S–S theory (a CS-to-US association); and the preparatory response theory (the CR-to-US relationship). Which explanation is correct? Although each is fine in some cases, none of the theories appears to be sufficient for all situations. Part of any resolution to this question goes back to the learning-versus-performance distinction: what has the participant

TABLE 3.4   **Comparison among Several Theories of What Is Learned in Classical Conditioning**

Theory	S–R	S–S	Preparatory Response
Associated elements	CS–UR	CS–US	CR–US
Example	Tone–salivation	Tone expectancy for food	Salivation–food
Evidence for	CR often similar to UR	Sensory preconditioning, US devaluation	Conditioned response reduces noxiousness of US
Criticisms	CR often different from UR	Does not specify what response will be made	Explicit reinforcement reduces, does not enhance, conditioning

learned versus what does the participant do? Cognitive (S–S) theory may accommodate the stimulus relationships that have been learned, but the S–R and preparatory response theories may describe how that knowledge is translated into behavior.

Contemporary approaches suggest that a conditioning procedure can produce multiple forms of learning. For instance, in the field of animal conditioning, Wagner and Brandon (1989) say that conditioning leads to both an emotional, affective response and a specific, localized response. For instance, if using a shock US, there may be a general or diffuse emotional conditioned reaction to the CS, such as fear evidenced by heart-rate changes or suppression of eating; and a specific motoric reaction, such as a leg flexion or an eyeblink. In a different context, studying brain-injured patients, neurologist Damasio and his colleagues (e.g., Bechera et al., 1995) found that a classical conditioning procedure led to a conditioned emotional reaction (fear to the color paired with a loud noise) and verbalizable knowledge (the subject could tell us which color was paired with the noise, and which color was not). As a final example, we can point to conditioning explanations of advertising. One claim has always been that conditioning associates an affective feeling with a product: By pairing the right images and sounds with the product name in a commercial, the viewer will come to associate the product with pleasure, excitement, action, or fun. However, the conditioning procedure may also associate factual information with the product, for example, that the product is fast, effective, or long-lasting (Kim, Allen & Kardes, 1996).

The Role of Awareness in Conditioning

If classical conditioning is considered to be a simple, possibly even primitive form of learning, then conscious cognitive factors are not necessary for conditioning to occur. If conditioning is considered to involve cognitive processes, then awareness may be a factor. What is the role of awareness in conditioning? Evidence from several different sources can be considered.

It is certainly the case that college student participants can often verbally report the CS–US contingency that they have experienced. This has been shown in eyeblink and GSR conditioning, and in some cases of evaluative conditioning (e.g., Shimp, Stuart, & Engle,

1991). But does this awareness of the CS–US contingency precede or follow the appearance of conditioned responses? Is it necessary for conditioning? The data from unaware participants are contradictory. In some cases, experimental participants who cannot report the CS–US arrangement did not make conditioned responses (see review by Dawson & Schell, 1987), but in another study, unaware and aware participants responded comparably (Papka, Ivy, & Woodruff-Pak, 1997). Interestingly, participants who can report that the tone was followed by the airpuff are not always aware that they were making eyeblinks during the tone (Papka, Ivy, & Woodruff-Pak, 1997).

Conscious awareness of the conditioning procedure can be minimized or excluded by using distracting secondary tasks, simpler organisms, or response systems beyond awareness. As examples, eye-blink conditioning occurs even when a second task is being performed simultaneously, such as reacting to words presented visually or watching a video (Papka, Ivy, & Woodruff-Pak, 1997). Many of the participants were still aware of the tone–airpuff pairings, but this awareness did not correlate with the amount of conditioning. Odor-aversion conditioning occurs in the common garden slug, even showing latent inhibition and blocking effects (Sahley, Rudy, & Gelperin, 1981). Finally, we can cite the case of a man with spinal cord injury who showed conditioned control over his bladder, even though neither the stimuli nor the responses involved could be detected by the patient (Ince, Brucker, & Alba, 1978). Together, these sorts of observations suggest that Pavlovian conditioning does not require conscious awareness.

Amnesic subjects, who are aware but are unable to recall experiences from day to day, have shown eye-blink conditioning. These individuals have suffered damage to certain areas of the cerebral cortex, which diminishes their ability to remember and recall events that they experience. When given repeated sessions over days, an amnesic might not be able to describe the previous training sessions, yet the sounding of the tone CS elicits a conditioned eyeblink (Daum, Channon, & Canavan, 1989).

In some instances, awareness of the CS–US relationship will affect responding to the conditioned stimulus. In a conditioning preparation such as the eyeblink or GSR, simply telling our human participants that extinction is about to begin, and reinforcing this belief by disconnecting some of the wires, leads to an immediate cessation of the CR. There is no reaction to the very next CS presentation. However, awareness that an aversive US will no longer occur does not always override all conditioned responses. Taste aversions, such as those incidentally learned during chemotherapy, and fear of phobic-type stimuli, such as pictures of spiders or snakes that were paired with a shock US, are persistent in spite of awareness (Dawson, Schell, & Banis, 1986; Ohman et al., 1976).

Extensions of Conditioning

Conditioning with Drug USs and the Development of Tolerance

Pavlov noted that after repeated injections of morphine, a dog would became nauseous simply at the sight of the hypodermic needle. Contemporary work on conditioned drug reactions has broadened our conception of classical conditioning in several ways: Drugs can act as unconditioned stimuli; diffuse contextual stimuli, such as the injection procedure, or the room in which drugs are administered, can function as CSs; and the conditioned response is sometimes opposite to the UR (see Table 3.1).

These factors are illustrated in the development of drug tolerance. Repeated administrations of a drug can lead to a reduction in the drug's effectiveness. Rats given a series of injections of opiate drugs such as morphine or heroin develop a tolerance, as measured by respiration, body temperature, and pain threshold. What role might classical conditioning play here? Is tolerance a CR?

One way to test for classical conditioning after drug exposure is to replace the drug in the injection with an inert saline solution. This could be labeled a placebo injection. The idea is to monitor the body's conditioned response to the injection procedure (the CS) in the absence of the drug (the US). What is sometimes observed are physiological reactions *opposite* to those initially elicited by the drug. For example, whereas morphine produces lethargy as an UR, the reaction to the placebo is increased activity. Morphine raises body temperature; the placebo injection lowers temperature. Morphine has analgesic effects, in reducing pain; the placebo increases pain sensitivity (see Siegel, 1991, for a review).

Why is the reaction to a saline injection opposite to that of the morphine? One theory proposes that conditioning can lead to the development of conditioned responses that are the opposite of the unconditioned responses. According to Solomon's *opponent process theory*, (e.g., Solomon, 1980), the UR to a stimulus stays the same over presentations. But a second response, the CR, gradually develops over trials, and is opposite in direction from the UR. Siegel (1991) refers to this conditioned response as a compensating response, one that counteracts the effects of the drug itself to maintain bodily homeostasis. Thus, the CR and UR are opponent responses. Overlaying an opponent CR on top of the UR leads to the *appearance* of tolerance.

Another feature of the drug conditioning experiments is the explicit acknowledgment that the context in which the drug occurs is a CS. Treating the context as a CS leads to several testable predictions. For one, the original reaction to the drug can be reinstated by giving the drug in a different context where the compensating response (or CR) is not evoked. An illustrative pattern of results is shown in Table 3.5. After animals had been given frequent morphine injections, they had the same threshold for pain as animals given

TABLE 3.5   Illustrative Pattern of Results in Testing the Effects of Morphine Tolerance

Test Situation	Hypothesized Elements Present	Pain Threshold
Saline control condition	No CR, no UR	Normal pain threshold
Morphine given in test room	CR and UR	Normal pain threshold
Saline given in test room	CR only	Lower pain threshold
Morphine given in different room	UR only	Higher pain threshold

Note: Several days of morphine exposure are first given to develop a tolerance, then testing occurs in the same room that morphine had been given in, or in a different room.

Source: Siegel, 1982.

saline injections. This demonstrates tolerance to morphine. Giving the morphine in a different room reinstated morphine's usual pain-suppressing property. The effectiveness of the drug returns simply by testing the rat in the "nondrug" room.

In one particularly dramatic demonstration of room-specific tolerance, rats were given heroin or saline in different rooms. Rats that had a tolerance to an otherwise lethal dose of heroin in the heroin room showed a 50 percent increase in the death rate when injected in the nondrug room (Siegel, Hinson, Krank, & McCully, 1982). This may explain why some drug users overdose when taking amounts they previously tolerated. If the drug is taken in a different environment from usual, the compensating responses may not be evoked, and so the drug has its full effect. In a retrospective interview study of overdose victims who lived to tell about their experience, 7 out of 10 reported changed environmental conditions associated with the overdose reaction (Siegel, 1984).

By extension, the compensatory-response model also addresses withdrawal symptoms. Say that an addicted individual is confronted with cues associated with drug taking: the place where opiates have frequently been used, at the time of day in which the drug was usually taken, or after the usual number of hours since the last administration. These characteristics define context, circadian, and temporal CSs, respectively. If the drug is not taken, then the compensating CRs are seen in unadulterated form. The responses may be a drop in body temperature, speeded respiration, cramping and nausea, and hyperactivity. These symptoms of withdrawal, evoked in the absence of the drug, are all opposite to the reactions typically elicited by opiate drugs. The conditioning theory also suggests that detoxification that takes place in a very different environment from the drug-taking environment, does not extinguish the context–drug association. Relapse occurs because on returning to the original living environment associated with drugs, withdrawal and craving are elicited (Siegel, 1982).

The theory of compensating responses has its share of criticisms. Only some drugs show CRs that oppose the UR. The challenge then is to predict which show compensation and which do not. Eikelboom and Stewart (1982) have suggested that possibly the URs have been incorrectly identified in the case of the opiates, as these drugs have different effects on the central nervous system than in other parts of the body. Thus, the reactions the drug produces in the bloodstream should not be considered to be the UR, since such effects occur without involvement of the central nervous system.

Research on drug conditioning illustrates three important points: first, that drugs can act as USs; second, that contextual stimuli can act as CSs; and, third, that the conditioned response does not have to mimic the unconditioned response.

Modification of Immune System Response

The basics of the immune system have become familiar to most of us, often reflected in our knowledge of immune system failures as in AIDS or in deliberate attempts to suppress immunity as a precursor to organ transplants. The immune system is the body's defense against foreign substances and microorganisms, such as viruses and bacteria. Although the immune system had been believed to function autonomously, in recent decades scientists have recognized the role of the central nervous system (CNS) in coordinating immune functions. CNS involvement opens the way for the possibility of conditioning immune reactions. In fact, a field of specialization has developed, called *psychneuroimmunology,* which is nicely defined by the subtitle of one review as "the interface between behavior, brain, and immunity" (Maier, Watkins, & Fleshner, 1994). For example, we have long known that asthmatic reactions can be conditioned. Human studies have shown that the pairing of neutral stimuli with allergens (used as USs) can lead to conditioned allergic responses (e.g., Dekker, Pelser, & Groen, 1957).

A discovery during a taste-aversion learning experiment led to even more surprising findings. Ader and Cohen (1975) paired a saccharin taste with the drug cyclophosphamide, which was being used as the US to induce illness. A side effect of the drug (from Ader's perspective) is that it is an immunosuppressant. Incidental to conditioning an aversion to the taste, the saccharin CS also developed the capacity to suppress immune functioning as a CR. Such conditioning of the immune system is now accepted as a well-demonstrated phenomenon, even if we do not yet fully understand the mechanism behind it (see Ader & Cohen, 1993).

Observations in humans suggest similar results. Bovjberg and colleagues (1990) found that women who had received a number of chemotherapy treatments (which can include drugs such as cyclophosphamide) displayed an immune suppression after being brought to the hospital, but before the next round of chemotherapy actually began. Their immune suppression may have been a conditioned response evoked by the conditioned stimulus of the context of the hospital.

Unlike morphine conditioning discussed in the preceding section, the conditioned and unconditioned responses in immune conditioning are alike. Could a placebo in this case have a practical application by mimicking the effects of the actual drug? In certain disorders, an overactive immune system attacks the body and so suppression becomes a desirable treatment. Ader and Cohen (1982) found that occasionally substituting the conditioned saccharine solution for the drug was as effective as giving the drug each time in treating an immune system disorder in mice. That is, the placebo reaction was sufficient to delay onset of the disease.

One other extension of classical conditioning is *modeling causality learning,* or the learning of cause and effect relationships. This application is described in Box 3.2.

Applications of Conditioning

The Conditioning Theory of Phobias

A *phobia* is an excessive and intense fear, usually of a specific object or situation, such as a fear of snakes and spiders, of heights, or of speaking in public. Where do phobias come from? Psychologists can offer a variety of explanations. Instinct theory states that some fears are innate reactions to certain stimuli; loud noises, sudden movements, or of certain animals. A psychoanalytic explanation states the things we seem to fear are symbolic of what we unconsciously fear. Freud concluded that 5-year-old Hans's fear of horses was actually displacement of the child's fear of his father, due to Oedipal conflict. There is one other explanation that psychologists point to whenever they want to demonstrate the significance of Pavlovian conditioning. Maybe fears and phobias originate through classical

BOX **3.2**

Detecting Causality

Pavlovian conditioning has sometimes been described as an example of causal learning: When an organism is being conditioned, it is learning cause-and-effect relationships among events (Hall, 1994; Young, 1995). From among a variety of stimuli, which one "causes" the US? Whatever stimulus regularly precedes the US could logically be thought of as having causal properties.

Interest in cause-and-effect relationships has a long history in philosophy and psychology. Some philosophers in the Rationalist and Nativist traditions said that we are programmed to perceive these sorts of patterns, just as with other innate categories of knowledge and perception. David Hume, a British empiricist philosopher, instead argued that our belief that one event causes another derives completely from our past experience with those stimuli, which is the frequent repetition of one event following another. "When we look about us towards external objects, and consider the operation of causes, we are never able...to discover any power of necessary connection.... We find only that the one does actually follow the other..." (Hume quoted in Jones, 1952). Hume argues that, logically, there need not be any connection between one event and another; and that our expectation and anticipation that the "cause" will be followed by an "effect" is simply an inference and not necessarily a fact.

Hume further listed the conditions for judging causes and effects. They must be contiguous in time and space, the cause must be prior to the effect, the cause always produces the effect, and the effect arises only from the same cause. These features well describe the ideal contingencies for producing classical conditioning: The CS and US are paired, the CS closely precedes the US, the CS is always paired with the US, and the US does not occur in the absence of the CS (Hall, 1994).

Researchers of human cognition have noted the parallel between classical conditioning and learning about other kinds of contingencies between stimuli. For example, in medical diagnoses, one may look for symptom–disease correlations. What kinds of information do you need to conclude that a particular symptom is diagnostic of the disease? First, look for the conjunction of the two stimuli. For example, a fever must be present in order to diagnose the flu. But, logically, we would need to tally the other possible contingencies between the two events. Does a fever occur without the flu? Can the flu be present without fever? If any of these were the case, then fever would be an unreliable indicator of the flu. This sort of contingency analysis can be set up in a 2 × 2 table: presence or absence of the symptom and presence or absence of the illness (see Table 3.6). In evaluating the information from these sorts of contingencies, we humans do a rather poor job. We seem to have a bias to overattribute cause based on the conjunction of two events and neglect the information obtained from the other cells of the table. Wasserman, Dorner, and Kao (1990) asked subjects about the relative importance of these four cells in making inferences about hypothetical problems, such as the effectiveness of a drug to cure skin rashes or the relationship of a symptom to an illness. For example, Cell A, in which the symptom and illness are both present, was judged to be the most important fact in making a judgment (by nearly 100 percent of the subjects). The other cells, in which the symptom occurs alone or the illness occurs alone, were judged less important, and the cell in which neither occurs was rated least important (by 50 percent of the subjects).

Studies of human contingency learning, using paradigms like symptom–disease learning,

TABLE 3.6   2 × 2 Tables to Assess Causality

	Effect Present	Effect Absent
Cause Present	Cause, effect	Cause, no effect
Cause Absent	No cause, effect	No cause, no effect

have found parallels to animal conditioning, such as the blocking effect and relative validity. For instance, first learning that a fever is associated with the flu may block subsequent learning that a second symptom, stomach distress is also a predictor (Chapman, 1991). Varying the relative validities among symptoms (one predicts the illness reliably while others have varying probabilities) leads to the more valid cue being selected as the most accurate (Shanks, 1991). Thus, given symp-

toms of fever and stomach distress, the one that best correlates with the occurrence of flu is better learned. In addition, the Rescorla-Wagner model of classical conditioning, originally derived from studies of animal conditioning, is often used as a model of human contingency learning (e.g., Shanks, 1995). The result of all this research has been a fertile cross-pollination of ideas between animal and human learning.

conditioning: An initially neutral stimulus becomes phobic because it has been paired with an aversive stimulus: something traumatic, painful, or frightening.

The initial statement of the conditioning theory of fear learning is embarrassingly simple. John Watson and Rosalie Rayner (1920) set out to condition an 11-month-old child named Albert to fear a laboratory rat. The first exposures to the rat showed that fear was not innate; Albert readily attempted to touch and grasp the rat. However, when exposure to the rat (used here as the CS) was followed by an unexpected banging of a steel bar with a steel hammer (the US), a change in Albert's reactions took place. Over the course of a few pairings, Albert became more tentative in his reaching for the rat, his lip began to quiver, and finally he would cry. This fear of the rat was conditioned fear, the CR.

Watson and Rayner's demonstration of fear conditioning was both powerful and influential. Where do phobias come from? No longer would we need to explain fears on the basis of instincts or unconscious forces. According to Watson and Rayner, they originate in conditioning experiences. This study has served as the basis for speculations in literature on the applications, mostly evil, of Watson and Rayner's theory to future societies. In *Brave New World,* for example, Aldous Huxley describes children who are conditioned to fear books by electrically shocking them when books are touched. The idea was to produce a working class that would not be distracted by ideas and education.

Although widely cited, Watson and Rayner's study leaves much to be desired as a valid scientific experiment. In an article entitled "Whatever Happened to Little Albert?," Harris (1979) describes how the story has been distorted over the years, like a rumor that becomes exaggerated with each retelling. In point of fact, fear of the rat dissipated between sessions, so that Albert had to be periodically reconditioned. Other researchers' attempts to replicate by conditioning fear to other objects (e.g., toy blocks) failed. And, Watson and Rayner's conditioning theory has been rightly criticized for being too simple. Its exclusive reliance on pairings, or contiguity, omits other factors known to affect conditioning. (Curiously, Harris's article does not tell us what happened to Albert. All that we do know is that Albert's family moved away, taking Albert and his phobia with them. Watson and Rayner had not deconditioned the child before he left the study.)

Hans Eysenck (1979) reviewed a number of other significant failings of the Watson and Rayner theory of conditioning. Not all or any stimulus that is paired with trauma becomes conditioned. The sensitive laboratory parameters (e.g., the exact timing of CS and US) typically do not occur in the real world. Phobias seemingly do not extinguish. And we cannot always determine that there was a traumatic experience that conditioned the fear. However, rather than discarding a classical conditioning model, researchers have attempted to refine it by incorporating contemporary knowledge of the learning process.

Do phobias originate because of an aversive or traumatic conditioning experience? Di Nardo, Guzy, and Bak (1988) found that two-thirds of dog phobics could recall a conditioning event involving a dog, mostly involving bites or other painful experiences. Unfortunately for conditioning theory, an equal percentage of nonphobic individuals could also recall traumatic and painful experiences with dogs. De Jonghand and colleagues (1995) found that over 90 percent of dental phobics reported one or more painful treatments that they characterized as "traumatic." In this case, the phobics reported more such experiences than did nonphobic participants, although again there was substantial recollection of painful dental treatments among those who now reported being relatively relaxed (!?!) during visits to the dentist.

One significant revision to the conditioning model is the addition of the notion of preparedness (Eysenck, 1979; Seligman, 1972). Earlier, we saw that taste-aversion learning might be an instance of prepared learning. Similarly, possibly evolution has prepared us to acquire certain fears that have high survival value. Phobias do not develop to any arbitrary object that happens to occur in proximity to trauma. Instead, people become fearful of the dark, heights, and enclosed spaces; of snakes and spiders; or of other people. According to preparedness theory, these are stimuli that have represented dangers in the evolutionary history of humans and our primate predecessors. There are other classes of stimuli with which we surely have more unpleasant contact but which do not become the object of phobias. Children fall off bicycles daily, but they do not develop bike phobias. How often do we get shocked by an electrical appliance? Yet there is no Greek-root word for vacuum cleaner phobia.

The theory of preparedness has itself evolved over time. Ohman and Mineka (2001) suggest that there is an evolved "module," or dedicated brain circuit for learning prepared fears. This module activates defensive behaviors and emotional feelings in response to a threatening situation or stimulus. (A learning module is a hypothesized specialization in certain areas of the brain that has evolved for a particular type of learning. For example, birds may have a song module, and possibly humans have a face-recognition module.) The prepared fear module has several characteristics.

1. It responds selectively to certain stimuli, particularly those that evolution has determined to be potential threats or dangers.
2. Responding is automatic and involuntary, much like a reflex reaction.
3. The fear response is relatively unaffected by other modules, in particular by cognitive operations. Thus, consciously realizing that this snake is not harmful does not reduce your fear.
4. There are specialized neural circuits. For fear conditioning, the amygdala of the central core of the brain seems to be centrally involved in fear conditioning.

The notion of preparedness explains the rapidity of fear learning, its persistence, and its acquisition under relatively poor conditions. As was shown with taste-aversion conditioning, prepared learning could occur in just a single trial, even with wide temporal separation between CS and US. The notion of preparedness seems like the salvation of the conditioning theory. But are the claims of preparedness valid?

Preparedness can be supported by evidence for selective conditioning of fear-relevant CSs. The rationale for these studies is the same as for demonstrating selective conditioning of tastes and illness. Marks (1977) anecdotally describes an incredible (but unfortunate) coincidence in which a young woman passenger was in a car crash while browsing through a book on snakes. Did the woman develop a fear of cars? No, she became snake phobic. Laboratory studies of preparedness compare GSR conditioning to fear-relevant CSs, such as pictures of snakes; or fear-irrelevant CSs, such as pictures of flowers. According to preparedness theory, if these pictures are paired with a mild electric shock US, we should more quickly learn fears to snakes than to flowers. For example, in one study, discrimination conditioning was used, with a CS+ paired with a shock US and a CS– presented without shock. One group of college student participants received fear-relevant CSs, specifically, pictures of snakes and spiders were the CSs. A second group of students received fear-irrelevant CSs, pictures of flowers or mushrooms. The fear-relevant CS paired with shock evoked a greater skin conductance reaction than did a fear-relevant CS not paired with shock, and also a greater reaction than to an irrelevant CS that had been paired with shock. This use of fear-relevant stimuli as both CS+ and CS– is particularly nice because it controls for the possibility that the shocks simply sensitized the participants to all fear-relevant stimuli in the experiment (Ohman et al., 1976).

Additional evidence for preparedness comes from studies of fears in monkeys. Cook and Mineka (1990) studied monkeys reared in captivity that had never been exposed to snakes, and therefore should not have a learned bias toward them. These monkeys were not fearful of snakes at first exposure, indicating that the fears were not innate. In a conditioning study, young rhesus monkeys watched a videotape in which footage of phobia-relevant stimuli (snakes) or unprepared stimuli (flowers) were spliced together with footage of other monkeys showing fear and fright. That is, the participant monkeys saw another animal apparently exhibiting fear to a snake or to some daisies. In conditioning terminology, the snake and flowers are the CSs, and seeing the fearful monkey on film is the US. The participant animals were later tested for fear of snakes by requiring them to reach over or go around a toy snake in order to get a food treat. Those monkeys who saw the snake film were more fearful of the snakes than those who saw flowers. Those who saw flowers did not acquire a fear of the flowers. Thus, monkeys are more likely to learn to fear snakes than to fear unprepared stimuli such as flowers.

Alternatives to the preparedness theory of evolutionary predispositions have been offered. Could the fear relevance of snakes and other potentially phobic stimuli be attributed to knowledge acquired during the life of the individual organism? Maybe exposure to negative information about snakes during our lives is what actually facilitates fear learning later. It simply seems likely that the college students in psychology experiments already have some fear or trepidation about snakes but not flowers. This is the notion of a *learned associative bias,* in contrast to a prepared associative bias. These preexisting biases can then be magnified through aversive conditioning. In one experiment, human participants are told they would receive shocks. From this moment on, these experiment participants have a higher expectation that shocks will follow the prepared CSs than the unprepared CSs, even if no shocks are actually given (see Davey, 1995). In another case, if a sequence of fear-relevant and fear-irrelevant stimuli are randomly followed by nothing, a tone stimulus, or a mild shock, the participants overestimated the frequency with which the shocks occurred with the prepared stimuli (Tomarken, Mineka, & Cook, 1989; see also Mineka, 1992).

The preparedness hypothesis has received other criticisms as well. Not all studies find that fear-relevant stimuli are selectively conditioned (see McNally, 1987). People do develop fears of nonevolutionarily prepared stimuli, such as dental anxiety. Many people become afraid to drive after having a car accident. Some categories of human fears tend to be more age-related than evolutionarily determined, for example, 3- and 4-year-old children develop animal fears, whereas 13-to-18-year-old adolescents have social fears (Miller, Barrett, & Hampe, 1974).

Overview of the Conditioning Theory of Phobias.   A conditioning theory suggests that an initially neutral stimulus becomes phobic when it has been paired with a traumatic or aversive event. Mineka's research on monkeys, as well as other research on what is known as observational learning, shows that phobias can be learned secondhand, through observation of others' traumatic experiences with the eventually phobic stimulus. However, not everyone develops a phobia from adverse experiences: Many of us have had painful dog bites or dental treatments, but few of us develop a phobia of dogs or dentists (some fear or trepidation maybe, but not a phobia). Some phobic learning may occur readily because it is biologically prepared. On the other hand, maybe cultural and social influences determine the readiness of learning to fear bugs and snakes.

Systematic Desensitization

If fears can be conditioned, it is reasonable to suppose that they could be unlearned. One method of reducing conditioned responses is through extinction. Simply presenting a feared stimulus repeatedly and ensuring that no traumatic or unpleasant US follows should extinguish classically conditioned fear. Unfortunately, extinction poses several difficulties. People try to avoid phobic stimuli thus preventing the exposure necessary for extinction to occur. Extinguished responses spontaneously recover over time. And extinction tends to be context specific, that is, fears extinguished in one context recur to the stimulus in different contexts (Bouton, 1994).

Apparently a more forceful approach is necessary. *Systematic desensitization,* developed by Joseph Wolpe, is one such method. The phobic stimulus is treated as a CS, and it is paired with a US or a response that is incompatible with fear. The idea is to *countercondition* the phobic CS. In an early instance of counterconditioning, Mary Cover Jones (1924) removed a fear of rabbits in a young child (Peter this time, not Albert) by pairing ice cream with presentations of the rabbit.

Wolpe's method of systematic desensitization has several distinctive features. He most often uses muscle *relaxation* as the response to pair with the phobic CS. His patients are first taught how to relax their muscles, to the point where they can do so quickly. You may be familiar with some techniques of progressive relaxation and the use of relaxation audiotapes to control breathing and muscle tension. Also, Wolpe does not present actual phobic stimuli, but instead has his clients imagine the feared stimuli, which is frightening enough for phobic individuals. He constructs an *anxiety hierarchy,* or a series of graded imaginal stimuli related to the fear, ranging from less to more fearful items. The items are actually prompts for scenes the clients are supposed to imagine. For example, the hierarchy for snake fears might start with "imagine you see a promo for a TV show on snakes" to "imagine you are watching a snake pass by your feet." (In contemporary practice, exposure to actual phobic situations in vivo are added later in the treatment.)

The counterconditioning phase involves pairing items from the fear hierarchy (the CSs) with instructions to relax (the US). The least fearful scenes are imagined first and paired with relaxation, followed by progressively more fearful items as they become tolerated. The patient cannot be anxious (meaning "tense") and relaxed at the same time. These are incompatible responses. Wolpe seeks to have relaxation dominate over the tension.

Systematic desensitization is a mix of conditioning theories. The basis is in S–R theory, by trying to attach the relaxation response to the phobic stimulus. But the method is also obviously cognitive, in having the participant imagine the fearful stimuli.

Is desensitization effective? Some now classic studies found it was more effective than "insight" or psychoanalytic therapy (Paul, 1967). Several literature summaries suggest it is the method of choice for fears involving specific, identifiable referents, such as insects and snakes, heights, public speaking, and so on (Kazdin & Wilcoxon, 1976; Linden, 1981). Is the effectiveness due to the counterconditioning? Maybe fear reduction is due to extinction, since desensitization includes nonthreatening exposure to phobic stimuli. There is evidence pro and con on the effectiveness of exposure alone. One study of snake phobias found that pairing items from the anxiety-hierarchy with relaxation was necessary for fear reduction. Training in relaxation alone or exposure to the anxiety-hierarchy items alone was not sufficient to reduce dear (Davison, 1968). Alternatively, recent reviews have distinguished between facilitative components, which may enhance the therapeutic outcome, and essential components, those that are necessary for the therapy to be effective. The essential component of desensitization is "repeated exposure to anxiety-evoking situations without the client actually experiencing any negative consequences" (Spiegler & Guevremont, 1993, p. 205). Contemporary treatments for phobias, as well obsessive-compulsive and panic disorder, seem to regularly include exposure as part of the therapy. This is supplemented with cognitive therapies that attempt to give the patient a sense of control, self-confidence and self-competence, and some understanding into the disorder.

Summary

Classical conditioning, also called Pavlovian conditioning, is not the simple form of reflex learning portrayed in popular stereotypes. It is a flexible and adaptive form of associative learning.

The Definition of Classical Conditioning

In classical conditioning, an initially neutral conditioned stimulus, or CS, is presented with a biologically significant unconditioned stimulus, or US. The US elicits an unconditioned response, the UR. After a number of pairings, the CS comes to elicit a conditioned response. Contemporary examples of conditioning allow for indirect measures of learning other than the traditional CR.

Methods of Studying Classical Conditioning

A variety of specific procedures are used in studying conditioning, including salivary conditioning, eye-blink conditioning, and galvanic skin conductance responses (GSR). Tones and lights serve as CSs, and the USs are significant stimuli such as food, airpuff, or shock. The learned CR often resembles the UR, such as salivation or an eyeblink. Some other methods of conditioning include taste-aversion learning and evaluative conditioning. The CR in these cases is indirectly assessed, through aversion or avoidance of the CS, for example.

Various kinds of stimuli can serve as CSs, including external and interoceptive stimuli, and contextual and temporal stimuli. The unconditioned stimuli are often reflex-eliciting, but stimuli with acquired values are sometimes used.

Basic Phenomena of Conditioning

Acquisition refers to the development of a CR across pairings of the CS and US. Control procedures, such as unpaired CS and US presentations and randomly scheduled CS and US presentations, are needed to evaluate nonconditioning sources of responding.

Extinction refers to the presentation of the CS alone after conditioning, and to the decline in responding to the CS that then occurs. The CR spontaneously recovers after a period of time without stimulation, indicating the CS–US association has been suppressed but is still present. Conditioned responding generalizes to stimuli that are similar to the CS. A discrimination can be trained by presenting one CS with the US and another CS without the US.

The Role of Contiguity

Conditioning is affected by the temporal contiguity, or spacing, between the CS and US. Forward pairings, in the sequence CS then US, produce more conditioning than do the simultaneous presentations of CS and US, or backward pairings of US followed by CS. There are optimal CS-to-US intervals, but the exact time interval varies across species and responses, and conditioning effectively occurs within a range around this optimal interval.

Other Factors Affecting Conditioning

Usually, a number of potential CSs are available on any trial. Through stimulus selection, only certain of these stimuli become associated with the US. Prior exposure to a potential CS, without the US, reduces the conditionability of the CS. This is called latent inhibition. In a compound made up of two or more CSs, the amount of conditioning is divided among stimuli. A more intense CS will overshadow a weaker CS; and the more informative or valid predictor of the US will condition better.

Conditioning to a CS can be blocked by presenting it simultaneously with another CS that has already been trained with the US. Blocking suggests that the occurrence of the US must be surprising for conditioning to occur.

The Rescorla-Wagner model describes the trial-by-trial acquisition of conditioning with multiple stimuli. The increment in conditioning on each trial is a function of the difference between the maximal amount of conditioning possible with a given US and the associative strengths of whatever CSs are present at the start of a trial. In the blocking procedure, this difference will be smaller because of the high associative strength of the pretrained CS.

Conditioning is affected by the relevance of the CS to the US, also referred to as CS and US belongingness. Certain interoceptive CSs, such as taste and odor, easily condition with certain types of USs, such as poison, and condition slowly if at all with other USs, such as electric shock. Correspondingly, exteroceptive CSs, such as tones and lights, quickly condition with external USs, such as shock, and poorly if at all with internal USs, such as poison, as shown in Garcia and Koelling's experiment using a bright-noisy-tasty CS. Taste-aversion learning may occur readily because organisms are biologically prepared to form associations between certain classes of stimuli. Alternatively, there may be an associative bias to form these associations, based on previous learning history.

Conditioned inhibition occurs when there is a negative correlation between the CS and the US: The US is more likely to occur without the CS than with it. Inhibition can be conditioned through discrimination training (CS–), contrast training of an inhibitor that is paired with an excitor (CS+/CSx-no US), or through backward conditioning. Inhibition is assessed by summation tests or retarded excitatory conditioning.

What Is Learned in Classical Conditioning?

Stimulus–response (S–R) theory states the CS comes to elicit the unconditioned response, or some portion of the UR. However, an overt UR is not necessary for conditioning to occur, and sometimes the CR is not the same as the UR.

The stimulus–stimulus (S–S) theory states that conditioning produces an association between the learned, internal representations of the CS and the US. This theory specifies that knowledge of the US is learned, not a specific conditioned response. S–S theory is supported by studies of sensory preconditioning, in which an association is sometimes demonstrated between two neutral CSs that have been paired. The size of the CR after conditioning also changes in reaction to devaluation of the US.

The preparatory response theory (R-S) theory states that the conditioned response is reinforced by making the US more palatable or less aversive. However, counterproductive CRs are sometimes acquired.

What is the role of awareness in conditioning? Participants can often verbally report the CS–US contingency that they have experienced, but conscious awareness can be excluded by using distractor tasks, simpler organisms, or response systems beyond awareness.

Extensions of Conditioning

Repeated exposure to a drug can lead to the development of tolerance: The drug seemingly loses its effectiveness. Research on drug conditioning shows that drugs can act as USs, that contextual stimuli can act as CSs, and that the conditioned response may be opposite to the UR. Thus, tolerance may develop due to compensating CRs that counteract the UR.

Immune system reactions may become conditioned. A taste (the CS) paired with an immune-suppressing drug (the US) may itself acquire immune system–suppressing properties. Unlike tolerance with morphine, the immune CRs mimic the URs.

Applications of Conditioning

How do fears and phobias originate? A classical conditioning theory says that an initially neutral stimulus becomes conditioned (phobic) because it has been paired with fear, pain or trauma. In Watson and Rayner's study, a child became fearful of a rat (used as the CS) that was paired with a loud noise (the US). The conditioning model has been updated by the addition of vicarious learning (learning fears through observation of other's fears) and preparedness (evolution has prepared us to readily acquire certain fears that have high survival value, such as fear of darkness, heights, or snakes). However, previous learning may bias our expectancies that certain stimuli (such as snakes) are dangerous.

If fears can be conditioned, it would seem reasonable to suppose that they could be unlearned also. The counterconditioning technique of systematic desensitization, developed by Joseph Wolpe, is one such method. The phobic stimulus is treated as a CS, and is paired with a response that is incompatible with fear, usually relaxation. Desensitization is effective in treating phobias, possibly due to extinction of fear to the phobic object or situation.

Instrumental Conditioning

Reward

Many of us engage in various behaviors we wish we didn't: vices such smoking or drinking too much, dangerous actions such as speeding, or so-called nervous habits of nail biting, hair pulling, and teeth grinding. These bad habits are seemingly automatic, pervasive, and beyond remediation. Why do we do these things? There are other behaviors we wish we did perform habitually: studying, exercising, and controlling our diets. Why are they so difficult to start and maintain?

     Self-behavior modification attempts to deal with such behaviors. The idea is to modify our own behaviors, either to decrease unwanted behaviors (such as smoking or speeding) or increase desired behaviors (such as studying or exercising). Drawing on the basic research from the laboratory, behavior modifiers have identified two elements influencing habitual behaviors: stimuli that seem to trigger the behaviors and consequences that seem to reinforce the behaviors.

As a starting point, our bad behaviors are probably reinforced, or rewarded, by some positive outcome that followed. Maybe nail biting is calming. Speeding certainly gets you where you are going faster, and beyond that there may be the thrill of fast driving. Smoking is rewarded with peer approval and maybe a little rush from the nicotine. Habitual behaviors are also associated with stimuli in the environment that trigger, evoke, signal, or set the occasion for the habitual behavior. Smoking becomes attached to too many eliciting stimuli: after eating, after class, after a meeting, while socializing. Nail biting or hair pulling are triggered by ever more nervous situations: scary movies, talking to instructors or bosses, working out conflicts with roommates, and ruminating about tomorrow's assignment.

On the other hand, desirable behaviors are not immediately reinforced. Studying is daily, but the opportunity to earn a good exam grade happens only occasionally in the semester. Exercising has long-term consequences, but little in the way of immediate gratification (at first) for all that expenditure of energy. Nor are these behaviors connected to any triggers. There is not yet a habitual time or place to evoke exercising, or studying, effortlessly.

The remedies are, first, change the consequence of the behavior. Fine yourself for smoking, speeding, or cursing. Schedule positive consequences for studying or exercising. Next, establish set stimulus conditions to be associated with the desired behaviors: a time and place exclusively devoted to exercise or study. Such prescriptions sound like exercises in self-control, which is what we believe we are lacking to begin with. After all, if you had the will power, you would stop smoking and start exercising. The self-modification perspective shies away from explanations based on personal weaknesses, and instead replaces them with eliciting stimuli and reinforcing consequences, objective conditions that can be manipulated and that do influence behavior.

The topic of this chapter is instrumental learning. *Instrumental learning* is learning the connection between a behavior and its consequence. The behaviors of individual organisms are instrumental in producing various outcomes, some positive and some unwanted. The chapter deals more broadly with behavior than just our bad habits. Our intention is to derive some systematic principles that apply to eliciting stimuli, instrumental behaviors, and the consequences arranged.

Definition and History

Thorndike and Trial-and-Error Learning

Learning evolved as a means for organisms to adapt to changing environments. Whatever the underlying mechanisms involved in learning, they need to be universal and applicable across the phylogenetic scale. Learning occurs in animals that are not conscious and rational, and so the mechanisms need not involve conscious deliberation and reflection. In his research, Edward Lee Thorndike sought to observe the development of an adaptive behavior in order to systematize the principles involved (Thorndike, 1898, 1911).

Among the many learning tasks he employed, the best known is "cats in a puzzle box." Here, cats are placed in a wooden crate having a hinged door in the front and a trip mechanism somewhere in the box. Some disguised mechanism would open the door, allowing the cat to escape. For example, pushing a pole that sticks up through the floor or pulling a loop of wire hanging in the back of the box would open the door. Thorndike chose responses that were not already in the cats' repertoire, to study how the response developed with practice. Each time the animal tripped the mechanism and escaped, the cat would be replaced in the box to try again. Learning could be measured by the time required to escape the box across trials.

Thorndike observed and named a number of characteristics of what we now call instrumental learning. First, he described the animal's efforts to escape as *trial and error.* The cat tries many behaviors at first, such as clawing and scratching at the door. Gradually, over trials, ineffective responses drop out. Another response becomes more frequent, the one that immediately precedes the door opening. If the cat was brushing against the pole, the animal comes to do this more frequently. In fact, these behaviors become repetitive and *stereotyped:* The same form of the response occurs trial after trial.

Thorndike explained the learning by his *law of effect:* "Of several responses made to the same situation, those which are accompanied or closely followed by satisfaction to the animal will, other things being equal, be more firmly connected with the situation, so that, when it recurs, they will be more likely to recur; those that are accompanied or closely followed by discomfort to the animal will, other things being equal, have their connections to the situation weakened.... The greater the satisfaction or discomfort, the greater the strengthening or weakening of the bond" (Thorndike, 1911, p. 244). The law of effect is a statement of the *principle of reinforcement:* Behavior, in its form, timing, and probability of occurrence, is modified by the consequences of the behavior.

The escape response comes under the control of the environmental stimuli present at the time the response occurs, in this case, the stimuli of the puzzle box. These stimuli later would be called *discriminative stimuli.* They signal when (or where) reinforcement is available. The response would be called an *instrumental response;* it is instrumental in producing reinforcement. Learning, according to Thorndike, is the formation of a *stimulus–response* (or S–R) connection, from discriminative stimulus to the instrumental response, and reinforcement is what conditions or strengthens this S–R connection.

Thorndike's conception of learning was that reward exerted its effect mechanistically, meaning automatically and without conscious thought or reasoning. In opposition to this was the view that learning occurred through intelligent problem solving, or insight. Insight implies that the animal suddenly comprehends the door-opening mechanics. The light bulb flashes overhead, the cats slaps its forehead and says to itself, "Oh, now I get it! The pole is connected to the door." As intelligent as many animals (including humans) are, much of their learning is nevertheless governed by trial and error. In one example of what should have been easy learning, food was placed beyond a gorilla's reach outside of the cage. A stick was nearby, within reach. Would the gorilla insightfully realize that the stick could be used to pull in the food? Or would a slower process of trial-and-error learning occur? In fact, learning by the gorilla showed many similarities to that of Thorndike's cats. Sometimes the gorilla would bump the stick while reaching for the food. Other times, the gorilla would pick up the stick and slap the ground in frustration. Only eventually was the stick used as a tool (Peckstein & Brown, 1939). Learning to use the stick to retrieve the food was a gradual process.

Although the fact of instrumental conditioning is now well established, some of the responses learned by Thorndike's cats may have appeared for reasons apart from trial-and-error learning. What does a cat do when you come near? Sometimes it rubs up against your leg. Behaviors such as pole rubbing can be elicited by the presence of a human observer, rather than because they were reinforced by escape (Moore & Strunkard, 1979). For this behavior, instrumental conditioning was confounded with another preexisting cause of the response. Fortunately, Thorndike also studied learning of unconfounded escape responses.

Skinner and Operant Learning

Beginning in the 1930s, B. F. Skinner began to develop techniques, terminology, and principles of learning by reinforcement. Skinner first developed a small experimental chamber in which to condition animals such as rats or pigeons (Skinner, 1938). This "operant conditioning chamber" allows precise experimental control over the presentation of discriminative stimuli and reinforcers, and the recording of responses. (The term "Skinner box," which is now in some dictionaries, has generally replaced operant conditioning chamber in everyday language; see Figure 4.1.) A contingency is arranged between an operant response, for instance, pressing a handle or bar, and a reinforcer, usually a small round food pellet delivered through a chute. Skinner coined the label *operant response,* as a contrast to the Pavlovian conditioned response, to indicate that the subject's response operates on the environment to produce a certain outcome. The bar press-to-food contingency should lead to an increase in bar pressing, known technically as *positive reinforcement* (and informally as *reward training*). Once conditioned, operant responses also can be extinguished. In *extinction,* the reinforcer is withheld, which should lead to a decrease in the frequency of responding. Extinction in operant or instrumental learning is a parallel operation to extinction in classical conditioning.

(Skinner [1956] later recounted how he came to invent the operant bar-press task. He was running rats in a straight alley, in which rats ran from the start end to the goal end for food reward. Skinner soon tired of retrieving them and so added a return alley for the rat to run back to the start box on its own. Skinner then wondered, why bother having the rat go somewhere to obtain the reinforcer? Why not let the rat stay in one place and do something else? And so the bar-press response was invented. Extinction was "discovered" one day when the food-delivery mechanism jammed and so the unrewarded rat stopped responding. Partial reinforcement schedules were invented as a practical solution to the problem of going through too many food pellets, which in those days were hand-made by the experimenters.)

The distinction between *instrumental conditioning* and *operant learning* is significant among researchers of each, but may be less obvious to outsiders. One difference is that in instrumental learning, discrete trials are often used: The subject is given separate occasions during which the response may be performed, for example, a trial in a maze or puzzle box. In operant studies, the subject is allowed continuous availability to the re-

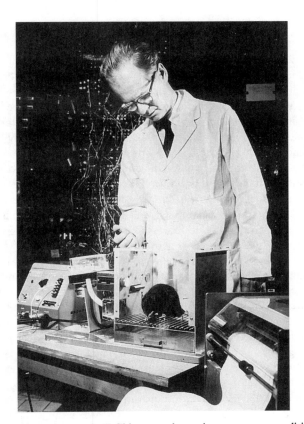

FIGURE 4.1   B. F. Skinner and a rat in an operant conditioning chamber (a.k.a. the "Skinner box").

Source: From *A History of Modern Psychology,* 6th ed. (p. 299), by D. P. Schultz and S. E. Schultz, 1996, Fort Worth, TX: Harcourt Brace. Reprinted courtesy of B. F. Skinner Foundation.

sponse. The rat is placed in the Skinner box for a 50-minute hour and can perform the response whenever. The instrumental approach averages out individual variations in performance by using groups of subjects, whereas the operant approach seeks to demonstrate lawful relationships in a single subject.

A more important distinction is that the instrumental approach tends to adopt a particular form of theorizing in its attempts to explain learning, often postulating unobservable theoretical constructs. For instance, Tolman said that rats develop "cognitive maps" of mazes. These hypothesized maps cannot be observed directly, and can be inferred only from behavior. Skinner eschewed this form of theorizing and opted instead for a strictly functional approach: The frequency of responding is a function of the amount of reinforcement, or of its delay, or its schedule, and so on. These functions sometimes take the form of mathematical formulas to describe the lawfulness and regularity of response patterns.

Methods of Study

Instrumental learning is studied through a variety of methods. Although the puzzle box is unused these days, rats and pigeons are still frequently trained in Skinner boxes. With pigeons, a round Plexiglas disk placed at eye level can be pecked. This response is called key pecking and is reinforced with pieces of grain or seeds. This is primarily an operant task.

Mazes are once again popular now that spatial learning and memory are topics of renewed interest. The simplest mazes are T-shaped or Y-shaped, with a start alley leading to a choice point and left and right goal boxes. Entry into the correct goal leads to food or some other reinforcer. (Maze learning is discussed in detail in Chapter 11.) One frequently used instrumental task is the straight alley, or runway. Basically, this is a maze simplified by the removal of turns and choice points. It is simply a long alley, with a start compartment at one end and a goal compartment where reward is available at the other end. The rat is released from the start box and the time to reach the goal box is recorded. Learning is shown by the speed of running, which increases across rewarded trials.

Several interesting methods have been developed to study instrumental learning in human infants. The response of head turning can be reinforced by the opportunity to suck milk or juice from a bottle. Trials can be initiated by a discriminative stimulus, such as a tone, which signals the availability of milk if the baby turns to the right (or left, whichever is selected as the target response). Somewhat older infants learn to move their legs in order to shake an overhead mobile tied to the limb via a ribbon, as illustrated in Figure 4.2. During acquisition training, leg movements increase when they are rewarded. After untying the ribbon, extinction occurs: The flexions decrease when they are no longer rewarded (Rovee-Collier et al., 1980).

With older children or college students, the instrumental response task can be embedded in a computer game, with certain letters of the keyboard as the response. For instance, students may be told that they are playing an investment game; each press of the space bar invests some of their money; the computer occasionally displays the profit or interest earned as the "reward" (Reed, 2001).

Positive Reinforcement

What we call reward in everyday language is a simplified and somewhat imprecise description of positive reinforcement. Positive reinforcement is defined by the presence of a response-to-reinforcer contingency. A contingency is essentially a rule, in this case one that relates performance of an instrumental behavior to a particular outcome, the positive reinforcer. In *positive reinforcement,* the reinforcer is contingent on performance of the instrumental response. Positive reinforcement is indicated when there is an increase in the performance of the response when the contingency is in effect. Who establishes and maintains the contingency? It may be the experimenter, but it could also be a parent or teacher, or even society. Are contingencies stated explicitly? In teaching our children, we more often tell them the contingencies, or rules, between behaviors and consequences. In other cases, the contingencies are simply put into effect for the subject to discover. A rat must

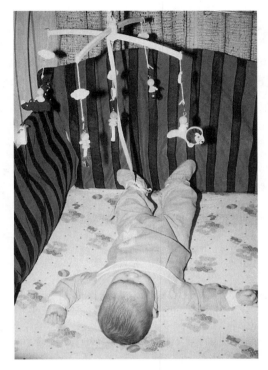
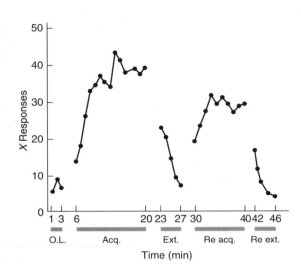

FIGURE 4.2   The left panel shows the experimental arrangement for infant conditioning of leg movements to elicit movement of the mobile as the reinforcer. The right panel shows acquisition and extinction of leg movements.

Sources: (*Left panel*) Rovee-Collier et al., 1980. Photo courtesy of Carolyn Rovee-Collier. (*Right panel*) From "Conjugate Reinforcement of Infant Exploratory Behavior," by C. K. Rovee and D. T. Rovee, 1969, *Journal of Experimental Child Psychology, 8,* p. 36. Copyright 1969 by Academic Press. Reprinted with permission.

discover what response is required to obtain food. Here we see the link back to Thorndike's trial-and-error learning.

The notion of "contingency" is important to defining instrumental conditioning: The reinforcer is contingent on, or dependent on, the occurrence of a response. Control conditions are required in an experiment to assure that the responding we observe is due to the contingency and is not incidental to some other aspect of the experiment. If I attempt to "reward" my dog's tail wagging with a food treat, tail wagging will surely increase. But this is not due to the contingency of wagging-leading-to-food, and in fact it is probably the reverse (food causes wagging!). A noncontingent control condition is sometimes used, in which the rewards are programmed independently of the subjects' behavior. That is, reinforcers do not require a bar press or keystroke; rewards just occur randomly. The control can tell us how much more responding occurs when the instrumental contingency is in effect. Figure 4.3 diagrams response-contingent and -noncontingent reinforcement.

When college students play the investment game, an instrumental condition arranges for a profit to occur after every so many presses of the space bar. A noncontingent control group receives the same profits, but they are dispensed randomly by a computer program and are not dependent ("contingent") on bar presses. The rewarded group makes many more presses than does the noncontingent group. If you question the students, the reward subjects will believe their responses lead to reward; the control subjects will not perceive a connection between response and reward (Reed, 2001; Shanks & Dickinson, 1991).

Reinforcement Variables Affecting Acquisition

Positive reinforcers can be varied along several dimensions, each of which affects how quickly a response is acquired and the final level of performance that is attained. These variables include the amount and delay of reinforcement and the consistency with which reinforcement is administered.

Amount and Quality of Reinforcement

As a general principle, larger rewards produce better performance (i.e., more responses or faster responding) than do smaller rewards. For instance, rats will run faster in a straight alley for larger rewards than for smaller rewards. Illustrative data are shown in the top left panel of Figure 4.4. The reinforcer was either 1 gram of food or 0.05 gram. The large-reward animals ran faster than did the small-reward animals (Spence, 1956). (The other panels of Figure 4.4 show the effects of two other variables, the number of hours of food deprivation and the delay of reward, both of which are considered later.) Children offered points for completing school work accomplished more when more points were offered (e.g., Wolf, Giles, & Hall, 1968). The points are later exchanged for a toy, stickers, play time, and so on. The effect of reward magnitude needs to be qualified somewhat: Obviously, care must be taken not to satiate the subject with too large a reward.

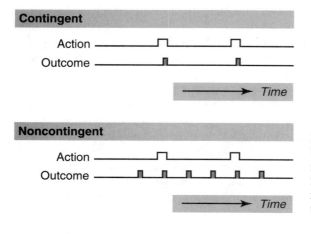

FIGURE 4.3 **The Contingent Relationship between Action and Outcome.** In the contingent relationship, each instance of the action is followed by the outcome. In the noncontingent relationship, outcomes occur independently of the actions.

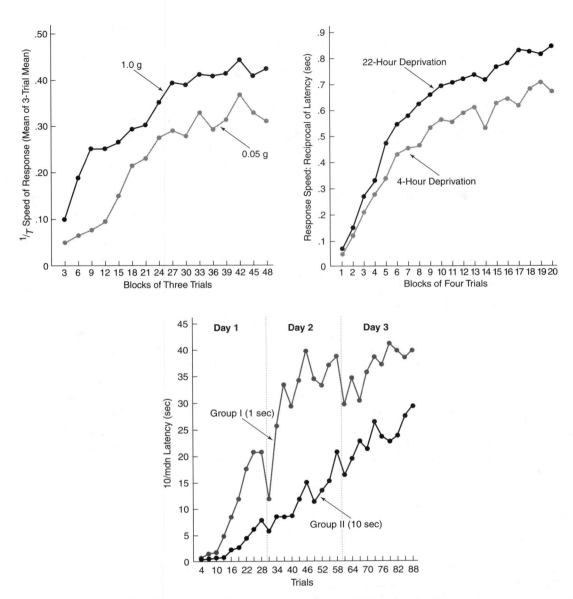

FIGURE 4.4   Effects of Three Reward Variables on Instrumental Learning by Rats.
(a) Amount of food reward, 1 gram versus 0.05 gram; (b) number of hours of food deprivation, 4 hours versus 22 hours; and (c) delay between response and reinforcer, 1 second or 10 seconds.

Sources: (a) and (c) from *Behavior Theory and Conditioning* (pp. 131 and 157), by K. Spence, 1956, New Haven, CT: Yale University Press. Copyright © 1956 by Yale University Press. Reprinted with permission. (b) from "Performance in Selective Learning as a Function of Hunger," by C. K. Ramond, 1954, *Journal of Experimental Psychology, 48,* pp. 265–270.

   Similarly, reinforcers that are qualitatively better, or are more highly preferred, produce better performance. Rats will respond more for a flavored water having a higher concentration of sucrose than a lower concentration. (Squirrels have been seen choosing peanut M&Ms over real peanuts. My guess is the M&Ms would be more potent rewards.)

Contrast Effects.   The effectiveness of a current reward is influenced by experience with previous rewards that differed in amount or quality. This is called a reinforcer *contrast* effect. Crespi (1942) demonstrated contrast in rats running a straight alley for food pellets. After switching from a larger to a smaller reward, the rats ran more slowly than animals trained with the small reward throughout. Crespi called this a depression effect, otherwise called *negative contrast* today. It is as if the small reward is perceived as really meager in contrast to the previous amount. Conversely, after switching from a small to a large reward, the rats ran even faster than animals given the large reward from the beginning. Crespi called this an elation effect, otherwise known as *positive contrast*.

   Contrast also occurs between qualitatively different rewards. In one early demonstration of negative contrast, rats ran more slowly after the reward was switched from bran mash, a more preferred reward, to sunflower seeds, which are less preferred (Elliott, 1928). These switched animals also ran more slowly than did rats reinforced throughout with the less-preferred sunflower seeds.

   Contrast in human instrumental learning is also readily shown. In one study, infants made instrumental sucking movements, recorded through an artificial nipple, that were reinforced with either water or sucrose. There was more sucking for sucrose, indicating that it was a qualitatively more effective reinforcer than was water. When water was substituted for sucrose, sucking decreased dramatically, to a level even less than that obtained by using water as the reward throughout (Kobre & Lipsitt, 1972). This is negative contrast.

   The occurrence of contrast implies a comparison between the value of the old and a new reinforcer. This suggests that contrast could be reduced if a long delay intervenes between experience with the old and new reinforcers (Riccio, Rabinowitz, & Axelrod, 1994). The delay may affect whether the amount or quality of the previous reward is accurately remembered. If you do not remember the previous reward, then the new reinforcer will not be perceived as being so different.

Drive

Drive can be described as a motivational need or desire for a given reinforcer. The level of an appetitive drive is usually manipulated by depriving the subject of access to the reinforcer for some period of time. For example, depriving a rat of food or water overnight increases the hunger and thirst drives, respectively. Drive increases responding to reinforcers that are relevant to the drive. The data from the top right panel of Figure 4.4 are from a study of rats that were food deprived for 4 hours or 22 hours before training sessions. The rats trained under a state of longer deprivation ran faster during the acquisition trials.

   Social interaction can be used as an effective reinforcer in a school setting. To build up a drive for this reinforcer, socializing could be blocked for a while. "Isolation," often called time-out, increases the effectiveness of a teacher's attention as a reinforcer. The longer the period of social deprivation, the greater the effectiveness of attention.

Do variations in drive, reward amount, and reward quality affect learning, or do they instead affect the motivation to respond? Contrast effects and changes in deprivation level produce rapid shifts in performance that are consistent with a motivational interpretation. When Elliott's rat ran more slowly for sunflower seeds, does this mean the rat knew less than on the previous trial? No, sunflower seeds are less motivating and so performance declined. This illustrates the learning-versus-performance distinction made earlier in this text.

Clark Hull (1949) acknowledged the coexistence of conditioning and motivation to instrumental performance in his theory of learning. Instrumental conditioning was represented in his theory by the factor of Habit Strength, which was determined by the number of reinforced training trials and the delay of reinforcement. Motivation was separately represented by the theoretical variables of Drive (e.g., the number of hours of food deprivation) and Incentive (e.g., reinforcer amount and quality). The actual degree of responding was determined by the combination of Habit Strength (H), Drive (D), and Incentive (K), as

$$\text{Response strength} = H \times D \times K$$

Put informally, the rat runs quickly in the straight alley because these three factors take on high values. The rat has received prior reinforced training to run (H). The rat is hungry now (D). The reinforcer is really appealing (K). (Hull used K to refer to incentive because I was already used for another variable.)

Schedules of Reinforcement

In his early research, Skinner discovered that reinforcement need not be given for each response, but instead could be given after some number of responses according to various schedules of reinforcement (Ferster & Skinner, 1957). A *schedule of reinforcement* refers to the specific contingency between the number, timing, or frequency of responding on the one hand and the delivery of reward on the other. In general terms, reinforcement can be given for each occurrence of the instrumental response or for only some. This is a distinction between continuous and partial reinforcement schedules. Reinforcing each instance of the response would be *continuous reinforcement*. In a *partial reinforcement* schedule, some percentage of the responses are reinforced.

During the initial training of a behavior, a continuous schedule of reward generally produces more rapid conditioning or a higher level of responding than does a partial reinforcement schedule. If one considers instrumental learning to be a form of trial-and-error learning, then the occasional nonrewards of the partial schedule may lead the subject to try other responses in an attempt to be more successful. Such strategies can lead to paradoxical results. Stevenson and Zigler (1958) compared children of average and below-average levels of intelligence in a button-pushing task. The instrumental contingency arranged by the experimenters was that only one of three buttons produced reward (a light flashed and points accumulated), and for different groups that button was reinforced 100, 66, or 33 percent of the time. The other two buttons had no effect whatsoever. The results nicely showed a schedule effect within each group of children: There was a higher frequency of pushing the correct button when reinforcement was given on a continuous rather than on a partial schedule. The surprising finding was that the supposedly less intelligent children obtained more rewards on the partial schedules than did the more intelligent children. The optimal strategy in this task is to discover which button produces reward, and then push only that button. The children of average intelligence tried patterns involving all three buttons, thinking there must be a better solution, and thus earned fewer reinforcements.

The rule that continuous schedules are better than partial schedules is not absolute. As we will see in the next chapter, partial schedules during *acquisition* produce more persistent performance during *extinction*. Also, in learning a motor skill, continuous reinforcement can block the subject's learning to judge whether the response was correctly performed or not (see Chapter 11).

Given that a partial reinforcement schedule is used, there are various ways of arranging the response–reward contingencies. In a *fixed-ratio* schedule, reinforcement occurs after a fixed number of responses (e.g., every fifth or seventh response). Fixed-ratio schedules lead to very high response rates: Reinforcement is determined purely by the participant's effort. By contrast, on a *fixed-interval* schedule, reinforcement is given for the first response that occurs after a set interval of time. For instance, during a fixed-interval, 30-second schedule, once 30 seconds has passed since the last reward, the next response will be reinforced. On this schedule, responding is infrequent immediately after each reward and then gradually increases in frequency as the time for the next available reinforcement approaches.

The occurrence of reinforcement can be made less predictable by varying the number of responses required for a reinforcer between trials, a *variable-ratio* schedule, or varying the time interval between trials, a *variable-interval* schedule. Thus, reinforcement on a variable-ratio 5-second schedule occurs after different numbers of responses that averages to 5 over trials. On a variable-interval, 30-second schedule, reinforcement occurs following the first response after intervals that average 30 seconds. Variable schedules produce relatively constant rates of responding because the occurrence of reinforcement is less predictable.

Schedules are important because they demonstrate that the rate and patterning of responding is sensitive to the exact reinforcement contingencies. Skinner challenged the critics who argued that behavior is too complex to be predictable (Skinner, 1953). Instead, by controlling the application of a reinforcer, at least some forms of behavior can be shown to be precisely predicted and controlled.

Delay of Reinforcement

Not surprisingly, reinforcement timed to occur immediately after the correct response is generally more effective than reinforcement that is delayed for some interval of time. The delay of reinforcement effect is like the CS-to-US interval effect in classical conditioning. There, as here also, we are emphasizing the importance of contiguity in association learning. The lower panel of Figure 4.4 shows the results of an experiment with rats trained to run a straight alley and given food reward 1 second after reaching the goal box or 10 seconds after entering the goal box. The short-delay group ran faster in the runway.

Delaying reward can impede learning in several ways. One explanation can be understood in terms of discovering the response–reinforcer contingency from trial-and-error behavior. If reinforcement does not immediately follow the instrumental response, other behaviors may occur during the delay interval, and they might inadvertently become conditioned. For instance, a pigeon pecks at a key but reward does not occur, so the animal starts turning around, and the food tray suddenly pops in after the delay times out. From the pigeon's perspective, the reinforcer occurs after turning, not after key pecking!

Another explanation for delayed-reward effects is that the response has been forgotten by the time reinforcement occurs. Have you ever been thanked by someone, but you forgot what you were being thanked for? Delay effects should be reduced if memory for the response could be made to persist across the delay interval. To increase the likelihood of remembering, Lieberman, McIntosh, and Thomas (1979) presented a distinctive stimulus after the response, a "marking stimulus," to make the response more memorable. In their experiments, rats ran a T-shaped maze, but were held in the end boxes for a delay interval before reward was given for a correct turn or withheld for an incorrect turn. Not surprisingly, these rats were slow to learn which turn was correct, possibly because the subject had forgotten which turn it had made. In the marking condition, when the rat made a turn in the maze, a tone sounded. The tone marked the response in memory, making the response memory more distinctive, so it could be connected later with the outcome.

Learning is also improved if the interval between the response and the delayed reinforcer can be bridged by a mediating behavior or stimulus, or by a reminder at the end of the delay interval of what the reinforced behavior was.

Self-Control.   Instrumental tasks can be expanded to allow several responses. For instance, two levers could be available in the Skinner box, each having a different reinforcement contingency. One response (say, the right lever) produces a small reward and the other lever a large reward. Similarly, immediate and delayed rewards can be assigned to certain buttons. Not surprisingly, the response producing the larger or more immediate reinforcer is selected more often.

What if the choice offered is between a small immediate reward and a delayed large reward? This sort of choice defines *self-control:* the capacity to inhibit immediate gratification in preference for a larger reward in the long run. Impulsiveness, then, would be choosing the small but immediately available reward. Reward amount and delay can be combined in experimental situations that allow the subject's pattern of responding to essentially express a preference. Whether self-control or impulsiveness occurs depends on the exact combinations of amount and delay. Self-control decreases if the delay is too long or the reinforcer too small. Self-control, or the delay interval that will be tolerated, can be increased by gradually lengthening the delay intervals before the larger rewards.

Self-control is affected by other factors. In children, age is one determinant: Self-control shows a developmental trend. For example, 3-year-olds choose the immediate small reward, whereas 5-year-olds display more self-control (Logue, Forzano, & Ackerman, 1996). Adolescents and adults are quite able of exercising control and choosing the response associated with a delayed large reward, as long as the reinforcers are points or tokens. When food is the reinforcer, even adults sometimes break down and select a response producing immediate reinforcement.

Secondary Reinforcement

So far in this chapter we have cited a variety of different reinforcers, such as food, accumulating points, or the opportunity to socialize. Some of these can be labeled as primary reinforcers, or events that are innately reinforcing. *Primary reinforcers* reduce biological needs of the organism, such as food does for a hungry subject. Other primary reinforcers include water, or relief from excessive heat or cold, or from pain. Other stimuli that function as reinforcers are derived from primary reinforcers. A *secondary reinforcer* is a neutral stimulus that has been paired with a primary reinforcer and thus has acquired the capacity to reinforce on its own. For example, a stimulus such as a tone that has been paired with food may then function as a reinforcer for the instrumental response of bar pressing. Animal trainers will often develop secondary reinforcers, such as whistles or clickers, to reinforce from a distance or to reward correct performance without having to interrupt the animal's routine. Using this conditioned stimulus to reinforce instrumental responses is known as *secondary reinforcement* (also called conditioned reinforcement), in contrast to primary reinforcement.

This procedure of pairing a neutral stimulus with a primary reinforcer sounds like classical conditioning, and indeed the goal is the same in both: to develop an association between the neutral and unconditioned stimuli. The classical conditioning comparison also suggests some procedural details that affect secondary reinforcement. For instance, the secondary reinforcer should extinguish if it is not regularly followed by the primary reinforcer. Thus, some periodic reconditioning of the secondary reinforcer is necessary.

One form of conditioned reinforcement uses tokens as rewards, which can later be exchanged for other reinforcers. In an early study, chimps were trained to bar-press for poker chips, which could be redeemed occasionally for grapes and other foods (Wolfe, 1936). The chips apparently became valued possessions in their own right, as animals hoarded them and even stole from one another.

Token reinforcement was used in one study of elderly nursing home residents in order to increase the demands on their memories and, it was hoped, their everyday memory functioning (Langer et al., 1979). The residents were encouraged to seek out and remember useful nursing home facts (e.g., events scheduled by the social director). Tokens were given for correct recall of these facts. The demands were increased weekly in terms of the number of facts to be remembered or how long they had to be remembered, and the tokens were redeemed for a gift at the end of the study. The token group was able to provide more correct answers than did the control group, and also showed some improvement in other measures of general memory.

Social Reinforcement

An especially powerful class of reinforcers for human behavior is *social reinforcement*. Praise, attention, physical contact, and facial expressions given by parents, teachers, or peers can exert considerable control over our behavior. As an obvious example, in a demonstration using a single subject, a teacher praised an otherwise recalcitrant seventh grader for completing math problems. Math-work performance increased, suggesting that the attention in this case was a positive reinforcer. The importance of the response-to-reinforcement contingency was demonstrated when praise was then withheld, leading to a drop in math work, and reinstatement of praise brought performance back up again (Kirby & Shields, 1972). In another case, a student would talk too softly to be heard, complain about illnesses, and remain apart from the other children during recess. This withdrawn behavior was reinforced by attention from the teacher and other adults nearby, who would spend time with the student. (Attention is not always rewarding; on some occasions, we might actually seek not to be noticed.) Rearranging the reinforcement contingencies to provide attention to social behavior and ignoring the other behaviors led to a change in the student's socialization. Classroom social reinforcers not only improve academic responses, but often generally improve attentiveness to possible social reinforcers for other behaviors, and decrease disruptiveness that leads to social disapproval (Kazdin, 1994).

Why do social reinforcers have such power? Some theorists argue that social reinforcers are primary reinforcers, deriving from social drives inherent in humans and other animal species (Harlow, 1959). Other learning theorists classify them as secondary reinforcers. Approval has been paired with primary reinforcers such as food or protection from danger (Miller & Dollard, 1941; Skinner, 1953).

Social reinforcers have several advantages in behavior modification over natural reinforcers such as food. Praise can be immediately given, and it does not usually disrupt ongoing behavior. Satiation is less likely a problem, and there are fewer unhealthy consequences of giving too much praise as opposed to too many M&Ms. Attention also has robust transsituationality: It can be given for all sorts of appropriate behaviors.

Summary of Some Reinforcement Variables. Positive reinforcers can be primary reinforcers, such as food or water; secondary reinforcers, or stimuli that derive from primary reinforcers, such as a tone, token, or gold star; and social reinforcers, such as praise. A positive reinforcer is more effective in conditioning and maintaining instrumental responding when the reinforcer is large; when the reinforcer is highly preferred; when the organism has a drive or need for the reinforcer; when given immediately; and when given after each response. Deviations from these general rules do occur. Contrast effects show that a given reinforcer may be more or less effective, depending on the comparison to previously given reinforcers. In self-control procedures, the characteristics of delay, amount, or quality of the reinforcers can be opposed. For example, one response produces a large but delayed reinforcer, whereas another response produces a small immediate reinforcer.

Theories of Reinforcement

What makes reinforcers reinforce? We have seen a variety of things that function as reinforcers: food or water for animals, moving a mobile for infants, tokens and stickers for young children, and accumulating points for button pushing by college students. Do these events have something in common that makes them act as reinforcers? Over the years, a number of descriptions of reinforcement have been offered. Thorndike defined a reinforcer as that which produces a satisfying state of affairs, but this is a vague and subjective description, and does not offer much guidance. Skinner adopted a very pragmatic definition: A reinforcer is whatever works to increase the frequency of the operant response. We still do not know why a reinforcer reinforces, and this definition is potentially circular. How do I know that **X** is a reinforcer? Because it increases contingent responding. Why does responding increase? Because **X** is a reinforcer. One way around the potential circularity is to show that something works as a reinforcer in other situations, not just in the context originally used to demonstrate reinforcement. This is the principle of transsituationality

(Meehl, 1950). Food acts as a reinforcer for bar pressing, but also for maze learning, or any of a variety of tricks we may teach an animal. Unfortunately, even generally acknowledged reinforcers may have limited applicability across contexts. Food will reinforce bar pressing but not face washing or scent marking by hamsters (Shettleworth, 1975). Food will reinforce maze learning by hungry organisms, but not for animals motivated by fear.

A number of theories have been offered to explain reinforcement. The major categories describe reinforcers as stimuli (things such as food, tokens, and points); reinforcers as activities (e.g., consuming, exploring); and reinforcers as information (the response was correct versus incorrect). To anticipate the conclusion derived from the following discussion, reinforcers will ultimately be found to work for several different reasons. A single explanation may not subsume all instances of reinforcement.

Reinforcers as Stimuli

Drive Reduction.   We may first attempt to define reinforcers as stimuli, such as food, water, and gold stars. Hull (1943) postulated that, at the most basic level, reinforcers are stimuli that reduce drives based on biological needs. Thus, food reduces hunger, water reduces thirst, and so on. This *drive-reduction* theory makes good sense in accounting for many of the reinforcement variables mentioned earlier. More potent reinforcers are those that reduce drive more effectively. Thus, larger (rather than smaller) rewards should reduce drive better, as will immediate reward (rather than delayed) and the more frequent rewards of a continuous schedule (versus a partial schedule).

But what about reinforcers that have no obvious relationship to drive reduction, such as tokens, points, or even money? Here, conditioned reinforcement enters in. Stimuli may acquire secondary reinforcing properties through their association with primary, or biological, reinforcers. Presumably, secondary reinforcers could transfer their reinforcing power to other neutral stimuli, thus extending to stimuli farther removed from the primary reinforcer. The many stimuli that reinforce human behavior may be said to have acquired reinforcing properties.

Hull's drive-reduction theory was an enormous influence on learning theory for many years. It nicely tied psychological explanations of learning to biological ones, and it offered a precise and testable theory. Unfortunately, numerous instances of learning without apparent drive reduction began to accumulate in the research literature. As examples, rats would learn perfectly well a variety of instrumental responses for saccharin reinforcers (Sheffield & Roby, 1950). Saccharin, a nonnutritive substance, does not satisfy hunger but is still highly reinforcing. Male rats learned an instrumental response when access to a receptive female rat was the reinforcer. This was still the case even if the rats were separated prior to ejaculation, preventing reduction of the sex drive, and if anything should have been frustrating rather than reinforcing (Sheffield, Wulff, & Backer, 1951).

A variety of other stimuli have been found to act as reinforcers, although what drive they were reducing was unknown. Rats would learn to run through one maze in which the reinforcer was the opportunity to enter—another maze. Monkeys learned to open containers to see what was inside or to press levers to unblock a window to see outside (reviewed by Eisenberger, 1972). When juvenile monkeys are made fearful, they seek out something soft and comfortable to cling to, rather than something that has previously provided food reinforcement (Harlow, 1959). In the face of these contrary results, one way to salvage drive-reduction theory was to postulate more drives: curiosity and exploratory drives, achievement motives, drive for contact–comfort, and so on. An alternative was simply to redefine reinforcement.

Incentive Motivation. Instead of reducing drive, maybe reinforcers actually increase drive. Saccharin and novel stimuli are reinforcing because they arouse and stimulate the organism. The ideas of Sheffield, Crespi, and Tolman evolved into the theory of *incentive motivation:* Reinforcers are incentives that elicit responding. This corresponds well with the way we talk of rewards in everyday language: We perform in order to get the reward. The difference between drive reduction and drive induction is the difference between push and pull: Drives push us into action, whereas incentives entice us on to obtain them.

The distinction between drive reduction and incentive motivation is illustrated in studies of *reinforcer priming.* Giving a free reinforcer, one that need not be earned, can enhance instrumental responding to obtain more of the reinforcer. Imagine giving a rat a small portion of the food reward before it enters the maze. What would drive-reduction theory predict? There should be slower maze running because drive had been lessened. Actually, a pretrial reinforcer can increase running speed by rats (Terry, 1983) or induce some people to work harder (Johnson, 1974). Hebb (1949) referred to this as the "salted peanuts" effect. You have no thought or desire for eating peanuts until someone offers you one; then, you have to have more!

One difficulty with an incentive theory of reinforcement is that instrumental responding will sometimes persist even though there is no longer any incentive. As will be noted later, satiated rats will persist in responding even though they no longer consume the accumulating food pellets.

Brain Stimulation. A third approach to defining reinforcers as stimuli seeks the underlying physiological basis of reinforcement. Possibly there is a common area of the brain that is activated by those stimuli that work as reinforcers. James Olds and Peter Milner (1954), working in Hebb's lab at McGill University, discovered that stimulation of the reticular formation in the rat's brain was reinforcing. Rats were trained to make bar-press responses in which brief bursts of electrical stimulation were given as the reinforcing stimulus. Stimulation of the hypothalamus, which is involved in regulating motivation related to hunger, thirst, and sex, worked well as reinforcement. This result suggested the possibility that a final common path had been discovered for all reinforcers.

Subsequent research has discovered brain areas involved with other reinforcers, such as those for the opiate drugs or alcohol. There has even been the suggestion that a genetic anomaly is associated with a reward-craving syndrome (Blum et al., 1996). Individuals with a certain version of the gene too easily become addicted to any of several compulsive behaviors, including smoking and gambling.

However, reinforcing brain stimulation has several properties that differentiate it from conventional reinforcers. No deprivation is needed, and satiation does not occur. Responding maintained by brain stimulation dissipates rapidly once reward ceases, whereas behavior reinforced with conventional rewards typically persists longer before extinguishing.

Reinforcers as Behaviors

As an alternative to characterizing reinforcers as stimuli, we could think about reinforcers as activities or behaviors. That is, it is not food that is a reward, but rather the activity of eating that is reinforcing. This at first seems just a matter of semantics, but the altered perspective expands the category of positive reinforcers to include all sorts of other activities that we know function as such.

The major proponent of the reinforcement-as-activity approach is David Premack (1962, 1965). His notion, generally speaking, is that behaviors can be ranked in terms of their preference or value to an individual. Some activities are highly preferred by many of us, such as going to the movies or eating ice cream, and other activities are less preferred, such as studying or mowing the lawn. These preferences can be established by observing the relative probability with which the various behaviors occur. According to what we now call the *Premack principle,* a higher-probability activity will reinforce a lower-probability activity. Thus, going to the movies will reinforce studying, but not vice versa.

A simple statement of the Premack principle glosses over some important technical details. Preferences sometimes have to be determined individually, ideally under conditions allowing unrestricted opportunity to engage in all of the relevant activities in order to determine their baseline frequency of occurrence. Timberlake and Allison (1974) noted that the probabilities of occurrence of different behaviors can vary over time, because the activities are subject to deprivation or satiation. Thus, after watching the *Star Wars* Film Festival, movie watching becomes temporarily less likely and it may thus temporarily lose its reinforcing property.

The Premack principle was neatly demonstrated in a study of two behaviors in rats: running in an exercise wheel and drinking water. Rats that were thirsty would rather drink than run. So, wheel running could be used as the instrumental response that was reinforced by the opportunity to drink. So far, this is no big deal. But what if the rats were exercise-deprived but not particularly thirsty? Given an unrestricted opportunity to engage in running or drinking, these rats would more likely run in the wheel. In this case, the order of preference for the two behaviors was reversed. Drinking water could be treated as the instrumental response that is reinforced by the opportunity to run (Premack, 1962).

The generality of this finding is shown in a parallel study of children, who were allowed access to candy and a pinball machine to first assess individual preferences for each. In the next phase of the study, each behavior was used either as an instrumental response or a reinforcer for different subsets of children. The children who had originally preferred pinball now increased their eating of candy (used here as the response) in order to get access to pinball (used here as the reinforcer). Children who initially preferred eating candy now played pinball (the response) to gain more candy (the reinforcer) (Premack, 1965). One more oft-cited example of the Premack principle was the school teacher who allowed students a few minutes of running and carrying on in the classroom as a reward for a period of studious activity. What appeared to be unruly behavior (e.g., kicking a waste basket, pushing the teacher around the room in his desk chair) was actually the systematic application of a learning principle (Homme et al., 1963).

Reinforcers as Strengtheners

We speak casually of reinforcers as rewards or incentives, but there is an alternate sense of the word *reinforce:* to strengthen. This is the original sense used by stimulus–response theorists such as Thorndike and Hull. The reinforcer strengthens the association between a discriminative stimulus and an instrumental response. For instance, when a stimulus light is followed by a bar-press response, the food reinforcer strengthens the association between the light and the bar press. Contemporary research has validated this strengthening role.

The potential strengthening effects of a reinforcer are usually confounded with its reward or incentive effects, both of which lead to improved performance. One way to distinguish the two roles that a reinforcer can take is to oppose them. Huston, Mondadori, and Waser (1974) conditioned mice to remain on a platform in a Skinner box. Stepping down off the platform, which is in fact the first thing mice do, results in a foot shock. When returned to the chamber the next day, the control mice remained on the platform for some time, the latency to step down being a measure of fear learned on the previous day. The experimental animals were fed in their home cages immediately after stepping down and being shocked. What effect would food have on learning to stay on the platform? If the food did have a "rewarding" effect, this would be to reward stepping down, the last response made, so the mice should step down more quickly the next day. However, if food took on the role of a strengthener, it could enhance the association between stepping down and receiving shock, leading to longer latencies to step down. And, in fact, the mice given food after the training trial stayed put on the platform longer than animals not fed. In a replication, sucrose given after stepping down increased learning about the shock, but saccharin did not (Messier & White, 1984). Reward effects should have been comparable between the two sweet-tasting substances. Recall that Sheffield showed that saccharin was an effective reward, so either taste should have rewarded stepping down.

Reinforcers, being stimuli of significance to the organism, produce neural arousal that possibly aids consolidation of recent experiences into permanent memory. According to the theory of memory consolidation (e.g., Hebb, 1949), a learning experience produces transient activation within certain areas of the nervous system. Reinforcers may reexcite those neural units, allowing additional opportunity for permanent changes to occur in the nerve cells to encode the learning experience (Landauer, 1969). In the experiments mentioned in the previous paragraph, sucrose and other sugars seem to affect neurotransmitter substances in the brain and produce the neural arousal needed to act as a strengthener in a way that saccharin does not (Gold, 1992). Reinforcers do not have to be rewards like food, water, or gold stars in order to strengthen learning. The critical feature is that the reinforcer enhances excitation of those neural units involved in the learning experience and in memory consolidation. This means that strengthening effects can be produced by other means than simply presenting a reinforcing stimulus. Administering, as examples, stimulant drugs or hormones shortly after a learning experience, or electrically stimulating certain areas of the brain (White & Milner, 1992), also seem to facilitate learning, and by implication, consolidation.

Reinforcers as Information

One difficulty in applying a reinforcement theory to human behavior is that in many situations there is no obvious reinforcer such as food or water, or even gold stars, present. In maze learning by humans, the outcome is simply tracing the route to the goal box. In a motor skill task, the outcome may be that the skill comes to be performed more accurately or efficiently. In such cases, we might say the reinforcer is information: "yes, I did it right" or "no I didn't." Even in those situations in which the reinforcer acts as an incentive or as a strengthener, it also conveys information as to whether the response was correct.

Biofeedback is an example of the informational role of reinforcement. A subtle, usually undetectable bodily reaction is monitored by an electrode attached to the body, such as muscle tension in the forehead. In *biofeedback,* this bodily response can be converted into an external signal, such as a tone. Changes in muscle tension are converted into increases or decreases in the volume or pitch of the tone. The goal is to learn to control the tone, thereby also controlling the muscle tension. The tone provides information about muscle tension, information that we otherwise did not recognize (see Box 4.1).

So, What Is Reinforcement?

Several theories of reinforcement have been reviewed. Although one or another explanation can be adopted exclusively, many theorists accept that reinforcement plays multiple roles. In some cases, a reinforcer is a significant stimulus that the organism needs to learn about for survival. In other cases a reinforcer can be well described as a reward or an incentive for certain behaviors. In still other cases, reinforcement is information about whether a response is correct. Reinforcers are events that elicit affective reactions of pleasure or displeasure, provide information about the world, and stimulate certain forms of neural activity. Thus, there may be no one answer to our question.

Is Reinforcement Necessary for Learning?

Much of human learning goes on without any apparent reinforcement. Memory occurs without a deliberate intention to remember in the absence of explicit rewards. Although animal studies routinely use reinforcement, and very obvious reinforcers such as food, water, or relief from shock, is reinforcement even necessary for learning by animals?

The classic test of this question was Tolman and Honzik's study of latent learning by rats (1930). Three groups of animals were trained in a maze. One group received food in the goal box on each daily trial. Across 11 days of training, these animals learned to run faster and to enter fewer blind alleys. A second group never received food in the goal box. Their performance improved only slightly over days. So far, this looks like a fairly standard study showing that reinforcement affects learning. But is it likely that the nonrewarded rats did not learn anything about the layout of the maze in 11 days? Maybe they did learn the route, but had no reason to run promptly into the goal box. After all, it really wasn't a "goal" box for the nonrewarded animals, was it? Tolman and Honzik included a third group that was first trained without reward. On day 11, food was placed in the goal box for the rats to discover when they eventually got there. On the next opportunity, day

B O X **4.1**

Biofeedback

At one time, psychologists distinguished the voluntary and controllable aspects of our body, or the skeletal muscle system, from the supposedly unconscious activity of internal organs innervated by the autonomic nervous system. This division between voluntary and involuntary has weakened with the modern emphasis on mind–body medicine, and the realization that supposedly unconscious body functions can indeed be controlled. Meditation, relaxation, and behavior change all influence the state of our physiological reactions to stress.

One difficulty in modifying an unconscious response is being able to detect changes. How do you know your blood pressure is elevated at that moment? _Biofeedback is the procedure of giving feedback about the activity of an internal response._ This feedback is a first step in allowing an individual to modify and control the responses of internal organs, muscles, brain waves, and so on. An external monitor, connected to electrodes taped to some part of the body, tells the current level of activity of the response. For example, blood pressure or muscle tension would be indicated by the loudness or pitch of a tone feedback stimulus. The individual undergoing biofeedback is instructed to try and change the tone. Lowering blood pressure or muscle tension decreases the tone. People do learn to control their internal activity when given this external feedback, learning to raise or lower heart rate, or raise or lower blood pressure (Schwartz, 1975).

As noted in this chapter, reinforcement can play several roles, from reward to incentive. In biofeedback, the information role predominates. The feedback acts as a signal to inform the subject whether and how much the behavior has changed.

In addition to practical benefits, biofeedback research has influenced basic and theoretical ideas about learning. Responses of the autonomic nervous system were once thought to be modifiable only through classical conditioning (remember Pavlov and salivary conditioning?), whereas responses of the skeletal nervous system were controlled through instrumental conditioning (e.g., Skinner and bar pressing). Biofeedback demonstrates instrumental training of autonomic responses, breaking down one division between the two supposedly different forms of learning. We also know that skeletal responses, such as paw flexion, are modifiable through classical conditioning.

How exactly are autonomic responses changed? We really are not sure. It is possible that we do it indirectly by working the voluntary, skeletal muscle system. For example, heart rate could be increased by pinching yourself, or decreased by controlling breathing. But this wouldn't really be conditioning of the autonomic system. This is why the animal studies of biofeedback by Neal Miller and his students were so important (e.g., Dicara, 1970; Miller, 1969). They instrumentally conditioned rats to increase or decrease heart rate. Correct responses were reinforced with bursts of electrical stimulation to the reward areas of the brain. To ensure that the muscle system was not mediating heart rate changes, the rats were paralyzed with a curare-like drug. Heart rate changes could not be mediated by changes in tensing, breathing, or other skeletal responses. The rats were still able to change their heart rates, to an extent that was life threatening. Thus, instrumental control of the autonomic nervous system seems to be genuine, even if yet unexplained.

12, the rats in this third group quickly traversed the maze, entering few wrong alleys en route to the goal box (see Figure 4.5, upper panel). Tolman said that these rats had learned the maze during those first days without reinforcement, but that this knowledge was "latent" (or hidden) until a reason to display the learning was present.

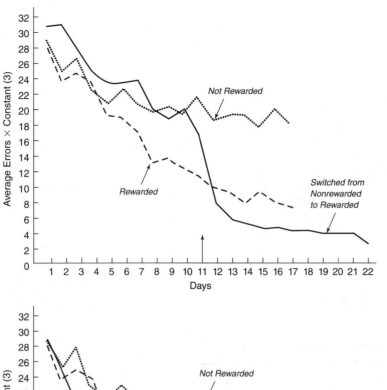

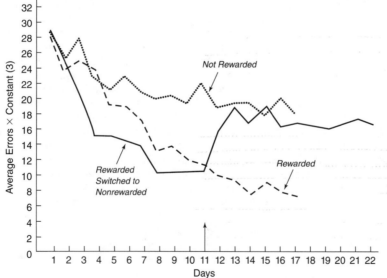

FIGURE 4.5 Results of the Tolman and Honzik Latent Learning Experiments. Both graphs show the number of maze errors made over days. The upper panel shows the effect of switching from nonreward to reward on day 11; the lower panel shows the effect of switching from reward to nonreward on day 11.

Source: From "Introduction and Removal of Reward, and Maze Performance in Rats," by E. C. Tolman and C. H. Honzik, 1930, *University of California Publications in Psychology, 4,* pp. 257–275. Copyright © 1930, The Regents of the University of California. Adapted with permission.

In a second experiment, Tolman and Honzik employed a symmetrically opposite manipulation: After training with reward, on the eleventh day, food was omitted in the goal box. On day 12, the rats, who obviously knew their way through the maze, suddenly started taking wrong turns (see the lower panel of Figure 4.5).

Traditional reinforcement theorists at first disputed Tolman's interpretation of latent learning. Maybe actually there was reinforcement on the no-food days: Removal from the goal box reduced the fear of this unknown place in which the rats had been placed. Possibly 10 days of acclimation and adaptation to the experimental procedure eliminated irrelevant behaviors and motives, and so the single reinforcement on day 11 was sufficient to condition the correct maze choices. However, even granting the contribution of these other factors, the now-accepted conclusion is that learning can occur without explicit rewards.

Other examples of learning without reinforcement were cited in earlier chapters. In perceptual learning (Chapter 2), rats exposed to shapes such as squares or triangles in the home cages were later quicker to learn discriminations to these stimuli.

Conscious Awareness in Human Instrumental Learning

In the 1950s and 1960s, several experiments were reported that seemed to demonstrate subtle shaping of human verbal behavior apparently without any awareness by the subjects that they had been conditioned. At the same time, claims were being made that subliminal learning could occur: Subthreshold stimuli would command us what to do and we would automatically respond. This possibility of unconscious learning raised the spectra of manipulation of human behavior by unscrupulous individuals. In reaction to such fears, the U.S. Congress passed legislation forbidding embedded subliminal commercial messages in films (Moore, 1982). For a decade afterwards, the scientific claims and data went back and forth over the possibility of learning without awareness. What role does conscious awareness of the response–outcome contingency play in learning?

In one of the first demonstrations of unawares conditioning, Greenspoon (1955) simply told his subjects to say out loud each word that came to mind. Greenspoon would mutter "umm humm" whenever a plural noun was emitted and make no response to other words. The subjects were not told of this contingency. The students began to use more plural nouns during the course of the session. This is *verbal conditioning*: The use of a certain verbalization is followed by an outcome that affects the frequency of the verbalization. In another version of the procedure, Taffel (1955) asked his subjects to make up sentences using any of the pronouns on a list he provided (I, YOU, HE, SHE, IT, WE). A certain predetermined pronoun, the exact one varying from subject to subject, would be followed by an "un humf." Use of the selected pronoun increased across the session. In postexperimental interviews, Greenspoon's college student participants claimed to be unaware of the contingency between the words they spoke (the response) and the experimenter's mumbling (the reinforcer). These results were taken to suggest that unconscious conditioning had occurred. Such claims were readily accepted at first, given also that animals, infants, and psychotic mental patients were already assumed to learn without conscious awareness.

Our contemporary reaction to the claim for unconscious learning is both "yes" and "no." Other research discussed throughout this text shows that learning occurs without our awareness or recollection. The effects of experience often can be subtly detected using implicit rather than explicit tests of learning. You may recall Zajonc's demonstration of the acquisition of a preference for familiar stimuli, even though those stimuli had been initially presented subliminally (Chapter 2). So, yes, learning can occur without our awareness that we have learned.

But does unawares learning occur in verbal conditioning studies? Self-reports are too often inaccurate measures of awareness. The subjects may be reluctant to report an awareness of which they are not quite certain or they give the answer for which they think the experimenter is looking. More detailed interviewing revealed that many participants were indeed aware of the response–outcome contingency or they guessed a rule that coincided with the actual contingency (DeNike & Spielberger, 1963; Dulany, 1968). For example, one student thought the experimenter was interested in hearing her talk about her roommate, and so "she" pronouns were used more often. In general, the participants who were aware showed conditioning. Participants who were unaware of the contingency did not increase their use of the target words. Interestingly, an occasional participant decreased using the selected words as a reaction to awareness ("No psychologist is going to mess with my brain!").

It is also clear that normal instrumental performance can be enhanced through verbal instruction of the contingencies. We tell children the "rules" relating behavior to consequences. Systems of reward for appropriate behaviors are more effective even with psychiatric patient groups, when the contingencies are first described verbally (Ayllon & Azrin, 1964).

Criticisms of the Use of Reinforcement

The application of reinforcement principles to everyday behavior has been a spectacular success for psychology. Behavior modification is applied in schools, institutions, workplaces, and the clinic. However, behavioral technology has been criticized both for its underlying philosophy and its long-term effectiveness. One objection is a moral one: that the use of reinforcement is manipulative. Granting and withholding reward is a form of control. A second criticism argues that certain behaviors should be performed regardless of inducements. Appropriate behavior should be expected, should be the norm, and should not depend on bribery or rewards. Proponents of behavioral psychology, such as B. F. Skinner, reply in return that our behavior is already controlled by its consequences, although we are not always aware of it (Skinner, 1971). Parents, peers, schools, churches, employers, and governments all use rewards or sanctions to control human behavior. Even if explicit rewards are not given, internal reinforcement may be present. Self-praise, or feelings of self-esteem from doing good, could derive from secondary reinforcement, or what in the old days was called conscience.

Another objection is that reinforcement undermines intrinsic motivation, or an internally motivated desire to perform a given behavior for its own sake. With *intrinsic motivation,* in contrast to the extrinsic motivation produced by rewards, the incentive to perform comes from the activity itself. In one study of the undermining effects of explicit rewards (Lepper, Greene, & Nisbett, 1973), nursery school children were first observed while they drew and colored with markers, something kids like to do anyway. Drawing is said to be intrinsically motivated. Then, in one condition, the children were offered reinforcement for doing more drawing, and in another condition there was no reinforcement. Later, the children were again allowed to play with the markers. Those who had been reinforced now colored less than did those not previously reinforced. Reward had provided an explicit reinforcer for the behavior, replacing intrinsic reasons for using the markers, such as doing it for fun.

This belief that rewards undermine intrinsic motivation has become a widely accepted argument against reward programs, in fields ranging from education to business management (Kohn, 1993). However, the detrimental effects of external rewards may be explained by mechanisms already discussed in this chapter. For example, children in the experimental groups who were rewarded for drawing may have satiated on the activity. If I reward you for going to the movies, and then offer you the chance to go to the movies again, you might reasonably decline because you have had enough for now. The decline in drawing after reward might also be due to negative contrast effects. The intrinsic rewards of the activity may appear less to the children in contrast to the explicit rewards they had recently received. Thus, rewards can sometimes inhibit behavior, but for reasons unrelated to changes in intrinsic motivation (Eisenberger & Cameron, 1996).

Finally, some critics challenge the effectiveness of reinforcement, saying that all too often, reinforcement produces transient changes in responding, which disappear when reinforcement ceases or becomes infrequent. In one sense, this should be anticipated, given our knowledge of the importance of incentive to performance as shown by Tolman and Honzik's latent learning experiment or the contrast experiments. On the other hand, learning is supposed to produce relatively permanent changes in behavior, as noted in the definition of learning given in the first chapter ("Learning is a relatively permanent change in behavior..."). We could expect more durability to learned habits.

The counterargument by those who use behavior modification is that the use of explicit reinforcers is often intended to be temporary. Once appropriate behavior starts to occur with some regularity, other reinforcers in the individual's environment may take over. A person will be praised for good behavior or feel satisfaction in accomplishing a task. And some behaviors simply have little intrinsic motivation to begin with. Not many of us find real satisfaction in cutting the grass or doing calculus. External motivation in the form of rewards may be better than not doing the work at all (Chance, 1992). (The literature on the disadvantages of reward is summarized in a book titled *Punished by Rewards* [Kohn, 1993].)

Response Learning

Some of the instrumental responses described so far were chosen by researchers for their experimental convenience. However, a significant use of instrumental conditioning is in shaping a particular form of the response. The contingencies we arrange between the exact response desired and presentation of reinforcement can be used to create new behaviors and modify existing behaviors precisely.

Shaping

Say we want to train a behavior that is not presently in the organism's repertoire. How can we reinforce something that does not occur? Skinner offered the method of response shaping. We start by reinforcing a response that is performed and that approximates the desired behavior. Once this response occurs at a higher frequency, we reinforce certain deviations in the direction of the target behavior. To teach a rat to bar-press, the rat is first reinforced for being near the bar, then touching the bar, then pawing the bar, then bearing enough weight on the bar to depress it. Shaping uses differential reinforcement, as one behavior is reinforced and other behaviors are not. Step by step, the reinforced response is slightly changed from those that will no longer be reinforced. By this process of *successive approximations,* reinforcement is used to create a new response. An analogy is to molding a figure from clay. In this case, we are molding behavior.

Some remarkable examples of shaping are evident in the work of Mary Joan Willard, a former research assistant to Skinner. She founded an organization called Helping Hands: Simian Aids for the Disabled, which trains capuchin monkeys to assist quadriplegics. The monkeys are trained to open and shut doors, turn lights on or off, change books in a reading stand, switch cassette tapes, or get and hold beverages for their owners (MacFadyen, 1986). Shaping was used to train novel and complex behaviors that certainly were not present in the animals' repertoires to begin with.

Chaining.   Instrumental conditioning can be used to construct a sequence of behaviors, with reinforcement occurring only after the final response in the sequence. This process is called *chaining,* the notion being that each response is like a link in the chain. Some explanations of chaining attribute dual roles to each link in the chain. One hypothesis is that each response also acts as a discriminative stimulus for the next response in the series. Another description is that each response also acts as a secondary reinforcer for the previous response (Grant & Evans, 1994; B. A. Williams, 1994).

In the classic demonstration of chaining, a laboratory rat named Barnabas learned to perform a sequence of eight behaviors before receiving a reward. He had to climb a stairway and a ladder, lower and cross a platform, go through a tunnel, and eventually enter a little elevator to take him to the bar-press lever. The terminal response of bar pressing produced the food reinforcer. Other examples of chaining range from teaching a sequence of steps in manufacturing assembly (Walls, Zane, & Ellis, 1981) to learning to play notes in sequence on a keyboard (Ash & Holding, 1990).

Chains can be trained in the forward direction, that is, by practicing the first response in the chain and then adding successively the next elements; backwards, beginning with the last element; or by training the entire chain simultaneously. No one method is clearly better than another in all situations. Starting from either of the ends will lead to overtraining of that response, whereas the opposite end will receive less practice. Training by the whole-chain method produces more total errors, but also more practice on all links. If either the first or last response is more difficult than the other links in the chain, then starting with that end may be the best strategy. For example, pilot trainees who were practicing landings in a flight simulator were trained with backward chaining, by practicing the landing first, then adding the runway approach, and so on (Wightman & Sistrunk, 1987). The landing itself is the most important element in the chain and one that benefits from overtraining.

Forward chaining was used by physical therapists to teach disabled individuals and stroke patients to transfer themselves from a wheelchair to another chair or bed (Wilson, 1984). The procedure was divided into a series of steps: positioning the chair, putting the brake on, removing feet from the foot rests, and so on. In this instance, the first steps needed to be accomplished safely before moving to the next steps.

Limitations of Response Learning

As powerful as reinforcement is for conditioning behavior, not all responses can be modified through reinforcement. Skinner himself noted this when he distinguished between respondent conditioning (what we have called classical conditioning) and operant learning (what we have called instrumental conditioning). Some reflex responses could be modified only through classical conditioning, whereas certain voluntary responses were modifiable through reinforcement. (We now recognize that supposedly involuntary behaviors can be self-controlled through biofeedback; see Box 4.1 on page 109.)

There are also species-specific limitations on what can be modified. Simply stated, not any arbitrarily selected behavior can be shaped using reward in any given species. As Shettleworth (1975) demonstrated using golden hamsters, behaviors such as digging and standing up were readily conditionable with food reinforcement. Other behaviors, such as face washing and scratching by the hamsters, were not readily modifiable with reinforcement. That is, giving food for each instance of washing did not increase washing.

Species limitations on instrumental learning were nicely shown in the field of animal training by two of Skinner's students, Keller and Marion Breland (Breland & Breland, 1961). They titled their paper, "The Misbehavior of Organisms," a play on Skinner's book title, *The Behavior of Organisms*. The Brelands found that certain behaviors seemed to be resistant to modification with food rewards. For example, they tried to teach a pig to put wooden coins in a piggy bank (this is just too cute!). If the pig did this, it received food. Instead, the pig persisted in rooting the coins, rubbing the coins on the ground with its snout as if digging them up. Rooting delayed and even prevented reward, behavior that is contrary to the reinforcement contingencies applied by the animal trainers. Yet, as training continued, rooting became even more frequent. Rooting is a species-specific behavior that interfered with the coin-dropping behavior.

One explanation for species limitations on response learning that has been offered is evolutionary preparedness. Through their evolutionary history, animals are prepared to learn certain response-to-outcome associations, such as which behaviors might lead to food or which behaviors lead to escape from danger. A related explanation links responses and reinforcers in terms of behavior systems. A *behavior system,* such as a feeding system or a mating system, is a related set of perceptual, behavioral, and motivational elements that function together as a unit. The activation of a given system, say, the food system, predisposes sensitivity to food-related stimuli (the perceptual elements), food-searching responses (the behavioral elements), and food-related reinforcers (the motivational elements) (Timberlake, 1994). In the case of the Brelands' rooting pig, the behavior systems approach suggests that hunger combined with food-related stimuli to instigate species-typical behaviors. In this case, the coins became associated with food, maybe as conditioned stimuli or as secondary reinforcers, and so elicited rooting behavior.

Discriminative Stimulus Control

We have discussed two of the elements of instrumental learning, the response and the reinforcer. The third critical element is the discriminative stimulus. Learning involves not only what response to make, but also when to make it. A *discriminative stimulus* signals the availability of reinforcement. In the bar-press situation, a tone or a light can be used as the discriminative stimulus, or S^D, signaling that the reinforcement contingency is in effect. Responses during S^D (pronounced "S-dee") are reinforced. Responses in the absence of the S^D are not reinforced. So, bar presses would only produce food when the S^D tone was present.

Stimulus control refers to conditioning a response to occur more often in the presence of the discriminative stimulus than in its absence. A response is brought under control of a stimulus. Stimulus control is an important aspect of instrumental learning. For us, many of these stimuli are contextual stimuli of time and place. Behaviors that are acceptable at a frat party are not appropriate in the classroom. A student may have difficulty studying because there is no time and place associated exclusively with studying. Sitting at your desk is also associated with listening to the radio, talking on the phone, paying bills, or even daydreaming. Cigarette smoking may be under the control of many stimuli. It is cued by a variety of situations, places, and people, thus making elimination of smoking difficult.

Generalization and Discrimination

Responding initially trained in the presence of a particular discriminative stimulus will generalize to stimuli that are similar to the trained S^D. This is basically the same idea as generalization of conditioned responses found to Pavlovian CSs. Figure 4.6 shows responding by pigeons and humans to a discriminative stimulus, in this case a particular color, and generalized responding to test stimuli of colors of different wavelengths. In each case, the subjects were first trained to make a response in the presence of one stimulus. Testing involves presenting other stimuli and recording the number of responses to each.

Stimuli that are similar but not identical to the S^D typically evoke fewer responses than does the trained stimulus. Generalization may be one reason why learned behaviors do not always transfer from one situation to another. That is, the stimuli in a new situation are different and therefore less effective in evoking the correct response. Imagine having taught some young children the difference between a circle versus an oval. Generalization may not occur when we use different objects to test the discrimination than the ones used to teach it. Generalization may fail to transfer when testing takes place in a different school or room, or the discrimination is not correctly produced for different tutors. These several examples point to the multiplicity of stimulus dimensions that enter into defining the discriminative stimulus.

Paradoxically, in some circumstances, responding to novel stimuli can equal or exceed that to the trained stimulus. If some attributes of the S^D are forgotten, a different stimulus will be responded to much like the initially trained stimulus. Figure 4.7 shows generalization gradients of pigeons originally trained to respond when the key light was illuminated green. Testing immediately thereafter led to more responding to green and less responding to other colors. But when tested a week later, responding decreased during the green light and increased during presentation of other colors (Thomas et al., 1985). We can hypothesize that during the delay interval there was some forgetting of the exact color trained. This may be why we sometimes mistakenly recognize someone for an acquaintance whom we have not seen for awhile. We have forgotten our friend's appearance somewhat, and so we misidentify someone else.

The complementary process to generalization is discrimination. In *discrimination training,* responses are reinforced in the presence of S^D, but these responses are not rein-

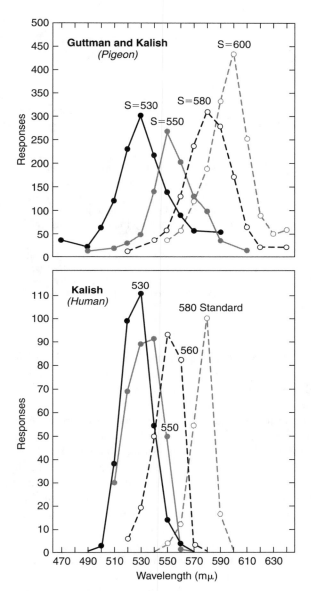

FIGURE 4.6   Gradients of Generalization to Color Discriminative Stimuli. Frequency of response by four pigeons (upper panel) and four humans (lower panel) who were reinforced for responding in the presence of colored lights of 530 nanometers (basically green), 550 nm, 580 nm (yellow), or 600 nm (orange), and then tested with colors above and below the trained stimulus.

Source: From Learning, Memory, and Conceptual Processes (p. 301), by W. Kintsch, 1970, New York: John Wiley & Sons. Copyright © 1970 by John Wiley & Sons. This material is used by permission of John Wiley & Sons, Inc.

forced in the presence of S^Δ (pronounced "S-delta"), a stimulus signaling that the reinforcement contingency is not in operation. For example, a pigeon's key pecks will be rewarded while a red light is present, but not during a blue light. A child may be reinforced by praise or attention for doing homework in the presence of one parent, but is not reinforced in the presence of the other parent.

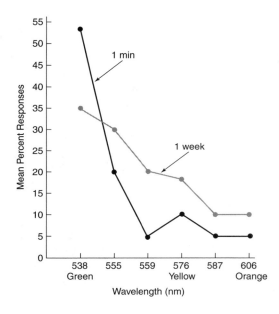

FIGURE 4.7 Generalized Responding after Two Different Delay Intervals Following Training with a Green Stimulus (538 Nanometers). There was more generalized responding to the untrained stimuli 1 week after training than 1 minute after training.

Source: From "Long-Term Memory in Pigeons: I and II," by D. R. Thomas et al., 1985, *Learning and Motivation,* Volume 16, pp. 464–477. Copyright 1985, Elsevier Science (USA). Reproduced by permission of the publisher.

Discrimination training has the effect of restricting generalization to stimuli similar to S^D. The generalization gradient can be sharpened by training between highly similar stimuli, for example, different shades of red as S^D and S^Δ, versus red and blue as the two stimuli. Thus, there will be less generalized responding.

Responding sometimes occurs during S^Δ, particularly early during discrimination training and when there is generalization from S^D. Nonreinforced responses can produce emotional reactions, such as frustration, and the S^Δ itself may become aversive through association with these negative emotions (Terrace, 1971). Imagine teaching a child a difficult discrimination. A large number of mistakes is upsetting, making the task aversive and something to be avoided in the future. Herbert Terrace introduced a conditioning method that produces less emotional reaction to S^Δ, called *errorless discrimination training* (e.g., Terrace, 1974). The idea is to minimize responding to the S^Δ (i.e., errors), and thus the negative emotional reactions that accompany nonreinforced responding. S^Δ is introduced in such a way that the subject is not likely to respond to it. The stimulus, S^Δ, then can be gradually changed, a process called stimulus fading, making it more like the S^D.

In one demonstration study, developmentally retarded preteens were taught to distinguish between circles and ellipses. A circle was projected onto one panel of an eight-cell display, and the boys were rewarded with chimes and candy for touching that panel when the instructor said "circle." Faint ellipses were occasionally projected in the other cells at the same time that the circle was shown. The ellipse was gradually made darker and more distinct as training progressed. Eventually, selection of the circle occurred with few errors (i.e., choices of the ellipse). Errorless learning was quicker and produced a better discrimination than did standard trial-and-error learning (Sidman & Stoddard, 1967). Another example involved children who had difficulty discriminating speech sounds. Via an animated computer game, sounds were presented that had certain components exaggerated by making them longer and louder (e.g., "baaaa"). The speech sounds were gradually normalized over trials as the children were able to identify them correctly, leading to nearly errorless learning (Merzenich et al., 1996).

Discrimination training can have a paradoxical effect on the generalization gradient around the reinforced stimulus. Sometimes response rates are higher to stimuli slightly different from the S^D than to the S^D itself. For example, after learning that a 350-gram weight is the S^D, and a lighter 250-gram weight is the S^Δ, a weight of 375 grams is more likely to be (mis-)identified as the S^D than the actually trained 350-gram weight (MacKinnon, 1972). The highest response frequencies, or the peak responding, shifts to a value above the rewarded S^D and away from the nonreinforced S^Δ. This phenomenon is called *peak shift*. Why does this occur? One possibility is that choice of the 350-gram weight receives generalized inhibition from the nonrewarded 250-gram weight (Spence, 1937). The still heavier weight is farther away from S^Δ on the generalization gradient and so is less subject to generalized inhibition. Alternatively, maybe the participant first learned the rule "choose heavier," and so a yet heavier weight is chosen because it fits the rule.

Summary of Response Learning and Stimulus Learning

Instrumental learning involves three elements: a discriminative stimulus, a response, and a reinforcer. By specifying exactly the form of the response that will be followed with reinforcement, the response can be shaped, or molded. By the process of successive approximations, reinforcement is used to create a new response. In addition, a series of behaviors can be linked together in series by a process of response chaining, so that only the terminal behavior is itself followed by a reinforcer. As powerful as shaping and chaining are for producing novel behaviors, not all behaviors can be modified through reinforcement. There may be species-specific limitations on which response–consequence sequences can be learned, such as digging for food rewards and running when shock is administered. Alternatively, the notion of a behavior system suggests that certain behaviors and motivational states need to match in order to function together as a unit. Thus, food searching by a hungry organism can be conditioned by food reinforcers.

Stimulus control achieved through discrimination training can determine precisely when the response is made. Just as with response learning, stimulus control is subject to limitations such as species-specific or behavior system limitations, or to generalization decrement.

What Is Learned in Instrumental Conditioning?

In the previous chapter on classical conditioning, we asked which elements, from among the CS, US, CR, and UR became associated. We can ask a similar question with respect to instrumental conditioning. Given the three elements of discriminative stimulus, instrumental response, and reinforcer, what are the associations that are acquired? All combinations have been seriously considered.

Response–Reinforcer Learning

The obvious answer to "what is learned in instrumental conditioning?" seems to be that the response becomes connected to the reinforcer. Speaking casually, we say that the organism performs the response in order to get the reward. Rats bar-press for food, young school-children read books for stickers, and so on. Responding often seems to be under exquisite control of the reinforcement conditions: Larger and tastier rewards provoke more vigorous response, delayed rewards weaken responding, and satiation of drive leads to a reduction in responding.

The theory of *response–reinforcer* association predicts that changes in the reinforcement conditions should lead immediately to changes in the response. This has been studied by changing reinforcement expectancies. An example is the earlier-cited latent learning experiment of Tolman and Honzik. Rats would run faster or slower, corresponding to their changed expectations of what would be found in the goal box. Introducing food in the maze led to immediate improvement in performance; omitting food led to an immediate decrement.

Unfortunately, behavior is not always so sensitive to the changes in outcome produced, as we will see in what follows. In addition, the response–reinforcer theory accepts the incentive theory of reinforcement. As noted earlier, reinforcers take many roles, such as providing information or reducing drives, and are not always incentives.

Stimulus–Response Learning

Theorists such as Thorndike and Hull said that a connection was learned between the discriminative stimulus and the response. The reinforcer acts to condition this association, but is not itself part of the learned sequence. We earlier saw a contemporary example of the strengthening effect of reinforcement in considering what it was that made reinforcers reinforce.

Some of the strongest evidence for *stimulus–response* (or S–R) conditioning are cases in which the response seems to have become separated from its reinforcing consequences, and has become an automatic reaction to the stimulus. For example, the instrumental response sometimes persists even though reinforcement is freely available and the response is no longer needed to obtain reward. Singh (1970) demonstrated the effects of "free rewards" in a pair of experiments using rats and children. He first trained rats to bar-press for food on one side of the apparatus, and then, in the next phase, food pellets were simply delivered on the other side. In a parallel study, 6-year-old children first learned to button-press for marbles while standing along one side of a large box (in which the experimenter was concealed, dispensing marbles), and later free marbles were given from the other side of the box. When allowed to obtain reward from either side, both rats and children more often choose the response side over the free side. Rats will press the bar, go over and eat some from the dish, and then go back and bar-press some more. This phenomenon has been referred to as the Protestant Ethic effect: Rewards should be earned through hard work.

Other evidence supporting the disconnection of responding from outcome comes from studies of habitual behavior in mazes. Well-trained rats will run through a pile of food pellets placed in the middle of a maze alley on their way to the goal box. The rats go through food, slipping and sliding, pellets flying everywhere, on their way to get food (Stoltz & Lott, 1964).

In still other cases, responding does not change to match changed reward conditions. In an early study, Tolman (1933) first trained rats to run a maze for food. Then he placed them in the goal box and gave them a strong foot shock. What did the rats do the next time they were in the maze? Tolman reported that the rats "dashed off…just as usual…and bang whack into the very food compartment in which they had just been shocked." In a contemporary example, rats first trained to bar-press for sucrose solution were then given sucrose–poison pairings in a taste-aversion learning procedure. The result of this second treatment was that the rats would no longer drink sucrose. Still, the rats continued to bar-press even though they did not drink the sucrose they earned (Adams, 1982).

What's wrong here? These outcomes appear contrary to common sense. Behavior should sensibly change in response to changed reinforcement conditions. However, persistence in the old mode of behavior is comprehensible in light of the habits acquired over many (sometimes hundreds of) trials. S–R theory predicts that the discriminative stimuli come to elicit the previously reinforced instrumental responses.

Clearly, however, behavior is not always so inflexible and S–R theory is not always correct. Sometimes the animals do react according to our commonsense notions. In other versions of the previously described experiments, Rescorla's rats did stop bar-pressing after the sucrose was associated with poison, and Miller's rats refused to enter the recently shocked goal box (Miller, 1935; Rescorla, 1987). The point is that organisms, both rats and humans, do sometimes act out of habit and in accordance with S–R theory (see Habit Slips in the Applications section).

Stimulus–Reinforcer Learning

A typical sequence of events in an instrumental trial is discriminative stimulus, response, and reinforcement. Because of this, the S^D is paired with reward. Thus, classical conditioning can occur between the stimulus and the reinforcer, or in Pavlovian terminology, between the CS and the US. The S^D then elicits conditioned responses in anticipation of the reinforcer (such as conditioned arousal, excitement, or fear), which increase performance of the instrumental response. One source of evidence for a *stimulus–reinforcer* association comes from studies in which a separately trained Pavlovian CS is presented during the instrumental task. For example, a tone CS conditioned with a food US would increase bar pressing reinforced by food. Bar pressing would increase during the tone.

Another forceful example of stimulus–reinforcer learning occurs in the pigeon key-pecking task. Illumination of the Plexiglas key, followed by a key peck, is reinforced with grain presentation. However, keylight–grain presentations alone are sufficient to condition key pecking. If the pigeon is at first blocked from key-pecking (e.g., by a transparent barrier), and simply observes the light being followed by the grain tray opening, the pigeon will immediately key-peck when given the opportunity. This *autoshaping* shows conditioning in the absence of response–reinforcer training, but which followed stimulus–reinforcer experience.

What Is Learned? Stimulus–Response–Reinforcer

Rather than concluding that any one of the preceding explanations is exclusively correct, we might instead suggest that each may make a contribution to instrumental learning. Combining the several associative relationships is possibly the best descriptor of what can be learned in instrumental learning (Rescorla, 1987). As Skinner noted, the discriminative stimulus sets the occasion for when a response will be reinforced, but the stimulus does not elicit the response. And as Tolman noted, the subject may learn a set of expectancies, some being means-to-ends sequences (e.g., bar pressing to obtain food), others being stimulus–reward expectancies (the goal box signals food or shock). The question of what is learned is also addressed in the context of animal training (see Box 4.2).

Applications

Habit Slips

As we noted earlier, a discriminative stimulus can evoke the instrumental response even though changed reinforcement conditions suggest that a different response is now more appropriate. Persistence in habitual behaviors is not restricted to animals in laboratory experiments. Humans are creatures of habit also, and often enough, we perform a habitual response instead of an intended response. How often have you driven into a construction tie-up, only to remember then that you were stuck there yesterday and had resolved to detour that road today? James Reason (1990) describes numerous errors due to habits that intrude when a new response had been intended: putting sugar in your cereal when you meant to cut back; driving past the intended stop only to realize you don't have dinner when you arrive home; and, nearly tragically, a military pilot flying in an air show who momentarily forgot he had live missiles that day and shot down another jet (the other pilot bailed out safely). Sometimes we act no differently than our rats who ran through food pellets on the way to the goal box to get food.

These sort of errors are called *habit slips:* the intrusion of a habit when an alternative behavior had been intended. Reason suggests that habit takes over when we are in familiar places, and we are distracted or preoccupied. While driving a familiar route, your mind is elsewhere and so habit takes you past the intended stop or turn on your way home. For the fighter pilot, the momentary distraction to a warning gauge allowed the habitual response, practiced in hundreds of hours of training, to occur. Under such conditions, the pilot unconsciously and automatically reacted to a stimulus with the habitual response.

Other errors are what D. A. Norman (1981) categorizes as capture errors: If two behavior sequences have identical starting elements, the more habitual behavior may capture the less frequent behavior. William James (1890) described a gentleman who intended to change for dinner, but instead changed into pajamas and got into bed. Reason reported the same slip nearly 100 years later. Both behaviors, changing for dinner and changing for bed, have identical discriminative stimuli and starting sequences: It is evening, you go to your bedroom, start to undress, and so on. As Reason notes, if your thoughts are elsewhere, your habits put you to bed.

Behavior Modification

In this chapter, we have frequently cited examples of reinforcement in everyday behavior. This ready applicability is no better demonstrated than in the field of behavior modification. *Behavior modification,* or behavior mod as it is known, seeks to apply the principles of operant learning to changing behaviors in a variety of settings. An important demonstration

---

BOX **4.2**

How to Train a Dog

People assume I am an expert on animal training because I have done research on learning using animals as subjects. But animal learning and animal training are entirely different fields, roughly corresponding to the basic-versus-applied distinction. Scientists who study learning in animals are not necessarily good animal trainers, and I suspect the reverse is also true. When my dog eats another door, I just tell people I am more interested in animal mind than in animal behavior.

Do animal trainers use the same learning principles discovered by psychologists in the laboratory? A journalist who spent time with some dog trainers found there were several approaches to training animals (Lenehan, 1986). Some trainers use instrumental aversive learning (described more in the next chapter). Response–outcome contingencies are established, as is usual in instrumental learning, but in this case, one response leads to an aversive outcome, whereas alternate behavior does not. For example, a dog on a leash tends to wander far and wide, sometimes wrapping itself around a tree or a pole. The corrective in this case is for the person holding the leash to keep walking while the leash drags the dog back around the tree. The dog is supposed to learn to stick close by the leash holder to avoid being choked, dragged, or entangled. Another avoidance learning technique sounds like a precursor to "invisible fencing." The dog wears a collar; a tone sounds if the dog goes too close to a boundary line; and shock is remotely triggered if the dog crosses the boundary. Again, the dog can avoid the shock by avoiding the tone (and therefore the boundary).

A different approach is adopted in training for obedience trials. These are formal competitions (some sanctioned by the American Kennel Club), that demand perfect, prompt, and precise responses. One trainer of national champions advocates repetition of the correct behavior so that it becomes second nature. To train a dog to walk close by you, the leash is kept as short as possible. The dog has no other choice but to walk closely, and will develop this habit after extensive practice over weeks and months of training. This procedure is reminiscent of S–R learning theory, which says that responses become habitual through repetition. The short leash prevents incorrect responses from occurring, as in errorless discrimination training.

An entirely different philosophy has been adopted by trainers of seeing-eye dogs. Reward and punishment are used, but seemingly only in the form of enthusiastic praise or verbal reprimands. The trainers assume that the dog is motivated to please its owner. Training also involves vicarious learning: The dog learns through seeing the outcome of its actions and mistakes. In our example of walking on a leash, now the dog must do the guiding. In one instance, the trainer allowed himself to walk into a pole that the dog (naturally) walked around. The trainer exaggerates his discomfort, as the dog looks "sheepish" about what it has done. They then turn around and try it again.

What is common to all these training philosophies is, first, an emphasis on practice, and, second, on outcomes (whether reward or punishment). So, there are some basics in common between the laboratory researchers and trainers. Now if I can just get my dog out of my chair....

project was reported by Ayllon (1963), who was called in to assist with problem patients in a psychiatric hospital. One patient, a 44-year-old schizophrenic woman, engaged in a number of disruptive behaviors. Ayllon first assessed the frequency of each and then applied a behavioral remedy. One problem was stealing food from other patients in the cafeteria. Ayllon used a reward-omission procedure. Each time the woman took food she was removed from the cafeteria and that meal was forfeited. (Today, this would not be allowed, because it violates the patient's rights.) The effects of this procedure are shown in Figure 4.8. Within a week, she ceased stealing food, and (with only an occasional lapse) did not regress during the year-long follow-up. During the year, her weight also dropped to healthier levels.

Another problem was towel hoarding. The psychiatrically trained staff attributed this to childhood deprivation, and the towels were substitute satisfiers for some other inner need. Ayllon treated the unwanted behavior directly. He suggested a novel procedure of "stimulus satiation": If towels are reinforcing, then a larger number of towels should produce satiation (analogous to satiating the hunger drive by giving a large amount of food). He instructed the staff to give the patient towels every day, which the patient at first appreciated, until 600 towels had accumulated in the patient's room. At that point, she no longer wanted any more; she asked the staff to remove them and, in fact, she began to take them out herself. She eventually reduced the number to just a few towels, a level that remained stable thereafter.

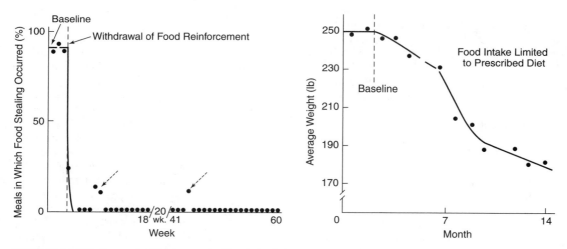

FIGURE 4.8 (*Left panel*) The response of food stealing decreases when it results in the withdrawal of food reinforcement. Occasional regression to food stealing is marked by arrows. Weeks 20–40 are omitted, as no stealing occurred then. (*Right panel*) Reduction in body weight that paralleled the suppression of food stealing.

Source: Reprinted from *Behavior Research and Therapy, 1,* by T. Ayllon, "Intensive Treatment of Psychotic Behavior by Stimulus Satiation and Food Reinforcement," pp. 53–61, copyright 1963, with permission from Elsevier Science.

Ayllon's methods were considered radical. Schizophrenics were not considered to be reasonable enough to show learning. Their symptoms were thought to be due to childhood problems that had to be resolved before any improvement could occur. Ayllon suggested that many patients are institutionalized not because of mental but for behavioral difficulties. If the goal of therapy was behavioral rehabilitation, these problems could be treated and the individual could return, or remain, in the community.

An application of secondary reinforcement in institutionwide systems is known as a *token economy*. For example, the staff of a psychiatric institution is faced with the problem of motivating patients and residents to perform a number of daily living behaviors: dress and groom in the morning, arrive at the cafeteria on time, clean their rooms, and so on. The patients can be given tokens for each desired behavior or for completion of several behaviors if a partial reinforcement schedule is used. The tokens can then be exchanged for various reinforcers such as candy, movie tickets, outdoor activities, and so on (Ayllon & Azrin, 1968).

Cognition in Animals

Humans possess many sophisticated cognitive capacities, such as assessing differences in number, judging the passage of time, and mentally viewing objects from different perspectives. Do other animals possess these conceptual capacities? Interestingly, the way to test for more complex abilities is to use a task involving simpler instrumental learning techniques: discrimination and generalization.

Can animals accurately judge the passage of short intervals of time, say 20 seconds versus 40 seconds? Roberts (1981) trained rats on two fixed-interval schedules. The onset of a light as a discriminative stimulus signaled that bar presses after 20 seconds would be rewarded; when a tone came on instead, a bar press after 40 seconds would be rewarded. Basically, we are asking the subject to judge and differentiate two intervals of time. As is typical of fixed-interval responding, the rats made few bar presses when either stimulus came on. As time passed, responding increased, as if the animals were timing out 20 or 40 seconds. (We sometimes do this with the microwave: "That feels about 40 seconds.") On test trials, reward was withheld. Responding increased in frequency as time passed after stimulus onset, peaking at just over 20 seconds during the light and just over 40 seconds during the tone. The rats were responding most frequently at about the time when food normally became available.

To test another capacity, the sense of number, rats were trained to eat three, four, or five small pieces of food from a larger pile available (Davis & Bradford, 1991). If the rat ate the correct number and then returned to the start area, it was rewarded with more food. If the animal ate more, the experimenter shouted "No!" and the rat scurried back to the start area. Across 200 training trials the rats learned to eat just the correct number of pellets (on 50 percent of the trials). Following training, the experimenter left the room and observed the animals through a video link, to show that stopping at three (or four or five) was not due to the menacing presence of the experimenter.

These are but two examples of the use of discrimination training to assess cognitive capacities. Neither of these examples used monkeys or apes. We might be less impressed with timing and counting among the so-called higher animals. The methods of discrimination form the basis of much current research on timing, counting, and sequencing in animals, as well as the work on animals' learning human-like languages.

Summary

Edward Lee Thorndike sought to systematize the principles involved in the development of adaptive behavior. Acquisition was governed by the law of effect: Responses that produced a satisfying consequence became connected to the situation. Thorndike's learning by trial and error, or instrumental conditioning as it is now called, consists of three elements: the discriminative stimulus, the response, and the consequence.

B. F. Skinner used the label operant learning to indicate that the response operates on the environment to produce a certain outcome. Skinner described extinction of the operant response and patterned behavior by providing reinforcement according to certain schedules.

Positive Reinforcement

Positive reinforcement is defined by the experimental contingency, or rule, relating performance of a target behavior to a particular consequence. A consequence is shown to be a positive reinforcer if the behavior then increases in frequency or vigor.

Instrumental-response learning is influenced by several reinforcement variables. In initially training a response, reinforcement is usually more effective if it occurs immediately after the response than if it is delayed for some time; if reinforcement is administered for each response than if only given after some of the correct responses; and if larger or more preferred reinforcers are used rather than smaller or less preferred rewards. (There are important exceptions to these principles if responding is assessed during extinction instead of during acquisition.) Response-contrast effects, or changes in the level of responding, can occur when the reinforcer is changed from what was previously used.

Drive level, often manipulated through reinforcer deprivation, also affects responding. Given the learning-versus-performance distinction, variables such as drive, amount, and quality of reinforcement each clearly determine the motivation to respond, but they may also affect learning.

A schedule of reinforcement refers to the specific contingency among the number, timing, or frequency of responding, and the delivery of reinforcement. A partial reinforcement schedule reinforces the response only some of the time. The basic schedules involve reinforcing a certain number of responses (ratio schedules) or reinforcing responses after certain amounts of time have passed (interval schedules); these ratios and intervals may be fixed or varying.

A neutral stimulus, such as a tone, may become a secondary reinforcer by pairing it with a primary reinforcer, such as food. For example, token reinforcers are used to reinforce human behaviors in a variety of situations.

Theories of Reinforcement

Skinner pragmatically defined a reinforcer as being whatever works to increase the frequency of the operant (or instrumental) response. But what makes reinforcers reinforce?

Reinforcers can be described as stimuli. Hull said that reinforcers were stimuli that reduce biological needs or drives. However, some stimuli, such as saccharin, are reinforcing but do not reduce drive, or the drive is unknown, such as for novelty or contact comfort. According to incentive motivation theory, reinforcers are stimuli that elicit responding. A final stimulus approach shows that electrical brain stimulation can serve to reinforce instrumental responding, suggesting that certain neural areas are the final common denominator for all reinforcers.

A powerful class of reinforcers for human behavior is social reinforcement, in the form of praise, attention, physical contact, or facial expressions. It is unclear whether social stimuli are primary reinforcers or learned secondary reinforcers.

An alternative approach defines reinforcers as activities or behaviors. According to the Premack principle, an activity that has a higher probability of occurrence will reinforce a lower-probability activity. Preferences for activities are not fixed, but can vary due to deprivation and satiation, and vary across individuals.

A third approach suggests that reinforcers strengthen the association between a stimulus and a response, in the sense of bonding or cementing the connection. Reinforcers are significant stimuli that produce neural arousal that aids memory consolidation.

Finally, reinforcers convey information about correct performance of a behavior. Biofeedback, for example, uses an external signal to provide information concerning the performance of otherwise unobservable bodily responses.

Is reinforcement necessary for learning? Tolman and Honzik's classic study demonstrated that maze learning by rats occurred in the absence of reward. The learning was latent until motivated by reward.

What role does conscious awareness of the response–reinforcer contingency play in human instrumental learning? In the verbal conditioning paradigm, an experimenter "reinforces" ("umm humm") the emission of a target word, causing an increase in the frequency of the target word. However, conditioning seems to be limited to those participants who are aware of and can report the contingency.

The real-world application of reinforcement procedures has been criticized on several grounds. The effects of reinforcement are said to dissipate when it is discontinued. Reinforcement can be characterized as manipulative and controlling. And, it may supplant intrinsic motivation with an external, materialistic motivation for performance.

Response Learning

A significant use of instrumental conditioning is to shape particular forms of the response. By the use of differential reinforcement and successive approximations, new behaviors are created. In response chaining, a sequence of behaviors is constructed and reinforcement is given only after the final response.

As powerful as reinforcement is in modifying behavior, not all responses can be altered through reinforcement. For example, there are species-specific limitations. Hamsters can be reinforced with food for standing but not for washing. These limitations may be due to an evolutionarily determined preparedness to learn certain response–reinforcer associations. Alternatively, a behavior systems approach (e.g., feeding or mating systems) emphasizes that a related set of stimulus, behavior, and motivation elements function together as a unit.

Discriminative Control

Learning involves not only what response to make but also when to make it. A discriminative stimulus, or S^D, signals the availability of reinforcement if a response is made. Responding initially trained in the presence of a particular S^D will generalize to similar stimuli. Through discrimination training, S^Δ comes to signal that reinforcement is not available, and so responding may then be inhibited. In errorless discrimination training, errors (i.e., responding to the S^Δ) are minimized, reducing the negative emotional reactions that otherwise accompany nonreinforced responding.

What Is Learned in Instrumental Conditioning?

One possibility is that the response and the reinforcer become associated. The response is seemingly sensitive to variations in reinforcement, and sometimes changes immediately in reaction to altered conditions of reinforcement, as shown in the latent learning experiments.

Thorndike and Hull instead said a connection was learned between the discriminative stimulus and the response, with the reinforcer serving to strengthen this bond. Behavior sometimes persists in the face of altered reinforcement conditions, taking on the character of habitual responding in the presence of certain stimuli.

Because the S^D is frequently followed by reinforcement, classical conditioning can occur between this stimulus and the reinforcer. In conclusion, we acknowledge that associations among any of the three elements of an instrumental trial are possible, with one dyad or another predominating in a given situation.

Applications

Habit slips are unconscious intrusions of a habit when an alternative behavior had been consciously intended. Environmental stimuli elicit well-practiced habits when we are in familiar places, and we are distracted, and we had intended to deviate behavior from the usual. For example, if two behavior sequences have identical starting elements, the more frequent behavior may capture the less frequent behavior.

Behavior modification is a professional field that seeks to apply the principles of operant learning to changing unwanted or inappropriate behaviors in a variety of settings, such as schools, institutions, workplaces, and everyday life. For example, Ayllon used reward omission to eliminate food stealing by a patient in a psychiatric institution. He then used satiation to decrease towel hoarding.

Another instance of behavior modification is the use of token economies in institutional settings. Tokens are given for certain behaviors or for completion of several behaviors, and the tokens then can be exchanged for other reinforcers.

5 Instrumental Conditioning

Nonreward, Punishment, and Avoidance

Experimental psychologists are often asked (only half-jokingly) whether we use electric shocks on people. Shock is occasionally used with humans, both in the laboratory and in behavior therapy. In an example of therapeutic significance, shock was given in the treatment of an unusual feeding disorder in an infant, called ruminative vomiting. Rumination means habitual regurgitation of the food into the mouth after it has been swallowed. Usually no physical causes are found, such as disorders of the digestive system or allergic reactions to the food. Psychiatrists sometimes suggest that a disturbed mother–infant relationship induces tension during feeding (Marlow, 1969). The condition can require hospitalization for life-sustaining intravenous feeding. For example, one infant's weight dropped from 17 pounds at 6 months of age to 12 pounds by his first birthday. As a last resort a psychologist tried using electric shock to punish vomiting (Lang & Melamed, 1969). A daily series of 1-hour sessions was given. Excessive peristaltic activity (monitored by electromyograms) after feeding was followed by an electric shock to the infant's leg. The incidence of vomiting decreased dramatically during the first two sessions, and shocks were rarely needed to be given thereafter. Weight gain occurred rapidly, beginning even on the shock days, and the child was soon released from the hospital.

This example shows how a behavior can be modified by aversive learning procedures. The example also raises moral and ethical questions that must be considered in the use of aversive conditioning. Is punishment justified, especially with individuals who are otherwise powerless in the situation? Is it justified if it works? Could the same results be obtained using reward and extinction rather than punishment?

Defining the Contingencies: Nonreward, Punishment, and Avoidance

Instrumental conditioning was defined in the previous chapter as the contingency arranged between a particular response and an outcome. In the case of positive reinforcement, the instrumental response led to a rewarding outcome and an increase in instrumental responding. Response–outcome contingencies also define the three aversive-outcome learning procedures that are the topics of the current chapter.

In several *nonreward* contingencies, the response is not followed by a positive reinforcer. In *extinction,* reward is omitted after those responses that once produced positive reinforcement. Another nonreinforcement procedure is *omission,* in which a selected response prevents a positive reinforcer from occurring. An omission contingency usually implies that doing something else will lead to positive reinforcement. A procedure used in schools is *time-out:* The child is temporarily removed from the situation and so is deprived of the opportunity to earn reinforcement (such as attention or playing with the other children). The intention with the several nonreward contingencies is to decrease the frequency of the response, or its intensity or strength.

In *punishment,* a response is followed by an aversive stimulus, which should act to decrease the frequency of this response in the future. Technically speaking, punishment is often defined as any outcome that decreases responding, which would therefore include the nonreward procedures described in the preceding paragraph. Here, we are restricting the meaning. Punishment is more than just withholding reward, but is instead the application of an aversive event. If you misbehave and your allowance is withheld, this is omission. If you misbehave and you are spanked, this is punishment.

In *avoidance learning,* an instrumental response prevents the aversive stimulus. The intention is to increase the frequency of the response. Avoidance is also called *negative reinforcement:* reinforcement because the instrumental response increases in frequency, just as in positive reinforcement; negative because the response removes or prevents the (aversive) reinforcer. Negative reinforcement is one of those often-misused terms in psychology, frequently being misapplied to punishment. Learning psychologists themselves often use more descriptive phrases such as avoidance learning as synonyms.

The basic instrumental contingencies of reward, omission, punishment, and avoidance learning are summarized in Figure 5.1.

There is a symmetry between pairs of contingencies. Reward and omission are often used together. Among several potential behaviors in a situation, one response is rewarded (positive reinforcement) but another response is not (omission). In the behavior modification technique of "praise and ignore," a teacher praises certain appropriate classroom responses and ignores (or at least tries to ignore) inappropriate responses.

Reinforcing Consequence

	Pleasant, Appetitive	Unpleasant, Aversive
The response *produces* the reinforcing outcome	**Reward Training** *(positive reinforcement)* (response increases)	**Punishment** (response decreases)
The response *prevents* the reinforcing outcome	**Omission, Extinction, Time-Out** (response decreases)	**Escape, Avoidance** *(negative reinforcement)* (response increases)

FIGURE 5.1 The Four Basic Instrumental Conditioning Contingencies.
The columns list the outcome, or reinforcing event, as appetitive or aversive.
The rows designate the response–reinforcer contingency: The response is, or is
not, followed by the reinforcer.

The two outcomes involving aversive reinforcers, punishment and avoidance, also
pair up. A certain behavior leads to punishment, and so this response should decrease.
Some alternative behavior prevents the punishment, and so that response should increase.
We saw this in the example that introduced this chapter: Vomiting was punished, but re-
straint avoided punishment.

Sometimes the same response could be described by either of two contingencies, depending on the motivation. Do you study to get high grades (positive reinforcement) or to
prevent low grades (avoidance learning)?

Nonreward

Extinction

If a behavior is maintained by reward, then the elimination of reward should lead to a dim-
inution of the response. In *extinction,* positive reinforcement is simply withheld following
each occurrence of the instrumental behavior, with the expectation that the response will
extinguish. Behavior modification practitioners typically advocate extinction as an alternative to punishment. In practice, however, extinction produces certain side effects that
discourage its use. First, extinction can produce unpleasant emotional effects, primarily
frustration. The organism becomes frustrated because the expected reinforcers are no
longer forthcoming. This might be evidenced by increased activity or aggression. Second,
to make matters worse, extinction can temporarily increase the nonreinforced behavior.
This is referred to as an *extinction burst.* An example is shown in Figure 5.2 for infants conditioned to make arm movements that activated an overhead mobile (Alessandri, Sullivan,

& Lewis, 1990). Movements increased during extinction instead of decreasing, which could be attributed to frustration. If you put your money in the soda machine and no soda comes out, what do you do? You push the button several more times, an example of an extinction burst. (Kicking the machine is frustration-elicited aggression.) In our earlier infant example, arm movements would eventually decrease. Then comes the third side effect. After a delay interval, the response recovers, a reaction known as *spontaneous recovery,* the same phenomenon we mentioned in classical conditioning. Repeated extinctions are often necessary to thoroughly suppress a response. Extinction really does work. But given extinction bursts, frustration behavior, and spontaneous recovery, you can see why some practitioners might be put off.

Although withholding a reward can elicit undesirable reactions such as frustration, there can be beneficial effects of extinction-elicited behavior. When the old response no longer produces reward, the organism engages in new behaviors to try to restore reward. Behavioral variability increases. In one demonstration, Neuringer, Kornell, and Olafs (2001) first trained rats to press three levers (of five levers present) in a particular sequence. Pressing the three in correct sequence was rewarded with a food pellet. Then food was withheld during the extinction phase. The animals tried the old three-lever sequence, but also tried other sequences and included the other two levers among their repertoire. This makes obvious sense in terms of real-world adaptation: If food (or water, or safety) is not obtained with the old behavior, the organism must select a new behavior, and will probably choose one similar to the old response that once worked. Whereas one might think of instrumental conditioning as inducing repetitive, stereotyped responding (which is one interpretation of Thorndike's cats in the puzzle box), in some cases it may lead to creative and novel behavior.

The Partial Reinforcement Extinction Effect

Resistance to extinction refers to how persistent a response is, even though the response is now nonrewarded. The specific conditions of reinforcement used during acquisition have a

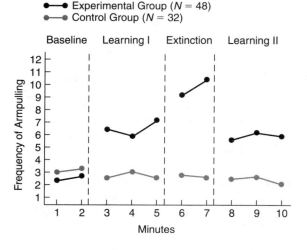

FIGURE 5.2   Mean Rate of Arm Movements. During the learning phase, arm pulling activated the mobile, producing an increase in movements from the baseline phase. During the extinction phase, when arm movements no longer affected the mobile, responding paradoxically increased, illustrating an extinction burst of responding.

Source: From "Violation of Expectancy and Frustration in Early Infancy," by S. M. Alessandri, M. W. Sullivan, and M. Lewis, 1990, *Developmental Psychology, 26,* p. 740. Copyright © 1990 by the American Psychological Association. Reprinted with permission.

significant effect on the ease or difficulty of extinguishing a response. Many of the reward variables that slow or retard acquisition of an instrumental response actually lead to sustained responding during extinction.

The *partial reinforcement extinction effect* (initially referred to as the PREE, but often shortened simply to the PRE) is the most studied of these factors that affect extinction. After instrumental training with a partial reinforcement schedule, say, reinforcement for half of the correct responses instead of reinforcing all of them, extinction is slower. The data in Figure 5.3 show a PREE in running speeds by rats in a runway (Weinstock, 1954). During acquisition, the continuously reinforced animals ran faster. During extinction, when none of the rats was being rewarded, the (previously) partially reinforced animals ran faster. Similar effects are found in human tasks in which button pressing is only sometimes rewarded. We can ask our human participants to estimate their perceived likelihood of being "correct" (i.e., reinforced) on the next trial. Often, the 100 percent reward group has higher expectations of success during acquisition, but during extinction the partially reinforced groups maintained higher expectations (Lewis & Duncan, 1958).

The PREE at first may seem paradoxical because the response should have been conditioned better after 100 percent reinforcement and therefore should be more persistent. There are several explanations for why a partial schedule produces more resistance. According to the *discrimination hypothesis,* the onset of extinction is readily discriminated from the previous continuous schedule of rewards. Every previous response has been rewarded; the response is suddenly not rewarded; something has obviously changed. After experience with partial reinforcement, the first extinction trial (from the experimenter's perspective) is not necessarily so for the participant. Only after several nonrewarded trials does the participant notice that conditions are changed from before.

Two other theories focus on the sequence of rewarded and nonrewarded trials during acquisition training as determiners of persistence during extinction. According to

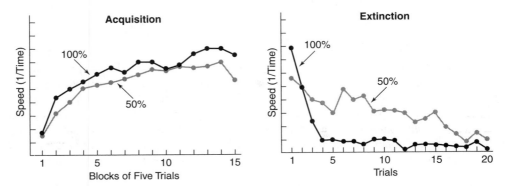

FIGURE 5.3   Speed of Running by Rats in a Straight Alley. During the acquisition phase, reinforcement occurred either every trial (100%) or on half of the trials (50%). No reward occurred during extinction, yet the previously partially reinforced group ran faster.

Source: From "Resistance to Extinction of a Running Response following Partial Reinforcement under Widely Spaced Trials," by S. Weinstock, 1954, *Journal of Comparative and Physiological Psychology, 48,* p. 319 (*left*) and p. 320 (*right*). Copyright © 1954 by the American Psychological Association. Reprinted with permission.

the *frustration hypothesis* (Amsel, 1962, 1994), the frustrating aftereffects of nonreward become associated with the subsequent occurrence of reward. That is, the frustration experienced after nonreward on one trial is followed by reward on the next trial. Frustration thus becomes a discriminative stimulus for reward. The subject who is reinforced on every trial does not experience frustration and so does not come to associate it with eventual reward. The frustration hypothesis requires that there be frequent transitions between nonrewarded and rewarded trials during acquisition in order to condition these associations.

A related theory suggests that the PREE occurs because the memory of nonreward on one trial becomes associated with the occurrence of reward on a later trial. According to the *sequential hypothesis* (Capaldi, 1971, 1994), at the start of a new trial, the participant remembers the outcome of the previous trial and associates it with the outcome of the current trial. The sequential theory, though similar to frustration theory, makes some different predictions. Fewer acquisition trials are required: a single nonrewarded (N) trial followed by a rewarded (R) trial is sufficient to produce the PREE. The assumption made is that memories can become associated quickly, whereas the conditioning mechanism of frustration theory takes more trials. Another difference from frustration theory is that trials can be spaced farther apart because the memory of nonreward is hypothesized to persist longer than the frustration produced by nonreward. The frustration from the soda machine failure lasts a few minutes. The memory will be recalled the next day when you think twice about trying that machine again. Also, sequential theory says that the sequence of N and R trials can be arranged to produce different degrees of persistence during extinction. Specifically, longer strings of N trials preceding an R trial produce more resistance than do shorter strings of N trials. Given the sequence N–N–N–R, the animal may remember that several nonrewards occur before reward eventually comes. Thus, responding should persist more during extinction, which also presents long strings of nonrewarded trials.

These last two accounts of the PREE, the frustration and sequential hypotheses, say something interesting about the effects of nonreward. Whereas our initial reaction to being nonrewarded might be to give up, the absence of reward can instead become a cue for continued efforts in the hope that they eventually will be reinforced. This notion will form the basis for teaching persistence (discussed later).

Extinction: An Overview.   The frequency of a given behavior should decline when that behavior is no longer followed by a positive reinforcer. This expected decrease is interrupted by extinction bursts of responding and by spontaneous recovery. What is interesting is that the course of extinction is affected by the previous reinforcement history. Responding during extinction may be more persistent if reward during training is intermittent rather than continuous. This partial reinforcement effect has been attributed to initial learning that nonreward is eventually followed by reward. That is, different things are learned during acquisition with partial versus continuous reinforcement schedules.

Punishment

In punishment, a target response is followed by the presentation of an aversive stimulus. In our everyday language, punishment refers either to the application of a noxious outcome, such as spanking, or to withholding a positive outcome, such as your allowance. These two uses are similar in intended outcome, which is that the punished behavior should decrease in frequency. Some psychologists distinguish the two contingencies by referring to Punishment 1 and Punishment 2 (the latter being reward omission). In our usage here, punishment is being distinguished here from extinction or omission.

There are claims that punishment does not work, or at least does not work as well as extinction. The evidence goes back to some early experiments by Thorndike, and later Skinner. For example, Thorndike had students learn vocabulary via a multiple-choice format. In the reward condition, Thorndike said "right" when the correct word was chosen. In the punishment condition, he said "wrong" when the incorrect word was chosen. Vocabulary was learned better with reward than with punishment. (Of course, "right" conveys more information than does "wrong," since the latter does not indicate which of the remaining choices is the correct one.)

Estes (1944), in his Ph.D. dissertation under Skinner, attempted to suppress bar pressing in rats by extinction and by punishing the response with electric shock. Notice the distinction between nonreward and punishment. The rats were first trained to bar-press for food reward. Then, bar pressing was no longer rewarded (i.e., extinction), or bar pressing was followed by shock. During the single treatment session, the shocked rats did indeed bar-press less than did the nonrewarded rats. This is shown as the first point in Figure 5.4. But on succeeding test days, when shock was no longer given, bar pressing gradually returned. In the short run, punishment suppressed responding more than did extinction; in the long run, it was no more effective than extinction. This finding led to the conclusion that the same end result can be accomplished by simply withholding reward.

Staddon (1995) has characterized Skinner's advice with respect to punishment: First, it is not effective as positive reinforcement in altering behavior; second, positive reinforcement is more effective in the long run. Staddon, another of Skinner's students, notes that contemporary research discounts each of these premises. Punishment is indeed quite effective in altering behavior, if it is applied correctly (see what follows). In fact, the

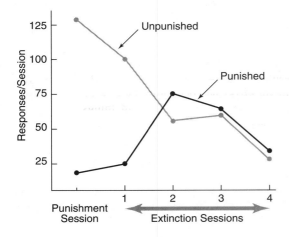

FIGURE 5.4   A Comparison of Two Means of Suppressing Bar Pressing by Rats. On day 1, the animals in one condition were punished with shock for each bar press. Extinction was used with both conditions in the next 4 days.

Source: From "An Experimental Study of Punishment," by W. K. Estes, 1944. This figure is from *Conditioning and Associative Learning* (p. 131), by N. J. Mackintosh, 1983, New York: Oxford University Press. Copyright 1983. Reprinted by permission of Oxford University Press.

most persistent responding seen in the laboratory is motivated by punishing consequences. And behaviors maintained by reward can cease when reinforcement stops; the long-term effect of positive reinforcement is no more enduring than is the effect of punishment.

When Does Punishment Work?

Punishing Stimuli. In laboratory research with animal subjects, electric shock has been the most typically used punishing stimulus, mainly because the timing and intensity of shock are readily controllable. (Note that this is *not* the electroconvulsive shock discussed in other places in this text.) Loud noise has also been used. Shock is occasionally used with human subjects as well.

Other aversive reinforcers do not have the stigma that shock has. Nail biting can be punished by painting the finger tips with a bad-tasting substance. A sudden loud noise can punish teeth grinding. Snapping a rubber band on your wrist can self-punish bad habits (I once tried this for swearing, but that damn rubber band…well, never mind). Applying noxious odors, spraying water mist in the face, or squirting lemon juice in the mouth have all been used to punish undesirable behaviors (see Table 7.1 in Spiegler & Guevrement, 1993).

Response-Contingent Punishment. Punishment is defined by a response–consequence contingency. It is important to demonstrate that the response suppression we observe is truly due to the punishment contingency and not to nonspecific effects of punishment. Once again, a control group is needed to assess the effect of presenting punishment non-contingently, that is, in no particular relationship to the response, versus the effect of punishment that is delivered contingent on a specific response.

Why would noncontingent punishment suppress responding? The administration of a noxious stimulus can arouse emotional or motivational states such as fear and avoidance. We may mistakenly think that punishment is suppressing some specific response, when in fact it is suppressing a range of behaviors. A child reprimanded in school stops talking to other children during class, but also ceases to volunteer answers to questions in class.

Intensity. An intense punisher is more effective than a mild punisher. Numerous studies have shown that a stronger shock will suppress bar pressing more quickly and more permanently than will weaker shocks.

This immediately poses a problem, because our tendency is to start with mild punishment and gradually increase the intensity if the weaker punishment doesn't work. Unfortunately, this actually decreases the effectiveness of the intense punishment. J. Brown (1969) introduced shock in a short segment of a maze that the rats ran through on their way to the goal box. By gradually increasing the shock level from 0 to 40 volts across days, running was essentially unaffected. Beginning with the intense shock would have immediately stopped running. When punishment gradually increases in intensity, habituation can occur, or adaptive responses are learned to minimize its aversiveness.

Delay of Punishment. Punishment is more effective if it is applied immediately after the target behavior, and decreases in effectiveness the longer it is delayed. Solomon,

Turner, and Lessac (1968) punished dogs by hitting them with a rolled newspaper for eating food placed next to the experimenter. Punishment was given immediately after the dog began to eat, after 5 seconds, or after 15 seconds. The dogs all learned not to eat under these conditions. The challenging test of delayed punishment was a series of trials in which the dogs were returned to the room, with the experimenter absent, to see how long they would resist eating. The 15-second-delay animals lasted about 3 minutes before eating. The 5-second-delay dogs avoided the food for 7 test days before breaking down. The immediately punished dogs resisted eating for the whole 2 weeks of the test.

In many circumstances, punishment is necessarily delayed. Corporal punishment in schools, trials in the legal system, and waiting in your room until your parent comes home all involve delayed punishment. There are means of reinstating the inappropriate behavior closer to the time of punishment. We sometimes do this with our pets. We show them the shoe they chewed or drag them back to the room they trashed earlier. The time gap also can be bridged verbally by reminding someone why they are being punished. Alternatively, one may be able to reenact portions of the previous behavior and then punish. The previous chapter mentioned Tolman's study in which he placed rats in the goal box of the maze and shocked them, yet sometimes they still ran back into the goal box. Miller (1935) redid the experiment, but allowed the rats to run the last few inches into the goal box and then shocked them. Reinstating a portion of the response (i.e., running to the goal box) made punishment effective, and the rats now avoided the goal box.

Schedule of Punishment.   Punishment can be presented following each instance of the unwanted behavior, or according to a partial schedule. Punishing each instance is generally more effective in suppressing the behavior than punishing only some instances of the behavior.

However, once punishment ceases, the response may recover, much like spontaneous recovery during extinction. We saw an example of recovery earlier when Estes' rats resumed bar pressing when the shocks stopped (Figure 5.4). The punished response may recover more after a continuous schedule, whereas a partial schedule of punishment produces more persistent response suppression.

Incompatible Responses.   The punishing stimulus can elicit behaviors that are incompatible with the desired outcome. Have you ever seen a harried parent trying to quiet a crying child by yelling at the child? Neal Miller relates a folksy example about trying to punish a dog's leaving the house by the window. (Apparently, this was a problem in the old days. Lassie and Timmy did this all the time.) As the dog is about to jump, swatting its tail only intensifies the jumping. Swatting the dog on the snout causes a rearing back, the opposite of jumping, and is a more effective punisher. (In case you want hard data on this and not just a cute anecdote, see Sheffield, 1948. In an activity wheel, shock stops a running animal and starts a stopped animal.)

Concurrent Reinforcement.   The effects of punishment can be neutralized if positive reinforcement of the inappropriate behavior occurs along with punishment. In one sense, this occurred in Solomon's study cited earlier. Dogs that received delayed punishment also received more food before being hit. The opposing outcomes, reward and punishment, may arouse approach–avoidance conflict. Or, the punishing event may inadvertently become a secondary positive reinforcer by virtue of pairing punishment with reward.

Anyone who uses punishment should assess the alternative sources of reinforcement in a situation. For instance, punishment administered by a teacher in a classroom may be counteracted by the positive social reinforcement of attention from the student's peers.

Individual Differences.   Finally, we should mention the possibility that there are individual differences in susceptibility to punishment's effects. Introverted persons may be more reactive to punishment, whereas extraverted persons may be less reactive (but more influenced by rewards). The evidence for this is only suggestive, because punishing stimuli were verbal reprimands, often as mild as the experimenter saying "incorrect" (Gupta & Shukla, 1989).

Individual differences have been demonstrated in comparing breeds of dogs. Freedman (1958) used the Soloman procedure mentioned earlier. Dogs were slapped with a newspaper and told "no" when offered a bowl of food in the laboratory room. Shetland sheepdogs refused to eat during subsequent tests, whereas basenjis and beagles (the latter, depending on rearing conditions) ate in spite of punishment.

Unwanted Side Effects of Punishment

Whatever beneficial effects punishment holds for changing behavior, it also produces unwanted side effects. These include fear, aggression, and avoidance of situations associated with punishment.

Conditioned Fear and Avoidance.   The punishment situation is exactly that used to condition fear through classical conditioning: A neutral CS is paired with an aversive US. The place in which punishment occurs or the person doing the punishing may become a conditioned stimulus that evokes fear as a conditioned response. To give a concrete example, say a child is punished in school. The school, and maybe the teacher or the principal, becomes conditioned to elicit fear. The child is then fearful in school, which likely interferes with academic performance. The child may avoid school altogether, behavior we otherwise call truancy or dropping out.

Aggression.   Punishment can elicit aggression as an unconditioned response or as a conditioned response. In some early studies of the "punishment–aggression" hypothesis (e.g., Miller, 1948), pairs of rats confined within a conditioning chamber were given electric shocks. The rats began to nip at one another, what is called shock-elicited aggression. The parallel to the human case is obvious: Physically punishing someone may provoke aggression. If the punishment is for aggression in the first place, then we have perversely designed a method to increase, rather than decrease, the undesired behavior.

In one recent example, some of the college student participants were first "punished" by receiving highly critical comments on an essay they wrote. The students then "played" a competitive reaction-time game in which whoever pushed a button more quickly gave a punishing loud noise to the other person. Students who received critical evaluations chose to administer louder noises and pressed the buttons longer (thus giving a longer-duration noise) (Bushman & Baumeister, 1998).

Matters get worse. The aggressive behavior might be inadvertently reinforced. Each time the shocked rats attacked one another, Miller turned off the shock, thereby reinforcing biting. (This is negative reinforcement. The response of biting increases because it causes shock to be terminated.) A child's aggression against siblings could be reinforced by a decrease in their annoying or disturbing behavior (Snyder, Schrepferman, & St. Peter, 1997).

Finally, the learned aggression may generalize. If the original target in the shock-elicited aggression situation (i.e., another rat) is not present, the lone rat may attack something else. (Ask any graduate student or professor who has attempted to pick up a rat after shocking it.) What has been called "displaced aggression," attacking someone who is not the source of our woes, may be an example of generalized aggression.

The punishment–aggression relationship is presented as a plausible hypothesis to encompass several related findings. However, there are exceptions to its generality. Punishment usually first provokes attempts to escape rather than to aggress, and the aggression elicited appears to be more defensive than offensive. Also, as we will see later, overexposure to shock produces learned helplessness, which decreases aggression in animals.

The aggression hypothesis has been tested in human studies, although with milder forms of punishment. In some cases, college students are exposed to mild electric shocks, loud noise, foul odors, and high room temperatures as the aversive stimuli. The students are then asked to perform some other task in which aggression might be displayed, such as a cooperative game with others who are present, to earn points or money. The prior aversive conditions evoke a tendency to "punish" others by withholding points or imposing loud noises on the other players for poor performance. Displacement can even occur when some innocent other student is punished merely for being present (Berkowitz, 1983).

Paradoxical Rewarding Effects of Punishment.   The pairing of a punishing stimulus with a positive reinforcer can convert the punisher into a secondary reinforcer. The punishing stimulus then could inadvertently reinforce behavior rather than suppress it. In one study, Pavlov presented a mild shock and followed it with food. After several shock–food pairings, the dog subsequently salivated when shocked. Would shock trained in this manner work as a conditioned, secondary reinforcer?

The psychiatrist and researcher Jules Masserman described the induction of masochistic behavior. Imagine visiting his lab and seeing a cat lever pressing and then receiving unpleasant blasts of air to its face. Bar press, air blast. Where did this perverse behavior come from? If we had visited the lab earlier, we would have seen Masserman first training the cat to lever-press for food. Then the air blasts were added, only occasionally and mild enough so as not to disrupt lever-pressing. By gradually increasing exposure to the air blasts, and tapering off the food rewards, he eventually had the cat bar pressing for punishment (Masserman, 1943). This study nicely demonstrates several points. First, a punishing event (here, the air blast) may become a conditioned reinforcer by virtue of pairing with a positive reinforcer (food). Next, the gradual increase in the intensity of punishment minimizes its power to suppress behavior. Finally, knowing the learning history of an organism can sometimes explain behavior that appears irrational.

Punishment or Nonreward?

The preceding research could suggest that a humane alternative to punishment (again, here defined as the application of an aversive stimulus) would be to withhold reward as a means of suppressing unwanted behavior. Extinction, time-out, or omission are each alternatives to punishment. But are nonreward and punishment all that different in their side effects? Both function similarly in several ways. The frustration provoked by nonreward can elicit aggression, just as does punishment. Animals seek to escape from stimuli associated with nonreward, just as they attempt to escape from stimuli that have been paired with punishment (e.g., Terrace's 1971 paper, "Escape from S-"; see also Wagner, 1969). There is some substitutability between the nonreward and punishment, in that one can replace the other in inducing persistence (Brown & Wagner, 1965, described in what follows). Maybe the deciding difference between the two is that withholding reward is categorically different from the application of aversive stimuli as used in punishment.

Should Punishment Be Used?   The answer requires a consideration of both efficacy (i.e., does punishment work?) and ethics (should it be used?). In the first case, we can ask whether punishment in a particular case will be applied according to parameters that are effective. Punishment is effective when it is intense and given immediately and consistently after the inappropriate behavior. Punishment's effectiveness is reduced if the punishment elicits responses incompatible with the punished behavior or if a given response is both punished and rewarded. Punishment can produce potentially undesirable side effects such as aggression, fear, and avoidance.

   The answer in the second case is that punishment involves moral and ethical issues as much as it involves scientific ones. As a behavior modifier, you could decide not to shock a child who engages in self-injurious behavior no matter how well it works. Or you might abstain from punishment if you conclude that the conditions under which it is being administered are known to be ineffective (see Box 5.1).

Persistence

Partial reinforcement during acquisition can make a response more resistant to extinction. The partial reinforcement extinction effect (the PREE) is an instance of a more general principle: Experience with any of a variety of what we might call "trying" experiences can induce persistence. Experience during the acquisition phase with delayed rather than immediate rewards, or with smaller rather than larger rewards, also increases the resistance of the response to extinction. Notice that these are opposite of the effects of these same variables during acquisition: Initially learning a response proceeds faster with continuous, immediate, and larger rewards (Mackintosh, 1974).

   Persistence may also transfer across different kinds of aversive outcomes. For example, say we have a response that is reinforced by food. Occasional presentations of a mild shock during acquisition increases persistence later when we attempt to extinguish the response by withholding reward. The reverse is also true: Occasionally omitting the food reinforcer during acquisition can maintain responding in the face of shock that is introduced later (Brown & Wagner, 1965).

B O X **5.1**

Punishing Self-Injurious Behavior

Self-injurious behavior (or SIB) occurs occasionally among developmentally disabled, autistic, or brain-damaged children. These children will bite themselves, scratch their skin, or bang their heads, in some cases with incredible frequencies. One case study reported extrapolated counts of hundreds of hits per minute (extrapolated because someone intervened and stopped the child before a full minute of such self-injury passed). Therapists have tried to control SIB with drugs, restraints, or the behavioral methods of reward, extinction, and omission. Most of these methods have proved to have limited value.

One promising, but controversial, treatment is the use of electric shock as punishment for head banging. The apparatus for this, called the *Self-Injurious Behavior Inhibiting System* (SIBIS) was developed collaboratively by parents, physicians, psychologists, and engineers. SIBIS consists of a lightweight headgear that senses sudden movements typical of head banging and triggers an electric shock, and an arm or leg band, powered by a 9-volt battery, to deliver the shock. The shock is response-contingent, immediate, consistently delivered, and can be intense, all of which are conditions conducive to effective punishment. The alternative behavior of not head banging avoids shock and thus fulfill a negative reinforcement contingency.

There are other self-injurious behaviors. Children may bite themselves or stab themselves repeatedly, or pick at their skin. For example, a brain-damaged 6-year-old would literally "climb the walls": she climbed up (and fell off) furniture, window sills, and roofs. The child suffered repeated physical injuries from falls. The therapist tried shock as a punishing stimulus for climbing. Climbing virtually disappeared in the therapist's office after three sessions (yes, the kid climbed there also), and in the home after almost 3 weeks (Risley, 1968).

Taken out of context, the SIBIS procedure sounds pretty immoral: shocking defenseless, dis-abled children. A number of advocacy groups have protested the device, and its use was legally banned (temporarily) in Massachusetts where it was first employed. Officials of the federal Department of Education questioned "whether society can sanction for use with disabled citizens forms of punishment, such as electroshock, that would never be tolerated for use with non-handicapped children and adults" (Landers, 1988, p. 22). In addition, many behavior modification specialists cited Skinner's research as expert testimony on the ineffectiveness of punishment.

The issue of whether to use shock is not clearly one-sided. Proponents argue that the effects of a small number of shocks more than outweigh the potential physical injury that results from SIB. SIBIS dramatically reduces the incidence of head banging. Linscheid and colleagues (1990) report several single-case experiments in which SIBIS virtually eliminated SIB. Skinner felt compelled to enter the debate to clarify his own position on punishment. "Punishment is usually used to the advantage of the punisher" and "I believe that there is no longer any use for corporal punishment in schools and much to be gained by suppressing it." But Skinner also said: "If brief and harmless aversive stimuli, made precisely contingent on self-destructive behavior, suppress the behavior and leave the child free to develop in other ways, I believe it can be justified. When taken out of context, such stimuli may seem less than humane" (Skinner, 1988, p. 22).

Why does one type of pain, that from shock, suppress SIB, when the pain from the self-inflicted injuries does not? Some have suggested that SIB is a form of compulsive behavior. Once engaged, there is no end point and so it continues. The shock is both different enough and intense enough to break the cycle temporarily. Further research is needed on the causes of SIB, and why SIBIS works.

This interchangeability of aversive consequences suggests a hypothesis of *generalized persistence:* that certain types of training conditions will maintain responding in the face of increased demands or challenging circumstances. A nice demonstration of generalized persistence is shown in a pair of parallel studies that test persistence in performing chores and school work (Eisenberger et al., 1979). In the first experiment, adult, institutionalized, depressed patients were asked to perform some ward chores (picking up, putting things away, making coffee, etc.). In the continuous-reward condition, a single chore was requested, for which the patient was thanked. In the partial-reward condition, three or four chores were performed before the patient was thanked. Later, a different person asked for some help in sorting computer punch cards. Persistence was measured by the number of cards sorted and the amount of time spent sorting. On both measures, patients in the partial-reward group were more persistent. Persistence generalized beyond the initial task of doing ward chores, and generalized to requests by another person. In a second study, similar procedures were used to reward learning disabled children. Those who were first reinforced for doing several math or several spelling problems were more persistent on the alternate task than were the children first rewarded for every problem.

The similar effects induced by punishment, delayed reward, nonreward, or increased effort suggest a common underlying factor. Possibly transfer occurs across aversive consequences that share similar negative emotional effects. (The expected outcomes in generalized persistence are illustrated in Table 5.1.)

TABLE 5.1   Generalized Persistence: The Relationship between Acquisition Conditions and Subsequent Persistence during Extinction or Punishment

Partial Reinforcement

Phase I: Acquisition	*Phase II: Extinction*
100%: Rewarded for each response 50%: Rewarded for some responses	The 50% group is more persistent

Partial Punishment

Phase I: Acquisition	*Phase II: Extinction*
Food: Food given after each response Food + shock: Food after each response, and shock after half the responses	Food + shock is more persistent

Delayed Reinforcement

Phase I: Acquisition	*Phase II: Extinction*
Immediate: Reward immediately after each response Delay: Reward given after a delay	Delayed reward is more persistent

Why is the study of generalized persistence important? For two obvious reasons: Bad habits are often persistent, even in the face of unpleasant consequences, and good habits are ones we would like to persist in spite of unpleasant consequences.

Avoidance Learning

In a negative-reinforcement contingency, an instrumental response escapes or prevents an aversive outcome. That response should then increase in frequency. Negative reinforcement includes both escape and avoidance learning. In *escape learning,* you learn a response to terminate an aversive stimulus. For example, you click your seat belt to turn off the reminder buzzer. Most research has concentrated instead on *avoidance learning,* acquiring a response that prevents the aversive outcome. Avoidance would be clicking your seat belt before the buzzer, to prevent its sounding. Avoidance learning is theoretically more challenging than is escape learning, because when the subject makes a correct response, nothing happens. Stated in this manner, how can "nothing" be reinforcing?

A typical avoidance learning task begins with a warning signal, which is followed a few seconds later by an aversive stimulus. On succeeding trials, the performance of a selected instrumental response during the warning signal prevents the aversive stimulus and terminates both the warning signal and the trial. A standard task in animal experiments uses a two-compartment, or shuttle-box, apparatus. When the warning tone sounds, the animal has to move from one compartment to the other to avoid being shocked by the electrified metal bars that form the floor of the apparatus. Another trial begins shortly, and the animal hops back to the first compartment to avoid shock.

Responses such as shuttling are *active avoidance* responses: Active performance of a certain response prevents the aversive stimulus. Studying can be an active avoidance response to avoid a bad grade. In *passive avoidance,* withholding a response prevents the aversive outcome. For example, young hatchling chicks peck at nearly anything in their search for food. If a distinctively colored piece of grain is painted with a foul-tasting substance, the chicks will learn to avoid eating grain of that color. This is passive avoidance. A familiar example of passive avoidance is the scene in every horror movie in which someone is confronted with a door. We all know, "Don't open the door!" Not opening it would be passive avoidance, although passive avoidance seems to occur rarely in films.

The infant ruminator introduced at the beginning of this chapter was exposed to both punishment and avoidance contingencies, depending on which behavior we focus on. Whereas peristolic activity was punished with shock, holding food down avoided shock. Interestingly, early during training, the child figured out an active avoidance response that prevented punishment: simply raising his leg a bit took it off the shock plate. The researcher then had to change the method of shock delivery.

(Animal participants often figure out ways to prevent being shocked, showing that they are at least as clever as their experimenters. The walls of conditioning chambers are smooth sheet metal or Plexiglass. Otherwise, rats and mice would jump off the shocked floor and cling to a seam, ledge, or even a screw head until the warning signal went off. If the grid bars of the floor were far enough apart, the animal would squeeze between them and escape. Some rats discovered that by standing on their hind legs and balancing on one bar, they would interrupt the electrical circuit between adjacent bars [Broadhurst, 1963]. One rat rolled over on the grid floor and used its fur as an insulator while it continued to bar-press for food rewards [Schwartz, 1978]!)

Avoidance learning may play a role in the development and maintenance of socially aggressive behavior of children. Children sometimes become aggressive as a way of dealing with conflict, anger, or arguments with their parents. If the child's aggression resolves the conflict, by forcing the parent to cease arguing back in an attempt to keep the peace, then aggression is reinforced. Field observations of families of children referred for conduct disorders show a strong relationship between reinforcement of aggression and subsequent behavioral problems 2 years later (Snyder et al., 1997).

A parent's use of physical punishment also can be negatively reinforced. If a parent's yelling and hitting (the instrumental response in this example) leads to a reduction in the annoying behavior of the children (the aversive stimulus), the parent's use of punishment is reinforced and will likely increase in the future (Kazdin, 1987).

Theories of Avoidance Learning

A seminal and influential theory of avoidance learning is the two-process, or Watson-Mowrer, theory (Mowrer, 1947). The pairing of the warning signal with shock conditions fear to the signal via classical conditioning. This is exactly the mode of fear and phobia learning we discussed in Chapter 3. Little Albert learned to fear the white rat after it was paired with a loud noise, and this is the Watson part of the two-process theory. Once the warning signal (or the CS in Pavlovian terminology) is conditioned, escape from the signal is reinforced by fear reduction. Albert would get away from the rat, and doing so reduced the child's level of fear. Escape from the warning signal is instrumental conditioning, the second process, which was added by Hobart Mowrer. Note that according to the two-process theory, the subject is motivated to escape the warning signal, rather than avoiding what the signal signals. That is, Albert is said to escape from the rat rather than avoid the loud noise that had been paired with the rat.

The two-process theory makes several testable predictions. One major prediction is that termination of the warning signal after a correct response is critical for avoidance learning. After all, escape from the warning signal is what is important. Albert is afraid of, and is seeking to get away from, the rat and not the noise that had been paired with the rat. The data are consistent with this prediction. If warning signal termination does not occur promptly, avoidance conditioning is markedly impaired (Kamin, 1956).

If avoidance responding is motivated by a fear-eliciting stimulus (e.g., the warning signal), then the presentation of other conditioned stimuli that similarly evoke fear should increase responding (Rescorla & Solomon, 1967). Thus, if little Albert also feared a tone, then presenting the tone and the rat should increase his running speed.

In spite of these successful tests, the two-process theory has some weaknesses. One of the remarkable features of avoidance behavior is its persistence. Phobic individuals will avoid their feared target for years. Well-trained animal subjects will make the avoidance response for hundreds of trials. This is interesting because on all these occasions, the response prevents the aversive outcome. Fear to the warning signal should extinguish, since it is not being followed by an aversive outcome. Remember, the warning signal is a Pavlovian CS.

It seems obvious to us that avoidance occurs because you have acquired a pair of expectations: Responding prevents an aversive outcome, and if you do not respond, you can expect to be punished. The first expectation is continuously verified: If I respond, I don't get shocked. The second expectation is never subjected to a reality check: not responding to see what happens now. (There was an obsessive-compulsive who snapped his fingers to keep from being eaten by tigers. When asked why he believed this, he snapped his fingers and said, "You don't see any tigers here, do you?") This explanation is the basis of a *cognitive theory* of avoidance learning (Bolles, 1972; Seligman & Johnson, 1973). We can illustrate this theory with the example of an acquired fear of germ infection. Say that an individual learns a stimulus–outcome belief (e.g., handling a contaminated object can lead to illness) and a response–outcome sequence (e.g., washing your hands is not followed by illness). Deciding whether to respond requires the integration of the two expectancies: Objects lead to infection, but washing will prevent the illness. Eliminating avoidance behavior therefore requires modifying both expectations. That is, the subject must learn that the warning stimulus no longer signals danger, and that not responding will not lead to punishment. This is the goal of some behavioral therapies for certain anxiety disorders that include avoidance responses (see Box 5.2).

Summary of Avoidance Learning. In avoidance learning, a response is acquired that prevents an aversive outcome. This is also called negative reinforcement: An instrumental response escapes or prevents an aversive outcome ("negative") and that response should then increase in frequency ("reinforcement"). For example, in a home security system, a warning beep is followed a minute later by the alarm sounding. Performance of a selected instrumental response during the warning signal, keying in your security code, prevents the aversive alarm and terminates the warning signal. According to the two-process theory, the warning signal first becomes associated with the aversive outcome. Thereafter, termination of this signal is reinforced by fear reduction. The cognitive theory of avoidance learning states that pairs of expectancies are learned: the belief that nonresponding leads to the aversive stimulus, whereas responding prevents the aversive stimulus.

Approach–Avoidance Conflict

Why would anyone persist in behavior that is punished? The sensible thing to do is cease and desist. The answer is that a given behavior might have other sources of motivation. Perhaps it was previously reinforced, as in the case of Masserman's cats, and reinforcement may still be available. Children misbehave because the misbehavior is fun.

When a behavior has two opposing outcomes, one positive and one aversive, conflict may result. A child is drawn to a parent who often provides nurturance and security, but the child also fears outbreaks of anger. A dog that has been punished is simultaneously drawn by anticipation of food or petting, and repelled by the threat of further punishment. Although either approach or avoidance may predominate, the two can be equated in a way that balances them. Miller (1959) described the intersection of these tendencies in terms of the distance from the goal. There is a point where the strength of the approach tendency is about equivalent to the strength of the avoidance tendency. Here, vacillation of behavior occurs between the two competing learned motives. This overall pattern of behavior is called *approach–avoidance conflict.*

BOX **5.2**

Repression and Avoidance

Our thoughts and memories can sometimes provoke anxiety. Think of your most embarrassing moment or recollect an instance of danger in your life. To prevent distress, we could simply try not to think about these things. Repression is a more extreme version of "not thinking" about something. Although initially developed within Freud's theory of psychoanalysis, learning theorists such as Dollard and Miller (1950) suggested that repression might be an instance of avoidance behavior: The avoidance of certain thoughts is reinforced by a reduction in fear.

You are probably familiar with the word-association test: I give you a word and you say the first thing that comes to mind. The psychological defense mechanism of repression sometimes occurs to repress, or inhibit, an association. Avoidance learning could suggest a means of "suppressing" associations. Anderson and Green (2001) first taught their subjects 40 pairs of words. They then had their subjects practice some of the associations, by showing the first item and requesting recall of the second. For other word pairs, the subjects were instructed not to reply with, or even think about, the response to the cue word. That is, the subjects were to suppress those associations. After up to 16 practice suppression trials, the subjects were asked to recall the associated items. The subjects were less able to recall the suppressed associations, even though the word pairs were well known after preliminary training. Anderson and Green suggest that we can learn to deliberately keep memories from entering consciousness. When people encounter a cue to an unwanted memory, repression keeps the unwanted associate from being retrieved.

Everyday memory lapses are sometimes attributed to a motivated desire to forget. Forgetting an appointment or an upcoming exam, for example, is motivated to avoid thinking about something that is unpleasant. But do we really suppress memory for appointments or do we remember and simply decide not to keep them? There is little direct data on this question. Self-reported reasons for forgetting may not be the real reason. After all, when asked why an appointment was missed, the all-too-ready reply is "I forgot." Meacham and Kushner (1980) surveyed women about remembering planned or intended ac-

tivities, and found they forgot mostly trivial things. Important plans were remembered, but if they were unpleasant they were less likely to be carried out. "People are not likely to forget unpleasant intentions; they may, in fact, think about them obsessively...but they may very well not carry them out when the time comes" (Kvavilashvili, 1992, p. 514).

Extreme cases of repression fall under the category of the psychogenic amnesias (discussed further in Chapter 7). The memory for a traumatic experience, such as a near-death accident, a physical assault, or a childhood sexual trauma, may be seemingly forgotten. They are not forgotten in the sense of being lost from memory; instead, they remain unrecallable or repressed. Remembering such traumas would provoke considerable distress and psychological pain. Although the notion of repressed memories often raises skepticism among research psychologists, 100 years of clinical observations document cases of amnesia for wartime experiences, crimes, natural disasters, and abuse (van der Kolk & Fisler, 1995).

Amnesia may be a form of dissociation in which some mental experiences are separated out, or dissociated, from ongoing consciousness. A traumatic memory becomes inaccessible to conscious memory, as a coping reaction of avoidance. To avoid remembering is to avoid the distress the memory inevitably provokes. (This is just one interpretation. In later chapters, we will consider other explanations of dissociation and amnesia.)

Recently Bremner and colleagues (1995) studied posttraumatic stress disorder (or PTSD) in Vietnam War veterans. The researchers documented gaps in memory lasting from minutes to hours to days. For instance, some soldiers have no explicit recollection at all of a battle they were in. At the same time, remembering is a central problem with PTSD more often than is forgetting. Vivid memories return as flashbacks, in nightmares, or during periods of intense emotional arousal. Why are some traumas repeatedly remembered, and others simply repressed? Why do some people experience posttraumatic stress and others do not? These are some of the challenging questions awaiting research answers.

Given that a behavior has been both rewarded and punished, what determines whether approach or avoidance occurs? Two obvious factors are the amounts of conditioning with each outcome, and their relative intensities: the magnitude of the reward versus the severity of the punishment. The distance from the punished goal, either physical or temporal, is another factor. There is a stronger tendency to avoid the punished goal the closer you are to the feared alternative.

Conflict can be reduced if reward and punishment are experienced in the presence of different contextual stimuli. This is illustrated by teaching rats a discrimination that at first provokes conflict: In one experimental room, shock is avoided by running from one compartment to the other in the shuttle box; and in another experimental room, shock is avoided (in the same piece of apparatus) by staying put. This is the distinction between active avoidance and passive avoidance mentioned earlier. Amazingly, the animals learn the discrimination between experimental rooms, responding appropriately in each room (Spear et al., 1980).

Approach or Avoidance as Coping Responses

The distinction between approach and avoidance has been extended to characterize individual styles of coping with stressful situations. In dealing with traumatic stressors, such as the aftereffects of a natural disaster or an accident, some people attempt to cope with distress by not thinking about the situation, whereas others confront the stressor. The avoidant coping style has been variously labeled as blunting, selective inattention, repression, and denial (see Roth & Cohen, 1986). These words well describe behaviors used to minimize the arousal of distress. For example, when confronted with a frightening medical diagnosis, one could avoid talking about the illness, deny its severity, or engage in distracting activities to block thinking about the illness. The approach-coping style has been labeled as monitoring, selective attention, sensitization, and intrusion (opposites of the corresponding avoidance responses listed earlier). The approach orientation might lead one to seek out more information about the illness, talk about it, or join a support group.

Approach and avoidance styles of coping were experimentally demonstrated in college students who participated in a shock-avoidance experiment (Averill & Rosenn, 1972). The students listened to an audiotape that had two tracks: One track played music and the other track would sound a tone warning of an upcoming shock. The subjects could switch between tracks. Whereas some subjects switched back and forth between the music and the warning, other subjects actually chose to listen to the music exclusively and ignore the warning signal. Sometimes the anticipation of unpleasantness is worse than the actual aversive stimulus.

Is one coping style better than another? There is not one answer to this question. The answer partially depends on whether the aversive outcome is controllable or not. In one study, students who were anticipating midterm exams used "problem-focused" coping, which was an active preparation for the exams. The students expected the outcomes to be positive. After the exams but before grades were posted, distancing and avoidance coping strategies were used. At that point, the stressor was beyond their control and the outcome was unknown (Folkman & Lazarus, 1985).

Is one style more effective in relieving distress? It depends on when distress is measured. To approach a stressor provokes more immediate fear, whereas avoidance reduces fear. Imagine having to return to the scene of an accident or an assault. However, approach allows habituation and counterconditioning of the fear, and possibly the acquisition of instrumental behaviors that control the stressor, and so may lead to more long-term reduction of anxiety. Assault victims who had more postassault exposure to the location had significantly less distress after 6 months (Wirtz & Harrell, 1987).

The avoidant coping style has been implicated in the development of posttraumatic stress reactions, more so than the approach style. Following a severe stressor such as combat experience or even a motor vehicle accident (Bryant & Harvey, 1995), individuals who avoided thinking about the experience may paradoxically have more intrusive thoughts and memories. Their denial of symptoms may also delay the diagnosis of potentially treatable disorders.

Learned Helplessness

Punishment and avoidance represent symmetrical, and opposite contingencies between instrumental responses and an aversive outcome. In a given situation, there is one response that leads to punishment and another that avoids it. But what if the aversive stimulus is not controllable? What if no response can be discerned that either produces or prevents the punishing stimulus? _Learned helplessness is learning that there is an explicit lack of contingency between responses and an aversive outcome._ Experience with uncontrollable stressors can lead to passivity in the face of subsequent stressors, even though they might be controllable.

Learned helplessness in animals was initially demonstrated using a two-phase experimental design: one phase to induce helplessness and a second phase to assess the effects of helplessness training. As illustrated in Table 5.2, during the first phase some rats are given tail shocks. The escapable-shock group is given shocks that can be escaped by performing an instrumental response, such as turning the wheel to terminate shock. The helplessness group is first exposed to unavoidable and uncontrollable shocks. These two groups receive the same duration and sequence of shocks, the only difference being whether there is a response that could terminate the shocks. A third control group is left untreated in this phase of the study. In the next phase of the experiment, all three groups are trained on a new avoidance response. Typically, animals are conditioned to shuttle between two compartments in reaction to a warning signal of impending shock. Three groups are used in order to separately assess the effects of shock in Phase 1 (the escapable-shock versus the untreated group), and experience with escapable shock (the inescapable- versus escapable-shock groups).

TABLE 5.2   Design of the Learned-Helplessness Experiment

	Phase I	Phase II
Control group	No training	Avoidance training
Escapable group	Escapable shock training	Avoidance training
Inescapable group	Inescapable shock	Avoidance training

The results of one study of learned helplessness are shown in Figure 5.5 (Maier, Seligman, & Solomon, 1969). The animals that were not shocked and those that received escapable shock during Phase 1 rapidly learned to shuttle in Phase 2. That is, they responded more quickly over successive trials. The animals given helplessness training in the first phase showed no learning, and their latencies remained at the ceiling, the 60 seconds maximum allowed in each trial.

Helplessness-like phenomena can be readily demonstrated in humans in simple laboratory tasks. For example, college student participants are exposed to loud tone pulses that are "unpleasant but not harmful." The students are seated in front of a small box with a push button on it. The students are told "when the tone comes on, there is something you can do to stop it." Actually, only those in the escapable-shock group could turn off the tone with a button press. For the inescapable-shock participants, the button did not work. After 30 tones, the subjects are escorted to a different apparatus, a version of a shuttle box. This is a box with a knob on top that obviously slides from side to side. The participants are again told there is something they can do to terminate the tones. This is the crucial task, the one used to measure the effects of helplessness training. Prior exposure to inescapable tones in the push-button phase of the study leads to slower reactions in the second phase when the tones are now avoidable (Hiroto, 1974). Students exposed to escapable loud tones or not exposed to the tones (the control group) both responded more quickly in Phase 2.

What causes learned helplessness? Seligman (1975) suggests that the experience with uncontrollable stressors produces emotional, motivational, and cognitive deficits. Emotional deficits are shown by various psychosomatic illnesses, such as ulcers (e.g., Weiss, 1977). Motivational deficits are shown by a lack of initiative to respond, thus producing the maximal response latencies shown in Figure 5.5.

Cognitive deficits are beliefs that no matter what responses are attempted, they will be unsuccessful. With our college students, we can ask them to estimate their expectation

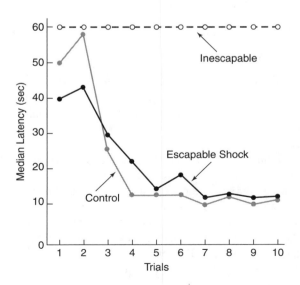

FIGURE 5.5   Average Latency to Escape Shock during the Second Phase, after a Previous Experience with Escapable Shock, No Shock, or Inescapable Shock. The maximum allowed latency of 60 seconds was reached by the helpless animals.

Source: From "Pavlovian Fear Conditioning and Learned Helplessness," by S. F. Maier, M. E. P. Seligman, and R. L. Solomon, in *Punishment and Aversive Behavior* (p. 328), edited by B. A. Campbell and R. M. Church, 1969. Reprinted by permission.

for success on their next attempt at a task. For example, if solving anagrams is the task, then each successful solution should increase the expectation that more success will follow. However, the expectations of students exposed to helplessness conditions are unchanged by success. They do not believe they will do any better.

The cognitive belief in uncontrollability may be more important than the actual experiences with uncontrollable stressors. That is, helplessness might be induced through altering the subject's beliefs about controllability, regardless of the actual experience with the aversive stimuli. This was nicely demonstrated in a study of the effects of uncontrollable noise on psychological performance (Glass & Singer, 1972). College students were exposed to aversive noise presented via headphones. The sound was a 100-decibel mix of office machine noises and people speaking in several languages. One group was told there was a panic button they could hit to briefly turn off the noise, but were asked to resist using it. Thus, these participants believed they had some control over the noise, although in fact they did not exercise this control. (We might call them the "potentially" escapable-noise group.) The inescapable-noise participants were not told about a panic button. After termination of the noise-exposure phase of the study, both groups were given puzzles to solve. The panic-button students were more persistent in working at puzzles, whereas the inescapable-noise group gave up more quickly. This study shows that it is the perception of control, acquired in the first phase, that is important.

Evans and Johnson (2000) studied further the potential debilitating effects of office noise. Clerical workers were assigned to a condition in which they heard low-intensity office noise for 3 hours, during which time they performed a number of cognitive tasks. Although the women did not report feeling stressed, an elevated level of the hormone epinephrine indicated more stress than a non-noise control. The noise group was less persistent in working a cognitive puzzles, just as were Glass and Singer's (1972) helplessness group. One other interesting finding was that the noise subjects made fewer ergonomic or postural adjustments to the work station. Could it be that a feeling of lack of control extends to attempting to make workplace accommodations that increase comfort and ease during work?

Extensions of the Learned-Helplessness Concept

Learned helplessness is one of several important psychological conceptions that had its roots in the animal lab (Domjan, 1987) and has since entered the vocabulary of everyday discourse. Several extensions of helplessness have particular relevance to human learning, in applications to psychopathology, personality, and classroom education.

Depression.   In laboratory studies with human participants, depressed and helplessness-induced individuals in the same experiments perform in a similar fashion (e.g., Klein & Seligman, 1976). Seligman (1975) noted the similarities between helplessness and depression in their symptoms, cause, and treatment. (After completing his degree in animal conditioning, Seligman moved on to clinical psychology. We could define his field of work as experimental psychopathology.) The symptoms of both helplessness and depression include reductions in activity, aggression, and motivation. Depressed people and inescapably shocked animals suffer disruptions in eating, sleeping, and sexual behavior. Helplessness and some depressions have similar etiologies: They can be caused by traumatic experiences that are uncontrollable (and often unpredictable).

One type of cognitive-behavioral therapy for depression is a form of assertiveness training. Depressed individuals are forced into action, both to demonstrate that responding leads to reinforcing outcomes (the behavioral component) and to alter the belief that all efforts are useless (the cognitive component). A therapy for helplessness is to force exposure to the fact that escape is possible. In one study, dogs that acted helpless in the presence of shock were physically dragged from one side to the other in the shuttle box, as shock terminated coincident with each shift (Seligman, Maier, & Geer, 1968). This procedure of forced exposure to shock escape was successful in teaching the avoidance response.

Acknowledgment of the parallel between helplessness and depression has been useful in the fields of experimental psychopathology and clinical psychology. But learned-helplessness theory may oversimplify depression. For instance, not all depression is traceable to uncontrollable traumatic events as the source, and not all individuals who suffer trauma become depressed.

Causal Attribution Theory.   In a revision of helplessness theory, Abramson, Seligman, and Teasdale (1978) described further the complex role of beliefs in the production of helplessness. Helplessness is ultimately determined by the belief that our behavior is ineffectual in determining what happens to us. This description of helplessness overlaps with attribution theory, a concept from social-personality theory in psychology. *Causal attributions* are the beliefs, or attributions, we use to explain why things happen. Attributions can vary along a number of dimensions. One dimension is labeled the locus of control (e.g., Rotter, 1990): Are the consequences we experience under our control or beyond our control? People who have an *internal locus of control* believe that they control what happens to them through their own efforts and abilities, or lack thereof. People with an *external locus of control* believe that things happen for reasons outside of themselves, and thus beyond their control: situations, chance, or the whims of others. In Hiroto's experiment mentioned earlier (Hiroto, 1974), in which college students tried to terminate a loud noise, the subjects had completed a locus-of-control inventory as part of the study. External locus-of-control individuals performed like students who had received helplessness training. If an aversive-noise stimulus occurs, it is perceived as being beyond their control, and so it seems that they do not try as hard to escape. By contrast, internal locus-of-control individuals act more like the group trained with escapable noise. Internals responded quicker than did externals.

In addition, attributions can be *stable or transient.* For example, academic failure could be attributed to lack of ability, a stable and enduring characteristic, or to lack of study, a transient cause that could be reversed. Finally, attributions can be *specific* to certain areas ("I'm not good at math") or *global* evaluations ("I'm not good at academics"). The potential for helplessness to develop depends on the particular combination of attributions we use to explain failure. Attributing failure to a transient and internal attribution ("It's my fault; I didn't study") will not be as demotivating as accepting a stable and external attribution ("No one in this school is going to give me a break").

Classroom Education.   The hypothesis of varying causal attributions has been used to explain why some school children lack motivation, persistence, or self-confidence. Dweck and Reppucci (1973) categorized school-aged children as helpless or persistent (the latter were called "mastery oriented") on the basis of the children's attributional style. Helpless children blamed their failure on lack of ability, which is an internal and stable cause. These fifth graders with reading difficulties had little expectation for future success at reading. Retraining them to attribute their poor school performance to lack of effort, an internal but transient attribution, offered a remedy: Work harder, rather than giving up.

What kind of experiences should reverse helplessness? At first thought, success would seem the obvious answer. Provide the child with a series of solvable problems to virtually guarantee successful completion. But Dweck pointed out that children realize when the problems are too easy, and attribute their success to the teacher being too easy on them (an external attribution) and not their own efforts. Dweck (1975) instead used a training procedure that ensured some problems were not solved, mixed in with a number the child could solve. This procedure was more successful in reversing helplessness than giving the child only problems that could be solved correctly. We earlier saw a related idea of using partial reinforcement schedules as a way of inducing persistence (e.g., Eisenberger et al., 1979).

Attributions affect the performance of teachers as well as that of their students. Teachers who have internal attributions believe that their efforts matter: They control the classroom, the learning that occurs there, and the success of their students. Teachers with external attributions believe that their efforts really do not matter because the important student influences (good or bad) are things that happen outside of school (Woolfolk & Hoy, 1990).

Physical Health.   Helplessness is intimately associated with emotional reactions of the body to stress. For example, inescapably shocked rats develop more and larger ulcers in the stomach than do escapably shocked rats (Weiss, 1977). It was first reported that monkeys who could control shock developed ulcers and the monkeys who passively received shock did not. This was known as the "executive monkey" study, the idea being that the executive who makes decisions is the one prone to ulcers (Brady et al., 1958). In a major reversal, this classic research finding was later shown to be incorrect, and probably was due to factors used in assigning monkeys to the different conditions. The accepted result today is that the *controllable shock is less stressful,* contrary to the executive monkey finding, and the helpless organism gets the ulcers.

Correlational findings from human research indicate that a cluster of negative attitudes, which includes pessimism, cynicism, helplessness, and depression, has been linked to a variety of physical health problems, from the common cold to cancer (Scheier & Carver, 1993). It seems logical to assume that an opposite, positive set of traits would lead to better health. Indeed, an optimistic orientation does seem to convey psychological and physical health advantages. Aspinwall and Taylor (1992) studied the adjustment of new freshmen to college. At the beginning of their first semester, the students completed an inventory assessing the trait of optimism. Three months later, the more optimistic students were experiencing less distress, even after equating academic performance.

How else do optimists and pessimists differ? The optimistic individuals are more likely to confront and deal with stressful situations, which is essentially the approach mode of coping discussed earlier. Pessimists tend to deny stressors or try to avoid them, essentially what we described as the avoidance mode of coping (Scheier & Carver, 1993).

Correlations between traits of optimism or helplessness and health have to be interpreted cautiously. Does optimism lead to better health or does good health promote optimism? Do previous illnesses and diseases predispose someone to now be pessimistic about the outcome of future illness?

Challenges to Learned-Helplessness Theory

Meanwhile, back in the laboratory, researchers were developing alternative explanations for helplessness effects. The important distinction to make here is between the observed effects, often labeled helplessness, and their interpretation, specifically Seligman's theory of cognitive, emotional, and motivational deficits thought to underlie helplessness. Could other factors account for the observed behaviors of helplessness in animals?

Learning Incompatible Response.   During helplessness induction, maybe the subject learns a response that conflicts with the to-be-learned avoidance response in the second phase of the study. For example, if the rat happens to be standing still when the shock terminates, it will associate passivity with relief from shock. This learning may be accidental, or "superstitious." Nevertheless, having learned to stand still, a passive avoidance response, will certainly interfere with learning to shuttle back and forth, an active avoidance response, in the next phase of the experiment (Anisman, deCatanzaro, & Remington, 1978).

Neurochemical Changes.   The stress induced by inescapable shock has been hypothesized to produce neurochemical changes that affect learning. In animals, inescapable shocks may induce a short-term depletion of norepinephrine, which leads to a transient form of helplessness. In rats, these short-term effects persist for a day or so, after which norepinephrine levels recover, returning the animal's capacity to learn (Glazer & Weiss, 1976a, 1976b).

Alternatively, repeated painful stimulation can lead to the secretion of endorphins in the brain that suppress pain (Bolles & Fanselow, 1982). Inescapable shock seems to be more effective in producing these endorphins. If so, the animals could respond less during avoidance learning because the shocks are not perceived to be as painful.

The Significance of Learned Helplessness

An older psychiatric literature refers to the notion of hopelessness, or of psychologically giving up in the face of stress or adversity. The laboratory and experimental work on learned helplessness gave a firm scientific basis to these ideas. Helplessness is learning that there is an explicit lack of contingency between responding and an aversive outcome. Helplessness produces behavioral, motivational, and cognitive deficits. A behavioral approach to learning emphasizes the first two categories, such as acquisition of passive behaviors or reduced motivation as the sources of helplessness. A cognitive approach emphasizes the beliefs and expectancies that are acquired, such as a belief that aversive stimuli are uncontrollable or the expectation that responding is useless. Learned helplessness has merged with other ideas in the areas of health, educational, personality and abnormal psychology to help explain the origins of illnesses, school failure, depression, and attributional style. In one sense, helplessness has come full circle, from clinical observations through the laboratory and back to the applied areas.

Applications of Aversive-Learning Contingencies

Aversion Therapy

Aversive and noxious stimuli may be explicitly incorporated in therapeutic treatments known broadly as *aversion therapy.* The intention here is to condition an association between some behavior deemed inappropriate and a noxious outcome. Aversion therapy is an application of the Watson-Mowrer two-process theory of avoidance learning. Classical conditioning is used to form an association between a target stimulus (e.g., cigarettes, alcohol) and an aversive stimulus (shock or nausea), the first process. Thereafter, avoidance of the target stimulus is instrumentally reinforced by a reduction in fear or discomfort, the second process.

Aversion therapy has been used for two classes of unwanted behaviors in particular, addictions and sexual deviancy. In aversion therapy for smoking, for example, cigarette smoking is paired with electric shock or a drug that induces nausea. In aversion therapy for inappropriate sexual behavior, a sexually arousing stimulus (e.g., women's shoes for someone with a fetish) is paired with an aversive stimulus (electric shock).

Does aversion therapy work? This is one of these questions with a "yes, but…" answer. First, it depends on the methods employed. In treating alcohol or smoking problems, electric shock is usually not effective (Nathan, 1976), whereas a drug that induces nausea is. This may be because the drug produces a more intense aversion than does shock, or because of the relevance or belongingness of the CS (e.g., the taste of alcohol) to the US (drug-induced nausea). You may recall that taste-aversion learning occurs selectively between taste and illness, but not between taste and electric shock (Chapter 3).

A second difficulty in assessing aversion therapy is that it typically occurs as part of a larger treatment program. The therapy may occur in an inpatient setting in which the individual is also receiving social support, individual counseling, group therapy, social skills training, and so on. The patients are also likely to be highly motivated, having reached a point where their personal and professional lives are in danger. The therapy "package" may work, but due to the contributions of multiple components rather than simply due to the aversion therapy alone.

A detailed evaluation of an inpatient program in Portland, Oregon, was provided by Wiens and Menustik (1983). Treatment usually extended over 2 weeks and contained five aversion-therapy sessions. During these sessions, the smell and taste of alcohol were paired with the drug emetine, which induces feelings of nausea several minutes after injection. The therapist has the client taste an alcoholic beverage at about the time that physical distress induced by the drug begins. "The approach response to alcohol is punished immediately by an aversive reaction, and the patient is expected to transfer the resulting avoidance of alcohol from the clinical situation to all other occasions" that present the opportunity to drink (p. 1090). Other social-support therapies are employed during treatment. A novel aspect of this program is the use of periodic refresher aversion treatments, in which patients are brought back to the clinic and given reminder pairings of alcohol with nausea. This procedure provides spaced repetitions of conditioning, a factor we know benefits retention. This clinic's success rate, defined as 1-year abstinence, is about 63 percent. Abstinence over 3 years falls to about 33 percent. Older, married, and better-educated clients do better, which likely reflects motivation and desire to be cured. These results are both discouraging, given the high rates of relapse, and encouraging, given the low levels of success of other treatment programs for alcoholism.

Treatment of Obsessive-Compulsive Disorder

The *zeitgeist* (or spirit of the times) in contemporary psychology certainly favors cognitive over behavioral approaches to psychotherapy. However, the behaviorist two-process learning theory offers a fruitful application to certain disorders. In obsessive-compulsive anxiety disorders, individuals have an excessive fear of something or compulsive behaviors that need to be performed. An excessive (or obsessive) fear of getting germs from objects that others have handled, leads to compulsive behaviors such as washing, wearing gloves, or disinfecting objects. Cognitive therapy might examine the irrationality of this behavior, and the thoughts and beliefs behind it. Behavioral therapy would try to recondition the specific behaviors.

From an avoidance-learning perspective, which should be more effective for eliminating obsessive-compulsive behavior: (1) providing safe exposure to the feared object to extinguish the fear? or (2) preventing the compulsive behavior to prove that no adverse consequences follow? A parallel is seen in the experiments on eliminating an avoidance response in rats: (1) extinguish the fear to the warning signal or (2) prevent the avoidance response. Studies that have assessed the separate contributions of *stimulus extinction* versus *response prevention* have sometimes shown a desynchronization between the two. That is, fear to the warning signal can be extinguished by prolonged exposure to it. The stimulus seemingly no longer provokes any fear. When given the opportunity, however, the subject will still perform the avoidance response during the warning signal. On the other hand, prolonged experience with response prevention, by blocking the avoidance response, reduces the need to perform the avoidance response. Yet the warning signal is still feared (see Mineka, 1979).

The same thing happens in humans. We have two methods to reduce obsessive-compulsive behavior. For example, individuals who have an intense fear of dirt and germs use excessive hand washing as a means of decontaminating themselves. Foa and colleagues (1984) found that therapy involving just exposure to contaminants indeed reduced fear to dirt, garbage, or public telephones. Alternatively, preventing hand washing (response blocking) reduced the worry that something bad would happen if the response was not made, and it decreased the need to engage in this obsessive behavior. However, neither alone was as effective as the combination of treating both the obsessive fear of contaminants *and* the compulsive hand washing behavior (i.e., extinguish fear to contaminants *and* prevent hand washing).

This is not to say that behavioral therapy is the only or even the most effective treatment for obsessive-compulsive disorders. Cognitive therapies are often packaged along with a conditioning therapy, and pharmacological treatments are sometimes suggested.

Summary

Instrumental conditioning is defined by the contingency arranged between a particular response and an outcome. In addition to positive reinforcement, instrumental learning includes three aversive-outcome procedures, which are the content of this chapter: nonreinforcement, punishment, and avoidance.

Nonreinforcement

One category of contingencies uses nonreinforcement: A target response is not followed by a positive reinforcer. In extinction, the reinforcer is omitted after those responses that once produced positive reinforcement. In omission, a selected response prevents a positive reinforcer from occurring. In time-out, the subject is temporarily removed from the situation and so is deprived of the opportunity to earn reinforcement.

Extinction produces side effects that sometimes discourage its use: unpleasant emotions such as frustration, an extinction burst of responding, and spontaneous recovery of the extinguished response after a delay interval.

The specific conditions of positive reinforcement present during acquisition affect the persistence of responding during extinction. The *partial reinforcement extinction effect* (PREE) is the most prominent of these factors. Extinction is slower following instrumental training with a partial reinforcement schedule rather than a continuous schedule. The PREE may arise because of failure to discriminate the onset of extinction, because frustration has been counterconditioned, or because nonreward was eventually followed by reward during acquisition. Other reward variables that slow or retard acquisition, such as small or delayed reinforcers, can also lead to sustained responding during extinction.

Punishment

In punishment, a response is followed by an aversive consequence, which acts to decrease responding. There have been claims that punishment does not work (Thorndike) or it only temporarily suppresses responding (Estes and Skinner). However, punishment is effective when it is given contingent on a particular response, and is intense, immediate, and consistently applied. The punishing stimuli should not elicit responses that are incompatible with the desired outcome.

Punishment can produce side effects of learned (or conditioned) fear and avoidance of the punisher or the punished situation. Punishment can elicit aggression, which may be inadvertently reinforced and thus strengthened. The punishment (or the punished behavior) may become a secondary reinforcer through association with a positive reinforcer.

Nonreward and punishment share some common features: They both produce negative emotional reactions, and behavior may transfer between these two types of outcomes.

Persistence

Response persistence in the face of extinction or even punishment can be enhanced by previous exposure to partial reinforcement, small and delayed rewards, or even mild and occasional shock during acquisition. Responding in the presence of the same or other adverse consequences (nonreward, punishment, shock, lean reward schedules, etc.) is called generalized persistence. The study of response persistence is significant because bad habits are often so persistent and because good habits are not persistent enough.

Avoidance Learning

In avoidance learning, or negative reinforcement, a response prevents the occurrence of the aversive stimulus. The increase in the frequency of the response (i.e., reinforcement) leads to a decrease in the frequency of punishment (i.e., negative reinforcement).

How do we explain avoidance responses that are reinforced by the occurrence of "nothing" as the consequence? Mowrer said the pairing of a warning signal with shock conditions fear to the signal via classical conditioning. Escape from the warning signal is reinforced by fear reduction, which is instrumental conditioning. Some difficulties for the two-process theory are the facts that avoidance behavior is exceptionally persistent, and the warning signal does not seem to extinguish even though it is not followed by shock on successful avoidance trials.

A cognitive theory of avoidance states two sorts of expectancies are acquired: a stimulus–outcome expectancy (e.g., tone is followed by shock) and a response–outcome sequence (e.g., the avoidance response is not followed by shock). Successful avoidance responding requires the acquisition of two expectancies: Tone means shock, and a response in time will prevent the shock. Eliminating avoidance behavior requires modifying both expectations.

When a given behavior has two opposing outcomes, one positive and one aversive, approach–avoidance conflict may result. Approach or avoidance also characterize styles of coping with stressful situations. In attempting to deal with traumatic stressors, some people try to handle anxiety by not thinking about the situation, whereas others confront the stressors. The approach response provokes more immediate fear, but may be more adaptive in the long run for controllable stressors.

Learned Helplessness

Learned helplessness is learning that there is an explicit lack of contingency between response and an aversive outcome: There is no response that is causing punishment, nor is there one that prevents it. Helplessness is demonstrated using a three-group design. During the first phase of an experiment, one condition is exposed to escapable shocks, a second condition is exposed to inescapable shocks, and the third condition receives no shocks. In the second phase of a study, the inescapable-shock subjects fail to learn an avoidance response.

Uncontrollable stressors produce emotional, motivational, and cognitive deficits. Emotional deficits are shown by various psychosomatic illnesses, such as ulcers. Motivational deficits are shown by a lack of initiative to respond. Cognitive deficits are shown by beliefs that whatever response made will be unsuccessful. Causal attributions are the beliefs, or attributions, we use to explain why things happen. Helplessness is ultimately determined by the attribution that behavior is ineffectual in affecting what happens to us. For example, people with an external control attribution believe that things happen for reasons external to themselves and are thus uncontrollable. External locus thus predisposes to helplessness.

Learned helplessness has been extended and applied to explaining depression, failure in classroom learning, proneness to stress-related illnesses, and to an opposite disposition, learned optimism. Laboratory studies have challenged the explanation of helplessness in the initial animal experiments, arguing instead that inescapable stressors lead to incompatible responses, neurotransmitter depletion, and endorphin secretion.

Applications

Aversive stimuli may be incorporated into therapeutic treatments known broadly as aversion therapy. The intention is to condition an association between some behavior deemed inappropriate and a noxious outcome. One application is to reduce the frequency of unwanted addictions to alcohol or cigarettes. In aversion therapy for smoking, for example, cigarette smoking is paired with electric shock or a drug that induces nausea.

In obsessive-compulsive disorders, individuals often have an excessive fear or phobia, and compulsive or ritual behaviors that need to be performed. The two-process theory suggests that eliminating obsessive-compulsive behavior requires (1) safe exposure to the feared object to extinguish the fear and (2) prevention of the compulsive behavior to prove that no adverse consequences follow. An effective behavioral treatment uses both stimulus-extinction and response-prevention components of the two-process theory.

CHAPTER

6 Verbal Learning

The previous chapters described the methods of classical and instrumental conditioning, areas of learning that were heavily influenced by the behavioral approach to psychology. Later chapters will focus on the area of memory, which is more influenced by the cognitive approach. The current chapter is transitional between behavioral psychology, with its emphasis on stimuli and responses, contiguity, and association learning; and cognitive psychology, with its emphasis on rehearsal, elaboration, and mental imagery. _Verbal learning_ is usually identified with the learning (or memorization) of lists of words. It is concerned with the acquisition and retention of such items in an effort to describe the basic laws of learning. Work on verbal learning follows in a tradition begun by Herman Ebbinghaus, a German psychologist working in the 1880s, who introduced some of the methods. Early verbal-learning researchers studied the effects of such variables as the number of repetitions, the spacing of the repetitions, or the transfer of learning from one list to another. Although verbal learning as a term now sounds old-fashioned and not as contemporary as _cognitive psychology,_ the topics studied are still very much in vogue and have a decidedly applied nature.

Two caveats are in order. First, *verbal* learning is somewhat of a misnomer because often we study learning of nonword materials: faces, pictures and objects, places and locations, odors, and action sequences are just a few examples. Second, *rote* learning implies a passive, uninvolved subject who is attempting to memorize information. Our subjects are rarely passive. "The image of the subject in a verbal-learning experiment as being a tabula rasa upon which the investigator simply chisels associations, and quite against the S(ubject)'s wishes, is archaic. The S(ubject) is far from passive and the tablet has already impressed upon it an immense network of verbal habits. A more accurate description of the verbal-learning experiment is one in which the subject actively 'calls upon' all the repertoire of habits and skills to outwit the investigator" (Underwood, 1964, p. 52). Therefore, over time, cognitive variables have been added to our studies: the effects of rehearsal, imagery, and organization. In verbal-learning experiments, we may not be dealing with "raw" learning; we study the formation of associations influenced by associations the subject already possesses.

The Ebbinghaus Legacy

In 1879, a twenty-something German scholar named Herman Ebbinghaus began a remarkable series of experiments on himself. Ebbinghaus had still not yet decided on his life's work. Although 6 years beyond his Ph.D., he had worked as a tutor for a wealthy family, traveling with them to teach their children. On a visit to a Paris book shop, he found the textbook *Elements of Psychophysics* by Gustav Fechner, which portrayed an experimental approach to the study of perception. Ebbinghaus became convinced that a quantitative approach to memory was also possible. Until this time, memory was not thought to be amenable to the methods of science. Although there was a long history of the memory arts, who could say whether their memory was better or more accurate? Ebbinghaus's research was summarized in his classic (and brief) book *On Memory,* published in 1885 (reprint edition, 1964).

Ebbinghaus's procedure involved *serial learning,* or memorizing lists in sequence until they could be recalled perfectly. The learning materials were three-letter syllables, each composed of a consonant, vowel, and a consonant, referred to in English as *nonsense syllables.* Most of the syllables were not words, but some were. Ebbinghaus used this material to produce sequences of syllables that would not be meaningful prose. Beyond this, possibly Ebbinghaus's greatest contributions were his methods for objectively measuring learning and retention. Learning (or acquisition) could be measured by the number of study trials that were necessary to repeat the list back without error. For instance, a list of 10 syllables might be memorized after 4 study and test trials, whereas a list of 15 syllables might require 8 study trials.

Ebbinghaus would later attempt to recall the list. Failing perfect recall after a delay interval, he would relearn the list. His measure of memory (or retention) was the number of trials needed to *relearn* the list to a perfect recitation. By comparing the number of trials initially needed to learn a list with the number of trials needed to relearn the list, Ebbinghaus derived a measure of *savings:* how many trials were saved in relearning. If a list originally took 10 repetitions to learn, but could be relearned in 4 repetitions the next day, there was a savings of 6 repetitions. This could be converted to a percentage savings: 10 – 4, divided by 10 (and multiplied by 100 to eliminate decimals), or a 60 percent savings. The significance of the savings measure is that it allows the detection and measurement of memory even in the absence of the ability to recall or recollect an experience.

Suppose you are studying for finals, and you run across some material that is unfamiliar. You have no recollection whatsoever of it, even though you must have learned it at one time for an earlier exam. Savings would be evidenced if, in fact, you can now learn it faster than you had originally learned it.

A savings measure was used in a study of the effects of electroconvulsive shock (or ECS) on forgetting. ECS is administered by psychiatrists in a hospital setting as a treatment for depression. It involves passing electrical current through the brain of an anesthetized or sedated patient to provoke a seizure. Although controversial as a procedure, it is apparently effective in relieving depression. Individuals who receive ECS typically later claim to be amnesic for events that immediately preceded ECS. Is the memory really gone, or is there some residual memory that cannot now be recalled? Talland (1968) attempted to answer these questions by having patients learn narrative passages before ECS and then relearn the passages after ECS treatments. Even though after ECS the patients said they had never read these passages before, they relearned them more quickly than they learned new control passages. These results suggest that ECS did not eliminate memory, but did affect retrievability of memories.

Another of Ebbinghaus's contributions to quantification was his description of the *curve of forgetting.* After learning a list, Ebbinghaus would test his relearning of the list after various intervals: immediately, hours later, days later, a month later. In the first minutes and hours after learning, the amount retained dropped dramatically. After longer retention intervals, the rate of loss of the remaining memory decreased and eventually leveled off. Figure 6.1 shows Ebbinghaus's data. The Ebbinghaus curve of forgetting shows that most forgetting occurs shortly after the initial learning. Whatever persists past this early phase is better retained, and is forgotten at a slower rate.

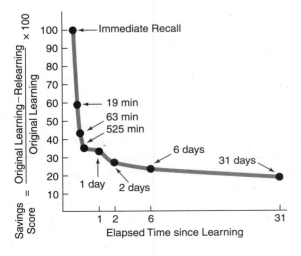

FIGURE 6.1   The Curve of Forgetting across an Interval of 31 Days. Derived from Ebbinghaus's own recall data, retention is plotted in terms of the percentage savings in relearning.

Source: From *Memory: A Contribution to Experimental Psychology,* by H. Ebbinghaus, 1885/1964, New York: Dover. Copyright © 1964 by Dover Publications, Inc. Reprinted with permission.

Ebbinghaus studied how acquisition and retention were affected by variables such as the length of the lists, the meaningfulness of the material, the spacing of practice trials, and the amount of savings after different numbers of study trials. In summary, Ebbinghaus's contributions included methods for performing controlled verbal-learning experiments; means of quantifying the results; and describing the empirical effects of several variables on learning.

This chapter will consider three basic verbal-learning methods. Serial learning requires recall of a list in the same sequence in which the items were presented. Free recall also refers to remembering lists, but the items can be recalled in any order. The method of paired associates refers to learning lists of pairs of items, in which the first item is used as a stimulus for recall of the second.

Serial Learning

In *serial learning,* a list of items is learned and reproduced according to their sequence of occurrence within the list. Ebbinghaus's experiments were serial tasks, although serial learning is prominent in life outside the laboratory. Everyday examples include learning the alphabet by young children, poetry by middle schoolers, and statistical formulas by college students ("Sum and then square, or square and then sum?"). There are many numerical codes we need to memorize, such as those for the ATM, voice mail, or computer access. Other examples of serial learning involve actions: the series of steps in programming your VCR or calculator, or putting together a bicycle. Learning to go from one place to another in a new town, for example, is an instance of spatial serial learning.

In a serial-learning task, study trials in which the list is presented are alternated with test trials in which the subject attempts to recall the list. Learning can be quantified by counting the number of correctly recalled items at each serial position or, conversely, by the number of errors made. Another measure of learning is the speed with which a list can be recalled or performed.

Serial-Position Effect

One of the most prominent factors affecting serial learning is the position of each item within the list. The beginning and end portions of the list are typically learned faster and with fewer errors, whereas middle items are learned with more difficulty. This is the *serial-position effect.* Some prototype serial-position curves are shown in Figure 6.2. In each case, a list was presented and tested until the subject could reproduce it in sequence without error, and the curves show the average number of errors made at each position during learning. Graph A shows the number of errors rats made at each of the seven choice points in a maze (McLaughlin, Cicala, & Pierson, 1968). Graph B shows errors made in learning lists of nonsense syllables by college students (Hovland, 1938/1951). Graph C shows errors students made in learning to point to a series of blocks in a certain sequence (Jensen, 1962). Plotting errors, the reverse of plotting correct responses, was standard at one time. In each case, there is an inverted U-shaped curve: More errors were made in learning the

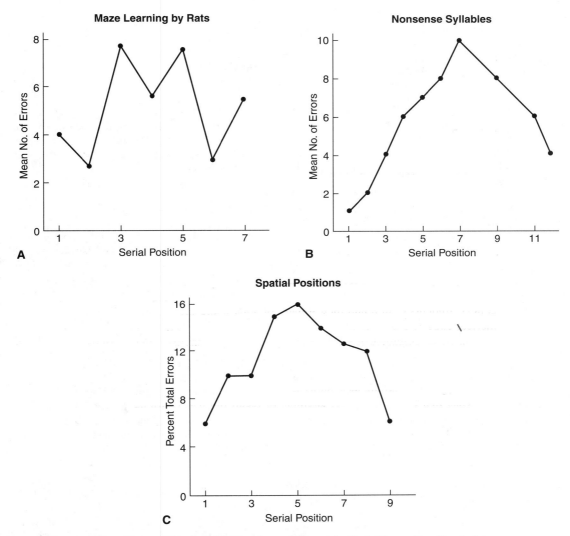

FIGURE 6.2   Three Curves Showing the Numbers of Errors in Serial Learning. Graph A is for rats learning a seven-choice-point maze. Graph B is for memorization of a list of 12 nonsense syllables. Graph C is for location of objects.

Sources: (Graph A) From "von Restorff Effect in Rat Maze Learning," by J. P. McLaughlin, G. A. Cicala, and D. K. Pierson, 1968, *Journal of Comparative and Physiological Psychology, 66,* p. 428. Copyright ©1968 by the American Psychological Association. Reprinted with permission.

(Graph B) From "Human Learning and Retention," by C. I. Hovland, in *Handbook of Experimental Psychology* (pp. 613–688), edited by S. S. Stevens, 1951, New York: Wiley. Copyright © 1951 by John Wiley & Sons. This material is used by permission of John Wiley & Sons, Inc.

(Graph C) From *American Journal of Psychology.* Copyright ©1962 by the Board of Trustees of the University of Illinois. Used with permission of the University of Illinois Press.

BOX 6.1

The Ubiquitous Serial-Position Curve

By plotting correctly recalled items, the serial-position curve is often U-shaped (the opposite of the inverted-U found by plotting errors, as in Figure 6.2). The classic U-shaped curve is seemingly ubiquitous: It can be found in many different situations. Like Ebbinghaus's Curve of Forgetting, it is a general principle of learning to which we can point. This chapter illustrates the curve with data from serial learning of nonsense syllables, mazes, and object locations; and free recall of word lists. Some other examples of the U-shaped curve are the following.

■ *Short-Term Memory.* Murdock (1968) found the U-shaped curve in the immediate recall of short strings of digits.

■ *Long-Term Personal Memory.* Sehulster (1989) attended the New York Metropolitan Opera for 25 years. He tested his own recollection of over 260 performances he had attended. In attempting to date given performances, and in remembering who sang which role, he obtained U-shaped curves, with more accurate recall (e.g., month, week, day, and matinee versus evening performance) for the first and last 5-year blocks.

■ *Long-Term Factual Memory.* Roediger and Crowder (1976) asked college students to name all of the U.S. presidents. The first few and the most recent presidents were better recalled than the presidents in the middle. There were several jogs in the curve, where some presidents were especially well remembered (e.g., Lincoln, FDR). (See Crowder [1993] for an updated recall curve from a later generation of students.)

■ *Long-Term Skill Retention.* Gymnasts were asked to reproduce a 12-step floor routine, either immediately or after a delay of up to a week. U-shaped reproduction curves were seen, subject to several modifiers. Expert and older gymnasts recalled more elements of the routine than did novices and younger participants. Also, the experts could recall much further into the list before forgetting a step; that is, they could recall the first 6, 7, or 8 steps before making an error (Tenenbaum, Tehan, Stewart, & Christensen, 1999).

■ *Animal Memory.* Wright and colleagues, (1985) tested recognition by students, monkeys, and pigeons of lists of four briefly presented visual stimuli. The stimuli for the students were kaleidoscope patterns, to minimize verbal rehearsal. After each list was shown, a single test stimulus was presented and the participant had to indicate whether it had been on the list. A remarkably parallel set of curves was produced across the three species. After a moderate delay interval of 2 to 25 seconds, the U-shaped curve appeared.

Sometimes either primacy or recency occurs. Pillemer and colleagues (1988) asked alumni to recall five events from their freshman year of college, 5 to 20 years earlier. More events were recalled from early in the academic year (a primacy effect) than later. On the other hand, when college students attempted to name all of their teachers since first grade, a recency effect was seen: The more recent teachers were recalled better (Whitten & Leonard, 1981). Recency effects also appear in many subject populations in which primacy is impaired, such as individuals with amnesic syndrome, children, and the elderly.

The serial-position curve poses a theoretical challenge, both to explain why the same phenomenon occurs under so many different conditions and to explain those exceptions that do occur.

middle positions than either the starting or ending serial positions. Serial-position curves are found in many situations, both in laboratory and naturalistic research. A number of these are described in Box 6.1.

Several hypotheses have been proposed for position effects in a serial task, in particular explanations based on anchoring, rehearsal, and interference. Possibly, the subjects in serial-learning experiments latch onto some distinctive items in the list that serve as sort of anchors from which the rest of the list is attached. The end points are typically these anchors. Middle items in the list are more likely to become associated to one another rather than to the context (Bower & Hilgard, 1981).

The anchor point can be modified by making some other item within the list distinctive. For instance, in a continuous presentation procedure, the end of one presentation of the list simply continues immediately onto the next (1–2–3–4–5–1–2–etc.). If one item is of a different sort than the others in the list (1–2–3–A–5–etc.), it may be learned rapidly and thus become the anchor. In this case, if the distinctive item is plotted in the first serial position, regardless of actual position within the list, a typical serial position curve is obtained, with faster learning of the anchor and the items preceding and succeeding (Coppage & Harcum, 1967).

An analogous finding is our tendency to organize personal memories around various temporal anchors. Students, not surprisingly, anchor their memories with respect to the start and finish of the academic year. Their recall of personal experiences will sometimes produce a serial-position curve, with more recollections from early and late in the school year and fewer from the middle of the year (Kurbat, Shevell, & Rips, 1998).

Another explanation for the serial-position effect is that rehearsal patterns differ across serial positions. The first items have less competition with other items for rehearsal, and the last items have some extended rehearsal after the list is completed before the next trial commences. The middle items share more divided rehearsal. (Differential rehearsal is considered in more detail in Chapters 7 and 9.)

An interference hypothesis argues that learning some list items can interfere with learning others. Proactive interference occurs when early learning disrupts later learning. Items at the beginning of the list will not be subjected to much proactive interference; items in the middle and at the end of the list will. Retroactive interference occurs when later learning disrupts earlier learning. The end of the list will not be subject to much retroactive interference, but the beginning and middle of the list will. However, the middle items suffer maximal interference, both proactive from the learning the early list items and retroactive from learning the end items.

Zhao (1997) recently contrasted proactive and retroactive interference effects in the recall of commercials broadcast during several Super Bowl football games. Zhao compared recall of commercials that were preceded by different numbers of commercials, thus varying the potential amount of proactive interference; or that were followed by different numbers of commercials, thus varying the potential amount of retroactive interference. The first commercials in a string were typically better recalled than other commercials and were relatively uninfluenced by following commercials. However, the last commercials in a block were poorly recalled, and recall of these was worse the more commercials had preceded.

Remote Associations

One possible explanation of list learning is that item-to-item associations are formed. Each item in the list serves as a cue for the next. In learning the alphabet, A triggers B, which in turn triggers C, and so on. As sensible as this notion sounds, Lashley (1951) pointed out that a theory of item-to-item associations would be much too slow to accommodate quick, skilled, and unified behaviors. Lashley argued that there must be earlier anticipation and activation of responses prior to their being performed than would occur from the immediately preceding items.

Ebbinghaus contrasted item-by-item associations with an alternative hypothesis that *remote associations* are learned among nonadjacent items. The letter A can be associated with C and D, albeit with less strength than A's association to B. Ebbinghaus tested this notion of "connections at a distance" by first learning one list and then deriving new lists in which successive items had been two, three, or more positions away in the original lists. For example, the list A–B–C–D–E could be transformed to A–C–E–B–D, in which every other item from the first list now follows in the transformed list. This defines a second-degree transformation. A third-degree list would have every third item now follow one another. Ebbinghaus found savings in learning the derived list as compared to original learning, and the amount of savings was a function of the number of steps removed from the original lists. For example, second-degree lists showed 11 percent savings, whereas seventh-degree lists showed only 3 percent (Hovland, 1951).

In long-term recall of material such as prose, poetry, or speeches, lines and phrases in the middle are sometimes forgotten, yet we can recall portions that come later and continue to the end (Rubin, 1977). Remote associations may account for our ability to continue later in the sequence even though some previous sections are forgotten.

Lashley also criticized item-to-item association theory by noting that well-learned items are seemingly grouped, or unitized. An accomplished pianist does not play one note at a time; rather, whole groups of notes are played as if they were a single unit. Listen to children recite the alphabet and hear the groupings: the letters H–I–J–K form one group, and L–M–N–O–P form another. This grouping notion is captured in Estes's theory of hierarchical associations: Lists or sequences are divided into sections, and those into subsections, and so on (Estes, 1972; Lee & Estes, 1977). For example, at the top of the hierarchy might be the code for "list," the next level codes for segments within the list (e.g., "beginning," "middle," "end"), and the lowest level contain the items within the segment ("A, B, C"). Carrying out a sequential activity involves activating the higher-order code, which then activates the lower-order segments in sequence. The idea is that single items are not activated via associations from the immediately preceding item, but instead all the items contained within a segment are activated. As one item in a segment is translated into behavior, succeeding items are already primed and ready to go. This can be shown by recording the time intervals, or latencies, between responses. Latencies are shorter from within a segment than between segments. Items within a unit may be run off relatively quickly (ABCDEFG), whereas there may be pauses between units (between G and the next segment, HIJK). The hierarchical theory also predicts that when errors occur, they will mostly be transpositions of the activated items from within a segment, rather than anticipations from a later group. Thus, in learning the alphabet, M and N might be exchanged in sequence, but not M and R.

Learning Items and Learning Their Positions.   Serial learning is complicated by the fact that both the items themselves and their serial positions must be remembered. Partial forgetting occurs when, for example, an item is remembered but not its position. This mimics a memory problem in real life: We remember that something happened, but misrecall when. This can be a crucial error in eyewitnesses' recall of the sequence of events. An alternative error is remembering the correct position of an item, but misplacing the item in the wrong list. Hintzman, Block, and Summers (1973) presented four lists in succession, and then asked their subjects which list a given test item had been in and the approximate serial position (e.g., "Was TABLE in the middle of the second list?"). Subjects sometimes misrecalled which list an item had been in, but they accurately recalled the position the word had occupied. Similarly, I can sometimes accurately recall where students sat in my classroom, but I misrecall which course they were in.

Learning item positions within a list has been demonstrated in animals (Chen, Swartz, & Terrace, 1997). Monkeys were first trained to respond to four photographic slides in a certain sequence. After several such lists were learned, new derived lists were created that took one item from each list, but preserved the original serial position of each. Thus, the first item from one list would be followed by the second item from another list, and so on. The animals learned these derived lists more quickly than they learned lists that placed items in changed serial positions.

Serial Learning: An Overview

Serial tasks include learning items in sequence, and testing the recall of items as a function of their position within the sequence. Serial-learning phenomena have generated considerable interest, both empirically, for example, in describing the shape of the serial position curve, and theoretically, in terms of explanations of serial position effects in terms of differential rehearsal or interference. In addition, the starting point for other research on items that occur in sequence, from television commercials to memory for personal events distributed in time, has been to plot serial memory.

Paired-Associate Learning

The method of paired associates was described in the 1890s by Mary Whiton Calkins, a student of William James, later a faculty member at Wellesley College, and eventually president of the American Psychological Association (Madigan & O'Hara, 1992). In *paired-associate learning,* two items are presented for study, labeled stimulus and response (abbreviated S and R). Study trials in which both S and R are presented alternate with test trials in which the stimulus alone is presented and the subject attempts to recall the response. For example, I could pair the stimulus word TABLE with the response AARDVARK; when you next hear TABLE, you should respond with what? AARDVARK, of course. This description of paired-associate learning resembles that of classical conditioning, each having an emphasis on stimulus–response pairings and association learning. In fact, this may have been what made paired-associate learning appealing to many psychologists.

Examples of paired-associate learning abound in our everyday lives. Learning the vocabulary in another language is heavily dependent at first on paired-associate learning: Spanish to English, English to Russian, and so on. So is learning the names of people (see Box 6.2). The many numerical codes we must now memorize are paired associates: Various number sequences are responses to stimuli such as an ATM code, voice mail code, home security code, and so on. And don't forget those many hours of your youth spent memorizing multiplication tables.

In typical paired-associate learning experiments, a list of S–R pairs is presented. The sequence of pairs is varied over trials to prevent serial learning of the responses. In studies of immediate or short-term memory for paired associates, a single presentation of the list is given. Calkins herself often used lists of 7 to 12 pairs and tested memory after a single presentation of the list. Following in the Ebbinghaus tradition, the to-be-recalled items have often been nonsense syllables or other materials of low meaningfulness, such as letter or number strings. However, many other sorts of materials can be used as stimuli and responses: words, pictures, movements, odors, and so on.

Analysis of Paired-Associate Learning

One useful approach to organizing the variables that affect paired-associate learning is to partition such learning into a series of stages or tasks: stimulus discrimination, response learning, and S–R associating (McGuire, 1961). The stage approach attempts to determine the contribution of certain variables to different aspects of paired-associate learning.

Stimulus Discrimination.   The several stimuli used in a paired-associate learning task can vary in their similarity to one another. High similarity will reduce the discrimination of one stimulus from another or, conversely, increase the (inappropriate) generalization of a response item from one to another. How can you give the correct response if you can't tell the stimuli apart? In foreign language learning, for example, some words may be alike in spelling and pronunciation. The Latin phrases *in vitro* and *in vivo* are often confused; in vitro means "in glass" and in vivo means "in life." The similarity between the two phrases used as stimuli may cause the wrong English response to be recalled. In art appreciation class, there is the discrimination between the French painters Manet and Monet.

Stimulus discrimination can be facilitated by finding ways to differentiate among the items. For example, preexperimental exposure to the stimuli may produce familiarity with the differences among them (Ellis & Muller, 1964). Children who play with blocks that are square, rectangular, or octagonal in shape will be more ready to connect the correct word labels. In Chapter 2, we saw that rats learned object discrimination faster if there had been preexposure to the stimuli in their living cages, a phenomenon called perceptual learning.

There are other ways to increase stimulus discrimination. When young children are first learning to read, they have a difficult time with similar-looking letters: the pairs *b* and *d*, *p* and *q*, and *m* and *n*. Lockhead and Crist's (1980) starting point was that certain fonts (typefaces) are easier to read than others. What we might call old-fashioned type was especially elaborated with serifs: a line or a bar at the end of the main strokes of a letter. Serifs contribute to readability by making the letters distinctive. Lockhead and Crist translated this notion into a test of children's ability to discriminate between pairs of similar stimuli. They

BOX **6.2**

Name Learning

Surveys of everyday memory problems always find that forgetting names is a common complaint (e.g., Crook & Larabee, 1990). Why are names so difficult? As with many such questions asked in this book, there is no single answer. To begin with, I suspect that there could be a sort of cognitive helplessness when it comes to remembering names. Because we expect to forget them, we just don't try. Also, names may not receive the kind of attention that other aspects of people receive. A name is spoken, it fades quickly from memory, and it is gone. A face can be continuously inspected while we converse with someone.

Are names in fact unusually difficult to learn? They are in comparison to learning other things about people, such as their occupations or interests. Cohen and Faulkner (1986) presented lists of sentences about fictitious individuals to a sample of older adult subjects (e.g., "In Glasgow a policeman named James Gibson recently won a prize for ballroom dancing"). These sentences list names, places, hobbies, and occupations. On later testing, the names were the least recalled class of facts. Names and occupations differ along several dimensions. Many names are less familiar, meaningful, or imageable. Occupations have extensive preexisting associations to other knowledge. Interestingly, even if we equate the words used as names and occupations, the names are still poorly learned. In what has been called the Baker/baker paradox, we remember that a person *is* a baker but not that his *name* is Baker (McWeeney et al., 1987). In a similar fashion, nurses could recall a disease named after a person (such as Hodgkin's disease or Bell's palsy), but could not remember a person named Mr. Hodgkin or Ms. Bell (Terry, 1995).

Our analysis of paired-associate learning suggests that S–R associating can be difficult. Connecting names to particular people is a difficult step for several reasons. Many first names (e.g., John, Chris, Susan) apply to several people. Names are generally paired arbitrarily with faces, the only limiting factor being gender specificity of some names.

Various mnemonics have been promoted to overcome our name-learning weakness. Names can be made meaningful by trying to relate the names to already known words, or by activating our existing knowledge the way we do to remember other things (e.g., the next time you meet someone named George, think of five things you know about Georges).

Memory-improvement books advocate a technique that is a version of the keyword mnemonic. The trick is to find a verbal link between the person's name and some distinctive facial feature. For example, a dimple in Mr. Wellman's chin could be pictured (in an exaggerated fashion) as a "well." Seeing the well on his chin would then remind us that his name is Wellman. Abstract names could be associated with concrete words that sound like the name: silver for Silber or garden for Gorden. In one study that compared this method to various controls, name recall was maintained better after a 1-week delay (Groninger, Groninger, & Stiens, 1995). These techniques even work with individuals suffering dense amnesia who are impaired at name learning. Wilson (1987) successfully had her patients use images to connect names and faces, such as imagining Sue eating soup or Mike speaking into a microphone.

As important as encoding strategies are for name learning, name *retrieval* also needs to be practiced. One mnemonic method, the "name game," encourages frequent retrieval of newly learned names. Given a small group of people, each person gives his or her name. However, the person must also repeat the name of each person who went before him or her in the introductions. Thus, the third person repeats the name of the first two. After the final introduction, the cycle repeats, but now the first person must repeat the names of everyone else. This name game method uses practice at retrieving names from memory. An experimental test of the name game using several hundred seminar students found significant retention even after 11 months (Morris & Fritz, 2000).

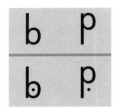

FIGURE 6.3   Example of Letters Given Distinctive Features.

Source: From "Making Letters Distinctive," by G. R. Lockhead and W. B. Crist, 1980, *Journal of Educational Psychology, 72,* p. 485. Copyright © 1980 by the American Psychological Association. Reprinted with permission.

gave 5-year-olds sets of cards to sort into piles of *b*'s and *d*'s, or *p*'s and *q*'s. In some decks, a distinctive element was added to one or both letters—for example, a line might pass through the descending arm of the *q*, or a dot might be placed within the *b*'s lower loop (see Figure 6.3). The children were able to sort these letters more quickly and more accurately than those without distinctive markings (i.e., sans serif). Lockhead and Crist suggest that adding distinctive elements might facilitate learning the names of letters, and once learned, the serifs could be gradually faded out.

Response Learning.   The ease or difficulty in learning the paired-associate response items can also vary. Again, using our example of learning a new language vocabulary, using your native language to respond to foreign word stimuli is easier than learning the foreign language words as the responses. When definitions are to be learned, it is easier to learn the word as a response to the definition as a stimulus than to memorize the (usually longer) definition as a response to a given word.

Response learning is affected by several factors. Meaningful response items are learned more easily, that is, responses that already have many associations, that are familiar, or that are encountered frequently in language. The modality of the to-be-learned material is important also. Presenting the response as a picture item generally leads to it being learned more quickly than as a word, even though the subject's response is to name the picture verbally.

Stimulus–Response Associating.   In addition to discriminating among the stimuli and learning the individual responses, stimulus and response items need to become connected (the term most often used is *associated*). Among variables that are known to affect the efficiency of S–R associating are prior knowledge, stimulus–response mapping, and cognitive elaboration.

Prior knowledge could take the form of already existing associations. Preexisting associations could either facilitate or inhibit learning new associations. For example, learning a list of paired associates that contained S–R pairs such as TABLE–KITCHEN and WHISTLE–TRAIN would be facilitated by the associations that already exist between these words. However, pairing TABLE–TRAIN and WHISTLE–KITCHEN in the same list would slow learning, because the responses have existing associations to other stimuli in the list. Interference is readily illustrated in learning new behavioral associations. Having first learned that the power window switch is on the door of one car will interfere with learning that it is on the center console in another car.

S–R mapping refers to ways in which the response items map onto the stimuli. One example of mapping is learning to make different responses to two stimuli. Given a pair of light stimuli, one on the right and one on the left, the task is to quickly push a response button when each lights. Responding to a stimulus with the corresponding hand movement (i.e., right with right) is faster than when the stimulus–response requirements are crossed. If the stimuli and responses are drawn from several obvious semantic categories (e.g., tools, flowers, foods), learning will be faster if a given category of stimuli is paired with a category of responses. For instance, conceptual S–R mapping occurs if tools are paired with cities as responses, or foods are paired with flowers as responses (Bower, Thompson-Schill, & Tulving, 1994).

S–R mapping also occurs in animal learning. Dogs readily learned to raise the right paw when a buzzer sounded in front, and the left paw when a metronome sounded from behind (in each case, the dog received a food reward for raising the correct paw). But the dogs could not learn the discrimination when the buzzer and metronome were both in front of the dog (Dobrzecka, Szwejkowska, & Konorski, 1966).

S–R associating can also be facilitated by what is known as *cognitive elaboration.* Additional information, or elaboration, can help link the stimulus and response terms. In a study by Pressley and colleagues (1987), stimulus–response pairs were presented in the form of sentences, such as the "the short man bought the broom." The to-be-learned associations are between the actions engaged in as stimuli (e.g., bought a broom or read the sign) and the different men as responses (e.g., the short man or the poor man). For one group, labeled the precise elaboration condition, an additional phrase was given to suggest a reason why a particular man and action are related. Thus, the short man bought the broom "to sweep out the crawl space." Or, the large man read the sign "warning about thin ice." When tested later with a series of "who" questions (Who read the sign? Who bought the broom?), more person–action sequences were recalled by participants who studied sentences with the elaborations. Instructors realize that sometimes students resist additional information, fearing it would only overload memory. Precise elaboration is a case in which the added information is beneficial.

Instead of an experimenter (or a teacher) providing the elaborations, the learner may be prompted to generate cognitive mediators that relate stimulus and response. For example, how might TABLE and AARDVARK be related? Wang (1983) found that those college students who were better paired-associate learners generated more mediators than did the slow learners. The fast learners also more accurately recalled those mediators on later test trials. We will see this idea of mediators recur when we discuss mnemonic devices.

Direction of Associations.   The clinical psychological method of free association calls for a person to respond with the first word that comes to mind in reaction to a stimulus word. Given the stimulus word BUTTER, many people would respond FLY, a usual and typical association. However, these normative associations are elicited in a single direction, from stimulus to response. When tested in the reverse sequence, FLY will rarely elicit BUTTER. Similarly, the association from BABY to BOY is strong, but BOY will less often evoke BABY.

Does paired-associate learning also produce a connection in one direction, from stimulus to response? Typically, if subjects are given the response items, the backward association of the response to the stimulus appears much weaker than the forward association that was practiced. The possibility of unidirectional association learning has important implications for academic learning. Studying language vocabulary in one direction, for example, from Spanish to English, does not guarantee recall in the opposite direction, from English to Spanish. Practicing multiplication tables, for example, $8 \times 6 = 48$, does not ensure that reverse sequences will be available during division drill, for example, 8 goes into 48 how many times?

When preschool children were taught letter–sound pairings, one group was shown the letter as the stimulus and the children had to say the letter as the response; the children in the other group heard the letter named (the stimulus), and the children responded by pointing to the letter. When the children were then presented the response and asked to name or select the stimulus, both groups showed difficulty: They could not go from response to stimulus as readily as they could go from stimulus to response (Speidel, 1978).

This failure to recall the stimulus when given the response could indicate that the association has been formed in just a single direction. However, because participants mostly practice making the response, maybe they are not facile at producing the stimulus. The stimulus word has never been searched for in memory. The appearance of backward associations from response to stimulus can be increased by prior experience in recalling the stimulus items alone.

Factors Affecting Paired-Associate Learning: A Summary

Paired-associate learning has been described as a series of steps: learning the responses, discriminating among the stimuli, and associating the responses to the stimuli. Learning is facilitated by S–R mapping and cognitive elaboration. Recall of the stimulus, given the response, is sometimes poor, but backward associations benefit greatly from practice in recalling the stimulus items.

Free Recall

The *free-recall task* is as simple as it sounds: A list of items is presented and the subject attempts to recall as many of them as possible. Unlike serial learning, ordered recall is not necessary, which is why recall is called *free* (meaning *unconstrained*). Retention can be tested after a single presentation of a list, or repeated presentations and tests can be given to assess learning across trials. Multitrial free recall is used in some standardized tests of learning ability, such as the California Verbal Learning Test (Delis et al., 1987). In this test, a 15-word list is presented, and recall tested, five times in succession. The average number of words recalled can be derived for various groups, by age, gender, educational level, or medical status. Figure 6.4 shows the average numbers of words recalled in multitrial free recall as a function of age groupings (Davis & Bernstein, 1992). A delayed test of memory for the list was given 30 minutes later. College students recalled nearly 9 words on the first trial, and over 13 on the fifth, whereas the oldest participants recalled fewer than 6 words after the first reading and only 10 after five trials.

Free recall is a tremendously interesting task because it is affected by so many variables, and it illuminates many processes that occur during learning. By way of illustration, we can describe three widely studied factors: serial position, rehearsal, and organization.

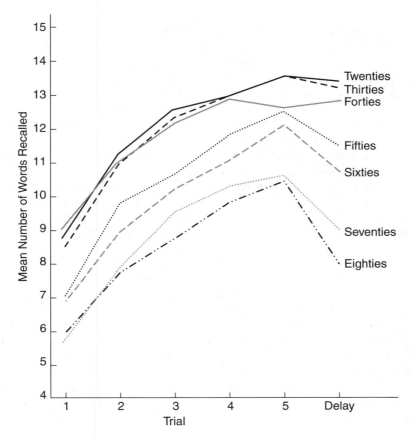

FIGURE 6.4   Age effects on free (unordered) recall of 15 word lists across five presentation and test trials, and on a final test after a brief delay.

Source: From "Age-Related Changes in Explicit and Implicit Memory," by H. P. Davis and P. A. Bernstein, in *The Neuropsychology of Memory,* 2nd ed. (p. 252), edited by L. Squire and N. Butters, 1992, New York: Guilford. Copyright © 1992 by Guilford Publications, Inc. Reprinted with permission.

Serial-Position Effects

Even though the subjects are free to recall the words in any order, we can tabulate recall as a function of each word's position in the list during presentation. Just as with serial-learning tasks, a *serial-position effect* is sometimes found. That is, more words are recalled from the beginning and the end of the list, and fewer words are recalled from the middle. The enhanced recall of the first items in the list is called the *primacy effect.* The enhanced recall of the last items in the list is called the *recency effect.* So, the serial-position effect actually can encompass two subeffects, primacy and recency.

This serial-position effect in free recall is one of the most investigated phenomena in the field of learning. Much of this research has endeavored to separate or dissociate the two end points. Recency is generally affected by different variables than those that affect primacy (see Glanzer, 1972). For instance, recall of the first items (primacy) is increased by a slower rate of presentation of the list items or by using familiar rather than unusual words. Recall of the final items (recency) is enhanced when testing occurs immediately after the list presentation and may be entirely absent if a delay or distraction occurs before recall is tested.

Some of the theoretical explanations offered for the serial-position curve in free recall are similar to those given for serial learning discussed earlier, in particular the roles of position stimuli and interference. Thus, the first and last items may be more accessible to recall because they are associated with the distinctive stimuli of position within the experimental context. That is, not only are the words in the list remembered, their relative positions are retained as well. The distinctive position information may aid item recall. Middle items in the list have less distinctive positional cues. Alternatively, the end positions are exposed to less interference from other items as at least one interval, either the one preceding or the one following the list, is empty (Greene, 1986).

One more widely influential explanation actually encompasses two explanations. Serial-position effects may result from the influence of two separate memory stores, a long-term memory and a short-term memory (Atkinson & Shiffrin, 1968). Primacy is said to be due to the added rehearsal that the first items receive, thus increasing the likelihood that they are retained in long-term memory. Rehearsal is typically subvocal and so is unobservable. But if the participants are instructed to rehearse out loud, the beginning words do indeed receive more rehearsals than do the middle and last words (Rundus, 1971). The end items of a list do not, however, receive extra rehearsals, so the number of rehearsals does not account for recency. Recency instead is attributed to the fact that the final items are still in short-term memory when testing begins and are recalled first during output, before forgetting has had a chance to occur. (This dual-memory interpretation of the serial-position effect is discussed further in Chapter 7.)

Rehearsal

Recall capacity seems to develop with age, from childhood into young adulthood. The increased recall by older children is especially evident for items in the beginning and middle a list, and is less so for the last items of a list, the recency segment (Ornstein, Naus, & Liberty, 1975). If primacy is due to the extra rehearsals some items receive, possibly age differences between younger and older children, and between children and adults, are due to differences in the amount or pattern of rehearsal.

In an early study of rehearsal, Keeney, Cannizzo, and Flavell (1967) monitored self-talk of 6- and 7-year-old children. The subjects were shown six photographs of objects. The experimenter would point to three of the pictures, and after a 15-second delay, the child would have to reproduce the sequence. The child wore a toy space helmet during the experiment, and during the delay interval, the visor would be lowered over the eyes. The visor prevented the child from seeing the pictures during the delay, and allowed the experimenters to watch unobtrusively for mouth movements indicative of rehearsal. Children who were observed to rehearse also recalled more. In a follow-up phase, the nonrehearsers were in-

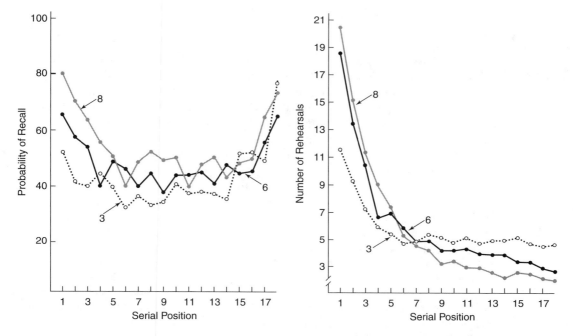

FIGURE 6.5   The left panel shows the mean number of words recalled by serial position for third, sixth, and eighth graders who were instructed to rehearse out loud. The right panel shows the mean number of rehearsals each word received.

Source: From "Rehearsal and Organizational Process in Children's Memory," by P. A. Ornstein, M. J. Naus, and C. Liberty, 1975, *Child Development, 46,* pp. 818–830. Copyright © 1975 by the Society for Research in Child Development, Inc. Reprinted with permission.

structed to rehearse, and then they also recalled more. The implication of these results is that rehearsal facilitates retention.

Another study compared recall of 18-word lists by third, sixth, and eighth graders. The left panel of Figure 6.5 shows that most of the age superiority occurred in recall of the first three words of a list—the primacy portion of the curves. Eighth graders recalled more here than did sixth graders, who in turn recalled more than third graders (Ornstein et al., 1975). These children had been instructed to rehearse out loud. (The researchers insightfully realized that the space helmet procedure was not going to work with eighth graders.) The right panel of Figure 6.5 shows the number of rehearsals recorded for words at each serial position of the list. Older children rehearsed the first words of the lists more often than did the younger children, which is consistent with a rehearsal interpretation of the primacy effect. In addition, rehearsal patterns differed by age. The younger students simply rehearsed each word as presented, whereas the older students would alternate rehearsal across several items. For example, given the partial list APPLE, HAT, STORY, the younger children would rehearse "apple, apple, hat, hat, hat…," whereas the older kids would rehearse "apple, hat, story, hat…." The latter form of rehearsal, sometimes called *distributed rehearsals* (Modigliani &

Hedges, 1987), is more beneficial to learning, possibly because it better interassociates the list items. Age differences in recall can be reduced somewhat by instructing the younger children in more effective rehearsal strategies (Naus, Ornstein, & Aivano, 1977).

Is rehearsal purely a developmental trend or is it stimulated by environmental influences such as schooling and the demands school places on memory? In a study done in Mexico's Yucatan Peninsula, separate participant groups who differed in age and education were compared (Sharp, Cole, & Lave, 1979). In a free-recall experiment, children and adults were read a list of 20 common nouns from several categories (e.g., animals, clothing). Adults and adolescents who had attended school recalled more of the words than did unschooled individuals of the same ages. In this case, the best predictor of recall was not age but rather education.

Organization

Memory for longer word lists is far from perfect after a single presentation. For example, high school students listened to lists of 12, 24, and 48 words, and remembered about 8, 11, and 15 words, respectively (Tulving & Pearlstone, 1966). The number of words that can be recalled increases dramatically if the words can be organized in some fashion. *Organization* refers to using existing knowledge to group together items that are similar or are related. For example, maybe the words in a list can be grouped by categories of related items, such as all the words referring to tools, that name animals, or that are foods (Mandler, 1967). Hypothetically, organization occurs in the way people store the words in memory, but in practice, an individual's organization of learned material is detected during output, for example, the animal words are first recalled, then the tools. Items that are recalled together are thought to be grouped together in memory. Organization might better be labeled *reorganization,* because the subject changes the organization from that provided by the experimenter to one that the subject imposes. Organization has several effects: It seems to reduce memory load, it influences the sequence in which items are recalled, and it directs memory search during recall. Three forms of organization have been studied in the context of free recall: associative clustering, categorical clustering, and subjective organization.

If the to-be-recalled words have preexperimental associations, subjects can use this information to organize the list. We see this in *associative clustering* during output: Associated words are recalled together (Jenkins & Russell, 1952). If BLACK, TABLE, STOP, WHITE, CHAIR, and GO are presented sequentially in a list, the words will likely be recalled in a sequence that groups the already associated word pairs, such as BLACK, WHITE, STOP, GO, TABLE, and CHAIR.

Lists can be constructed so that there are several words from the same semantic category, such as types of animals or foods. The related words will tend to be recalled together even though they were separated in the list during presentation. This *categorical clustering* (Bousfield, 1953) increases the number of words recalled. Instead of remembering 15 unrelated words, it is easier to remember 5 categories, each containing 3 related words.

The power of categorical organization was shown in a study by Bower, Clark, Lesgold, and Winzenz (1969), who employed a multilevel organizational scheme. There were 112 total words from four basic categories (PLANTS, MINERALS, etc.), each of which was further subdivided. For example, MINERALS included STONES and METALS; STONES was further subdivided into MASONRY and PRECIOUS STONES. The students who were shown the hierarchical organization learned and correctly recalled all 112 words after only four study trials. A control group not given the organizational scheme remembered about 70. These results also make the point that it helps to know what the organization is. The control subjects likely perceived that the 112 words were related by some categories, but they had not been shown the complete outline.

Tulving and Pearlstone (1966) suggested that organization improves recall overall by increasing access to categories of items that might otherwise be forgotten. Once at least one item from a category is recalled, usually a constant number of items is recalled from that category. Tulving suggests that recall involves a two-stage process, recalling the categories and then the items within each category. The more categories that are recalled, the more words are recalled overall.

What if the lists are not associatively or categorically organized? People will tend to impose their own organization on the lists. This *subjective organization* (Tulving, 1962) will be idiosyncratic, varying from person to person. But if participants come up with their own organization of a list of unrelated items, how can we decode the organization? One solution is to use a multitrial task: The same list is presented, and recall is tested, several times in succession. Words that are consistently recalled adjacently from trial to trial, with a frequency greater than expected by chance, indicate subjective organization. For example, a list may include the words APPLE, BELL, TABLE, COFFEE, and SCHOOL. Someone might consistently recall BELL and SCHOOL together across several test trials, even though these words are separated in the list. This pattern of output depicts one person's subjective organization. Another person might recall COFFEE and SCHOOL together, or APPLE and SCHOOL, because of their subjective associations.

Does clustering really aid recall? The literature seems to show that high clustering correlates with better recall. But could it be that the causal direction is reversed, and the more words you can remember the more likely you are to cluster them? Brown and colleagues (1991) pretested students on recall of categorizable lists to identify those subjects who were high- and low-clusterers. In the next phase of the experiment, everyone was encouraged to group words by categories during recall. The category names were provided one at a time, and the participants recalled as many words as possible before proceeding to the next category. If clustering determines how much is recalled, this testing procedure should help the low clusterers catch up to the high clusterers. They did not. Those who began the experiment with the organizing strategy continued to recall more than those who had to be encouraged to group words at output. Although organization undoubtedly increases recall, there may still be individual differences in remembering that are not easily eliminated by instructional manipulations.

Organization in recall has been used to measure the development of sophisticated knowledge schemes, for instance, as one progresses from being a novice to becoming expert within a given discipline. As one example, psychology students taking a statistics and experimental-design course were asked to judge the relatedness of 30 concepts taught in the course. The students' progression in their major could be measured by how well their groupings of concepts matched that of their instructors (Goldsmith, Johnson, & Acton, 1991).

In contrast to a standard hierarchical outline, other formats for organizing material have been tried. For instance, a matrix style offers two dimensions of organization: An item is categorized by both column and row labels (see Table 6.1). Broadbent, Cooper, and Broadbent (1978) found that a matrix was as good as a hierarchical organization for word-

TABLE 6.1   Alternative Means of Organizing a List of Names, either within a Hierarchy or in a Matrix

Hierarchy

	Politicians		Writers	
	British	American	British	American
	Gladstone	Lincoln	Chaucer	Twain
	Disraeli	Van Buren	Tennyson	Longfellow

Matrix

	Politicians	Writers
British	Gladstone	Chaucer
	Disreali	Tennyson
American	Lincoln	Twain
	Van Buren	Longfellow

Source: Broadbent et al., 1978.

list recall, and either mode of organization produced better recall than did no organization. Kiewra and colleagues (1991) found that experimenter-provided matrix outlines provided a better study aid in a classroom lecture situation than did hierarchical outlines.

The notion of organization has been applied to improving real-world memory. The recall of medical information is one example. Patients can forget much of what a doctor tells them, sometimes because the information is technical, or distressing, or because there is simply too much. Ley and colleagues (1973) manipulated how physicians presented information, and interviewed actual patients immediately after their visits. In the control condition, the doctor told the patients whatever was appropriate for that case. In the organization condition, the doctor presented the material in the following format: Here is what is wrong with you; these are the tests we are going to carry out; this is what I think will happen to you; here is what you must do to help yourself. The doctor's statements were tape recorded to verify that control and organization conditions were equal in the number and kind of medical facts presented. The patients who received categorized information recalled significantly more statements than did the control patients. Although the trend today is to provide written information sheets to patients, doctors still first verbally go over their findings. Organizing the facts appears to aid the patient's recall.

False Recall

In a now often-cited paper, Deese (1959) described an experiment in which all the words in the list were associated with one other word that was *not included* in the list. For example, the words BED, REST, AWAKE, SNOOZE, SLUMBER, and SNORE were read to the subject. When asked to remember this list, many subjects recalled the word SLEEP, which was not on the list. As many as half of the subjects will make this intrusion error, recalling the unstudied but highly associated word. The to-be-remembered items themselves determined the frequency and nature of misrecalls that occurred.

(The Deese paradigm has become an important tool for studying false memories and memory distortion, and is discussed again in Chapter 10.)

Organization in Animal Memory

Animals also remember related or organized information better, and will even cluster similar items at output. For example, Menzel (1973) tested young chimpanzees in an outdoor enclosure, in which he first showed them the hidden locations of 18 pieces of fruit and vegetables. Shortly after, he released an animal to retrieve as many pieces of food as could be remembered. The animals clustered by food type: They first retrieved the fruit pieces and then went back for the vegetables. Dallel and Meck (1990) tested rats in a maze in which food was placed in eight locations, with three different types of foods instead of just one. The rats clustered recall by reward: First, they retrieved the cereal pieces, then the seeds, and so on.

Free-Recall Summary

The study of unconstrained recall of lists has shown several variables to be influential. The three major variables discussed here all suggest that human learners are not passive participants in our experiments, but actively try to learn. Serial-position curves can indicate the use of strategies in learning: rehearsing the first items to increase learning and quickly reporting the last items before they fade from memory. Recall is enhanced by rehearsal, which seems to develop during childhood, and which indicates a conscious attempt to remember. Finally, participants attempt to impose organization on to-be-recalled lists, reordering items from the sequence of presentation to increase retention.

Available versus Accessible Memories

As noted earlier, the significant contribution of Ebbinghaus's savings test is that it can show the presence of memory that cannot be recalled. Tulving and Pearlstone (1966) elaborated on Ebbinghaus's idea with their distinction between available and accessible memories. *Available memories* are those present in the memory store; although, as we well know, not everything in memory can be recalled. *Accessible memories* are those that can actually be recalled or retrieved. This distinction is readily appreciated by students: It is the difference between having learned the material for the exam (it is available) and actually being able to recall it during the exam (it is accessible). Too often, it seems, known information is not accessible during the exam, but is recalled after the test has been turned in. The distinction also applies to the *tip-of-the-tongue* experience (Brown & McNeil, 1966). You are searching for a name or a word, and you know that you know it, but you just can't recall it right now. The item is temporarily inaccessible. You would recognize the lost word if someone else said it, and it likely will come to you later, thus showing that the word was available in memory all along.

Given that more memories are available than are usually accessible, are there some alternative ways of probing memory to retrieve those currently inaccessible items? Maybe different ways of testing offer more sensitive measures of what has been learned, provide better reminder cues, or access different aspects of memory.

Cued Recall

A simple and direct method to facilitate access to unrecalled information is to provide additional retrieval cues in an attempt to prompt memory. For example, in assessing memory for a categorized list of words, category names can be given to "cue" recall. In Tulving and Pearlstone's (1966) study, some participants were first simply asked to recall as many of the 48 words from a categorized list as possible. During a second recall attempt, the category names were given, and these helped to retrieve additional unrecalled categories of words. (A student might be given the cue CITIES and then recalls a few cities from the list.) This effect of category prompting indicates that more was available in memory than could be accessed by unassisted free recall.

Given the advantage of cued recall, one might assume that the more cues the better, right? If either TABLE or SOFA helps to retrieve the target word CHAIR, both cues should help even more. Unfortunately, our naive belief is true only up to a point. There can be such a thing as too many cues, what is known as the *cue overload effect.* Roediger's (1973) participants studied lists of categorized words. During testing, the category names and some of the list items from that category were given. All that the participants had to do was recall the remaining words from that category! But the participants actually recalled fewer remaining items than if the extra cues had not been provided. That is, noncued participants recalled those "remaining" words better than did the cued subjects (see also Roediger, Stellon, & Tulving, 1977). Why does cue overload occur? One interpretation is that the cue words strengthen their own activation in memory. Then, as memory is searched during testing the cue words, which are currently the most active and the strongest traces in memory, are repeatedly retrieved. In effect, the cues compete with retrieval of the remaining words, and bottle up the retrieval process. The phenomenon is analogous to what happens when you are trying to remember a word on the tip of your tongue. A wrong word comes to mind, but then the more you search, the more that wrong word keeps popping up, blocking retrieval of the sought-after word.

Recall versus Recognition versus Relearning

A *recall test* requires the subject to reproduce, or recall, the studied information. A *recognition test* presents studied items, along with unstudied or distractor items, to see if the previously studied item can be detected. In a *relearning test,* the initially studied material is relearned and the amount of savings is assessed. Do these different testing formats differ in their sensitivity to detect learned information? We need to be careful in making comparisons among these methods. The tests are not comparable, and each produces a different type of measurement. Simply put, recalling 50 percent of the responses is not the same as a 50 percent savings (i.e., taking half as many trials to relearn the list).

In a contemporary study, college professors were tested for memory of their former students' names (Bahrick, 1984b). Faculty members were given tests of name recall to students' pictures, name recognition, and savings in relearning names to faces as compared to learning new name–face associations. The students were from classes from different semesters, ranging from courses just completed a few days before testing to some 8 years earlier. Bahrick's results are shown in Figure 6.6. In this case, recognition and savings are superior to recall. It is also of interest that forgetting apparently occurred within 11 days of the end the semester! (It's sad but true: I forget students' names after the fall semester ends and have to relearn them in January.) Bahrick does not directly compare one type of memory test to another. Rather, much in the Ebbinghaus tradition, he argues that more may be available in memory than is accessible with a given form of testing.

Nelson (1978) used a different procedure to compare the several methods of assessing retention. College students learned lists of number–word pairs and were tested 4 weeks later. During the test session, first the stimuli were presented to see which responses could be recalled. Many were unrecalled, as expected after a month-long delay. Responses that could not be recalled were then tested by matching recognition: The participants attempted

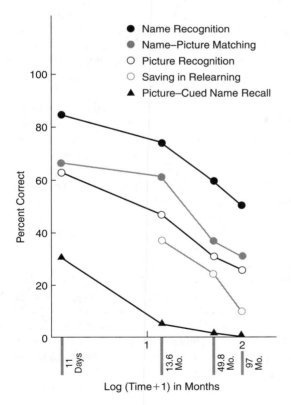

FIGURE 6.6   College Professors' Memory for Their Students. Name recognition, picture recognition, recall of names to student's photos, name and photo matching, and relearning of names to student photos.

Source: From "Memory for People," by H. P. Bahrick, in *Everyday Memory, Actions, and Absentmindedness* (p. 27), edited by J. E. Harris and P. E. Morris, 1984, New York: Academic Press. Copyright © 1984 by Academic Press. Reprinted with permission.

to match each response with the correct stimulus. Responses that were matched incorrectly were then relearned and compared to learning of new pairs. In sum, items that could not be recalled were sometimes recognized; and items that were neither recalled nor recognized showed savings during relearning. This suggests that the several tests could be ranked: The relearning test detected learning that the other tests could not.

The difference between recall and recognition is illustrated by a comparison of the two methods in a study of Alzheimer's and age-matched control subjects (Shimamura et al., 1987). Alzheimer's disease produces ongoing memory problems, as exemplified by the forgetting of daily events seemingly as they occur. Lists of 15 words were presented and tested. One such list was tested by the method of free recall, the other by recognition. In the latter case, the 15 studied words were presented along with 15 distractors in each test trial. After a single presentation, the Alzheimer's subjects recalled about 15 percent of the words, whereas age-matched control subjects recalled 40 percent. On testing recognition, the Alzheimer's subjects were over 60 percent correct and the controls about 85 percent. Thus, this study demonstrates two major effects: Both control and Alzheimer's participants recognized more words than could be freely recalled, and control subjects did better than the Alzheimer's subjects on both sorts of tasks.

One interpretation of the recall–recognition difference is that recognition is a more sensitive test, detecting learning that a recall test does not. An alternative interpretation is that the effectiveness of any type of test depends on its ability to reinstate the original context in which the material was learned. Tulving named this hypothesis the *encoding specificity principle,* which states that items are learned (or encoded) with specific meanings, and these meanings need to be reinstated in order to retrieve the memory (Tulving & Thompson, 1973). The idea is analogous to being able to identify a familiar actor who plays a different role in a new setting: Success at identification seems to depend on recalling the more familiar role played by the actor.

Tulving suggested that the usual superiority of recognition over recall might actually be reversed if the recognition test minimizes the subject's capacity to reinstate the original encodings of the to-be-recalled words. To test this notion, college student participants were given words to remember and at the same time were provided cues to aid memory for each word. For example, a to-be-remembered word JAM was presented with the cue *traffic.* Free recall (instructions to try to recall as many of the studied words as possible) was compared to a recognition test in which either the same or different cues were given. That is, the subject is shown either JAM–*traffic* or JAM–*strawberry* and asked, "Was JAM one of the studied words?" Subjects often recalled words (in the absence of cues) that were not recognized if presented with different cues. In our example, JAM would be recalled without any prompts, but would not be recognized if cued with "strawberry." In this case, free recall proved to be a better test than recognition. Tulving suggests that how we test may be less important than the capacity for any test to reinstate the context that was present at learning.

Maybe we are not too surprised that a word is not recognized when cued differently. In Tulving's procedure, we could argue that in fact the participants were being asked to recognize a different word. After all, a traffic jam is different from the jam one spreads on bread. However, the notion of encoding specificity will be supported by other studies in which the same words are studied and tested, but the general contextual conditions between the study phase and the test phase either match or vary, for instance, when studying and testing occur in the same—or in different—rooms, drug-induced states, or moods. Generally, recall is better when testing occurs in the same context in which learning occurred. (These studies are reviewed in Chapter 10.)

I suspect that a common belief among students is that multiple-choice tests are easier than essay exams: Recognition of the correct answer is believed to be easier than recalling it. But sometimes a multiple-choice question seems difficult because it is worded differently from the text or the lecture and does not lead to the answer that we otherwise (believe) we know. In this case, an essay-type question might have tapped the unrecognized fact.

Implicit Learning

Implicit tests of knowledge can present evidence for memory that explicit tests, such as instructions to recall or recognize previously studied items, do not. *Implicit learning* refers to learning that seemingly occurs without awareness or intention to learn, and often cannot be articulated verbally. Have you ever found that you could perform a skilled series of actions, but you could not describe it in words? Try telling someone how to tie a necktie or shoe laces versus actually demonstrating it. Instead of requesting verbal recall from our subjects, their implicit learning might be shown by faster or more skilled performance of a task (tying your shoe laces or necktie). The notion of implicit learning follows naturally from Ebbinghaus's work. Remember that he was interested in learning that was not recallable, but that could otherwise be shown via relearning tests. So also attempted verbal recall of a sequence may not adequately demonstrate learning that is detected implicitly.

An example of an implicit *serial* learning task is the serial-reaction-time task. For example, the computer screen is divided into number of compartments, and a "list" is presented by marking boxes in sequence with a star. As each box is marked, the subject pushes a corresponding button on the keyboard. The subjects are not informed that the sequence of locations repeats, but in fact the 16-position sequence repeats 20 times, although without a break between repetitions. We measure how quickly the subject responds as each marked location is presented. Learning is indicated by faster reactions across trials. Both college-aged and elderly adult subjects showed faster reactions as the sequence repeated, as if they were able to anticipate which box was next in sequence. When the repeating sequence was changed without warning, the reactions times lengthened, as if the learned anticipations now interfered with the altered sequences (Howard & Howard, 1992). Many subjects cannot verbally reproduce the sequence or cannot even guess the next position better than at chance levels, yet they nevertheless show quicker reactions across trials (Willingham, Nissen, & Bullemer, 1989).

Paired-associate learning can be tested implicitly also. In a word-fragment completion task, the subjects are shown a series of word pairs, such as BOOK–FOREST. The subjects are not instructed that this is a learning or memory task. Sometime later, the subjects are given a string of letters and blanks and asked to complete each with the first word that comes to mind. The instructions make no reference to the previously seen words. Some of the word fragments are presented with the same words they were previously paired with, e.g., BOOK–FOR___, whereas other fragments now appear with different words, for example, WINDOW–FOR___. Implicit learning of the new association is shown when the fragments are more often completed with the studied response word in the same condition than in the different condition. The idea is that the previously seen cue word unconsciously primes the response word that had been paired with it.

Because college students are likely to be aware of the relationship between the study and fragment lists, this procedure may not be a pure test of implicit learning (Bowers & Schacter, 1990; Graf & Schacter, 1989). In addition, implicit recall of the new associations is only sometimes found, and some investigators report negative findings. A stronger case for implicit association learning can be made by using amnesic individuals who do not consciously recollect the study list but nevertheless still complete the word fragments with the study list words (Graf, Squire, & Mandler, 1984).

Is an implicit test of learning simply a more sensitive test of knowledge, the way that cued recall or relearning taps otherwise unrecallable information? The indication instead is that implicit learning represents a different form of learning from the conscious and deliberate forms of learning we have otherwise been discussing in this chapter. The evidence for a distinction between implicit learning and explicit learning is presented in detail in Chapters 7 and 11.

Relationships among the Verbal-Learning Tasks

Do serial learning, paired-associate learning, and free recall all tap the same underlying processes? Does proficiency at one ensure ability on the others? Underwood, Boruch, and Malmi (1978) tested 200 undergraduates on 28 different memory tasks, which were spread across 10 sessions. Several versions of each verbal-learning procedure were included. For example, free recall was tested with lists of imageable words, abstract words, associatively related words, and categorically organized words. The statistical procedure of factor analysis was used to determine which tests were correlated. Underwood and colleagues found that paired-associate learning and serial-learning tests were positively correlated: Individuals tended to do well on both types of tests, poorly on both, or average. This could suggest that paired-associate and serial tasks require a common type of ability. The most obvious is association learning, between stimulus and response or among items in a list. Free-recall performance was statistically separate. That is, performance on serial learning or paired associates was unrelated to free recall. Unlike paired-associate and serial learning, which are typically multitrial learning tasks, free recall is usually single-trial. This suggests that the capacity to remember once-presented information may be separable from multitrial learning.

The importance of this correlational approach is to determine whether verbal learning is a single ability or process, or involves multiple processes. The evidence suggests that, even among these simple learning tasks, different abilities or strategies are being tapped.

Do these laboratory tests predict the ability to remember in the real world? Surprisingly, there is little evidence here. One difficulty is finding measures of everyday remembering that are valid and uncontaminated by confounding variables. For example, older adults were better than young adults at remembering an appointment or calling the experimenter at a future time (cited by Harris, 1984). Is this because older adults remember better? Because their lifestyles impose fewer demands on their memories? Or do older persons make better use of reminders and sticky notes?

A few comparisons of laboratory and everyday memory are available. Wilkins and Baddeley (1978) used adult women, ages 35–50, as participants. They first were tested on free recall of several 16-word lists. The women were then given a task analogous to remembering to take medicine on schedule: pressing a button on a wrist timer at scheduled intervals for 7 days. Those women who recalled fewer words in the laboratory tests were more accurate on this prospective memory test. They pushed the button closer to the correct time and had fewer instances of forgetting completely. Yet these tasks are different in many ways. The lab task requires memory for verbal material from the (recent) past, whereas the other task involves remembering to perform an action in the future.

Kurtz-Costes, Schneider, and Rupp (1995) tested 5- to 9-year-olds with tasks meant to simulate everyday remembering, school-related memory, or traditional laboratory tests of memory. For example, list recall could be measured in the "shopping game," in which the children had to remember a list of items to get in the "store" across the room. Recall could also be measured by the more standard task of presenting and testing recall of a list of words. "Geography" was a school-related paired-associate task, requiring remembering facts about different countries. Learning names and faces was considered an everyday paired-associates task. The researchers found that there were low correlations among the several tasks; good performance on an everyday simulation was unrelated to performance on a school-related or laboratory task. There was little evidence of consistency across tasks within individuals. That is, a child's remembering would vary from one paired-associate test (remembering names/faces) to a second (remembering countries and products) to a third (remembering arbitrarily chosen stimulus and response words in the laboratory task). Kurtz-Costes et al. suggest that the child's use of strategies, such as whether to rehearse or not, can vary with the familiarity of the material and the child's knowledge base. Any one test might not be representative of what the child could potentially remember.

Application: Mnemonics

Mnemonic devices are various schemes, strategies, or procedures used to aid encoding and retrieval. Students are probably most familiar with first-letter and *acronym* mnemonics: remembering a list of things by their first letters. For example, the first letter of each of the Great Lakes makes the acronym HOMES. First-letter mnemonics encode both item and order information. Thus, the planets can be remembered in order from the sun by the sentence "My Very Educated Mother Just Served Us Nine Pizzas," where the first letter of each word is the first letter of a planet's name (Mercury, Venus, Earth, etc.). Prior to the invention of the printing press, mnemonic methods were used to retain large bodies of knowledge. In high school, we learned that epic tales such as the Iliad and the Odyssey were transmitted orally for hundreds of years before being written. In the European Middle Ages, elaborate schemes, often based on imagery, were devised to organize, store, and retrieve whole books of information. "Memory was needed by the entertainer, the poet, the singer, the physician, the lawyer, and the priest" of the Middle Ages, says the historian Daniel J. Boorstin (1983, p. 482).

The Keyword Mnemonic

One mnemonic technique, the *keyword method,* was developed by Atkinson and Raugh (1975) to aid foreign-language acquisition. The idea is to find a mediating word to link the to-be-associated words. In learning Russian–English vocabulary, for example, a mediating word is chosen that sounds like the Russian word, but that can also be visualized interacting with the English translation. The Russian word for "bell" is *zvonok,* pronounced "zuahn-oak," which sounds like the English word "oak," and so oak can be the mediating word. One can imagine an oak tree containing "bells" for acorns.

Atkinson and Raugh (1975) found that subjects using the keyword method learned nearly twice as many Russian vocabulary words as did control subjects on the first study day. The keyword subjects were still superior after 3 days of practice. Pressley and Dennis-Rounds (1980) found that school-aged children who were studying Spanish as a second language learned twice as many vocabulary words as did controls. Pressley and Dennis-Rounds also tested backward recall. As noted earlier in paired-associate learning, recall from the response back to the stimulus is often poor. Similarly, keyword-trained participants had very poor backward recall in going from English back to the Spanish words. The keyword groups eventually exceeded the controls, but only after several days of study.

The keyword method can be applied to learning other school-related materials that fit a paired-associate format, such as linking the names of famous people with their accomplishments (Jones & Hall, 1982) and cities with their products (Pressley & Dennis-Rounds, 1980).

Another mnemonic for remembering lists of words is the *narrative story method* (Bower & Clark, 1969). The idea is to fabricate a story that includes each word in sequence. For example, the following student-generated sentence includes six to-be-remembered words (capitalized): a LUMBERJACK DARTed out of a forest, SKATEd around a HEDGE past a COLONY of DUCKs. College student participants studied 12 lists of 10 words each. One group was instructed in the narrative procedure, and the other group was simply told to memorize the list. When each list was studied and tested immediately, both groups did equally well, which is no surprise given the level of ability of the participants (Stanford undergraduates). The interesting results occurred at the end of the session, when the students were asked to recall *all* of the lists, given only the first word of each and asked to recall the rest in the correct order. The narrative subjects remembered about 93 percent of the words, whereas the control subjects recalled only 13 percent.

Imagery Mnemonics

Many mnemonic systems are based on visual imagery. Imagery is otherwise known to enhance memory, and pictures or even simple line drawings are typically better remembered than are the names of the objects depicted. Some people with exceptional memories claim to use visual imagery.

The *method of loci,* or *locations,* is an ancient mnemonic based on imagery. It is sometimes described as taking a mental walk. In the method of locations, you first learn a fixed series of places. You must be able to readily form an image of each, the same image each time, and go through the locations in the same sequence each time. Later, when you have a list of things to remember, you mentally follow the route, imagining one (or more) of the to-be-recalled items at each location. When you want to recall the items, you rewalk the route and look to see what is stored at each location. In medieval times, scholars were said to recall thousands of facts by locations spread through churches, theaters, or even cities (Yates, 1966). The Jesuit missionary Matteo Ricci devised a Memory Palace to provide sufficient locations for teaching scripture (Spence, 1984). The Russian mnemonist *S* reported using locations along familiar city streets, but also described "losing" objects that he "placed" behind objects or in the dark away from the street lights (Luria, 1968). In modern times, the method has been adapted for memory-impaired individuals. The visual modality is useful for brain-injured individuals who have verbal-learning deficits and cannot benefit from narrative or keyword mnemonics (Wilson, 1987). Instead of remembering a person's name as "Mike," the person is imaged as a "microphone."

Another imagery technique is the *peg word*. As with the method of locations, the first step is to memorize a series of images. In this case, the numbers 1 to 10 and their rhymes are the pegs on which to-be-recalled items will be imagined. Thus, "one is a bun, two is a shoe, three is a tree," and so on. The subject practices forming an image of each rhyming object. Later, the to-be-remembered items are imagined interacting with the pegs. As with the method of locations, the peg-word system allows recall of the list starting from either end, or for individual items. What was the sixth item in the list? Well, 6 is sticks, so what image is stored with sticks?

Are bizarre and unusual images better memory aids than more common images? Our everyday theories about distinctiveness might suggest that the unusual should be better remembered. Generally, this is true with the imagery mnemonics. However, bizarre images are prone to interference from other bizarre images. Similarly, common images may be fine, but they suffer interference from other common images. This means that the repetitive use of one form of imagery might lead to more forgetting than mixing kinds of images. Also, bizarre images might be less effective in paired-associate tasks, in which one item is used to cue recall of the other (Einstein, McDaniel, & Lackey, 1989). It may be difficult to reinstate what you had associated with the bizarre stimulus. A similar rule applies to storing objects in unusual places: The association of objects and their locations is worse when unusual locations are chosen (see Box 6.3).

Analysis of Imagery Mnemonics.   What are the essential components of a mnemonic system such as the peg-word or location method? Bower (1970) reviewed the research findings with respect to these two, and noted the following important features:

1. There is a known list of cues (the numbers or locations) that need to be present at encoding and at retrieval.
2. The to-be-remembered items need to be associated with the cues during input.
3. Imagery that is unusual, bizarre, or striking is better.
4. The cues used at recall must be the same as those thought of while studying.
5. Multiple items can be stored at each location or with each peg.
6. Surprisingly, the systems are reusable with little interference from trial to trial.

Do mnemonics really work? A simple answer is "yes"; they can be quite effective, as noted earlier for the keyword method. In one experimental comparison, three imagery techniques (location, peg word, and linking pairs of items in an image) were used to memorize

BOX **6.3**

Forgetting the Location of Stored Objects

One particularly annoying lapse of everyday memory is forgetting where you last put something. Something is put down, but not in its usual place, and later we cannot recall where we left it. Or items that have some value to us, such as keys, jewelry, important documents, or letters, are likely to be hidden in special places to ensure future access or to hide the objects from others. All of the respondents to Harris's (1980) survey reported doing this. Rather than leaving a letter in a desk drawer, an unlikely place is chosen, for example, in a book, behind a photograph, or under the couch. A certain logic prevails at the time that makes us think this location will be readily recalled in the future. But, of course, weeks or months later, this logic cannot be reconstructed and the object remains lost. Winograd and Soloway (1986) cited a friend who put his passport in a suitcase pouch. This seemed to make eminent sense, except that their friend could not remember this and only stumbled on the lost passport long after it had been replaced.

Winograd and Soloway (1986) asked their participants to imagine in what locations they would hide a series of items. In paired-associate terminology, the objects were the stimuli (e.g., a camera) and the locations were the responses (in the closet). Both likely and unlikely hiding places were used (e.g., hide the camera in the closet or under the couch). When the subjects were tested a few minutes later, there was already significant forgetting for the unusual locations of objects. Even people who strongly believed that the unusual locations were more memorable still recalled only half as many objects in unusual as in usual locations.

Why do we forget unusual locations for objects? Winograd and Soloway say we mistakenly apply the "distinctiveness" principle of memory. Our commonsense belief is that distinctive events are better remembered than are plain and common events. This is the same logic that applies to using bizarre images in visual mnemonics. But distinctiveness applies to memory for items, such as objects *or* locations, but not necessarily to associations, the connection between the object *and* its location.

Thinking of either item alone (the camera or the couch) may not be sufficient to trigger an association to the other item, especially a weak, infrequently used, and atypical association. (Your association between TABLE and CHAIR will be much stronger than the unusual association I have offered earlier in this chapter, that between TABLE and AARDVARK. Although AARDVARK is a bizarre and distinctive item, fat chance you will remember it 6 months later as an associate to TABLE.) Putting objects in unusual places is an instance where our everyday belief about how to remember proves to be incorrect.

To increase the likelihood that one item will retrieve the other may take a different form of mnemonic preparation. The imagery mnemonics that stress interacting images, such as peg-word and location methods, may help us to recall unusual locations of hidden objects.

Object locations are forgotten for other reasons. Absentmindedness occurs when we unconsciously put something down while our attention is directed elsewhere. For example, in the library, I put down my key ring because I needed two hands to peruse a bound periodical. How do we later find these objects? Mentally, we try to replay or reconstruct our actions and behaviors, or retrace our earlier route (see Cohen, 1996).

Objects are also lost because we make *updating* errors. Where did I leave something last, as opposed to the location before that? The changing nature of knowledge sets up ideal conditions for interference. Bjork and Landauer (1978) simulated updating in a paired-associate task by constantly repairing the stimuli with new responses. Some subjects were instructed to try and eliminate the old responses, such as by mentally erasing them from a blackboard, but this was not very effective. The most successful updating technique was to concentrate on elaborating the current pairing, for instance, by forming an image or using a story to link the two. From what we know about mnemonic devices, they seem to be reusable without interference carrying over.

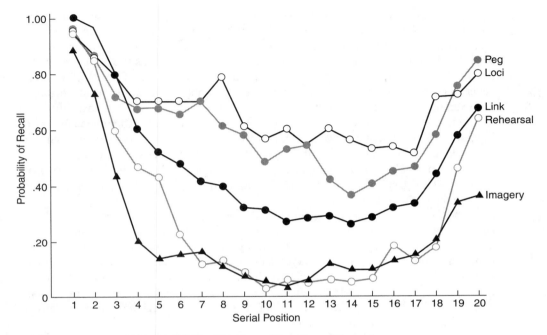

FIGURE 6.7   Serial Recall of 20-Word Lists as a Function of Several Mnemonic Strategies. Strategies are rehearsal (repeat each word), imagery (vividly picture each word), a linking story, the peg-word system, and the method of loci (locations).

Source: From "The Effectiveness of Four Mnemonics in Ordering Recall," by H. L. Roediger, 1980, *Journal of Experimental Psychology: Human Learning and Memory, 6,* p. 565. Copyright 1980 by the American Psychological Association. Reprinted with permission.

20-word lists. The college student participants recalled more 1 day later than did control subjects who were told to simply rehearse each word, or form a mental image of what each referred to (Roediger, 1980). The results of one test are shown in Figure 6.7. The data here are words recalled in the correct serial position. These results show that the method of location and the peg-word system produced better recall of items in sequence. Mnemonic training procedures among elderly and gerontological populations have also been found to be effective (Verhaeghen, Marcoen, & Goossens, 1992). There is apparently also a motivational component to using mnemonics. Student users claim that the mnemonics make learning more enjoyable and interesting, factors that would contribute to their use and maintenance (Higbee, 1994).

A more complex answer to the question of whether mnemonics work is that different mnemonic systems may be more appropriate for different memory tasks. Herrmann (1987) reviewed the literature on mnemonic effectiveness and found that for paired-associate learning, linking imagery (as is used in the keyword method) was the most effective. For free-recall tasks, in which order of recall is not important, the narrative story method was superior. For serial recall of items in sequence, the narrative method and the method of locations were best.

So, who really uses mnemonics? Generations of college and professional students have used first-letter mnemonics to remember lists of facts, from memorizing the 12 cranial nerves (On Old Olympia's Towering Tops, A Finn and German Vault and Hop) to ROY G BIV (the colors of the visible spectrum). Nursing students use acronyms such as RICE for the treatment for a sprain (rest, ice, compress, and elevate; Beitz, 1997). Of relevance to psychology majors are mnemonics for the symptoms of various mental disorders. For example, Generalized Anxiety Disorder is coded as FIRST: fatigue, irritability, restlessness, sleep disturbance, and tension (Reeves & Bullen, 1995). The mnemonic for the Mental Status Examination is Como Estas: concentration, orientation, memory, and so on (Astrachan, 1991). A variation of the keyword technique was developed for art classes to assist students learning artists and their paintings (Carney, Levin, & Morrison, 1988), and a combined imagery and hierarchical method for learning taxonomic classification in biology (Levin & Levin, 1990).

Whatever their value, mnemonic techniques take time to learn and use. It is frankly simpler to write a list before going to the store. Harris (1980) surveyed a sample of students and adults concerning their use of memory aids. Most people reported using external reminders: notes, lists, writing on their hands, or setting a timer. The only true mnemonic used was the first-letter mnemonic: Seventy-three percent of students used it "once or twice in the last 6 months." Hardly anyone reported using other formal mnemonic systems. A survey of psychologists who work in the field of memory research found essentially the same thing (Park, Smith, & Cavanaugh, 1990). The mnemonic devices that we teach in our classes, such as peg-word, location, and story methods, were ranked last. Electronic memory aids, such as the pocket organizers now available, will likely replace even written notes. Artificial-intelligence researchers are devising newer memory "prostheses" that will be more sensitive to what needs to be remembered in different situations (Lamming et al., 1994).

Perhaps the contemporary value of mnemonic techniques is in their demonstration of which variables most affect learning: imagery, meaningfulness, organization, and retrieval cues. We may not use formal mnemonic systems to remember, but we use the components in smaller ways in everyday remembering.

Summary

Verbal learning refers to a body of research that followed in the Ebbinghaus tradition and that seeks to determine the effects of certain independent variables on learning primarily verbal items. The older verbal-learning tradition reflects the behavioral stimulus–response tradition, but the newer research is heavily cognitive.

Herman Ebbinghaus, in his 1885 book, *On Memory,* introduced quantifiable measures of learning (i.e., the number of repetitions to criterion) and memory (i.e., the number of repetitions to relearn, or savings). He described the Curve of Forgetting, which showed most forgetting occurs shortly after learning, with further losses occurring at a slower rate. Ebbinghaus also devised new learning materials (the nonsense syllable) and introduced methods of experimental control in his research.

Three basic tasks have been developed to study verbal learning: serial learning, paired-associate learning, and free recall.

Serial Learning

In serial learning, a list of items is presented in a fixed order on each trial, and the subject is required to reproduce items in order. A serial-position curve often occurs, as the first and last items in the sequence are learned more quickly than are the middle items.

In addition to learning item-to-item associations in a list, remote associations may also be acquired between separated items. List items may be learned in groups, which are remembered or forgotten together. Remote associations and grouping allow us recall the remainder of a list after some intervening sections are forgotten. In serial learning, the item and its location within the series are separate bits of information. A sequence can be learned implicitly, such that it can be performed accurately even if it cannot be explicitly recalled and described.

Paired-Associate Learning

In paired-associate learning, two items are presented for study, labeled stimulus and response (abbreviated S and R). The task is to recall the response when presented with the stimulus alone. Paired-associate learning can be analyzed into the components of stimulus discrimination, response learning, and S–R associating.

The stimuli used in a paired-associate learning task may be similar, and so we must learn to discriminate one from another. Learning will be faster if the stimuli are made more discriminable from one another, as through familiarization or adding distinctive features.

Response learning is affected by the difficulty in learning the response items, the meaningfulness of the responses, their familiarity, and prior knowledge of them.

Associating the stimulus with the response is affected by preexisting associations among items in the to-be-learned set and by cognitive elaboration. Generating mediators that relate the stimulus to the response facilitate learning.

Paired-associate connections are typically stronger from stimulus to response and weaker in the backward direction from response to stimulus. The backward association benefits from increased practice at retrieving the stimulus item.

Free Recall

In the free-recall task, a list of items is presented and the subject attempts to recall as many of them as possible. Unlike serial-learning procedures, ordered recall is not necessary.

As in serial learning, free recall produces serial-position effects. Enhanced recall of the first items, the primacy effect, is often attributed to the added rehearsal that the first items receive. Enhanced recall of the final items, the recency effect, has been attributed to the fact that these items are often recalled first before forgetting has had a chance to occur.

Free recall is influenced by rehearsal or repeating the items until they are tested. Rehearsal shows a developmental progression in children. Rote repetition is not as effective as some sort of elaborative rehearsal, which seeks meaning or associations among the to-be-remembered items.

Free recall improves if the material can be organized, that is, if items can be grouped or chunked. Associative clustering occurs when items that have preexisting associations are grouped together during recall. Categorical clustering occurs when items from the same semantic category are grouped together. Subjective organization occurs when subjects devise their own grouping of items and is detected by analyzing the sequence of recalled items across successive tests.

Do serial learning, paired-associate learning, and free recall tap the same underlying learning processes? Correlational studies suggest that there are different abilities or strategies involved instead of a single verbal-learning ability. Do these laboratory tests predict everyday remembering? The correlations are generally low, but this may be because laboratory and everyday memory tasks differ in kind, interest levels, and ecological relevance.

Available versus Accessible Memories

One of Ebbinghaus's significant contributions was to show the existence of memory (through savings during relearning) that could not be recalled. This is the distinction between availability and accessibility. Available memories are those present in the memory store, whereas accessible memories are those that can actually be recalled or retrieved. This distinction is illustrated by the tip-of-the-tongue phenomenon, in which you know that you know a word or name, but you can't recall it right now. Presenting additional memory prompts during cued recall makes more information accessible. Cue overload occurs when too many prompts actually block recall of an item that otherwise would have been remembered.

How do tests of recall, recognition, and relearning differ in their sensitivity to available memories? Items that are not recalled are sometimes recognized; and savings occurs for items that are neither recalled nor recognized correctly. Tests of implicit memory, such as word-fragment completion, detect memory in amnesic individuals who otherwise do poorly on recall and recognition tests of explicit memory. Recall, recognition, and implicit memory may differ in sensitivity to detecting memory, or they may be assessing different aspects of what is remembered.

Mnemonics

Mnemonic devices are various strategies or procedures used to aid encoding and retrieval, such as using the first letters to form an acronym for the to-be-remembered items. In the keyword mnemonic, first developed to assist learning foreign-language vocabulary, a mediating word is chosen to link the to-be-associated words. In the narrative chaining method, a string of unrelated words are connected through a made-up story. In the method of loci, or locations, items are imaged in certain locations along a fixed mental route. The peg-word system uses number and imaged pegs ("one is a bun…") on which to attach the target items. Mnemonics work because there is a list of cues that the to-be-recalled items are associated with during study and that can be used to guide retrieval.

The various mnemonic systems do indeed work, although some are better for serial-learning tasks (such as the method of loci) than for paired associate (linking images) or free recall (narrative chaining). However, mnemonic techniques are time-consuming to learn and to use. Few students use more than acronyms. Most people instead use external cues such as lists, day planners, PDAs, and sticky notes.

7 Human Memory

Conceptual Approaches

Forgetting is the bane of every student's existence. It is bad enough to forget course material, but forgetting continues beyond the classroom. Students who kept a diary of memory lapses reported all too frequently forgetting meal cards and keys, appointments, classes, and even exams (Terry, 1987). There is the story of one student who worked all night to complete a history paper, only to realize the next morning that the *test* was that day and the paper wasn't due until next week. That's not the worst part. In his next class, he realized that his English paper *was* due then. Students actually report more instances of forgetting than did an elderly sample, even though the popular stereotype is that the latter are the forgetful ones (Reason, 1993).

We are all subject to memory lapses. One news clipping describes someone who took a break while moving into his new apartment in the city. After lunch, he couldn't remember his new address, and was still looking days later. The alumni notes of a 90-year-old reports that not only does he forget what he was going upstairs to get, but while pausing to consider, he forgets whether he was going up or coming down. Stephen Jay Gould, a noted scientist and essayist, recalled weekly breakfasts eating bagels with his grandfather, sitting outside of the Forest Hills Tennis Stadium in Queens, New York. When Gould retraced his steps 30 years later, he found they actually had been sitting on the steps outside of a moving and storage company (Gould, 1990).

When students ask why they have trouble remembering, I have to respond that this is too broad a question to be given a single answer. Memory is better explained when partitioned into separate components, rather than treating it as a unitary capacity. The realization that forgetting is due to a failure of one type of memory or another, or of one stage or another, offers a more helpful answer.

This chapter considers several theoretical approaches to memory, each of which partitions memory along different dimensions. One approach postulates different types of memory, such as personal memories versus general knowledge. Another approach divides memory into a series of steps: forming, retaining, and retrieving memory. A third approach emphasizes differences in how memories are processed. These approaches are outlined in Table 7.1. A final approach attempts to model memory in the nervous system by describing the formation and activation of neural connections.

This chapter's theories generally derive from cognitive psychology, but two other fields also offer insights into the nature of memory. The field of neuropsychology, with its emphasis on brain and behavior, seeks to distinguish those areas of the brain associated with the different components of memories. Case studies of individuals with brain injuries provide important means of testing our theories and for generating new conceptions of memory. In addition, connectionist models merge the physiological psychology of the neuron with cognitive theories of memory.

Partitioning Memory

Why do we hypothesize multiple memory systems instead of a single general memory? Tulving (1985) considered several reasons. Among the most surprising is his belief that we cannot assert many generalizations about memory as a whole, although statements about

TABLE 7.1   Three Approaches to Memory

Memory Components	Stages of Memory	Processes of Memory
Short-term memory	Encoding into memory	Depth of processing
Long-term memory	Storage in memory	Shallow rehearsal
Episodic	Retrieval from memory	Elaborative rehearsal
Semantic		Transfer-appropriate processing
Procedural		
Priming		

particular forms of memory are valid. Thus, there may be general principles for long-term memory and for short-term memory, or for personal memories versus knowledge, but just not the same principles. To the degree that the hypothesized memory components do function differently, the multiple systems approach is sound. However, we need to be careful not to partition memory into too many too small units, each with its own set of laws.

Another compelling reason is the heuristic value in postulating multiple memory systems. A heuristic is a sort of rule of thumb. It is a guideline that often works, although it may not be perfectly accurate and it does not explain what is going on. The hypothesis of multiple memory stores has heuristic value in simplifying our theories. The several components, each with different characteristics, may be simpler to construct and to use than a single memory system that has many discordant facts.

A third reason for postulating multiple memory systems is that the empirical results of our studies suggest multiple processes are involved. This is part of the research strategy of uncovering dissociations. *Dissociation* occurs when an experimental variable (or variables) has different effects on different tasks or measures. For example, are verbal learning and spatial learning encompassed by a single memory system, or are they separate? Injury to the left hemisphere of the brain can impair learning of verbal items, such as word paired associates or free recall of word lists. Spatial learning of a maze or a new route is unaffected. Because only verbal learning is affected by left-brain injury, this could suggest the two types of materials are learned by different brain areas.

A simple difference between verbal and spatial learning could occur for reasons other than a specialized learning capacity in the left hemisphere. The tests of verbal and spatial learning likely differ in many ways: the to-be-remembered materials, the task demands, the sensory modalities used, and so on. A more convincing demonstration would be a *double dissociation,* in which the experimental variables differentially affect performance on two or more tasks. If we can also show that right-hemisphere lesions impair spatial memory but not verbal learning, then we would have a double dissociation.

Figure 7.1 shows the results of one such study. The subjects had to remember, in one case, whether a test word had been recently presented on the video screen, and in the other case, whether an X had been presented at a certain location on the screen. The subjects were individuals who had surgical lesions of one hemisphere of the brain to control epilepsy. Those with lesions to the language hemisphere (usually the left side of the brain) did worse on the word-recognition test; those subjects with lesions to the nonlanguage hemisphere (usually the right) were more impaired on the spatial location test (Kesner, Hopkins, & Chiba, 1992). This finding suggests that the two cerebral hemispheres play different roles in verbal and spatial learning.

Dissociations may be produced in several ways: by using different experimental manipulations (e.g., the length of the retention interval before testing), different memory tasks (such as recalling words or completing words when some letters are missing), neurological differences (as in comparing people with injuries to the left or right hemisphere), and different subject populations (such as younger versus older subjects).

Each uncovered dissociation should be cautiously interpreted. A dissociation does not automatically imply that there are separate underlying memory systems or abilities. Two tasks could vary in their procedures, difficulty, or familiarity (Hintzman, 1990). For example, Hanley-Dunn and McIntosh (1984) gave college students and elderly adults lists

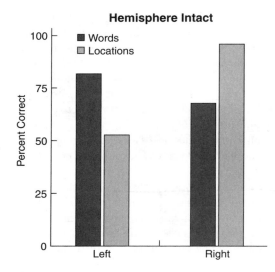

FIGURE 7.1   Example of the effects of lesions to one side of the brain on recognition memory for words or spatial locations.

Source: Kesner, Hopkins, & Chiba, 1992.

of names to remember. The students did better than the elderly when the to-be-remembered names were those of rock music performers; the elderly did better when the names were of Big Band musicians. This pattern of results does not indicate that separate memory systems or brain areas are involved in remembering different categories of names. Nor does it show different memory processes in older versus younger people. As the authors pointed out, in this case there were differences in the meaningfulness of the to-be-learned materials to the two age groups.

Components of Memory Approach

One of the major approaches to partitioning memory divides memory into different stores or types. The primary divisions are sensory memory, short-term memory, and long-term memory.

Sensory Memory

Sensory memory is the first step in information processing. Information passes through the sense receptors and is briefly retained in a sensory memory before being recoded into short-term memory. Most research has focused on the visual and auditory sensory memories, although sensory memories may exist in other modalities. The visual store, or *iconic* memory, holds a great deal of information but only for at most 1 second's time. This can be demonstrated by flashing a matrix of a dozen letters for about 1/20th of a second and asking people to report what they had seen. Participants can usually report three or four letters. The subjective experience is as if they were reading the letters off a vanishing image.

More letters seem to be available than can be reported, but they are forgotten over the few seconds time it takes to report the letters. The image of the letters fades from iconic memory. This problem was neatly bypassed in the partial-report method developed by George Sperling (1960). After the letter matrix is presented, a cue signals which row in the matrix is to be reported: first, middle, or last. The subject does not know in advance of presentation, and so attention cannot be focused on one or another row. By sampling different rows or positions in the array over trials, much as we sample people in survey research, we can estimate iconic memory's capacity immediately after stimulus presentation. Testing one row at a time usually shows nearly perfect recall of any row of three to four letters. The iconic memory capacity is therefore estimated to be about 10 items, a dramatic increase from the 3 to 4 items found with the whole report method first described. However, delaying the row cue by a fraction of a second diminishes even partial recall.

Dual-Store Theory: Short-Term and Long-Term Memories

Although the starting point for information processing is the sensory memory, the emphasis within many theories has been on the next two memory systems, short-term memory and long-term memory. Thus, these models are often referred to as dual-store theories, even though they may also include a third memory, the sensory store. The dual-store theory, particularly the detailed theory of Atkinson and Shiffrin (1968), has become the prototype of other theories and so is sometimes referred to as the "modal model."

(A note on terminology is needed here. Atkinson and Shiffrin referred to short-term *store* and long-term *store*. Others have adopted the terms short- and long-term *memory,* or short- and long-term *retention,* or *immediate* memory instead of short-term memory, as alternative generic labels to the theoretical short-term and long-term stores of Atkinson and Shiffrin's theory. I will use short-term and long-term memory here and in the next chapter. But be aware that different terms are preferred by different authors.)

Short-term memory (or STM) and *long-term memory* (or LTM) are theorized to have different characteristics, thus distinguishing the two memory systems. First, and most obvious, STM is brief. Unless maintained by rehearsal, information in STM lasts 15 to 30 seconds under laboratory testing conditions. If you look up a new phone number, you will forget it quickly, maybe before you even reach the phone, in the absence of rehearsal. Memories in LTM are more durable. You won't likely forget your current phone number overnight.

STM has a limited capacity, holding at most a few items, whereas LTM is assumed to be virtually limitless in size. Retaining one seven-digit number is plenty for STM; retaining the many numerical sequences we use in everyday life is possible with LTM.

STM codes items in a verbal form. Introspectively, we seem to verbally rehearse in STM. Memories in LTM can be encoded in other modalities: an image, a smell, a touch, or an emotion.

Forgetting occurs from STM when the contents of storage are displaced (and replaced) by later-occurring items. Reading a second phone number can displace a first number from STM. Forgetting does not easily occur from LTM. Forgetting your phone number does not usually occur, although memorizing a new phone number can interfere with recall of your old one.

Finally, STM serves to transfer information into LTM. Specifically, rehearsal in STM keeps information available longer for encoding into LTM. The more you rehearse a phone number in STM, the better you should remember it in LTM.

The preceding listing includes the modal properties of short- and long-term stores. In the next chapter, we will consider the validity of these statements, and developments since Atkinson and Shiffrin's original theory.

What sorts of evidence suggest that there are two memory storage systems? Short-term and long-term memory are dissociated in several ways. The *serial-position curve* that is obtained in free-recall tasks is differently affected by several independent variables. In remembering a list of words presented a single time, recall of the first words, also called the *primacy effect,* is enhanced if the list is presented at a slower pace and is reduced if the list is presented at a faster rate (Glanzer & Cunitz, 1966). The slower pace allows more opportunity for rehearsal in STM, allowing a stronger encoding into LTM. Representative results are shown in the left panel of Figure 7.2. As can be seen, fast or slow presentation does not particularly affect recall of the last items of the list. Recall of the final list items, called the *recency effect,* is enhanced if testing is immediate and recall is impaired if testing is delayed (Glanzer & Cunitz, 1966). This is shown in the right panel of Figure 7.2. After a delay interval before testing recall, recency disappears but the primacy effect is still there. Immediate recall of the last items is from STM. The delay is usually occupied by distractor activity, which prevents rehearsal and thus transfer to LTM.

Short-term and long-term memories are also dissociated by the patterns of memory loss observed in individuals rendered amnesic by injuries to different areas of the brain. The amnesic subject H. M., known now to generations of students (and better known than many of the psychologists who have studied him), has damage to the interior of his temporal lobes. Specifically, as a result of experimental surgery in 1953 for the relief of epilepsy,

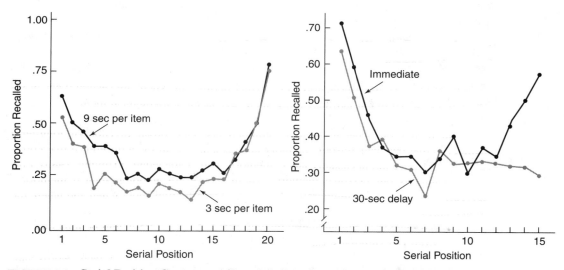

FIGURE 7.2   Serial Position Curves, as Affected (*left*) by Rate of Presentation of the Items, Fast or Slow, and (*right*) Immediate or Delayed Testing.

Source: From *Experimental Psychology: Contemporary Methods and Applications* (p. 214), by I. P. Levin and J. V. Hinrichs, 1995, New York: McGraw-Hill. Copyright 1995. Reprinted with permission of The McGraw-Hill Companies.

the hippocampus and other nearby structures on both sides of his brain were removed. Remarkably, little about H. M. changed. His epilepsy was controlled; his IQ went up a bit; his personality was unchanged. But over time, his doctors realized that his postsurgery memory problems, which had been expected to resolve, instead became permanent. Basically, H. M. cannot form new long-term memories. He cannot learn new facts, vocabulary, place, faces, or mazes. (Some forms of learning are spared, as will be described later.) However, his short-term memory is preserved. He can remember short strings of letters, digits, or words, and he can remember long enough to carry on a conversation. H. M.'s pattern of what is remembered and forgotten, and that of other amnesic syndrome patients like him, suggests a dissociation between short-term memory, which was spared, and the ability to acquire long-term memories, which has been lost to the brain lesions (Hilts, 1995; Scoville & Milner, 1957).

The case of K. F. provides a symmetrical and opposite comparison. K. F. cannot repeat back even the shortest strings of words. If read two or three items, likely only one will be recalled. However, K. F. can form long-term memories. Curiously, if read longer lists of 7 to 10 items, K. F. shows a serial recall curve with primacy; that is, he recalls more of the first items than middle items (Shallice & Warrington, 1970).

(These descriptions of H. M. and K. F. are overly broad. As will be shown later in this and other chapters, H. M. can learn classically conditioned responses and motor skills, or what will be called "procedural learning." Individuals like K. F. may have short-term memory in other sensory modalities. K. F.'s impairment seems to be with his verbal short-term memory.)

Finally, a dissociation between short-term and long-term memory is suggested by the effects of other types of brain trauma, such as electroconvulsive shock. This research is discussed in Box 7.1.

Divisions of Long-Term Memory: Episodic versus Semantic

In contrast to STM, long-term store is relatively permanent. There are several types of information retained in our permanent memory, such as autobiographical memories, factual knowledge, and various skills and habits, which suggest to theorists that LTM itself is made up of several separate memory components. One broad division of long-term memory is that between episodic memory and semantic memory, a difference that corresponds to what we might casually label "memory" and "knowledge" (Tulving, 1985). *Episodic memory* is our personal memory system. These are autobiographical memories. Episodic memories retain temporal and contextual information about when and where the events represented occurred. We can use time of occurrence to retrieve episodic memories, and retrieved memories can be approximately dated. An example would be remembering moments from last summer's vacation. *Semantic memory* is our store of general knowledge. It is more like dictionary or encyclopedic knowledge. It includes facts, words, language, and grammar. It has sometimes been referred to as generic memory, or knowledge that many of us have in common, in distinction to the unique and personal episodic memories. Semantic memory includes knowledge, but not the memory of how or when it was learned. For example, you have a great deal of generic knowledge about dogs in semantic memory—they make good pets, they bark, they are related to wolves, and so on. You probably

BOX **7.1**

Electroconvulsive Shock and Amnesia

Electroconvulsive shock (ECS) is sometimes used as a treatment for severe depression. Memory loss is one prominent side effect of *electroconvulsive therapy* (ECT). Most patients will report some retrograde amnesia for events that preceded ECT. These reports are difficult to evaluate in the absence of corroborating evidence. Forgetting may be due to pretreatment depression, antidepressant drugs, or the unreliability of informal reports. However, controlled studies indicate that ECS does affect memory.

The development of retrograde amnesia for real-life memories was assessed in a seminal study by Janis and Astrachan (1951). During a pre-ECT interview, the patients were questioned in detail about their life histories: schools attended, jobs held, places lived, and so on. The purpose of the pretest was to determine what was recallable before treatment. A second interview occurred 1 month after the completion of the ECS treatments. Every one of the subjects forgot some facts that they could recall before ECT. For example, one patient had first reported being unemployed for several months prior to treatment. Afterwards, he was unable to recall this, and claimed to have worked right up until the time of hospitalization. Interestingly, some of the forgotten material was for events many years prior, things that certainly had been in long-term memory. Janis and Astrachan suggested that ECT affected retrieval, reducing access to certain memories.

Squire, Slater, and Miller (1981) also sought objective assessments of the loss of naturalistically acquired memories. Their subjects first answered questions about public events, or TV shows that had aired for a single season. Forgetting these facts would indicate the precise time periods encompassed by the amnesia. In the first week following ECT, the patients showed some retrograde amnesia that extended back 1 to 3 years for some personal events and a decade for public and political events. However, a second test given 7 months after ECT showed that much of what had been forgotten on the first post-ECT test could then be remembered.

One early hypothesis for the retrograde-amnesic effects of ECS was that it disrupts the consolidation of short-term memories into long-term memories (Hebb, 1949; McGaugh, 1974). Supporting evidence came from animal conditioning experiments in which the timing of a learning trial and ECS administration could be precisely controlled. For example, rats were first given minimal training in how to avoid a foot shock. They then received ECS at delays ranging from seconds to hours after the avoidance training. The results of one study are shown in Figure 7.3 (Chorover & Schiller, 1965). The closer the ECS was to training, the more forgetting occurred. Delaying ECS supposedly allowed more time for consolidation of the training experience into long-term memory (Duncan, 1949).

Consolidation theory was challenged by several observations. For one, memory of the avoid-

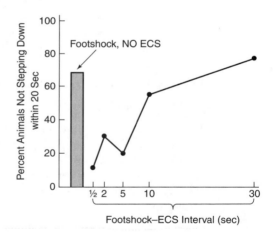

FIGURE 7.3 Memory Disruption as a Function of the Delay between Learning and Administration of ECS. The graph plots the number of subjects who avoided the shocked floor when the single training trials had been followed by ECS after different intervals or no ECS.

Source: From "Short-Term Retrograde Amnesia in Rats," by S. L. Chorover and P. H. Schiller, 1965, *Journal of Comparative and Physiological Psychology, 59,* p. 76. Copyright © 1965 by the American Psychological Association. Reprinted by permission.

ance-learning experience would return after "reinstatement" treatments were given that reexposed the animals to some portion of the training experience as a reminder treatment (Miller & Springer, 1973). If ECS had blocked consolidation, there should be no memory to reinstate. Consolidation theory is also questioned by memory recovery in the human studies cited earlier and the temporary amnesia for items that have already been consolidated into long-term memory. Squire suggests that ECS may affect both retrieval of already stored memories and their continued consolidation. The return of supposedly "forgotten" memories supports the retrieval-failure hypothesis. The persistent loss for other memories suggests that some material in long-term store is still susceptible to disruption.

ECS may have different effects on other forms of learning. Studies on animals have shown a dissociation between an instrumentally learned response that avoids a foot shock, which is forgotten after ECS; and a classically conditioned fear of the warning signal for shock, which is not forgotten after ECS (Naitoh, 1971). In humans, word-fragment completion, an example of implicit memory, may be unimpaired in ECS patients, even though they are impaired in tests explicitly requesting recall (Graf et al., 1984).

---

don't recall how or when you learned each fact. By contrast, a specific memory of an event in your life involving a dog at a particular time and place would be episodic recall. Our everyday use of the phrases "I remember" versus "I know" parallel episodic and semantic memory.

Many of the laboratory experiments on human memory presented in this text are tests of episodic memory: memory for words and pictures that occurred in a particular context (the lab) at a particular time (often just a few minutes ago). In a free-recall task, you might be asked to recall the most recent list of words but not the previous lists presented in the day's session. The unremembered words are forgotten from episodic memory, but they are not forgotten in the sense that the student is no longer able to use or comprehend those words. These word are retained in semantic memory.

The episodic-semantic distinction is evident in certain types of amnesias. Schacter (1983) reports a case of impaired episodic but spared semantic memory in an Alzheimer's patient. Alzheimer's victims often have trouble with ongoing memory, or remembering events as they occur, and so are forgetful about the recent past. Rather than simply reporting data from laboratory tests, Schacter assessed memory during a couple of rounds of golf. Schacter's friend remembered the rules of the game and knew which club to use and when. For example, realizing he probably could not drive the ball over the water hazard, he selected a short iron to safely lay up before the pond. He correctly used an extensive vocabulary of technical terms, for example, birdie, bogey, divot. This is knowledge stored in semantic memory. Yet after a brief delay, the man could not remember which direction his ball had gone, or which of two balls on the fairway was his. After moving on to the next tee, he could not recount any details of the previous hole. This is failure of episodic memory, an inability to form ongoing memories of personal life.

A dramatic case of episodic memory loss involved a man who received a head injury in a motorcycle accident (Tulving, 1989). The young man can remember all sorts of facts about his life. These generic facts, about where he lived and worked, where he went to school, or how to play chess are in semantic memory. Note that not all of knowledge about ourselves is episodic. We can have semantic knowledge about ourselves, just as we have generic knowledge of the world. However, this young man could not remember a specific episode involving himself in any of these known events. He could not remember a single episode of having vacationed in the family cabin, or having been at work, or having ever played chess. This is loss of episodic memory.

Attempts to functionally dissociate episodic and semantic memories in laboratory experiments have had mixed success. One difficulty is that testing the two hypothesized forms of memory requires different materials, procedures, or tasks. For example, two types of words might be presented to subjects in an experiment. Some words are frequently encountered in reading and speaking and so are called high-frequency words. Others words have low frequency of usage in everyday language. Later, half of our subjects are given a recognition test of episodic memory: A long list is presented from which to select the words studied earlier. More of the *low*-frequency words are recognized. (This sounds paradoxical. But, in the *word-frequency effect,* the subject is not sure of the source of familiarity of the high-frequency words because they are encountered so often; low-frequency words occur so rarely they can only be familiar from their recent occurrence in this experiment.) The remaining subjects are given a test of semantic memory. Strings of letters are briefly flashed on the screen, and the task is to decide which strings form real words (e.g., CAT) and which do not (e.g., ATC). Here, the high-frequency words that were studied earlier are identified more quickly than are the low-frequency words. We have a dissociation between the low-frequency words, which are recognized more accurately in an episodic recognition test, and the high-frequency words, which are identified faster in a semantic word-identification test. The problem is we are confounding the type of test with type of memory. Maybe the difference is not episodic versus semantic, but recognition memory versus identification (Neely, 1989).

Attempts to dissociate the two memory systems via laboratory experiments have faced these sorts of confoundings, and some theorists downplay the episodic–semantic distinction. However, others defend it for its heuristic value. The distinction between forms of long-term memory is useful in describing the development of semantic or generic memories. In children, for example, a child's first experience with a cow leads to an episodic memory. Repeated experiences lead to the formation of a generic memory of cow-related facts and lore. The same logic applies to our autobiographical memories. Your first college class meetings produce distinct episodic memories. The day-by-day episodic memories are eventually supplanted by generic memory of what a typical class is like, and rapid loss of memory for individual class meetings (Linton, 1982). This process could be described as the transition from episodic to semantic memory.

Another application of the episodic–semantic memory distinction is in describing *source amnesia.* You know something, but not how or where you learned it. For instance, if I tell you some odd fact of history, for example, that the name of Robert E. Lee's horse was Traveler, you might later remember this fact but not where you learned it. The fact seems to have been incorporated into your semantic store of information about General Lee, but you have lost the episodic reference (the who, what, when, and where of first hearing this fact).

Divisions of Long-Term Memory: Procedural Learning and Priming

Explicit versus Implicit. Direct questioning about the contents of memory is an *explicit task.* Explicit tests tap the episodic and semantic knowledge that we can report on. An *im-*

plicit task assesses the effects of prior experience indirectly, by measuring performance on some task that does not requires explicit recall. For example, a stimulus is reacted to more quickly the second time it occurs than during its first presentation. Performance improves regardless of whether you recall the previous experience. Implicit memory is performance that occurs independently of conscious attempts to recall.

The meaning of the terms explicit and implicit has evolved in their short history in the psychology lexicon. Some of the contrasting terms used to distinguish between implicit and explicit memory are shown in Table 7.2. The terms are sometimes used to refer to separate types of memory, that is, explicit memory systems such as episodic and semantic memory, and implicit memory systems as demonstrated by procedural learning and priming (described in the sections that follow). Today, the terms implicit and explicit are more often used to refer to how knowledge is assessed: Does the procedure make explicit reference to the prior experience with the tested material, or is knowledge elicited implicitly? In this use, the terms are neutral with respect to whether or not there are independent memory systems underlying explicit and implicit memory. However, there are two classes of implicit procedures hypothesized to be mediated by different neural systems from the explicit memory systems of episodic and semantic memories. These tasks are called procedural learning and priming.

Procedural Learning. *Procedural learning* is the acquisition of knowledge of how to do things and includes perceptual skills, motor skills, and cognitive skills. Procedural knowledge has been characterized as "knowing how" rather than episodic and semantic's "remembering that." I know *how* to skate versus I remember *that* I once fell (Squire & Cohen, 1984). Procedural learning is characterized by the acquisition of generalized rules for performing a task or procedures. Unlike episodic and semantic memory, however, the knowledge may not be accessible to conscious verbal recall.

The procedural learning tasks most commonly used in research have different combinations of perceptual, motor, and cognitive skills. For instance, mirror star tracing combines perceptual and motor skills. Subjects trace the outline of a printed star, but by watching their hand movements through a mirror reflection. This requires reversing the direction of hand movements from the direction seen in the mirror. Learning to read text that has been inverted or mirror-reversed is another procedural task, one that combines a cognitive skill and

TABLE 7.2   Some of the Contrasting Terms Used to Distinguish Implicit and Explicit Memory

Explicit Memory	Implicit Memory
Fact memory	Skill memory
Declarative	Procedural
Knowing that	Knowing how
Autobiographical	Perceptual
Memory	Habit
Conscious recollection	Skills

Source: Squire, 1987, p. 169.

a perceptual skill. As a final example, learning a sequence of spatial locations can be procedural. Markers are sequentially flashed in a grid on a computer screen. Subjects follow along, hitting response keys corresponding to each location. The sequence repeats, although the subjects are not told this, and many claim not to have detected a pattern. Nevertheless, the subjects come to anticipate the next location and respond more quickly to the repeated sequence, even if the sequence cannot be described verbally. Again, procedural knowledge is knowing how to perform well rather than knowing verbally what the sequence is.

Repetition Priming. Priming refers to the facilitated response to a stimulus that has been recently experienced or has been "primed" in memory. For example, the identification of a word stimulus is facilitated by prior exposure to that stimulus. A typical word-priming experiment has two stages. First, participants are shown a list of words. They need not be presented in the context of a memory experiment. Rather, using incidental learning procedures, the participants may be simply asked to read the words as they are visually presented. In the second phase, the stimuli are presented again along with other distractor items, but in a task that imposes some perceptual or cognitive difficulty in discerning the stimuli. Priming is demonstrated if identification is facilitated by the previous exposure. Note, the participants are not explicitly told in the second phase that the words were previously seen.

Several tests of the effects of the priming presentation are available for the second phase in these experiments. Say, for example, the word TABLE had been presented in the first phase. In a word-stem completion test, the first several letters of a word are given (TAB_) and the subject is asked to complete it with the first word that comes to mind. In the word-fragment test, some letters are missing (T_B_E) and the subject needs to fill in the blanks to form a word. Priming occurs when the stem or fragment is completed with words studied during the first, priming phase, as opposed to other words that may fit. For instance, in one study, the stem TAB_ was completed with TABLE about 30 percent of the time in the unprimed control condition, whereas in the priming condition, TABLE was the solution 49 percent of the time (Rajaram & Roediger, 1993). The letters might be presented scrambled as an anagram (e.g., BETLA) for the subject to solve. Priming is shown by the solution of primed versus unprimed anagrams. Thus, the preceding anagram was solved as TABLE 52 percent of the time in the unprimed condition, but 63 percent of the time after a priming exposure (Rajaram & Roediger, 1993).

Yet another test identifies the effects of a priming exposure through a perceptual identification task. In perceptual identification, the subject attempts to read a target word flashed on a screen for a fraction of a second (say, 25 to 30 milliseconds), a duration that makes conscious recognition difficult. Primed words are more likely to be identified than unprimed words. The control comparison in each of these priming procedures is to words that were not exposed during the first phase. These provide a baseline for stem or fragment completion, anagram solution, or perceptual identification with which to compare the pre-exposed items.

In some cases, performance on an implicit test is better than that on an explicit test. For example, college students attempted to explicitly recognize words they had studied 7 days previously or complete word fragments based on those words. In the latter condition, the students were not reminded, at testing, that these words were from those presented a week earlier. Recognition declined dramatically over time, from about 60 percent immediately after studying to about 20 percent a week later, but fragment completion held steady at around 50 percent (Tulving, Schacter, & Stark, 1982). In other research, amnesic subjects (those having amnesic syndrome like H. M.) simply cannot recall many of the words they have studied earlier, and they perform only a little better in a recognition test. Yet amnesics do as well as nonamnesic individuals in completing word stems or word fragments (Shimamura et al., 1987).

Visual Object Priming.   Priming can occur with stimuli in other modalities. For example, drawings of objects or scenes can be presented and then tested later through a method of fragmented pictures (see Figure 7.4). Subjects attempt to identify the object from the fragmented picture. On each trial, one drawing is shown at a time, from most fragmented to least, until the subject can identify the object or word. Across trials, identification can be made with ever more degraded images. Previously seen pictures are easier to identify from the fragments than are new pictures. This technique of fragmented pictures was actually one of the first used to show that amnesics could in fact learn and remember implicitly (Warrington & Weiskrantz, 1968a). Subjects like H. M., who could not recall the pictured objects when explicitly asked to do so, could nevertheless identify objects more quickly from fewer and fewer fragments.

The priming effects of picture exposure can persist over long intervals of time. Cave (1997) presented 200 object drawings to her college student subjects (simple line drawings of a dog, piano, tree, lamp, etc.). The students simply named each object as shown. After delays of 6 to 48 weeks, the students were brought back and were given the same object-naming task, but some of the pictures were new and some were repeated from the initial priming session. The students were faster at naming repeated pictures than novel pictures, even after nearly a year had passed.

The Role of Conscious Awareness.   Implicit memory is often said to reflect recollection without awareness that one is remembering. "An increasingly large literature from both patient and nonpatient populations indicates that people can display implicit memory without having any conscious recollection of the experiential basis of the effect" (Kihlstrom, 1987, p. 1449). But can we objectively assess the degree to which implicit priming reflects nonaware retention? The contribution of explicit memory to an implicit test cannot readily be discounted. By testing amnesic subjects, we have somewhat more assurance that awareness of a previous study trial is not a factor in an implicit memory test. Yet even amnesics are not completely devoid of new memories. They will explicitly remember some of the studied items.

With college students as participants, there is a likelihood they may notice the relationship between the test items and the words presented in the first phase, and then perform the task explicitly. Although this is a possibility in specific instances, in general, the argument is refuted. Awareness of the relationship between the first list and the tested items has been assessed by postexperimental interview. The incidence of priming in one series of studies did not differ between test-aware and -unaware subjects (Bowers & Schacter,

FIGURE 7.4   Fragmented-Pictures and Fragmented-Words Implicit Learning Task.

Source: From "A New Method of Testing Long-Term Retention with Special Reference to Amnesic Patients," by E. K. Warrington and L. Weiskrantz, 1968, *Nature, 217,* pp. 972–974. Copyright © 1968 Nature/Macmillan Publishers Ltd. Reprinted with permission.

1990). In other experiments, more of the previously seen words are produced by an explicit request to recall than by implicit instructions (Graf, Squire, & Mandler, 1984). That is, subjects complete more stems with studied words when they are told it is a memory test than when they are not. If the implicitly instructed subjects had realized this was a memory study, implicit memory scores should have converged with explicit scores. Finally, if an independent variable affects implicit and explicit memory differently (and examples are presented in what follows), then subjects are treating the tasks differently.

Dissociating Priming and Explicit Memory.   In order to argue that implicit priming represents a different memory system than that accessed by explicit tests of episodic or semantic memory, we need to demonstrate that the two classes of tasks are dissociable. Tulving and Schacter (1990) categorized several types of evidence that dissociate implicit and explicit memory.

1. Performance on explicit and implicit tests are sometimes statistically independent; that is, performance on the two is uncorrelated.
2. Certain experimental treatments affect explicit memory but not implicit memory. For instance, the serial position of the words presented during priming has little effect on later word-stem completion, although serial position has large effects on whether the words are recalled explicitly (Brooks, 1994).
3. Individual differences such as age affect explicit memory but not implicit memory. Parkin and Streete (1988) tested picture-fragment identification and explicit recognition of pictures in children. They found increases across ages 3 to 7 in recognition of previously shown pictures, but the younger children did as well as the older ones on the implicit test.
4. Neurological and psychopharmacological treatments affect explicit and implicit memory differently. For instance, we have already noted that amnesics recall poorly on explicit tests of memory, but do as well as non-memory-impaired individuals on priming tests.

The Organization of Long-Term Memory

What is the relationship among the several hypothesized components of long-term memory? Various organizations of memory have been proposed. Tulving (1985) suggests that three of the memory systems form a "monohierarchy" in descending order of inclusiveness: Procedural learning includes within it semantic memory as a subset, which in turn includes episodic memory as its subset. This memory system would appear as follows:

Memory System Hierarchy
Procedural
|
Semantic
|
Episodic

Priming effects are attributed to still another memory system (or set of systems associated with different sensory modalities) that overlaps both the procedural and semantic memory systems. This other memory Tulving calls the *perceptual representation system* (or PRS; Tulving & Schacter, 1990).

In a different hypothesized organization of long-term memory, Squire (1987; Squire, Knowlton, & Musen, 1993) divides memory into two major categories, declarative and nondeclarative:

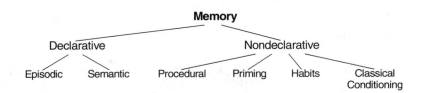

Declarative memory can be consciously recalled and reported verbally. That is, we can "declare" these memories. Instructions that explicitly request recollection from memory are accessing declarative memory. Declarative memory includes episodic and semantic memory.

Nondeclarative memory is defined by exclusion. It is whatever types of memory that are not declarative. Nondeclarative memory includes procedural skill learning, priming effects due to recent exposure to a stimulus, habit learning, and classical conditioning. Nondeclarative knowledge, as is obvious from its label, is often assessed implicitly and not by direct or explicit verbal recall.

Stages of Memory

A second approach to memory separates it into a series of stages. A memory must first be formed, then retained, and later retrieved. These stages are usually labeled *encoding, storage, and retrieval.* Forgetting could arise from problems at any one of these stages. For example, if you cannot remember the answer to an exam question, it may be because (1) you never really learned the material, (2) you learned it but it has since been lost from memory, or (3) you learned it, it's there, but you can't recall it right now (although you will probably remember shortly after turning in your exam). The stage approach is not so much a theory about memory, but rather a set of assumptions or "givens" about memory. It is also not an alternative to the separate-memories approach discussed earlier, or the processing approach discussed later. Some researchers combine multiple approaches, for example, studying the retrieval stage of short-term store or encoding of information into semantic memory. The goal of the stage approach is to identify the effect of certain variables on one stage of memory or another.

The stages of encoding, storage, and retrieval cannot be perfectly isolated from one another. For instance, to study retrieval failure requires prior encoding, so that something can be (temporarily) forgotten. Also, some variables influence more than one stage. Categorizing or grouping items aids encoding, and this organization also facilitates retrieval by providing a systematic means for searching memory.

Dissociating Stages

Experimental Dissociations.   Functional dissociations of the stages are shown when an experimentally manipulated variable primarily affects either encoding, storage, or retrieval. This can be illustrated by a study of the effects of alcohol on memory (Storm & Caird, 1967). College student participants were given word lists to learn either while sober or after consuming alcohol. When these two conditions were compared later, after the drug had worn off, the studied-sober group remembered more words. This finding could suggest that alcohol impaired encoding. But you might object that the change in conditions from intoxication to sober made the memories of the alcohol group less retrievable. This is the notion of state-dependent retrieval: Memories encoded in one state of consciousness (sober or intoxicated, in the present example) are more accessible when retrieval is attempted while in that same state of consciousness. That is, maybe both groups encoded equally well, but the intoxicated group experienced retrieval failure when tested sober. To test for changes in retrieval conditions, two additional groups could be run that are tested while intoxicated. Now we can see whether the group given alcohol at both study and test remembers as much as the group that was sober at study and test. The results from this experiment are shown in Table 7.3. The data are presented in terms of the number of trials to relearn the list, so lower scores mean better retention. The participants who were sober at both study and test did better than the subjects who were intoxicated at both times. Each of these groups was tested for relearning under the same drug condition that had been present when studying, so the deficit in the alcohol group is not due just to retrieval failure. We would conclude from the comparison of these two groups that alcohol impaired encoding.

However, there is also evidence for a retrieval deficit. Switching conditions between study and testing increased the number of relearning trials, as compared to staying in the same condition. Although alcohol often impairs memory, the specific pattern of results shown here, of alcohol affecting both encoding and retrieval, is not always found (Maylor &

TABLE 7.3   Effects of Alcohol before Studying and/or before Testing on Relearning Word Lists

		Study State	
		Sober	*Alcohol*
Test	*Sober*	5.8	11.2
State	*Alcohol*	7.5	8.5

Note: The data are presented in terms of the number of trials to relearn the list; lower scores mean quicker relearning.

Source: Storm & Caird, 1967.

Rabbitt, 1993). However, this study nicely illustrates the logic of attempting to experimentally separate stages. (See Chapter 10 for further discussion of state-dependent learning.)

Retrieval failure can be shown to have occurred when a change in testing procedure reveals memory that was not evident in an earlier test. One means of facilitating retrieval is to provide some "reminder" cues, or prompts to aid recall. This concept has been useful in studying forgetting in animal studies. Poor performance in a conditioning experiment might at first be attributed to an encoding deficit, that is, a failure to learn. The stage analysis offers the possibility that conditioning occurred but the learning now cannot be readily retrieved. Possibly, the seemingly forgotten conditioned response could be reinstated by "reminding" the animal of the earlier conditioning experience. For instance, just prior to a test trial, the participant could be given a brief exposure to, as examples, the reinforcer alone, the experimental apparatus, or the conditioned stimuli (e.g., Deweer & Sara, 1984; Spear, 1973). The intention is to expose the participant to enough information to reinstate the initial learning experience in memory, but not enough information to promote additional conditioning. An analogy might be to return you to some classroom on campus as a means of reminding you of the course(s) you attended in that room. Testing animals after a reminder usually shows better conditioned responding than without the reminder treatment, presumably due to enhanced retrieval of otherwise forgotten learning.

This same rationale applies to efforts to maintain memory availability in human infants. After babies had learned to move their legs to shake a mobile, the behavior would normally be forgotten a month later. However, exposure to the overhead mobile, unconnected to the infant's leg, about 2 weeks through the delay interval prevented forgetting at the 1-month interval (Rovee-Collier et al., 1980).

Neuropsychological Dissociations. The neuropsychologist attempts to dissociate certain stages by finding individuals with impairment at one or another stage. H. M., the amnesic discussed earlier, is believed to have an encoding deficit: He cannot form new memories. H. M. can still retrieve many of his older memories from before his operation: He can relate much of his early life history.

Actually, one could logically argue that for individuals like H. M., who continuously forget recent experiences, the failure could be at any stage of memory. One could say H. M. has a storage deficit: Newly learned material rapidly disappears from long-term storage. It is also possible that information is encoded and stored, but it becomes unretrievable. Indeed, this latter hypothesis has been offered. For example, in experiments using amnesic subjects, several different lists are presented and tested in succession. Although few words are recalled from the just-heard list, the amnesics sometimes recall words from earlier lists. These are intrusion errors. If words from a previous list intrude during recall of the current list, then there obviously must be some memory for the other lists. This suggests the amnesic has difficulty, not in forming memories, but in discriminating a recent memory from those of earlier lists (Warrington & Weiskrantz, 1968b).

Other aspects of amnesics' performance also suggest that their forgetting may be a retrieval rather than encoding problem. Amnesics sometimes recall if tested implicitly, but not if tested explicitly. For example, amnesics first read a list of words and then later are tested with word fragments. If tested explicitly by being asked to complete letter stems with words from the previously seen list, the amnesics perform poorly. ("What lists?" they ask. After all, they are amnesic.) However, if the task is presented as a diversion or game ("Can you think of a word that begins with these letters?") without reference to the previously studied lists, the amnesics complete the stems with previously studied words. Whereas earlier we said that the amnesics had encoding deficits, implicit recall via a word-priming manipulation suggests that some form of encoding did in fact take place.

Another dissociation strategy is to compare amnesic individuals who have different brain pathologies. Some amnesic individuals are able to encode and retain new memories, although with great difficulty. The subject N. A., who suffered damage to his thalamus (a structure near the hippocampus), at first appears to be just as amnesic as H. M. Both have difficulty retaining new memories. Yet N. A. can attain nearly normal levels of recall or recognition with sufficient practice. He must spend considerably more time studying than do nonamnesic subjects. However, once learning has occurred, forgetting occurs at a normal rate (Squire, 1981). Thus, amnesia associated with the hippocampus (which characterizes H. M.) and amnesia associated with the thalamus (which characterizes N. A.) may dissociate the encoding stage (Squire, 1987).

Processing Approaches

Depth of Processing

A third major approach to memory emphasizes how the kind or quality of processing determines memorability. *Depth of processing theory* (Craik & Lockhart, 1972) was initially offered as an alternative to the theory of separate short-term and long-term memories. A single memory system is hypothesized, and variations in the degree of cognitive processing determines whether something is remembered. Rapid forgetting is due, not to a loss from a transient short-term storage as Atkinson and Shriffrin suggested, but rather to shallow processing. Sustained retention is due not to transfer from one memory store to another, but rather to deeper or more elaborate processing. In either case, remembering or forgetting occurs within a single memory system, with variations in retention reflecting variations in the cognitive depth to which information is processed.

The idea of shallow versus deep processing is illustrated by two kinds of rehearsal. When we try to remember something, we are sometimes subjectively aware that we are rehearsing the to-be-remembered information. *Maintenance rehearsal* is the passive repetition of information, repeating something over and over. This exemplifies shallow processing. We use maintenance rehearsal to remember a phone number just long enough to dial it or to recall a message long enough to write it down. *Elaborative rehearsal,* on the other hand, is a more active form of processing. It involves meaningful analysis and comprehension of the material, and thus represents a deeper level of processing. Elaborative rehearsal of a phone number could include looking for a pattern among the numbers (a date, your ID number or pin number). Many learning strategies are instances of elaborative rehearsal: using mnemonic devices, forming mental images, and relating the to-be-recalled material to existing knowledge. Elaborative rehearsal should lead to longer retention than does maintenance rehearsal.

Deeper processing does not necessarily require a deliberate intention to learn. Remembering is due more to the quality of processing than the goal of the processing. Craik and Tulving (1975) demonstrated this in experiments on *incidental learning,* in which college student participants were shown a list of words but without instructions to remember them. Instead, the students answered a question about each presented word, with different types of questions used to elicit different levels of processing. In one condition, the participant decided whether the word contained the letter *e* (this requires processing the surface form or appearance of the word); in a second condition, a rhyme for the word had to be generated (which requires processing the sound of the word); in the final condition, the participant could be asked whether the word fits a given category, such as "animal" (which requires processing the meaning of the word). Later, the subjects were given a surprise test of memory for the words. Words that had received deeper processing during presentation were better recalled. Interestingly, the incidental learning in the deep-processing condition led to memory as good as that found in an intentional learning condition, one in which participants were explicitly instructed to remember.

Neuropsychologists have considered whether the forgetting characteristic of amnesia is due to deficient processing. Individuals with anterograde amnesia like H. M. have been tested in the depth-of-processing procedure of Craik and Tulving. Like normal-memoried people, amnesics show better retention after categorizing a word than after rhyming it (Graf et al., 1984). However, the amnesics are still severely impaired. Getting them to deep process material does not eliminate their amnesia. Schacter (1983) reports some observations on his Alzheimer's golfing partner. While playing a particularly challenging hole, the man was asked to elaborate on his actions: why he chose the club he did, why this shot was difficult, how it turned out. These elaborations certainly exemplify deep processing. Still, after moving on to the next tee, the man could not recall any details of the just-elaborated hole.

Soon after its introduction, depth-of-processing theory was challenged on several grounds (e.g., Baddeley, 1978). One criticism was that there were no independent measures of depth. Processing depth was instead inferred on the basis of manipulations that led to good or poor memory, the thing we were trying to account for. There are now independent measures of processing. In one procedure, participants attempt to perform two cognitive tasks at once, such as remembering words and adding numbers. If the primary task requires deeper processing, this leaves less capacity left over for the other task. Thus, deeper processing on the first task is shown by poor performance on the second task.

A second criticism was that the term "depth" is unclear, taking on different meanings. It was sometimes interpreted as elaboration of an item in memory, and other times it referred to a more distinctive representation in memory. We now acknowledge that deep processing can produce either elaboration or distinctiveness, and that both are beneficial to memory. (See Chapter 9.)

The notion of qualitative variations in processing at encoding has now been incorporated into the other approaches to memory. Thus, dual-store theorists distinguish between the two forms of rehearsal in STM, maintenance and elaborative. Elaborative processing is accepted as a significant factor that enhances encoding, and the distinctiveness of a memory is a significant factor facilitating retrieval. Depth-of-processing theory was so successful that, in a sense, it no longer exists as a separate approach to memory but has been assimilated into other approaches.

Transfer-Appropriate Processing

Our everyday knowledge of memory tells us that to facilitate retrieval, we should attempt to reinstate the cues or conditions present at encoding. In retrieving a forgotten memory, we try to remember where and when the event originally occurred or what we were doing. We realize that retrieval is importantly linked to the environmental conditions that were present at encoding. Another processing approach also links the two stages of encoding and retrieval, and takes this idea a step further. *Transfer-appropriate processing* theory (e.g., Kolers, 1975; Morris, Bransford, & Franks, 1977; Roediger, 1990) states that to retrieve memory, we need to reinstate the cognitive operations that were used at encoding. That is, how were we perceiving, manipulating, thinking about, or interpreting the stimuli at the time of input? Reproducing those same cognitive operations at output will best retrieve the memory.

The starting point for transfer-appropriate theory is the difference between implicit and explicit tests of memory. One possible difference between them is that they are based on distinct memory systems, the declarative and nondeclarative systems, and are localized within separate neurological structures in the brain. Transfer-appropriate processing theory suggests that implicit and explicit memory are not separate systems, but that the kind of processing each uses is different. Explicit tests, such as instructions first to study and later to recall the studied items, rely on elaborative operations at study and recall. At input, images may be formed of the to-be-remembered material or associated information is activated. At output, we attempt to recall those images or reactivate those associations. There is a match in the mental operations at the two stages. Implicit memory tasks rely instead on a match between perceptual operations at encoding and retrieval. For example, in a word-priming study, participants are asked to read a list of words without any instructions regarding memory testing. Retention is tested by giving participants word fragments to complete. In this case, the retrieval operation (trying to perceive what the word could be) more closely matches the encoding operation of reading. The general notion is that either an implicit or explicit test might detect memory, depending on whether the cognitive operations activated at testing mirror those operations performed during study. A change in the cognitive operations performed on the material between two phases of an experiment could lead to poorer performance.

A study by Weldon and Roediger (1987) illustrates the strategy of dissociating operations. Their college student participants studied lists of both pictures and words, and then attempted to recall the studied items (an explicit test) or complete word fragments (an implicit test). Pictures are typically better recalled than are the names of the pictured objects, and that occurred here. That is, the target item *dog* was recalled better after seeing a line drawing of a dog than after seeing the word DOG. (The pictures are better remembered in an explicit test because their memory is more elaborated, or possibly more distinctive.) On the other hand, the cognitive operations of visually inspecting words, rather than inspecting pictures, should be more similar to those involved in word completion. Indeed, more word fragments were completed for words the participants had studied than for pictures they had studied. That is, the participants more often completed d_g as *dog* after having seen the word DOG than after seeing the dog picture.

In another experiment, pictures and words were again presented for inspection in Phase I. In Phase 2, either a picture fragment or a word-completion test was given, as illustrated in Figure 7.5. When a word-fragment completion test was given, studied words were

Phase I: Study either 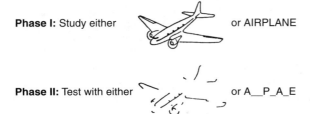 or AIRPLANE

Phase II: Test with either   or A__P_A_E

Phase I

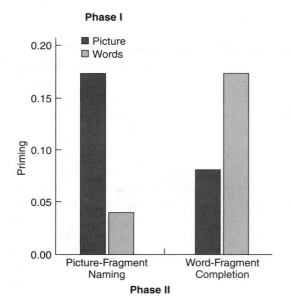

FIGURE 7.5   Design and Results of Weldon and Roediger. Studying pictures produced more priming than did words on the picture-fragment test; studying words produced more priming on the word-fragment test.

Source: From "Implicit Memory: Retention without Remembering," by H. L. Roediger, 1990, *American Psychologist, 45,* p. 1051. Copyright © 1990 by the Psychonomic Society. Reprinted with permission.

more often completed than were the names of studied pictures. Reading words is a cognitive operation similar to completing words, but inspecting pictures is not. When a picture-fragment test was given, studied pictures were more often completed than were pictures representing the studied words. Inspecting a picture is similar at both encoding and retrieval, and dissimilar to word reading (Weldon & Roediger, 1987).

Summary.   The processing theories presented here, depth of processing and transfer-appropriate processing, emphasize the cognitive processing information receives rather than separate memories stores. Memory, and conversely forgetting also, depend on the nature of the processing an item receives rather than which store or which stage is involved. However, the processing approach need not preclude the other approaches presented in this chapter. For instance, the stage approach is illustrated in the retrieval failures that occur when encoding and retrieval operations do not match (as in some conditions in the Weldon and Roediger experiments presented earlier). The types-of-memory approach is consistent with the fact that priming occurs with real words, which are stored in semantic memory, but not with nonsense words, which are not. The several approaches could be viewed as complementary rather than as exclusionary.

Connectionist Models

Research on learning has historically proceeded on several levels. On the behavioral level, researchers attempt to describe the relationships relating independent to dependent variables. For example, what is the effect of massed versus spaced practice on the number of words recalled? On the physiological level, researchers study behavior–physiology relationships, such as the effects of electrical or chemical stimulation on memory. On a neural level, researchers search for the most basic changes in neurons and synapses that underlie memory. Connectionism attempts to unite these levels by modeling the neural changes that underlie learning and memory. Connectionism offers a framework for theorizing, much as cognitive psychology or neuropsychology offers frameworks within which different specific theories can be developed.

Because the underlying basis of memory is believed to be the activity of neurons in the brain, connectionist models attempt to simulate various memory phenomenon in a network of hypothetical neurons. D. O. Hebb's comment that the abbreviation CNS, standing for the *central* nervous system, might be reinterpreted as the *conceptual* nervous system is quite appropriate here (Hebb, 1955; B. F. Skinner, 1938, p. 421, earlier offered this interpretation tongue-in-cheek). A hallmark of connectionism is that this conceptual nervous system can be modeled on a computer. This allows precise predictions to be made, but also demands that the model be precisely specified.

Older psychological theories offered simple models of neural connections in the brain. Classical conditioning occurred, for instance, when a tone stimulus activated auditory neurons at the same time that the motor cortex activated a leg flexion. From such a starting point, modern connectionist theories offer more sophisticated elaborations. To anticipate the following discussion, the connectionist approach makes certain assumptions. These include the following.

1. Each neural unit, or hypothetical neuron, can potentially have connections to many other units. Each can also participate in multiple knowledge representations, analogous to the way a given letter can be used in many words. These models are therefore sometimes called neural network models.

2. The strength of connections increases with "pairings" of active neural units, and weakens when activation of one unit occurs without activation of the other. The increase or decrease in strengths over trials is often described mathematically by a learning algorithm, or formula, such as the delta rule or back propagation.

3. A neural unit, or a network of units, can be activated much as a neuron is activated. This activation gradually fades back to the prestimulation baseline or resting level over a brief period of time.

4. Activation of a particular neural unit may require stimulation from multiple input units. This is the concept of a threshold for activation.

5. There can be multiple layers of neural units. The outer layers correspond to input and output, and thus only they are observable. Inner layers, called hidden units, combine and summate activation from units in the previous layer.

Each of these assumptions is elaborated in what follows.

Modeling Person Identification

Connectionism can be illustrated by modeling person knowledge: the connections between names and individual identities. In a connectionist model, each neural unit has multiple connections to other neural units. As an analogy, for many of us the name JOHN can apply to several individuals. JOHN specifies a particular person when it occurs in combination with certain other features (e.g., a classmate, a fellow worker, a relative). Thus, there is not a simple one-to-one connection between JOHN and a specific individual.

One can always make up a set of connections post hoc to describe memory. Just draw connecting lines between items that we think are associated (e.g., TABLE → CHAIR) and leave out the lines between items that are not associated (TABLE   AARDVARK). The challenge is to simulate the formation and strengthening of those associations. In connectionist models, the starting point is the presence of potential interconnections among the neural units. Simultaneous activation of two units leads to a strengthening of the connection between them, whereas the activation of one without the other leads to a weakening of this connection. This feature parallels synaptic changes in the nervous system, in which synaptic junctions are strengthened by repeated use.

To illustrate, we can have one set of "nodes" (or neural units) represent names, for example, John, Fred, Bill, as shown in Figure 7.6. The system needs to learn which name goes with which person. To start with, each name could potentially connect to any or all of the person identity nodes. The latter are representations of particular individuals and have themselves been formed through learning. On each trial, one name and the corresponding person are presented. Activating a name causes activation to flow to all of the person nodes. However, because only one person node is active at a time, the strength of only the connection between that name and that person node is increased. (In some models, inhibition actually accrues between the activated name and the other *in*active person nodes.)

The Delta Rule

Connections between nodes can vary in strength. The increase or decrease in strength represents the effects of experience, or learning. One formula for computing the trial-by-trial increases in strength is the *delta rule*. (Delta, and its symbol Δ, often stands for "change" in mathematical formulas.) The increment from each trial is a constant proportion of the difference between the maximum possible activation and the current level of activation. Usually, some constant number is given for delta, such as .02 or .10. At the start of training,

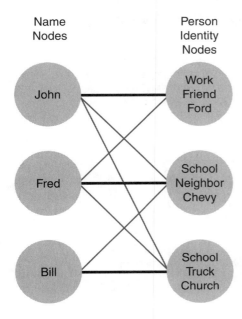

Name Nodes

Person Identity Nodes

John

Work Friend Ford

Fred

School Neighbor Chevy

Bill

School Truck Church

FIGURE 7.8   Possible Connectionist Name–Person Identity Model. The potential name–person connections are shown with the thinner lines. The darker lines show the stronger connections eventually learned.

the strength between any name and a particular person is probably some low value, but often 0 will be arbitrarily assigned. The maximum amount of activation is set at the number 1 (or 100 percent). If delta is .10, then each pairing of the name with the person increases the connection by .1 (or 10 percent) of the distance remaining to 1. For example, at the start of training, the difference between the maximum allowable activation and the current level of activation is 1 (or 1 minus 0, which is 1) times delta, or .1. Thus, after the first pairing, the strength of the connection between a name and the person nodes has increased from 0 to .1. On trial 2, the difference between maximal activation and the actual strength is $1 - .10$, or .9. This difference is multiplied by delta, giving a trial 2 increase of .09 (i.e., $.9 \times .1 = .09$). The strength of the connection is then .19, or .09 added to the existing .10.

The delta rule, specifying that increments are a constant proportion of the distance between the existing strength and the maximal possible, produces a classic learning curve. As described in Chapter 1, such curves are characterized by relatively large increases in learning on the early trials. On later trials, the increments become smaller and smaller in absolute size, although the delta proportion stays the same. This is illustrated with hypothetical numbers in Table 7.4, which continues the example started in the preceding paragraph. (For further detail on the delta rule, see Shanks, 1995.)

An alternative formula works backwards by comparing the desired outcome with the actual output from the connectionist model. The output is determined by the combined strength of activation that arrives at the output nodes. If the output is incorrect, it can be altered by assigning different weights to the connections leading up to the output. If a name leads to recollection of the wrong person, than the weighing of different facts needs to be

TABLE 7.4 Trial-by-Trial Learning of a Name–Person Connection with Delta Set at .1

Trial Number	Increment on That Trial	Strength at End of Trial
1	$(1 - 0) \times .1 = .10$	.10
2	$(1 - .1) \times .1 = .09$	.19
3	$(1 - .19) \times .1 = .081$	.271
4	$(1 - .271) \times .1 = .073$	.344
5	$(1 - .344) \times .1 = .066$	.410
6	$(1 - .410) \times .1 = .059$	.469
7	$(1 - .469) \times .1 = .053$	.522
8	$(1 - .522) \times .1 = .048$	.570
9	$(1 - .570) \times .1 = .043$	.613
10	$(1 - .613) \times .1 = .039$	.652

Note: Each increment is computed using the formula (maximal – existing) × delta. The maximal, or asymptotic, strength is 1.00. The starting strength of the connection is 0. The increment in each trial is then added to the strength at the end of the previous trial, giving the strength in the last column.

altered so the connections lead to the correct person. As a rough analogy, in learning the names of a man and a woman, gender information is informative in narrowing the search set of possible names for each, so gender should be weighed more heavily. Gender is less helpful if the two people are both male, because both men will likely share the same name set to be searched. A discrepancy formula, similar in conception to the delta rule, is used to adjust the weights of the nodes connected to the output across trials.

There is a final feature of connectionist models to mention. The activation of a node may require a certain degree of input strength. Thus, activation of the person identity node does not occur automatically even though it is stimulated by the name node. Activation may need to be summed across input from several nodes, possibly those representing time and place, which help push the person node above some threshold for activation. We have all had the experience in which a name by itself is not enough to trigger recognition of the person referred to. A reminder of where we know this person from, or when we last saw him, combined with the name, may trigger recollection. This connectionist feature also parallels activity in synaptic transmission among neurons in an actual nervous system. Multiple synaptic input pulses are often required to trigger the next neuron in the chain.

What other sorts of knowledge can be represented by connectionist networks? Neural models have been proposed for semantic memory, spatial learning in the hippocampus, instrumental response–outcome contingencies (see, e.g., McNaughton & Smolensky, 1991; Shanks, 1993), and the development of classically conditioned associations between conditioned stimuli and an unconditioned stimulus.

Distributed Memory

Some connectionist models have the property of distributed memory. Memory is not localized to specific neural units. Knowledge is coded by the pattern of active and inactive units, and any group of neural units could thus represent the memory to the degree that they exhibit the pattern. For example, one event might be represented in memory by a pattern of active (signified by a + sign) or inactive (a − sign) neural units as +−+−. A different pattern of these same units, maybe ++−− or −+−+, corresponds to a different memory. Different specific neural units reproduce the memory if they reproduce this same pattern of activation. Memory can be distributed, in the sense of being in various locations within the brain, wherever the pattern appears.

Connectionism and the Other Approaches

How does connectionism relate to the other approaches described in this chapter? Items in short-term memory are, in connectionist models, those items that are currently active in the neural network. Asking you to briefly retain the words TABLE–DOG–GRASS results in the activation of their neural representations above threshold. These units are now "in" short-term memory. Activation will gradually decay back to resting or baseline levels, corresponding to forgetting from short-term memory.

Elaborative rehearsal in short-term memory could be described as the activation of other units concurrently with those already active. The name JOHN can be elaborated by activation of connected units, such as the image of John's face, other knowledge about John, and so on. In the stage model, encoding is the strengthening of connections between nodes, whereas retrieval is the activation of the retrieval cue's neural units, which in turn activate the units connected to them.

Applications

Aspects of the approaches presented in this chapter have, in a general and nondetailed manner, become incorporated into the public's general knowledge about memory. Popular magazine treatments of memory regularly refer to short-term and long-term memory, or to retrieval failure. The finer details of the several approaches presented here have more precise implications for memory outside the laboratory.

Repetition Priming

Priming effects can be manifested in many ways. Priming can increase the liking or preference for unfamiliar stimuli. As you may recall from Chapter 2, Zajonc found that "mere exposure" to stimuli increased the liking of those stimuli, even if the stimuli were not remembered. In his experiments, nonsense shapes and drawings were flashed for a fraction of a second, too quickly to be consciously perceived. This could be considered as a priming presentation. On a later test with above-threshold stimuli, the participants preferred the primed shapes to novel shapes.

Similarly, a priming exposure to a name can affect later judgments about the name. The presentation of invented names (i.e., novel pairings of first and last names) in one session leads to these names being identified as those of famous people a day later. Even though explicit recollection of the names fades over the 24-hour delay, participants misattribute later familiarity of the names to fame (the "becoming famous overnight" effect;

Jacoby et al., 1989). If the name sounds familiar, it must be someone famous. Curiously, this effect is greater for male than for female names; that is, male names are more likely to be judged famous (cited in Greenwald & Banaji, 1995).

Another example of priming involved judges who watched video clips of gymnastic performances. The judges were more accurate in detecting errors when these same moves had been viewed earlier (Ste-Marie & Lee, 1991). The implication here is that judging bias can result due to priming. A gymnastics judge could more likely detect an error if the judge saw an athlete make that same error earlier, say, in a previous round or during warm-up.

The Study of Abnormal Memory: Amnesia

Cognitive neuropsychology combines the theoretical approaches of experimental psychology with the study of the functioning of normal and brain-injured individuals. Neuropsychology has contributed substantially to testing theories developed in the lab. As we have noted by examples in this chapter (e.g., H. M. and N. A.), case studies of brain-injured individuals are used to dissociate components, stages, or processes of memory. The influence works in the opposite direction also. Our understanding of amnesic disorders has benefited from the laboratory-based theories of memory.

We all have some familiarity with the concept of amnesia. Yet most amnesias do not match the stereotype depicted in soap operas and films. Amnesia is actually too broad a term, as an amnesia can originate from one of many causes and can take many forms. To appreciate the give and take between the cognitive psychologists and the neuropsychologists, an understanding of the nature of amnesia is a useful starting point.

Classification of Amnesias.   The amnesias can be described along two major dimensions, one of cause (physical or psychological) and the other time (loss of memory about events that preceded or followed trauma) (Kopelman, 1987). Most amnesias have a physical or *organic* cause, due to injury or damage to the brain. This might be head trauma; a brain infection such as encephalitis or meningitis; brain-cell death due to stroke or anoxia, the loss of oxygen; exposure to toxic substances and chemicals, such as solvents; or prolonged alcohol abuse. The resulting amnesia can vary in severity depending on which areas of the brain are damaged and the extent of that damage.

Amnesia can also result from psychological trauma. *Psychogenic* amnesias (or "functional" amnesias, to use a medical term for disorders of unknown causes) are the stuff of film and soap operas, but are nevertheless real enough. Someone witnesses a grisly murder, but then becomes amnesic for the crime.

The second dimension of amnesia is the dichotomy between forgetting the past versus an inability to form new memories. *Retrograde amnesia* is forgetting of events that occurred before the onset of the disorder. This is our everyday conception of amnesia: the forgetting of some portion of the past that was once recalled or should be recallable. The extent of retrograde forgetting may be limited to the few minutes or hours preceding trauma, or it may be extensive, in some cases extending back months or years. For example, after a traumatic head injury, retrograde amnesia can be extensive, but the time span of forgotten material gradually shrinks, leaving a residual permanent amnesia that is usually fairly limited. In other disorders, such as Korsakoff's (described in what follows) and Alzheimer's diseases, an opposite pattern occurs. Retrograde amnesia increases over time as more and more of the past becomes unavailable. The memory loss is likely permanent in these disorders.

Forgetting can proceed in the opposite direction. From the moment of trauma onward, the formation of new memories can be impaired. This is *anterograde amnesia,* the inability to form new memories or acquire new knowledge. Anterograde amnesia is less familiar to many of us, but it is a common and serious outcome of brain trauma. The anterograde amnesic individual cannot report the events of the previous hours or days because those memories either have not been formed or are not accessible. The inability to keep a running memory of our lives can often be a more serious problem than that of retrograde amnesia.

Retrograde amnesia and anterograde amnesia can be represented as forgettings that proceed in different temporal directions from the trauma that provokes forgetting:

$\leftarrow$ Retrograde amnesia — TRAUMA — Anterograde amnesia $\rightarrow$

Retrograde and anterograde amnesias can occur separately, although commonly both are present. H. M. has learned very little since his operation over 40 years ago. This is the result of anterograde amnesia. He also has some retrograde amnesia: He has forgotten things that happened in the few years that preceded the operation, memories that were available up until the operation (Ogden & Corkin, 1991). Tulving's motorcycle accident patient has both retrograde and anterograde amnesia. He cannot recall episodic memories from before the accident and he cannot acquire new episodic memories since the time of the accident (Tulving, 1989).

Types of Amnesias.   *Amnesic syndrome* is the label given to individuals like H. M. They are characterized by the inability to form and retrieve new long-term memories, but they still have reasonably normal short-term memory. Amnesic syndrome individuals have difficulty acquiring new general knowledge, or what we earlier called semantic memories, as well as impairment in forming episodic memories. However, these amnesics often can demonstrate new learning via procedural learning. For example, amnesic syndrome individuals can be classically conditioned and acquire an eyeblink CR (Daum et al., 1989). Amnesics can learn other perceptual, motor, and cognitive skills as well. The hippocampus is usually the damaged brain region in amnesic syndrome, although naturally occurring brain traumas rarely damage a single region of the brain.

Korsakoff's syndrome is an amnesic disorder named after the Russian psychiatrist who described it over 100 years ago. This syndrome is associated with prolonged alcohol abuse (literally, decades long) and the thiamine vitamin deficiency that accompanies such use. (Evidence has been produced for the contribution of each factor to producing Korsakoff's-like symptoms.) Damage to the diencephalon of the brain, which includes the thalamus and mammilary bodies, is evident, but not necessarily the hippocampus. The disease has an insidious onset, meaning that it develops gradually over months and years. Korsakoff's is characterized by both anterograde and retrograde amnesia. Tests of general knowledge may show profound amnesia that extends back over decades. Some memory loss is retrograde (forgetting of information that was once known) and some is anterograde (forgetting of the period in which memory ceased to function).

The neurologist Oliver Sacks (1985) described a 50-year-old Korsakoff's patient who believed he was 20, and thought the date was 30 years earlier, at the end of World War II.

Once the disease set in, older memories began to disappear (this would be retrograde amnesia) and new memories stopped forming (this is anterograde amnesia). This patient could not comprehend pictures of Earth taken from space, and was startled by his own reflection in the mirror of what appeared to be a much older man. The distress passed quickly as these perceptions faded from memory. In fact, Sacks was not recognized when he reentered the room several minutes later.

Psychogenic Amnesia. Amnesias caused by psychological traumas are almost always retrograde: forgetting the past, or some part of the past, that preceded the trauma. There are three main categories of psychogenic amnesia: limited amnesia, fugue state, and dissociative disorder.

Limited amnesia is the forgetting of a specific traumatic episode, as when a soldier forgets a terrifying battle. In an older psychiatric terminology, these were referred to as hysterical amnesias. The French psychiatrist Janet recounted a case from the turn of the last century of a woman who was told her husband had just died. She was immediately devastated with grief. The report turned out to be a malicious prank. Afterwards, she became amnesic for the whole episode, but forgot nothing else. Interestingly, memory of the event would recur in nightmares (described in Nemiah, 1979).

A more profound instance of psychogenic amnesia is forgetting one's entire past life and identity. In a *fugue* reaction, the person literally does not remember who he or she is. For example, one young man developed fugue after the death of his grandfather, to whom he had been particularly close. For a week afterwards, the young man was unaware of who he was, and could not recollect any personal (episodic) memories (Schacter et al., 1982). Note that the fugue individual retains language and other sorts of general knowledge. In this case, the fugue ended when a funeral scene in a television show reinstated the lost memory. The entire fugue period, which had lasted about a week, was itself no longer remembered. Fugue reactions generally resolve after a week or so, although some may persist for months. They are sometimes characterized by the amnesic wandering off and adopting a new identity, hence the derivation of the word *fugue* from the Latin *to take flight*.

In dissociative disorders, a person exhibits multiple personalities or identities. These different personalities are often unaware of, and so are amnesic for, each other. Nemiah (1979) recounts a Reverend Bourne, who alternated between being a preacher and a gambler, and each personality was unaware of the other and what the other did. (Imagine the Freudian interpretation of this case!)

In the psychogenic amnesias, the memory is not lost from the brain as it may be with some organically caused amnesias. It instead becomes inaccessible to conscious retrieval. In our stages of memory terminology, the amnesic is experiencing retrieval failure. The memory may return later under various conditions: sometimes spontaneously; possibly in a dream, as it did for Janet's patient; through hypnosis; or after the administration of anxiety-relieving drugs.

One interpretation of psychogenic amnesia is the repression hypothesis. This originally derived from a Freudian psychoanalytic theory, but does have some intuitive appeal. Traumatic memories are repressed into some unconscious part of the mind as a way of relieving anxiety and fear. Fugue is an extreme version of repression, by escaping a distressing life situation full of reminders. An instrumental learning (or reinforcement) theorist might agree with the notion of repression, but argue that repression occurs because it is reinforcing, in the sense that it reduces fear just as does any avoidance response (Dollard & Miller, 1950). Just as I might avoid a place that arouses fear, I could avoid recollecting memories that elicit fear.

Another explanation suggests the memory has become dissociated or separated from conscious awareness (Janet, 1907). But how does this occur? One answer in contemporary terms is to say that forgetting traumatic events is an instance of state-dependent or mood-dependent forgetting (see Chapter 10). If the episode were one of intense arousal and fear, the memories could become difficult to retrieve during normal consciousness when the strong emotional states are absent. There are claims that reinstating the intense emotional arousal of an original experience under hypnosis can lead to memory recall. Diamond (1969) reports that Sirhan Sirhan, who murdered Robert Kennedy (the brother of President John Kennedy), denies having committed the murder. However, with hypnosis, he gradually reexperiences the anger and emotion felt at the time and recalls the crime.

Another possibility is that psychogenic amnesia is an instance of implicit memory. As such, the memories are not available to conscious recollection, although they may be expressed in other ways. In one case of fugue, a woman could not recall any details about her life, but she did show skin-conductance changes (used to assess emotional reactions) to familiar stimuli. When presented with some true and some false statements about her life, such as her birth date, she showed stronger reactions to the correct facts than to incorrect ones (Gudjonsson, 1979). We have seen examples before of a separation between conscious memory and unconscious knowledge. Priming effects in picture-fragment completion have also been found between dissociated personalities. Exposing one personality to a picture facilitated identification of the picture from fragments by an alternate personality. However, explicit recall of the list of pictures did not transfer from one personality to the other (Eich et al., 1997).

Everyday Forgetting and the Models of Memory

Surveys reveal that many of us are concerned about everyday forgetting. An ABC News Poll (reported on February 10, 1997) showed that 46 percent of respondents worried more about failing memory than about failing health. The numerous memory-improvement self-help books that are available attest to a market for advice. Much of our worry over everyday forgetting is unjustified—our memories are just not that bad. However, we have become sensitized to the issue of memory lapses and we overreact. Some British psychiatrists have described an "mnestic hypochondria," an excessive concern about memory problems among middle-aged individuals who nevertheless test fine on memory (Berrios, Markova, & Girala, 2000). These "worried but well" individuals are characterized as bright, educated, ambitious, and perfectionistic. One could suppose that such people, working and living busy and stressful lives, might become anxious about perceived declining memory abilities.

Accurate data on everyday forgetting is difficult to obtain. Nevertheless, certain forms of everyday forgetting are more frequently mentioned than others. What follows are some items from the *Short Inventory of Minor Lapses* that were rated with the highest frequency of occurrence by two samples of participants in England: college students and other adult visitors to the Applied Psychology Unit (Reason, 1993). As noted at the start of this chapter, the several approaches presented in this chapter may offer ways to understand why forgetting occurs, and offer means for remediation and prevention.

1. How often do you forget to say something you were going to mention?

2. How often do you have the "what-am-I-here-for?" feeling when you have forgotten what it is you came to do?

3. How often do you forget to do something that you were going to do after dealing with an unexpected interruption?

At first glance, each of these seems to be a failure of short-term memory. The intention to say or do something was displaced during a brief time interval by ongoing events and so was not remembered. Consciously repeating (via maintenance rehearsal) the intention to say or do something should keep it in mind until it can be acted on. Alternatively, the stage approach suggests that retrieval failure is the source of the forgetting here. At the moment of action, nothing reminded you of what you wanted to say, do, or get. You realize that it was retrieval failure when your intention is suddenly remembered, or retrieved, sometime later.

Research on prospective memory, or remembering to do things in the future, suggests the importance of reminder cues (Harris, 1984). Such cues need to be active, like an alarm clock, and not passive, like a note in your pocket that can itself be forgotten. Also, the cue needs to be timely, to remind you at the right time. A morning reminder about an afternoon meeting is not an effective cue for when to leave for the meeting. Finally, the cue needs to be specific. The proverbial "string tied around your finger" does not remind you what it is you need to remember.

4. How often do you find yourself searching for something that you've just put down or are still carrying with you?

This could be an example of absentmindedness: Your mind was occupied elsewhere and so you did not deeply or elaboratively process where you placed the object. The interesting next question is: When you find the lost object, do you then recall having mislaid it? If you still have no recollection, then maybe you did have an encoding failure. If you do recall putting down the object, then you were earlier experiencing retrieval failure. (One final possibility is that this is not a memory failure at all, but instead you have kids who misplace things when you aren't looking.)

5. How often do you find you cannot recall the name of a familiar person or object?

6. How often do you find that you cannot recall a word or name at that moment? You know the word; it is on the tip of your tongue.

Remembering names is important and forgetting them often has serious social and professional implications. Sometimes names are known but they cannot be recalled at will, an example of retrieval failure. In this case, additional retrieval cues may help prompt the memory. We incidentally do this anyway, running through an alphabetical listing of names to see if any seem to fit (Harris, 1978; Reason & Lucas, 1984).

When we see a familiar person, their name is often the most difficult thing about them to remember. Figure 7.6 showed a connectionist model for associating names and people. Young, Hay, and Ellis (1985) have proposed a model, based on everyday forgetting, that places these steps in the reverse direction. First, we recognize someone's face. Then, we recall all the other things we know about the person, such as their occupation, where we know them from, and so on. This is person identification. Only after these steps are successfully completed do we recall the name. Ellis, Hay, and Young point to everyday memory studies that show we often remember everything except a person's name, but we never remember the name and nothing else.

In attempting to recall a name or word that is on the tip of your tongue, some other word or name may repeatedly come to mind. The problem is, once this wrong word is retrieved, it seems to block recall of the sought-after item. Connectionist theory offers an explanation here. These blockers are often more familiar or more frequently used, as compared to the less familiar word on the tip of your tongue (Reason & Lucas, 1984). Partial information places us near the target in memory, but then triggers items that are closer to threshold or that have stronger connections to the cues. The blocker's level of activation is temporarily elevated and so it pops into consciousness. Each subsequent recall attempt finds the most active item, which happens to be the blocker. How can blocking be overcome? *Stop trying to remember.* Let the blocker fade back to its resting level. The sought-after word will come to you later. (Or, as most people reported doing, go to an external source: Look up the word, or ask someone else.)

Certain other memory distortions fall between the amnesias and everyday forgetting. Some of these are discussed in Box 7.2.

Summary

Partitioning Memory

Memory may be better understood when partitioned into separate components, stages, or processes than when treated as a unitary trait. We hypothesize multiple memory systems because generalizations about memory as a whole are not always valid; and for the heuristic value in simplifying our theories of memory. The dissociations that are produced when a variable has different effects on different tasks also suggest separate systems. Dissociations may be produced by different experimental manipulations, memory tasks, neurological disorders, or subject populations.

Components of Memory Approach

One approach divides memory into different stores, or types. One division is between sensory memory, short-term memory, and long-term memory. In sensory memory, information passes through the sense receptors and is briefly retained before being recoded into short-term memory.

The dual-store conception of short-term and long-term memory is referred to as the "modal" model. Short-term store has a limited duration and capacity, stores items verbally, and is subject to disruption. Long-term store retains indefinitely, has virtually unlimited capacity, and retains information in many forms. The distinction between two memory stores is suggested by the serial-position effect. Different experimental variables affect the primacy and recency portions of the curve. Short-term and long-term memories are also dissociated by the patterns of memory loss in amnesic individuals. H. M. cannot form new long-term memories, but his short-term span is normal. K. F. is impaired in short-term verbal span.

B O X **7.2**

Anomalous Forgetting Phenomenon

The theoretical approaches we have covered in this chapter can also be applied to some unusual memory experiences, such as cryptomnesia, déjà vu, or reality monitoring.

There are times when you think you have come up with an original idea, only to realize later it was actually suggested by someone else. This lack of awareness that the idea is a memory has been called *cryptomnesia*. (Or in plain English, inadvertent plagiarism.) Freud once thought he had an original insight into the origin of the neuroses, only to be reminded that his friend Wilhelm Fliess had suggested the idea to Freud a year earlier (Freud, 1901/1960, p. 143). George Harrison was sued because four notes of his song "My Sweet Lord" resembled an earlier song, "He's So Fine," by the Chiffons. B. F. Skinner described the phenomenon well: "One of the most disheartening experiences is discovering a point you have just made—so significant, so beautifully expressed—was made by you in something you published a long time ago" (Hostetler, 1988).

One possible explanation of cryptomnesia is that it is an instance of implicit memory. An initial experience produces a memory that later comes to mind without our awareness that we are remembering. Alternatively, cryptomnesia may be an example of *source amnesia*. You know something, but without an episodic trace to identify the source (the where and the when) of the learning (Brown & Murphy, 1989).

An opposite experience is that of *déjà vu,* French for "never seen." Déjà vu is the sense of familiarity evoked by a present experience, even though you believe the experience is novel. For instance, you feel like you have been here before, but you have not. Penfield and Jasper (1954) called this an illusion of familiarity. If cryptomnesia is remembering without awareness, then déjà vu is awareness without a memory to validate the feeling.

A Freudian or psychoanalytic theorist might suggest that you are just repressing the memory of an earlier experience (Reed, 1979). A conditioning theorist might explain déjà vu on the basis of generalization across stimuli: There may be sufficient resemblance between the new and some previous situation to remind you of the old. Sno and Linszen (1990) expressed this idea within an analogy to holograms. Any portion of a holographic negative can be used to reproduce the entire picture, unlike a regular photographic negative. However, the smaller the piece of the holographic negative, the less resolution is present. Similarly, as an older memory weakens, losing resolution and detail, it becomes easier to confuse with other memories. Thus, a new experience may "match" the fuzzy image of an older memory, one that is actually not of an event similar to the present's. Figure 7.7 shows how a degraded image of Lincoln might be mistaken for that of a young Sigmund Freud.

Seeing yourself in memory is another type of memory distortion. Nigro and Neisser (1983) asked college students to remember some personal experiences, such as giving a speech or being in an accident. Most of the students recalled at least a few memories from the perspective of observing themselves. These *observer memories* were reported more often in older rather than recent memories, and in memories rated as emotional and self-conscious, such as giving a public presentation. How do observer memories originate? Nigro and Neisser suggest that some memories are rehearsed more often, as would occur for emotional events. This rumination leads to a change in orientation, from the self looking out to the self being looked on.

One final anomaly to consider is the distinction between memories for things that we did versus those that we only thought about doing. We certainly remember actions we performed or things we said. But actions that were planned but not carried out, or words considered but never spoken are also remembered. Distinguishing between memories of real and imagined events is called *reality monitoring.* How do we tell the difference? Johnson and Raye (1981) believe that we evaluate the attributes of the memories. Memories of actual events have a greater sense of time and place, and more sensory detail. Internally derived memories are more schematic, less coherent, and have fewer traces of sight, sound, or feel.

FIGURE 7.7   Degraded-Memory Theory for Déjà Vu. As memories for two different people, in this case, Lincoln and a young Freud, fade in memory, they become more alike. Possibly, déjà vu is due to the misperceived similarity between some present stimulus situation and the faded memory of a different situation.

Source: From "The Deja-Vu Experience: Remembrance of Things Past?" by H. N. Sno and D. H. Linszen, 1990, *American Journal of Psychiatry, 147,* p. 1593. Copyright © 1990, the American Psychiatric Association; http://ajp.psychiatryonline.org. Reprinted by permission.

One reason for considering these anomalous memory experiences is to show they may not be so odd after all. Although multiple interpretations have been offered for several of these phenomena, the explanations all derive from principles of learn-ing and memory otherwise discussed in this text. The usefulness of a science of memory is not just to explain basic research findings, but also to explain the unusual in everyday life.

Long-term store can be further divided into episodic and semantic memories. Episodic memory is our personal or autobiographical memory system. Semantic memory is our store of general knowledge. It is more like dictionary or encyclopedic knowledge. Although not always separable in laboratory experiments, the distinction is useful in describing the development of memory from episodic to semantic or generic memories.

Two other hypothesized divisions of long-term memory are considered to be instances of implicit memory. Procedural learning is knowing how to do things: perceptual, motor, and cognitive skills. Procedural tasks include mirror star tracing, reading reversed or inverted text, or learning recurring sequences of numbers or locations. Priming refers to the facilitated response to a stimulus that has been recently experienced, or has been "primed" in memory. For example, the identification of a word from a few letters, or fragments, is facilitated by recent exposure to that word.

Explicit and implicit memory are terms used to refer to how we test memory. Direct questioning about the contents of memory is an *explicit* task, as in recall and recognition tests of episodic and semantic memory. Indirectly assessing the effects of prior experience by measuring performance rather than recall is an *implicit* task, as in the skill learning of procedural tasks. Procedural learning and priming effects are both examples of implicit memory, although explicit recall may influence performance on these types of tasks.

Stages of Memory

Another approach to memory separates it into several stages: encoding, storage, and retrieval. The stages are experimentally dissociated when a variable primarily affects one stage or another. For example, alcohol primarily affects the encoding stage.

Neuropsychological dissociations are demonstrated by individuals with impairment at one or another stage. H. M. is believed to have an encoding deficit: He cannot form new memories. However, some amnesics misrecall words from previous, supposedly forgotten lists, which suggests that encoding occurred, but the amnesics have trouble directing retrieval.

Processing Approaches

Remembering and forgetting can be attributed to the type of processing information receives. Depth-of-processing theory hypothesizes only a single memory store, and variations in the degree of cognitive processing determines whether something is remembered. Rapid forgetting is due to shallow processing, whereas sustained retention is due to deep processing. The distinction between shallow and deep processing is illustrated by two kinds of rehearsal. Maintenance rehearsal, or the passive repetition of information, is shallow processing. Elaborative rehearsal involves meaningful analysis and comprehension of the material, and thus represents a deeper level of processing. According to depth-of-processing theory, robust incidental learning occurs due to the cognitive involvement and interest in the target material.

Transfer-appropriate processing theory states that retrieval is facilitated by reinstating the cognitive operations that were used at encoding. These operations include reading, finding words or objects to complete fragments, associating items with others in memory, and so on. Either an explicit or an implicit test of memory could produce better performance, depending on the match of operations used at encoding and at testing.

Connectionist Models

Connectionism attempts to combine cognitive and biological approaches by modeling the neural changes that underlie learning and memory. Each neural unit can have connections to many other units. The strength of connections increases when neural units are simultaneously active. Inner layers, or hidden units, may combine and summate activation from units in the previous layer. A neural unit can be activated much as a neuron is activated, and activation gradually fades back to the prestimulation baseline or resting level over a brief period of time.

The trial-by-trial increases in connection strength are described by the *delta rule*. The increment on each trial is a constant proportion of the difference between the maximum possible activation and the current level of activation. The application of the delta rule in simulations produces a classic learning curve characterized by relatively large increases in learning in the early trials and smaller increments in later trials.

The Study of Abnormal Memory

The amnesias are described along two major dimensions, one of cause (physical or psychological) and the other time (loss of memory of events that preceded or that followed trauma). Most amnesias have a physical or organic cause due to injury or damage to the brain. Psychogenic, or functional, amnesias result from psychological trauma. Retrograde amnesia is forgetting of events that occurred before the onset of the disorder. Anterograde amnesia is the inability to form new memories or acquire new knowledge.

Amnesic syndrome, caused by injury to the hippocampus, is characterized by the inability to form and retrieve new long-term memories (anterograde amnesia), some retrograde amnesia, and a reasonably normal short-term memory. Amnesic syndrome individuals, like H. M., are impaired in acquiring semantic as well as episodic memories. However, new learning occurs via procedural learning.

Korsakoff's syndrome is an amnestic disorder associated with prolonged alcohol abuse and vitamin deficiency, and is characterized by both anterograde and retrograde amnesia. Tests of general knowledge may show profound amnesia that extends over decades. Damage to the thalamus and mammilary bodies in the brain is usually present.

Psychogenic amnesias are retrograde: forgetting the past, or some part of the past, that preceded the trauma. They fall into one of three categories: limited amnesia, fugue state, or dissociative disorder. In psychogenic amnesia, the memory is not lost, but it becomes inaccessible to conscious retrieval. The lost memories sometimes spontaneously return, are accessible through hypnosis, or are demonstrated by implicit memory testing. Psychogenic forgetting may be due to repression, avoidance, or dissociation in the form of state-dependent remembering.

Many forms of everyday forgetting can be described within the approaches covered in this chapter. Understanding where a breakdown occurs offers a better chance for prevention and remediation. Examples of forgetting from an inventory of memory lapses include momentary forgetting, prospective forgetting, absentmindedness, and temporary forgetting of common words and names.

Short-Term Retention

In the previous chapter we discussed the amnesias, which for the most part involve forgetting from long-term memory. In our everyday lives, forgetting over short time intervals is also troubling. Absentmindedness, a common label for everyday lapses, occurs when people forget what they were doing, were about to do, had intended to do, and so on. You go upstairs to get something but become distracted by something else. You wonder what you were looking for, wander around looking for something that needs getting, and likely return empty-handed. The fretting about age-related memory decline so often discussed in the popular press is often in reference to something forgotten from just a few minutes earlier.

This chapter is about remembering over brief intervals of time. *Short-term memory* (STM) refers to memory that is limited both in its duration and its capacity. As assessed in laboratory tests, STM retains on the order of five to seven items, for several seconds to less than a minute in the absence of rehearsal. Short-term memory is distinguished from *long-term memory* (LTM), which in the laboratory is typically any memory more than a few minutes old, and in the real world, our memories of a lifetime.

The distinction between (at least) two memory systems has long been a part of psychology's history, both in cognitive and biological theory. For example, William James (1890) wrote of the primary memory of consciousness, and the German psychologist G. E. Muller (Muller & Pilzecker, 1900, in German; see Lechner, Squire, & Byrne, 1999, for an English summary and discussion) hypothesized a transient "perseveratory activity" in the brain that could eventually consolidate into a permanent long-term memory. In contemporary theory, short-term memory has been the subject of some controversy. Is there really a memory separate from long-term memory? In the interest of parsimony, maybe a simpler theory of a single memory system would suffice. Alternatively, maybe a single short-term memory is not sufficient, and, instead, our theories should include multiple short-term stores. Other researchers use the label *short-term retention* to distinguish their research on retention over short intervals of time, but without implication that there is a separate short-term memory store (e.g., Spear & Riccio, 1994).

Whether short-term and long-term remembering take place within a single memory or in separate memories, remembering over short intervals has important implications for our everyday cognitive functioning. "Without it, you couldn't understand this sentence, add up a restaurant tab in your head, or even find your way home" (Wickelgren, 1997, p. 1580). Short-term, or working memory as it is increasingly being called, has been referred to as our mental blackboard: a temporary, reusable workspace in the mind used for comprehension, reasoning, and planning.

Definitions

Some History

"When deeply absorbed, we do not hear the clock strike. But our attention may awake after the striking has ceased, and we may then count off the strokes" (Exner, quoted by William James, 1890, p. 646). This quote captures well the subjective feel of short-term memory. In quoting Exner, William James was making a distinction between primary memory and secondary memory. Something in *primary memory* has never left consciousness and is part of the psychological present. Something in *secondary memory* has been absent from consciousness and therefore belongs to the psychological past.

The concept of an "immediate" memory, or what can be recalled from the immediate past, lay dormant in psychology for many years before Waugh and Norman (1965) reintroduced the primary–secondary memory distinction. Primary memory holds only a few items and for only a few seconds, and forgetting occurs rapidly if rehearsal is prevented. The capacity limitations of primary, or short-term, memory mean that a small number of items can be retained at any one time, and the addition of a new item requires displacement of some other item already in STM. In fact, forgetting from primary memory is due more to displacement by subsequent items than the passage of time. Information can be maintained for longer durations in primary memory through rehearsal, which also allows increased opportunity for transfer of information to secondary memory.

Waugh and Norman suggested an important concept for memory testing: that recall could come from primary memory, from secondary memory, or both. This idea has implications for the timing of assessments of learning. The fact that you can recall something immediately after its presentation (e.g., a name, a definition, a list) does not mean that the information has entered secondary memory and will therefore be available for future recall. Wilson (1987) illustrated this idea in a study of patients with memory impairment due to brain injuries. The patients did as well as the unimpaired control participants in remembering short lists of words, if tested immediately. The memory deficit of the head-injured was only revealed when testing was repeated 24 hours later, when they remembered far less than did the controls.

The next step in theory development was the multistore system of memory of Atkinson and Shiffrin (see Figure 8.1). As noted in the previous chapter, this has developed into a "modal" model of memory, or the schematic that serves as the outline for other theories of memory. Atkinson and Shiffrin (1968) refer to three kinds of memory: the very transient sensory registers; short-term store (a primary topic in this chapter); and long-term store. (Note: Atkinson and Shiffrin refer to types of memory *stores,* or places for memory storage. We will continue to use the generic terms short-term *memory* and long-term *memory* in this chapter.) This model incorporates several of Waugh and Norman's notions about primary memory, including those of capacity limitations, rehearsal, and transfer to LTM. Atkinson and Shiffrin made the important suggestion that active control processes are employed in STM. Examples of control processes are where to direct attention, how to code new inputs, when to rehearse, and which retrieval cues to use. This control over how memory is used is a fundamental characteristic of STM, which defines it as an active rather than passive store (Shiffrin, 1993).

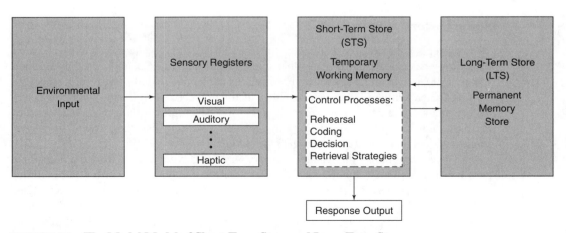

FIGURE 8.1 The Modal Model of Short-Term Store and Long-Term Store.

Source: From "The Control of Short-Term Memory," by R. C. Atkinson and R. M. Shiffrin, 1971, *Scientific American,* 152–161. Copyright © 1971 by Allen Beechel. Reprinted with permission.

Atkinson and Shiffrin's hypothesis that there are separate short-term and long-term memory stores provoked two markedly different reactions from some other psychologists. A few argued that postulating two kinds of memory was excessive and unparsimonious (i.e., complicated), an interpretation to be considered later. The other reaction was that two memory stores was not enough! Baddeley and Hitch (1974) proposed the evolution of a single short-term memory into *working memory*. Working memory has a *phonological loop* that is responsible for the brief storage and rehearsal of verbal information. There is also a *visuospatial sketch pad* for retaining and manipulating visual images and spatial information. These two subsystems are coordinated by a *central executive* that controls the limited resource of attention, deploying attention to one or more tasks. Working memory certainly bears similarities to the modal model, in having a verbal rehearsal store and the control processes exercised by the central executive. The important difference is in separating STM into two stores. Two tasks could potentially be performed at once, as long as they use different stores. Such dual-task performance is less well accommodated in the single STM of the modal model. (The working memory model is discussed later in this chapter.)

Working memory is the focus of much current research, but the terms "working memory" and "short-term memory" are often used interchangeably. What follows in this chapter is first a consideration of the characteristics of short-term memory, second of working memory, and finally some applications of each.

Short-Term Memory Tasks

Short-term retention is often assessed by one of two tests. The *distractor task* attempts to quantify the duration of immediate memory over brief delay intervals. The *memory span* attempts to quantify the capacity of immediate memory. STM is also indirectly inferred on the basis of other tasks, such as from the recency portion of the serial-position curve.

The Brown-Peterson Distractor Task

The Brown-Peterson distractor task was described by British researcher John Brown in 1958, and the Americans Lloyd and Margaret Peterson in 1959 (but see Pillsbury & Sylvester, 1940). In this task, a few items are presented for retention, usually three letters or words. This number can be recalled accurately if the subject is tested immediately, and therefore is well within the capacity of short-term memory. However, the subject is instructed to perform a distractor task, such as counting backwards by threes, until told to recall the target items. Thus, the sequence of events in a trial might be a visual presentation of the to-be-remembered items (e.g., DOG–CAT–TREE), a number (e.g., 933), counting backwards ("…933, 930, 927…"), and finally the experimenter's instruction to attempt to recall the target items. Representative data are shown in Figure 8.2 for the retention of three consonants or three words. The amount recalled drops off dramatically after as little as 9 seconds of distractor activity.

The rapid forgetting found with the distractor technique was thought to be significant for two reasons. First, it seemed to demonstrate how brief STM was in the absence of

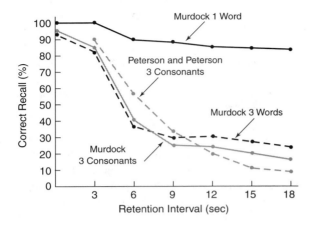

FIGURE 8.2   Mean Percent Recall of Words or Letters in the Brown-Peterson Distractor Task.

Source: From "Implications of Short-Term Memory for a General Theory of Memory," by A. W. Melton, 1963, *Journal of Verbal Learning and Verbal Behavior, 2,* p. 9. Copyright 1963 by Academic Press. Reprinted with permission.

rehearsal, assuming rehearsal is precluded by the distractor activity. Memory for the to-be-remembered items faded quickly. However, the absence of rehearsal was more apparent than real. If forgetting is due simply to the decay of a memory trace, the nature of the distractor task should not have any effect. But it does. A difficult distractor task, such as answering arithmetic problems, produces more forgetting than does an easy task, simply reading numbers (see Crowder, 1976). Thus, some surreptitious rehearsal does seem to occur during distraction, and more difficult tasks block rehearsal more effectively.

The second reason for interest in the rapid forgetting was that it seemed to occur in the absence of interference. This may sound odd because it is obvious to us that there is distraction from the counting task. However, interference referred to a particular theory in which forgetting was attributed to competition between similar memories. One type of interference is called *retroactive interference,* in which the retention of earlier learned information is interfered with by later-occurring material. Since interference was believed to be primarily determined by similarity between competing memories, digit counting should not have caused retroactive interference with the recall of words or letters. (If verbal distractors had been presented instead of counting backwards, then retroactive interference would have been a plausible cause for forgetting the target items.)

Retroactive interference is only one potential source of interference in the distractor task. Another significant source of interference comes from earlier or preceding material. Imagine participating in one of these experiments. You are given list after list of three words to remember, for as many as 50 lists. Is it really the case that each list is forgotten, totally and completely, at the end of each trial? After all, the assumption is that this is an STM task. Or is it likely that there is some cumulative memory, and that recall of the current list is affected by memory from the previous lists? This is called *proactive interference:* Material presented earlier interferes with retention or recall of the most recent information. The current list of to-be-remembered items cannot be recalled due to competition from the memories of earlier lists.

There are several bits of evidence supporting the proactive interference hypothesis. Curiously, performance in the Brown-Peterson distractor task is often perfect on the very first trial: Subjects remember the word triplet or consonant triplet perfectly after delays of 15 seconds. This may be because there is no previous material to offer proactive interference. Forgetting does develop as the number of trials increases, consistent with the notion of proactive interference building up across trials. Also, closely spaced trials in the Brown-Peterson task produce more forgetting, by increasing the opportunity for interference from a previous trial. These findings are consistent with the idea that memory from earlier trials can interfere with recall on subsequent trials (Crowder, 1976).

Interference is increased by the similarity of the items to be recalled. If the to-be-remembered words across adjacent trials come from the same semantic category (e.g., names of foods) rather than being unrelated words, performance declines even more rapidly across trials. Proactive interference seems to build up. If after several trials the category of target words is shifted, say, to professions, recall of the changed triplet increases dramatically, a phenomenon labeled *release from proactive interference.* This buildup and then release from proactive interference is illustrated in the left panel of Figure 8.3 with data from Wickens (1972). Recall of word triplets that came from the same semantic category (names of fruits) declined across the first three trials. Changing word categories on the fourth trial from fruits to professions or flowers, but not to vegetables, led to an increase in accurate recall, as compared to maintaining the initial category.

Another illustration of the buildup and release of proactive interference is in memory for television news stories (Gunter, Berry, & Clifford, 1981). A series of brief news reports from the same thematic category (e.g., domestic politics or foreign affairs) was presented as the to-be-remembered items. Recall of story triplets from within a category decreased over trials, consistent with the hypothesis of the buildup of proactive interference. If the category of stories then changed, release occurred and the final list of stories was recalled better (see the right panel of Figure 8.3).

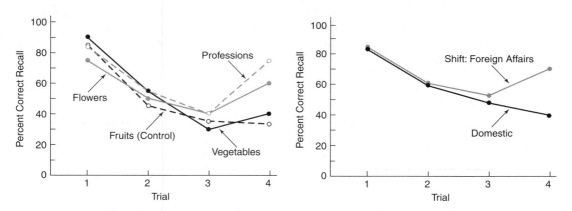

FIGURE 8.3   Buildup (across Trials 1 to 3) and Release (Trial 4) of Proactive Interference for Words (*left panel*) and News Stories (*right panel*).

Source: (Left panel) From "Characteristics of Word Encoding," by D. D. Wickens, in *Coding Processes in Human Memory* (p. 207), edited by A. W. Melton and E. Martin, 1972, Washington, DC: Winston/Wiley. Copyright © 1972 by Taylor & Francis. Reprinted with permission. (*Right panel*) Gunter, Berry, & Clifford, 1981.

The Distractor Task: An Overview.   The distractor task attempts to assess the retention of a few items across several seconds of distracting activity. The distractor task was initially thought to be a pure measure of decay of short-term memory, one that was uninfluenced by either rehearsal or interference. It turns out instead to be influenced by both of these factors. Rehearsal occurs surreptitiously, although more difficult distractors reduce the amount of rehearsal. Retention is also affected by proactive (items from preceding trials) and retroactive (material following the target items) interference. Interestingly, these same factors, rehearsal and interference, are known to influence the strength of long-term retention (see Chapters 9 and 10).

Memory Span

The *span* of immediate memory is defined as the longest sequence of items that can be recalled in correct order after a single presentation. Recall is attempted immediately, without a delay or a distractor. Memory span is usually tested by presenting somewhat longer lists than are used in the distractor task, often five to nine items for college students, to assess the maximum length than can be recalled correctly. The to-be-recalled items are typically letters, numbers, or words. Our spans seem to be limited to about seven items, or "the magical number seven, plus-or-minus two," as George Miller titled it in a famous article in 1956.

Memory span is relevant to our remembering outside of the laboratory. Seven digits is the length of a standard telephone number, exclusive of area codes. Conrad (1958) asked his participants, experienced postal workers, to listen to and then dial eight-digit numbers. Only about 50 percent of the numbers were dialed correctly. When a constant prefix was added (such as the "9" often needed to get an outside line), recall dropped even further. Memory span is also measured as part of some intelligence tests. The Wechsler Scales have a digit span as one subtest. For more fun, there is the digits-backward portion, in which the numbers have to be recalled in reverse order.

Memory span seems to be a straightforward measure of short-term memory capacity. However, span is not fixed and invariant, but is affected by numerous variables. For example, nonrhyming items are recalled better than rhyming words; digits are remembered better than words; shorter words are remembered better than longer words; and drawings of objects are remembered better than the names of the objects (Brooks & Watkins, 1990). Word span in college students correlates with verbal SAT scores, suggesting that memory capacity is partially determined by word knowledge (Engle, Nations, & Cantor, 1990). Span increases with practice on a given type of material. In one study, adolescent boys with severe learning disabilities were given 10 minutes of daily practice at recalling digit and word strings. After 2 weeks there was a significant increase in span length, although memory span remained below average for the children's ages (Hulme & Mackenzie, 1992).

An important determinant of memory span is the *word-length effect:* More items can be remembered when shorter words are the to-be-remembered items. Baddeley, Thomson, and Buchanan (1975) found that college students' spans were dramatically shorter for lists of words that were each five syllables long (such as ASSOCIATION, CONSIDERABLE, or UNIVERSITY) than for lists of one-syllable words. Five one-syllable words could be remembered 75 percent of the time, yet barely 30 percent of five five-syllable word sequences could be recalled.

Do longer words take up more space in short-term memory? Or is it that they take longer to rehearse, and therefore cannot be repeated as often? Baddeley and colleagues (1975) found that span correlated with articulation rate, which is a measure of how fast you could simply pronounce the target words. Longer words take longer to vocalize than shorter words, and so maybe longer words also take longer to (mentally or subvocally) rehearse. The word-length effect may also contribute to age differences in the capacity of STM: Articulation rate increases through childhood and into adulthood, as does memory span (Nickolson, 1981).

Further support for the articulation hypothesis comes from a study of Welsh bilingual speakers, who could recall more digits in English. English has shorter words for numbers than does Welsh (Ellis & Hennelly, 1980). Similarly, more numbers were recalled in Chinese than in English, using both bilingual and single-language speakers. This result is nearly entirely accounted for by the faster articulation rate for digit names in Chinese (e.g., Stigler, Lee, & Stevenson, 1986). Later work extended these findings across a range of different languages (English, Hebrew, Arabic) and showed a consistent relationship between memory span and the amount of time it takes to articulate digits in that language (Naveh-Benjamin & Ayres, 1986).

An interesting practical question is to analyze the reasons why there are differences from person to person in the size of the memory span. Does a poor digit span necessarily imply a limited STM? Estes (1974) considered several hypotheses from cognitive theory. First, there may be insufficient familiarity with ordinal numbers, such as counting and using numbers in sequences. Next, an individual may not have developed the strategy of parsing a string into smaller blocks or groups of digits. We do this with phone numbers: 1-800, then 123–4567. Instruction in this grouping strategy increases span. Finally, the digits must be sequenced correctly during recall. There is no partial credit for remembering the digits correctly but forgetting their order. This means that as each digit is spoken, the remaining numbers must be temporarily inhibited from being spoken until their turn. Some individuals may have difficulty with this temporary inhibition. Thus, poor span performance can occur for several reasons that are not directly related to the actual capacity of STM.

Characteristics of Verbal Short-Term Retention

Short-term memories seem to have a different character from long-term memories. "This primary memory image is…an extremely lively one, but is subjectively quite distinct from every sort of after-image or hallucination…. It vanishes, if not caught by attention, in the course of a few seconds. Even when the original impression is attended to, the liveliness of its image fades fast" (Exner, cited by James, 1890, p. 646). Recent memories are rich in sensory quality, such as sound, color, and texture. In addition to these subjective impressions, certain objective features have been attributed to short-term memory, which have been cited to differentiate it from long-term memory:

Acoustic encoding
Limited capacity

Limited duration
Susceptibility to forgetting
Transfer to long-term memory

These characteristics are those typically attributed to short-term memory, particularly in Atkinson and Shiffrin's theory, but they also apply to the phonological store in Baddeley's working memory. As we will see, some of the features may not in fact uniquely discriminate short-term from long-term memory, thus blurring any ready distinctions between the two hypothesized memory systems.

Acoustic Encoding

In a typical laboratory task, words, letters, or digits are read or shown to the participant, and the items are recalled out loud. Not surprisingly, the words are remembered as they sound, as if they were being verbally rehearsed. Long-term memory, on the other hand, has been characterized as involving semantic encoding. That is, we remember the meaning or interpretation of a word rather than the exact word or its sound. One way of demonstrating this difference is to attempt to remember words that sound similar but that have different meanings (e.g., MAN, CAN, MAD, CAP, MAP). If the words are encoded by sound, they will be very confusable and errors should occur as sound-alike substitutions are remembered. If recall is requested immediately after list presentation, this indeed is what happens (Baddeley, 1966; Conrad, 1964). If the words are encoded semantically in LTM, they are not confusable: A MAP is different from a MAN and a CAP. On a delayed test of recall, the errors in recall are synonyms of the presented words: HAT is remembered instead of CAP.

Technically, the confusions in short-term memory seem to be more articulatory (i.e., how the sounds are pronounced) rather than acoustic (how they sound). Confusions occur among voiced consonants (*p, t,* and *k*), but not between voiced and unvoiced (*p* is not misrecalled as *b* or *d*) (Hintzman, 1967). This finding is consistent with the relationship between articulation and memory span, noted earlier.

The verbal–semantic distinction helps explain why we can sometimes recall a just-heard sentence verbatim, but in recalling later from long-term memory we paraphrase the sentence into somewhat different words. Sachs (1967) demonstrated this idea in memory for sentences that were embedded in short prose pieces, testing sentences either immediately or after a brief delay. The participants listened to the paragraphs, which were occasionally interrupted to test for a discrimination between verbatim and paraphrased versions of recently heard sentences. If the sentence was one just heard, the subjects could usually identify a verbatim copy and discriminate it from a paraphrased version. If the sentence had occurred about 30 seconds earlier (or two to three sentences back) in the passage, verbatim test sentences were often confused with paraphrased versions that had the same meaning.

There are exceptions to the acoustic-in-STM versus semantic-in-LTM distinction. Short-term memory is certainly facilitated by the meaningfulness of the to-be-remembered material (e.g., CIA and FBI). Conversely, long-term memories are sometimes encoded acoustically. As examples, poems are often retained verbatim in LTM; and exact wording is sometimes remembered in long-term memory, not just the gist. As poor as our verbatim recall of prose often is, distinctive sentences heard in conversations can be discriminated from their paraphrases, even 2 days later (Keenan, McWhinney, & Mayhew, 1977).

The acoustic–semantic difference most likely reflects various combinations of the task demands, the to-be-remembered material, and the strategies people adopt to remember. When the task is to retain short lists of words or numbers for brief periods of time, one list after another, subjects may use speech-based codes, and adopt a passive and repetitive rehearsal strategy, much like when we rehearse a phone number just long enough to dial it. When meaningful material is used and the task requires retention over a longer interval, the subjects may use semantic coding and adopt an elaborative rehearsal strategy. Thus, a person might try to form associations among list items, organize the items, or relate the items to existing knowledge.

Limited Capacity

Short-term memory has a limited capacity to hold information, in contrast with the virtually unlimited capacity of long-term memory. The span of short-term memory is said to be limited to about seven items (plus-or-minus two; G. A. Miller, 1956). Waugh and Norman's estimate of primary memory ran less than this, on the order of two or three items. But what exactly is an item? The data from the Brown-Peterson procedure shown in Figure 8.2 show equivalent retention of three letters or three words, even though the words contain more letters. So, is an item a letter, a word, an idea? One answer is that an item is a unit already existing in long-term memory. Letters, digits, and words are each represented in permanent memory; each is an already known item.

Miller (1956) suggested that our limited span could be enlarged by increasing the amount of information contained within each item. For example, the apparent capacity of memory span can be increased by parsing and encoding the material in terms of meaningful units, called chunks. Remembering the string FBIATMCIA is more difficult than remembering FBI–ATM–CIA. Simply dividing a string of to-be-remembered items into smaller units can facilitate recall. (Allen and Crozier [1992] found that grouping digits by threes was an optimal chunk size versus larger or smaller chunks, a finding that held across several age groups.)

This chunking strategy can allow remembering strings much longer than seven digits or words. Miller describes one subject, Sydney Smith, who could recall lists of 20 randomly sequenced 1's and 0's. Had Smith enlarged his short-term memory capacity to 20 items? Not at all. A code was created and memorized that translated three-digit strings into letters. Thus, 100 = A, 101 = B, 110 = C, and so on. As Smith listened to a list, he parsed it into triplets, converting each to a letter, and remembered the letter. Thus, he would actually remember something like A–D–F–C–C–B. In reproducing the "digit" string, he decoded the letters back into 1's and 0's.

Other examples of coding schemes have been described in the years since. Chess masters have been found to encode meaningful arrangements of pieces as a single familiar setup. A professional gambler nicknamed "Bubbles" was able to convert numbers into meaningful items. For example, the sequence "205" might be a reasonable running time for a race horse (cited in Schacter, 1996). In my classes, I often read out lists of proverbs (e.g., "A penny saved is a penny earned"). Students rehearse a code word or two for each proverb (e.g., "penny") and use these to re-create the five to seven proverbs that are then recallable, equivalent to 25 to 30 words.

There are two points to emphasize here. One is that STM capacity is indeed limited. Apparent enlargements of STM are often accomplished by recoding items into more encompassing units. The second point is that short-term memory uses long-term memory. We can remember several items in STM when they are already represented somewhere in long-term memory. By contrast, our capacity drops drastically for unfamiliar material, as in the case of digits presented in an unfamiliar language.

Limited Duration

Short-term memory is short, although the answer to "How short?" varies. Estimates of primary memory when rehearsal is limited are on the order of seconds (Waugh & Norman, 1965). As we saw earlier, forgetting occurred after 15 to 30 seconds of distraction in the Brown-Peterson task. Clinical usage of terms like "recent memory" among physicians and neurologists often refers to something on the order of one to several minutes.

The persistence of long-term memories is several orders of magnitude greater. If you remember back to the first chapter, an instance of long-term remembering in itself, research by Bahrick was cited that showed excellent retention of names and faces of high school classmates even 50 years after graduation.

Forgetting: Short-Term Memory Is Sensitive to Disruption

Forgetting from short-term memory was believed to be due to spontaneous fading of the memory trace over time (Peterson & Peterson, 1959) or to displacement of old items by new items (Atkinson & Shiffrin, 1968).

It does not take much to disrupt STM. You look up a phone number, someone asks you a question, and before you get to dial, the number's gone. One well-studied form of disruption of STM is the *suffix effect*. At the end of each list of to-be-remembered items, a recurring item is added that need not be remembered (e.g., the phrase "okay, now recall"). This suffix reduces recall of the last item, or sometimes the last few items. Some studies have found the suffix must be a language sound, such as a letter or a syllable. For instance, the word "zero" presented after a list of nine items caused more forgetting of the final item in the list than did presenting a buzzer after the list (Crowder, 1972). At least, the subject must believe it is a language sound. Speech syllables ("ba") interfered with recall when they were used as suffixes, but animal sounds ("moo") and musical instrument notes did not. This held even when the exact same sound was used and subjects were told it was either a language syllable ("ba") or the sound of a sheep ("baa") (Ayres et al., 1979; Neath, Surprenant, & Crowder, 1993). Interestingly, when deaf subjects remember lists presented via sign language, a suffix effect can be produced with an added sign (Shand & Klima, 1981).

Schilling and Weaver (1983) demonstrated an application of the suffix effect to the recall of simulated phone numbers. In the suffix condition, each number was followed with the phrase, "Have a nice day!" The researchers were testing a phone company policy for directory assistance calls. The suffix did not affect numbers with familiar prefixes (the first three digits). Maybe these were encoded as a single item, just as 1–800 is, functionally reducing the length of the to-be-remembered number. However, the suffix interfered with recall when unfamiliar prefixes were used. Ironically, the phone company's attempt to be friendly could have the perverse effect of causing you to forget the number!

One problem with the displacement-from-STM hypothesis is that distractors do not always cause loss of information from memory. For instance, in some cases, there is more "forgetting" after a short delay filled by distractor activity than after a longer interval. In the Brown-Peterson distractor task, fewer items were recalled after 8 seconds of counting than after 16 seconds (Peterson, 1966). Obviously, 8 seconds of distraction could not have cleared STM if the items were back in memory again after 16 seconds. What was the distractor's effect during the shorter interval? It likely was affecting the retrieval of items from memory rather than necessarily displacing them from STM. An analogy might be those instances in which you temporarily forget what you were about to do or say, but then shortly afterwards, the intention is recalled. We would likely attribute this absentmindedness to momentary retrieval failure. Similarly, the variable effects of distractors suggest that they are momentarily affecting the retrieval of items from memory, rather than clearing information from memory.

Short-term retention in the real world often takes places in the context of a divided-attention task. Instead of the quiet background conditions of the laboratory, other sounds occur simultaneously with the to-be-remembered list (e.g., you look up a phone number and then attempt to dial it while the television is on in the background). This background noise should impair short-term memory, and it does, particularly when the exact sequence needs to be recalled. One seemingly obvious factor, the loudness of the background sound, turns out to be less influential that the pattern of background sounds. A constant, unvarying noise causes less distraction that a varying pattern. Speech varies: It varies in sounds, loudness, and pauses. Memory span is worse if the background sound is other speech, even speech in an unknown language, than if the background is white noise, an unvarying sound. Even alternating two simple tones as background can be distracting, *if they vary enough*. For instance, a pair of similar tones, "beep–bip," is not as distracting as the dissimilar "beep–bop" (Banbury, Macken, Tremblay, & Jones, 2001).

Transfer to Long-Term Memory

The potential role of STM in transferring information to LTM is an explicit assumption of several theories, and this characteristic has some commonsense appeal. When we decide we really need to remember something in permanent memory, we seem to process information in a certain way in STM. We rehearse a name or number, try to form an image, or devise a mnemonic to aid later recall. According to several multistore theories, retention in short-term memory allows the opportunity for information to be transferred, or copied, into long-term memory. In Atkinson and Shiffrin's model, rehearsal allows more opportunity to encode into long-term store. Canadian psychologist D. O. Hebb reasoned that a temporary form of memory was necessary to hold information long enough to allow consolidation into the physical representation of permanent memory in the nervous system (Hebb, 1949).

Several different sorts of evidence seem to support this transfer function of STM. If subjects are asked to rehearse out loud when attempting to remember a list of words, we find that words receiving more rehearsals are generally recalled better (Rundus, 1971). That is, more rehearsals correlate with better long-term memory for those words. (An exception occurs for the recency portion of the list, which receives few rehearsals, but these items are retrieved first during recall and so are retrieved from STM.) A related finding is that as children grow older, they tend to rehearse more, and with increasing age comes better long-term recall.

Verbal rehearsal may be necessary in acquiring some kinds of knowledge, such as learning new vocabulary words. New words need to be first remembered by sound, since a representation cannot be retrieved from LTM. This process can be experimentally simulated by asking children to remember nonwords. There is a strong correlation between this form of auditory memory (i.e., remembering the sound of the nonwords) and the size of the children's already existing vocabularies. Adults attempting to learn paired associates, in a simulation of foreign language learning, are impaired when articulation is suppressed. Suppression is produced by having the subjects repeat nonsense speech sounds, such as "da, da, da…," to prevent rehearsal (Gathercole, 1994). Taken together, these studies suggest the role of rehearsal in transferring knowledge into LTM.

There is other evidence, however, which suggests that residence in STM is neither necessary nor sufficient for LTM formation. One telling observation comes from brain-injured participants like K. F., who are impaired in the immediate recall of auditory information. K. F. has a limited verbal short-term memory, often restricted to recalling a single item in the Brown-Peterson distractor task. If read two numbers, "4, 7," K. F. will recall the 4 but not the 7. Nevertheless, he can learn and retain long-term memories at normal rates (Shallice & Warrington, 1970). If a 10-word list was repeated until memorized perfectly, K. F. learned just as quickly as normal control participants. K. F. was able to learn a list of 10-word pairs (paired-associate learning), showing no difference from unimpaired subjects. K. F. shows a dissociation between poor performance on a STM task and normal performance on LTM tasks.

Can we rightly conclude that K. F. learns in the absence of short-term memory? A slightly different explanation says that K. F.'s condition is better described by a theory that has multiple short-term memory stores, such as Baddeley's working memory model. K. F. may have an impaired verbal (or phonological) short-term memory, leading to poor distractor task recall. But he may have a normal visual-spatial short-term memory. His inability to verbally rehearse might be compensated for by processing in the visual-spatial sketchpad as an alternative route into long-term memory.

It is also the case that maintenance of information in short-term memory does not guarantee entry into long-term memory. Football players who had just suffered a concussion could remember the events leading up to the head injury. These memories gradually became less available as time passed, and were essentially gone after 4 hours. Even though the information had been in STM and was rehearsed, as shown by the players' reproductions of their stories during the first several posttraumatic minutes, eventually forgetting occurred (Lynch & Yarnell, 1973).

Finally, we can point to the fact that a high level of exposure to material does not ensure retention in long-term memory. For example, how many people can reproduce either side of a Lincoln-head penny or know the matchup of letters and numbers on the phone dial? The answer is, "not many." Morton (1967) found that 1 in 150 participants was completely correct in describing the phone dial. Few U.S. college students could correctly name the eight features on both sides of a penny (Nickerson & Adams, 1979). When British radio (the BBC) was preparing to change frequencies, several weeks of announcements, jingles, and newspaper advertisements were used to inform the listening public. However, virtually none of the listeners surveyed could tell what the new channel locations were, although 84 percent knew the exact date of the change (Baddeley, 1981).

Overall, the evidence suggests that processing in short-term memory does aid long-term learning. Activities such as forming mental images and actively interassociating or organizing to-be-recalled material are control processes employed within short-term memory that do benefit long-term retention. (These encoding strategies are discussed further in Chapter 9.) However, simple passive residence in STM may not suffice to transfer information to LTM.

Summary of the Features of Short-Term Memory

The just-reviewed characteristics suggest that there are few absolute distinctions between verbal short-term memory and long-term memory. Either acoustic or semantic encoding can occur in both memory stores. The capacity of STM, although indeed limited, is expandable by using coding schemes to draw on what is already stored in LTM. Although distracting activity can cause forgetting, some of this may be due to retrieval failure rather than actual displacement from memory. Finally, rehearsal in STM does not necessarily ensure entry into LTM. Thus, not all of the supposed characteristics of verbal STM neatly dichotomize it from LTM. Interestingly, many of these same features have been found in research on animal short-term memory. This work is reviewed in Box 8.1

Other Modalities of Short-Term Memory

The research and theory described so far has focused on memory for auditory and verbal material. This bias derives partly from the use of college students and word lists in our experiments, and partly from our tendency to equate short-term memory with verbal rehearsal. However, short-term retention occurs in other sensory modalities and with other types of materials.

Visual Short-Term Memory.   To study visual short-term memory, stimuli are presented as short lists of images, via pictures, slides, and so on. The images may be meaningless, such as nonsense shapes, or the pictures may be meaningful, for example, scenic mountain views. Retention is tested by a recognition procedure: A test picture is presented and the subject decides whether it was in the previewed list.

The use of picture stimuli does not necessarily exclude verbal encoding of the images. Short-term retention of words and pictures are affected in a similar way by some variables. For instance, longer presentation times (e.g., 3 seconds versus only 0.5 second) and longer intervals between images (6 seconds versus 2 seconds) both lead to better recognition of the correct item. These results are consistent with a verbal encoding interpretation: Maybe subjects recode the pictures into words and then rehearse these descriptions. To reduce the likelihood of rehearsal, one could use nonverbal organisms (see Box 8.1) or use

Read

BOX **8.1**
Animal Short-Term Memory

The study of animal short-term memory has a long history, going back to Walter Hunter's studies of delayed responding in the 1920s. Most tests used today are variants of Hunter's delayed response. A stimulus or cue is presented that tells where food is hidden, but the animal is not allowed to retrieve it until a delay interval has passed. For example, the animal watches as food is hidden in one corner of the room, or in one of several dishes that have distinctive covers. In a contemporary application, Coren includes the delayed response as part of a test battery in his popular book *The Intelligence of Dogs* (1994).

Delayed responding can tell us many things about animal memory. Hunter's interest was in comparative psychology: comparing memory in different species. Rats and racoons could remember where the food was hidden for several seconds, dogs and cats for 2 to 3 minutes, and monkeys and young children for a few minutes. Maier and Schneirila (1935) also report a gorilla that remembered the food location 2 days later. (I wouldn't want to be the research assistant who tells the gorilla "no, not now; later.") Clearly, the latter value is due to long-term memory for the food location, but some of the other retention intervals also seem long for "short-term memory."

Control procedures are necessary to assure that correct choice after the delay is due to memory rather than some alternative strategies. For instance, some animals will simply stare at the baited location until released to retrieve the food. Konorski (1967) reported that dogs' performance declines somewhat when such bodily sets are disrupted, by walking the dog around, for example, but is still above chance levels of choice. Similarly, odor cues from the food reward need to be neutralized or eliminated.

The delayed-response procedure is also useful for studying human memory, particularly that of infants who cannot be tested with verbal procedures. For instance, a toy could be hidden in one of three covered wells, and after a brief delay, the infant would be allowed to retrieve the toy. Nine-month-old infants choose correctly, whereas

7-month-olds do not (Reznick, Fueser, & Bosquet, 1998).

We can also ask detailed questions about the animal's memory. In addition to remembering *where* food was hidden, do animals remember *what* was hidden? Tinklepaugh (1928) would sometimes hide lettuce and sometimes pieces of fruit. Monkeys performed well with either, retrieving the food at the end of the delay and immediately consuming it. What happened if the food type was switched during the delay? Monkeys, particularly chimps, quickly realized that Tinklepaugh had pulled a fast one on them. They sometimes refused to eat the changed food, and they would search the other containers. One chimp hurriedly stuffed the food into her mouth, but then spat it out, as if realizing this was not the expected taste!

Another task is the delayed matching-to-sample procedure, or DMTS. A to-be-remembered stimulus (called the "sample") is presented, and after a brief delay, several choice stimuli are given. When the subject chooses the one that "matches" the sample, reward is given. DMTS is often used with pigeons, who can remember various color, line, shape, and pattern stimuli over a period of a few seconds. In one study of a dolphin, Herman and Gordon (1974) found perfect matching of tone stimuli presented via underwater speakers in the pool, even after 2-minute delays. In a more recent study, dolphins matched objects (cylinders, balls) perceived through echolocation that could not be seen visually (Roitblat, Penner, & Nachtigall, 1990).

The preceding are fairly basic memory abilities, and the fact that animals can display what appears to be STM may not be surprising. The really interesting findings are those similar to the *control processes* of human memory. For example, a stimulus that is "surprising" is remembered better in STM than is an expected stimulus (e.g., Terry, 1996; Terry & Wagner, 1975). A surprising stimulus is one whose occurrence, at that moment, is not predicted or expected. How is a stimulus occurrence made surprising? Through stimulus discrimination learning, certain stimuli are trained to signal the occurrence (S+) or absence (S–) of a target event, such as

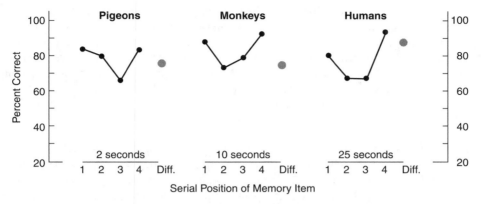

FIGURE 8.4   Serial-Position Curves for Pigeons, Monkeys, and Humans.
Participants were shown sequences of four pictures on each trial. After a delay interval, a single picture was presented for participants to identify as having been from the list or as being a different picture (the points above "Diff." in the graphs).

Source: Reprinted with permission from "Memory Processing of Serial Lists by Pigeons, Monkeys and People," by A. A. Wright et al., 1985, *Science, 229,* pp. 287–289. Copyright © 1985 American Association for the Advancement of Science.

food. The occurrence of food would then be surprising if it followed the S–. If food is the to-be-remembered stimulus, surprising food is better remembered than is expected food.

Control processes are well illustrated by studies of "instructed forgetting." After reading a list of words, the experimenter might tell you: "Forget it; I'm not going to test you on these." The control process of rehearsal ceases as soon as you realize the words do not have to be remembered. (Sometimes, after explaining something, the professor says, "but this won't be on the test," and instantly the material disappears from your memory.) If you are later asked to recall those words, fewer are recalled than after instructed remembering.

There are parallel effects in rats. A target stimulus is presented, but followed by a "forget tone" meaning that the rest of the trial has been canceled and memory for the target will not be tested. Every once in a while, however, the trial is completed. The animal's memory for the target stimulus on "forget" trials is worse in comparison to "remember" trials when they expected to be tested (e.g., Grant, 1982).

Other parallels between humans and animals have been noted. Serial-position curves for visual short-term memory by pigeons, monkeys, and humans are shown in Figure 8.4 (Wright et al., 1985). A common set of procedures was developed in which subjects were shown a sequence of four pictures on each trial. After a delay interval, and these intervals varied across species, a single picture was presented for subjects to identify as having been from the list or as being a different picture. The shape of the curves are remarkably similar across species. At intermediate delays of 2 to 25 seconds (across species), there is the U-shaped curve having both primacy and recency.

Studies of animal STM are important for several reasons. They are widely used in comparative cognition, a field that compares the cognitive capacities of different species from an evolutionary perspective. Neuroscientists use animal STM to investigate the effects of brain lesions, neurotransmitter substances, and brain chemistry. Finally, pharmacologists use animal memory as a sensitive assay of the potential cognitive side effects of new drugs and compounds.

materials that are not verbalizable. Wright and colleagues (1990) compared memory for scenic slides and kaleidoscope images. Lists of 10 images were presented and the "off" time (or blank screen time) between images was varied between 0.5 and 6 seconds. Longer off times facilitated recall of the scenic pictures, as if subjects were verbally rehearsing between pictures ("tree, brook, snow,...") during the longer intervals between pictures. Memory for the kaleidoscope images, on the other hand, did not improve with longer off times between images, suggesting they were not being verbally rehearsed. Remembering these images thus seemed to depend on a visual memory.

Spatial Short-Term Memory.   Short-term memory for spatial positions can be illustrated using a grid on a computer screen, something like a tic-tac-toe board. An asterisk is presented in one square at a time, in a random sequence, to mark locations. After presentation of this list of positions, the participant attempts to point to the locations in the same order in which they had appeared.

Dark and Benbow (1991) tested spatial memory in the preceding manner using mathematically or verbally gifted seventh graders. Strings of three to nine items were presented, using lists of spatial positions, digits, or words. The mathematically gifted performed better than did the verbally gifted students on the spatial and digit spans. On the word span, the verbally gifted kids did better. These results are shown in Figure 8.5, which also includes data from children who were both mathematically and verbally gifted.

Short-Term Memory for Actions.   STM for movements has been tested using short lists of hand and arm actions. In a version of the distractor technique, Kausler, Wiley, and Lieberwitz (1992) presented movement triplets to adult subjects. Example actions might include clapping, waving, or pressing a button, although not all of the movements were so readily described in words. For example, Kausler and colleagues (1992) tested movement memory span in both college student and elderly adult participants. After delays of 15 seconds, there was little forgetting if the participants did nothing or if they counted backwards. There was significant forgetting among both age groups if the participants performed interfering actions or if they watched the experimenter perform distracting actions during the 15-second delay. Thus, just as in the Brown-Peterson task, retroactive interference occurs when the distracting material was in the same sensory modality as the target material.

Short-Term Memory for Odors.   Olfactory memory is so robust that it is virtually a contradiction in terms to link "short-term memory" and "odor memory." Engen, Kuisma, and Eimas (1973) presented their participants either a single smell or a list of five odors. These were chosen from a pool of 100 odorants being used. After distractor intervals of from 3 to 30 seconds spent counting backwards, the participants were given a test odorant and asked whether it was the same as one just presented (or one of the five presented, in the list version). Overall accuracy averaged around 80 percent, with no significant forgetting between 3 and 30 seconds. Although a short-term memory procedure was used, there was little evidence of short-term forgetting. Later research showed no significant forgetting of odors across intervals of months (Engen, 1987).

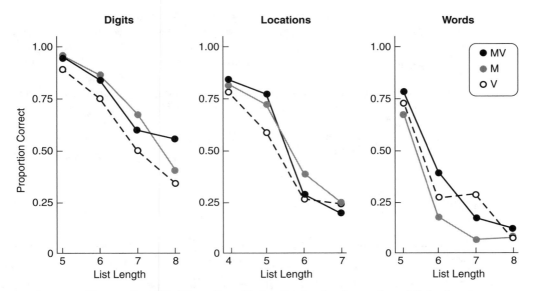

FIGURE 8.5   Correct Recall in Three Span Tasks. Graphs plot the number of digits, locations, and words recalled by the mathematically gifted (M), verbally gifted (V), and mathematically and verbally gifted 13-year-olds (MV).

Source: From "Differential Enhancement of Working Memory with Mathematical versus Verbal Precocity," by V. J. Dark and C. P. Benbow, 1991, *Journal of Educational Psychology, 83,* p. 52. Copyright © 1991 by the American Psychological Association. Reprinted with permission.

More recent research has shown some forgetting across intervals of seconds to minutes, particularly if the odors are unfamiliar and not easily encoded verbally (deWijk, Schab, & Cain, 1995). Familiar odors were remembered better, but this could be due to facilitation by verbal encoding. An odor can be encoded as a word (e.g., *talcum powder*) and then after the delay interval, the subject decides whether the test stimulus is talcum. However, recognition of unfamiliar odors, which depends more on memory for the sensory attributes, was still excellent after a delay of 100 seconds.

Short-Term Memory in the Hearing Impaired.   As we have seen, people sometimes recode from one modality to another; that is, visual images or odors are recoded and then remembered as words. One interesting population in which to study this possibility further is hearing-impaired individuals. What is the nature of their encoding in STM? Although numerous studies have been done, the results are complicated by a number of factors: varying levels of hearing impairment, amount of training in oral speech, and facility with one or another type of sign language (signing versus spelling words). Hearing-impaired children who have learned some spoken English make phonological confusions, just as do hearing children. Deaf children without spoken language more often make confusions based on visual similarity of the printed words and similarity in the form of manually presented signs (Conrad, 1970). Bellugi, Klima, and Sipple (1974–1975) found that word span was slightly longer in hearing participants for words they heard than in hearing impaired subjects for signs they saw. This finding may be analogous to the word-length effect: Signed words may take longer to "rehearse" than spoken words. Another difference is that hearing subjects tend to encode sequentially, whereas hearing-impaired subjects may encode by location. In one study, numbers were presented one by one in a spatial grid. Hearing subjects tended to recall in the sequence in which the numbers appeared, thus skipping around on the grid. Hearing-impaired subjects more often systematically went cell by cell in the grid, recalling the digits according to spatial position (Rodda & Grove, 1987).

Working Memory

Working memory is an advancement and elaboration of the earlier theory of short-term memory. *Working memory* includes both memory storage in at least two sensory modalities, and a component that controls the use of those memory stores. Specifically, the working-memory model (e.g., Baddeley & Hitch, 1974, 1994) divides a single STM into phonological and visuospatial substores (see Figure 8.6). One reason for doing this is that people can indeed do two things at once. This contrasts with performance on the Brown-Peterson distractor task, in which two things cannot be done simultaneously: remembering the to-be-recalled items and counting backwards. However, both of these tasks are verbal. As long as two tasks involve different working-memory substores, mutual interference between the two may be reduced. For example, we can typically drive a car and carry on a conversation simultaneously. Thus, one prominent feature of the working-memory approach is to assess dual-task performance. If the two tasks use different STM stores, there will be less interference than if the two tasks involve the same store.

Several lines of research support the separability of the two subsystems. Remembering a string of words is disrupted by simultaneously repeating irrelevant speech sounds (the suppression technique mentioned earlier). Remembering a picture or a nonsense shape is impaired by simultaneously performing a visual tracking task (e.g., keeping a stylus on a moving dot of light). In each of these cases, a single short-term store (the verbal or the visual) is performing two tasks at once, and so interference occurs. On the other hand, if the two tasks use different stores, interference is reduced. Remembering a word list is not se-

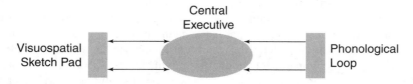

FIGURE 8.6   Working-Memory Model.

Source: Reprinted with permission from "Working Memory," by A. D. Baddeley, 1992, *Science, 255,* p. 557. Copyright © 1992 American Association for the Advancement of Science.

verely affected by a visuospatial tracking task: Each can be performed at the same level alone as when done together (Shah & Miyake, 1996; see review by Gathercole, 1994).

In addition to two memory stores, working memory includes a third component, the central executive. The central executive acts as a sort of manager between the two memory stores, which manipulates and coordinates information stored in the buffers, directs attention, and engages in problem solving and planning.

The phonological store of working memory has several of the characteristics described earlier for the modal model of short-term memory. The visual-spatial store corresponds to the visual and spatial short-term memories described earlier. One of the significant interests in the working-memory model has been its application to other memory conditions, such as reading and prose processing, or to aging and dementia.

Aging and Working Memory

Memory over short retention intervals, as assessed by the distractor or span tests, decreases with age. Is this decline due to a reduction in the duration or the capacity of short-term memory? The working-memory model suggests that there could be other, less obvious factors of aging that adversely affect memory. One factor associated with aging is slower processing. On certain tasks, older adults take longer to achieve the same level of performance as younger adults. For example, older adults can remember as well as do younger participants if the to-be-remembered stimuli are presented for longer durations. This suggests that the older participants encode into memory more slowly. Once the stimuli are in memory, the rate of forgetting across delay intervals is the same in older and younger participants. In another example, participants performed a reading and an arithmetic task concurrently. The older participants took longer to respond to questions about what they had read, suggesting that they are slower at switching from one task to another (Salthouse, 1994).

A second factor has been associated with aging. Hasher and Zacks (1988) studied working memory in the domain of language processing: listening, reading, and comprehension. They believe that older participants have particular trouble inhibiting extraneous associations that are activated by the target material. These tangential thoughts can be triggered by the material itself (such as personal associations or reminiscences) or by the external environment (noticing the room, maybe the lecturer, but not the lecture). Working memory's capacity is taxed by this irrelevant content. One result may be attentional: failure to keep up with the conversation or not being aware of what you have just read. Another effect is that unrelated thoughts can foster weaker encodings of the target material and interference among target and irrelevant memories.

Dementia and Working Memory

Alzheimer's disease is a particularly devastating form of cognitive dementia. Although some studies show unimpaired verbal and spatial memory in mildly affected patients (Baddeley, 1992a), other reviewers conclude that genuine Alzheimer's victims show profound memory impairments across the board (Kopelman, 1994). One reason for this discrepancy may be the degree of impairment of the experimental participants. Alzheimer's is a progressive dementing disease, and so not all individuals are equally affected. Another possible resolution of the discrepancy between experimental reports is whether a single task is being performed or two tasks. In one study, Alzheimer's patients were found to be impaired at doing two tasks at once, even though each alone could be performed competently (Baddeley, 1992a). The difficulty of each task alone, a visual tracking task and verbal memory span, was adjusted so that each could be performed well. However, when both tasks needed to be performed simultaneously (tracking a moving light while remembering a string of words), performance dropped off dramatically. Unimpaired control participants would be able to perform both tasks simultaneously with little cross-interference. As with normal aging, we can point to the difficulty that Alzheimer's patients had in alternating between the tracking and word-memory tasks. This may reflect impairment in the coordination of attentional resources by the central executive.

Is There Really a Separate STM?

Is there a really a separate short-term or working memory? It seems perfectly obvious that some things are forgotten quickly and others slowly if at all. Some researchers are seeking the biological basis of STM and the neural areas involved with it (e.g., Desimone, 1996; Goldman-Rakic, 1996). Their view presumes the physical reality of STM. However, the existence, or even necessity, of hypothesizing a STM remains unproven to other theorists. As noted earlier, there are few features that absolutely differentiate short-term from long-term memory. Maybe STM could be considered as purely theoretical, a metaphor or an idea that has generated much useful research.

Neuropsychological Dissociations of Two-Memory Systems

Neuropsychological studies of individuals with impairment of auditory-verbal short-term memory indicate that they have different sites of brain injury than do patients without STM losses. In the last chapter we described H. M., who has an intact STM. His digit span has declined somewhat over the years to about 5—not bad for an older gentleman. K. F. is just the opposite, being grossly impaired on memory span and distractor tasks, particularly for verbally presented items (Shallice & Warrington, 1970). H. M. and other "amnesic syndrome" patients have damage to the hippocampus and related structures deep within the temporal lobe. K. F. suffers from injury to a different area, one roughly on the border between the temporal and the parietal lobes of the left hemisphere. The discovery of other patients like K. F. has led to the naming of a "short-term memory" syndrome, referring specifically to impaired auditory-verbal STM (Shallice, 1988).

Studies of animal memory also show a dissociation between brain areas necessary for remembering over the short term versus the long term. In a nicely matched set of comparisons, Mishkin and Appenzeller (1987) showed that damage to the combined hippocampus and amygdala impaired short-term retention of objects recently shown to a monkey, but did not prevent long-term learning of objects. In both experimental tasks, food was given as a reward for choice of the correct object and withheld for choice of the incorrect object. In the short-term memory task, the lesioned animal could not remember which of two objects had been shown most recently. However, in the long-term memory task, the animal could learn which of two objects was consistently paired with food.

Counterpoint: A Single-Store Approach?

One critic of two-store memory theories argues that many variables have the same effect on retention after short intervals and after long intervals, rather than these variables showing different effects as is characteristic of a dissociation (Crowder, 1993). For example, STM and LTM are each susceptible to proactive and retroactive interference. There are also exceptions to the experimental dissociations that are said to distinguish the two forms of memory. For example, STM is said to be indicated by the recency effect, or enhanced recall of the final items of a list, that is present in immediate testing but not after a delay. However, we can find recency in recall from long-term memory also. As just one example, there is a serial-position curve, including a recency effect, in college students' recall of U.S. presidents (Roediger & Crowder, 1976; updated data from a more contemporary sample of students is shown in Crowder, 1993). If STM and LTM are similarly affected by experimental variables, maybe a simpler explanation would be to hypothesize a single memory store.

Can the evidence that favors a separate STM be parsimoniously accommodated within a single memory system? One alternative to hypothesizing separate short-term and long-term memory stores is to suggest that there is a single set of memories, but memories can differ between those that are currently active and those that are inactive (Lewis, 1979). Suppose I ask you to recall the name of your third-grade teacher or your favorite pet's name. What you have just done is taken an inactive memory and made it active. The latent memory corresponds to what we have called long-term memory, and its activation is what we have called short-term memory.

Shiffrin (1993) elaborated on this idea with an analogy from neural connectionism (discussed in Chapter 7). STM can be thought of as the temporary activation of neural elements above resting or baseline levels. This activation contributes to synaptic changes in conductivity, leading to strengthened connections with other items in long-term memory (i.e., transfer from STM to LTM). The fading or return of the active neural elements to their resting levels corresponds to forgetting from STM.

One Memory, but Multiple Traces

Another single-memory hypothesis reminds us of two facts: Memories are multidimensional, and each dimension could have a different rate of forgetting.

The memory for an item or an event may be encoded in multiple dimensions, such as sight, sound, touch, emotion, and so on. In a *memory-attribute* model, memories are complex representations containing several attributes (Tulving & Watkins, 1975; Underwood, 1983). When we are introduced to someone, we may later recollect attributes that are auditory (e.g., hearing a name or the sound of his or her voice), visual (appearance), olfactory (a fragrance), tactile (a handshake), and emotional (tension, e.g., if this is your new boss). The rate of forgetting of each attribute may differ. Thus, the forgetting curve for different memories can vary, such as acoustic versus semantic, but not because they were in different memory stores (Wickelgren, 1970). The several attributes may be forgotten from a single memory store, but forgotten at faster or slower rates relative to each other (see Figure 8.7).

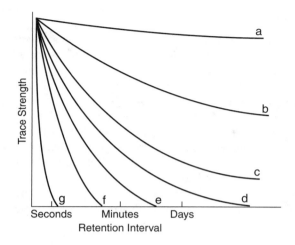

FIGURE 8.7 Hypothetical Curves of Forgetting for the Different Attributes that Make up a Memory. Different dimensions (e.g., auditory, visual, tactile, emotional) may be forgotten at different rates, corresponding to what is otherwise described as short-term memory (e.g., attribute f) or long-term memory (e.g., attribute a).

What otherwise appears to be forgetting from short-term memory may instead be the rapid forgetting of certain stimulus modalities, such as sound. What appears to be more persistent long-term memory may be the slower forgetting of other stimulus modalities, such as sight or smell.

One Store or Several?

We have considered the hypothesis of a single memory system as an alternative to postulating two memory systems, STM and LTM. Which model is correct? Combining different rates of forgetting with multiple-memory attributes provides a sophisticated single-memory alternative to the dual-store theory. However, the single-memory hypothesis has not achieved acceptance as has the dual-store theory (Healy & McNamara, 1996). The modal model embodying STM and LTM provides the basis of much physiological research (Zola-Morgan & Squire, 1993). Neuroscientists are delineating brain areas that are active during short-term retention, which are separate from those involved in long-term memory. Finally, the concept of STM has provided valuable insights into learning and memory in general (see Box 8.2). A familiar phrase attributed to the psychologist Kurt Lewin is, "There's nothing so practical as a good theory." Any single experiment or observation does not prove the existence of separate memory systems. The usefulness of the multiple-memory concept may be in how readily it allows us to think about, and advance, our knowledge of memory.

Applications

What Is Short-Term Memory For?

What purpose does a primary, short-term, or working memory serve? Does it do or allow certain functions that are not easily accommodated by long-term memory? McCarthy and Warrington (1990) discuss several possible roles for short-term memory. Two potential

B O X **8.2**

Short-Term Memory Deficits in Medical and Psychological Disorders

Short-term memory is frequently used to measure the neurological impact of various diseases and psychological disorders. Impairment can be a subtle, but quantifiable, indication of cognitive dysfunction. Memory loss has been associated with conditions as diverse as Lyme disease, toxic poisoning from bad shellfish, and overexposure to high altitudes (Hornbein et al., 1989; Logigian, Kaplan, & Steere, 1990; Teitelbaum et al., 1990).

In some cases, impaired memory is secondary to the disease process and is simply used as an indicator of general cognitive impairment. Sherwin (1988) found a decrease in short-term and long-term memory following hysterectomy in women, but no loss in those who received estrogen-androgen administration.

In other cases, memory deficits are anticipated on the basis of the known physiology of the disorder. For example, diabetes could be expected to disrupt remembering due to blood sugar imbalance. The latter is important to normal functioning of the brain. Glucose administration has been shown to facilitate memory in animals and humans (Gold, 1987). Children and adolescents with early-onset diabetes do have lower digit span scores, as well as some long-term memory impairments (Hagan et al., 1990). Among elderly diabetics, deviations in digit span have been inconsistently found (Tun, Nathan, & Perlmuter, 1990). Similarly, the administration of glucose to nondiabetic elderly in an attempt to improve memory has sometimes facilitated long-term memory, but not specifically the length of digit span (Manning, Hall, & Gold, 1990).

Memory impairment is studied in certain psychological disorders also. One aspect of obsessive-compulsive disorder is repetitive checking behavior: looking to see whether something was done or not; for example, is the oven off, the light out, and the door locked? One hypothesis is that compulsive checkers simply do not remember well. In fact, Sher and Mann (1984) did find some memory deficits among their checkers, including lower scores in forward and backward digit recall.

Another possibility is that compulsive checkers cannot discriminate whether they have actually done something, or only thought of doing it. To test this idea we could ask experimental participants to perform a series of actions (e.g., plugging in an iron) or just imagine doing another action (e.g., turning off a lamp). Later we ask our subjects whether they remember which of the actions they had performed. This procedure is used to study "source monitoring," remembering the origin of a memory. Obsessive-compulsive individuals do not have poorer discrimination between performed versus imagined actions, in comparison to matched control participants. In fact, the more anxious checkers had even better memory for actually performed behaviors. However, they did report they had less confidence and trust in those memories (Constans, Foa, Franklin, & Mathews, 1995).

Finally, memory may be studied in an attempt to understand the neurological nature of a disorder. Schizophrenia, a severe disorder of thinking, is believed to involve frontal-lobe dysfunction, as evidenced by increased distractibility (among other symptoms). Short-term verbal and spatial memory are both reduced in schizophrenic individuals, consistent with similar impairments found with frontal-lobe injuries (Park, Holzman, & Goldman-Rakic, 1995). Those who are researching the genetic basis for schizophrenia have found similar working-memory deficits among close relatives of schizophrenic individuals, relatives who are themselves free of the disorder.

One difficulty that experimental psychologists encounter in reviewing the medical and psychiatric literature is the many different uses of "short-term memory." As used in the clinic and the real world, it can refer to intervals of a few minutes to a few hours. One reference distinguishes among immediate memory (Atkinson and Shiffrin's STM), recent memory (minutes or hours), and remote memory (the latter two corresponding to LTM) (Salisbury, 1991). Another guide for clinical practice refers to short-term memory as the ability to name the current U.S. president and vice president,

(continued)

Box 8.2   Continued

or recall a word list after 5 minutes (Crigger & Forber, 1997).

A film critic's review of *Memento,* directed by Christopher Nolan and based on a short story by his brother Jonathan (Nolan, 2001), claims the amnesic central figure suffers from a loss of short-term memory. But the whole point of the story is that the character has only short-term memory, and cannot maintain an ongoing episodic long-term memory.

Not all of these memory lapses should be labeled STM. Many people that I have talked to refer to any forgetting of recent events as a short-term

memory problem. What is often implied, however, is forgetting that takes place over hours or even days. These could be described as problems with recent memory, which is a nontechnical term, but technically not STM or primary memory as discussed in this chapter.

The study of memory concepts is valuable both to clinicians (in medicine, psychiatry, and psychology) and to experimentalists. Insights from the lab may inform real-world practice and vice versa. The application of memory concepts and findings also justifies the work of basic research.

functions are language comprehension and problem solving. A third, which we have already considered in one context, is as a gateway to long-term memory.

Comprehending and Using Language

Language comprehension, through reading, listening or watching signed symbols, takes time. The first words and phrases of a sentence need to be remembered until the end of the sentence is produced in order to comprehend the entire thought the speaker (or writer) is expressing. For example, given the sentence HE STRODE ACROSS THE COURT AND PROTESTED VIGOROUSLY TO THE JUDGE THAT HIS OPPONENT WAS INFRINGING ON THE RULES BY USING _____. What is the meaning of this sentence? You have probably formed some idea even without the missing last words, but that meaning could be different from your expectation. One ending is (*he protested*) AN ILLEGALLY STRUNG TENNIS RACKET. Another is (*he protested*) INADMISSIBLE EVIDENCE. Each ending gives a different meaning to the first part of the sentence. Comprehension of the meaning of either requires the memory for the lengthy early portion of the sentence. Maybe this is what short-term memory is for: to provide continuity in reading and listening.

Several studies have shown a correlation between working memory and reading comprehension. Daneman and Carpenter (1980) used a dual-task procedure in which students read a series of unrelated sentences out loud and also tried to remember the last word in each sentence. This is a dual-task procedure, in which both tasks (reading and remembering) use a single verbal memory store. For example, the following sentences might be read by the students:

THE POLICEMAN ATE THE APPLE.
THE GIRL SANG THE SONG.
THE RAIN BEAT ON THE WINDOW PANES.

After a few sentences (the exact number varies over trials), a question is asked about one of the sentences to ensure comprehension ("Who sang?"), and at other times, the experimenter requests recall of the final words. In this example, these are APPLE, SONG, and PANES. Good readers had a longer memory span (i.e., recalled more final words from more sentences) than did poor readers. Dual-task performance in older students also correlates with their verbal SAT scores and standardized reading scores (Daneman & Merikle, 1996). In contrast to the correlation of working memory with reading ability, simpler measures of STM capacity, such as the digit span and word span, do not correlate highly with measures of reading comprehension. However, Daneman and Carpenter (1980) argue that simple span assesses only the storage capacity of STM and not the combination of capacity and processing that occurs during reading. Perfetti and Lesgold (1979) offered an analogy of reading comprehension to a conveyor belt. As words come down the line, the meaning must be abstracted and transferred into long-term memory. Some students simply cannot keep up: Accessing the meaning of some words on the "conveyor" takes too long, causing some other words on the conveyor to be missed or forgotten.

The role of STM in language comprehension has been questioned. Some individuals with impaired auditory-verbal spans due to brain damage are not necessarily impaired in coping with conversations. K. F. can repeat meaningful sentences, even though he cannot repeat back two unrelated words in the distractor task. Indeed, McCarthy and Warrington (1990) report that some individuals with impaired verbal STM still hold demanding jobs requiring good language skills.

A compromise position suggests that the phonological component of working memory acts as a sort of backup memory. When sentences are short or easily comprehended, it is not needed. With syntactically more complex or lengthy sentences processing may lag behind the input and so the representation in the phonological store needs to be consulted (McCarthy & Warrington, 1990).

Problem Solving

Mental problem solving requires attention, encoding, storage, and manipulation of information, all processes for which *working memory* is well designed. Dark and Benbow (1990) studied memory for arithmetic word problems in mathematically and verbally gifted seventh graders and correlated these scores with several measures of memory span. An example problem might read: "The entertainment portion of a 30-minute TV show on Tuesday night lasted 4 minutes longer than four times the portion devoted to commercials. How many minutes of commercials were there?" Solving such problems requires retention and manipulation of the numerical facts. The academically gifted children, who as we noted earlier had longer word- and digit-memory spans than did average children, were better at remembering word problems. Gifted children seem to form what Dark and Benbow refer to as more "compact encodings," which is much like Miller's idea of chunking to pack more information into an item.

Problem solving also requires translating relational statements into a mathematical proposition (the "4 minutes longer than 4 times the...commercials" portion). In the preceding example, commercial duration could be expressed as x, and the entertainment duration as $4x + 4$, and the sum of these two equals 30 minutes. Or $5x + 4 = 30$. Relational statements pose particular difficulties for students, including college students. Undergraduates who had longer memory spans accurately recalled more relational statements in math word problems (Cooney & Swanson, 1990).

Efficient use of working memory also means deciding what not to rehearse. Capacity can be freed by excluding irrelevant facts, such as the fact that the show in the problem aired on Tuesday evening. Students with longer memory spans were able to forget more of the irrelevant statements (Cooney & Swanson, 1990).

Dark and Benbow's work with precocious children illustrates the complexity of working memory. We started this chapter with the suggestion that short-term memory simply held information briefly. Now we are led to consider several distinct processes, each of which contributes to individual differences in performance. Information must be encoded, but capacity is affected by coding or chunking schemes, and by familiarity with the material. Rapid retrieval from long-term memory is important: Word meaning must be accessed in semantic memory and temporarily maintained. Information is manipulated, as in the translation of word problems into an algebraic form, and then the substitution of numbers into the formula. Finally, irrelevant information must be discarded and extraneous associations inhibited. Just as problem-solving ability is considered to be a defining feature of intelligence, so now working memory is being considered as a link to intelligence (Wickelgren, 1997).

Working memory's central executive is accorded a prominent role in problem solving. The central executive allocates attention to the submemory systems and is involved in planning and decision making. These traits appear to be disturbed in frontal-lobe-damaged and Alzheimer's individuals. Frontal-lobe injury is characterized by excessive distractibility, perseveration, and lack of planning, a set of symptoms that has been labeled the "dysexecutive syndrome" (Shallice, 1988). Short-term memory is impaired because these individuals are easily distracted. Perseveration, or persisting in one mode of behavior, is manifested by a difficulty in switching between concurrent tasks (e.g., from a verbal to a spatial task) or difficulty in adopting new rules of behavior (e.g., first sorting a deck of cards by color, then sorting by suit).

Shallice and Burgess (1991) described a naturalistic example of executive dysfunction by frontal-lobe-injured patients. Their participants were given a list of errands in a shopping mall (actually, since the researchers are British, the location was a "pedestrian precinct"). These tasks required memory retention (e.g., of what to buy), planning (to sequence errands efficiently), retrieval (remembering when and where each task occurs), and information manipulation (there were limits on spending and on time to complete the errands). The patients made many more errors than did the control participants. Memory failures often occurred as a by-product of planning errors: failing to sequence activities efficiently, or establish retrieval cues (e.g., remember to deposit a letter in the mailbox that is just outside the bakery).

The Role of STM in Theories of Long-Term Memory

We have already mentioned the possible role of STM as a gateway into long-term memory. This idea is not universally accepted, as noted earlier in this chapter, yet numerous theories of long-term learning have postulated a role for STM.

Both consolidation theory (Hebb, 1949) and dual-store theory (Atkinson & Shiffrin, 1968) state that interference with short-term processing will likewise interfere with the formation of long-term memory. For example, electroconvulsive shock (ECS) interferes with memory for events that just preceded ECS. This is an instance of retrograde amnesia (Chapter 7). According to consolidation theory, the electroshock "clears" a neural short-term memory and thus prevents sufficient opportunity for consolidation into long-term memory. The longer that ECS is delayed after the to-be-remembered event, the better is long-term memory. Presumably, the longer delay before shock allows more time for consolidation. A similar explanation is offered for the retrograde amnesia that head injuries cause: Events immediately preceding the trauma are displaced from a short-term memory before they can be transferred into long-term memory.

To cite a similar effect but produced by a milder manipulation, the occurrence of surprising events can cause a retrograde amnesic-like effect. For example, Ellis and colleagues (1971) tested free recall of lists of line drawings. The surprising occurrence of a nude photograph in the middle of one list zapped memory for the picture that just preceded the photo, maybe by displacing that item from short-term memory. The nude was well remembered, but not the picture before it in the list. Note that in each of the preceding cases, those involving ECS, head trauma, and surprising stimuli, recall from STM was not tested directly. Disruption of short-term memory was inferred on the basis of poor performance on a test of delayed memory recall, that is, a test of LTM.

Summary

Short-term memory (STM) refers to memory that is both brief (lasting from several seconds to less than a minute in the absence of rehearsal) and of limited capacity (with estimates ranging from two to seven items). STM is distinguished from long-term memory, which in the laboratory is typically any memory more than a few minutes old.

The distinction between these two memory systems has long been a part of psychology's history. First William James, and then in modern times, Waugh and Norman, distinguished between primary memory and secondary memory. The next step was the development of the multistore theory of Atkinson and Shiffrin. According to this model, STM has a limited capacity, old items can be easily displaced by new items, rehearsal facilitates transfer to LTM, and control processes are employed in STM. The most recent stage in the evolution of STM is Baddeley and Hitch's working memory, which has a phonological loop for the rehearsal of verbal information, a visuospatial sketch pad, and a central executive to control the limited resource of attention over one or more tasks.

Short-Term Memory Tasks

Short-term memory is often studied through the distractor technique and the memory-span task. The Brown-Peterson distractor task is used to measure the duration of STM. To-be-remembered items are presented, the subject performs a distractor task such as counting, and then attempts to recall the target items. The amount recalled drops off dramatically after as little as 9 seconds of distraction. This rapid forgetting was thought to be significant for two reasons. First, it seemed to demonstrate how brief STM was in the absence of rehearsal, and, second, that forgetting seemed to occur in the absence of interference. However, short-term retention is influenced by both of these factors: Surreptitious rehearsal occurs in spite of the distractor activity and interference, particularly proactive interference, affects distractor performance.

Memory span is a measure of the number of items that can be recalled in correct order after a single presentation. It is essentially the capacity of short-term memory. Span is limited to about seven items (plus-or-minus two). Span is increased by chunking, by familiarity, and by practice with the to-be-remembered material. An important determinant of span is word length: Span is greater for shorter than for longer items. Memory span correlates with articulation rate, and longer words take longer to speak than shorter words.

Characteristics of STM

The verbal short-term store of Atkinson and Shiffrin and the phonological store of Baddeley's working memory are characterized by acoustic encoding: Words are remembered as they sound. STM has a limited capacity, although apparent capacity can be increased by chunking or coding to increase the amount of information contained within each item. STM is of limited duration in the absence of rehearsal. Forgetting from short-term memory occurs due to displacement of the memory trace.

Rehearsal of information in STM allows transfer to LTM. Verbal rehearsal may be necessary in forming some kinds of long-term knowledge, such as in vocabulary learning. However, residence in STM is neither necessary nor sufficient for LTM formation. Brain-injured subjects like K. F., who have a limited verbal short-term memory, can nevertheless learn and retain long-term memories at normal rates. Maintenance of information in short-term memory does not guarantee entry into long-term memory. Thus, in sum, there are few absolute distinctions between the features of verbal short-term memory and long-term memory.

Short-term retention can be demonstrated for visual and olfactory stimuli, for spatial locations, and for actions.

Working Memory

The working-memory model divides STM into phonological and visuospatial substores. A prominent feature of the working-memory approach is to assess dual-task performance. If the two tasks use different STM stores, there will be less cross-interference than if the two tasks involve the same store. In addition, the central executive acts as a sort of manager between the two memory stores and manipulates, organizes, and plans information and actions.

Working-memory tasks have been employed to study aging and dementia, which in turn helps illuminate working memory. Aging is associated with slower processing, as shown by slower encoding of target items into memory or slower switching between tasks. Alzheimer's patients are impaired at doing two tasks at once, even if each can be performed competently alone. This finding illustrates the distinction between the single store of STM and the dual stores of working memory.

Is There Really a Separate Short-Term Memory?

Can memory be parsimoniously accommodated by a theory of a single-memory system? The existence, or even necessity, of hypothesizing separate STM and LTM remains unproven to some theorists. For instance, some variables similarly affect retention after short and long intervals.

One alternative hypothesis is that there is a single set of memories, but memories can differ between those that are currently active (STM) and those that are inactive (LTM). Another hypothesis is that memories are multidimensional and that each dimension has a different rate of forgetting. What appears to be forgetting from short-term memory is rapid forgetting of certain stimulus modalities, such as sound. What appears to be long-term memory is the more enduring retention of other stimulus modalities, such as sight or smell.

Evidence in favor of a STM–LTM distinction comes from neuropsycholgical studies. Individuals with impairment of verbal short-term memory have damage to different areas of the brain than do patients without STM losses. Studies of memory in animals also show a dissociation between brain areas necessary for remembering over the short term versus the long term.

Applications

What is the purpose of short-term memory? One possibility is that it is necessary for language comprehension. The span of working memory correlates with measures of reading comprehension. Dual-task performance, such as reading sentences and remembering the final words, correlates with verbal SAT scores and standardized reading scores.

STM may be necessary for problem solving. Several distinct working-memory processes contribute to problem solving. Information must be encoded into working memory, other information must be retrieved from LTM, steps in problem solution must be sequenced, and irrelevant information must be excluded. Working memory's central executive seems to play a central role in organizing these types of activities necessary for problem solving. By contrast, injury to the frontal lobes produces a "dysexecutive syndrome," characterized by excessive distractibility, perseveration, and lack of planning.

Finally, numerous theories of long-term learning have hypothesized that STM is a sort of gateway into long-term memory. Both consolidation theory and dual-store theory state that interference with short-term processing would prevent long-term memory formation. Studies involving ECS, head trauma, and surprising stimuli as interfering events show impaired long-term learning.

9

Encoding

Encoding refers to the acquisition of information: the initial formation of a memory trace. A textbook such as the one that you are now reading can cite references to learning under idealized conditions: simple materials, minimal distractions, and students physically and mentally prepared to learn. Yet how often will such controlled learning conditions occur in the real world? Recall your first year of college, taking what seemed like too many courses, each requiring a different form of studying. Long hours and lots of stress. Or consider having to learn under particularly trying conditions: the U.S. Marine Corps boot camp at Parris Island, South Carolina. The physical training and emotional pressure the recruits experience are well known from film and television. What many of us are not aware of is the academic learning that occurs over 11 weeks of training. Each recruit attends classes and is issued a set of textbooks totaling over a thousand pages. Studying occurs at odd times of the day (or night)—whenever opportunity allows. The recruits are typically physically fatigued when they need to study. They are under intense emotional pressure and stress (read: FEAR). The recruits are certainly motivated to learn, but the material is so foreign as to appear more like Ebbinghaus's nonsense syllables than meaningful prose. How do variables such as time of day, emotional arousal, incentive, and meaningfulness affect learning? This chapter will consider these and other more usual laboratory variables that affect encoding.

Separating Encoding from Retrieval

This chapter focuses on variables that are thought to influence encoding into memory. One means of separating the contributions of each stage is to vary the conditions of learning, or encoding, while holding constant the conditions of storage and retrieval. Still, the division of information processing into stages of encoding, storage, and retrieval is in some ways arbitrary. After all, better encoding implies that both storage and retrieval will improve also.

The methods of neuroscience offer another means of separating encoding of ongoing experiences into memories, from the storage of memories over time or the later retrieval of memories. Functional neuroimaging studies, the various brain scans, can be used to assess brain activation at each stage of memory. For instance, a tracer element is injected into the blood and a positron emission tomography (PET) scan maps where this element travels to in the brain during the performance of a cognitive task. The difference in activity levels in areas of the brain during performance of different tasks, such as studying a list of words versus recognizing previously studied words, may indicate which brain regions are implicated in each stage. Grady and colleagues (1995) found that the certain areas in the left hemisphere were more active during the encoding of face pictures than during subsequent recognition. Interestingly, older subjects (age 69 versus the younger 25-year-olds) generally did not have higher activation in these left-brain areas and were less accurate on the memory test. Thus, the deficit in remembering sometimes seen in older individuals could be due to weaker encoding as opposed to faster forgetting or difficulty in retrieving memories. In another type of imaging study, the brain activity during study of individual items was measured. This activity was then correlated with whether those items were recalled or forgotten. Certain areas in the left hemisphere were found to be more active during the study of verbal items that were recalled and were less active during study of items that were later unrecognized (Wagner et al., 1998). Similarly, certain areas of the right hemisphere were more active during encoding of photographs of scenes that were subsequently recognized than during the study of photographs that were not recognized (Brewer et al., 1998). So far, the technology does not exist to routinely scan the brains of learning and remembering subjects, so we will continue to differentiate storage and retrieval based on more traditional methods of dissociation.

Some Basic Variables in Encoding

In the laboratory, encoding into episodic memory is often studied. Episodic memory is remembering information based on its occurrence at a particular time and place. Free recall of lists of words, sentences, or pictures are tests of episodic memory: recalling the items you just saw, here in the laboratory. As students and learners, we may have a more practical interest in learning that occurs outside of the lab. Yet in order to better study the effects of encoding, the researcher needs to have control over the task from presentation until testing.

A number of factors are reviewed in the several following sections: rehearsal, imagery, serial-position effects, and arousal, just to name a few. Several of these factors are summarized for quick reference in Box 9.1.

BOX **9.1**

Summary of Some Factors Related to Encoding, and Their Definitions

Characteristics of the to-Be-Learned Material

Word Meaningfulness. Meaningful words are ones having some combination of the following: a high frequency of occurrence in language and print, are easily pronounced, have many associations to other items, and are more imagable.

Concrete/Abstract Words. Words that refer to actual, physical things, and that tend to be imagable and have a number of associations versus words that refer to nonphysical abstract ideas.

Imagery. The degree to which items can be mentally imaged. Pictures or objects actually seen are better remembered than if their names are simply read.

Factors in the Presentation of to-Be-Remembered Materials

Serial Position. The sequence in which items are presented; the classic serial-position effect is a U-shaped curve in which the first items and the last items in the list are well recalled.

Spacing of Repetitions. Two presentations of an item can be massed, one immediately after another, or spaced, with some interval of time or some other items occurring between repetitions.

Isolation Effect. An unusual or distinctive item that stands apart from the other items in a series.

Cognitive Strategies

Maintenance Rehearsal. Somewhat passive, repetitive thinking about to-be-remembered material.

Elaborative Rehearsal. Thinking about the material in such a way as to require more cognitive effort, to activate more associations, or to produce a more distinctive memory representation.

Subject Factors

Arousal. Mental or physiological arousal, associated with circadian rhythms, stimulant and depressant drugs, or emotional arousal.

Incentives. The provision of explicit rewards for learning or remembering.

Incidental versus Intentional Learning. The participants are instructed to remember the material ("Please try to remember this") or the participants are simply asked to process the material in some other way ("Is the word a food or an animal?") without mention of a later test of retention.

Elaborative Rehearsal

The role that rehearsal plays in remembering has been considered in several previous chapters. The number of words that are recalled from a list typically correlates with the number of rehearsals the words receive (Chapter 6). This is consistent with the dual-memory distinction, which asserts that rehearsal in short-term memory promotes better long-term representation of the rehearsed information (Chapters 7 and 8). However, enforced rehearsal does not always lead to better recall (e.g., Wixted & McDowell, 1989). All rehearsal is not the same; there seems to be some qualitative differences in rehearsal.

One important distinction that we can make is between elaborative rehearsal and maintenance rehearsal. The two terms derive from the levels-of-processing approach of

Craik and Lockhart (1972), which posits that information can be processed to a greater or lesser extent, and thus by analogy to different "depths" along a continuum from shallow to deep processing. *Maintenance rehearsal* is a form of shallow processing, a recycling of information in order to keep it available in short-term memory or the phonological store. We use maintenance rehearsal to remember a phone number long enough to dial it, simply repeating the number over and over until it is no longer needed. Maintenance rehearsal can be effective for short-term retention, and our research participants will choose to use maintenance rehearsal if they know they will be allowed uninterrupted rehearsal until the time of recall (Wixted, 1991).

Elaborative rehearsal is processing in which to-be-remembered material is related to other information. There is an active or deliberate attempt to cognitively interact with, reflect on, or use the to-be-remembered information, which is why elaborative rehearsal represents deep processing. We use elaborative rehearsal to memorize a phone number by, for example, looking for meaningful patterns in the numbers. The two forms of rehearsal also produce qualitative differences in memory: Elaborative rehearsal produces more of an episodic memory, a recollection of having studied the material at a particular time and place. Maintenance rehearsal does not: The facts seem familiar, but you cannot remember how or where you learned them (Gardiner et al., 1994).

The idea of elaborative rehearsal is a central theme in this chapter: Many of the variables that affect encoding in one way or another can be interpreted as instances of elaborative processing.

What Exactly Is Elaborative Processing?

A typical procedure for manipulating processing depth is to present a list of items and have the students answer a question about each item as they occur. Different types of questions require different levels of processing of the target items. For instance, given the target word BONE, the various questions asked might be, "Does the presented word contain the letter *e*, does it rhyme with *train*, is it an *animal*?" These questions require different levels of processing: the surface form or appearance of the word; the sound of the word; or the meaning of the word. Later, the subjects are tested for memory of the list. Items that received deeper processing during presentation are more likely to be recalled (Craik & Tulving, 1975).

The analogy of elaborative processing to deep processing may be a useful description, but this does not specifically define what elaboration is. At least three hypotheses have been offered: elaboration, distinctiveness, and effort (Horton & Mills, 1984). *Elaboration* refers to expanding a newly formed memory trace. Something is remembered better if it can be related to other known facts. If you have to remember the word AARDVARK, you might try to think of any associations to the word or any facts you know about aardvarks. Figure 9.1 illustrates the sets of possible associates that could be activated by the target words CRAB, FACT, and LAMP (Nelson & Schreiber, 1992). The words CRAB and FACT have larger sets of associations that could be activated than does the word LAMP. (CRAB and LAMP, however, could evoke specific mental pictures or images, whereas FACT does not. Imagery in encoding is discussed in a subsequent section.) Elaborated traces have more connections or associations to other memories. This increases the number of possible retrieval cues, and so elaboration affects both encoding and retrieval.

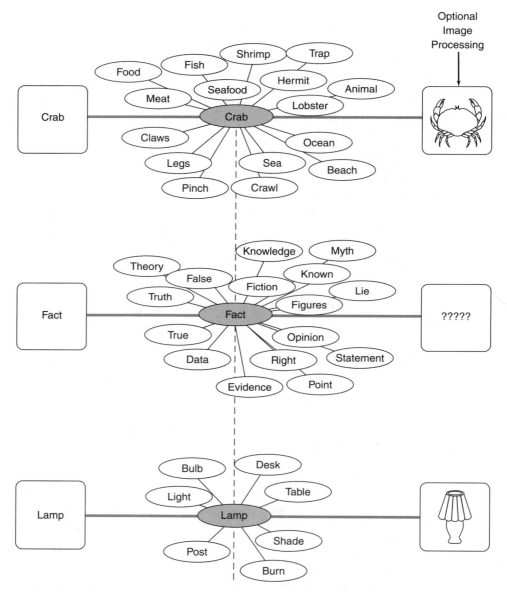

FIGURE 9.1 Hypothetical Elaborative Encoding of Three to-Be-Remembered Words, CRAB, FACT, and LAMP. Each word activates associated words and ideas, although the size of the associated sets vary. In addition, some words may evoke a mental image of the word's referent.

Source: From "Word Concreteness and Word Structure as Independent Determinants of Recall," by D. L. Nelson and T. A. Schreiber, 1992, *Journal of Memory and Language, 31,* p. 240. Copyright © 1992 by Academic Press. Reprinted with permission.

Alternatively, elaborative rehearsal may increase the *distinctiveness* of the memory. A distinctive memory is one that stands out, is more easily discriminated from other memories, and will suffer less interference from other memories during retrieval. Unlike elaboration, the distinctiveness hypothesis allows that shallow processing may sometimes lead to good retention, as long as the memory representation is distinctive. For instance, orthographically distinct words, that is, words that are unusual looking (such as LYMPH or AFGHAN) are recalled better than are orthographically common words (such as LEAKY or AIRWAY), even when the words are matched for meaningfulness and frequency of occurrence in language (Hunt & Elliot, 1980).

The third possibility is that elaborative processing requires more effort, and it is actually the amount of effort expended that determines retention. *Cognitive effort* can be measured by the impairment in performance on a second task done simultaneously with the memory task. For example, as a to-be-remembered list of words is presented, the subject must also push a button every time a tone stimulus sounds. Increasing the cognitive effort required in the memory task will lead to a corresponding slowing of reaction time to the tone (Eysenck & Eysenck, 1979). Elaborative rehearsal in the memory task leaves less capacity available for the stimulus-detection task. The results of such a dual-task procedure are shown in Figure 9.2. More words were recalled when the participants had to make a deep judgment ("Does the word name something that is edible?") rather than a shallow judgment ("Does the word contain a letter *e*?") about the word, but it took them longer to react to a tone or light stimulus that occurred during or near to the deep judgments. The slowed reaction times are an indicator of the cognitive effort being expended on the judgment task.

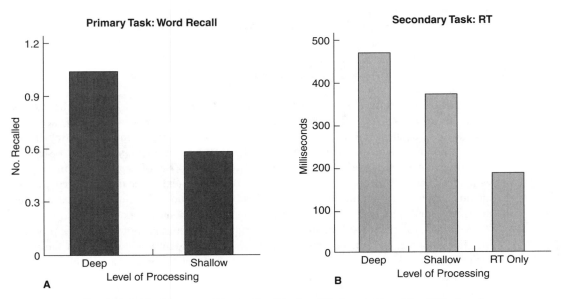

FIGURE 9.2 Dual-Task Performance Illustrating Trade-off between Cognitive Effort and Reaction Time.

Source: Eysenck & Eysenck, 1979, p. 479 and p. 481.

The various definitions of elaborative rehearsal can be illustrated by applying the notion of processing depth in several studies of memory for faces. Subjects in Bower and Karlin's (1974) study were shown high school yearbook photos. In one condition, the subjects made simple judgments about the faces (e.g., identify gender). In the other condition, they were asked to make character judgments for each face (e.g., "Does this person look honest?"). The first condition presumably requires shallow processing and the second condition deeper processing. When tested afterwards, the character judgment participants correctly recognized more faces than did the group that made shallow judgments. If you want to remember a face, ask yourself, "Would I buy a used car from this person?" Following on Bower and Karlin's study, Winograd (1981) had participants study faces for distinctive features. For instance, "Does this person have a large nose? Is he wearing glasses?" This turned out to be an effective means of increasing retention, and the more features searched, the better memory for the studied faces was. Looking for distinctive facial features could be considered shallow processing because it focuses on surface features, but it does increase distinctiveness. What about the role of cognitive effort? Given deep-processing instructions, participants make more eye movements when inspecting the pictures, implying more processing effort (Bloom & Mudd, 1991). Deep-processing subjects also report more interest and involvement in the task, whereas the shallow-processing groups find their task boring and undemanding (Sporer, 1991). So, why does elaborative processing enhance face memory? There is experimental support for all three hypotheses of elaboration, distinctiveness, and cognitive effort.

The theoretical concept of elaborative rehearsal has received its share of criticism (e.g., Baddeley, 1978). One criticism is that elaboration can refer to several different processes. One response here is to design experiments that contrast the alternate definitions to determine which meaning of elaboration is more appropriate (e.g., Waddill & McDaniel, 1998). Another concern was the lack of independent measures of cognitive elaboration, measures separate from the hypothesized effects on memory. Dual-task procedures, such as trying to remember a list of items and reacting to a stimulus, or measuring eye movements during processing, offer independent measures of elaboration.

How Can Elaborative Processing Be Enhanced?   The techniques used in the various mnemonic devices discussed in Chapter 6 exemplify elaborative processing. In the keyword mnemonic, a mediating word is selected to connect two target items. How can you remember that Pittsburgh is a steel-producing town? Link Pittsburgh to the Steelers, and then to steel. In the narrative method, a story is fabricated to link together a series of target words. In the peg-word and location mnemonics, images are formed of the target and the mnemonic cue. These methods require meaningful analysis of the targets, the creation of distinctive representations in memory, and cognitive effort. Not surprisingly, the mnemonics work.

Organizing the to-be-remembered material is another means of elaborative processing. For example, in remembering a list of words from identifiable categories (animals, tools, foods, etc.), the words can be more readily interrelated in memory, which is what elaboration is.

Conclusions about Elaboration.   "People will probably learn more if we can find ways of making them work harder at encoding and if they are encouraged to deal with new information in terms of its meaning and semantic content. Getting students to simply repeat material or spend more time looking at it is not the most efficient way to ensure they will learn and remember the content" (Kulhavey, Schwartz, & Perterson, 1986, p. 122). This summary reminds us of several aspects of elaboration: effort, meaningfulness, and active rehearsal.

Imagery and Memory for Pictures

Verbal encoding is not the only way of learning material, and it may not be the best. Visual coding can be extremely effective. We see this both through the use of imagery and in the recall of pictures versus words.

If words are presented for study, *concrete* words are typically recalled better than *abstract* words. Concrete words refer to things that physically exist and objects that can be experienced through the senses (such as the word CRAB), whereas abstract words refer more to ideas (such as the word FACT). Concrete usually refers to words that easily arouse a mental image or picture of the word's referent. Concrete words show a memory advantage over abstract words, as shown in a variety of learning situations (reviewed by Nelson & Schreiber, 1992).

Memory for pictures is often remarkably good. In one study, subjects were shown over 2,200 photographs presented in 2-hour sessions on 4 days. During testing, 280 pairs of slides were presented and the participants had to decide which picture in each pair had been seen before and which one was new. Correct choices were made over 90 percent of the time (Standing, Conezio, & Haber, 1970). Granted, this procedure is not comparable to that typically used to test word memory. Photographs have much more detail than a printed word, allowing many cues to discriminate old from new photos. Still, the number remembered is impressive.

Objects are recalled even better than pictures. Given stimuli displayed in one of three ways, actual objects were better recalled than were photographs of the objects, which were in turn better remembered than the printed name of the objects. This is also one case in which younger students did as well as older ones: fourth graders were as good as college students in recalling objects (Bevan & Steger, 1971).

Instructing participants to visually image to-be-remembered items such as words often increases recall (e.g., Roediger, 1980). In a variation of this instruction, memory for classical music pieces was improved by giving the participants a concrete label for each piece and having the participants create imagery as they listened to the music (Delis, Fleer, & Kerr, 1978). A musical selection might be given the concrete label, "Winter Forest," as opposed to the more abstract, "Rebirth of Justice." In fact, concrete and abstract labels were assigned to the same piece, for different participants of course. The college students described more vivid images being evoked during the music that had a concrete label, and when given a surprise test of recognition, they were better able to identify snippets from music that had concrete labels.

Why would picture memory be so much better than word memory? One reason is that pictures can be remembered with two encodings, one visual and the other a verbal translation of the picture. This is referred to as *dual coding* (Paivio, 1969). Another advantage for pictures is that the memory is more specific and distinctive than is the memory for an unelaborated word. As shown in Figure 9.1, the words CRAB and LAMP can take on specific images. For example, imagine remembering the word DOG versus a simple line drawing of a dog. The drawing cannot be too generic; it must show some kind of dog. (A large dog or small? Pointy or floppy ears?) This image may activate other knowledge of dogs, possibly unique facts that the word DOG does not retrieve, or it may remind us of a particular dog.

The recall of pictures benefits from organization just as does the recall of words. A number of objects can be shown in a picture, either organized in some fashion or individually. For instance, in one study that used children as participants, the target items were grouped in a picture (e.g., a doll sitting in a chair holding a ball) or the items were pictured separately (e.g., a doll next to a chair, next to a ball). A later test picture left one object out. The children who had originally seen the grouped picture were better able to supply the missing item (Horowitz, Lampel, & Takoniski, 1969).

Picture memory benefits from elaborative processing, just as does word memory. Bransford, Nitsch, and Franks (1977) showed students a photograph of a living room, and gave orienting instructions to induce different forms of processing. Some were told to try and find small hidden *x*'s within the picture. Another group was told to think about the kinds of actions they could perform with the objects. The students were then unexpectedly asked to recall as many objects from the picture as possible. The *x* group remembered only about 8 objects, but the action group remembered over 20. What is nice about this manipulation is that the *x*-searching subjects did closely attend to and scan the picture. Even so, their recall was poor.

Meaningfulness

Ebbinghaus compared his retention of poetry versus nonsense syllables. He found that the meaningful material was remembered better than the nonmeaningful, a conclusion that has been repeated for 100 years now. But what exactly is meaningfulness? And how can we increase it?

The starting point for analyzing meaningfulness was to discover those variables that correlated with ease of learning (reviewed in Gordon, 1989). If we think of meaning as something we already know something about, then meaningful words should be familiar words. Words rated as being meaningful do have a high *frequency* of occurrence in the language: we hear them, read them, and use them often.

Meaningful words are high in ease of *pronounceability*. This may be related to familiarity and frequency. This may also involve the phonological store of working memory: New words are rehearsed there during acquisition.

Meaningful words have more *associations* to other ideas and knowledge. We can use these associative links to activate related knowledge. This gets at one definition of elaboration: A meaningful item can be elaborated better in memory by drawing on an extensive network of interassociations. This network can involve semantic memory (general knowledge) and episodic memory (personal recollections).

Finally, meaningful words are often more *imagable*. A mental image or a remembered picture can often be generated for meaningful words (DOG versus LIBERTY). (In attempting to remember an abstract idea such as LIBERTY, you might try to make it concrete, possibly by remembering it as the Statue of Liberty.) The meaningfulness of a word can overlap with its concreteness and imagability.

The preceding listing of characteristics suggests that meaningfulness has to do with prior knowledge: Meaningful material is stuff you already know about. Generally, learners use knowledge they already possess to relate new items to this existing knowledge. The implication is that the more you know, the more you can learn. This truism has been substantiated in comparing people who are experts in certain domains and novices. For example, if shown various arrangements of chess pieces on a board, chess masters will remember them more accurately than less experienced players. This is particularly true if the pieces are in a meaningful arrangement (Gobet & Simon, 1996). When given 31 lines of a computer program to memorize, advanced student programmers learned them more readily than did students of intermediate ability. Again, the advantage for the experts was dependent on the program lines being in a logical sequence, and the advantage virtually disappeared when the program lines were scrambled (McKeithan et al., 1981).

This expertise in remembering does not indicate exceptional memory ability per se, but rather *domain-specific knowledge.* There are certain subject areas (domains) in which we each possess detailed and specific knowledge. You can recall information well from areas with which you are familiar. College students who were knowledgeable about baseball could remember fabricated baseball facts better than less knowledgeable students. Students knowledgeable about music remembered more fabricated facts about music than about baseball. A general memory ability does contribute. In this same study, the ability to memorize meaningless associations was related to learning about either topic. But apart from this, there was a significant contribution of domain-specific knowledge (Kuhara-Kojima & Hatano, 1991).

How Can Meaningfulness Be Used to Increase Learning?   One suggestion is to use existing knowledge to make new information more meaningful. Learners themselves may attempt to create meaningfulness in otherwise unfamiliar material. We saw one example of this in the studies of memory span (Chapter 8): Given a lengthy, random series of items, one strategy is to chunk them into more meaningful units. For example, one 38-year-old savant (otherwise described as having a mental age of 11; people like this were formerly called idiot-savants) had exceptional numerical memory ability. He would memorize things like city populations, distances between cities, or the number of rooms in various hotels. He could readily remember strings of numbers, such as 4836179621. How? "When I saw this number, I read it as 4, 836, 179, 621. I remembered 4 because of the fourth of July…836 was the Chinese population of the State of Texas in 1910…179 is the number of miles from New York to Harrisburg, and 621 is the number of a house I know in Denver" (Treffert, 1989, p. 74). Another mnemonist, Hans Eberstark, has exceptional language-learning abilities and, in fact, spent his working life as a translator. He readily picks up words in new languages, mainly by looking for similar-looking or -sounding words in other languages with which he is familiar (Bernstein, 1993).

Meaningfulness can also be provided to the learner. Bransford and Johnson (1973) found that a list of vaguely worded instructions could be more readily recalled when a label was given (Flying a Kite or Washing Clothes). Without the label, the list of instructions seems fairly random. Similarly, we saw earlier that classical music pieces were remembered better when they had been given concrete labels (Delis et al., 1978).

Presentation Variables

Serial-Position Effect

Events happen in time. This applies to individual words in a list or events in life. Their sequence is often a major determinant of what is recalled. The classic *serial-position effect* is a U-shaped recall function, in which *primacy* reflects the enhanced retention of the beginning of the sequence and *recency* is the enhanced recall of the end of the sequence. According to the modal model of memory, the serial-position effect reflects the independent contributions of two types of memory (Atkinson & Shiffrin, 1968). Primacy is said to be due to long-term memory for first list items, which typically are rehearsed more and have more opportunity to be elaborated on in memory than later items. Recency is due to short-term memory for the final items, which are typically recalled first during output, before forgetting can occur. This explanation matches our earlier discussion of the distinction between elaborative rehearsal (of the primacy items) and maintenance rehearsal (of the recency items). Thus, the serial-position effect may be due to differential encoding.

However, serial-position curves can be readily obtained under experimental conditions that are not in accord with the dual-memory model. For instance, recency effects are sometimes found in recall of lists from long-term memory. Recalling events from the previous school year, or naming the U.S. presidents, produces a U-shaped curve with both primacy and recency. In each, the recent items are indeed recalled from long-term and not short-term memory. (Serial-position effects are discussed in Chapters 6, 7, and 8.)

Isolation Effects and Vividness

One commonly held belief about memory is that unusual or distinctive material is better remembered. Helena von Restorff, a Berlin Ph.D. of the 1930s, studied this phenomenon. In presenting a list of to-be-remembered items, the manner of presentation of one item was made distinctive. For example, if the other words were printed in black, one word would be printed in red. If the list consisted mostly of words, one item would be a number. The distinctive item, distinctive in the context of the list, was usually learned more quickly or remembered better. This effect has been called the *von Restorff effect,* or the *isolation effect,* in reference to isolating one item in the list. A nice example of the isolation effect is a television commercial that contains no sound whatsoever; the message is signed by an actor, and printed at the bottom of the screen. The sudden silence is the midst of the other attention-seeking ads certainly stands out.

The von Restorff effect is typically attributed to enhanced encoding of the distinctive item. Perceptually, an isolated item stands out from the others. It should garner more attention, be rehearsed more, and possibly be more elaborated in memory. Such explanations define a "differential processing" view (Waddill & McDaniel, 1998). Brain-wave measures of orienting indicate subjects notice and attend to the isolated item (Fabiani & Donchin, 1995). However, enhanced recall of the isolated item might be because it is more distinctive during retrieval. Against a blur of memories of many similar items, the isolated item may be distinguished and thus recalled (Hunt, 1995).

Something of an isolation effect can occur in remembering characteristics of individuals. Atypical behavior from someone we know well would stand out and might then be well remembered. This notion was demonstrated in a study by Hastie and Kumar (1979). Hypothetical individuals were described by trait labels to induce a personality impression in the participants. For instance, someone would be described as intelligent, clever, quick, and smart. After this, a list of 20 to-be-remembered behaviors of this hypothetical person was presented. Most were congruent with the initial personality labels, for example, the person was said to have won a chess tournament, attended a symphony concert, or liked reading history. In addition, one or a few incongruent behaviors were presented: He failed math twice, or he was always getting lost. When the participants tried to recall the list of behaviors, the incongruent ones were usually recalled better than the congruent behaviors, especially when the incongruent behaviors were few in number. For example, whereas about 50 percent of the congruent behaviors were recalled, a single incongruent behavior in the list was recalled 77 percent of the time.

Isolation effects occur in animal memory also. Rats were trained to make the correct sequence of turns in a maze with seven choice points. One choice point was made distinctive by painting stripes on the wall and putting sandpaper on the floor. Separate groups of rats had the second, fifth, or seventh choice made distinctive in this manner. Fewer errors were made in learning the correct turn at the distinctive choice point than in the others (McLaughlin et al., 1968).

Other research has shown a more complex and interesting pattern of results when memory for the whole list is considered. Whereas the isolated item is well recalled, this may come at the expense of memory for items before and after it in the list. For example, suppose the following partial list of words is presented: table, dog, tree, grass, COLUMBUS, school, coffee, and soup. The enhanced recall of the distinctive item (COLUMBUS) can impair recall of the words just before it (GRASS and TREE). Tulving (1969) called this a *retrograde amnesic effect*. Retrograde amnesia is defined as forgetting for the past, and is usually used in the context of a traumatic cause for the amnesia. In Tulving's experiment, the participants did not actually experience trauma from the word COLUMBUS, but the unusual word was surprising enough to have a retrograde amnesic-like effect.

In addition, the distinctive item may impair memory for the words that follow it. Detterman (1975) found an *anterograde amnesic effect,* in which words after the distinctive one were forgotten. In the preceding example, SCHOOL and COFFEE might not be recalled. The results of one of Detterman's experiments are shown in Figure 9.3. A list of 15 words was presented auditorily, with the distinctive item in the eighth position being presented much more loudly than the remainder of the words. The graph nicely illustrates the enhanced retention of the von Restorff item, the corresponding retrograde amnesic effect (the shaded portion before the distinctive item), and the anterograde amnesic effect (the shaded portion after). Note also that the first and last items of the list are recalled better than the middle items, which we earlier labeled primacy and recency effects.

A related question concerns the effect of *vividness*. Information that is presented in a way that is attention grabbing, emotionally interesting, and image provoking should be remembered better. However, in contrast to the isolation effect, vivid presentation does not necessarily lead to better memory. The advantage to vivid presentation tends to be small and inconsistent, as found in various comparisons of TV versus audio presentation, video versus reading, or film versus still-picture modes of presentation (Taylor & Thompson, 1982). One difference between successful demonstrations of isolation effects and the absence of such effects in vividness experiments is mainly one of procedure. In studies of the isolation effect, the subjects are given one distinctive item in an otherwise homogeneous list. In terms of a differential-processing hypothesis, the isolated item can be selectively attended to, rehearsed, or elaborated on at the expense of other items that suffer reduced processing. In many vividness studies, separate groups of participants are presented the same target information in more vivid or less vivid presentation formats. The participants can

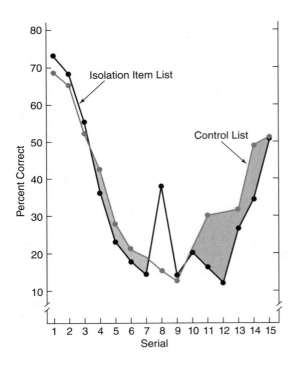

FIGURE 9.3   The Isolation Effect in the Recall of a List of 15 Words. A distinctive item occurs at the eighth position in the experimental list. The distinctive item is well recalled, but there is some forgetting of the items that preceded and followed it in the list.

Source: From "The von Restorff Effect and Induced Amnesia: Production by Manipulation of Sound Intensity," by D. K. Detterman, 1975, *Journal of Experimental Psychology: Human Learning and Memory, 1,* p. 626. Copyright © 1975 by the American Psychological Society. Reprinted with permission.

devote all of their attention to the material at hand, whether it is vividly presented or not. Attention and rehearsal need not be divided between vivid and nonvivid material. The point is that if several presentations are made to an audience, a single vivid presentation likely would be remembered better than the less vivid ones. If the audience sees only a single presentation, a vivid one would necessarily not be preferentially remembered.

For instance, Bretz and Thompsett (1992) studied the effectiveness of different formats for a 3-day training program on "manufacturing resource planning" offered to employees at Kodak Corporation. A "traditional" method of training involved mostly lectures. An "integrative-learning" format included several manipulations that would seem to define vivid presentation. Sessions began with activities to create a positive relaxed atmosphere, posters summarizing the basic principles of the program were displayed on the walls, the concepts were reinforced through group activities (fabricating games, simulations, discussions, or group presentations on the course content). After the training sessions, factual information that was presented during the program was assessed with recall and multiple-choice-type questions. The integrative-learning subjects performed no better than did the traditional group on these tests. This is surprising given what we know about encoding variables. There are several lessons here. One is that our commonsense expectations need to be tempered by actual research applications. Second, given what we know about vividness effects, possibly any one of the integrative-learning manipulations would have been effective alone. But 3 days of varied activities nullifies the distinctiveness of each. We should note that participants rated the integrative program as more enjoyable than the traditional format. So even if integrative learning was not more effective in promoting learning, there may be other reasons for choosing it.

Spacing Effects

Hardly any student has not heard the admonition, "Study every night, don't wait and cram at the last minute." Thus, you are already familiar with the *spacing effect:* Spaced practice (or distributed practice, as it is sometimes called) leads to better retention than does massed practice. If something is to be studied two (or more) times, it is better to distribute the repetitions than to mass them close together. Like the serial-position curve, this is an amazingly general observation of learning (Dempster, 1996).

Why does spacing repetitions produce better retention? Several theories have been offered over the years. No single explanation seems to accommodate all of the available data, so contemporary theories often advocate two-process accounts. (According to the principle of parsimony, when the simpler explanation won't suffice, we can adopt a more complex one.) Each explanation has led to novel experimental tests that offer insights into the effects of spacing.

Hypothesis 1.   A second massed presentation of an item interferes with ongoing processing of the first presentation. One sense of this is that short-term memory for the first presentation is displaced by the second presentation. Processing the first presentation (referred to here as P1) is terminated prematurely by a massed repetition (or P2), and so the massed practice decrement is due to poorer retention of P1. We might refer to this as the *retrograde amnesia* hypothesis.

One way to assess whether P1 is less remembered during massed, as opposed to spaced, trials is to tag P1 and P2 differently. That is, present some slightly different information along with the two presentations and see which is remembered better. By presenting the target word in different modalities at P1 and P2, and then asking participants to recall not only the items, but whether they had been auditory or visual, we find that it is the second item that is less well remembered (Hintzman, Block, & Summers, 1973). This fact, and other evidence, weighs against this hypothesis that the first item suffers interference with massed repetitions.

Hypothesis 2.   Participants attend less to a second presentation when it is repeated too soon. The idea here is that participants are attempting to remember a list of items, and so processing must be distributed across the items. A massed P2, seeming so familiar, is skipped through to devote more time to other items. Shaughnessy, Zimmerman, and Underwood (1972) actually let participants pace themselves through the list by giving them the remote control to the slide projector. They skipped through immediate repetitions, but spent more time on repetitions that occurred after longer delays. Thus, this can be labeled an *attention-deficit* hypothesis.

Further support for the attention-deficit explanation of massed repetitions comes from monitoring eye movements across a photograph. The number of fixations decreases to pictures that are presented again in a list, as compared to novel pictures. Eye movements are reinstated by a slight change in the image, such as changing the location of objects in the picture (Ryan, Althoff, Whitlow, & Chen, 2000).

Hypothesis 3.   Spacing repetitions of a target item leads to slightly different encodings. Long-term recall is enhanced by having multiple retrieval cues, or routes, to the target. When the two occurrences are more widely spaced, they might be encoded somewhat differently into memory. For example, given the list TABLE, FORK, SCHOOL, BOOK, TABLE, the first TABLE may be encoded as a kitchen item and the second as a classroom item. Recalling either FORK or BOOK might aid retrieval of the target word TABLE. This explanation is known as the *encoding variability hypothesis.* Back-to-back TABLEs are likely to be encoded similarly, both as kitchen items, for example.

Encoding variability suggests that massed repetitions might not be so bad if P1 and P2 are encoded differently, just as they supposedly are when repetitions are spaced. Different encodings can be simulated by using homographs, or words that have two different meanings, as stimuli and biasing their encodings. For example, the homograph FOOT is first presented in the context of "inch," and the second time in the context of "toe." Words presented in this fashion do not show a massed-practice decrement (e.g., Gartman & Johnson, 1972). That is, using our previous example, FOOT is well remembered even though the two presentations were massed. This is a contrived manipulation, and some have argued that the homographs are actually different words (Martin, 1975), but it does illustrate the reasoning behind encoding variability. The general idea is that items may be encoded differently when they are encountered on separate occasions.

Variable encoding can be manipulated in other ways. Bellezza and Young (1989) compared different encodings in a paired-associate learning study. In the consistent encoding condition, a given stimulus–response (or S1–R) pair was presented twice. In the variable encoding condition, the response word was presented twice, each time paired with a different unrelated stimulus word (S1–R and S2–R). When the S–R pairs were massed, variable stimulus encodings led to better learning that did the consistent encodings. Switching stimuli in the massed pairs reduced the decrement otherwise seen when the same S–R pairs repeated. However, if the repetitions are spaced, recall of the response was more likely when the stimulus–response pairs were the same each time.

One consensus idea that has emerged from all the research on distributed practice is that "a little forgetting may be good for learning" (Cuddy & Jacoby, 1982; Krug, Davis, & Glover, 1990). With a massed second presentation, there is a false feeling of knowing when in fact the material is not known well at all. After a longer spacing between the two presentations, the participant may recognize that the item has been temporarily forgotten, which should heighten processing of the repetition. In addition, longer spacings give an opportunity to practice recalling the target material from long-term memory.

Effect of Retention Interval.   As universal as the spacing effect is, there is one deviation to the spaced-is-better rule: If retention is tested after a short delay interval after the second presentation, massing is sometimes better. The general design of studies that combine spacing interval and retention interval is illustrated in Table 9.1. For example, Balota, Duchek, & Paullin, (1989) used a modified paired-associate procedure with college-aged and elderly adult subjects. Spacing varied from having back-to-back presentations to pre-

TABLE 9.1   Schematic Design of Massed (M) and Spaced (S) Presentations Followed by Immediate Testing or Delayed Testing

		Test Results
Massed presentations, immediate testing	P1–P2–Test	
Spaced presentations, immediate testing	P1–––P2–Test	M > S
Massed presentations, delayed testing	P1–P2–––Test	
Spaced presentations, delayed testing	P1–––P2–––Test	S > M

sentations separated by 20 other items. Item pairs were sometimes tested immediately, or after a delay of about 20 items. A portion of their results are shown in Figure 9.4. Both younger and older subjects recalled more massed items on the immediate test and recalled more spaced items on the delayed test.

Other examples can be cited from several diverse procedures, using animals or humans, and involving shorter or longer time spans. In the Brown-Peterson short-term memory distractor task (Chapter 8), a triplet of to-be-remembered words is presented twice in immediate succession, or 8 seconds apart. The participants are distracted for several seconds and then attempt to recall the words. Immediate repetition led to better recall after 2 or 4 seconds; spaced presentations led to better recall after 8- or 16-second delay intervals (Peterson, Hillner, & Saltzman, 1962). Medin (1974) found a similar effect in monkeys using a delayed matching task. The animals were shown some food placed beneath one of two objects, and the monkeys had to remember which object concealed food. The correct object varied from trial to trial. Two massed presentations were better when the monkey only had to remember for 6 seconds, but spaced presentations were better if the animal had to wait a full minute before being allowed to retrieve the food.

The spacing of repeated television commercials also shows a retention-interval interaction. Subjects watched a TV news show containing commercial breaks. A target ad was

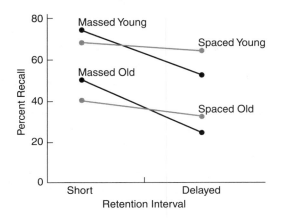

Spacing × Delay

FIGURE 9.4   Mean Percent Correct Recall in a Continuous Paired-Associate Procedure by Younger and Older Subject Groups. Items were presented either massed (presented 1 pair apart) and spaced (presented 20 items apart), and tested shortly after (2 items later in the list) or after a longer delay (20 items later).

Source: From "Age-Related Differences in the Impact of Spacing, Lag, and Retention Interval," by D. A. Balota, J. M. Duchek, and R. Paullin, 1989, *Psychology and Aging, 4,* p. 7. Copyright © 1989 by the American Psychological Association. Adapted with permission.

repeated, with either one or four other commercials between the repetitions, thus defining the massed versus spaced manipulation. Two participant groups, college students and elderly adults, remembered more after massed repetitions when they were tested immediately after the show. If memory was tested a day later, spaced commercials were recalled better (Singh et al., 1994).

There is a significant implication from these sorts of results. One can arrange a situation to make learning appear to be easy or one could arrange it to make learning lasting. Imagine having several things to learn (facts, vocabulary words, or skills as examples). Practicing a single fact or skill in a massed fashion should lead to rapid improvement. With massed practice, you may attain a superior level of performance during the study phase. Intermixing the facts or skills in the practice sequence will slow learning, as you apparently forget from one trial to the next. Yet in the long run, learning and transfer will be increased by intermixing rather than massing the study items (Schmidt & Bjork, 1992).

The previously mentioned facts and speculations suggest that there may be an optimal arrangement of massed and spaced repetitions. One novel approach is to start with massed repetitions and gradually increase the length of the spacings. Landauer and Bjork (1978) put the method of "expanded rehearsal" to good use in teaching names, and Rea and Modigliani (1985) used it to teach multiplication tables and spelling lists. Bahrick advocates this spacing pattern as a preferred means of entering academic information into a lasting long-term memory (see, e.g., Bahrick & Phelps, 1987). Bahrick compared the learning of Spanish vocabulary in daily, weekly, or monthly study sessions. The more massed conditions seemed to produce better recall, for example, from one day to the next as compared to from one month to the next month. However, 30 days after learning was completed, the massed practice conditions showed a huge loss, whereas the spaced group had virtually no forgetting (Bahrick, 1979).

Although we are all familiar with the spacing effect, at least one researcher claims it is not practiced enough in education (Dempster, 1988). For example, textbooks could be written that repeat certain ideas from chapter to chapter, thus ensuring repetition and spacing. Semester and quarter systems do not allow for the widely spaced repetitions (over intervals of months) that Bahrick thinks are effective.

Generation Effect

In most of the experiments presented so far in this book, the researcher presented the to-be-remembered material. The participant looks or listens and tries to remember. An alternative means of presentation is to have the participant involved in presenting the to-be-recalled items. Slamecka and Graf (1978) described a procedure in which their participants generated the target items in response to certain cues. For example, in the following word pairs, fill in the blanks with a word that is opposite in meaning: HOT: _____; STOP: __. Participants who generated the words COLD and GO were more likely to recall these words later than did subjects who simply read the word pairs. Numbers that are answers to simple math problems are remembered if participants do the arithmetic themselves rather than simply reading the results (Crutcher & Healy, 1989). The *generation effect* is increased memory performance on study material that is generated by the participant rather than being externally provided. The generation effect has been shown in a variety of situations. Enhanced memory occurs in free recall of the generated words, in cued recall in which the first word of each pair is presented as a cue for the second, and by recognition in a multiple-choice format (Burns, 1990, who also notes some complications).

Participant generation of the target material seems to induce elaborative processing that the read-only condition does not. The words must be meaningfully comprehended, and the participant must attend to the relationship between the cues and generated items. Having the participant generate the target word also mimics what will be required later during testing: Produce the to-be-remembered item in response to some cue. This is exactly what the transfer-appropriate processing account discussed in the last chapter would predict: Recall is improved when the encoding and retrieval (or testing) requirements are more nearly alike.

Limitations of Elaborative Processing

I have described several variables that can lead to improved recall and that support the general claim that elaborative processing leads to better encoding. Are there any limits to the benefits of elaborative processing? Are there tasks for which elaboration does not help, or maybe even interferes with learning?

Implicit memory may be one such exception (Schacter, Chin, & Ochsner, 1993; see Chapter 7). Implicit memory refers to tests of retention that occur without reference to the previous learning task, and therefore in the absence of explicit awareness. For example, after subjects have read a list of words, instead of asking for explicit recall of the words, we might test recall implicitly with a word-fragment completion test. Some letters and blanks are given, for example, C_A_K. The missing letters can be filled in several ways (e.g., CHALK or CRACK). A priming effect occurs when the previously seen words are offered as solutions in the word-completion task: The studied words are "primed" in memory, and so are readily "seen" in the fragments. Implicit tests of memory are often coupled with incidental learning at the input stage. The participants are not told to learn the material, and at the output, we do not remind the participants of their previous encounter with the material. As it turns out, many of the variables that enhance explicit memory have little or no effect on implicit memory.

1. *Depth of processing.* During the study phase, the subjects can be requested to make shallow or deep judgments about the list items. Deep processing leads to better explicit memory, but does not affect the likelihood of completing word fragments with the studied items (Bowers & Schacter, 1990; Graf et al., 1984).
2. *Serial position.* Word completion can be tested explicitly by asking the subjects to complete the stems with words from the study list. In this case, a serial-position effect was obtained: More words from the beginning and end of the study list were recalled. Given implicit memory-test instructions ("Complete these word fragments with the first words that come to mind"), there was no serial-position effect (Brooks, 1994).
3. *Generation effect.* Explicit memory is better for target items the participant generates than for items simply read. Thus, if given HOT: C__D to study, COLD will be remembered better than if the blanks had been filled in. This *generation effect* occurs with

implicit testing, but only if the same fragments are tested as were used during the generation stage. Testing with HOT: C_L_ will not produce priming facilitation (Gardiner, 1987).

4. *Modality–specific–learning.* Implicit memory is reduced if the words are presented auditorily and then the word fragments are visual. Explicit memory is less affected by changes in sensory modality. Also, a picture is recalled better than a word (i.e., a picture of a dog versus the word DOG) in an explicit-memory test. Word-fragment completion is better after studying the word DOG than after seeing a picture (Weldon & Roediger, 1987).

Another potential limitation of elaboration is particular to verbal elaboration. Sometimes verbal encoding of nonverbal information, such as pictures or faces, leads to less accurate retention. In essence, we remember the words we used to encode an event rather than the event itself. A prime example of this *verbal overshadowing* is memory for faces (Schooler, Ryan, & Reder, 1996). In trying to describe a face, people tend to focus on those features that are verbalizable (such as eye color or the shape of the lips) and not on features that are difficult to articulate (such as the configural arrangement of facial features) but that may be more important for face recognition. Verbal overshadowing occurs in other tasks, such as remembering the taste of specific wines. Novice and expert wine tasters were asked to taste and verbally describe several wines. Later, they were given a recognition test to distinguish the tasted from new wines. The untrained tasters did worse when they had verbally described the earlier wines. Not having a sophisticated vocabulary for describing wine, the participants tended to remember what they said rather than what they tasted. Expert tasters were not impaired by verbalization; presumably, their vocabulary matched their subtle taste discriminations (Melcher & Schooler, 1996).

Learner Variables

The learner brings a number of characteristics to the learning situation. Factors such as age, gender, personality, and learning style are discussed in the final chapter of this text. Here a number of other learner variables that can influence encoding are considered, including the intention to learn, the presence of incentives, interest in the target material, and the level of arousal.

Incidental versus Intentional Learning

A paradox involving everyday memory is that often we just seem to spontaneously remember things without any deliberate intention to remember and without any mnemonic preparation. You can probably remember what you had for breakfast this morning and something you read earlier in the newspaper. This is *incidental learning*. At other times, in order to remember, we need to deliberately study, rehearse, and so on. This is *intentional learning*. How necessary is intention to remember? To anticipate the discussion that follows, how much we learn and remember is more a function of how we think about the material and less about our intention to remember it.

The general experimental design used to demonstrate incidental learning is to present a series of words with instructions to the subjects to process the words in different ways. They might be asked to state whether the word has an *e* in it or is typed in uppercase or lowercase letters. These orienting tasks involve little cognitive work, what we earlier called shallow processing. Alternatively, the participants might be asked to rate the pleasantness of the words or to assign the word to a semantic category (Craik & Tulving, 1975; Hyde & Jenkins, 1969). These orienting tasks require deeper processing. (We earlier saw a different example of shallow and deep processing in Bower and Karlin's study of face memory.) After this, the participants are given a surprise test of memory. More of the words are recalled that had received semantic analysis, and the participants who performed the deeper processing recalled as many words as participants who were told in advance about the memory test. Incidental recall can be as good as intentional. Sample results from Hyde and Jenkins's (1969) study are shown in Table 9.2.

Incidental learning occurs as a function of a variety of cognitive operations. Several examples have already been presented in this chapter. Faces were remembered better when students made personality judgments about them (Bower & Karlin, 1974), and objects in a photograph were remembered better when subjects thought about using the objects (Bransford et al., 1977). These studies employed the incidental learning design. Even experts sometimes remember better incidentally. Medical students and medical school faculty were given patient protocols containing about 20 bits of information, mostly laboratory test results. The participants were asked to diagnose the patient or to try to memorize the case data. The medical specialists who made a diagnosis recalled more specific facts than did the students who diagnosed or memorized. Paradoxically, the physicians actually recalled less when they tried to memorize (Norman, Brooks, & Allen, 1989).

This is not to say that the intention to learn is without effect. An intention to learn can bring to bear additional cognitive resources, such as rehearsal, imaging, or elaboration,

TABLE 9.2   Number of Words Recalled by Participants Given Intentional or Incidental Learning Instructions Combined with Different Processing Instructions

Group	Instruction	Number Recalled (of 24)
Incidental learning groups		
	1. How pleasant is the word?	16.3
	2. Is there an *e* in the word?	9.4
	3. How many letters are in the word?	9.9
Intentional learning groups	"Try and remember these words"	
	1. How pleasant is the word?	16.6
	2. Is there an *e* in the word?	10.4
	3. How many letters are in the word?	12.4
	4. (No other task)	16.1

Source: Hyde & Jenkins, 1973.

that might not otherwise be engaged. Research on incidental learning makes the point that a variety of ways of processing information will facilitate remembering.

Incentives

The psychology literature on reinforcement clearly shows that reward can increase responding (e.g., Bolles, 1975; Spence, 1956). Can reinforcers also be used to increase performance in memory tasks? The experimental data indicate that once a subject has committed to learn, reward has little additional effect. When separate groups of college students were offered different sums of money for each word recalled, 10 cents versus 1 cent, there was no difference in the number of words recalled. Out of 40 words, the dime group recalled 55 percent whereas the penny group recalled 51 percent (Nelson, 1976). In another study, offering $10 to participants if they were among the best in the experiment did not produce any better memory than not offering an incentive (Nilsson, 1987). Given that the participants were motivated and were trying to remember to begin with, as is typical of college student participants, the amounts offered had no additional effect.

There is an important limitation to the preceding generalization, based on whether each participant received a single reward amount or was offered different amounts for different items. In instrumental conditioning with animals, contrast effects occur when the rat experiences different reward amounts. A given reward is more effective when offered in contrast to a smaller reward (see Chapter 4). Something similar occurs when human participants experience multiple reward amounts. If students are informed that some of the to-be-remembered words are worth more money and some less, they now remember more of the dime words and fewer of the penny words (66 percent versus 49 percent; Nelson, 1976). Cohen (1983) found a similar effect by designating some words as important: Again, more of the important words were recalled. In these cases, a rational strategy is employed: Given a fixed amount of time for rehearsal, devote it to the high-value words and not to the low-value words. This is not unlike what students do in juggling their work load among courses: Devote more time to the important courses (maybe psychology of learning) and less to other classes.

What about incentives offered after learning, at the time of testing? Again, differences in reward amount have little effect here. In one study, a list of 75 words was studied. One week later, the students came back to the lab and attempted to recall as many words as possible. After this first test, some participants were offered $1 for each additional word they could recall. The average number recalled was 5, the same as by the participants not offered the incentive but simply asked to try and remember some more (Nelson, 1976; see also Nilsson, 1987).

A few caveats are in order here. The promise of an incentive for remembering does not affect memory itself but rather behaviors that will lead to better retention (such as rehearsal or cognitive elaboration). Also, the previously described experiments used college students, who were probably intrinsically motivated to try their best regardless of incentive. There may have been little room for further improvement in the incentive conditions. The use of incentives has even been criticized as undermining intrinsic motivation (Kohn, 1993). Incentives may be more important in the real world, where rewards might motivate individuals who are not even attempting to learn or recall.

Interest

Having a personal *interest* in the to-be-learned material will usually increase retention. Interest affects attention and contact with the material, and it may lead to deeper cognitive processing of the material.

People with interests in certain topics seem to readily acquire new information within that domain. Some of this is because prior knowledge facilitates acquiring new knowledge. Experts more easily acquire new information in their field of expertise than do novices. However, interest also contributes in other ways. In one study, British soccer (they call it football) fans were asked to memorize lists of football scores. The fans were informed that some scores were real and some were simulated. The degree of expertise of the fans predicted memory for actual scores but not for simulated scores. Emotional involvement with favored and rival teams led to better recall of the real scores. Simulated scores did not evoke this interest because they had no implications for real standings among the teams. This is a nice example of when even expertise in a field does not guarantee better memory (Morris, Tweedy, & Gruneberg, 1985).

Arousal

We could expect arousal to facilitate learning, and generally it does. One can almost always find this commonsense result, but equally as often, the findings must be qualified by interacting variables. One limitation is that the term *arousal* is ambiguous and has different meanings as a variable in psychological research. Arousal can refer to a psychological state of attention or alertness; to physiological arousal as assessed by measures of heart rate, galvanic skin response (GSR), or EEG; or to a trait, such as anxiousness or impulsivity, indicated by self-report ratings.

Another important qualification is that the optimal level of arousal for any given task varies. Performance is usually better at some intermediate level of arousal and is less efficient at both lower and higher levels. A corollary to this is that different tasks have different optimal levels. These two statements together define the *Yerkes-Dodson law* (1908): Performance follows an inverted U-shaped curve, with peak performance occurring at intermediate levels of arousal and decreased performance at higher or lower levels (see Mandler [1992] for a contemporary discussion). As a hypothetical example, remembering facts from a classroom lecture might be inhibited if you are either too fatigued or too hyper. It is also likely that taking an exam or demonstrating video game skills requires different optimal arousal levels than does classroom learning. The difficulty that this poses for research is that any arousal we introduce as experimenters must be added to an existing baseline level of arousal present in the individual, which is often unknown.

A real-world example of the Yerkes-Dodson law is the recall by 3- and 4-year olds of a hurricane they had experienced (Bahrick, Parker, Fivush, & Levitt, 1998). Arousal was defined by the amount of damage to the house produced by the storm: High arousal was assumed in cases where the house was penetrated, moderate arousal if there was extensive outside damage, and low arousal if the damage was minimal. The number of facts recalled as a function of arousal level are shown in Figure 9.5. More was recalled by the moderately stressed children than by those presumed to have experienced lower or higher levels of arousal.

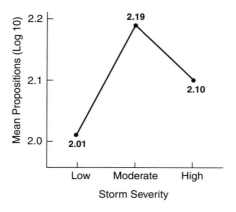

FIGURE 9.5   Mean number of facts recalled (the means are log-transformed) by 3- and 4-year olds as a function of hurricane damage.

Source: From "The effects of stress on young children's memory for a natural disaster," by L. E. Bahrick, J. F. Parker, R. Fivush, & M. Levitt, 1998, *Journal of Experimental Psychology: Applied, 4,* p. 318. Copyright © 1998 by the American Psychological Association. Reprinted with permission.

There are several kinds of evidence that suggest arousal is important for learning. Arousal has been manipulated directly through the administration of stimulant drugs and indirectly through correlations with circadian rhythms. We can also consider the effects of extremely low levels of arousal, such as sleep (see Box 9.2), and extremely high levels of arousal, such as that produced by strong emotions (discussed separately in a following section).

Stimulant Drugs.   Stimulant drugs that increase central nervous system arousal should also increase learning. The stimulant strychnine, a poison when taken in higher doses, was an ingredient in tonics once prescribed for memory loss and forgetfulness (Essman, 1983, p. 131). The behaviorist psychologist John Watson claimed the only reason he passed his final exam in Greek was that he drank a quart of cola syrup, which contains caffeine, while cramming overnight (Watson, 1936). There is some experimental evidence to support these anecdotes. Low doses of strychnine increase conditioning and maze learning (e.g., Leccese & Grant, 1980). Human eye-blink conditioning is enhanced when the stimulant amphetamine is administered (and retarded by the depressant amobarbital; Franks & Trouton, 1958). However, it is unclear whether such stimulants actually increase learning (e.g., by facilitating encoding) or simply affect performance (e.g., reducing fatigue) (Essman, 1983).

Unfortunately, there are no simple effects of most stimulants on learning. Caffeine, a drug commonly consumed outside of the laboratory, has produced complex interactions with other variables such as personality, gender, age, the time of day, and the type of memory task (Hogervorst et al., 1998; Revelle et al., 1980). Immediate free recall of word lists by women was, in one case, impaired following a dose of caffeine (Erikson et al., 1985), and, in another study, enhanced (Arnold et al., 1987). Caffeine had little consistent effect on men in either study. Why were women affected? In one case, a cognitive explanation was offered suggesting that caffeine-induced arousal interfered with rehearsal. In the other case, a biological explanation said that caffeine combined with estrogen levels to enhance arousal. Arousal is the common theme, but at two different levels of explanation.

Glucose and certain other sugars can increase remembering. Such effects have usually been obtained in elderly adults tested for recall of a prose paragraph but not with other tests such as the digit span or paired-associate learning (Hall et al., 1989). College students

B O X **9.2**

Sleep Learning

Does learning occur while we are asleep? An entire industry has developed around the promotion of sleep-learning tapes. Simply play the tape through a pillow speaker during the night and wake up the next morning refreshed and fluent in Spanish! But if the sleep state is one of low arousal, can anything really be learned then?

The results of many early studies were inconsistent, sometimes showing learning and sometimes not (see Aarons, 1976). The discrepancy seemed to be due to whether the participants were actually asleep when the tapes were played. No learning occurred if the material was presented when the participants were truly asleep, as verified by EEG and REM recordings (not REM the band, but rapid eye movements). For example, Emmons and Simon (1956) presented a 10-word list *46* times during the night. The list was played only when EEGs indicated the participant was in deep sleep. The tape otherwise was stopped. When tested with a five-option multiple-choice test the next day, the participants recognized a hardly encouraging 25 percent of the target words, as compared to a chance level of 20 percent. On the other hand, researchers who adopted a pragmatic philosophy about instruction would simply play the tapes from lights-out until wake-up the next morning. Some learning did occur under these conditions, but most probably occurred when the participants were drifting off to sleep or during awakenings during the night.

Some forms of learning do occur during sleep. Simple classical conditioning and habituation (a decrease in orienting reactions to an irrelevant stimulus) have been demonstrated to occur in sleeping animals and humans (see Badia, 1990).

Why are dreams so poorly recalled? If you are awakened during REM sleep, often a dream is recalled. If you are awakened minutes after leaving REM the dream has already slipped away. One theory is that dreams are briefly retained in short-term memory, but in the absence of sufficient arousal, the dream is not encoded into long-term memory (Koulack & Goodenough, 1976). Of course, dreams may be forgotten for other reasons discussed in this chapter: the images and events in our dreams are not always meaningful; they are not logically organized; and they do not conform to our waking schemas. There seem to be gender differences in dream recall: Women report higher frequencies in dream diaries (Martinetti, 1989). We can only speculate as to the reasons for this. Possibly, women's dreams are more organized and meaningful.

Sleep *after* learning has a different effect than sleep during learning. A classic study by Jenkins and Dallenbach (1924) showed that 8 hours spent sleeping after learning was more beneficial than 8 hours spent awake. One interpretation of the results is that sleep protected the newly learned material from interference due to waking activity. Recent research has suggested a different explanation: Sleep is an important time for consolidation of the memory traces into permanent memory. During sleep, those neural elements that were active during learning become reactivated during sleep. This has been referred to by analogy to "off-line processing" (Stickgold, Hobson, & Fosse, 2001). In back-to-back articles published in the journal *Science,* researchers showed that postlearning REM sleep enhanced learning of spatial mazes by rats (Wilson & McNaughton, 1994) and an eye movement motor skill in humans (Karni et al., 1994). Disruption of the REM stages of sleep impaired later retention. So, in a sense, learning does occur during sleep—the learning that began before sleep commenced.

Remembering under Anesthesia?

Learning while anesthetized poses similar research problems to sleep learning, primarily knowing whether the subject is truly unconscious. Different anesthetics affect different parts of the body, and so there may be some consciousness even though pain and movement are blocked (Andrade, 1995). In experimental tests of the effects of low doses of inhaled anesthetic drugs, memory on verbal tasks such as the digit span and free recall, was poorer (Adam, 1979). Interestingly, in one well-controlled study, implicit memory was found after surgical anesthesia (Kihlstrom et al., 1990). Pairs of moderately associated words (such as TABLE and KITCHEN) were

(continued)

Box 9.2   Continued

repetitively read to patients during surgery, with the intention of strengthening the words' associations. Half of the participants heard one list of word pairs, and the other half heard a second list. Thus, the unheard lists provided baseline rates of free associations later. On two occasions after surgery, the participants were given free-association instruc-

tions. The first word in each pair was presented and the participants were asked to respond with the first word that came to mind. More of the moderately associated words presented under anesthesia were recalled than if these associations had not been heard. Thus, implicit memory may be one form of learning that can occur under low levels of arousal.

did not benefit from the extra sugar. One explanation for this difference is that the elderly are more likely to have poor regulation of blood glucose levels (Reige et al., 1985).

Does arousal facilitate memory formation, or does it simply increase alertness and attention to the task? We would not be surprised if attentive participants remembered more. An arousal hypothesis suggests a more central role for these stimulants, that of enhancing memory formation in the brain. One way to separate the potential effects of stimulants on attention versus memory is to administer the drug *after* the learning trial is over. The drug cannot enhance attention to a task that is already completed, but it could enhance encoding of the memory into a long-term trace. Elderly humans given glucose after they studied the prose passage had improved retention a day later. The control group that received saccharin after studying, a sweet taste but without the sugar to boost arousal, performed less well (Manning, Parsons, & Gold, 1992). In another study, mice were shocked after drinking from a water tube (Stone, Rudd, & Gold, 1990). Glucose was given after this conditioning trial. The mice were tested the next day for their willingness to drink from the water spout. The latency scores showed a dose–response curve characteristic of the Yerkes-Dodson law: A moderate dose of glucose promoted better retention (i.e., longer avoidance of the spout) than did either lower or higher doses.

Circadian Rhythms and Learning.   Arousal varies during the course of the waking day. Do circadian variations influence learning ability? In one study of digit span, a measure of short-term memory, performance peaked at about 10:30 A.M. and declined thereafter into the early evening hours (Blake, 1967; see right panel of Figure 9.6). Immediate recall of specific facts from a 1,500-word science article peaked even earlier in the morning: Correct recall was maximal at 8 A.M. and steadily declined thereafter, with a slight bump back up after lunch (Folkard & Monk, 1980; left, Figure 9.6). (These studies both used British students. I would be surprised to see U.S. students peaking at that hour in the morning.)

One difficulty in linking levels of arousal to circadian rhythms is the assumption that everyone has the same cycle. If people differ in their levels of alertness at different times of day (i.e., so-called morning "larks" and evening "owls"; Guthrie, Ash, & Bendapudi, 1995), there may be parallel differences in recall at different times of day. Indeed, one study found that morning people were more accurate in paragraph recall when tested at 9 A.M. than at 8 P.M., whereas evening people did better at the later testing time (Petros, Beckwith, & Anderson, 1990).

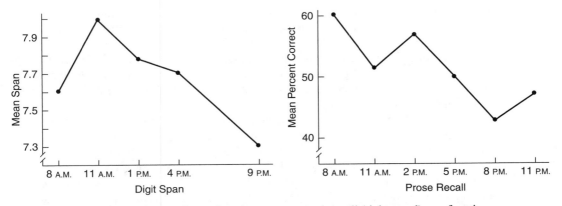

FIGURE 9.6 Digit-span recall (left panel) and prose-paragraph recall (right panel) as a function of time of day of testing.

Source: (*Left panel*) Blake, 1967. (*Right panel*) From "Circadian Rhythms in Human Memory," by S. Folkard and T. H. Monk, 1980, *British Journal of Psychology, 71,* pp. 295–307. Reprinted with permission from the *British Journal of Psychology,* copyright © 1980 by The British Psychological Society.

Some Conclusions about Arousal.   An implicit assumption of arousal theories is that an aroused brain simply works better at consolidating information into a stable memory. It is as if once the brain is cranked up, anything thrown in will be remembered better. Apart from any hypothesized neural effects, we need to consider the broader influence of arousal on cognition. Arousal affects what we attend to and what is ignored, what and how we encode, and how efficiently we retrieve. The source of arousal will also have different effects. Arousal elicited by a startling unknown sound will affect learning differently than arousal produced by loud but familiar background noise.

Emotions and Encoding

Are highly emotional events remembered better than neutral events? This question seems too easy and the answer seems too obvious. However, getting objective data to support our subjective impressions is not so easy. The two basic problems are determining whether what we recall is accurate and exactly how emotions influence remembering.

How Do Emotions Affect Memory?   First, emotional arousal will focus attention on certain aspects of a situation. Given our limited capacity to divide attention, this means that peripheral details may go unnoticed. In an experimental simulation of memory for an emotional event, a vignette (or story) was presented via a series of seven slides, and, simultaneously, the participants' eye movements were recorded. When one slide depicted an emotional outcome to the story (a child hit by a car), there were more fixations on the central details of the picture. These details were also recalled better than in the neutral condition, but peripheral details were not recalled as well in the emotional condition. Does this mean that overt attention alone explains memory for detail? No. In another version, the critical slide was presented for 180 milliseconds: long enough for a single eye fixation, but not long enough for eye movements to differ between emotional and neutral slides. Nevertheless, central detail memory was better for the emotional slide (Christianson et al., 1991).

A second effect of emotion is to produce bodily arousal that could contribute to long-term memory formation. Epinephrine is released from the adrenal medulla during and after an emotional stressor, which activates receptors in the body, which in turn lead to stimulation of the amygdala in the brain. The amygdala has been implicated in the formation of long-term memory for emotional events in animal conditioning studies (McGaugh, 1991; Thompson & Gluck, 1991). Incidentally, glucose is hypothesized to be involved in an intermediate step in this process. We noted the effects of glucose on memory earlier.

Third, emotional events are distinctive. Often, they are not everyday experiences. Emotional events are talked about and thought about, and so they are well rehearsed and elaborated in memory (Heuer & Reisberg, 1992). In the extreme example of posttraumatic stress disorder, the memories replay and intrude into thoughts and dreams.

Thus, emotions incorporate several themes from this chapter: attention, arousal, distinctiveness, and elaboration. (Emotions may also affect retrieval, either to facilitate or inhibit recall. These latter possibilities are discussed in the next chapter.)

Flashbulb Memories.   One striking memory phenomenon that most of us have experienced is that of having a vivid memory for a surprising, emotional, and consequential event. For many of us, the precipitant is particular to our own lives, for example, a phone call conveying tragic news or a letter bringing unexpected good news. Others are for events that are shared by a community or a nation, such as the news of the attacks on September 11, 2001, or hearing of the death of Princess Diana or John Kennedy, Jr. Brown and Kulick (1977) used the term "flashbulb memories" to capture the essence of such memories. It is as if a picture of that moment when we heard the news is encoded into memory. This image is assumed to be complete, detailed, and accurate. Brown and Kulick proposed the existence of a special memory mechanism, triggered by surprising and emotional events, that immediately creates a record of the contents of consciousness at that moment. These memories are immune to forgetting. Presumably this mechanism evolved as a means of survival in primitive humans (and animals) to handle memory for consequential events that might recur.

The method introduced by Brown and Kulick to study flashbulb memories was to ask people if they remembered when they first learned of a significant news event, such as the assassination of President Kennedy or Martin Luther King. Even 13 years after the assassination of Kennedy and 8 years after the assassination of King, people reported photolike memories. These included details of where they were when they heard the news, what they were doing at the time, from whom or how they heard the news, their immediate affective reactions, and what they did next. Interestingly, among both black and white respondents, John Kennedy's death was an event that most frequently provoked a flashbulb memory. Martin Luther King's death was more often remembered in this manner by black Americans than by whites.

Neisser (1982) criticized the Brown and Kulick procedure on several grounds. What people claim they remember is not necessarily true, no matter how vivid the memory seems to be. Piaget distinctly remembered being kidnapped as a young child and often retold the story, although he later learned this had not happened (cited in Loftus & Ketcham, 1994).

Neisser also argues that the memories may be formed, not in a flashbulb instant, but in the hours or days afterwards, when people tell and retell their story. Indeed, people's recollections do have a news-reporting quality to them: when, where, why, who, and what.

Researchers next moved to questioning subjects soon after a traumatic experience and then retesting them months later. The accuracy of memory on the delayed second test is verified by comparison to the first memory test, a method which presupposes people remembered accurately during the first test. McClosky, Wible, and Cohen (1988) questioned people about flashbulb memories for the space shuttle *Challenger* explosion 1 week afterwards and again 9 months later. The participants evidenced remarkable consistency (94 percent overall) in their answers to specific questions about where they were, who told them, and so on. Over time, the memories did become more general and contained fewer details. But about 9 percent of the "facts" remembered 9 months later were inconsistent with the 1-week recollections, and about 6 percent of facts were forgotten. One could be impressed by the robustness of the memories: These are very good memories. Or, like McClosky and colleagues, one could focus on the forgetting: These memories were not perfect, unchanging, or immune to forgetting.

Is there a separate flashbulb mechanism? Maybe instead we should view memory as a continuum, with different factors such as surprise, emotionality, consequentiality, or rehearsal acting to push memories toward one end point or the other.

Eyewitness Memory and Emotional Arousal. Eyewitness recall may offer another source of data on the effect of emotional arousal on memory. Are witnesses to a crime or an accident, who have been exposed to an emotional event in a realistic situation, more or less likely to recall significant details? Once again, there is no simple answer, because recall is determined by a complex set of interacting variables. Emotional arousal may lead to focusing and retention of central details, but poorer retention for peripheral and unattended details. One example of this is labeled *weapons focus:* Victims or witnesses focus attention on a weapon, but possibly do not remember other details of the situation, such as the face of the perpetrator (Loftus, Loftus, & Messo, 1987). In one study of weapon focus, participants who thought they were waiting for an experiment heard an argument in the next room. Someone emerged from the room carrying either a pen or what appeared to be a bloody letter opener. The participants were then tested for face recognition of this person, which was the real purpose of the study. The perpetrator's picture was less often identified in the weapon condition than in the pen condition (cited in Loftus, 1979). An emotional witness and a nonemotional person might remember equal amounts of information, but different details of the situation.

Another variable in witness remembering is that of differential elaboration; some aspects of the situation are rehearsed and elaborated more than others. We saw an example of this with the von Restorff (or isolation) effect, in which enhanced learning about one item comes at a cost to memory for adjacent items.

A final variable to consider in comparing memory for emotional versus less emotional events is the length of the delay before recall is tested. Emotional stimuli are sometimes poorly recalled immediately after exposure to them, but are remembered better than nonemotional events on delayed tests days and weeks later; that is, unemotional stimuli are forgotten faster. In a laboratory demonstration of this effect, participants were given a list containing both emotional and neutral words. Emotionality was verified by GSR measures taken during presentation of the words. Fewer emotional words were recalled during a test given immediately after list presentation, about 80 percent versus 90 percent of the neutral words. On testing a week later, fewer of the neutral words were recalled, about 60 percent, as compared to nearly 70 percent of the emotional words (Parkin, Lewinsohn, & Folkard, 1982).

A traumatic experience may also produce retrograde or anterograde amnesic effects (or both), so that certain details will be forgotten due to their temporal placement relative to a startling event. Loftus and Burns (1982) showed a 2-minute video depicting a bank robbery, a film used by banks to instruct their employees on how to handle this kind of situation. Toward the end of one version of the film, a bank teller is shot, but this does not happen in the control version. Participants who viewed the first version of the film did not recall a critical fact shown just before the violent act: the number on a bystander's football jersey. Only 4 percent of those seeing the violent film remembered it, whereas 28 percent of the control participants did. Christianson and Nilsson (1984) found forgetting on the other side of the traumatic event. Their participants did not recall a critical detail that followed the arousing stimulus. These two studies thus show effects like those of Detterman's (1975) placement of a surprising word in the middle of a list of words: forgetting for information presented before (i.e., retrograde) and after (i.e., anterograde) the surprising stimulus.

Conclusions about Emotions and Memory.   Emotional arousal can facilitate encoding into memory. But knowing this fact will not tell us what details will be encoded. Remembering a suspect's face would be helpful to the police, but the victim's attention may have been focused on a weapon. Significant details that preceded or followed a startling moment may be forgotten. Rehearsal may elaborate some of the memories, but at the same time can introduce distortions. To this list, we can add other forgetting factors. Details may be remembered, but their temporal order is not, leading to misrecall of the sequence of events. Forgetting the source of what is remembered, some facts that were heard about or thought of, can lead to misrecall of these details as having been actually perceived (Johnson & Raye, 1981). We are therefore limited in our ability to make broad statements about the effects of emotion on the accuracy of memory.

Schemas

Schemas are outlines of general knowledge that are stored in semantic memory. Schemas, also called scripts, scenes, or frames, are ways of organizing knowledge. Schemas are often hypothesized to have a hierarchical structure, with packets of information stored at each level. One often-cited example is the "restaurant script," as listed in Table 9.3. At the top of the hierarchy is the label "going to a restaurant." The next level down has subordinate categories, such as entering, ordering, eating, and exiting. Within these categories is general knowledge about each step: Ordering involves reading the menu and telling the server what you want; exiting involves paying the bill and leaving a tip.

Alba and Hasher (1983) noted that there are several ways a schema can influence what is learned in a given situation.

TABLE 9.3   Restaurant Schema

1. Entering
    Customer enters
    Looks for table
    Sits down
2. Ordering
    Looks at menu
    Signals server
    Orders food
3. Eating
    Server brings food from kitchen
    Food brought to table
    Customer eats
4. Leaving
    Server brings check
    Customer leaves tip
    Customer pays cashier

1. *Selection.* Schemas guide selection of what is to be encoded, usually details that are relevant to the schema.
2. *Storage.* A schema can organize memory for events, providing an outline of where each new piece fits.
3. *Abstraction.* Common features across a number of similar experiences are abstracted and stored in the schema; specific details from any one event need not be retained.
4. *Retrieval.* A schema provides retrieval cues to guide and direct memory search.
5. *Normalization.* The schema may lead to memory distortion, in that we remember what usually happens, as recorded in the schema, rather than what actually happened.

There are some nice examples of schema influence in studies of remembering the objects in a room. Rooms used for different purposes, say, an office, a classroom, or a dorm room, typically contain different items. Brewer and Treyans (1981) allowed their participants to view an office for 35 seconds, and then asked them to recall as many of the 61 objects it contained as possible. Having a schema for this sort of room guides encoding of the objects when the participants are inspecting the room, for example, by major categories such as furniture items and then subcategories such as items likely to be on a desk versus in a bookcase. The schema also aids retrieval later: What would be in an office? What sorts of furniture? What would be on a desk? Not surprisingly, the students recalled many of the schema-relevant items, such as a chair, desk, and books, and fewer of the schema-irrelevant items.

Pezdek and colleagues, (1989) extended these findings by showing two rooms: a graduate student office and a preschool classroom. Each contained schema-consistent objects (books, beer bottle, and a desk; or toys, games, and blocks); or schema-inconsistent objects (simply exchanging some things between the office and preschool room). The results of this study make several important points about what is and is not remembered. Items highly relevant to the schema are remembered, for example, books and a chair in an office. Unusual or unexpected items were recalled even better, for example, a toy truck in a graduate student's office. However, objects that are neither schema-relevant nor unexpected seem to get lost. There was a clock radio in the office. We don't expect it to be there, yet its presence is not surprising either. It is forgotten.

(I was once surprised to see a playpen in an associate dean's office. He had been babysitting his grandchild that day. This is a schema-inconsistent item and was thus memorable.)

The organization of items can determine whether a schema is activated during learning. For example, a picture could show a TV, a door, a clock on the wall, a child reading, and so on. The items could be arranged in an organized scene, maybe depicting a family room, or they could be randomly arranged in a single picture. More items are recalled 1 day and 1 week later from the organized pictures. Rearrangements of the objects were better detected in the organized pictures, even when testing occurred 4 months later (Mandler & Ritchey, 1977).

Schemas unfortunately can lead to misencoding. When students in a speech-and-hearing course were shown a list of symptoms that led them to make a diagnosis of a specific hearing disorder, they later misrecalled some symptoms that had not been presented but that were consistent with the diagnosis. They remembered what is typical for this disorder. On the other hand, making the diagnosis improved recall in one way: On a recognition test, the participants were able to correctly reject symptoms unrelated to the diagnosis that had not been seen before. There was a trade-off between the memory-improving and memory-distorting effects of the schema (Arkes & Harkness, 1980).

Another example of distortion arises when sex-role stereotypes affect what is remembered. If the target material is schematized as being male-oriented or female-oriented, then men and women may remember the same material differently. Separate groups of college students were read a vaguely worded, nonspecific prose passage of several hundred words that was titled "Making a Shirt" or "Building a Workbench." Sentences included: "First you rearrange the pieces into different groups.... Work slowly on one part at a time.... Make sure they are the right pieces.... At first they may not seem to fit." On testing, women recalled more ideas from the shirt example than did the men, but men recalled more of the workbench story. Yet everybody had heard the same sentences. The titles apparently activated different schemas (or no schema at all) within which to encode the vaguely worded instructions (Hermann, Crawford, & Holdsworth, 1992).

Distortion effects are also found in young children's recall of scripts. Children were read a story about a birthday party in which some facts were grossly misordered (e.g., the cake was eaten several sentences before the candles were blown out). When reconstructing the story, the children either omitted the misordered sentences or inserted them where they should have fit according to a schema (Hudson & Nelson, 1983).

As memory for repeated events becomes schematized, specific details may become lost. Linton (1982) kept an index card diary of personal events in her life for 6 years. She periodically tested herself by sampling items and trying to determine whether she really remembered the events. She reported forgetting specific details when an event was repeated. For example, early in her study, Linton could recall details of the first meeting of a committee to which she was appointed. As more meetings accumulated, details of each became blurred, and, instead, a more generic memory (or schema) developed. Now, specific events that differentiated one meeting from another (where they had lunch one day or who missed a given meeting) were lost. A similar finding was seen in kindergarten children who attended a series of workshops. They could recall more of what typically happened during the sessions after four visits than after one. They had by then formed a generic memory of the sequence of events. However, they began to lose memory for details, such as misrecalling events from one week to another (Hudson, 1990). Once a schema is formed, memory for specific details declines.

Strict adherence to a schema would allow recall of only those events that conform to the schema. However, exceptions to the rule are remembered, especially if they are unusual or surprising. Vividness or von Restorff effects can still occur. And schemas can undergo change, as new examples are assimilated into the schema. The restaurant schema you first developed as a child, likely based on fast-food outlets and Happy Meals, is modified as you experience different types of eating establishments.

Metamemory

In this chapter we have presented many factors that affect learning. In addition, learning will be importantly influenced by our knowledge of when and how these factors work and our beliefs that they will indeed work. *Metamemory* refers to our knowledge about memory. It includes our estimates about the difficulty of learning certain materials, which strategies we think will be most useful, monitoring our progress during learning, awareness of what we know and do not know, and beliefs about how our own memories differ from memory in general. (Metamemory also includes knowledge about retrieval, which will be discussed more in the next chapter.)

Metamemory is usually assessed by a self-report questionnaire, the scores on which can then be correlated with actual memory performance. For example, students can be asked to make "ease-of-learning" judgments, possibly using a 10-point scale, prior to actually attempting to learn material. U.S. students should predict that their learning the capitals of former Soviet republics will be more difficult than learning the county seats of a U.S. state. When the students subsequently attempt to learn a set of facts, they actually spend more time on the items they had predicted would be more difficult (Nelson & Leonesio, 1988). "Judgments of learning" are ratings taken after studying, but before testing, when subjects rate how well they think they have learned the material. These estimates often predict how much of the material is recalled on an actual test.

What factors guide a student's decision that they have studied sufficiently or not? *Judgments of learning* (JOLs) are primarily affected by characteristics intrinsic to the material. In the case of remembering lists of words, the imagery value of words affects JOL ratings. For paired associates, the degree of associative relatedness between members of a stimulus–response pair affects JOL ratings. JOL ratings made after studying high- or low-imagery words, or related versus unrelated paired associates, accurately predict later recall of the words or associates. Interestingly, extrinsic conditions of learning, such as increasing the number of repetitions or spacing the repetitions, do not increase JOL ratings. Under these study conditions, later recall was much better than the students predicted. Certainly, students are aware that spacing and repetition facilitate learning, yet having studied under these conditions does not increase the belief that more learning has occurred (Koriat, 1997).

Metamemory perceptions show a developmental progression. The use and elaborateness of rehearsal increases as children age, as does their metamemory belief that rehearsal is beneficial. Five-year-olds realize that teenagers have better memories and that the five-year-olds have better memories than do their younger siblings. Older children can predict better when they are ready to be tested (judgment of learning) than younger children (Kail, 1990). On the other hand, even very young children have accurate perceptions of when memory might fail. When asked how they could remember to bring something to school tomorrow, they offered reasonable strategies such as placing the object near the door or in their school bags or asking Mom to remind them (Kreutzer, Leonard, & Flavell, 1982).

Individuals thus possess some general knowledge of learning and remembering. In addition, they have knowledge of how good their own memories are. This is referred to as *memory self-efficacy:* Judgments about how effectively we think our memory will function in a particular situation. Self-efficacy can be assessed through self-report inventories, such as that presented in Box 9.3. Individual differences in self-efficacy beliefs are dramatically shown in comparisons of younger and older adults (Ryan, 1992). Participants aged 25 to 85 rated self-perceived memory for such things as conversations or names, and the incidence of absentmindedness. Both older and younger participants believe that, in general, memory declines with aging. However, most people, young or old, did not think their memories are as bad as those of others their age. Personal self-efficacy, in this case, was rated better than the perceived effectiveness of memory in general for an individual's own age group.

The direction of cause and effect between self-efficacy beliefs and actual performance is debatable. Certainly, low expectations will limit effort devoted to trying to remember. I often hear students complain that they just cannot learn some type of material (foreign languages or statistics as examples). These beliefs can be as detrimental as any lack of ability. On the other hand, our self-perceptions may be accurate representations based on our actual experiences. If I constantly forget names, I should correctly believe that I have a name–memory problem.

Conclusion.   To understand how new learning occurs, we need to consider several factors: the material to be learned, the context in which learning occurs, the cognitive resources available in different memory structures, the task demands, the existing knowledge base of the subject, the strategies selected, and our beliefs about how learning occurs. The point of this lengthy list is to remind you, once again, of the complexity of obtaining a scientific understanding of the learning process.

Applications

Academic Learning and Encoding

Elaboration.   Consider some student-learning techniques in light of elaborative processing. Underlining in textbooks, taking notes during lectures, and writing summaries are often used by students, but actually may contribute little to learning (Snowman, 1986). Although each could be done in a manner that promotes elaborative processing, students may instead become accomplished at passive underlining and transcribing. For example, Hirst and colleagues (1980) had college students extensively practice taking dictation while

BOX **9.3**

Example Metamemory and Self-Efficacy Items from *Motivated Strategies for Learning Questionnaire*

This is a self-report inventory illustrating aspects of metamemory. Retention is affected by the strategies we use, how well we regulate our learning, our beliefs in our own abilities, the importance of the subject matter, and test anxiety. Students were instructed to respond to these items using a 7-point scale (1 = not at all true of me, to 7 = very true of me).

Cognitive Strategy Use

- When I study, I put important ideas into my own words.
- When I study for a test, I practice saying the important facts over and over to myself.
- When reading, I try to connect the things I am reading about with what I already know.

Self-regulation

- I ask myself questions to make sure I know the material I have been studying.
- I work on practice exercises and answer end-of-chapter questions even when I don't have to.

Self-Efficacy

- I'm certain I can understand the ideas taught in this class.

- My study skills are excellent compared with other students in this class.
- Compared with other students in this class, I think I know a great deal about the subject.

Intrinsic Value

- It is important for me to learn what is being taught in this class.
- I prefer class work that is challenging so I can learn new things.
- I think I will be able to use what I learn in this class in other classes.

Test Anxiety

- I worry a great deal about tests.
- I have an uneasy, upset feeling when I take a test.
- When I take a test, I think about how poorly I am doing.

Source: Pintrich & DeGroot, 1990.

---

reading unrelated material simultaneously. The students became proficient at doing both tasks at once, with little cross-interference. This suggests that students might in fact be able to take lecture notes without really attending to the content of the lecture. Some studies of note taking found that students who take notes recall no more than do students who simply listen to the lecture (Kiewra et al., 1991). *Taking notes* might not be as important as *having the notes later,* to review and study.

Other student study techniques promote shallow processing. Students tend to underline too much when reading or include too much verbatim copying while summarizing, which in either case is a passive rather than active strategy. Both underlining and summarizing improve recall when students are limited in the amount of each: for example, only three lines of underlining per page or summaries restricted to three sentences (Kulhavy,

Dyer, & Silver, 1975). Note taking improved recall of lecture material when the students were instructed how to organize their notes to promote interrelationships across the material (Kiewra et al., 1991). In these cases, the students have to process the material better to select the most important ideas.

One means of getting students to think about facts they are asked to remember is to prompt them with a question: Why would this be so? These questions force elaboration of the to-be-learned material. In one demonstration of this method of *elaborative interrogation,* Canadian college students studied short paragraphs about universities. In the interrogation condition, they were asked why each fact might be true. A sample fact might be "McGill University stands on land donated by a fur trader." These students recalled more facts and correctly associated them to the universities than did control participants who simply read the paragraphs. Elaboration helped whether subjects knew they would be tested or if the test was a surprise (Woloshyn et al., 1990). Elaborative interrogation forces subjects to integrate the given facts with existing knowledge.

Meaningfulness.   Meaningfulness is enhanced in textbooks that use text adjuncts such as headings, titles, or theme statements to help organize and interpret the to-be-remembered information. As mentioned earlier in this chapter, labels or titles affect recall of prose passages, possibly by activating existing knowledge or schemas that can guide encoding and subsequent retrieval. Other text techniques are advance organizers and analogies. Advance organizers are longer introductory statements that act as a bridge between what the student knows and the new material. Analogies activate prior knowledge to facilitate the understanding of new material that is being presented. Each of these adjuncts can produce meaningful learning that increases retention over longer intervals (Royer, 1986).

Generation Effect.   What are the educational implications of the generation effect? Suppose you are required to memorize a series of facts. (For example: Who was the first person to fly solo across the Atlantic? Answer: Charles Lindbergh.) The teacher could present a list of questions and answers for you to read. Or the questions could be followed by some clues for you to generate the correct answer. These clues could be, for instance, an anagram made up of the letters spelling the correct answer, or the answer with certain letters omitted. In either case, you must generate the correct answer. De Winstanley (1995) tested college students in the preceding manner, and found that the generate condition produced better recall of the answers. What was also notable was that this effect was present 2 days later, when the participants were given a surprise test on the answers to the questions.

Self-Efficacy.   A motivational factor related to metamemory is the belief that a strategy works and is worth the effort. Teaching students a mnemonic technique that we know from our research should work will not be of much benefit unless the students are convinced it will make a difference in their learning. In the standard intervention design, someone is first taught a mnemonic technique; the method is tested once to show it works; and then you hope the students will continue to use it. Pressley, Levin, and Ghatala (1988) added another step after teaching an imagery mnemonic to assist foreign-language vocabulary acquisition. The students attempted to learn some other vocabulary words using their own methods, whatever those were. The most beneficial training condition was one in which the participants first learned well using the imagery mnemonic, but then learned poorly with their own techniques. Those participants who had clearly seen its power went back to using if for subsequent trials in the study. Other students who were taught the mnemonic simply dropped it when given the opportunity.

Circadian Rhythms.   Does time of day affect academic learning and retention? Ebbinghaus conducted an early study for a school system and concluded that the early afternoon was the worst time for academic instruction. N. F. Skinner (1985) found that course grades among Canadian college students at his university were higher in afternoon and evening sections than in morning sections. Unfortunately, enrollment in morning and afternoon sections is a mix of voluntary and involuntary assignments; for example, some courses may be offered only in the morning, or freshmen are forced to take early-morning classes that are the only ones left after everyone else has registered. It is also important to recall that there are individual differences in alertness at different times of day (the morning types, who are bright, chipper, and otherwise annoying at early hours; and the evening types, who are bright, chipper, and normal later in the day). Students who rated themselves high on a "morningness" scale had higher grades in their 8 A.M. classes than later in the day. Low-morningness people had their lowest grades in 8 A.M. classes (Guthrie et al., 1995).

Knowledge of the effects of various encoding variables is useful in other applied areas. Box 9.4 discusses some uses in advertising.

Summary

This chapter focused on variables that primarily affect the encoding of information into memory. However, encoding cannot be isolated from storage and retrieval factors. Most laboratory studies of encoding use episodic learning tasks such as free recall or recognition.

Some Basic Variables in Encoding

Encoding is affected by rehearsal, imagery, and meaningfulness.

A distinction can be made between elaborative rehearsal, a form of deep processing in which the to-be-remembered material is related to other information, and maintenance rehearsal, a form of shallow processing in which information is passively repeated. Elaborative rehearsal promotes better retention through associations to existing knowledge, the formation of distinctive memories, and the effortful processing that it entails.

Elaboration can be enhanced by organization, imagery, or mnemonics. Student study tactics, such as underlining and note taking, are often passive and do not promote much elaboration. The technique of elaborative interrogation, asking "why" questions about the to-be-recalled material, increases retention.

Material that is more *imagable,* or concrete instead of abstract, is better remembered. Pictures and objects are remembered better than are words. This may be because of dual coding of both an image and a word.

Meaningful material is better remembered. Meaningfulness is defined by the high frequency of occurrence in language, ease of pronounceability, number of associations to other

Memory for Commercials

In this chapter, concepts such as elaborative processing and the spacing of repetitions are illustrated in academic and school learning. Encoding is also relevant to the business world and to one field in particular: marketing. One purpose of advertising is to make sure the consumer remembers your brand. Several factors discussed in this chapter have been shown to affect memory for advertisements and television commercials.

Repetition Effects

Anyone who has seen the same commercial 10 times in one evening knows that advertisers believe in the power of repetition. Actually, Hugo Munsterberg, a Harvard psychologist and the founder of the field of industrial psychology, demonstrated 80 years ago that four small newspaper ads produced better product recall than one large ad.

Consumers today watch shows they have recorded earlier on videotape. Advertisers worry that VCR users zip through commercials in replaying taped shows, undermining the effects of repetition. Zipping through familiar commercials still enhances memory, although not as much as watching the same commercial at regular speed (Gilmore & Secunda, 1993).

Spacing Effect

The spacing of repeated television commercials affects retention. Generally, spaced presentations are better recalled than massed. However, the spacing effect depends on the length of the retention interval, just as it does for several other situations mentioned in this chapter. In one experiment, two participant groups, college students and elderly adults, watched a TV news show containing commercial breaks. A target ad was repeated, with either one or four other commercials between the repetitions, thus defining the massed versus spaced manipulation. The participants remembered more after massed repetitions when they were tested immediately after the show. But if memory was tested a day later, commercials that had been spaced were better recalled (Singh et al., 1994).

Serial Position

Commercials usually come in strings. Does their position within a list affect recall? Terry and Bello (1997) presented lists of 15 television commercials for students to remember. When tested immediately after the list, both primacy and recency effects were obtained, and more of the middle commercials were forgotten. After a delay, only commercials at the start of the list were well recalled. On the basis of these results, advertisers would be better advised to place their ads first at the beginning of a commercial break.

A market research company in the Netherlands collected data from 39,000 viewers across a 15-year period from a sample that included several thousand commercials that had been broadcast. The first commercials in a block were better recalled, a primacy effect (Pieters & Bijmolt, 1997). The researchers noted that some European networks allow advertisers to select early versus late positions within a block of commercials, although at extra cost.

Age, Vividness, and Depth of Processing

Cole and Houston (1987) combined several variables in a single study to show their influence on commercial memory. News and commercial information presented in a television format was better recalled than when the same or similar information was presented in a newspaper. This could be taken to show a vividness effect. Younger subjects (ages 18 to 45) recalled more than did older (60 and over) subjects. Processing depth was varied by giving instructions to focus on the meaning of the material, or its sensory qualities. Deeper processing did increase recall of the print-format advertisements, but had no effect on the televised versions. Of particular concern, from an advertising perspective, was that recall by the elderly was poor to begin with, and was generally resistant to improvement by television format or deep-processing instructions. Cole and Houston suggest that advertisers need to explore alternative manipulations to enhance brand memory in the elderly, a population that is increasing in size and affluence.

items, and concreteness or imagability. Basically, meaningful items are ones you are already knowledgeable about. Material can be encoded better if we can find some meaning to it, as in the case of finding a meaningful pattern in an otherwise random strings of numbers or letters.

Presentation Variables

Encoding is also affected by the way material is presented. This section of the chapter included several "effects": the serial-position effect, the spacing effect, the isolation effect, and the generation effect.

The *serial-position effect* shows that the first and last items in lists are usually recalled better. The primacy effect is often attributed to better long-term memory for the first items, and the recency effect is often attributed to recall from short-term memory.

A *von Restorff* or *isolation effect* occurs when an unusual item, embedded in an otherwise homogeneous list of items, is particularly well remembered. The isolation effect may be due to enhanced rehearsal or to the distinctive memory representation of the isolated item.

If a to-be-remembered item is presented two or more times, spaced or distributed repetitions produce better recall than do massed repetitions. This *spacing effect* may be due to the total amount of rehearsal that two widely separated items permit, the reduced attention to a closely spaced repeated item, or to different encodings of spaced repetitions. One exception to the spacing effect is that massed repetitions may be better if testing occurs immediately following presentation.

The *generation effect* is increased recall of study material that is generated by the participant rather than being provided by the experimenter. If the participant can be guided to produce the correct information during study rather than simply reading it, retention will be enhanced.

Learner Variables

A number of learner variables that can influence encoding were considered, including the intention to learn, the use of incentives, interest in the target material, arousal, and emotions.

Retention is often more a function of how information is processed rather than of explicit attempts to remember. *Incidental learning,* or remembering without any deliberate intention to do so, is sometimes as effective as intentional remembering.

Offering explicit *incentives* to remember, such as money or points, usually does not improve recall in laboratory experiments. Given that a student-participant is already committed to attempt to remember, incentives do not increase cognitive processing. However, trade-offs may occur if both high- and low-incentive items are presented, as the former are better rehearsed at the expense of the low-incentive items.

People with an *interest* in a particular topic, or knowledge domain, seem to readily acquire new information within that domain. Some of this is because prior knowledge facilitates acquiring new knowledge, but interest also arouses motivation for deeper processing, leading to better encoding.

We expect *arousal* to facilitate learning, and generally it can. However, there are no simple effects of arousal on learning. Each statement about daily rhythms, stimulants, and so on, must be qualified by interactions with multiple other variables. According to the

Yerkes-Dodson law, performance is usually better at an intermediate level of arousal and less efficient at both lower and higher arousal levels. The optimal level of arousal varies with task difficulty, such that more difficult cognitive tasks are more efficiently performed at lower levels of arousal than easier tasks.

Circadian rhythms affect arousal and thus possibly indirectly learning and remembering. Some studies have shown better memory in the morning than later in the day. However, there may be individual differences associated with circadian rhythms. Stimulant drugs such as caffeine and glucose can facilitate remembering. Posttraining administration of stimulants enhances remembering, suggesting the effects of arousal are on encoding or consolidation of memory.

Emotional arousal can enhance retention, first by focusing attention on certain aspects of the situation. The weapons focus of crime victims attests to their vivid memory for the central details of a situation and poor recollection of peripheral details. Second, emotion produces bodily arousal (e.g., epinephrine is secreted) that contributes to long-term memory formation. Third, emotional events are distinctive. They are talked about and thought about, and so they are well rehearsed and elaborated in memory.

A flashbulb memory is a particularly vivid memory for a surprising, emotional, and consequential event. It is as if a picture of that moment is encoded into memory. Some researchers have emphasized the persistence and apparent accuracy of flashbulb memories over time. Others have focused on misrecall and inaccuracy in these memories.

Eyewitness memory is affected by all the complexities involved in encoding, arousal, and emotion in memory. Because of their intense emotional arousal, one could expect witnesses to be good rememberers. Emotional arousal can facilitate encoding, but knowing this fact will not tell us which details are encoded.

Schemas

Encoding is affected by our extensive preexisting knowledge, often summarized in the form of schemas, and by our knowledge of the way memory works.

Schemas, also called scripts, scenes, or frames, are ways of storing and organizing general knowledge in semantic memory. New events are encoded into memory using the existing schema as an organizing guide. Schemas affect attention, selection, abstraction, and normalization. Schemas also influence retrieval, sometimes leading to the misrecall of schema-relevant events. Items that are consistent with a schema (what is expected) and items that are discrepant with a schema (what is surprising) can be well recalled, although for different reasons.

Metamemory

Metamemory refers to our knowledge about learning and remembering. Learning will be importantly influenced by our knowledge of which encoding factors work, our beliefs that they will indeed work, and our monitoring of progress during learning. Self-efficacy, or how effective we believe our memory will be in a given situation, correlates with memory performance, but it is not clear whether poor remembering lowers expectations or whether low expectations reduce performance.

CHAPTER

10 Storage and Retrieval

Why does forgetting occur? First, it is important to acknowledge that some forgetting is necessary, even adaptive. We do not need to remember everything perfectly. How would you determine where you parked your car this morning if you have perfect and equally strong memories of parking your car every past morning? Remembering needs to be selective. The mnemonist, or expert memorist, *S* was plagued by remembering too much (Luria, 1968). He could not follow a train of thought without every odd associated memory leading off on a tangent. Yes, remembering too well was a problem for him. Although remembering each and every pleasant experience would be nice, remembering every unpleasant experience from the past could overwhelm us with despair. At the same time that some researchers are working on drugs to maintain or enhance memory, other researchers are developing drugs to block memory (Hall, 1998). If individuals exposed to traumatic experiences could be treated, maybe the distressing memories associated with posttraumatic stress disorder, anxiety states, or depression could be minimized. So, not all forgetting is bad.

Experimental psychologists have traditionally considered two possible explanations for forgetting: interference and decay. The *interference* explanation suggests that forgetting occurs due to conflict from other memories. *Decay* corresponds to a commonsense intuition that memories spontaneously weaken and fade over time. As simple as the idea of decay sounds, it is difficult to test. The passage of time during which decay could occur is typically filled by other activities that could interfere with the target memory. In a classic experiment, student participants recalled more after sleeping for 8 hours than after staying awake for 8 hours (Jenkins & Dallenbach, 1924). Even though the passage of time, and presumably the opportunity for decay, was equal between groups, the awake group remembered less and so was hypothesized to have suffered more interference.

However, such findings are ambiguous. Performance by the sleep and awake groups could vary due to diurnal differences, sleeplessness, or even the possibility that sleep promotes consolidation, the opposite of decay. A fundamental problem with the decay theory is its suggestion that the passage of time alone somehow "explains" forgetting. McGeoch (1932), a proponent of interference theory, offered the analogy that iron rusts over time, yet time is not the cause of rust. Time alone does not account for forgetting, but something that happens during that time.

Interference theory argues that forgetting results from competition between memories. Interference could come from memories that preceded the target memory, called *proactive interference;* or from memories formed after the target memory, called *retroactive interference.* For instance, changed stimulus conditions at the time of retrieval may cause the interfering memory to be retrieved rather than the target memory. One question that we will consider in this chapter is whether misleading information given to witnesses simply competes with target memories or instead alters the target memories.

Although interference and decay explanations are still actively considered to explain forgetting (e.g., Bower et al., 1994), much new contemporary thinking has focused on retrieval deficits. Forgetting is increasingly being construed as a failure of retrieval, whereas forgetting due to encoding failure, decay from storage, or interference is seen to be less significant. One prospect for the future is a technology of retrieval cuing, or procedures for implanting or embedding retrieval cues at the time of initial input of material (Cofer, 1979). The bulk of this chapter will consider factors that influence retrieval.

Our first consideration, however, will be the duration of memory. How long are memories retained and in what form are they stored?

Storage

We can begin with an apparent contradiction: the dual observations that we seemingly forget so quickly and remember so long. According to Ebbinghaus's curve of forgetting (shown in Figure 6.1), a great deal of forgetting occurs shortly after learning is completed. (The correctness of this principle is demonstrated if you have forgotten Ebbinghaus's curve.) Yet our everyday experience suggests that many memories are in fact long retained. Is Ebbinghaus's curve wrong, or are we wrong about our own memories?

How Long Is Long-Term Memory?

Is forgetting as drastic as Ebbinghaus's curve suggests? The inability to recall does not necessarily mean a loss from memory, but could instead reflect an inability to retrieve what is still there. This was the point of Ebbinghaus's demonstration of savings during relearning. Material that could not be recalled could nevertheless be relearned quickly, indicating there was still some trace of memory to build on. What would be of particular interest are controlled studies that quantify retention for naturalistically learned information. A number of modern studies fulfill these criteria, assessing long-term retention of classmates, school-learned material, and even TV shows.

Long-Term Memory for Naturalistically Learned Material

Fifty Years of Memories for High School Classmates.   Bahrick has studied retention of school-learned materials, ranging from high school Spanish vocabulary to the grades obtained in those classes. In a seminal study, Bahrick and colleagues (1975) assessed memory for high school classmates by people who had graduated as long as 48 years earlier. Retention was tested in different ways: recalling names of classmates; recognition of their names from among a pool of distractor names; recognition of classmates' yearbook pictures from distractors; and name–face matching.

What difficulties are encountered in studying memory under these conditions? Primarily, there are individual differences among participants that may confound measures taken at different delays. For example, the amount and kinds of exposure to individual classmates are not exactly the same. There are differences in exposure to classmates since graduation. Some people remained in their home towns; others moved away. Some return to class reunions, or take out the old yearbook to reminisce, but others have had little occasion to refresh their memories over the years. Bahrick's participants answered detailed questionnaires about such variables so that he could statistically control for some of the differences from one person to another. Finally, the tests had to be individually constructed for each person to accommodate his or her own graduation class.

The results of several types of retention tests are shown in Figure 10.1. The number of names that could be free recalled ranged from about 15 percent for recent graduates down to less than 7 percent for the oldest graduates. But measures such as name or face recognition and name–face matching show basically no loss of information out to 14 years postgraduation, and, in general, memory does not severely decline until 47 years after. Even among the oldest graduates, recognition scores are in the 70 to 80 percent range. This is far better than would be anticipated from laboratory studies of Ebbinghaus's curve.

Why is memory so good here? Bahrick notes two factors in particular: Naturalistic learning of classmates involves repeated exposure, and spaced repetition of these exposures. For example, some exposures are spaced across holiday breaks and summer vacations.

Remembering Knowledge Learned in School.   One uninformed criticism of education is that so little is retained compared to what was initially learned. By contrast, several reviews of the literature suggest that, in some cases, the amount lost is relatively small. Semb, Ellis, and Araujo (1993) assessed learning 4 and 11 months after completion of a child psychology course. In comparison to end-of-term test scores, grades only fell about 20 percent on the delayed tests. Multiple-choice tests produced higher scores than did recall tests, just as they often do in laboratory tests of memory using much shorter delay intervals.

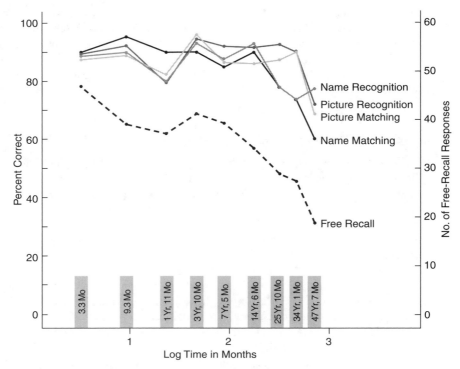

FIGURE 10.1   Memory for High School Classmates. The scale on the right shows the number of names in unaided recall; the scale on the left is for correct choices in name recognition, picture recognition, and name–picture matching. Recall was tested 33 months to over 47 years later in individuals from different graduating classes.

Source: From "Fifty Years of Memory for Names and Faces: A Cross-Sectional Approach," by H. P. Bahrick, P. O. Bahrick, and R. P. Wittlinger, 1975, *Journal of Experimental Psychology: General, 104,* pp. 54–75. Copyright © 1975 by the American Psychological Association. Reprinted with permission.

How much will be remembered from a course like the one in which you are using this text? Conway, Cohen, and Stanhope (1991) compared groups of students who had taken a cognitive psychology course up to 12 years earlier. The largest portion of forgetting occurred within the first 3 to 4 years. After that, knowledge retention stabilized at above chance levels. The shape of Ebbinghaus's curve was present (i.e., rapid initial loss followed by more gradual forgetting), but the time frame is of a different order of magnitude: in this case, years instead of days. Names, of theorists and researchers, were most likely to be forgotten, the same material we have trouble with outside the classroom as well.

Bahrick tested the retention of Spanish or algebra studied in high school. He compared people who had graduated different numbers of years previously. Most of the forgetting occurred within the first few years; whatever is then still remembered remains pretty stable for nearly the next 50 years. The primary determinant of persistent retention is the initial level of acquisition. Those students who took higher-level courses in high school and earned higher grades retained more (Bahrick, 1984a; Bahrick & Hall, 1993).

Memory for TV Shows.   Squire and Slater (1975) tested memory for TV shows that had aired for just one season and had not been repeated in syndication. Viewers had the opportunity to learn about these shows over an extended, but still restricted, time interval. By using a multiple-choice test format, recognition of titles of recent shows (those from a year or two earlier) averaged over 70 percent. Interestingly, show titles from 8 to 15 years earlier were still correctly identified 55 to 60 percent of the time. Control groups of junior high school students, who would not have been old enough to have seen these shows, and people who were living out of the country when these shows aired, scored at guessing levels.

Memory for Public Events.   Tests of knowledge of public events from past years and even past decades have been developed to assess forgetting in the elderly or among brain-injured individuals. Information about newsworthy events and celebrities is assumed to have been available to most people living at the time. We can use these tests to get an estimate of the pattern of forgetting across the lifespan. One example asks participants to identify faces of once famous individuals (Marslen-Wilson & Teuber, 1975). The people pictured were in the news during different decades. Older participants were good at identifying faces from the more recent decades and forgot more of the names from earlier decades. A major methodological difficulty is equating old events that are of equal salience to more recent events. Are the newer faces recognized because they are more recent or because they had more significance to the experimental participants? As with the other naturalistically learned materials described in the preceding paragraphs, exposure to presidents, generals, and film stars is probably frequent and distributed in time.

Long-Term Retention in Animals.   Most laboratory studies of memory in animals assess retention over relatively short intervals of minutes or days, although there are anecdotal reports of learned responses in pigeons (by Skinner) or dogs (by Pavlov) that persisted for years. A contemporary demonstration of long-term retention of visual information by pigeons was provided by Vaughn and Greene (1984). Their subjects were trained to discriminate between 160 nature slides that were discriminative stimuli for food availability and another 160 slides that signaled no food. That is, the pigeons were trained to key-peck during the positive slides but not during the negative slides. After retention intervals ranging from 235 to 730 days, the animals were still able to discriminate (i.e., remember) between the rewarded and nonrewarded slides.

The Permanent-Memory Hypothesis

Granted learning may be enduring, but how enduring? Loftus and Loftus (1980) informally surveyed individuals with graduate training in psychology. Eighty-four percent agreed with the statement that "everything we learn is permanently stored in the mind, although sometimes particular details are not accessible." This is the *permanent-memory hypothesis.* Forgetting is attributed to retrieval difficulties, not to decay of memory from storage.

The respondents offered several sorts of evidence for their belief in permanent memories. The most often cited finding was the claim that memories can be elicited through electrical stimulation of the brain. Wilder Penfield, a Canadian neurosurgeon, electrically stimulated areas of the cortex during surgery for the treatment of epilepsy. The patients were awake during this portion of the operation so that the surgeon could map out abnormal tissue that was the focus of the disorder. Electrode placements in the temporal lobes apparently caused patients to reexperience events from their past. The patients said these seemed like long-lost memories that could have not be recalled by other means. For example, one 26-year-old woman reported: "Yes, I think I heard a mother calling her little boy somewhere. It seemed to be something that happened years ago." When stimulated in another location several minutes later she said, "Yes, I hear voices. It is late at night, around the carnival somewhere—some sort of traveling circus. I just saw lots of big wagons that they use to haul animals in." Penfield concluded that all of our memories are permanently stored, a fact acknowledged in the title of his paper, "A Permanent Record of the Stream of Consciousness" (1955/1967). Penfield's notions of memory can be cast into a modern analogy to a video recording: There is a complete and continuous record of our mental experiences stored in the cortex. We just need a means of replaying those memories.

Although Penfield's findings are widely known in psychology, their support for permanent memory can be challenged. First, the majority of stimulated patients do not show recovered memories. Second, the mental experiences reported by the patients might not be memories, but instead could be imaginings, daydreams, or other phenomena created at the time of stimulation. Third, the validity of the memories is left unquestioned by the researchers, even though the patients themselves sometimes claim not to recognize the "remembered" events (Squire, 1987).

Other evidence offered for the permanent-memory hypothesis is the supposed recovery of memories through hypnosis and psychoanalytic techniques. Hypnotized crime victims or witnesses are said to be able to recall facts and details that were not reported before. However, hypnotized witnesses may be more willing to venture a guess about an uncertain memory, and they may be more susceptible to leading questions (see Box 10.1). The psychoanalytic technique of free association, or chaining through associations, reveals supposedly "repressed" memories. But, just as with the memories recovered by brain stimulation and hypnosis, how do we know these memories are of actual events?

The more pervasive difficulty with the evidence for permanent memory is the underlying logic: The successful recovery of *some* long-lost memories cannot prove that *all* of our life experiences are retained in memory.

The Nature of Storage

How are memories stored in long-term memory? Models have been proposed on both the psychological and biological levels. Psychological models often propose that knowledge is organized, possibly hierarchically, and that the different bits of information are linked. Biological theories hypothesize changes in the activity at the synapses between neurons. Examples of each of these approaches are described in what follows.

Psychological Models of Semantic Memory.   A number of network models have been proposed to illustrate the storage of general knowledge in semantic memory. The organization of material in semantic memory is likely to be common across individuals who share this knowledge, unlike our personal memories, which may be idiosyncratically organized. *Semantic network theories* assume that items of knowledge are interconnected via associations, relationships, or pathways. These connections can vary in strength or, in some models, in the distance separating one item from another. Thus, the memory representations of

BOX **10.1**

Enhancing Eyewitness Recall

As recently as a few years ago, a staple plot device in police dramas was to hypnotize a witness. Despite the popular stereotype, does hypnosis actually improve recall? There are several problems with hypnotically aided retrieval. First, witnesses do not necessarily remember more, but they are more willing to report information after being hypnotized. A witness may be unsure about a memory and so these uncertain details are not reported at first. When hypnotized, there may be a shift in the "response criterion." That is, the willingness to venture a guess shifts in a more lenient direction (see Smith, 1983).

Hypnotically aided recall is prone to distortion and misrecall, just as is normal memory. Given a few details, some leading questions, and some information learned incidentally while hanging around the police station waiting to be hypnotized, a hypnotized witness may inadvertently construct a memory. This idea is nicely described by an American Bar Association report entitled "Hypnotized Witnesses May Remember Too Much" (1978). The witness recalled details that could not possibly have been obtained through first-hand experience.

To avoid some of these problems, Geiselman and Fisher have developed the *cognitive interview* technique. Their method of interviewing applies many of the retrieval principles we cover in this chapter. Cognitive interviewing attempts to increase the similarity between encoding and retrieval contexts by having witnesses mentally reinstate the context that existed at the time of the crime. To minimize criterion shifts, subjects report everything, regardless of its perceived importance. Multiple retrieval paths are encouraged: Witnesses try recounting events in different orders and from a variety of perspectives.

Cognitive interviewing was compared to hypnosis in a study using college student "witnesses," who watched a police training film depict-

ing a crime (Geiselman et al., 1985). Two days later, the students were interviewed by trained forensic interviewers. Cognitive interviewing and hypnosis were both better than a standard interviewing technique in producing correctly recalled facts. Although cognitive interviewing was no better than hypnosis, there is less uncertainty about suggestibility and interviewer distortion.

Cognitive interviewing was also used with children. After viewing a 12-minute video, 6- and 10-year-olds were instructed to reinstate the context and to report all they could recall. These two components of cognitive interviewing led to recall of more details. Children who were exposed to misleading postevent information tended to misrecall details, and, unfortunately, the cognitive-interviewing strategy did not reduce or minimize these misrecalls (Hayes & Delamothe, 1997).

What do we know about eyewitness testimony? Are children really more suggestible? Are trained police officers better observers? A survey of 64 experts who have studied and testified on eyewitness memory showed strong agreement for a couple of beliefs (Kassin, Tubb, Hosch, & Memon, 2001). More than 80 percent of the experts believe that hypnosis increases suggestibility to misleading questions; that children are more susceptible to misleading information; and that exposure to a mug shot increases the likelihood of that person being chosen later in a lineup. The experts *did not* believe that hypnosis increases accuracy; or that violence necessarily distorts memory; or that police officers are necessarily better observers. Interestingly, the experts challenged a belief that seems to be common sense: The more confident witnesses are about their memory—the more sure they are—the more accurate their recall is. In fact, 87 percent of the experts agreed that this is *not* the case. Confidence does not predict accuracy.

TABLE and CHAIR could be said to have either a stronger connection between them or they are stored closer together in memory than are TABLE and AARDVARK.

An example of a semantic network model is illustrated in Figure 10.2. Collins and Quillian (1969) hypothesized a hierarchical arrangement of superordinate to subordinate knowledge. For example, the higher-order unit ANIMALS has subordinate categories such as FISH and BIRDS. Knowledge that is general to the entire category is stored at a higher level in the hierarchy. Information that is restricted or limited, as well as exceptions to the general category, is stored at the subordinate levels. Thus, the ANIMAL node includes information that is general to animals, such as that they breathe and they move. The BIRD node contains the facts that birds have wings and lay eggs. The OSTRICH node stores an exception to the generalization about birds—the fact that ostriches do not fly.

This hypothesized organization is tested by measuring True–False reaction times to statements that require accessing two elements in memory. Test items are selected to be at varying distances from one another in the hierarchy. For example, "BIRDS have WINGS" pairs two items from the same level; "OSTRICHES lay EGGS" pairs items that are a level apart. Faster responding to a statement indicates the two items are closer together, whereas slower responding suggests the two items are farther apart. For True statements, the farther

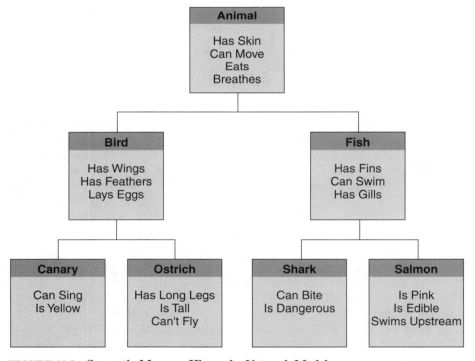

FIGURE 10.2   Semantic-Memory-Hierarchy Network Model.

Source: From "Retrieval Time from Semantic Memory," by A. M. Collins and M. R. Quillian, 1969, *Journal of Verbal Learning and Verbal Behavior, 8,* pp. 240–247. Copyright © 1969 by Academic Press. Reprinted with permission.

apart the two items are in the network, the longer it took to verify. This suggests that memory search begins with one item and then trees up or down the hierarchy to the second item in order to verify the truth value of the statement.

Reaction times to the False statements presented an intriguing finding. Some False statements contrast two items that are farther apart than any pair of True statements. For example, "OSTRICHES have GILLS" has two items that are widely separated in the hierarchy. Such statements took longer to reject than did the True statements, suggesting that the participants actually traced through the hierarchy from OSTRICH to GILLS before responding False. Other False statements, those obviously nonsensical, were quickly rejected, indicating that not every proposition gets thoroughly checked (e.g., "Statistics is a fun course").

Other models of semantic memory suggest that the organization is not strictly logical. Instead, items are distanced depending on frequency and contiguity in experience, although these would certainly overlap with a hierarchical model. In depicting such a model, as in Figure 10.3, the distance between nodes reflects the strength of the connection between items in memory (Collins & Loftus, 1975).

A common assumption among semantic memory models is that of *spreading activation:* Activation of one item in memory spreads to adjacent items, causing related knowledge to be activated. Spreading activation can be demonstrated by employing a *priming* manipulation in semantic memory judgments. A semantic verification task is again used, but simpler in format than that used by Collins and Quillian. The task is to rapidly decide whether a string of letters forms a word. Immediately before presenting the to-be-identified item, a related word is flashed on the screen to "prime" the target. For example, the word DOG is presented as a priming stimulus a fraction of a second before the test item COLLIE. Participants are then faster at identifying the string of letters COLLIE as being a word. The priming activation of DOG in semantic memory spread to related items, thus activating COLLIE before it was actually presented by the experimenter.

Other sorts of knowledge can be primed in semantic memory. Priming of gender stereotypes has been shown in a task that required naming the gender of target pronouns, for example, shown HE, the participant's response should be "male," or given SHE, the participant responds "female" (Banaji & Hardin, 1996). The priming stimuli were gender-related nouns (DOCTOR, NURSE). Male pronouns were more quickly labeled when preceded by male-stereotyped primes (e.g., DOCTOR—HE), and female pronouns were quicker when preceded by female primes (e.g., NURSE—SHE).

There are two factors that limit the spread of activation. First, activation weakens as it diffuses across the network. Second, activation spreading from an item having many associations will be divided across those many connections, resulting in weaker activation of each of them. This is known as the *fan effect.* An item with fewer associations will have its activation less divided, and so connected items will be more strongly primed.

The fan effect has been applied to a paradoxical observation about forgetting names: the momentary blocking of familiar and well-known names. (How often has your mother blocked in recalling your name?) Fanning occurs when the activation of a person node in memory triggers the many associations to that person, but each, including the name, are only weakly activated. Cohen (1990) found that reaction times to verify sentences (e.g., "Jeff is a musician") were slower the more facts were associated with a name. This is the fan effect. Activation of JEFF spread to several facts known about Jeff. When the same facts

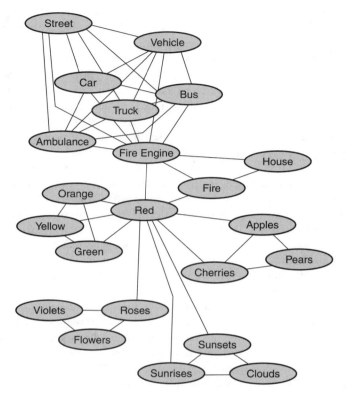

FIGURE 10.3   An Alternative Network Model in Which Knowledge Is Not Hierarchically Arranged. The strength of connections is illustrated by the distance between nodes.

Source: From "A Spreading Activation Theory of Semantic Processing," by A. M. Collins and E. F. Loftus, 1975, *Psychological Review, 82,* pp. 407–428. Copyright © 1975 by the American Psychological Association. Reprinted by permission.

are shared by several individuals, fans can become crossed, slowing retrieval even further. For example, if we know three things about Jeff (i.e., he is a musician, he attended UpState University, and he lives in Seattle), interference will occur if other names share these same facts (e.g., if George was also a musician), which is the cross-fan effect.

Neuropsychological Dissociations.   The patterns of memory loss found with neurological injuries also say something about the organization of semantic memory. A *modular approach* suggests that there are hypothetically separate memory modules in the brain, each underlying different sorts of knowledge (Shallice, 1988). For example, semantic memory may have separate modules for words of different grammatical classes, such as nouns and verbs. Caramazza and Hillis (1991) found two patients who were impaired at verb production. In reading (for one person) or writing to dictation (for the second), the verbs would be mispronounced, misspelled, misread, or go unrecognized as words. The interesting test was to present homonyms, two words that sound and are spelled alike but have different meanings. Thus, one patient could read "there was a CRACK in the mirror," in which the target word is a noun, but could not read "don't CRACK the nuts in here," in which the target word is a verb.

Another individual could not define spoken words that named living things, but could define nonliving objects. When the word "dolphin" was read to him, he could not tell what it was. The man was otherwise articulate, and could define much more difficult words that referred to nonliving things (McCarthy & Warrington, 1988). This finding suggests that there is not a single vocabulary (or dictionary) in semantic memory. Instead, categories of words are stored separately.

The modularity of semantic memory is also illustrated by other categories of knowledge impairments. Individuals with *prosopagnosia* no longer recognize faces that should be represented in semantic memory, including faces of famous people (George Washington, Elvis) and of family members. The latter can still be identified, but by their voices, posture, gait, or other cues. This is not strictly a perceptual difficulty. Prosopagnosics can accurately describe verbally a face they are inspecting. They simply cannot identify who it is (DeHaan & Newcombe, 1991). In one case, a dairy farmer with prosopagnosia not only failed to recognize family members, but also could no longer recognize individual cows by their faces (cited by McCarthy & Warrington, 1990).

Biological Substrates.   The search for the engram, or the neural representation of memory in the brain, has been ongoing since the beginnings of the field of learning itself. Researchers have explored various ways that learning could be physically represented in the brain. The theories are too numerous and too complex to be summarized here. Instead, a sampling will be offered.

Biochemical changes certainly occur in the brain during learning. For example, the synthesis of the protein ribonucleic acid (RNA) increases due to learning experiences. RNA, much like the genetic material DNA, can take a nearly infinite number of forms depending on the sequence of base chemicals. One theory was that a unique memory molecule is formed that encodes each new experience. The memory-molecule theory was consistent with a number of findings. Drugs that inhibit protein synthesis, such as antibiotics, seem to inhibit consolidation. A chemical was isolated in the brain of rats trained to avoid the dark alley in a maze, which seemed to encode this fear (it was called scotophobin, for fear of the dark). For a while, there were even speculations that knowledge pills would be developed, each containing the facts of a discipline (for reviews, see Rose, 1992; Sweet, 1969).

However, this early support for the memory-molecule theory fell apart. Protein production could have been stimulated by the general activity of the organism and not specifically by learning. The amnesias following protein inhibition were reversible, indicating that memory had been formed after all. And, some experiments could not be replicated (see Rilling, 1996).

A more promising mechanism for memory storage is change at the synaptic connections. Neurons, the cells of the nervous system, adjoin one another at junctures called synapses. Neural transmission is through stimulation of one cell by another. The number of synaptic connections between neurons is not fixed, but is affected by life experiences, at least in animals. For example, rats raised in enriched environments (toy- and playmate-filled cages) develop more synaptic connections in certain brain areas than do rats raised in pairs in empty laboratory cages (Greenough, 1985).

One model preparation for synaptic change that is being extensively studied is *long-term potentiation* in hippocampal cells (Lynch et al., 1991). Repetitive stimulation of one cell, or set of cells, potentiates or enhances the capacity for adjacent cells to be triggered. In a sense, something like spreading activation occurs from one cell to another. Repeated experience allows potentiation of one cell by another to occur more readily. On a gross level of description, this matches what we say occurs when one stimulus cues another, as exemplified in classical conditioning, paired-associate learning, or cued recall.

Eric Kandel and his research group have found evidence for two storage processes, a short-term and a long-term one (Kandel, 2001). Kandel started deciphering the synaptic changes that underlie learning in *Aplysia,* a marine snail with a simple nervous system, about 40 years ago (see Chapter 2). More recent work has included long-term potentiation in the mouse hippocampus. Kandel has found similar molecular chemical processes that subserve learning in both species. An intense stimulus, the kind that will produce either sensitization in *Aplysia* or long-term potentiation in the mouse hippocampus, leads to transient chemical changes at the synapses that allow subsequent stimuli to trigger a nerve impulse. This is the short-term process that lasts for a few hours. Repeated intense stimulation leads to chemical changes in the synapse, coding in the nucleus of the cell, and the growth of additional connections (synapses) between the cells. It is these later changes that characterize consolidation and the formation of a durable long-term memory.

Retrieval

A recurring theme in this book is the idea that much more is learned than is typically recalled. At one point, we distinguished between the *available* memories that are in storage and the *accessible* memories that we can actually recall (see Chapter 6). Tulving and Pearlstone (1966) illustrated this concept by presenting study lists of categorizable words to be remembered. Free recall was first tested without any prompts. Additional items were then remembered when the category names were given as a cues. Some of the "forgetting" during the initial attempt to recall was due to memories that existed but could not be retrieved. The idea of retrieval failure suggests an interpretation of forgetting that differs from a theory that memories spontaneously decay and disappear from storage.

Retrieval from Episodic Memory

What factors affect retrieval? As we will see, several variables are important, but three general factors can be offered: the distinctiveness of the memory, practice at retrieving the memory, and the presence of effective retrieval cues.

Distinctiveness. Events that are *distinctive,* or that stand out from a background of other events by being different, are generally well remembered. Flashbulb memories are well recalled, even if not perfectly accurate, because they represent events that are so different from others in our lives. In the isolation effect, or von Restorff effect, an item that differs from the remaining items in a list is better recalled (Chapter 9).

Why are distinctive events retrieved better? One explanation is that their retrieval cues uniquely target a single memory. When asked to recall an attempted presidential assassination in a flashbulb memory study, this prompt cues a very particular memory. By contrast, a retrieval cue might be too broad, potentially retrieving many items. In a sense, the cue is spread too thin. In remembering lists of categorized words, the category labels (foods, sports, etc.) are less effective as retrieval cues if too many items are subsumed in the category. The more items per category, the smaller the proportion of items within a category will be recalled (Roediger, 1973).

Testing Effects.   Retrieval is facilitated by previous retrieval. For instance, taking a test shortly after studying greatly enhances the amount that can be recalled on a later retest. The general design of studies of *testing effects* is to test shortly after learning, or not for the control condition, and then to test retention sometime later. It is recall on this later test that interests us. For example, the number of pictures recalled at the end of a 1-week delay nearly doubled when three other tests of memory had occurred, versus no other tests, immediately after studying the week before (Wheeler & Roediger, 1992).

Does testing improve retrieval by simply offering additional study opportunity? No, an additional study presentation is less effective than taking a test. Additional study primarily benefits information that is not recalled after first studying.

The effects of prior testing are greater if the same test is given both times. In Semb and colleagues' (1993) study described earlier, students took an end-of-course exam and then were tested 4 and 11 months after completing a psychology course. The scores on these later tests were about 10 percent higher to questions that had been on the final exam than to related questions. More difficult prior testing is also more effective. Glover (1989) found that an initial free-recall test produced better retrieval later than did an initial cued-recall test, which in turn was better than an initial recognition test. Again, "more effective" here means more recall on the retest given later.

A phenomenon known as hypermnesia offers a dramatic demonstration of testing effects. *Hypermnesia* is remembering that actually improves over successive attempts at reproduction of the studied material, in contrast to the forgetting that we expect to occur over time. Erdelyi and Kleinbard (1978) presented a list of 60 object line drawings for study (DOG, CAT, TREE, etc.). The participants were then repeatedly tested for recall of the pictured objects. The list was presented just once for study, but in some cases was tested 20 times over the following week. During each test, the participants were asked to name as many objects as they could recall. The total number of different items recalled across repeated testing is shown in Figure 10.4. Whereas just over 26 items were recalled on the first test, 38 were recalled on the final tests. This hypermnesia is the opposite of forgetting, or amnesia.

Bahrick and Hall (1993) reported that hypermnesia occurred for other test materials, including recall of general information, foreign-language vocabulary, and names. From one test to another, some items are indeed forgotten. But the number of newly recovered items on successive tests exceeded the number lost, leaving hypermnesia as a net gain.

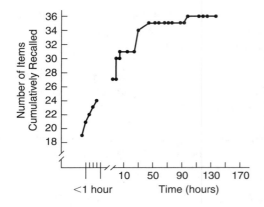

FIGURE 10.4   Hypermnesia. Number of different items recalled after a single presentation of the list. The list was tested more than 20 times over a period of a week.

Source: From "Has Ebbinghaus Decayed with Time? The Growth of Recall (Hypermnesia) over Days," by M. H. Erdelyi and J. Klein-bard, 1978, *Journal of Experimental Psychology: Human Learning and Memory, 4,* pp. 275–289. Copyright © 1978 by the American Psychological Association. Reprinted with permission.

Why would people remember more and not less across successive tests? One factor is that additional tests provide more time to retrieve. Another factor is that during "free" recall, people prompt their memories with subjective or self-generated cues (Roediger & Thorpe, 1978). The participants are thinking of one thing or another to help themselves remember. The self-prompting cues are likely to vary across successive tests as different things come to mind at different times, and so these later cues tap items that were not adequately cued on the earlier tests.

This capacity for additional recall of material across a series of tests has implications for eyewitness testimony. One assumption too often made is that the first recall is the most valid, and anything remembered later is suspect. Yet here we are asserting that additional accurate information can be elicited through repeated recall attempts. In a simulation study of witnessing, participants watched a film depicting a burglary. Memory recall was tested four times, and each time additional details were remembered without an increase in intrusions of incorrect facts (Scrivener & Safer, 1988).

In addition to distinctive memories and practice at retrieval, a third important factor in retrieval is to have effective retrieval cues. The consideration of such cues is taken up next.

What Makes a Good Retrieval Cue?

We will consider two answers here: cues that have strong preexisting associations to the target memory and cues that were encoded along with the to-be-recalled item when it entered into memory.

Associations.   One category of effective retrieval cues is those that are connected to the target by strong associations. Given the word TABLE, you might retrieve CHAIR as the first association that comes to mind, but not AARDVARK. TABLE is a good cue for CHAIR but not for AARDVARK.

In one illustrative study, participants were presented with a long list of words and then free-recalled as many as possible. After this, a second test phase was given to try and prompt recall of more words. The prompts were chosen to have varying degrees of association to the target word. For example, suppose the target word SKY was forgotten. Prompting elicited more of the forgotten words, and prompting was most effective with strong associates (e.g., BLUE) than with weak associates (e.g., CLEAR) (Bahrick, 1969).

Encoding Specificity.   An alternative theory for what makes an effective retrieval cue is that the best cues are those that were present at encoding. If you forget where you left an object, you mentally reconstruct where you were when you last had the object. If you want to recollect your childhood, go back to where you lived as a child. Being in the presence of cues that were also present long ago can aid retrieval.

This idea of matching cues between encoding and retrieval has been made explicit in Tulving's *encoding specificity principle.* In one demonstration, Tulving and Thompson (1973) varied the cues present at the time of studying and at testing. Their college student participants studied target words that were paired with weakly associated words as study aids. Thus, the to-be-remembered word LIGHT might be presented along with its weak associate HEAD. On recognition tests the target words were presented with the same cue words as before, or with cue words that had stronger associations to the target (e.g., DARK would be presented along with LIGHT). The participants' task was to choose which target words had been studied earlier. LIGHT was more often recognized in the context of the weak associate HEAD than when in the context of the strong associate DARK. This is because LIGHT had initially been encoded in the context of HEAD rather than of DARK (see the results in Table 10.1). According to the encoding specificity principle, recognition occurred when the test reactivated the same meaning with which the target words had been encoded.

(Why, then, did Bahrick find that strong associates were better than weak ones? Because in the absence of an explicit context, the participants spontaneously encoded the targets the same way they would have if the strong associates had been present.)

Tulving and Thompson in fact found that some words could be recalled, using free-recall instructions in the absence of any cues, which were not recognized later when presented with an unstudied cue. Thus, if the participants were asked to recall as many words as possible from the list, LIGHT might be recalled if no cues were given. But if the participants were given a recognition test with cues, LIGHT was not recognized when paired with (the supposedly helpful cue) DARK. Students sometimes have the similar experience of not recognizing the correct multiple-choice answer, although the answer would have been recalled in response to an essay question. Such findings show the reversal of the usual superiority of recognition over recall tests.

Contextual Learning.   The general notion that remembering will be better if the cues present at encoding are also available at retrieval has been discovered in several areas of research on learning. The encoding cues can be verbal, as in Tulving and Thompson's experiments. The cues can be also be contextual cues of time and place, internal cues of emotional or drug-induced mental and physical states, or cognitive operations the participant performs with the target material. The particular experimental arrangement of manipulating the encoding conditions in combination with the retrieval conditions is referred to as the encoding–retrieval paradigm (Tulving, 1983). The basic manipulation in any given experiment is that the cues present during encoding can be arranged to be the same, or different, at the time of retrieval. A sample listing of encoding–retrieval manipulations in the psychological literature is shown in Box 10.2.

TABLE 10.1   Variations in the Encoding–Retrieval Paradigm

A. Encoding-Specific (Tulving & Thompson, 1973, Table 1)

Study	Test	Percent of Words Recognized
head LIGHT	head LIGHT	65
	dark LIGHT	23

B. Context-Specific (Godden & Baddeley, 1985)

Study Context	Test Context	Percent of Words Recalled
Land	Land	38
	Water	24
Water	Land	23
	Water	32

C. (Drug-)State-Dependent (Eich et al., 1975)

Study Drug State	Test Drug State	Number of Words Recalled
Placebo	Placebo	11.5
Placebo	Marijuana	9.9
Marijuana	Placebo	6.7
Marijuana	Marijuana	10.5

D. Mood-Dependent Recall (Bower, 1981)

Mood at Study	Mood at Test	Percent Recall
Happy	Happy	78
Happy	Sad	46
Sad	Happy	46
Sad	Sad	81

You have probably been given the advice to study in the same room you will be tested in. There is some validity, with limitations, to this claim. For example, Smith (1979) had students study a word list in a college classroom. The students were then tested either in the same room or in a different room. (Both rooms had been made equally familiar in a preliminary phase.) More words were recalled when testing was in the same room in which the word list had been presented. Smith also found that the different-room deficit could be reduced if the students were instructed to "reinstate," or recollect, the study room prior to testing. You don't actually have to be there; just imagine you are there! This idea has been applied to a witness interview technique that emphasizes reinstatement of a crime or accident scene as an aid to retrieval (see earlier Box 10.1).

An everyday example of contextual forgetting might be the failure to recognize someone we encounter out of his or her usual context. This can happen when, for example, television actors appear in a different show or movie. The faces are familiar, but where do we know them from?

Examples of the Encoding–Retrieval Paradigm

Music as Context Stimuli
Mozart or jazz served as background music while the participants tried to remember a word list. Recall 2 days later was better when the same music was repeated (Smith, 1985). Interestingly, no context-dependent "quiet" effect was found when no music prevailed at study and test.

Odor as a Contextual Stimulus
Recall of faces after a 2-day delay was better when the same odor was present during studying and testing (Cann & Ross, 1989).

Temperature
Rats were first made hypothermic and then trained to avoid shock. When retested later, retention was better among animals that were rechilled than those tested at different body temperatures (Richardson et al., 1984).

Time-of-Day Dependency
Time-of-day effects have been found in animal conditioning studies. For example, rats performed better when they were tested at the same time of day at which they were first trained (Holloway, 1978). However, some attempts to find time dependency in human memory have not been successful (Folkard & Monk, 1985).

Bodily Kinesthetic Context
Subjects studied a word list while standing or lying down. Recall was better when tested in the same position than when positions were switched (Rand & Wapner, 1967). Similarly, state dependency was seen when studying and testing were preceded by either 5 minutes of exercise or of rest (Schramke & Bauer, 1997). Finally, one football coach complained about the NCAA requirement that pre-season workouts not be in full gear. "We teach them all their patterns and plays and as soon as they put on the shoulder pads they forget everything we taught them" (quoted by Green, 1991).

Ritalin and State Dependency
The drug Ritalin is sometimes used to treat hyperactivity in children. Swanson and Kinsbourne (1976) found state dependency in a sample of hyperactive children taking Ritalin, using a paired-associate learning task. However, in one other case, this effect only partially replicated (Shea, 1982).

Don't Phone in Your Answers
Canas and Nelson's (1986) participants studied a word list in the lab and were then dismissed. Those brought back to the lab a day later recalled more words than those called on the phone to be tested.

Pain-Dependent Learning
Subjects exposed to a list of words while experiencing experimentally induced pain (i.e., immersing their hands in ice water) later remembered more words when reexposed to the pain. Fewer words were remembered if the pain occurred only during list exposure or only during testing (Pearce et al., 1990).

Birth Order and Personality
Theories of sibling development often suggest that birth order affects personality: First children are supposed to be more responsible, conservative, and achievement oriented, whereas later-born children and more outgoing and rebellious. However, these predicted effects are not often seen in actual research. Harris (2000) argues that order effects exist, but only when siblings are together. Individuals have different personalities outside their family circle that would not be seen in research on individuals outside that context. Put the now-grown siblings back together again and watch birth order effects reassert themselves.

Memory for Personality Traits
In an incidental learning task, some participants were asked to judge whether certain adjectives described themselves (self-referent condition) or if the words described some other specific person, such as the president (other-referent condition). Referent-dependent retrieval was shown in that more adjectives were remembered when the same judgments were made at encoding and at retrieval (i.e., both self-referent or both other-referent) (Wells, Hoff, & Enzle, 1984).

State-Dependent Learning. *State-dependent learning* refers to better recall when testing occurs in the same drug-influenced state as was present during learning. A variety of drugs, including alcohol and marijuana, can produce state dependency in humans and animals. A study by Eich and colleagues (1975) illustrates the case for marijuana. Participants studied word lists either while under the influence of marijuana or not and then were tested after exposure to marijuana or a placebo. The use of controlled and illegal drugs imposes certain restrictions on the researchers. Government permission is needed to obtain and use the drugs for research purposes. Participants must be admitted users: Naive participants cannot be recruited from the Psych 101 participant pool for dope studies.

The design of this study and the results are shown in Table 10.1. There was a drug-state-dependency effect: Recall was better in the two groups in which the drug conditions at testing matched those present while studying. That is, recall was better in the group who studied and tested after placebos and in the group who studied and tested after the drug. Two limitations to this statement of drug-state dependency should be mentioned. If category cues were presented at testing, recall was then uniformly high (no pun intended) and state-dependent effects did not occur. So, drug-state retrieval cues can be overshadowed if better retrieval cues are available. It is also the case that human participants are sometimes aware of the drug conditions they are under. In Eich's study, self-reports showed that the marijuana was detected. Thus, the placebo may be a less than adequate control condition.

Mood-Dependent Recall. Just as external stimuli of time and place can act as retrieval cues, so can internal stimuli. Bower (1981) theorizes that stimuli arise from moods and emotional states, and that these mood stimuli can enter into associations just as do other sorts of stimuli that experimental psychologists more typically employ. Bower, Monteiro, and Gilligan (1978) demonstrated mood-dependent recall in an experiment in which happy or sad moods were induced in hypnotized college student participants. Recall of the to-be-remembered material was better when students were tested in the same mood state, whether this was happy or sad, as they were in when learning had occurred (see Table 10.1).

Mood-specific recall can have implications for depression and other affective disorders. Being depressed may lead to the retrieval of mostly sad memories, which only perpetuates the depressive mood. For example, if depressed individuals are given cue words and asked to recall any personal memory that comes to mind, they more often recall unpleasant experiences. This could be because they have had more unpleasant experiences to recall. However, in longitudinal research designs that tested the same individuals at different times, unpleasant memories were recalled when the individuals were more depressed and pleasant memories were retrieved when they were less depressed (Clark & Teasdale, 1982; Fogarty & Hemsley, 1983). This is sometimes referred to as *mood-congruent memory.*

The opposite of depression is the excited state of mania. In a parallel study to the one with depressed patients mentioned earlier, a word-association test was administered to manic patients. On succeeding days, the manic individuals were asked to recall the associations generated in that previous free-association phase. Recall was better when the mood state matched that of when the list was first generated (Weingartner, Miller, & Murphy, 1977). According to one anecdotal report, a man in a manic state withdrew a large sum of money from his bank and hid it. After being hospitalized and medicated, his mania abated, but he then had no recollection of where he had put the money. Six months later, the man became manic once again and went to hide something else behind a picture, whereupon he found the lost money. Although he still did not remember hiding the money, it is interesting that the same location seemed so sensible in the manic phase, but was not at all memorable in the normal state (Williams & Markar, 1991).

What do the several manipulations of context, drug-induced state, and mood have in common? One possibility is that they all reduce to mood-dependent memory. What is common when encoding and retrieval conditions are equated is "not *environmental* context dependent memory, but rather *experiential* context dependence, of the kind customarily associated with alterations of a person's affective, circadian, or pharmacological state" (Eich, 1985, p. 769, italics in the original). Eich found context-similarity effects using an indoor and an outdoor location as the two testing environments. More important, he found that matching the self-rated affect (i.e., feelings) between encoding and recall was more important than matching physical locations (1995). That is, being in the same mood was more important than being in the same place.

Limitations of Encoding–Retrieval Paradigm Effects.   We have presented several instances of the encoding–retrieval paradigm. Studies of encoding specificity, context-specific recall, drug-state dependency, and mood-dependent recall suggest that memory can be present but not always accessible to recall. However, we should not overemphasize the magnitude of these effects for several reasons. First, a number of studies have failed to find state-dependent or context-dependent effects. Second, state-dependent effects are more often found on recall tests but not on recognition tests, or not with tests presenting explicit retrieval cues (such as presenting the category names). State-dependent effects are also obtained after minimal amounts of exposure to the target material. These facts suggest that contextual cues are helpful when memory is poorly integrated and the participant therefore has few spontaneously produced retrieval cues to access the memory.

Third, contextual stimuli need to become connected to the target material or they will not facilitate retrieval. Not all contextual cues, moods, or drug-induced states necessarily become associated with the target. The distinction we are making here is between passive contextual stimuli and active stimuli that interact with the target information during encoding. If cues in the classroom do not become associated with the lecture material in some manner, such as inspecting some element of the room while thinking about a lecture point, the room should have no special retrieval power.

Finally, the environmental context becomes less influential when attention is focused on internal processes, such as mentally searching for associations among the to-be-remembered items. This overshadowing of the external by the internal can occur either during study or at testing (Smith & Vela, 2001). In either case, context-specific memory appears to be reduced, because the context is not being used during one phase, encoding or retrieval.

Emotional Arousal and Retrieval

Emotional arousal can have separate effects on the different stages of memory. It can aid encoding and facilitate consolidation of long-term memory. And as just noted, emotions also act as stimuli that can become associated with other events in memory. There is one other role not yet considered. That is, emotional arousal may impair our ability to retrieve memories.

High levels of an emotion, particularly fear or anxiety, can block retrieval of memories that otherwise would be recalled. In one particularly dramatic demonstration of emotional blocking, army recruits were tested in what they thought was a life-threatening situation. Prior to boarding a military aircraft, different groups of soldiers were given a sheet of emergency instructions to study. During the flight, the experimental treatment group was put under extreme emotional distress. One engine of the plane was stopped and the soldiers were told to prepare for an emergency ditching in the ocean. They were asked to complete a form noting the disposition of their personal belongings, and these forms were placed in a waterproof container to be jettisoned from the plane prior to ditching. Then the soldiers were given a written test on the emergency procedures. Would life-threatening fear interfere with retrieval? Compared to nonfear control groups, the crash-fearing group recalled significantly less of the emergency procedures (Berkun et al., 1962). (No doubt the soldiers recalled significantly more about this plane flight.)

Manipulating fear in this manner should provoke ethical concerns about the treatment of research participants. This study predated contemporary ethical standards and could not be repeated today. Yet the research addresses a significant question about whether emotional arousal interferes with the performance of critical duties. Individuals trained in emergency procedures might not be able to access the information under the stressful conditions of an emergency.

One recent study demonstrated a correlation between the level of stress hormones in the blood and remembering. Rats were first trained to swim to a submerged platform in the Morris water escape maze. The rats were then given electric shocks 2 minutes, 30 minutes, or 4 hours before being tested the next day. The shocks were used to induce emotional arousal. The rats could recall the platform location 2 minutes or 4 hours after the shocks. However, they did not recall as well 30 minutes after the shocks, a time when stress hormones were highest in the blood (deQuervain, Roozendaal, & McGaugh, 1998).

We have all experienced momentary forgetting. Maybe you temporarily forget your phone number or blocked on the answer to a simple question. Could emotional arousal cause momentary retrieval blockage? Luborsky analyzed transcripts of psychotherapy sessions during which patients reported they forgot what they were just about to say (Luborsky, 1988). The forgotten thought was recalled later in the session, indicating that the forgetting was only temporary. The analysis showed that emotional arousal and hesitancy about discussing certain topics preceded these momentary forgettings.

What if the emotional state is relieved? Will the forgotten material then return? In several older experiments, participants first studied and recalled some material such as word lists and then were given feedback designed to induce concern over their performance. The participants might be told they had not done well on the task or a personality test indicated abnormal traits. After this, the recall of the studied material was tested. Participants given upsetting feedback did not recall as many items as did those given neutral feedback. The important manipulation, from our perspective, is what happened after the emotional stress was relieved. The experimenters disclosed their deception, the distress was eliminated, and recall increased on a retest (Holmes, 1992).

Arousal in the form of test anxiety can interfere with retrieval in a student's life. Benjamin and colleagues (1981) found that highly test-anxious college students performed poorly on essay and short-answer questions, which make heavy demands on retrieval of information. These students performed better on multiple-choice tests, which are less demanding on retrieval. Later research by Naveh-Benjamin (1991) confirmed that some anxious students benefited from training to calm themselves in the test-taking situation, and their grades actually increased the following semester.

Remembering to Remember

One of the lessons learned from studying individuals who are expert at remembering is that they plan for retrieval at the time of encoding (see Chapter 11). That is, while they are rehearsing, elaborating, imaging, and all the other things people do when they try to remember, the experts are also devising strategies to retrieve the encoded material later. We can see this on a small scale if we think about what we do when asked to remember a list of categorized words, for example, some flowers, some foods, some animals. We rehearse the category names as we also rehearse the individual words, realizing the labels will be valuable later during testing.

Planning for retrieval is particularly important in *prospective memory,* or remembering to perform future actions. I have to remember to pick up dinner on the way home. Forgetting from prospective memory is likely to be forgetting to recall at the correct time or place, and less likely to be forgetting the intention. I will remember to get dinner; I just won't remember until I get home.

External cues and reminders reduce our dependence on spontaneous memory. This is why we have sticky notes, agendas, and shopping lists. An alarm tells you when to act or seeing someone reminds you to give her a message. Professional bartenders use external cues when they set out each type of glass needed to fill an order as reminders. Lamming and colleagues (1994) designed various electronic memory aids that would cue when to recall, so-called memory prostheses. In their work setting, electronic ID badges were worn, which also allowed tracking of individuals within the facility. A programmable pager could remind you not only of the time of a meeting or appointment, but also could remind you to tell someone else something when the computer noted you and the other person were both in the same room.

Other instances of prospective memory do not depend on an explicit cue to remember, but instead seem to involve spontaneous recall, or "remembering to remember." Remembering to take something out of the oven, to stop at the store on the way home, and to call someone later that day are examples. Such recall can depend on an internal prompt to remember at the correct time.

The distinction between external and internal prospective tasks is illustrated in laboratory studies using dual-task procedures. In one case, the research participants engage in a primary task that keeps their attention occupied. The secondary task is to remember to push a response button every time a tone sounds. This part of the task is prospective memory, remembering to do something later, and is cued by the tone, an external prompt. There is high accuracy on this sort of task, and prospective memory is unaffected by some of the variables that affect retrospective memory, such as aging (Einstein & McDaniel, 1990). On the other hand, prospective memory could be paired with an internal reminder, for example, requiring the participant to push the button every so many minutes. It is up to the participant to keep track of when to respond. More forgetting occurs in these self-initiated retrieval tasks, and in this case, younger participants do perform better than older participants (Einstein et al., 1995).

Metamemory and Partial Retrieval

Metamemory, our knowledge about memory, applies to retrieval. We know how to search memory, for example, by using active strategies to facilitate recall (see the section on Applications). We also know what is stored in our memories (or at least, we think we know what's there). This latter form of knowing has been studied in the two related phenomena of feeling of knowing and tip of the tongue.

Feeling of Knowing

Each of us has probably experienced occasions in which we cannot then recall something but we are sure that we know it. This *feeling of knowing* (FOK) is characterized by an "irritating mixture of surety and bafflement. The individual is convinced he knows but is frustrated by the inability to demonstrate his knowing" (Reed, 1979, p. 9). Related to FOK is *tip of the tongue* (TOT). This is a more intense experience in which we feel that not only do we know the sought-after word, but that we are so close to recalling it. In Brown and McNeil's (1966) classic study, tip-of-the-tongue "states" (as the authors labeled them) were elicited by reading definitions of unusual or infrequently heard words to their college students. If a word could not be recalled, often the participants could accurately name the first letters of the unrecalled word, the number of syllables it contained, and the stress pronunciation pattern across syllables. For example, an unrecalled street name in Boston led to recall of similar names that were rejected as not the sought-after one: CONGRESS, CORINTH, and CONCORD. The actual street name was CORNISH. What is interesting about FOK or TOT is how confident we are that we know, even though the item cannot be recalled to verify our feelings.

These partial recalls are also interesting because we can readily reject wrong answers. As William James said, "Suppose we try to recall a forgotten name…. There is a gap therein; but no mere gap. It is a gap that is intensely active…. If wrong names are proposed to us, this singularly definite gap acts immediately to negate them. They do not fit into its mold. And the gap of one word does not feel like the gap of another, all empty of content as both might seem…when described as gaps" (1890, p. 251).

Older people are more likely to report retrieval blocks, especially for names. In one diary study, 60- to 80-year-olds recorded twice as many name-recall failures as did middle-aged participants, and rated these names as ones that were familiar and usually easily recalled. Both age groups later recalled the sought-after names, showing that the initial failure was indeed one of retrieval (Cohen & Faulkner, 1986).

How do we know our feelings of knowing are correct if we cannot recall the item? Hart (1965) introduced a three-step procedure to assess FOK accuracy. The participants are first tested with some general information questions. For example, "Which planet is the largest in the solar system?" Second, for the unanswered questions, the participants rate their confidence that they really do know the answer. These are the FOK ratings. Finally, a recognition or multiple-choice test is given to see if the correct response to the previously unrecalled items is selected. For the example question given before, the alternatives might be "Pluto, Venus, Saturn, and Jupiter." Items that received high FOK scores are more likely to be answered correctly in multiple-choice tests.

High FOK ratings might suggest that people can somehow directly assess the strength of unrecalled memories or knowledge. People know what they know. However, high FOK ratings can occur for other reasons apart from actually having a memory for the sought-after information. Respondents often use other information to *infer* whether they should know the answer. The recall of related facts could lead you to believe the sought-for answer is also known. Familiarity with the topic in the question may mislead you into thinking you should know the answer. Past experience or education may suggest you should know (e.g., "I probably covered this in high school science"). In these cases, the FOK rating is something of a probabilistic judgment. The participant makes an educated guess that the answer is indeed known.

It is also the case that high FOK ratings sometimes correspond to flat-out wrong answers. "Who commanded the Union army at the Battle of Gettysburg?" People giving high FOK ratings to this question go on to select Grant or Sherman in the multiple choice. After selecting one of these choices, the participants are highly confident in the correctness of their choice. The correct answer is Meade. (Several explanations for the feeling of knowing are summarized by Nelson & Gerler, 1984.)

False Retrieval

A different sort of retrieval failure is the mistaken recall of some stimulus or event that had not actually occurred. False retrieval, false recall, or the controversial "false memory" are all terms used to describe mistaken recollection. Deese (1959) demonstrated false retrieval simply but effectively by presenting lists in which all of the words were associated with a target word that was not included in the list. For example, the list might include BED, REST, AWAKE, SNOOZE, SLUMBER, and SNORE. When subsequently tested, many participants believed that the word SLEEP had been on the list. It was not. Deese found that intrusions of the target (e.g., the word SLEEP) occurred 30 to 40 percent of the time, and Roediger and McDermott (1995) found intrusions in as many as 50 percent of their participants.

The false-recall effect is extremely robust. For instance, warning subjects about it only minimally decreases false recall (and by making participants cautious, decreases correct recall of real list items). The degree of false recall is similar in young and old age groups. Alzheimer's individuals recall many fewer of the studied list items, but surprisingly have false recall rates comparable to nonimpaired elderly. About the only factor that reduces false recall is to present the list items as pictures (i.e., line drawings). During testing, there is more certainty in recall of the specific images than of less detailed word memories (Israel & Schacter, 1997; see review by Roediger & McDermott, 2000).

Why are associated words recalled as having occurred? According to the notion of spreading activation discussed earlier, activation spreads from the representations of each list item in memory to associated items in memory, including the target. The cumulative effect of activation from several list cues is stronger activation of the related word. The more associates there are in the list, the more likely false retrieval becomes (Robinson & Roediger, 1997).

In some ways, the falsely recalled words are as real in the brain as are the actually presented words. If event-related potentials are recorded, a form of EEG recorded from electrodes placed on the scalp, the reaction to falsely recognized words (e.g., SLEEP) is no different from that to correctly identified words (e.g., SLUMBER), and differs from foil words presented during testing (e.g., DOG) (Johnson et al., 1997). Thus, calling this phenomenon "false retrieval" may be a misnomer. From the perspective of the neural reaction, the recognition of actually presented and associatively activated words does not differ.

Reality Monitoring

The distinction between items that were actually presented and those we falsely remember as having occurred has parallels in other false retrieval phenomenon. Have you ever been unable to remember whether you actually said something or had only intended to say it? Johnson refers to this distinction as one of *reality monitoring:* distinguishing between actually experienced events and those events that were imagined, thought of, heard about, or even dreamed (e.g., Johnson & Raye, 1981). Another label is *source memory.* A memory's origin can be external in the words we spoke, actions we performed, or objects we perceived, or the memory's origin could be internal in words thought of, actions planned, and objects imagined.

How do we distinguish between externally and internally derived memories? As with the feeling of knowing experience, the answer involves not simply remembering an event, but also making a judgment about the qualitative aspects of the memory. Johnson and Raye (1981) hypothesize that we inspect a memory for certain attributes and then make a guess about whether the memory seems to have originated externally or internally. Memories deriving from actual events seem to be more detailed. They are richer in sensory attributes: there are stronger traces of sight, sound, or texture. The memory is more firmly set in a context of time and place, as events preceding or following the target are also remembered. On the other hand, imagined memories seem to be more schematic and lacking in sensory detail. There is less recall of what came before and after the remembered event. Internally derived memories may also contain traces of the mental operations used to derive them. You may remember reasoning, inferring, or imagining, for example. For any given memory, you total up the number of attributes that suggests internal origin versus the number that suggests external origin, and then make a decision about the likely origin of the memory (see Figure 10.5). Some memories will be judged probably internal or external, and some memories we are just not sure of. (Did I do that, or did I just think about doing that? Maybe someone else did it and told me about it?)

Remembering dreams and remembering childhood are two areas that pose interesting contrasts between external and internal attributes. Dreams, though internally generated, can still be vivid, detailed, and clear, all attributes that make them seem real. Johnson et al. (1984) had subjects record their own dreams or listen to other people describe their dreams. On later testing, the subjects were actually poor at differentiating their own dreams from someone else's. As memories age, they lose their vividness, contextual details fade, and the order of events is forgotten. Not surprisingly, childhood memories based on actual events become difficult to differentiate from those memories that are not (Johnson et al., 1988).

Forgetting the source of a memory could lead to the false belief that the event really occurred. (Remember Piaget's vivid memory of having been kidnapped as a young child, when in fact he had not? He was only told that he had been kidnapped.) Loftus and Pickrell (1995) were able to implant childhood memories in several people (both children and adults) by get-

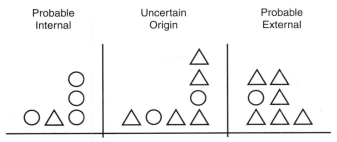

Strength or Amount of Contextual Information

FIGURE 10.5 Judging the origin of a memory is guided by decision rules based on the amount of contextual (time and place) information it includes. This dimension varies from memories with little contextual information (on the extreme left) to memories with high context (on the extreme right). The circles correspond to memories judged to be internally derived ("something I thought about doing"), and the triangles correspond to externally derived memories ("something I actually did").

Source: From "Reality Monitoring," by M. K. Johnson and C. L. Raye, 1981, *Psychological Review, 88,* p. 71. Copyright © 1981 by the American Psychological Association. Reprinted with permission.

ting family members to talk about fabricated events as if they had really happened. In one case, a 14-year-old boy was told how he had been temporarily lost in a shopping mall several years prior. Other family members went along with the story, adding details. After two days the boy really seemed to believe that he been lost, "remembering" more details, his feelings while lost, and even the man who eventually rescued him. (I suspect we now have a generation of young adults who vividly remember events from their childhood, when in fact what they are remembering are the videotapes of themselves that they saw later.)

Imagination Inflation

We have seen that there can sometimes be confusion between memories of actual events and imagined events. Goff and Roediger (1998) found that more thought leads to more confusion. Their subjects were asked to perform some simple action, such as knocking on the table or breaking a toothpick, or just imagine performing the action. During a later session the subjects had to recall whether they had performed or imagined the action. The more frequently an action had been imagined, the more likely it was to be remembered as one performed. This increase in the perceived reality of a memory is called *imagination inflation.*

Simply asking people to imagine a childhood event that did not occur can increase their belief that it could have happened. Garry et al. (1996) first asked subjects whether certain events had occurred during childhood, e.g., "Did you ever get stuck in a tree?" or "Did you win a stuffed animal at a carnival?" Two weeks later, in what the subjects thought was an unrelated study, they were asked to imagine some of the things that they had previously said had not occurred. After this, these imagined items were given higher ratings of belief that they had actually occurred.

Are some people more prone to imagination inflation? Imagination inflation correlates with hypnotic suggestibility, the capacity to respond to hynotic instructions (Heaps & Nash, 1999). One concern over imagination inflation is that psychotherapists use hypnosis and imaginal exposure (thinking about some distressing event) in therapy. Yet these are the same conditions associated with converting a thought into a memory for an actual event.

The Effect of Postevent Information

One of the more provocative issues about memory today is the role of postevent information on recall. Some seminal experiments demonstrated the effect of one type of postevent information, misleading questions. These experiments had three steps. First, the participants watched a short video depicting a minor car accident. Next, they were asked a misleading question to see if it would affect what was later recalled. Finally, the participants were asked questions about the video. For example, if the misleading question asked how fast the cars appeared to be going when they CRASHED, the participants later reported more car damage than did participants who were asked how fast the cars were going when they HIT (Loftus & Palmer, 1974). In another case, the misleading question asked about a traffic sign that was not present in the film. These participants later "recalled" seeing the sign in their reconstructions of the film (Loftus, Miller, & Burns, 1978).

Witnesses certainly can be led to misrecall events by misleading questions. Some of this may be due to acquiescence with the questioner's suggestions or an assumption that the questioner must be right about what appears (to the participant) to be an unimportant detail. The critical question concerns the fate of the original memory. Is it still there, but rendered less accessible to retrieval by the postevent information? Or has the misinformation actually changed the memory? Obviously, this distinction is important to evaluating eyewitness memory.

Explicit tests of recall sometimes cannot distinguish between these two alternatives. Possibly an indirect assessment of retention via an implicit memory test would reveal the original memory uninfluenced by the postevent information. To test this notion, participants in one study viewed a slide series showing a shopping episode and then read a narrative that contained misinformation, for example, the hammer in the slides was referred to as a screwdriver. When asked in an explicit test of memory what tool had been seen, the misinformation participants "recalled" the screwdriver. An implicit memory test was presented in the form of a picture-fragment test. The participants were shown a series of fragmented pictures of common objects, which included a hammer and a screwdriver. The participants were to name the object from the fewest number of fragments. The hammer was more readily identified, by virtue of its having been primed by an image of a hammer in the previous slide series. The misinformation presented following the slides did not affect priming in the picture-fragment test (Loftus, 1991). (*Note:* The screwdriver was also primed through its presentation during the misinformation phase. However, because priming effects are specific to modality or format, seeing the word "screwdriver" would not aid picture-fragment completion, although having seen a hammer would aid picture completion. See Weldon & Roediger, 1987, also described in Chapter 7.)

Target   Reproductions

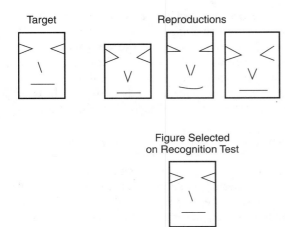

Figure Selected
on Recognition Test

FIGURE 10.6 In Zangwill's (1937) study, the participants first studied figures like those labeled TARGET (on the left); the participant then made several attempts to reproduce the target from memory, leading to successive distortions in their reproductions; finally, the participants were given a multiple-choice recognition test. The participants chose correctly even though the distractors were more like the participant's own reproductions.

Source: From "Processes of Memory Loss, Recovery, and Distortion," by W. K. Estes, 1997, *Psychological Review, 104,* p. 159. Copyright © 1997 by the American Psychological Association. Reprinted with permission.

Questions about postevent information are obviously related to interference theories of forgetting. A persisting concern in laboratory experiments is whether remembering one event retroactively interferes with retrieval of the earlier memory or whether it actually alters the earlier memory. Estes (1997) argues that some of both occurs. In an early study by Zangwill (1937), participants were shown a drawing, say, of an irregular figure and then produced a series of reproductions (see Figure 10.6). Systematic distortion appeared across the successive drawings, which became less like the original. However, when a recognition test was given afterwards, the original figure was more often correctly chosen and not some figure closer to the participant's own most recent reproductions. Memory for the original object was still there even after much potentially distorting interference.

Recovered Memory

Can memories of childhood abuse be repressed? Can memories of repeated and extended trauma remain hidden and unrecalled? These questions have placed research psychologists in the middle of a controversy. On one hand is the research showing that emotional events are well remembered, that false recollection occurs in laboratory tasks, and that misleading information or suggestion can lead to misrecall. On the other hand, there are psychotherapists who believe that memory repression is indeed a genuine psychological process, and that the denial of the existence of recovered memories on the grounds of "insufficient" or conflicting scientific evidence is tantamount to condoning the abuse of women or children.

The debate over "recovered" or "false" memories (depending on which side of the controversy you take) is a public one, unlike other controversies within cognitive psychology that arouse less outside interest. The conflict pits psychological experts against one another, frequently in court settings. (The local newspaper covers those cases in which a nationally recognized expert comes to town to testify.) Recovered memories of abuse can lead to accusations of a parent or relative as the abuser, and to countercharges of therapist suggestion.

Arrigo and Pezdek (1997) have tried to defuse the controversy surrounding recovered memories of childhood abuse by reminding us that amnesia occurs after other sorts of traumas as well. These include forgetting of accidents, natural disasters, combat, suicide attempts, or violent crimes. Unfortunately, as scientific evidence, claims for repression and subsequent recovery of memory for these traumas are often as weak as claims for recovery of childhood abuse memories. Many times we cannot independently verify the facts or events now being recalled. And we have only the victim's word that the event was truly unremembered for a period of time.

This does not mean that valid research on repressed and recovered memories is impossible. L. M. Williams (1994) confronted two problems frequently noted in repression research: Did abuse actually occur in the past, and did the victim forget that the trauma occurred? Williams first identified documented cases of childhood abuse that had occurred 17 years previously (on average). She then interviewed the (now) adult women for their recollections of the event. Williams found that 49 women (or about 38 percent of her sample) did not remember the abuse. Many of these women were old enough at the time of the abuse so that childhood amnesia was not a factor blocking memory. The present "forgetting" was not instead a reluctance to discuss something painful or embarrassing, because the women were willing to relate intimate details about other events. This study offers strong evidence that, indeed, forgetting of a traumatic experience can occur.

By what mechanisms could memories be unremembered yet still be in storage for later recall? Brewin and Andrews (1998) considered several. One explanation is in terms of repression: the mind suppresses recall of a painful memory. This could be an unconscious defense against the psychological distress produced by the trauma, or the repression could be conscious and deliberate. Alternatively, the traumatic memory might involve the implicit memory systems of the brain rather than the explicit systems. By definition, an implicit memory is less available for conscious recall. For instance, fear could be classically conditioned to be associated with a stimulus or cue without there being conscious awareness of that association. Finally, memory may not be accessible because adequate retrieval cues are not present. A memory formed during the intense emotional state of a traumatic experience could remain unrecalled as long as this strong and unique emotional state does not recur.

Retrieval versus Reconstruction

One misconception about memory is that it consists of static memory traces. This might be called a copy theory of memory. Our casual description of flashbulb memories fits the copy theory. We believe these memories persist unchanged over the years, almost like a photographic image. (In Chapter 9, we considered the evidence for accuracy of flashbulb memories.) An alternative conception of memory emphasizes less the retention of detailed memory images and more the *constructive* process of retrieval. That is, remembering is more like a reconstruction, on the basis of some stored fragments of information, of what must have happened. Neisser offered an analogy to the work of a paleontologist who reconstructs the appearance of a dinosaur from some fossil fragments (Neisser, 1967).

We have seen instances of reconstructive memory in considering the topic of schemas. Familiar and repetitive events, such as going to the movies or taking a trip, are represented in memory by schemas (or schemata, an alternative plural spelling). The schemas are standard outlines for such events. Schemas guide encoding of familiar events, the organization of information in storage, and retrieval cues that guide search of memory (Alba & Hasher, 1983). The use of a schema during retrieval of a specific event can lead to misrecall of what typically occurs (and is thus stored in the schema) rather than what actually occurred in a specific instance (e.g., Hudson, 1990; Linton, 1982). For example, you believe you bought popcorn on your last visit to the movies, when in fact you arrived late and so did not buy any snacks. Memory reconstructed according to the schema is not accurate in this instance.

Reconstruction is also illustrated in a study of sentence memory by Bransford and Franks (1971). Their college student participants heard a series of related sentences such as: "The car climbed the hill." "The hill was steep." "The car pulled a trailer." "The car was old." The participants shortly thereafter had difficulty discriminating old sentences from plausible but new test sentences. The several facts about the car appeared to have become unified into a single memory, and during testing individual facts could not be recovered. In fact, the test sentences that the participants judged as most familiar were ones never presented but that integrated all of the presented facts (i.e., "The old car pulling the trailer climbed the steep hill").

Instead of an either–or position of memory reproduction versus memory reconstruction, we could treat these two alternatives as end points on a continuum. Consider remembering a conversation you heard. Occasionally, verbatim memory for the exact wording is retained and later recalled: a particular phrasing or the wording of a joke. More often, we retain the general gist or meaning of the conversation and paraphrase the conversation when later recounting it. Finally, a highly stylized version might be retained, from which the conversation is reconstructed later. This later form involves going beyond the information given and includes inferences or interpretations that are added to the memory.

Automatic Retrieval

Sometimes retrieval of memory or knowledge seems automatic. You look at something and you know what it is. You are doing this right now in your reading: Comprehension seems to occur immediately and effortlessly. In fact, *not* reading words is more difficult than reading them. This is well illustrated by the *Stroop effect*. A list of color names is presented, the words being printed in different ink colors. The task is to name the color that each word is printed in. Color naming is impeded if the color names conflict with the color of ink in which they are printed (e.g., the word BLUE is printed in red ink). Our well-learned tendency to read words competes with naming a conflicting color.

The usual explanation of the Stroop effect is that reading is an automatic process. College student participants, who are basically professional readers, cannot help but read the words. The now-activated word representations in semantic memory interfere with color naming. In various theories, the interference is hypothesized to be central, blocking retrieval of the color name, or peripheral, setting up conflicting responses in output.

If word naming is automatic because it is overlearned, sufficient training with other materials might also produce Strooplike interference. MacLeod and Dunbar (1988) trained their college student participants to call certain shapes by color names (e.g., a square would be responded to as BLUE and a circle as RED; in fact, the shapes used were not so familiar or regular). When the shapes were then presented in colored ink, there was interference in naming the ink color because of the conflicting color name that had been associated with the shape.

Applications

Strategies for Searching Memory

What strategies are used in everyday life to aid retrieval? One survey found two frequently reported techniques (Harris, 1978). Retracing one's steps (mentally or physically) is used to retrieve mislaid objects or forgotten intentions, and alphabetical searching is used when names or words cannot be recalled.

The search strategies that people use can be uncovered using a thinking-out-loud protocol. Participants are given general prompts and are asked to think out loud as they attempt to recollect a specific instance (Reiser, Black, & Kalamarides, 1986). The strategies employed tend to direct and narrow the scope of the search. To recall, as examples, a chance meeting with someone or the date of the first exam this semester, you might ask yourself questions like: Where was I? What was I doing when this happened? Who was with me? What preceded or followed the event? Why would I have been doing that? Temporal landmarks are used to cue relevant information: At that time, where did I live, or go to school, or work?

Another retrieval strategy is to change your perspective or way of thinking about the to-be-recalled material. After searching fruitlessly for some lost memory, we sometimes realize we were simply thinking of the lost item in the wrong manner. For instance, maybe I should have been searching the category "people I know from school" and not "people I know from work." Changing perspective is illustrated in a study in which students read a paragraph-long description of a house. For some readers, the story was titled "Buying a House," and for others, the same story was titled "Burglary." Either version led to about the same amount of recalled details. However, if the participants were asked to think about the story from the perspective of the alternate title, additional details were recalled on a second test (in comparison to a second test without a changed title) (Anderson & Pichert, 1978). The alternate perspective lead to some different retrieval cues that evoked otherwise unrecalled information.

In a similar study, the participants were told they had been given the wrong title by mistake and were then given the correct title prior to testing (Hasher & Griffin, 1978). In this case, more correct ideas were recalled when the title was "corrected" than when the original title was re-presented. The participants in the corrected condition were likely using both perspectives to aid retrieval. Changing the perspective also reduced the number of intrusion errors or the misrecall of facts that were consistent with the theme but that were not part of the original story.

Studies of brain-injured patients suggest that controlled or strategic search of memory is associated with the frontal lobes of the brain. The recollective process can be thought of as an example of active problem solving, in which the participant selects plausible retrieval cues and evaluates the information each evokes. Unlike the amnesic syndrome patients for whom memories are absent, frontal-lobe-injury patients have trouble searching memory. Memories are haphazardly recalled, being accurately remembered on one occasion but not on another. There is difficulty generating specific personal memories from cues, such as recalling an event involving a DOG. The frontal patients might not evaluate the plausibility of what they do remember. For instance, one patient recollected that he had two brothers named Martin (Baddeley & Wilson, 1986).

Some researchers speculate that injury to the frontal lobe, when uncontaminated by damage to other brain areas, does not produce amnesia (Janowsky et al., 1989). Instead, the apparent memory problems stem from a deficit in the central executive of working memory, what Shallice (1988) called the *dysexecutive syndrome*. (When discussing the working-memory model in Chapter 8, we distinguished between the short-term memory stores and the central executive.) This is a failure to direct the voluntary aspects of retrieval. Frontal patients may have problems in establishing useful cues during the learning or encoding stage, in organizing retrieval later, and in evaluating what is retrieved for accuracy.

The notions of state-dependency and the dysexecutive syndrome are also relevant to understanding the effect of alcohol on memory. This is discussed in Box 10.3.

Context-Specific Learning

The possibility that learning is context-specific has important implications for training programs. If people are trained in one context, will they remember when tested elsewhere? As a specific instance, Baddeley noted that scuba diving students are taught emergency procedures in the classroom that might well be unrecallable under water during an emergency (a change in both context and emotional arousal). Godden and Baddeley (1975) assessed this possibility by having diving students study word lists on land or under water. Memory testing then occurred in the same or the opposite location. Their results, summarized earlier in Table 10.1, show context specificity of retrieval. More words were recalled when study and testing both occurred on the dock or under water. The implication of such findings is that training might be more profitably accomplished if done in the same location, or under the same conditions, as expected testing may occur.

How significant are context effects for classroom learning? Should you worry about forgetting everything you learned in this course when you leave the room? As we noted earlier, context effects are often subtle, requiring certain types of testing on poorly learned material. An extensive series of studies was carried out on 5,000 college students enrolled in five different kinds of courses. The students were told earlier in the semester that some would be taking their final exams in other rooms to relieve overcrowding and facilitate monitoring of finals. As it turned out, there were no significant effects of context change on final exam grades (Saufley, Otaka, & Bavaresco, 1985). Average grades of those students who took their finals in the course classroom did not differ from those who took their finals elsewhere.

Improving Accuracy of Recall in Surveys

Survey responses are an important part of the national decision- and policy-making process. Survey responses supplement government unemployment figures. The National

B O X **10.3**

Alcohol and Memory

As noted in this chapter, alcohol intoxication can produce state-dependent learning effects. However, alcohol affects memory in other ways. These effects can be organized in terms of the stage model of memory: encoding, storage, and retrieval.

Alcohol can inhibit memory encoding. Participants, usually volunteer college students, learn less well when they are intoxicated when they study than when they are sober. For example, recall of just-presented word lists was impaired in intoxicated participants (Weingartner et al., 1976). By using an immediate test, the participants are still in the same drug state during input and output, so the forgetting was not a state-dependent effect. Even when retested the next day in the intoxicated state, the alcohol participants recalled fewer words than did participants who were sober on both occasions (Miller et al., 1978).

This encoding deficit raises a question with respect to alcoholic amnesias for criminal actions. The notion of state dependency suggests that reentering the alcohol state could reinstate the forgotten memory. One attempt to do so did not lead to memory recall (Wolf, 1980). Thus, the memories may not have been encoded in the first place.

Alcohol particularly impairs spatial memory. Rats injected with ethanol have trouble recalling maze locations. The impairment is much like that seen with damage to the hippocampus. In fact, the activity of certain cells in the hippocampus seemed to be disrupted following ethanol injections and parallels the behavioral impairment in navigating the maze, both of which returned to normal after the alcohol wears off (Matthews et al., 1996).

Alcohol seems to be less detrimental to retrieval than to encoding. Introducing intoxication after studying does not significantly reduce recall from episodic memory, for example, recall of previously studied word lists (e.g., Birnbaum et al., 1978). However, retrieval from semantic memory is impaired, as assessed by reaction-time measures. Alcohol slowed comparisons between words (e.g., are these two words from the same category: DOG–CAT). This slowing was greater among women than men. The researchers note that blood alcohol levels are higher for women than for men, even though the dose of alcohol was adjusted for body weight (Haut et al., 1989).

Alcohol can impair the maintenance of stored memories, at least in extreme cases. Korsakoff's syndrome is a neurological degenerative disorder associated with prolonged (i.e., decades-long) alcohol abuse, producing lesions in the areas of the brain known as the thalamus and mammillary bodies. A characteristic of Korsakoff's patients is that memories that were clearly present in storage earlier are later lost. In one case study, a distinguished scientist completed his autobiography shortly before the onset of Korsakoff's. The manuscript provides a valid record of what could be remembered before, so that test questions could be constructed about his professional life (papers written, conferences attended, developments in his field) to quantify his memory loss. A retrograde impairment was found, showing profound forgetting for recent decades and sparing of memory for his earlier career (Butters & Cermak, 1986). (Korsakoff's syndrome is discussed in more detail in Chapter 7.)

Because Korsakoff's syndrome is also associated with frontal-lobe damage, there are metamemory deficits. For example, on tests of feeling of knowing (i.e., you cannot recall something, but you still think you know it), Korsakoff's amnesics, in comparison to matched alcoholic control patients, give inaccurate estimates of what they know that bear no correlation to actual recognition test performance (Shimamura & Squire, 1986).

What about non-Korsakoff's alcoholics? There also seems to be impaired learning and remembering as a function of the amount of alcohol consumption: a dose-impairment continuum ranging from social drinkers to alcoholics. The cessation of drinking may lead to recovery of normal cognitive abilities within a few weeks, particularly for nonelderly individuals (Goldman, 1983). The cognitive loss in Korsakoff's, however, is not reversible.

The adverse effects of alcohol on memory seem to occur at several stages, making it difficult to isolate alcohol's effects to any one stage in any one situation. One review of the literature suggests that alcohol has such a pervasive effect on information processing in general that a deficit at any stage of memory is bound to be found (Maylor & Rabbit, 1993).

Center for Health Statistics, a part of the Centers for Disease Control, uses surveys to help determine frequencies of illness and disease, eating and exercise, smoking and drug use, sexual behavior, crime victimization, and so on. Questioning is also part of a clinical interview. For example, a physician or an epidemiologist would ask about recently consumed foods in tracing an outbreak of food poisoning. Self-reports, as we all well know, are subject to inaccuracies. In addition to biased samples of respondents or response distortions, such as social desirability, inadequate memory retrieval is also a critical potential flaw in survey answers.

For example, we can ask people who are HMO members how often they have gone to the doctor in the last year. This is a useful question for research purposes because the accuracy of respondents' answers can be verified in comparison to actual records. The number of recalled visits is not that high, maybe 30 to 50 percent. The number recalled is especially low when multiple visits were made for the same problem. Why is it so poor? Possibly a sort of schematic memory develops, characterizing these visits in general, but making recall of specific ones, and thus their frequency, difficult.

One attempt to improve recall is to use a process of decomposition, to "decompose" a generic script memory into individual memories. The patients are questioned about details of each visit: What time was the visit, did someone accompany them to the office, which health provider was seen that time? The respondents try to locate individual medical visits temporally by noting their relationship to landmark dates (e.g., birthdays, holidays, vacations) on a time line. The decomposition and time-line procedures increased accuracy from a control level of 40 to 60 percent in the decomposition condition (Means & Loftus, 1991). An alternative strategy is to ask participants to recall each visit in a specific order, that is, working backwards from the most recent visit, which also sometimes enhances recall (Loftus et al., 1992).

A similar procedure is the *cognitive interview* (see earlier Box 10.1), used in one study to test recall of recently eaten foods (Fisher & Quigley, 1992). Students were invited to a little postexam party. Four days to 2 weeks later, the students were asked to recall what they had eaten. A cognitive interview procedure encouraged the students to re-create the context (environmental and psychological) of the eating session; to recall the foods available starting from each end of the table; to recollect their attitudes toward certain foods, both those selected and those not. The cognitive interview group recalled more of the foods they had eaten and were also able to recall more of the available but unchosen foods.

Summary

How Long Is Long-Term Memory?

Although Ebbinghaus's curve of forgetting seems to suggest rapid loss, a number of studies of naturalistic memory show substantial retention after delays of years and even decades. These include memory for names and faces of high school classmates, high school and college courses, one-season TV shows, and public events.

According to the permanent-memory hypothesis, everything we learn is permanently stored in the brain. Forgetting is due to the inability to retrieve some things. Often-cited support for this hypothesis comes from Penfield's use of electrical stimulation of the temporal lobes during surgery to elicit supposedly long-lost memories, and memories recovered through hypnosis or free association. However, these mental experiences are not necessarily memories, nor are they necessarily valid.

The Nature of Storage

How are memories organized in long-term memory? Semantic network theories assume that items of knowledge are interconnected in memory. Collins and Quillian used reaction-time measures to verify the hierarchical arrangement of knowledge organization. Statements related to more distantly separated facts took longer to verify than comparisons involving more proximal facts.

Activation of one item in memory spreads to other connected items. An item in memory can be identified more readily if it has been primed shortly before by a related item. This spreading activation is diluted if there are many connections from the activated item.

Case studies from neuropsychology illustrate the organization of memory, when whole categories of words (e.g., nouns or "living things") are lost following brain injury. The possible biological mechanisms of memory include protein changes, synaptic change, and long-term potentiation.

Forgetting is increasingly being construed as a failure of retrieval of memories that are potentially available, rather than attributing forgetting to either decay or interference.

Retrieval from Episodic Memory

Three general factors affect retrieval: the distinctiveness of the memory, the presence of effective retrieval cues, and prior practice at retrieving that memory. Distinctive memories are retrievable because they stand out against a background on otherwise similar memories.

Testing benefits memory more than does additional study. Hypermnesia is an increase in recall across successive tests in the absence of additional study and is the opposite of forgetting (or amnesia.)

What makes a good retrieval cue? One theory identifies cues that are strongly associated to the target. Thus, TABLE would be a good cue for CHAIR. Alternatively, the encoding specificity principle states the best retrieval cues are those that were also present and encoded with the target. Recall is facilitated when encoding and retrieval conditions are matched, as shown by studies of context-specific (or place-specific) retention; drug-state-dependent learning; and mood-dependent memory. However, context-specific memory is not always found. Contextual cues are sometimes overshadowed by more explicit retrieval cues, and interaction of the context with the to-be-remembered items may be required.

Retrieval can be impaired by high levels of emotional arousal, as is the case with test anxiety and momentary forgetting.

Establishing Retrieval Cues at Input

Prospective memory, or remembering to do something in the future, requires the establishment of retrieval cues that will prompt the desired behavior at the appropriate time. Prospective memory can be externally cued by reminders such as alarms or a list of instructions, or internally cued by intentions to remember.

Metamemory judgments include the feeling of knowing, the belief that we know something that cannot be recalled now; and the tip-of-the-tongue experience, an even more urgent feeling of knowing a word or name even though it cannot be recalled. The accuracy of our unrecalled knowledge can be verified by recognition tests. However, our intuitions are sometimes based on educated guesses about what we think we should know, and sometimes our intuitions are incorrect.

False Retrieval

Mistakenly recalling something that did not actually occur is referred to as false retrieval, false recall, or "false memory." Deese elicited false recall of a target word, such as SLEEP, by presenting a list of associates of the target. Reality monitoring refers to distinguishing between actually experienced events and those events that were imagined, thought of, heard about, or even dreamed of. External- and internal-originating memories are discriminated partly on the basis of memory attributes and partly on the basis of judgment. Similarly, one could forget the source of information, but correctly remember the information itself. False memories of childhood experience could be produced through combined failures of reality monitoring and source forgetting.

Witnesses can be led to misrecall an event after exposure to misleading postevent information. Although such effects readily occur, their interpretation is still uncertain. Does postevent information block access to the original memory? Or is the original memory replaced by the postevent misinformation?

In some cases, memory retrieval is a reconstruction based on some fragments of memory and schematic knowledge. Finally, some retrieval is seemingly automatic, as in reading, in which word meaning is accessed. In the Stroop effect, the color words interfere with naming the ink colors in which they are printed.

Applications

Retrieval can be a directed process, in which we employ strategies to direct the scope of memory search. One search strategy is to change your perspective or way of thinking about the to-be-recalled material. Neuropsychological studies suggest the frontal lobes are critical for initiating, directing, and evaluating retrieval.

If people are trained in one context, will they remember when tested elsewhere? An experiment using scuba diving students showed context specificity of retrieval, suggesting that training should occur in the same location, or under the same conditions, in which testing will occur. However, studies on 5,000 college students who took final exams in other rooms found there were showed no significant effects of room change on exam grades.

Survey data can be inaccurate due to incomplete retrieval of known information by the respondents. Proposed solutions are to use decomposition to "decompose" a generic script memory into individual memories for specific events; require episodic recall of particular events; and refer to temporal landmarks to more accurately date events.

11 Spatial, Motor-Skill, and Implicit Learning

Current psychological theories distinguish among different forms of long-term memory. One distinction is between declarative and procedural knowledge. _Declarative knowledge refers to memory for verbalizable knowledge or propositions._ It includes semantic memory, such as word meanings and general facts, and episodic memory, our autobiographical memory of specific events. In distinction, _procedural knowledge_ underlies skilled behavior and the ability to quickly perform various cognitive, perceptual, and motor operations. In contrast to declarative's "knowing that," procedural is referred to as "knowing how." Whereas declarative knowledge is typically shown by verbal recall of information, procedural knowledge is usually demonstrated by facilitated performance of behavior.

This chapter includes several forms of learning that correspond, in a general fashion, to the procedural description: spatial learning, or knowing how to get from place to place in an environment; motor-skill learning, knowing how to perform coordinated bodily movements quickly and accurately; implicit learning, knowing the underlying rules that govern complex sequences of behaviors; and expertise, or expert performance in a specific domain. All of these refer to fluent, quick, and skilled performance, whether running a maze or reading X-ray images. Each of these topics represents a subarea in the field of learning, and each separately has contributed to our knowledge of the general principles of learning. To anticipate what follows in this chapter, consider the following questions: Is spatial information remembered in the form of a route or a map? What is the role of feedback in learning skilled movements? Is the knowledge underlying skilled behavior accessible to conscious description, or is it outside of awareness? Is the skilled behavior of the expert due to practice or talent?

There is considerable current interest in procedural learning, which can be traced to the convergence of several influences: (1) There is renewed interest in Ebbinghaus's findings that even after conscious recall fails, memory can still be demonstrated in relearning; (2) amnesic individuals learn classically conditioned responses, motor skills, and strategies for problem solving, even though they have no recollection of having practiced the tests before; and (3) the effects of experience, or learning, can be detected in habits, attitudes, preferences, or the ease with which behavior and cognition occurs, and not just through explicit recollection.

Procedural learning is often referred to as a form of implicit learning, a term that parallels implicit memory. Explicit and implicit refer to the awareness and conscious accessibility of the knowledge learned. In some cases of procedural learning, we can perform but we cannot articulate how we do it. Some theorists have suggested that procedural learning is indeed unconscious, because it evolved earlier than conscious forms of knowledge representation (Reber, 1993). One important question we will consider is whether procedural learning is implicit or whether there is instead some explicit knowledge that can indeed be reported.

Spatial Learning

Spatial ability in our everyday lives is often taken for granted until we become lost. You become temporarily disoriented on leaving a movie theater, forgetting whether to turn left or right. You exit the mall at a different place from which you entered. You forget where you parked the car earlier. (On a really good day, you forget all three.) What sorts of experiences are necessary for acquiring spatial knowledge, and what exactly do we learn? In the following sections, we will consider alternative perspectives on whether spatial information is represented in memory as specific routes or as global cognitive maps.

In anticipation of what follows, several factors should be acknowledged. First, there are probably multiple kinds of spatial memories, just as there are with other forms of memory. Thus, there can be episodic memories for a particular trip or route, or semantic memory for a well-traveled route. In Chapter 8 we described spatial short-term memory, and in this chapter we will consider working and long-term spatial memories.

A second factor to acknowledge is that spatial memory tends to be very good. As one example, college students can well remember where previous semesters' classes met, even after the course titles, meeting times, and professors' names have been forgotten (Wittman & Healy, 1995). There are also individual differences in spatial ability, such as gender differences discussed in this chapter, and cross-cultural differences in people's spatial memory considered in Chapter 12.

Rats, Mazes, and Psychology

The rat and the maze seem to be two stereotypes that are inextricably linked to psychology's image. The use of rats as subjects began early in American psychology laboratories. Willard S. Small at Clark University first studied rats in mazes in 1900, capitalizing on the animals' burrowing and tunneling behavior. John Watson began research at the University of Chicago on the sensory cues used by rats in maze learning (Watson, 1907). At both Clark and Chicago, biologists were studying rat anatomy and physiology, so it was natural for biologically oriented psychologists to start studying rat behavior.

Route versus Survey Maps

An organism moving within a complex environment needs to develop some type of memorial representation of that environment. There are two broad conceptions of how spatial knowledge might be represented. *Route knowledge* is knowledge of a series of routes, directions, or paths through a spatial environment. For instance, we could describe maze learning as the memorization of a sequence of left and right turns in the maze. When you ask directions to an unfamiliar location, the response is likely to be in the form of a route: a specific series of distances and turns, with maybe an occasional landmark ("go straight 2 miles, turn left at the gas station"). In its extreme, a route is characterized by knowledge of sequential locations but not of general interrelationships. By contrast, a *survey map* or a *cognitive map* is a more abstract representation of an environment, placing specific routes in context with the surrounding area. The word *survey* implies an aerial overview of the area, and the phrase *cognitive map* implies that a schematic image is represented internally. Some of the terms that have been used to contrast survey and route maps are presented in Table 11.1 (from Cohen, 1989, p. 60). Given these two possibilities, route versus cognitive map, which form of representation does spatial knowledge take?

Place versus Response Studies.   According to one tradition in psychology, rats learn specific routes through mazes. Hull (1949) theorized that rats acquired stimulus–response as-

TABLE 11.1   Terms Used to Characterize Survey and Route Knowledge of Spatial Information

Survey Knowledge	Route Knowledge
Cognitive map	Paths
Global	Local
Semantic	Episodic
Bird's eye	Ground-based
Schematic	Concrete
Abstract	Detailed
Flexible	Sequential

Source: Adapted from *Memory in the Real World* (p. 60), by G. Cohen, 1989, Mahwah, NJ: Erlbaum. Copyright © 1989 by Lawrence Erlbaum Associates. Adapted with permission.

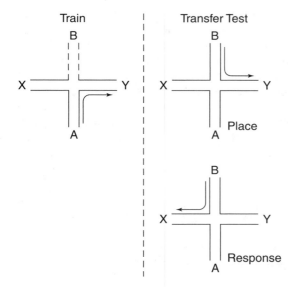

FIGURE 11.1   Maze Arrangements for Testing Place versus Response Learning.

Source: From "Mazes, Maps, and Memory," by D. S. Olton, 1978, *American Psychologist, 34,* p. 590. Copyright © 1978 by the American Psychological Association. Adapted with permission.

sociations in the mazes. The stimuli of each choice point became associated with a certain *response,* a left or right turn, for example. Tolman (e.g., 1948) hypothesized instead that the rats acquired a cognitive map of the maze and the surrounding environment. The rat learned the *place* where food was located in the maze, and importantly also within the room. The two views can be illustrated by reference to learning in a simple T maze (see Figure 11.1, left). Rats start at point A and are first trained to turn right at the choice point to get to the goal box (Y). What have the rats learned? Hull says they learned the *response* of making a right turn. Tolman says they learned the *place* where food is located in the maze. Each theory describes what the animal learns to do. How can the two hypotheses be separated?

Tolman proposed an experimental test to distinguish response learning from place learning (Tolman, Ritchie, & Kalish, 1946, 1947). He would simply rotate the maze 180 degrees, so that now the rat would be starting from a new location in the room (point B in Figure 11.1, right). Which direction would the rats turn according to the two theories? Hull's theory predicts that the rats will make a right turn as they have been trained to do, and now go away from where food had previously been located. Tolman's theory predicts the rats will check their cognitive map for the location of the maze within the room, and make a left turn to compensate for the change in starting location. The design of the place versus response experiment nicely contrasts route versus survey descriptions of learning and the differing predictions of the two theories.

What did the rats actually do? Most students guess that the rats turned left, consistent with the cognitive map theory and probably reflecting the cognitive bias we have in psychology today. It would be nice to say the data turned out clearly in favor of one theory or another. In fact, in some experiments the rats turned right as Hull predicted; in other studies, they went left as Tolman predicted. Stating the results in this manner does not seem to be helpful (and also leaves you wondering what will be the correct answer on the exam).

This simple and elegant experimental manipulation did not, in fact, resolve the controversy. Instead, the results told us something about the stimuli used in spatial learning. For example, in the studies done by Hull and his followers, the maze alleys were often enclosed by walls. The maze itself was surrounded by curtains, providing a homogeneous environment outside the maze. There were no prominent cues for the rat to orient itself within the room. This lack of external cues (or "landmarks") encouraged response learning. In the experiments by Tolman and his students, the mazes were "strip" mazes, being flat alleys with no walls and elevated off the floor. Distinctive features in the room (landmarks) were clearly visible from the maze. This procedure encouraged cognitive map learning. The place versus response controversy taught us is that either specific responses or cognitive maps may be learned: Rats, and people, are flexible in their use of whatever cues are available (Restle, 1957).

The distinction between response learning and cognitive maps is readily seen in our own experience. Interior hallways in large office buildings often lack visible external landmarks for orientation. People develop route maps from one location to another, maybe without realizing the spatial relationships between separate locations. After moving to a new town, we may learn a series of routes to various locations, for example, one route from home to school and another from home to the store. But can you get from school to the store? It is only after more experience that a generalized map of the town is acquired that allows you to take a more direct route between home and store.

The Radial Maze.   Cognitive mapping is convincingly demonstrated by performance in the *radial maze.* The prototype of this maze has eight or more arms radiating out from a central platform, as shown in Figure 11.2. The maze is usually elevated, often without side walls. Food is placed in recessed food cups at the end of each arm. The rat is allowed to enter any and all arms, which are baited at first, but food is not replenished once taken. The optimal strategy for a foraging animal, in terms of effort and energy expenditure, is to retrieve all the pieces of food without repeating an arm entry. Rats quickly learn this, achieving an accuracy level of entering 7.6 different maze arms among the first 8 choices (in an eight-arm radial maze) after only 15 trials of practice (Olton & Samuelson, 1976).

Why is this evidence that rats have learned a cognitive map? There are alternative explanations that do not require a process this sophisticated. One strategy is to enter the arms in sequence, proceeding in one direction around the circle of arms. This is a sensible strategy, one which we might use, and 50 percent of adults did in a human-sized version of the radial maze (Overman et al., 1996). However, the rats do not use any obvious pattern such as this (Olton & Samuelson, 1976).

A rat could depend on odor stimuli, either from its own previous perambulations or from the smell of food, to determine which arms have been entered and which not. Scents can be ruled out by several manipulations, ranging from surgically making the rats anosmic to dousing the maze in Old Spice aftershave to mask any scents (I believe this latter study was done shortly after Father's Day). Correct choices are relatively unaffected by such manipulations (Olton & Samuelson, 1976; Zoladek & Roberts, 1978).

Rats instead seem to use cues outside of the maze, or *extramaze cues,* to keep track of entered and unentered maze arms. One means of demonstrating this is by rotating the maze within the room between maze-arm choices. The subject is allowed to make four arm entries and then is removed from the maze temporarily while the maze is rotated slightly. The animal is then returned to the maze and allowed to complete its selection of arms. The rat mistakenly reenters previously chosen arms that are in the direction not yet visited and will avoid an unentered arm that is in the direction previously visited. The animal is responding to locations within the room and not to cues (such as smells) within the maze (Olton, Collison, & Werz, 1977). If detection of these extramaze cues is blocked, for example, by surrounding the maze with curtains, the accuracy of choosing different maze arms declines.

A note of caution is in order here. Even though rats might spontaneously focus on extramaze cues, other categories of cues might be adopted in some situations. If external cues are not available, rats can use internal, kinesthetic cues to help navigate the maze. Even when the maze and all its arms are completely enclosed and the rats are run in total darkness, the animals can learn to choose at better than chance levels (Brown & Moore, 1997). Although external environmental cues are obviously important, we must remember that there can be multiple types of cues available to navigate spatially. This is especially the case in long-distance navigation (see Box 11.1).

Morris Water Maze.   An ingenious test of spatial navigation is the Morris water maze (Morris, 1981). A rat is placed in a small swimming pool in which the water is clouded by the addition of powered milk. (Rats are very good swimmers.) There is a hidden platform

FIGURE 11.2   A Rat in a Radial Maze.

Source: © Hank Morgan, Science Source/Photo Researchers.

BOX **11.1**

Long-Distance Travel by Animals

A newspaper article from a few years ago told of a small dog, named Sam, who was left behind in Colorado when his family moved to California. The dog nevertheless showed up at their new home 10 weeks later, after apparently having traveled 840 miles across plains, deserts, and mountains of four states ("Dog Roams," 1983). The dog, tired and dirty from his trek, was also described as being nervous and suspicious. "He follows us everywhere," his owners say. (Hey, no kidding!) How does a dog find its way from Colorado to California?

Many feats of animal migration require extraordinary spatial abilities. But to state the obvious does not explain the causes of particular behaviors. Studies of animal way-finding indicate that there are several components to spatial ability: some means of determining direction, sensitivity to different kinds of stimuli, and possibly a cognitive map.

Take the example of homing pigeons. These birds can return to their home nests after having been released hundreds of miles away. The first thing the pigeon needs to do is determine direction. You cannot fly north, for instance, without knowing which way north is. Pigeons and other birds have several means of direction finding. Some can use the combination of sun position and time of day (i.e., the sun rises in the east and is in the southern sky at noon). Pigeons have been maintained indoors on a light–dark cycle that is advanced or delayed with respect to the actual day–night cycle. When released, these pigeons showed displaced homing, now judging the sun's position according to their altered circadian cycles.

Pigeons may also possess a magnetic sense. Basically, they can detect magnetic north as if possessing a built-in compass. This magnetic sense has been tested in natural homing situations by taping magnets to the pigeons' heads to disrupt orienting. Some cases of lost or disoriented homing pigeons have been attributed to anomalies in the local magnetic fields associated with mountains, iron fields, sun spots, and so on, that disrupt the birds' sense of direction (Walcott, 1989). There are occasional claims that humans have a similar sense. After being blindfolded, taken to a remote location, and spun around three times, people are supposedly able to point accurately to compass directions. Later experiments did not substantiate these earlier findings (Gould & Able, 1981).

Granted direction finding, homing pigeons also need to know where to fly to. Maybe pigeons, which have excellent visual memories, simply observe the outbound route, and can then retrace it when released. However, pigeons home even if prevented from seeing the route taken to the release point. (In one study, they were even anesthetized for the trip to the release point. They still found their way home!) Pigeons fitted with opaque eye cups, which allowed in light but not clear vision, were able to home to the general vicinity of their roost. Once there, the birds circled aimlessly and fluttered down anywhere. Apparently, visual landmarks are important for proximal homing, but not for long-distance travel. (Homing mechanisms are reviewed in Pearce, 1997.)

Other instances of way finding have been attributed to an ability to perceive and follow subtle sensory stimuli. For example, animals can return to a coastal region by following the scent of sea air carried by the wind over long distances. A "nuisance" wolf living near an airport in Alaska was captured and relocated several hundred miles away. When the wolf returned to the airport, it was hypothesized that it had followed low-frequency sounds from planes, which carry over great distances in Arctic regions. The proof was a second relocated wolf that found its way to an airport, but a different one from which it had been relocated (Rogers, 1989).

The place- versus response-learning controversy taught us an important lesson about spatial learning. Animals (and presumably, people too) can learn to use different kinds of stimuli: landmarks, magnetic sense, sun and star positions, olfactory stimuli, and so on. One researcher has suggested that homing pigeons are flexible in the strategies they use. Depending on where they were bred and trained, some may use magnetic sense, some olfactory stimuli, and others distinctive visual landmarks (Walcott, 1989).

Okay, so how did Sam find his family? I really don't think the dog could smell them 800 miles away. The family speculated that since they had once before made the trip from California to Colorado with the dog, Sam "remembered" the route and retraced it. This is a little far-fetched, and anyway, the previous trip had been to a different town in California. I think the Colorado people who took in Sam got tired of him, drove overnight to California, and left the dog on his owner's porch. That's my theory.

just under the surface of the water, and the goal is to learn the location of this platform. From trial to trial, the starting location in the pool is varied, so the animal learns the platform location on the basis of cues in the room. On the first trials, the animals spend considerable time searching for the platform. Over trials, the animals become faster and follow more direct paths in going to the platform.

The radial maze and the water maze have become commonly used laboratory tasks, particularly useful for testing theories about the anatomical basis of spatial memory. Performance in the radial maze is particularly impaired by lesions to the hippocampus. The radial-maze task differs from the mazes used earlier by psychologists, in which both food locations and the route through the mazes remained fixed over trials. The flexible use of working memory in the radial maze has been contrasted with habit learning by training animals with different rules in the radial maze. McDonald and White (1993) produced a triple dissociation among tasks and brain areas. Rats who received hippocampal lesions were impaired in learning the regular radial-maze task, which requires choosing all different arms in a trial. Rats with hippocampal lesions reenter already visited arms. A second task was a form of association learning, in which the rats were taught that only lighted maze arms contained food. Lesions of the amygdala impaired learning of this stimulus–reinforcer association. In the third task, the rats were trained to repeat choices of the reinforced arms, the opposite of the usual radial-maze alternation rule. Lesions of the striatum impaired learning this rule. In each case, the alternative lesions did not inhibit learning or performance. The pattern between lesions and impairments is summarized in Table 11.2.

The popularity of mazes once again to study animal spatial learning has extended to investigations in people. Virtual mazes have been developed in which participants "move" through a computer-presented maze by controlling a joystick. A Morris maze can be simulated in which distinctive cues are seen surrounding the maze, such as differently patterned and colored walls, to provide orientation information. The mazes have a progressively changing image, as if one were "swimming" (well, maybe wading) through the pool. The time to find the hidden platform, and the directness of the route from different starting points, can be recorded just as with mice and rats. In these virtual mazes, men typically perform better than women, although the males are usually more experienced with computer games (Astur, Ortiz, & Sutherland, 1998). In one case, college students were tested in a series of progressively more difficult virtual mazes, and were compared to mice trained in actual mazes. Not surprisingly, the humans learned faster than did the mice. But males of

TABLE 11.2   Dissociation of Three Learning Tasks Conducted in a Radial Maze after Lesions of Different Brain Regions

Tasks	Alternate Arms	Food in One Arm	Repeat Arms
Impairing lesion	Hippocampus	Amygdala	Striatum
Unaffecting lesions	Amygdala	Hippocampus	Hippocampus
	Striatum	Striatum	Amygdala

Source: McDonald & White, 1993.

both species performed better than did females (Shore, Stanford, MacInnes, Klein, & Brown, 2001).

As you may recall, damage to the hippocampus is significant in producing human amnesia (Squire, 1992). In humans, the left hemisphere exerts more control over verbal memory, whereas the right hemisphere exerts more influence over spatial memory. People with loss of right-side hippocampal tissue suffer greater impairments of spatial learning and memory. This includes tests of maze learning, remembering the location of objects, and learning to tap a series of blocks in sequence (Kolb & Whishaw, 1985). Patients with left-side hippocampal damage showed less difficulty on these tasks (Kesner, Hopkins, & Chiba, 1992).

The role of the hippocampus is clearly shown by H. M., the well-studied amnesic mentioned previously in Chapter 7. To refresh your memory, H. M. had portions of his temporal lobes removed, including the hippocampus on both sides of his brain, in an experimental procedure used to treat his epilepsy. H. M. is severely impaired at most forms of learning, including spatial tasks such as those mentioned before. His impairment is shown in the following passage reported by the researchers working with him:

> His limitations…are illustrated by the manner in which he attempted to guide us to his house, in June, 1966, when we were driving him back from Boston. After leaving the main highway, we asked him for help in locating his house. He promptly and courteously indicated to us several turns, until we arrived at a street which he said was quite familiar to him. At the same time, he admitted that we were not at the right address. A phone call to his mother revealed that we were on the street where he used to live before his operation. (Milner, Corkin, & Teuber, 1968, as cited in Kolb & Whishaw, 1985, p. 482)

This was 8 years after he had moved away from that address.

One recent study shows vividly the importance of the hippocampus for spatial navigation. London taxi drivers were found to have more development and greater volume in their hippocampi (the plural of hippocampus) than did matched control subjects (Maguire et al., 2000). This study used magnetic resonance imaging to obtain graphic images of the brain for comparison purposes. The researchers believe that the extensive use of spatial navigation skills led to the increased development in the hippocampus. However, the alternative possibility is that those who become taxi drivers had better spatial skills, and therefore larger hippocampi, to begin with, in comparison to the control subjects. If you cannot find your way around, you likely won't last long as a cabbie.

Route versus Survey Presentation

Spatial information can be presented either in a route format or in survey format. Do these produce differences in performance? Surprisingly, several studies have found little difference between route and survey descriptions of an area. Both Perrig and Kintsch (1985) and Taylor and Tversky (1992) gave their participants verbal descriptions of a town. The route versions were in the form of a series of directions one might follow in driving through. "On your left just after you cross the river you see a gas station…. Going left on Main Street after a few blocks you will see a church on your right." The survey description emphasized geographical layout. "Heading east across the river, you will see a gas station on the north side of the road. A few blocks north on Main there is a church on its east side" (from Perrig & Kintsch, 1985). Participants who studied either version were equally able to identify correct statements made about the town's layout and reject incorrect descriptions. Why didn't the route and survey versions produce different results? Both sets of investigators concluded that both groups of participants probably recoded the descriptions, likely into a visual image that in fact was not different from that encoded by participants who studied an actual map. Interestingly, this was especially so for male participants, who, given a route description, nevertheless encoded it as a spatial map.

Landmarks.   There are certain elements in an environment that by virtue of their distinctive features (e.g., size or shape) or their meaning (e.g., historical or social) stand out from other features in the environment. Because such elements are literally outstanding, these *landmarks* will be readily perceived, remembered, and used as reference points. When we give someone directions, or when asked where we live, we often start with some nearby landmark and describe a route from there. The extramaze cues used by rats in place learning or the radial maze, such as a door, window, or light fixture, can be considered landmarks. According to some theories of environmental cognition, we first learn landmarks, then routes around them, and finally we develop survey maps. Although spatial memory declines with aging, elderly participants can still recognize landmarks after traveling through an unfamiliar hospital building, even if they cannot reconstruct the route. College-aged participants could remember both routes and landmarks (Wilkins et al., 1997).

The capacity to recognize landmarks is apparently separate from that of learning routes. In certain neurological disorders, a person becomes impaired at identifying landmarks, such as individual buildings, but can follow a list of verbal directions, such as street names or a map. Other patients recognize landmarks but cannot learn routes. For example, one hospitalized but ambulatory patient could not learn her way from one ward to another and frequently became lost. She would recognize familiar locations, but could not conceive of how to get from one to another (McCarthy & Warrington, 1990).

Schemas in Spatial Memory

Schemas are ways of abstracting, organizing, and storing general knowledge (see Chapter 9). Spatial knowledge can be organized hierarchically in schemas. We may know the rough geography of the United States, and subsumed under that is the local geography of our home states, then towns, and below that the layout of our homes and workplaces. Some of this knowledge was learned through direct experience with places, some knowledge was learned indirectly through study, and some knowledge is inferential: We guess this must be so.

Spatial schemas can have two prominent effects on memory: They facilitate organization and they can distort recall.

Distortion in Cognitive Maps.   Spatial schemas distort recall due to the averaging, normalizing, or rounding off that occurs when a generalized map is acquired. For example, we tend to encode all turns as being 90 degrees, or right angles. Byrne (1979) asked people to draw some familiar road intersections. The intersections actually deviated from right angles by at least 20 degrees, yet the angles drawn averaged close to 90 degrees. This means that if in fact a series of left turns are consistently greater than or less than 90 degrees, going "around the block" will not return us to our starting point as we might predict from a schematic memory.

The tendency to normalize turns is seen in judging locations in a familiar city. The River Seine in Paris is more sharply curved than most Parisians imagine, producing misjudgments of distance and proximity (Milgram & Jodelet, 1976). Two locations are remembered as being on the same side of the river when they are not, and locations on the same side are remembered as being closer together than two on opposite sides, even though this is not actually the case.

This sort of distortion in spatial schemas is seen in other comparisons involving geographic locations. For example, which U.S. city is farther to the west, San Diego or Reno? We assume the correct answer is San Diego because California is farther west than Nevada. Which city named Portland is farther north, the Portland in Maine or the one in Oregon? Since Maine is the northernmost state on the east coast, then its Portland must also be farther north. In fact, Reno and Oregon's Portland are the correct answers. Our wrong guesses derive from the schematic spatial knowledge that leads to incorrect inferences. We may know the locations of the states, but not of the cities within them. In the preceding comparisons, state locations are used to infer the relative locations of cities (Stevens & Coupe, 1978).

Spatial schemas seem to have a preferred perspective. Much like a physical map, the picturelike image of a spatial environment has a top, or a "specific orientation" (Sholl, 1987). Aligning the image with the environment facilitates using the cognitive map as a guide. (Have you ever consulted a map and found yourself turning either the map, or yourself, to line up with nearby landmarks?) Judgments are easier and more accurate if forward in the environment corresponds to upward in the cognitive map (just as it is with a physical map). For example, we could ask college students to point in the direction of various unseen campus locations. The students could more quickly identify locations in front of them than locations behind them. When the students were asked to turn around, locations now in front were more quickly identified than were locations behind (Sholl, 1987).

Cognitive perspective can also distort distance judgments. When estimating distances between two locations, places closer to us are judged to be farther apart than are two locations that are more distant from the subject. For people in California, San Francisco and Los Angeles seem farther apart than they do to people in New York. The fascinating twist is when participants who were actually in Michigan were asked to imagine they were on the west coast or the east coast. These participants again exaggerated distances between cities closer to their imagined point of reference, relative to distant cities (Holyoak & Mah, 1982).

Organization in Spatial Memory.   The recall of verbal material is often marked by organization. Items that are semantically related (e.g., car, bus, and train) or which share preexperimental associations (table and chair) are recalled together during output. Spatial memory also shows organization as reflected by the presence of organization during output. This is nicely demonstrated in an animal parallel to the traveling sales representative problem: If you have a number of cities to visit, what is the most efficient route to take? Usually, going from one city to the next nearest, and then to the one nearest that, and so on. Juvenile chimps were used as participants in a study requiring them to remember the location of 18 pieces of food. As one researcher carried the chimp around a 1-acre enclosed field, the second researcher would show the placement of pieces of banana or lettuce. The experimenters criss-crossed the field distributing the food in a random fashion. (This probably mimics your class schedule: one class here, the next one is across campus....) When later released to retrieve the food, the chimps did not retrieve the food pieces in the same sequence in which the food had been hidden. Instead, the chimps organized their search routes to be more efficient in retrieving the food, employing roughly a principle of least distance in going from one piece to the next nearest piece (Menzel, 1973). (Incidentally, the animals remembered an average of 12.5 pieces per trial. Control animals that had not seen the placements but were simply allowed to search averaged less than one piece.) Locations were further organized by type of food. On some trials both fruit and vegetable pieces were hidden. The chimps first retrieved the fruit pieces, showing that the animals placed a priority on those rewards, and then went back for the vegetables. They would even pass by a vegetable on the way to the next piece of fruit!

The Development of Spatial Memory in Children

The distinction between response and place learning has been demonstrated in the development of spatial knowledge in children. Cornell and Heth (1979) arranged a learning task analogous to the place-versus-response procedure of Tolman and Hull. Infants ranging in age from 4 to 12 months old were seated in their mothers' laps. Small projection screens were placed on either side. Slides depicting random shapes were projected to one side every 10 seconds and a constant checkerboard pattern appeared simultaneously on the opposite side. Infants orient to novel stimuli and look less at repetitive stimuli (Chapter 2), and so the infants learned to look in the direction of the changing patterns. To test whether the infants had learned turn responses or a cognitive map, the mothers turned their chairs around to face in the opposite direction. Just as the starting location was rotated 180 degrees in Tolman's studies, the orientation with respect to the novel versus repeated slides was rotated. On these test trials, the youngest infants continued to turn in the same direction as before, which indicates response learning. The oldest infants correctly compensated for change of orientation within the room and now turned in the opposite direction.

Children have been tested in a human-sized radial-arm maze constructed outdoors (Overman et al., 1996). The eight arms were about 8 feet long and were enclosed by plastic mesh walls. Optimal performance in the radial maze requires entry into each arm without repetition. Children as young as 20 months were somewhat able to do this, selecting 40 to 50 percent different arms over the first eight choices. By 5 years of age, the children were as good as the adults, who achieved 97 percent accuracy. In parallel to the rat experiments, the provision of distinctive cues for each arm improved performance, and a delay interval between choices led to forgetting of the previously visited arms.

Motor-Skills Learning

In discussing spatial learning, we considered various forms of knowledge representation, such as route and survey maps, and cognitive schemas. Knowledge is one component of skilled performance in a spatial task. There is also the contribution of skilled motor (or movement) reactions. A well-trained rat, running through a maze at 4 feet per second, "generally look(s) like a piece of well-oiled machinery, moving smoothly through the maze with no hesitation or jerkiness, rounding off all corners, banking off the centrifugal walls, and generally moving at full tilt throughout" (Olton, 1979, p. 584). Maze times decrease over trials, not just because the animal learns the way, but because it also knows how to run the maze efficiently. To cite a human example, downhill skiers know the path and also have learned precise movements to traverse the route more efficiently.

Motor-skills learning can be defined as the acquisition of precisely adjusted movements in which the amount, direction, and duration of responding corresponds to variations in the regulating stimuli (Adams, 1987). The skill of playing tennis, for example, involves precise and accurate movements in response to momentary changes in stimulus conditions, often in anticipation of stimulus changes. Any given motor skill has perceptual, cognitive, and motor components, the relative contributions of which vary from skill to skill. For instance, the cognitive component is relatively more important in telegraphing Morse code, a laboratory task once frequently studied. Eye-to-hand coordination is obviously required in typing, but the cognitive component is also important in reading in advance of what is currently being typed (Inhoff & Gordon, 1997).

The combination of perceptual with motor skills is central in tasks such as the pursuit rotor and mirror drawing (see Figure 11.3). The goal of the pursuit rotor is to keep a stylus on a fixed point on a rotating disk (the latter being like a phonograph turntable). The speed can be increased over trials to increase difficulty, and time on target is measured. In mirror drawing, the subject attempts to follow the outline of an object, say, a star, with a pencil or stylus, but visual guidance is through a mirror. Eye–hand coordination must compensate for the difference in actual direction of hand movements from their perceived direction. The time taken to outline an object or the number of deviations from the outline can be taken as a measure of accuracy. (The relevance of mirror drawing can be illustrated by its use in one real-world occupation, dentistry. Dental students improved their mirror-guided movements after practicing with a finger maze that is mirror-guided; Kunovich & Rashid, 1992.) Each of these tasks requires eye–hand coordination, or perceptual (and) motor skill.

Is motor-skills learning an example of implicit, procedural knowledge or is it explicit, declarative knowledge? Motor habits are sometimes implicit: We know how to do something, but we cannot describe what we know. Try to verbally relay the steps involved in programming your VCR or performing a computer routine. Even manipulations intended to increase conscious control in mirror drawing, such as studying written instructions or having the experimenter verbally guide your drawing, do not improve tracking performance (Borresen & Klingsporn, 1992). On the other hand, motor learning does possess aspects of declarative learning. Conscious intention to learn, verbal self-guidance, and knowledge of the goal are indicative of declarative knowledge.

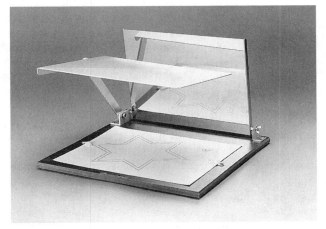

FIGURE 11.3   Pursuit Rotor and Mirror-Tracing Apparatus.

Source: Candland, 1962. Courtesy of Lafayette Instrument Company, Lafayette, Indiana.

The coordination of motor-skills learning capacity and declarative learning can be assessed by comparing them in various neurologically impaired populations. For example, mirror tracing occurs at a normal rate among Alzheimer's dementia individuals, even though they are grossly impaired in declarative memory tasks such as the recall of word lists (Gabrieli et al., 1993). Individuals with certain movement diseases of the basal ganglia, such as Huntington's or Parkinson's diseases, are impaired at pursuit rotor learning (Harrington, et al., 1990; Heindel, Butters, & Salmon, 1988, described further in what follows). Incidentally, old-style tasks such as mirror training and rotary pursuit have gained new life as tools for assessing motor-skills learning in various neurological subject populations.

Although the emphasis in this portion of the chapter is on the motor skill, these tasks also have a perceptual component that improves with training. Fendrich, Healy, and Bourne (1991) had participants copy random-number strings by typing them onto one of two keyboards that had different placements of the numbers, for example, a telephone touch pad and a calculator keyboard. Learning was tested 1 week later by having the participants copy old versus new number strings, using the same or different keypads. Old number strings were typed faster than new strings, indicating memory for the old sequences. Typing old strings on the original keyboard was faster still, indicating memory for the motor movements originally used.

Decades of research on motor-skills learning have emphasized two important controlling factors: practice and feedback.

Practice

Amount of Practice.   Motor skills improve with repetition. This does not mean that practice alone is sufficient for skilled learning. However, holding other factors constant, increasing practice does lead to better performance.

The relationship between practice and one measure of skilled behavior, the speed of performance, is well described by the *power law*. The idea of the power curve is much like that of the learning curve and the Rescorla-Wagner model, two concepts we have seen before (Chapters 1 and 3). In drawing a learning curve, we plot response speed on the vertical axis and number of training trials along the horizontal axis. Basically, responses become faster with additional practice, but not in a one-to-one fashion with the number of practice trials. Rather, performance increases as a function of the logarithm of the number of practice trials. The idea behind a log function is that ever greater amounts of practice are required to produce comparable increments in performance. That is, whereas the first 10 trials might produce a certain increment in speed, the next increment of that size may require 100 additional trials. Thus, the first point on the horizontal axis represents x number of practice trials, the next point is x^2 number of trials, and then x^3 number of trials. Plotting speed over the log number of trials produces a nice, straight-line increase in speed over trials.

This is essentially what we said about learning curves at the beginning of this book. Increments may be rapid at the start of training, but performance improves much more slowly as proficiency increases. You may have noticed something like this in learning a video game or a new sport. At some point, improvements in playing seem to have diminished. Frustration or discouragement may prevent the additional (and extensive) practice needed to further improve performance.

Schedules of Practice.   In learning verbal material, the general principle is that spaced repetitions lead to better memory than do massed repetitions. The spaced-practice advantage also applies to motor-skills learning. For example, in learning mirror star tracing, accuracy improves more quickly with 1 trial per day than with 10 trials—that is, if one counts trials, not days. Similarly, pursuit rotor learning improves as the intertrial interval increases from 1 minute to 3 to 11 minutes (Hovland, 1951).

The effects of the spacing of practice sessions on learning to type was studied by Baddeley and Longman (1978). The participants, British postal workers, were divided into four groups who received either one or two training sessions per day, with each session being 1 or 2 hours in length. After 60 hours of practice, the group receiving the most distributed practice, a single 1-hour session per day, had the best typists. They typed faster and made fewer errors. The group receiving the most concentrated condition, two 2-hour sessions daily, had the poorest performance on both measures. The acquisition curves for typing speed are shown in Figure 11.4. The groups are labeled with two numbers, the first number referring to the number of sessions per day and the second to the length of the session (e.g., Group 1 × 2 practiced once a day for 2 hours). The advantage for spacing persisted on tests given 1, 3, and 9 months later, even though all participants continued typing during these intervals.

Although spaced training produced better performance, training extended over many more days than it did in the massed conditions. The 1 × 1 group, training 5 days a week, took 12 weeks to complete the standard 60 hours of training, whereas the 2 × 2 group finished in 3 weeks. (I'll let you check the math.) Maybe the workers in the massed-practice conditions were affected by fatigue or boredom with long and repeated daily sessions of training. The postal workers were surveyed for their reactions to the training regimen. Surprisingly, the spaced groups were less satisfied and said they would not choose to train under those conditions. The extended number of training days did not appeal to them. As Baddeley and Longman note, if left to the participants, people would choose to train under the conditions that produced the slowest learning, the least accurate performance, and the poorest retention.

Another means of spacing trials is to intermix training on different items within a session. Given several items to learn, one could block trials on one at a time (mass practice on each) or alternate trials among the items (space trials). Goettl et al. (1996) compared a schedule of massed practice versus alternating blocks of practice on the acquisition of three very different tasks: "Space Fortress," an attention-demanding, spatial- and motor-skills video game; "Phoenix," a flight-simulator video game but using the keyboard instead of a joystick; and algebra problems, a cognitively demanding task that is not quite as much fun as the other two. Participants either practiced one task in a single day, or alternated tasks

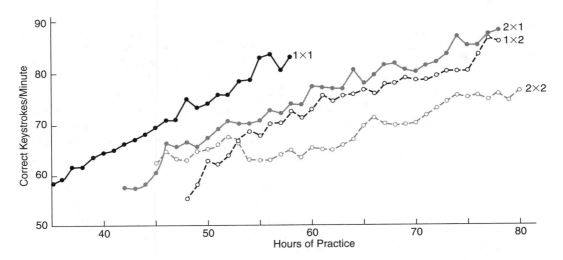

FIGURE 11.4 Learning to type as a function of the number of practice sessions daily (the first number) and length of practice sessions (1 or 2 hours).

Source: From "The Influence of Length and Frequency of Training Session on the Rate of Learning to Type," by A. D. Baddeley and D. J. A. Longman, 1978, *Ergonomics, 21,* p. 630. Copyright © 1978 by Taylor & Francis, Inc. Reprinted with permission.

within each day. Both schedules provided the same total amount of practice on each task over the several days of the experiment. The alternating schedule enhanced performance on two of the tasks, "Space Fortress" and algebra, and was no worse on the flight simulator. This is an especially nice demonstration, both because complex tasks were tested (rather than learning a simple skill like pursuit rotor); and for the pragmatic implication the findings suggest for organizational training. Organizations usually want to schedule training sessions over a day or two, especially if the employees need to be brought in from the field. Companies cannot afford to spread training over individual days spaced weeks apart, as the learning psychologists working for the organizations might recommend. The alternating module schedule might offer the benefits of distributed practice but in the same 2 or 3 days a company might otherwise devote to massed practice.

Massed repetition of practice trials can inhibit performance of skilled behavior, apart from any effects of massed practice on learning. This is our learning-versus-performance distinction again. Massing a large number of trials can lead to fatigue, loss of motivation, or attentional lapses that lower performance. That is, the participants may have actually learned more than is being displayed by their level of performance. Spaced trials allow time for recovery from the "work decrement," as it was called by Hovland (1951). Performance after a series of massed trials sometimes improves immediately if the next trial is delayed, presumably allowing opportunity for fatigue or other inhibiting factors to dissipate (Kientzle, 1949).

Knowledge of Results

Repeated practice will be of little benefit unless you know how well you are performing. Thorndike (1931) conducted a study in which students attempted to draw 4-inch lines. Actually, they drew 3,000 lines over 12 sessions. The student-participants were not given any feedback about how well they were doing, and having their eyes closed, the students could not see the lines they drew. At the end, they were no more accurate at drawing 4-inch lines than when they began.

Outcome information is called *knowledge of results,* abbreviated as KR. One form of KR is called feedback, which simply means externally provided information on the success or accuracy of the response that is given to the participant after a practice trial. This information serves as a basis for corrections on the next trial. Following in the Thorndike tradition, learning theorists long considered feedback to be analogous to reinforcement in instrumental learning, and therefore feedback was subjected to manipulations that paralleled reinforcement variations. For example, one could vary (1) the frequency with which feedback was given, in parallel to continuous versus partial reinforcement schedules; or (2) the immediacy of feedback, in parallel to delay of reinforcement. The commonsense expectation is that more frequent and more immediate knowledge of results should enhance learning. Practice trials without KR are either neutral or detrimental to learning.

Imagine learning to hit a golf ball. Without feedback after each stroke, how can you know whether you hit the ball well or not? If feedback is delayed, will you remember the exact movements you made that led to a good or poor shot? A long history of research clearly indicates that frequent, immediate, and detailed feedback led to faster learning of motor responses (see Adams, 1987).

Today, some researchers have questioned the benefits of using too much feedback during training, especially as it influences the retention and transfer of the response (e.g., Schmidt & Bjork, 1992). Granted that immediate and consistent feedback leads to superior performance (e.g., greater speed or accuracy) of a skill that is trained during a single session in the laboratory. However, will this skill still be better remembered if testing is delayed? Do these variables lead to better transfer when the skills demanded are altered slightly? Many studies indicate a "no" answer to both of these questions. We can cite examples involving both the frequency of feedback and the delay of feedback.

In one study, the participants learned a tracking response, basically using one finger to follow a curve projected on a screen that changes in speed and direction. Feedback was given after each trial or in summary form after every fifth or fifteenth trial. The group that received the most consistent feedback made smaller errors throughout the acquisition phase of the experiment. However, after only a 10-minute delay interval, the difference disappeared; all three frequencies of feedback conditions were then equivalent. Even more interesting was the fact that on a test given 2 days later, the leanest feedback schedule (that given every fifteenth trial) had the best performance (Schmidt et al., 1989). Although consistent feedback produced better performance during initial acquisition of the skill, a partial feedback schedule led to better performance on delayed retention tests of the skill.

Why would less frequent KR lead to performance as good as or better than more frequent KR? One explanation is the *guidance hypothesis*. Feedback has beneficial effects in that it guides the learner toward the correct movements. Information about errors and deviations from the goal can be seen. But consistent feedback may block the participants' learning to detect their own errors. That is, the participants become dependent on external KR for error information. They are less likely to attend to their own bodily kinesthetic feedback and thus do not learn to recognize good and poor performance. Athletes can know immediately whether a movement (e.g., a pitch or a hit in softball) was good or not, before seeing the actual outcome. Thus, frequent KR has both positive and negative effects. Optimal performance requires a balance between the two.

Is there a way to combine the beneficial effect of consistent KR on initial learning with the beneficial effect of partial KR on delayed retention? Wulf and Schmidt (1989) did so by initially providing feedback on each trial and then fading (or gradually reducing) feedback to a 50 percent schedule. In this case, acquisition was as rapid as it was for a continuous-feedback group, and the 50 percent KR group performed better on tests of novel versions of the required movements.

Delayed KR. In studies similar to those varying frequency of feedback, knowledge of results is given immediately or is delayed. There is good reason to expect that immediate feedback would benefit learning. After all, there is less likelihood of forgetting the just-made movements and less time for interference. However, just as with the partial schedules of feedback described earlier, delaying feedback allows the participants to develop their own error-detection capabilities. In comparison to participants given immediate feedback, participants for whom feedback was delayed for 3 seconds after each movement learned just as well during an initial training session. The delayed-feedback group actually did better on the second day, and this superiority persisted on a test given 2 days after that (Swinnen et al., 1990).

What is happening during the delay-until-feedback interval? We could imagine that there is a short-term memory for the motor response. During the delay interval, participants may be "rehearsing" the response they just made (although this rehearsal need not be verbal) and making a judgment about how accurate their response was. If this delay interval is filled by some distractor activity, then learning with delayed feedback is impaired (Swinnen, 1990). This is another parallel with learning of verbal materials: Distractors decrease retention of prior (similar) target material.

Some Concluding Comments on Learning Motor Skills.   The effects of some variables on motor-skills learning are sometimes the same as in other learning situations and sometimes different. Thus, spaced practice at a skill can be better than massed practice, just as it is in learning paired associates or in free recall of words. However, partial and delayed feedback do not exactly parallel the findings with partial and delayed schedules of reward in instrumental learning. However, even there, we found that partial reinforcement can have some beneficial effects on learning, particularly in inducing persistence in making the learned response. More will be said about skill learning in two other contexts: the relationship of motor learning to implicit learning and the development of expertise with extended practice.

Implicit Learning

Another form of "learning how to" is implicit learning. *Implicit learning* "is the process by which knowledge of the structure of a complex environment is acquired largely independent of conscious awareness of specific components of that environment" (Manza & Reber, 1997, p. 73). Implicit learning is exemplified in learning our first language. In first learning a language, we learn the often subtle rules of word order, word endings, pronunciation, and stress patterns. We come to speak (or sign) the language better than we can articulate the rules. Similarly, in laboratory simulations of implicit learning, participants are exposed to fairly complex cognitive procedures or rules. Skilled performance develops as a function of practice, but not necessarily because of declarative knowledge of the underlying rules. Learning can occur without an intention to learn and in such a way that the knowledge is difficult to express verbally. Learning is therefore said to be implicit.

Some Implicit-Learning Tasks

Many implicit-learning tasks are cognitive, or rule-based, tasks. One well-studied example is that of learning an artificial grammar. Human languages are guided by a set of rules, or the grammar, which we use even though we may not be able to articulate these rules. For example, the usual word order in English is subject–verb–object (e.g., dog bites man), a rule that guides both our production and comprehension of English. We readily reject ungrammatical strings of words (dog man bites). Reber (1967) devised an artificial grammar involving a set of letters instead of words, such as P, S, T, V, and X. The grammar determines which letters can follow which other letters. The allowable sequences are shown in Figure 11.5. To generate a grammatical string of letters, one moves through the system from S (for "state") 1 to S6. For instance, the first letter would be T or P and the last letter would be S or V. The

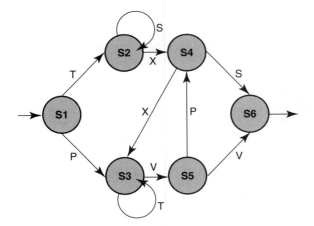

FIGURE 11.5   Artificial Grammar. Each "state" (S) represents a random choice: a certain proportion of the time the transition is in one direction (from S1 to S2, producing the letter T) or the other (from S1 to S3, producing letter P.)

Source: From *Implicit Learning and Tacit Knowledge: An Essay on the Cognitive Unconscious* (p. 28), by A. S. Reber, 1993, New York: Oxford University Press. Copyright © 1993 by Oxford University Press. Reprinted with permission.

arrows show the permissible transitions from letter to letter; recursive loops allow letters to be repeated. Strings of lengths of three to eight letters are usually studied, although longer strings could be generated. What is important is that there are ungrammatical sequences of these letters: TSXS is a grammatical string; PSXS is not.

Participants are first asked to memorize short sets of letter strings. The strings derive from the grammar constructed by the experimenter, although the participants are typically not told there is a grammar. For instance, a set of three strings of letters is presented, and recall tested, until the participants can repeat them back. Then another set of letter strings would be learned. If the rules that govern grammatical string formation are learned over trials, learning should become easier with practice. Indeed, participants who memorized grammatical strings made fewer errors across trials (a new set of letter strings) than did participants who studied letter strings that did not correspond to a grammatical sequence.

A direct means of determining whether the grammatical rules have been learned is to ask the participants to classify novel strings of letters as being grammatical or not. Participants who studied grammatical letter strings are about 60 to 65 percent accurate in classification, significantly better than a chance level of 50 percent.

The grammar learning is said to be implicit because it occurs incidentally, not deliberately. The participants are not informed that there is an underlying grammar from which the letter sequences are derived. The regularities of the letter strings are abstracted across memorized sets. Deliberate intention to discover and learn those rules can actually impede learning. Informing the participants that there are rules leads to more errors during set memorization and more mistakes in later classifying grammatical and ungrammatical strings (Reber, 1976).

Another example of an implicit-learning task is the serial-reaction-time procedure. A sequence of items is presented and the participant's task is to respond to each as it occurs. For instance, a light appears at one of four locations on a video screen and the participant pushes a corresponding key for each location. The sequence is seemingly random, although in fact it actually repeats. Sequence learning is indicated by reaction times that become faster over practice trials. The results from a representative study are shown in

Figure 11.6 (Nissen & Bullemer, 1987), in which the sequence is repeated after every 10 lights. Key-pressing reactions become faster across 80 trials, even for those participants who said they were unaware that the sequence repeated. Are people faster because they have learned something about the sequence, or have they just become practiced at more general aspects of the task? A control condition received the lights in a random sequence, and their speed of reaction improved little over trials.

Some implicit-learning tasks show very specific learning, as does the serial-reaction-time method, with little transfer to novel items. Other implicitly learned skills seem to be more general. After learning an artificial grammar with one set of letters, participants were able to perform better than chance when the grammar was applied to a different set of letters (Manza & Reber, 1997; Mathews, Richards, & Eysenck, 1989). Both specific and general learning effects are found in learning to read mirror-reversed words. Mirror reading of novel word triplets becomes faster across sessions, indicating acquisition of a skill of reading mirror-distorted text.

Figure 11.7 shows the mean time to read mirror-reversed text (Levin, Lilly, Papanicolaou, & Eisenberg, 1992). Some of the subjects were head-injured individuals who had disorders of explicit memory, and the other subjects were age-matched controls. When new mirror-reversed words ("unique" words) were presented daily, both groups read them faster when practice extended across 3 days. This general skill of reading mirror-reversed text persisted through a delayed test (session 4), which was given after recovery from the brain injury. Some words were repeated within each session and across sessions, and these were read even faster. This reflects a specific memory for those words. The results do show that the brain-injured read slower, overall, than did the control subjects, yet the pattern of general and specific implicit learning was the same.

Is Procedural Learning Unaware Learning?   Is implicit learning, such as the acquisition of the rules of an artificial grammar, unconscious learning? Is procedural knowledge inaccessible to conscious and verbalizable description? The difficulty in answering these questions is in determining whether the knowledge is actually unconscious. People may

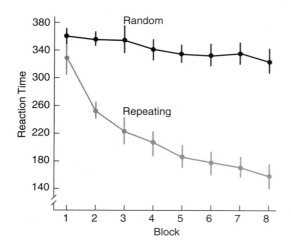

FIGURE 11.6 Mean reaction times in milliseconds to repeating versus random sequences of locations.

Source: From "Attentional Requirements of Learning: Evidence from Performance Measures," by M. J. Nissen and P. Bullemer, 1987, *Cognitive Psychology, 19,* p. 8. Copyright ©1987 by Academic Press. Reprinted with permission.

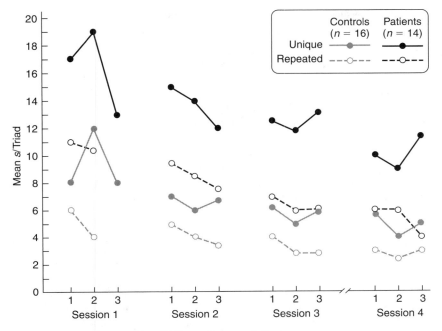

FIGURE 11.7   Times to Read Mirror-Reversed Text.

Source: From "Procedural Memory during Postraumatic Amnesia in Survivors of Closed Head Injury: Implications for Rehabilitation," by J. Ewert, H. S. Levin, M. G. Watson, and Z. Kalisky, 1989, *Archives of Neurology, 46,* p. 914. Copyright © 1989 American Medical Association. Reprinted with permission.

not be able to describe the rules or sequence of an implicit task, but this lack of verbalizable information does not convincingly demonstrate lack of awareness. Participants simply may decide not to report information of which they are unsure.

In some cases, participants are aware and can describe the underlying rules with some degree of accuracy. In one study of location sequence learning, 20 percent of the college student participants could report the repeating sequence. These participants also had faster reaction times by the end of training than did the unaware participants. However, even the 30 percent of participants who were not aware of the sequence still improved in speed over trials (Willingham et al., 1989). In artificial grammar learning, on the other hand, few participants can describe the rules governing acceptable letter sequences.

One criterion that has been suggested for determining whether learning is unconscious is to demonstrate a separation between direct verbal reports and some indirect measure of performance. For instance, maybe the participants can perform the implicit task but they cannot articulate the rules (Dienes & Berry, 1997). This definition conforms to one sense in which we think of unconscious: We know how to do something, but without insight as to how we do it. Another instance would be developing a "liking" for grammatical strings, even without awareness of the grammatical rules. Exposure to nonsense stimuli sometimes produces a preference or liking for those stimuli, as compared to novel nonsense stimuli. This is the mere exposure effect, first described in Chapter 2. Similarly, participants in artificial grammar experiments come to prefer studied grammatical letter strings over nongrammatical strings (Manza & Bornstein, 1995; Manza, Zizak, & Reber, 1998).

If participants cannot fully describe the rules governing procedural learning, they may nevertheless be aware of enough to aid successful performance. Maybe there are particular letter combinations that tell whether a sequence is grammatical. For the grammar illustrated earlier in Figure 11.5, a starting letter of P or T is allowable, as are ending letters S and V. Such knowledge can increase the accuracy of guesses at potentially grammatical strings and allow accurate rejection of ungrammatical sequences (Dulany, Carlson, & Dewey, 1984).

Even if explicit knowledge of the sequences is learned, how would this information relate to actual performance? Aware knowledge could develop after implicit learning occurs, or explicit knowledge could be learned coordinately with the implicit but still not determine moment-by-moment responding. Thus, the degree and influence of explicit knowledge on performance of an implicit learning task is still unknown.

Dissociating Categories of Implicit Learning

In previous chapters, we applied the term "implicit" to another type of memory task. Repetition priming is a form of *implicit-memory* testing, in which the identification of a stimulus is facilitated by prior exposure to that stimulus. As you may recall, in a typical word-priming experiment, a list of words is presented, often using incidental learning procedures. For example, the participants are asked to count the number of vowels in each word as presented or rate each word for pleasantness. In a second phase, the words are presented again in the context of a different task, such as completing word fragments. Priming is demonstrated if fragment completion is facilitated by the previous exposure. If, for example, the word TABLE had been presented in the first phase, then priming occurs when the participant completes the word fragment T_B_E with the word TABLE.

How is repetition priming related to implicit-learning tasks such as artificial grammar and serial reaction time? Theoretically, priming and implicit learning have sometimes been categorized together as one form of memory (Squire, 1987), or as overlapping types of memory (Tulving & Schacter, 1990; see Chapter 7). One methodological difference between repetition priming and procedural learning is the amount of experience required in order to demonstrate each. Priming occurs after a single exposure. Skill learning typically requires numerous practice trials.

Some tasks are not susceptible to both priming and implicit-learning effects. Word-fragment completion does not improve with practice. One does not become a skilled "fragment completer." Reading mirror-transformed words does improve with practice. But both fragment completion and inverted reading show a *priming effect:* Completion of the fragment with a preexposed word or identification of an inverted word is improved by prior exposure to the specific words being tested (Schwartz & Hashtroudi, 1991).

Priming and motor-skill learning have been dissociated in comparisons among individuals with various neurological disorders. Huntington's disease is an inherited disorder characterized by involuntary movements of the body and by progressive cognitive dementia. Average age of onset is in the 30s and 40s. Alzheimer's disease is evidenced by primarily cognitive deficits and usually has later onset. Individuals with these diseases have been compared in learning a motor skill, such as the pursuit rotor. The goal in this task is to keep a stylus on a fixed spot on a rotating turntable. The starting speed is adjusted so that everyone starts with the same time on target. Alzheimer's individuals improve across blocks of trials; that is, they become more skilled. Huntington's disease participants do not (Heindel et al., 1988). The reverse pattern is found on a priming task: The Huntington's patients completed more word fragments with the primed words than did the Alzheimer's participants (Shimamura et al., 1987). Note that the Alzheimer's participants were cognitively capable of performing the task; they just completed the stems with other words. (The Huntington's and Alzheimer's participants were both and equally impaired on explicit tests of memory, such as word recall and recognition.)

HIV infection is also associated with skill-learning impairments, a fact that is often unrecognized. For example, some HIV+ individuals were impaired in learning the pursuit rotor task (Martin et al., 1993).

Finally, there is other neurological evidence that word priming and skill tasks are dissociable. Behaviors having a motor component, such as mirror tracing, pursuit rotor, and prism adaptation, all seem to involve an area of the brain called the basal ganglia. Damage here, as occurs in Huntington's and Parkinson's diseases, impairs skill learning but leaves word priming intact (Saint-Cyr & Taylor, 1992).

Expertise

Expertise can be developed in many domains of knowledge or skill. One can become skilled at playing video games, programming a computer, speaking a foreign language, or reading X-ray scans. Where does expertise come from? What is it that differentiates chess masters from lesser players, or world-class musicians from others? One popular assumption is that an inherent talent is required. A particular ability is inherited that allows performance at an expert level, and not everyone has this talent. This inherent-ability conception is a popular stereotype about child prodigies who display talent early, and intellectually retarded "savants" who nevertheless display an exceptional talent in music, art, memory, and so on. (See Chapter 12 for further discussion of memory in savants.)

The notion of inborn talent has been challenged by Anders Ericsson (see particularly Ericsson & Charness, 1994), who argues that what separates the expert from the also-rans is the sheer amount of practice devoted to their skill. (A visitor to New York City asked, "How do you get to Carnegie Hall?" "Practice, practice, practice!") The difference between most participants in some activity and those who attain expert status is the amount of deliberate training and instruction. Individuals on their way to expert status maintain schedules of intense and prolonged practice, in some cases essentially engaging in the activity full time. Expertise can be acquired through training by otherwise unremarkable individuals. For example, college students developed digit spans of 80 to 100 numerals (Ericsson, Chase, & Faloon, 1980). The students did this through extended practice, learning various coding schemes and becoming adept at rapidly encoding number strings into long-term memory. Maybe child prodigies get an early start at practicing; savants have often spent years perfecting their talents.

How much practice is necessary to attain expertise? Ericsson, Krampe, and Tesch-Romer (1993) concluded that it takes about 10 years of full-time preparation, which corresponds to several thousand hours of practice or study. This 10-year rule applies to many domains of expertise, such as sports, chess, or music. For the most talented in the arts and sciences, more than 10 years may be required. Ericsson, Krampe, and Tesch-Romer's (1993) review showed that those who attained the highest levels of expertise had begun practicing 2 to 5 years before less accomplished experts and spent more time on deliberate practice. Top violinists at age 20 had spent more than 10,000 hours in practice, twice as much as that by those at lower levels of accomplishment (who were still experts themselves).

We might argue in response that without sufficient innate intelligence or athletic ability, no amount of practice could turn each of us into a Bobby Fischer or an Arthur Ashe. The point Ericsson wants to make is that when we look at the lives of experts, we see they have devoted an enormous number of hours to their craft. Ten thousand hours of training can account for a substantial amount of talent. Ericsson does allow a possible hereditary factor, but it is not a specifically inherited talent. What may be inherited is motivation: the drive and perseverance necessary to practice.

From Declarative to Procedural

In several points in this chapter, we have considered the role of conscious versus unconscious factors in the performance of skilled behaviors. Basically, we have been asking about the relative contributions of declarative and procedural knowledge. Recent theories of skill learning have incorporated both by breaking down skill learning into a series of steps or stages. First, factual knowledge is acquired: learning the nature of the task, rules, limits, exceptions, and so on. After additional practice, performance speed increases and less conscious guidance is required. With extended practice, a skill can be performed seemingly automatically. This succession of steps marks the transition from declarative knowledge to procedural knowledge.

Anderson's adaptive control of thought (ACT*) theory (1983) is designed specifically to describe this transition. The major variable that accounts for the development of proceduralization is practice: plain old repetition. Anderson proposes a two-stage model of skill acquisition, with a transitional step between stages. During the *declarative stage* of skill learning, information is learned. This stage involves conscious processing and attention, so there is heavy reliance on working memory. For example, you need to learn the different pieces in chess, their range of moves, and some strategies. This is declarative knowledge. If we introspect during the initial phase of skill learning, we notice a great deal of self-talk. We verbally encode and rehearse information or give ourselves verbal feedback and guidance. The declarative stage is followed by a transition phase in which knowledge application starts to become proceduralized. During this transition, groups of rules or operations that are frequently used together are chunked, or compiled, which increases efficiency. This transitional state is known as *knowledge compilation.* An analogy can be made to playing a complex piece of music. With practice, individual notes become combined into chunks. Playing then becomes the activation of groups of notes in sequence, rather than playing note by note. These chunks are stored in long-term memory. Performance now depends less on conscious control and more on long-term retrieval, thus freeing up working memory. The final stage, or *procedural stage,* is marked by skill refinement. Continued practice leads to further strengthening of the procedures. The procedural skills are refined as a result of generalization and discrimination. With generalization, the procedures are applied to new situations. Discrimination restricts the range of the procedures to only appropriate situations.

One small-scale example of skilled proceduralization is the performance of unintended actions when we are mentally preoccupied, also called *habit slips* (Reason, 1984). Some everyday motor routines are so well practiced that they can be run off with little conscious control or guidance. I decide to leave my office to go home; my body carries out a set of procedures while my mind is busy elsewhere. Some steps are compiled knowledge, such units as leaving the office (pack briefcase, empty coffee cup, get keys, turn out lights, etc.) or driving home (exit campus, turn right on boulevard, etc.). An action slip could occur when I had really intended to stop at the store on the way home, but instead I drive right past. Procedural knowledge is sufficient to get me home without conscious direction and, unfortunately, without intervention at the crucial moment when I passed by the store. Leaving an unfamiliar campus, one I had been visiting for a day, requires conscious deliberation and guidance of declarative knowledge.

Applications

Implicit Learning

Professionals in the field of cognitive rehabilitation help amnesics cope with everyday life in the face of memory deficits. The real frustration in this work is that amnesic individuals are, by definition, memory-impaired, so how can they learn new skills? With the realization that implicit-learning abilities are usually spared in amnesia, procedural and implicit-learning techniques can be used instead of explicit-learning methods in remediation.

Glisky and Schacter (e.g., 1989) used implicit learning to teach a woman with anterograde (or ongoing) amnesia to use a computer. She was first taught technical definitions using a "vanishing-cue" method. A word and its definition were first presented, and across repeated trials, a letter, then more letters, were omitted from the target word (e.g., DISK DRIVE, then D__K DR___E, then D___ D____). Eventually, the letters cues were omitted as the woman came to name the word given the definition. Similar "vanishing instructions" were used to teach the steps involved in operating the computer. Gradually, each line of instructions became abbreviated by omitting words, then whole steps were eliminated. This amnesic eventually learned enough to perform a data-entry job and was able to return to work with her former company. She eventually learned over 250 codes, symbols, and abbreviations. Through all this, her explicit memory remained impaired.

Why is implicit-memory training successful? We might say that because it uses a different memory system, different brain areas are involved. However, another explanation is that implicit methods minimize retrieval of the wrong information, which might later be mistakenly recalled as the correct answer. Baddeley (1992b) noted the similarity of implicit learning by vanishing cues to Terrace's errorless discrimination learning (see Chapter 4). In teaching a discrimination between stimuli, Terrace would ensure that responses were made only to the correct stimulus and not to incorrect stimuli. Similarly, the vanishing-cue method is easy enough at first to elicit just correct responses. Baddeley suggests that if errors were made, they, and not the correct words, might be recalled in future trials due to priming. Amnesics have a tendency to repeat recently made responses, not remembering whether that response was correct.

The errorless learning interpretation was tested in a word-stem completion task using 16 patients with severe memory problems (Wilson, 1992). In the error*less* condition, participants were shown a stem (e.g., BR___) and told what the correct word was (BREAD). In the error condition, the participants were first allowed to guess at a word that completed the stem (e.g., they might guess BREAK) and were then told the word for which the researcher was looking. When the participants were later tested with just the stems, more of the correct words were produced after the errorless study condition. In the error condition, more of the previous wrong guesses persisted.

Spatial Memory

Sense of Direction. In everyday concerns about spatial ability, what we are really talking about is sense of direction. Surveys of real-world memory often turn up a statistical factor associated with way finding, or, conversely, the ease of getting lost (Ryan, 1992). Individuals will readily volunteer self-estimates about their own sense of direction, and interestingly, these estimates are accurate. Kozlowski and Bryant (1977) had students rate their sense of direction on a simple seven-point scale. These estimates were significantly correlated with the accuracy in pointing to (unseen) campus buildings, judging the distance between pairs of buildings, and pointing in the direction of nearby cities. After being led back and forth through an underground utility tunnel on campus, students who rated themselves as having a good sense of direction showed improved accuracy in pointing to the end point, whereas students with poor sense of direction showed no improvement whatsoever.

Another potential source of differences in sense of direction is gender, discussed further in Box 11.2.

Remembering Where You Parked. The commonplace example of remembering where you last left your car nicely illustrates a number of spatial memory factors. First, remembering where you parked today is an example of memory updating. Because you need to recall the most recent placement of the car, and not yesterday's, forgetting of previous information is adaptive. Second, in testing memory for parking places, a recency effect is found: People recall where they left the car this morning and there is poor memory for previous days' parking spaces (Means et al., 1995). Parking memory seems to show little proactive interference from previous days' parking places. (I rarely confuse yesterday's and today's parking places. But if I move the car during the day, then I misrecall in the evening and return to the morning's place.) Certainly, one strategy to prevent confusion is to park in the same place every day. At the end of the day, you do not need to remember where you parked this morning, but instead where you park every day.

Improved Building Design. The principles of spatial learning can be applied to improving everyday navigation. One recommendation is to design spatial environments to make them easier for people to use. Hospitals, large public buildings, shopping malls, some university buildings, and residential complexes for the elderly all tax user-orientation skills. These are difficult environments to get to know because of size, infrequent exposure, or lack of external frames of reference.

One aid to negotiating large buildings is to use a color-coding scheme to distinguish different sections. Evans and colleagues (1980) took advantage of a projected repainting in

B O X **11.2**

Gender Differences in Spatial Cognition?

Do men and women differ in their spatial memory abilities? The popular answer is that men are better at spatial tasks (or more broadly, visual-spatial tasks) and women are better at verbal tasks. Unfortunately, this is another of those questions to which there is no simple answer. The difficulties begin with variations in the definition of spatial ability, are followed by disagreements about what the data actually show, and finish with alternative interpretations for whatever differences there appear to be.

To start with, spatial ability needs to be unambiguously defined. One might think that it encompasses the capacity to think about spatial relations of objects, persons, and space. However, spatial aptitude overlaps with, and may be confounded by, other abilities such as mental imagery, analytic thinking, arithmetic ability, and sound localization. Even if variously defined, there are some generally accepted measures of spatial ability. One is a test of mental rotation, which requires identifying what an object would appear like if rotated (mental rotation is illustrated in Chapter 12). Another measure is the embedded-figure test, in which a simple geometric form (say, a triangle) must be found when hidden in a more complex form.

Does the performance of men and women differ on such tests? Men generally perform better on spatial rotation tests (Halpern, 1989), although other visual-spatial tests show smaller differences (Caplan, MacPherson, & Tobin, 1985). However, these studies are sometimes criticized on methodological grounds. For example, children with learning disabilities may be excluded from samples on which some of the gender data are derived. More boys have such disabilities, and so will be disproportionately excluded. Also, the difference between men's and women's scores seems to be diminishing over recent years, a claim that is consistent with a social or cultural interpretation of gender differences (Feingold, 1988).

What about actual spatial way-finding performance? There is much less data here. In one study, men and women had to learn a route through a series of office corridors that formed a figure-8. (The middle corridor of the figure-8 was a blind alley.) Men and women made the same number of turns and took the same amount of time to complete the maze in each trial. But the men were more accurate in returning to the start point, and more men recognized a drawing of the maze than did women (87 versus 25 percent). Bever (1992) suggested that the men had learned a cognitive or survey map, whereas the women learned route maps.

In a questionnaire study, more women reported having spatial difficulties than did men in way finding, and the women expressed higher levels of anxiety about spatial situations. Example statements that women, more so than men, said provoked nervousness included finding their way back after making a wrong turn, and finding their way out of a complex office building. Also, women reported more often using route strategies rather than survey-map strategies (Lawton, 1994). Unfortunately, with self-report measures, it is difficult to separate expectancies and stereotypes from actual experience.

Memory for object locations is a spatial task in which men do not perform better. For example, men and women studied a picture containing line drawings of 30 objects. Women were better at later identifying objects that had been added and objects whose location within the picture had been changed (Silverman and Eals, 1992). In a second, naturalistic test, the subjects were questioned about the presence and location of objects that had been in the waiting room before the experiment. Again, women recalled more objects and their locations that did men. If the ordering of gender performance reverses between way-finding and object-location tasks, the notion of a unitary spatial ability is called into question.

If there are gender differences, what would be their basis? A social-cultural explanation posits there may be differences in life experiences, education, expectations, and/or stereotypes. Such differences could start early in life. Parents are more likely to restrict the exploratory opportunities of their daughters than of their sons. Other psychologists

(continued)

Box 11.2 Continued

have considered a hypothesis based on evolution, in which a division of labor between men and women led to different adaptive specializations (Silverman & Eals, 1992). Thus, those spatial abilities required for hunting and stalking prey (and are assessed in maze learning) are better developed in men. Abilities required for foraging for edible plants (possibly analogous to object-location tasks) are better developed in women.

Given that gender in humans confounds both biology and social-cultural learning, an alternative strategy is to study sex differences in animals. In a 17-arm radial maze, male rats did better than did female rats under a variety of rearing and cuing conditions. The males were better at remembering which arms had been visited and better remembered which arms were never rewarded (Seymoure et al., 1996). Male rats also performed better in the Morris water maze. But prior familiarization with the task eliminated sex differences (Perrot-Sinal et al., 1996). In animal studies, a need for acclimation to a task usually indicates different levels of emotionality, such as timidity or fear. Thus, maze differences between gender may be confounded with different levels of emotionality.

Another biological difference may be related to hormone differences. There are reports that verbal memory may be related to changes in estrogen levels. For instance, adult women showed fluctuations across the menstrual cycle on tests of speeded motor skills and on spatial-ability tests (Hampson & Kimura, 1988). This study does not show that women performed worse than men, only that performance of women varied across their cycle. In another study, women who received estrogen-replacement therapy following a hysterectomy maintained their preoperative levels of performance on prose paragraph recall and in paired-associate learning (Sherwin, 1994). It should be noted that estrogen did not increase memory, but rather prevented a decline.

Finally, we can note that differences in performance on spatial tasks do not necessarily mean differences in underlying ability. As noted earlier, women self-report more anxiety about way finding and getting lost (Lawton, 1994), and such anxiety could impair actual way finding. Self-fulfilling expectancies may come into play when the instructions for a task emphasize its "spatial" nature. In one case, women did more poorly than did men on a spatial task, the usually found result, when the usual spatial instructions were given (i.e., "this is a test of your spatial abilities"). However, when nonspatial instructions were given, men and women did not differ (Sharps, Welton, & Price, 1993).

Thus, although there may be gender differences in spatial performance, the evidence is less decisive in showing actual differences in spatial navigation or learning, and there is no shortage of possible interpretations.

a large university building to study color coding. Students in the "before" condition toured the four-story building when the interior surfaces were painted a monochromatic beige. They were then taken to a central point and asked to find their way back to a specific location (e.g., go to the chem lab). The interior walls on each floor were subsequently painted with different colors. The "after" group, who took the same tour and way-finding test, were faster in finding target locations and made fewer errors along the way.

"You-are-here" maps are another aid to orientation. However, careful placement and alignment with the environment is necessary for these to be effective. Judging direction from a cognitive map is faster and more accurate if the user is facing the same direction as the mental map. You-are-here maps are sometimes simply placed on a convenient wall, and so are reversed or inverted with respect to the surrounding environment (see Figure 11.8). This forces the user to make some cognitive rearrangements and leads to a greater number of direction errors (Levine, Marchon, & Hanley, 1984). Planners should choose the map location first and then design the map.

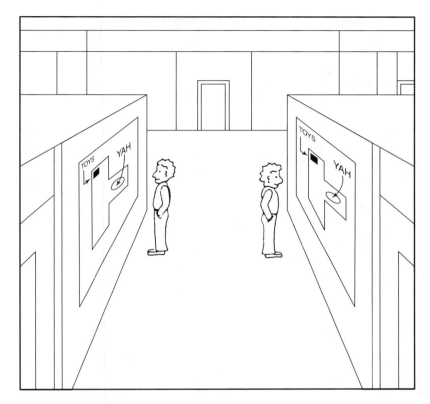

FIGURE 11.8   Placement of "You-Are-Here" Maps. Both maps are identical, but placed on opposite walls. The map on the right is correctly aligned with the layout of the corridors. The map on the left is misaligned.

Source: From M. Levine, I. Marchon, and G. L. Hanley, *Environment and Behavior, 16,* pp. 139–157, copyright © 1984 by Sage Publications, Inc. Reprinted by permission of Sage Publications, Inc.

Long-Term Retention of Skills

All too often, the goal of studying is to learn something "just long enough": long enough to get past the exam or the class presentation tomorrow morning. The real goal of education is permanent retention. Skilled performance in a job or occupation often depends on retention of skills and knowledge that are used infrequently. To take one extreme example, for many of us, certain emergency procedures are not needed every day, yet will need to be quickly recalled when an emergency does arise.

A research team at the University of Colorado at Boulder has been especially interested in long-term retention of skills (see, e.g., Healy & Bourne, 1995; Healy et al., 1993). The skills they studied ranged from detecting single letters to remembering math facts and foreign-language vocabulary, to performing in an army tank simulator (which is like the most awesome video game ever!). These researchers verified several guidelines that promote long-term retention. (*Note:* We are emphasizing long-term remembering, not just ease of acquisition.) Their recommendations are summarized in Table 11.3. Some examples are cited in what follows.

Optimize the Conditions of Training. There are numerous factors that facilitate encoding, many discussed in Chapter 9. Two examples may be mentioned again here: spacing and generation effects. If several arithmetic or vocabulary items are to be learned, it is better to intermix them within the study sequence rather than to mass study trials on each. This mixing schedule for spacing items will likely slow acquisition of the information at first, as compared to massed practice, but it leads to better retention in the long run.

The generation effect refers to getting the participants to generate to-be-remembered answers rather than simply having the experimenter provide the correct answers. Generation produces better retention than does simply reading the to-be-remembered item. In applying the generation effect to learning multiplication answers (e.g., $13 \times 8 = 104$), one should attempt to produce the correct answer rather than simply read it. One potential problem, as noted with the amnesics in errorless learning earlier, is that your previous wrong answers may be recalled later instead of the correct one. Prompts or cues might be provided to ensure the correct answers are generated, and thus remembered, rather than incorrect answers.

Optimize Learning Strategies. Healy and colleagues (1993) used the keyword mnemonic to teach language vocabulary in a series of studies. Each foreign word was paired with a soundalike English word, which in turn could be connected to the English translation. For example, the Spanish DORONICO and LEOPARD might be linked by a similar-sounding word DOOR. The keyword mnemonic facilitated acquisition and produced better long-term retention.

TABLE 11.3 Guidelines for Optimizing Long-Term Retention of Knowledge and Skills

Guidelines

1. Optimize conditions of training.
   Examples: Use spaced practice
              Intermix training of several components
              Encourage generation during practice

2. Optimize learning strategy used.
   Example: Mnemonics as mediators

3. Achieve automaticity.
   Example: Remembering rather than computing arithmetic answers

4. Optimize retention conditions.
   Example: Refresher and practice tests

Source: Healy et al., 1993.

Train until Retrieval Is Automatic.   As just noted, linking mnemonics that connect Spanish and English vocabulary words facilitated learning. But retrieval is indirect and slow: One must chain through the links. Practice should be continued until retrieval becomes direct: DORONICO comes to elicit LEOPARD directly, leading to faster response times and better long-term retention.

In solving novel arithmetic problems, students often will employ an algorithm, or shortcut. The multiplication problem 13 × 8 might be solved as 10 × 8 plus 3 × 8, each of which has already known solutions. However, these computations take time. Extensive practice of problems like 13 × 8 will make retrieval of the correct answer automatic and the computations will no longer be necessary. These overlearned answers will be better retained.

Optimize Retention Conditions.   This may be accomplished in two ways. One is to provide refresher trials or practice quizzes. As we noted in the previous chapter, practice at retrieval can be just as important as additional study. In one applied example, soldiers were first trained to disassemble and reassemble an M60 machine gun. One group was tested 8 weeks later, and they showed substantial forgetting. A second group received some refresher training midway through the retention interval. On the 8-week test, the second group showed significantly better performance (Schendel & Hagman, 1982).

Another way to aid retrieval is to maximize the similarity of training to testing conditions. Testing after a long delay is likely to require retrieval in the absence of many of the study cues present during studying. Studying should also be conducted under varied conditions, so that retrieval becomes practiced under varied conditions.

Developing Memory Skill

The study of individuals with expertise at remembering offers some learnable skills that will enhance our own memories. Individuals who are expert at remembering various types of material—numbers, maps, or scripts as examples—share a number of remembering techniques.

Skilled memory theory was developed to characterize the skill of those individuals who learned to remember long strings of random numbers (Chase & Ericsson, 1981). Three central features are postulated. First, during encoding, existing knowledge is used to organize and make target items meaningful. For instance, random numbers might be encoded as running times. Second, experts have well-developed retrieval routines. They can recall the cues (e.g., a fast mile, or 3:55). Third, with practice, both encoding and retrieval processes become faster.

Good map learners use several strategies during encoding. First, they partition the map into smaller sections and focus attention on one area at a time. This is comparable to partitioning a string of numbers or a list of words into smaller units. Good learners use visuospatial imagery to encode patterns and spatial relationships. Poor learners used more verbal rehearsal and naming of components. Finally, the good learners engage in more self-testing to assess whether they know the map yet (Thorndyke & Stasz, 1980).

In a study of *repertory memory,* both skilled drama performers and novices partitioned the lines into chunks, but the experts often chose smaller ones than did the novices. Experts selected certain words as landmarks (e.g., the starting words to a line or speech) and practiced these more often to establish them as retrieval cues. As with map and digit learners, their retrieval speeds was faster than novices (Intons-Peterson & Smyth, 1987).

Summary

Spatial Learning

Two types of memory representation are considered. Route knowledge is knowledge of a series of routes, directions, or paths in a spatial environment. By contrast, a survey or cognitive map is a more abstract representation of an environment, placing specific routes in context with the surrounding area.

Place versus response-learning experiments attempted to distinguish whether rats learned cognitive maps (Tolman) or specific turns (Hull) in mazes. The results were inconclusive with respect to the theories. Most organisms can learn flexibly about local cues to guide specific turns, and global cues to guide general orientation, depending on which sorts of cues are available.

Cognitive mapping is shown by performance in the radial maze and the water maze. In the radial maze, the participant must enter each goal arm once without repetition. Rats can do this in the absence of intramaze cues such as scents. Lesions of the hippocampus impair radial-maze and water-maze performance, just as hippocampal damage also impairs human declarative and spatial memory.

Landmarks are elements in an environment that by virtue of their distinctive design or meaning stand out. Landmarks are central to either route or survey maps. Landmark memory seems to be neurologically separable from route learning and cognitive mapping.

Spatial schemas can lead to distortion during recall due to the averaging and normalizing that occurs when knowledge becomes generalized. Errors in distance estimation, road-intersection angles, and relative proximity of geographic locations result from incorrect inferences from schematic spatial knowledge. Spatial information is organizable, just as is verbal information. For example, chimpanzees reorganized a search route to retrieve food efficiently, and by type of food.

Cognitive mapping shows a developmental progression. Human infants learn turn responses before place responses, and radial-maze performance increases from age 2 to nearly adult levels of accuracy by age 5.

Motor-Skills Learning

In motor-skills learning, the amount, direction, and duration of responding corresponds to variations in the regulating stimuli. Pursuit rotor and mirror tracing are exemplars of laboratory motor tasks.

One important determinant of skill is the amount of practice. The relationship between practice and the speed of performance is described by the power law. Plotting speed over the log of the number of trials produces a linear increase in speed (or a linear decrease in time required to make the response). As with verbal learning, spacing practice produces better learning than does massing trials.

A second factor affecting skill learning is knowledge of results. Outcome information or feedback on the success or accuracy of the response can be externally provided to the participant. Consistent feedback (given after each trial) and immediate feedback generally produce faster acquisition. However, partial-feedback schedules and delayed feedback can produce better long-term retention and better transfer to novel motor responses. According to the guidance hypothesis, occasional omitted or delayed feedback promotes attention to internal kinesthetic feedback, and thus learning to recognize good and poor performance.

Implicit Learning

Procedural knowledge is "knowing how" to perform a motor, perceptual, or cognitive act, rather than the factual "knowing that" of declarative learning. Procedural learning is often measured by an implicit test of learning. Implicit learning is the improvement in performance of cognitive, motor, or perceptual skills that develops with training. It is the process by which knowledge of a complex environment is acquired largely independent of conscious awareness of specific components of that environment. Artificial grammar and sequence learning are examples of implicit-learning tasks. Skill learning can be dissociated from priming in certain neurological conditions such as Alzheimer's or Huntington's disease.

Expertise

Although popular conception asserts that innate talent underlies exceptional ability, an alternative belief emphasizes the role of extensive practice. Expertise in many domains comes after years of deliberate and intensive training.

The acquisition of skilled procedural knowledge is marked by a series of stages: acquiring factual knowledge within the domain during the declarative stage; knowledge compilation, in which procedures are grouped into units; and proceduralization, in which operations become speeded and automatic.

Applications

Implicit training has been applied to teaching skills to amnesics, persons who otherwise could not acquire information explicitly. The vanishing-cue technique is one example of implicit training.

Our knowledge of spatial learning can be applied to understanding sense of direction, and improving the design of buildings. Long-term retention can be improved by applying several guidelines: optimize training conditions and strategies; train until retrieval is automatic; and optimize retention conditions.

Memory skills can be improved by partitioning material into smaller units, establishing retrieval cues at the time of encoding, and self-testing to assure that learning has occurred.

One of the goals of a scientific psychology is to describe general laws. This textbook, which includes the word "principles" in its title, attempts to specify some general, maybe even universal, principles of learning and memory. However, you and I realize that these generalities do not hold for each and every occasion. There are exceptions to the principles. Individual differences are one source of variations to the general principles of learning. Each person, and maybe even each organism, is unique. The combination of genes, physical constitution, environment, and life experiences causes each of us to react somewhat differently to what are seemingly the same situations. The remarkable thing, then, is that there are any general principles at all!

It would be impossible to describe the individual laws for each and every organism. Instead, researchers focus on broad categories of differences and try to describe the lawful principles that apply to these categories. Thus, how are children, adults, and the elderly alike or different in either learning (i.e., acquisition) or remembering (i.e., retention)? Are there gender, personality, or cultural differences that interact with the principles of learning?

Two distinctive approaches to research in psychology are the experimental approach and the correlational approach (Cronbach, 1957). Just as there are individual differences among our research participants, there are individual differences among researchers. The experimenters focus on those variables that can be manipulated by researchers, in order to determine what effects these variables have on learning. For instance, we can manipulate the spacing of repetitions to see how massed and spaced practice affects learning. The experimental approach seeks the general principles that transcend individual differences. A correlational approach focuses on variables that experimenters cannot control, such as gender, personality, or age, but that nevertheless may be important determinants of learning and memory in individuals. The correlational approach seeks the limiting conditions of the general principles. A complete theory of learning should provide two kinds of knowledge: the general principles governing acquisition, retention, and retrieval; and the contributions of individual differences to learning.

In some ways, what we are offering is a comparative psychology (although this phrase now refers to the field of psychology that makes comparisons among animal species). As Robert Yerkes said, "comparative psychology in its completeness necessarily deals with the materials of the psychology of the infant, child, adult whether the being be of human or infra-human; of animal or plant (!)—of normal and abnormal individuals; of social groups and of civilizations" (cited by Cronbach, 1957).

The Nature of Nurture: The Genetics of Learning Ability

The ability to learn (or the effect of *nurture*) is affected by the genetic makeup (or *nature*) of the individual organism. Genetic factors could directly affect the capacity to learn, for example, by affecting the structure or functioning of those nervous system regions involved in learning and remembering. Genetic influences also can indirectly affect learning, because people differ in their sensitivity to various stimuli, their intensity of reaction, or their level of emotionality, all factors that can influence learning and retention.

Animal Studies

The classic experiment on the genetics of learning ability was Tryon's breeding of rats for maze learning (e.g., Tryon, 1940). Tryon used the method of *selective breeding,* in which animals of similar learning ability were bred together over several generations. This is the same method used by animal breeders to produce specific physical traits. Fast race horses are bred with other fast horses in hopes of producing offspring that are faster still. Tryon first trained a large number of generic laboratory rats in a 17-turn maze. Some animals learned quickly; some learned slowly. Even among rats, there are sizable individual differences. Tryon selected the best maze learners and paired them for breeding. He also selected the worst learners and allowed them to breed. The offspring from these matings were then trained in the maze. The fastest-learning offspring from the faster-learning parents were selected for breeding; the slowest learners from the slowest learning parents are also selected for breeding. Tryon was careful to hold the environment constant across the successive generations of breeding, so that the differences could not be attributed to environmental changes.

After 18 generations of selective breeding, the two lines of descendants had diverged into what Tryon called the Maze Bright (MB) and Maze Dull (MD) rats. There was almost no overlap between the MB and MD lines of rats, although individual differences within the bright and dull strains persisted.

Do the MB and MD rats differ in their general learning ability? Subsequent research leads us to the more modest claim for a genetic influence on a *specific* learning ability, that of maze learning. The bright and dull rats differed in several ways: in their levels of emotionality, size and health, and reactions to being handled and to different types of mazes (Fuller & Thompson, 1978). However, improved research designs that control for these factors now routinely show that rats, mice, and fruit flies can be bred for differences in specific learning ability (e.g., Tully, 1996).

Genetic mutations can be induced by exposing organisms such as fruit flies to certain chemicals. Tim Tully tested chemically mutated fruit flies in a shock-avoidance learning procedure (Tully, 1996). The flies were trained in a T maze made of Plexiglas tubes. An odor is introduced into one arm of the T; after the flies enter that arm, they receive an electric shock. A different odor in the other arm of the T maze is not shocked. Tulley has found, and subsequently bred, flies that cannot learn this discrimination (so-called Dunce flies), or flies that learn but quickly forget (Amnesic flies).

Another method derived from molecular genetics is to introduce DNA that is thought to affect the brain areas involved with learning and memory into fertilized cells. Tang et al. (1999) produced strains of transgenic mice that had additional receptors in the hippocampus, an area I have frequently noted is implicated in learning. These additional receptor cells increase or lengthen the duration of hippocampal activity during a learning experience. This particular strain of mice, labeled Doogie (after Doogie Howser, MD, the character on TV who was a precocious child), did indeed learn better that normal mice. What was especially nice about this study is that the researchers used a battery of learning tests, not just a single task. The transgenic mice were better at detecting novel objects added to their environment; were better at learning the placement of the hidden platform in the Morris water maze; and were faster in acquisition and extinction of classical conditioning. This enhancement of general learning ability is important in ruling out genes that simply increased attention, emotionality, or activity levels.

To say that genes affect learning seems to imply that genetic makeup predetermines later ability. After all, how can environment affect what is genetic? In actuality, hereditary traits combine with environmental factors, such that the developmental outcome is more appropriately described as an interaction of genes and environment. For example, maze-learning capacity by both MB and MD rats is affected by the quality of social and environmental stimulation the animal experiences during rearing. Cooper and Zubek (1958) compared MB and MD rats raised in three different environments. In the restricted condition, the rats were housed individually in small cages. In the stimulating environment, several rats were housed together in a multilevel cage filled with toys and objects to manipulate (sort of a hamster habitat). The "normal" environment was something in between: a few rats living together, but with no toys. When later trained in the maze, the rats from the so-called normal living conditions showed the usual superiority of the MB over the MD (see Figure 12.1). Rats reared in the deprived environment were very poor learners, regardless of genetic background (i.e., MB or MD); rats reared in the stimulating environment were very good learners, again regardless of genetic background. Thus, expression of the genetic difference between strains depended on particular environmental conditions.

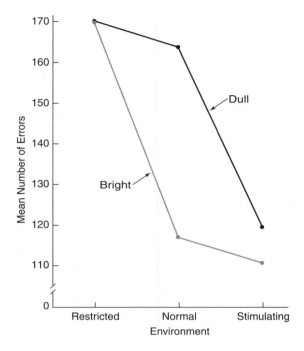

FIGURE 12.1   Number of maze errors made by Maze Bright and Maze Dull rats as a function of the rearing environment: restricted, normal, or enriched (stimulating).

Source: From "Effects of Enriched and Restricted Early Environments on the Learning Ability of Bright and Dull Rats," by R. M. Cooper and J. P. Zubek, 1958, *Canadian Journal of Psychology, 12,* pp. 159–164. Copyright © 1958 by the Canadian Psychological Association. Reprinted with permission.

These effects of environmental enrichment tie in nicely with the recent reports of the importance of early mental stimulation on intellectual development (e.g., Rosenzweig, 1996). One study showed that mice living in an enriched environment had an increased number of neurons in the hippocampus, an area known to be important for learning. These mice were tested in the Morris water maze, in which the mouse must learn the location of the platform hidden just under the surface of the water. The enriched-environment mice were quicker at learning the platform position (Kempermann, Kuhn, & Gage, 1997).

Human Studies

Assessing genetic differences in learning ability among humans is more difficult than in animals. The breeding histories and the environments that we are exposed to are not experimentally controllable. However, genetic influences are inferred from the results of methods such as the comparison of twins.

The *twins method* measures the similarity of identical twins (or monozygotic twins, referring to the production of two individuals from a single fertilized ovum) and the similarity of fraternal twins (or dizygotic twins, referring to two fertilized ova). Basically, we are asking whether identical twins are more alike in learning or memory than are fraternal twins. For example, in one study of 10-year-old twins, the identical pairs were more alike in the number of names and pictures recalled (the correlation was .43) than were fraternal pairs (the correlation was .31; Thompson, Detterman, & Plomin, 1991). At the other end of the age spectrum, elderly identical twins (mean age of 67 years) were more similar in the number of word lists they could recall and in memory for abstract figures (Finkel & McGue, 1993). Results such as these are taken to suggest that memory has a hereditary component.

However, the statistical estimates of the heritability of memory are often relatively small. This may be because memory is treated as a single ability, as opposed to partitioning it into different types of memory, such as short term versus long term or episodic versus semantic. For example, McClearn and colleagues (1997) pooled digit span and picture recognition into a single measure of memory. Partitioning memory could reveal different results. Thapar, Petrill, and Thompson (1994) compared 137 monozygotic twins pairs and 127 same-sex fraternal twins pairs on a battery of eight memory tests. The identical twins were more similar on tests of associative memory, such as learning names and faces. The identical twins were no more alike than were the fraternals on tests requiring brief retention, such as the digit span or remembering pictures for an immediate test. Thus, rather than concluding that memory, broadly speaking, is heritable, these results suggest there are genetic influences on certain kinds of learning or remembering.

A potential weakness of twins studies is that the identical twins may be more alike because their environments are more alike than are the environments of fraternal twins. The identical twins may be treated more alike by their parents, friends, and the world in general. They may also elicit similar reactions from others. A stronger case for genetic influence can be made if the twins happened to be raised separately and thus experienced clearly separate environments.

Age Differences in Learning and Memory

Changes in learning and memory across the lifetime have been studied experimentally using the same basic methods otherwise described in this text. Learning, the acquisition of information, has been studied using classical conditioning and habituation procedures, comparing age-related changes in behavior over trials. Memory, the retention of learned information, has been studied using episodic, one-trial procedures such as recognition and recall methods.

Classical Conditioning

Classical conditioning techniques have been applied across the age spectrum, from (literally) prenatal to elderly subject groups. Recall that classical conditioning involves pairing a CS and a US, and learning is indicated by the appearance of anticipatory responses being made to the CS. One major age-related change in conditioning is readily demonstrated: The very young and the very old do not condition as well as the age groups in between. Some examples of conditioning prenatally, in infants, and in the aged are reviewed in what follows.

Prenatal Learning.   Some especially provocative studies have suggested that classical conditioning can occur before birth. In one study of pregnant women, music was used as the CS and the mothers were trained in deep muscle relaxation as the US. After 24 pairings of music and relaxation during the thirtieth to thirty-seventh weeks of gestation, the activity level of the fetuses decreased when the music was again played. This calming effect persisted as a reaction to the music even after birth (Feijoo, as cited in Hepper, 1989).

The more general procedure for studying prenatal learning is to expose the fetus to some experience and then test after birth to see whether prenatal learning had occurred. For instance, in taste-aversion learning, a novel taste is paired with a noxious chemical that causes illness. Fetal rats can be exposed in utero, through a surgical procedure, to apple juice paired with an illness-inducing agent. When the rat pups are tested after birth, they show an aversion that is specific to the taste of apple juice (Smotherman, 1982).

Instrumental conditioning procedures can also be used to show the occurrence of prenatal learning. (Recall that instrumental conditioning is reinforcement or reward conditioning). For instance, a stimulus experienced *before* birth can function as a positive reinforcer *after* birth. In a study by DeCasper and Fifer (1980), infants' sucking on a pacifier was the instrumental response, which was reinforced by presentation of a tape recording of their mothers' voice. One- to 4-day-old infants increased sucking when this positive reinforcer occurred, but not when the "reinforcer" was a stranger's voice. DeCasper argues that these newborns learned the sound of their mothers' voices prenatally and did not have sufficient experience with the mother's voice after birth to make it reinforcing. In a later study, mothers-to-be read a specific story out loud during the last 6 weeks of the pregnancy. When the infants were later tested, they increased sucking to hear the particular story exposed during pregnancy rather than a different story read by the mother (DeCasper & Spence, 1986). (In these studies, the infants did not differentiate between their father's voice and another male's voice.) Anecdotally, Hepper (1989) reported that newborns apparently recognize soap opera theme music of the mother's favorite show. On hearing the theme, the infants stopped crying and became alert, whereas infants whose mothers had not watched this show during pregnancy did not react.

Conditioning in Infants.   Research with human infants has demonstrated classical conditioning of a number of responses such as eye-blink, head-turning, and sucking responses (Fitzgerald & Brackbill, 1976; Marquis, 1941). In some cases, the to-be-conditioned stimuli were olfactory stimuli. Newborns seem to quickly learn "scents" associated with their mothers. Such learning is important in helping to maintain mother–infant contact in any species, not just humans, and particularly for neonates, whose auditory and visual systems function poorly at birth. In one study of newborn infants, a neutral odor was accompanied with stroking their torsos (Sullivan et al., 1991). The experimental design included a number of control conditions missing in earlier investigations. Thus, other groups of newborns were exposed to just the odor, just the stroking, or the two unpaired. The next day (the day after their birth), the infants were tested for their reactions to the odor. Those infants who had received pairings of the odor with bodily contact turned their heads more often in the direction of the odor and were more active when the odor was presented. These infants did not respond to a different odor, one not previously presented.

Eye-blink conditioning, in which a tone CS is followed by an air-puff US, occurs in human infants as young as 10 days old (Little, Lipsitt, & Rovee-Collier, 1984). The amount of conditioning increased with age, although even the youngest group developed some conditioned responding over days. Infant conditioning does depend on the precise temporal arrangements between stimuli, even more so than is the case for adults. A different measured behavior or variations in the procedures used may preclude evidence of conditioning.

Aging and Conditioning.   At the other end of the age spectrum, classical conditioning begins a decline in humans after the age of 40 or so. Solomon and Pendlebury (1992) have studied eye-blink conditioning in both rabbits and humans, in each case using pairings of a tone and an air puff. The rabbits ranged in age from 6 months to 4 years; the humans, 25 years to over 70. The younger subjects in each species reached a higher level of responding to the CS, between 65 and 80 percent, whereas the oldest subjects responded to only about 20 to 30 percent of the CSs.

Memory Development in Children

The capacity to remember seems to develop from infancy, through childhood and adolescence, and into young adulthood. The interest for us here is not that children seem to remember less than adults, but why? As Flavel (1971) posed the question: "What is memory development the development of?" Several answers have been proposed, ranging from hypotheses that children have lesser short-term memory capacities to their having less knowledge of how memory works. What we will see is that much develops in children's memory.

Assessing Memory in Infants.   In infants, methods such as habituation, dishabituation, and classical conditioning offer nonverbal ways of assessing learning. Yet classical conditioning represents a form of learning different from what we usually apply to word memory. Episodic memory—remembering specific events or experiences—is most often assessed using verbal reports available in older children and adults. When adults are asked about specific events from their first years of life, such as the birth of a sibling, episodic memories are conspicuously absent. Adults' earliest childhood memories are typically from age 3 or so, occasionally a memory from before; often, our first memories appear later (Eacot & Crawley, 1998). Is it really possible that the experiences of our first years are not remembered? This phenomenon of *childhood amnesia* has been of interest since at least the time of Freud and the subject of many theories. One explanation is that key areas of the brain, particularly the hippocampus, have not yet matured in infants and so episodic memories are not formed (Nelson, 1995). Other explanations are that younger and older children differ in encoding, memory span, existing knowledge, use of learning strategies, and in metamemory.

Encoding Differences.   Possibly, memories in infants are encoded based more on sensory and movement dimensions, rather than verbally, and these former modes of encoding become inaccessible to retrieval when the child does become verbal. As we become more verbal with age, and particularly as schooling shapes the ways we think, we come to categorize the world differently. Adult schemata are different from those we had as infants. So, new retrieval or search cues simply do not work in retrieving nonverbally encoded memories (Neisser, 1967). An analogy would be a new computer software program that cannot access or open files encoded using a different software program.

If memories are there, maybe episodic recall in infants can be tested by nonverbal means, rather than waiting a few years for the children to become old enough to question. Bauer (e.g., 1996) has developed an elegant set of procedures in which children as young as 11 months can demonstrate remembering by imitating activities they have observed the experimenter performing. The procedure is called *elicited imitation.* The experimenter demonstrates an activity for the child, such as putting a teddy bear into a small bed, pulling the covers up, and reading the bear a bedtime story. The child is then encouraged to repeat the sequence. The number of target actions that the child reproduces and their sequence can be recorded, giving a measure of immediate memory. Even 11-month-olds correctly imitate two action sequences, and children of 24 to 30 months can repeat events of five to eight actions. After a delay ranging from a week to, in some cases, 8 months, the child is returned and shown the props used initially. Retention is demonstrated by these children spontaneously imitating the previous sequences. Apparently, quite a bit can be remembered during the early years of development.

Capacity.   Another explanation for what differentiates younger from older children is the capacity of their immediate memories. That is, maybe the short-term memory span or working-memory capacity is smaller in younger children. Processing, in terms of holding information briefly in memory, elaborating that information, and incorporating the new material into existing memories, is restricted and therefore limits what can be entered into long-term memory.

Memory span, the number of items that can be retained after a single presentation, is less in younger children. For example, children in first grade (about 6 to 7 years old) retained 3 or 4 digits; sixth graders had a span of 5 to 6 digits; and adults had a span of 7 ± 2 items (Engle & Marshall, 1983). Working-memory capacity, as assessed by requiring simultaneous performance of two tasks, also increases with age.

Developmental differences in short-term memory are less evident from the serial-position curve. What increases with age is memory for the early (or primacy) and middle positions of a to-be-remembered list. Children of most age groups recall the last item or two (a recency effect).

Knowledge.   As noted in discussing encoding (Chapter 9), a general rule is that the more you know, the more new you can remember. Maybe older children can remember more than younger children and infants because of the amount of preexisting knowledge they have.

This hypothesis predicts that younger children might do as well as, or even better, than older individuals if the younger children are more knowledgeable about the to-be-remembered material. This was nicely demonstrated by Chi (1978), who had 10-year-olds and adults remember arrangements of 20 chess pieces on a board and random strings of numbers. As expected, the adults had a longer span for digits. These particular children were chosen for the study because they were more knowledgeable about chess than were the adults. So, memory spans completely reversed for chess memory. Here, the children remembered the correct positions of more chess pieces than did the adults.

Simply knowing more does not completely account for age differences in memory ability, however. DeMarie-Dreblow (1991) explicitly taught her young participants information about the target material that was eventually to be used, names of birds. Even though the instructed children knew more about the birds, when it came time to remember lists of bird names, the children did nor recall any more than did uninstructed children.

Strategies.   Retention can be increased by the use of various mnemonic strategies: rehearsing the to-be-recalled material, forming mental images, grouping and organizing the items for later recall, and so on. Possibly, younger children do not use strategies, and therefore do not recall as well as older children. Indeed, there is strong evidence for this hypothesis.

In simple memory tasks, children of different ages are asked to remember a series of picture triplets. Four- and five-year-olds tend not to rehearse spontaneously, whereas older children, usually by age 8 or so, do rehearse. (We know this from watching their mouth movements; Locke & Fehr, 1971.) Teaching the younger nonrehearsers to rehearse does help them to remember more (Keeney, Cannizzo, & Flavell, 1967). With still longer lists and somewhat older children, more efficient rehearsal strategies develop. Younger children repeat one item at a time, usually the last item presented, whereas older children intermix rehearsal of several items, a pattern that increases recall (Ornstein, Naus, & Liberty, 1975; Ornstein, Naus, & Stone, 1977).

Metamemory.   Younger and older children seem to differ in their knowledge about memory, both their own in particular and how memory in general works. Metamemory, or knowledge about memory, is important in deciding what types of learning tasks will be difficult or when learning strategies should be used. For example, children were asked how they would remember to bring something to school with them tomorrow (Kreutzer, Leonard, & Flavell, 1975). This question asks children to tell something of what they know about memory. The children were very aware that they might forget if they simply depended on "remembering." Instead, the children suggested using reminders, such as placing the item near the front door or in their backpack, or writing themselves a note (or just asking mom to remind them). The children suggested more and more sophisticated solutions as age increased from kindergarten to fifth grade.

Although children are knowledgeable about memory in a general way, this knowledge is inaccurate in detail. When asked how many items of a given kind they could recall, children of most ages (including college students) overestimate. Practicing a memory test does not eliminate these overestimates. Pressley and Ghatala (1989), in a study spanning grades 1 to 8, asked students for three estimates of their performance on a vocabulary test: first, how well they thought they would do on a test; then, after taking the test, how well they thought they did; and, finally, how well they thought they would do on another test. Figure 12.2 shows the percentage of children who overestimated their performance. Before the quiz, 60 to 90 percent of the kids predicted they would do better than they actually did. The older children were most inaccurate in their predictions. After the quiz, the kids still thought they had done pretty well (though, on average, they only got 15 out of 30 items correct). The older children benefited most from their poor first test performance and were best able to lower their estimates of future performance, adjusting their predictions so that fewer fourth and eighth graders overestimated performance.

So What Is It That Develops?   There does not seem to be any one reason why memory improves from infancy to adulthood. Several factors, including encoding differences, pre-existing knowledge, memory span, and metamemory, contribute. As we will see later (i.e., cross-cultural comparisons), age alone is not the only determiner of memory. Schooling influences metamemory and the use of rehearsal strategies, two factors that affect recall independently of age.

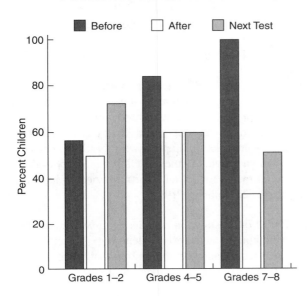

Percent Who Overestimate Quiz Scores

FIGURE 12.2   Percentage of children who overestimate performance before taking a difficult vocabulary quiz, estimating performance on the quiz they just took, and predicting how they will do on another quiz.

Source: From "Metacognitive Benefits of Taking a Test fro Children and Young Adolescents," by M. Pressley and E. S. Ghatala, 1989, *Journal of Experimental Child Psychology, 47,* pp. 430–450. Copyright © 1989 by Academic Press. Reprinted with permission.

Aging and Memory

Older adults, typically referring to those over age 60, do not remember as well as younger adults. In parallel to Flavell's question about memory development in children, Perlmutter (1978) asked: "What is memory aging the aging of?" A variety of explanations have been considered for the decline in memory with age, several of which are similar to those offered for the poorer memory found in young children. Thus, reduced memory capacity and metamemory failures are two hypotheses considered, as well as ones postulating encoding and/or retrieval difficulties.

Capacity.   Tests of working memory show a decline in performance with aging. For instance, there is an increased difficulty in doing two tasks at once, such as adding successively presented pairs of numbers and remembering the sums. This could indicate that the capacity of memory has been reduced (Charness, 1987; Light & Anderson, 1985). Others have suggested that there is a general cognitive slowing that accompanies aging (Salthouse, 1994). This slowing would be manifested at each step in performing a working-memory task: more time to encode the numbers, perform the addition, rehearse the accumulating sums, and then recall them. Thus, even if memory capacity was unchanged in the older adult, working memory still could be overtaxed by cognitive slowing.

Metamemory.   Possibly older adults have different or inaccurate beliefs about memory and how to use it. Having been out of school for a while, they have forgotten all those strategies they used when they were students. Maybe the elderly have unrealistic expectations about what can be remembered. Explanations such as these are not often supported by survey results. Perlmutter (1978) did not find any age effects in reported use of memory strategies, whether these were external aids such as lists and reminder notes, or internal methods such relating to-be-remembered information to already known information. Beliefs about how memory works (e.g., memory is better for organized, concrete, or interrelated material) also did not vary with age.

The belief that memory declines with age could influence performance. In one demonstration of this age stereotype, both young and elderly female subjects read vignettes (case examples) of everyday forgetting by people. The cases were accompanied by a picture of the person, which could be of an older or younger person, as a way of introducing age into the manipulation. The participants were asked to explain why forgetting had occurred. Memory failures in older people were attributed to their declining memory ability. Memory failures in younger people were attributed to lack of effort: They could have remembered well, but they just didn't try (Erber & Rothberg, 1991).

Noncognitive Sources of Decline.   Recall our distinction between learning versus performance. Performance could be poor even though the underlying learning or memory capacity has not declined. Aging is associated with a number of variables that, although not affecting memory directly, could nevertheless affect *performance* on a test of memory. Older individuals may suffer poorer health, take more medications that affect cognition, or experience mood impairments due to depression, grief, or life-style changes. Maybe the decline in memory is attributable to other factors associated with aging, but not necessarily to a decline in memory itself.

It is certainly the case that memory is impaired by many of these factors. Depression leads to poorer memory performance (Niederehe, 1991), and the side effects of combining many medicines is well recognized (e.g., Cammen et al., 1987). One survey found that general health, hearing and vision problems were good predictors of everyday memory problems (Cutler & Grams, 1988). On the other hand, a correlational study found that being healthier, educated, and intellectually active all predicted better memory performance (Arbuckle et al., 1992). However, even when the elderly participants selected for research purposes are uniformly healthy, the major factor in describing memory decline is age (West, Crook, & Barron, 1992). Holding other factors constant leaves a deficit that correlated with aging.

Intellectual Deficits

Mental retardation, increasingly referred to as developmental disability, describes a condition of lowered intellectual ability. The causes of retardation are many; genetic disorders and birth defects, head injury, anoxia, malnutrition, and exposure of toxic substances are just a few. In some cases, the specific cause is unknown. Mental retardation is defined by the level of intellectual ability present, which can be roughly characterized by an intelligence quotient (IQ) score. Given the score of 100 as the average for individuals of a certain age, IQ scores significantly below 100 are used to define categories from moderately to profoundly retarded.

Research on learning can make several contributions to the lives of the mentally retarded. One application is the use of reinforcement and behavior modification techniques to teach developmentally disabled individuals (Chapters 4 and 5). A second contribution is in applying principles of memory to enhancing learning, such as training in the use of rehearsal. We will consider here two other exemplar forms of learning, classical conditioning and verbal memory.

Conditioning

Individuals who have developmental disabilities learn through classical conditioning and, in some cases, perform at about the same rate as nondisabled participants. For example, in one study of eye-blink conditioning, institutionalized, retarded young adults (mean age of 25) and a sample of college students each required about 25 CS–US pairings to condition. Where the retarded and nonretarded diverged was in inhibiting responses to stimuli that were not paired with the air-puff US. During extinction, responding should decrease: The tone is now presented alone and is no longer followed by the air puff. However, the retarded individuals continued to respond after the control subjects had ceased (Lobb & Hardwick, 1976).

An important research tool is the study of retardation associated with certain genetic disorders. Down syndrome (DS), first described by Dr. John Langdon Down in the 1860s, is a genetic disorder in which an extra chromosome appears; in most instances of DS, one pair (the twenty-first pair) is replaced by a triplet (although there are other versions). The degree of retardation varies widely in DS children and adults, from mild to profound. Down syndrome is of particular interest because the brain pathology that develops in older DS individuals (in this case, over age 35) is similar to that which develops in Alzheimer's disease.

Down syndrome individuals were participants in a study of eye-blink conditioning (Woodruf-Pak et al., 1994), in which a tone was paired with an air puff. The researchers had a portable computer control and monitoring system that allowed them to take their laboratory with them. The participants could therefore participate within a familiar environment. The younger DS subjects (under age 35) developed conditioned eye blinks to the tone and responded more frequently to the tone than did the older DS participants, although the overall level of conditioning in each group was low. The results are shown in Figure 12.3, which shows the percentage of CRs from the final block of 16 trials. Conditioning in the older DS individuals did not differ from that of elderly Alzheimer's individuals. This response rate was much less than the 60 percent reached by unaffected young adult subjects.

How General Is the Learning Deficit? Is poor learning due to an overall intellectual impairment, or are there specific deficits in certain categories of learning, say, verbal versus spatial? Some research suggests that Down syndrome has a particular impact on spatial-learning ability. In designs that parallel the cognitive map-learning experiments discussed in Chapter 11, some DS infants (16 to 30 months of age) learned the location of a toy that was hidden in a familiar room. In the place-learning condition, the infants started from different locations within the room from trial to trial, but the toy remained in the same location. This is analogous to place learning by Tolman's rats or learning the platform location in the Morris water maze. The infant must learn a cognitive map of the goal in relation to multiple environmental cues within the room. DS children were particularly impaired at this task in comparison to non-Down children of a similar age (Uecker et al., 1993).

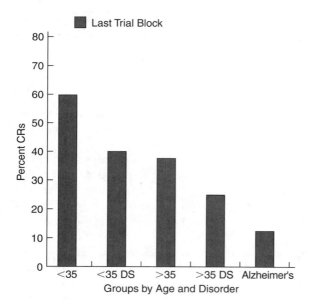

FIGURE 12.3 Mean Percent Conditioned Eye-Blink Responses at the End of Training. Graph shows results for young adults (under age 35), young adult Down syndrome, older adult and older adult Down syndrome (both over age 35), and Alzheimer's patients.

Source: Woodruff-Pak et al., 1994, p. 20.

The profile of abilities and disabilities differs among genetic disorders. Williams syndrome (WS) is a rare genetic disorder that produces mild to moderate mental retardation. In common with Down syndrome, Williams syndrome individuals are typically impaired on visual-spatial tasks, such as reproducing geometric designs with blocks. However, in contrast to DS, WS children are more articulate, fluent, and grammatical in their use of language. On verbal tests, such as word recall or digit span, WS perform significantly better than DS children. WS children cluster similar items during recall. This indicates an awareness of the categorical nature of the lists (Bellugi, Wang, & Jernigan, 1994).

Memory

Other research has investigated the roles of working-memory capacity, memory strategies, and metamemory in the retarded. One prevailing theme across several subtopics within this chapter is that strategies can play a beneficial role in remembering. Retarded children are less likely to use rehearsal spontaneously or to recall categorizable lists of items by category at output. This suggests a metamemory deficit or a lack of awareness of the effectiveness of memory strategies (see review by Kail, 1990).

Recall can be substantially increased by instruction in rehearsal. For example, retarded adolescents were trained to use rehearsal to aid remembering short strings of object names. The same items often recurred across lists over the 10 days of training, so the task required keeping track of the most recently presented items. As can be seen in Figure 12.4, children given rehearsal training remembered the list items better; those without such training remembered only the final items well (a recency effect). An interesting companion experiment used the same procedure with nonretarded children. One group received no formal instructions and they recalled nearly 90 percent of the items, presumably because they were rehearsing. When rehearsal was disrupted in a second group, their recall fell to less than 50 percent. This study shows that by manipulating rehearsal, the retarded and nonretarded individuals could achieve comparable levels of either good or poor performance (Brown et al., 1973).

If strategies such as rehearsal, organization, or elaboration can be acquired, will the use of a strategy be generalized beyond a particular experiment? Research on the transfer of strategy learning can be summarized on two levels (Kramer, Nagle, & Engle, 1980). On one level, the use of strategies tends not to be generalized to the learning of different types of materials. This is unfortunately characteristic of mnemonic training in children in general. Nondisabled school children who were trained to use a mediating keyword strategy to associate cities and their products did not generalize the procedure to assist in learning Latin vocabulary later (Pressley & Dennis-Rounds, 1980). On a more abstract level of transfer, retarded individuals have difficulty with a number of metamemory skills, including estimating their memory spans, making judgments of learning, apportioning study time, self-testing, or searching memory.

The previously reviewed findings suggest that memory performance by the retarded can be improved. Two caveats (or cautions) are in order here. First, most of the preceding research was done using mentally disabled individuals with relatively high overall levels of intelligence. The tactics of rehearsal or metamemory training will be less effective with more profoundly retarded individuals. Second, cognitive-skills training does not eliminate the gap between the retarded and the nonretarded, although such instruction can increase the adaptive functioning of both.

Learning Disabilities

A learning disability is an impairment of a specific cognitive ability, leaving other cognitive abilities unaffected. Learning-disabled individuals show a discrepancy between their poor performance in one area and adequate performance in other areas. The disability

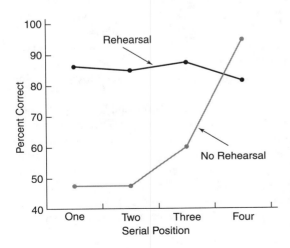

FIGURE 12.4   Effects of Rehearsal Training on Short-Term Retention in Retarded Adolescents. Without rehearsal training, only the final item in the list is well recalled.

Source: Brown et al., 1973, p. 126.

could be in reading (such as dyslexia), mathematics, or language. A learning disability is not due to general intellectual deficit.

A full consideration of learning disabilities would encompass much more than just cognition. There may be deficits in attention, perception, or language that affect learning. However, research on learning-disabled children has benefited from the various component approaches described in Chapter 7. For example, we can ask whether these disabilities are accompanied by deficiencies in working memory, or in the stages of encoding versus retrieval.

Learning-disabled children, when compared to control children of comparable intelligence, were found to process information poorly in short-term memory. They were less likely to rehearse, or if they did rehearse, they less often used organization or elaboration to facilitate encoding (Swanson & Cooney, 1991). We saw these same factors in comparing younger versus older children earlier in this chapter. There, as here with learning disabilities, the question is whether the failure to use effective rehearsal strategies underlies poorer recall. The answer, again, is that the use of strategies is not the entire cause. Instructing learning-disabled children in rehearsal usually increases recall, but does not eliminate the difference from the control group.

The learning-disabled may have difficulties at any of several stages of processing from attending to information, to encoding into long-term memory, to retrieval. Knee (1990) sought to discriminate among these several possibilities. Eight- to 10-year-old dyslexic children practiced a list of 15 words across five presentations and tests of recall. The dyslexic children recalled fewer words on each trial than did control children. An attention-deficit hypothesis might suggest that the dyslexic children are simply too distractible, which is the reason for slower learning. To test the distraction hypothesis, Knee presented the children a different list on the sixth trial to act as an explicit distractor and then retested recall of the original list. The distractor reduced recall of the original list somewhat, but affected the learning-disabled and control children equally, so the dyslexic were no more distracted than the controls. Another hypothesis is that poor list recall initially was due to retrieval problems: Maybe more words were learned than could be retrieved on command. Knee tested the retrieval deficit hypothesis by presenting cues during testing to reduce the retrieval burden. More words were recalled, but the cues also helped the nondyslexic children. Other measures showed that the dyslexic and nondyslexic children were essentially equal in their use of semantic organization of the lists (i.e., grouping words by category during recall) and in the number of words forgotten over a delay interval. By a process of exclusion, the slowed learning by the dyslexic children seems to reduce to an encoding deficit.

Studies like Knee's (1990) suggest that children with reading and language disabilities have a particular problem with verbal memory. What is their nonverbal memory like? Fein and colleagues (1988) tested dyslexic children on both verbal memory tasks and nonverbal tasks, such as reproducing abstract designs or remembering the sequence of a series of designs. Dyslexia is characterized by reading impairments, and so one could expect poor verbal memory performance. Actually, the dyslexic children had lower scores on both forms of memory than did the control children. However, not all dyslexics were equivalently affected. Neither verbal memory nor memory for designs correlated very strongly with reading ability.

Similarly, Swanson (1993) tested 10-year-olds with a math or a reading learning disability on a battery of working-memory tests. Each test required the child to remember a series of items (e.g., a story or the location of X's in a matrix) and also to answer a question about the material. Thus, this dual-task procedure exemplifies Baddeley's description of working memory as a place to hold information temporarily while simultaneously performing some mental operations. The math-disabled and the reading-disabled students had lower working-memory scores on both verbal and visual-spatial tests than did their nondisabled classmates. These results are surprising given that previous research has shown a correlation between verbal working memory and reading ability. Given the poor verbal working memory of the children with math disabilities in the present study, they should also have had a reading problem. The studies by Fein and colleagues (1988) and Swanson (1993) suggest that children with different disabilities, such as mathematics versus reading disabilities, have a generalized working-memory impairment that is not specific to verbal versus visual-spatial information processing.

Even though different disabilities may sometimes show similar deficits (e.g., poor verbal memory in both reading-disabled and math-disabled children), some researchers have argued that merging several groups together blurs the underlying patterns of ability and deficit. Others note that whereas cognitive approaches offer one means to describe what aspects of learning or remembering are disabled, it will not be a complete explanation. Learning-disabled children (and adults) experience social and emotional difficulties that interact with their learning disabilities.

Exceptional Memory: The Mnemonists

The psychology literature contains examples of individuals with truly exceptional memory abilities, some showing talents for remembering numbers or languages, others for memorizing the Bible, the Koran, or the *Iliad*. A Reverend Dr. Phelps claimed he could recall something specific about any day for the preceding 60 years of his life. If given the date March 6, 1879, "…in a few moments he will state the day of the week. Then he will give you the weather for that day, and describe some particular thing that happened" (Neisser, 1982, p. 413). Many such remarkable claims cannot be supported by documentation and so they fall in the category of anecdotes: interesting stories but ones that should not be accepted unquestioningly. However, other cases do include testing under controlled conditions, and here we can ask how good can memory be, and what causes it to be exceptional?

What may be the most remarkable case of exceptional memory is a man referred to as *S,* studied by the Russian neuropsychologist Luria (1968). *S* could apparently remember extraordinary amounts of verbal material. Long lists of names, numbers, and words could be recalled even years later. As examples, *S* memorized from a single presentation lines from Dante's *Divine Comedy* in its original Italian, a language with which *S* was unfamiliar. He also memorized the following meaningless mathematical formula:

$$N \cdot \sqrt{d^2 \times \frac{85}{vx}} \cdot \sqrt{\frac{276^2 \times 86x}{n^2 v \ \pi 264}} n^2 b \ = \ sv \frac{1624}{32^2} \cdot r^2 s$$

When given a surprise test 15 years later (that's right, 15 *years*), *S* was able to reproduce both the Italian verse and the formula. *S* worked as a mnemonist in clubs, doing several shows a night memorizing lists of words provided by the audiences. (Mnemonist is one name for people with exceptional memories. Neisser suggested "memorist" as an alternative label, but it doesn't seem to have caught on.) If *S* had any problem with his memory, it was that he remembered too much (you should have that problem!). *S* would occasionally make mistakes in recalling a given list, but this was because he was misrecalling lists from an earlier performance that evening. This is comparable to "forgetting" where you left the car this morning and instead going to where you parked it yesterday. *S* eventually learned how to forget these earlier-learned lists by "erasing" the lists from his mental blackboard.

Another mnemonist, discovered coincidentally during a search for visual imagers, had a truly remarkable visual memory. Reportedly, she could recollect whole pages printed in a foreign language years later (Stronmeyer & Psotka, 1970). Her most remarkable ability demonstrated in a laboratory was integrating two meaningless dot patterns to produce a three-dimensional image. Random-dot stereograms are patterns of tiny dots on a background. When the two images are fused, as occurs when viewed with glasses with red and green lenses, a three-dimensional object can be seen. This is analogous to the red and green printed images in the Magic Eye pictures. Stronmeyer's subject could fuse a currently viewed dot pattern with the memory of the other pattern presented 24 hours earlier and report the three-dimensional object (Stronmeyer & Psotka, 1970).

How do mnemonists remember so much? One factor for *S* was that a stimulus presented in one sensory modality was actually experienced in multiple modalities. This is called synesthesia, a condition of cross-modal perception. Spoken words would literally provoke visual images, smells, tastes, and tactile feelings. It is an inborn condition of the brain (Cytowic & Wood, 1982) and so may not be a trait that is learnable. If exceptional memory is biologically determined, of what benefit is there to the rest of us in studying memorists? One lesson from *S* is that memory is better for items presented in multiple sensory modalities. Another lesson is that even mnemonists use strategies to aid retention. For example, *S* would visually encode to-be-remembered material. Words and numbers would be converted into images to be retained. *S* also used the method of loci, or locations (Chapter 6). To remember a list, he would mentally place each object at some location during his mental walk down an imagined street.

Another strategy used by mnemonists is verbal elaboration. Nonsense syllables, random-number strings, or foreign words are mentally converted into meaningful items (e.g., JXS becomes "jacks"). The mnemonist VP could memorize lists of nonsense syllables by converting each to something meaningful. For example, his verbal associations to five to-be-remembered nonsense syllables were: a Latin proverb; the name of a familiar political scientist; the Latin word for swan; the Hebrew word for Gentile; and for the last, the word half-wit (from Hunt & Love, 1982).

Savants are individuals with an exceptional cognitive ability in the presence of otherwise low intelligence. Savants (formerly called idiot savants, indicating the contradictory nature of the abilities) can be calendar calculators (they can tell you what day of the week any date occurred on) or math whizzes. Some savants have exceptional mnemonic talents. The film *Rain Man* often defines the public stereotype of a savant: an individual who can memorize local phonebooks on an off night. But how good is memory in savants?

O'Conner and Hermelin (1989) studied savants who excelled at remembering bus information, such as routes, bus numbers, stops along the itinerary, and so on. Six savants were compared to six other autistic individuals of the same age and overall intelligence level, which was 23 years old and having an IQ of about 80. The savants were able to learn paired-associate lists of numbers (actually, London bus numbers) significantly faster than did the controls, thus showing the savants indeed did have better memory for bus-related information. Do savants have a better memory in general than do the controls? O'Conner and Hermelin gave both groups 10 tests, including both verbal and nonverbal memory measures (e.g., paired-associate learning of fruit and vegetable words). The savants and their IQ-matched controls did not differ overall, or on any of the single tests.

Two important points can be made. First, savants may have exceptional memories, but sometimes it is exceptional in comparison to that of others with low intelligence. Second, savants often have had years of practice with material within a certain domain, such as bus routes or songs. Treffert (1989) noted that parents may notice a talent in their autistic or retarded child early in his or her life, and heavily reinforce this talent thereafter. These individuals may come to possess prodigious skills, but due to years of practice.

Gender and Cognitive Abilities

Do men and women differ in their memory abilities? Most research has focused on cognitive abilities that are more inclusive than just memory. Verbal ability is defined by performance on a battery of tests, as, for example, by verbal SAT scores or on comparable tests of vocabulary, comprehension, and analogies. Spatial ability is most often measured by tests of spatial perception and of mental imagery, such as a test of mental rotation of objects (see Figure 12.5). At one time, the prevailing view was that men performed better on spatial tests and women on verbal tests. However, the differences in language and mathematics test scores seem to be declining over the years (Feingold, 1988). (See also Chapter 11.)

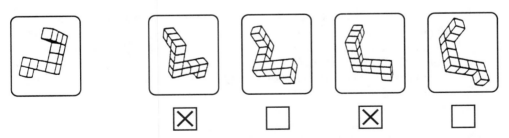

FIGURE 12.5   Mental Rotation Test for Spatial Cognitive Ability. A sample three-dimesional drawing of an object is given on the left. The task is to which two objects from the right are rotated version of the sample object.

Source: Reprinted with permission from "Mental Rotation of Three-Dimensional Objects," by R. N. Shepard and J Meltzer, 1971, *Science, 171,* pp. 701–703. Copyright © 1971 American Association for the Advancement of Science.

Comparisons between men and women are not easily interpreted. Recall our emphasis in the last few chapters that there can be several stages of memory. The range of potential interpretations for differential recall is nicely illustrated by a study of parents' recollections of milestones in their infants' lives. Robbins (1963) had access to families participating in an ongoing long-term study. The researchers had collected detailed records of developmental milestones in the infants' lives, such as when the child first stood or walked, when potty training began, when 2 A.M. feedings stopped, and so on. When the children were about 3 years old, Robbins asked both the fathers and mothers to date the occurrence of several of these events. Although both men and women significantly misdated most events by several weeks, fathers were off more often, and for 11 out of 13 milestones had greater deviations from the actual time than did the mothers. Is this because mothers are more interested in their children's early development, or are they more likely to have been actually involved when milestones were reached? Do sex-role expectations about memory focus attention differently? Maybe fathers would be better at recalling male-stereotyped activities that occur when the kids are older, for example, a first ball game. Did the mothers discuss their children's progress (possibly with their own mothers), thus rehearsing the information more? Or, were the mothers better at reconstructing when the milestones were reached? A simple finding of gender differences in recall is open to many possible explanations, ranging from differences in attention, encoding, to retrieval.

One recent study has attempted to match or control for potential incidental variables in gender research on memory (Herlitz, Nilsson, & Backman, 1997). The 1,000 subjects were randomly selected from the population of a region in Sweden, sampling ages from 35 to 80 years old. Education, intelligence, and general health were assessed so that any differences between gender could be statistically controlled. A battery of verbal episodic memory tests was administered to each subject, including tests of recall and recognition of word lists, sentences, new factual information, and names and faces. There were also measures of short-term memory and semantic memory (i.e., general knowledge and vocabulary). The women performed better, on the average, than men at word recall and recognition, learning new facts, and recognizing newly learned names and faces. Men and women did not differ in semantic memory or in short-term memory.

In some cases, gender differences in memory could be attributed to differential familiarity with the to-be-learned material. One generalization that has been mentioned several times in this book is that the more you know, the more new you can remember. If the target material is more familiar to one gender (e.g., chess pieces' positions) performance may be better. Davies and Robertson (1993) found that males were better at recognizing pictures of cars they had been shown earlier, and females were better at recognizing faces. This difference appeared as early as ages 9 to 11, and may be related to different interests of the two sexes. Gender differences may even appear if one *thinks* he or she knows more. When college students listened to a vaguely worded prose passage titled either "Building a Workbench" or "Making a Shirt," male students remembered more when given the workbench title, but female students remembered more when given the shirt title (Herrmann, Crawford, & Holdsworth, 1992). Yet everyone had heard the same passage.

Gender differences could also arise from expectations or stereotypes about how one should perform. Maybe men think they should be able to remember cars and sports facts, and so do better. Ceci and Bronfenbrenner (1985) conducted a study of prospective remembering in which children had to remember to perform some action 30 minutes later. Boys remembered better to check a battery charger (a stereotypically "guy" thing) and girls remembered better to check the oven. These effects were larger among the 14-year-olds than among the 10-year-olds.

Stereotypical gender expectations about performance might be manifested in self-handicapping. Our beliefs about the effectiveness of our own memories may affect how we actually perform. Women are expected to be better at remembering the kids' birthdays and men to be better at memory for locations or directions (Crawford et al., 1989). These expectations could influence the amount of effort put into a given memory task. After all, why try, when you are supposed to do poorly? When the instructions for a memory task emphasized its "spatial" nature, women did more poorly than did men. This is the usual result on a spatial task. However, when nonspatial instructions were given, men and women did not differ (Sharps et al., 1993).

Men and women might have different memory capacities because of inherent biological differences between the sexes. Differences in animal memory are sometimes found, particularly in spatial learning. And as we have seen before, there are socialization or experiential reasons for gender differences, such as differential knowledge or experience, interest levels, self-handicapping, or different expectancies about how one should perform. The point of mentioning these alternatives is to show the uncertain interpretation of any gender differences that are found.

Personality and Learning

Personality can be defined as an individual's characteristic mode of thinking, feeling, and acting. Personality is often described in terms of some relatively stable and enduring traits, such as the degree of extraversion, emotional stability, openness to new experience, impulsiveness, or conscientiousness (McCrae & DeCosta, 1986). Personality becomes relevant to learning if variations in one or another trait are associated with different behaviors or cognitions that affect learning. Two traits in particular that have been studied are extraversion and anxiety.

Introversion and Extraversion

Extraversion is one personality trait that may affect both learning and remembering. This trait is usually conceptualized as a continuum running from introversion at one end to extraversion at the other. It is assessed by a self-report inventory, in which participants respond to questions such as: "Would you rather work on a group project or an individual project?" "Would you rather go out with friends, or stay home with a good book?" What does sociability have to do with learning ability? Actually, it is not sociability that is important. Rather, other hypotheses suggest that introverts and extraverts differ in arousal, impulsiveness, or susceptibility to reward.

The British psychologist Hans Eysenck (1981) suggested that introverts have higher usual levels of central nervous system arousal than do extraverts, and this higher arousal can often facilitate learning. This at first seems counterintuitive, because extraverts seem to be more active and stimulated. But, Eysenck says, this is why extraverts are the way they are. Having lower arousal to begin with, they seek external stimulation, just as some of us drink coffee to perk up. Extraverts score higher on measures of thrill seeking and desire for stimulating experiences than do introverts. This natural difference in arousal suggests that in situations when arousal benefits learning, introverts should learn better. For example, the introvert's higher level of cognitive arousal would counteract boredom, fatigue, or lack of interest. On difficult tasks, ones that engage the subjects' attention and motivation, too much arousal would be detrimental and so the introverts might do poorly here (Howarth, 1969).

As noted in Chapter 9, arousal theory has difficulty reconciling the many alternative sources of arousal present in the real world. People are exposed to stress, caffeine, variations in diurnal arousal, different levels of anxiety, all of which produce mental and physiological arousal. This makes predictions of behavior in any given situation difficult.

Another concern with Eysenck's theory is whether the word "extraversion" accurately describes the central personality variable that is involved. Revelle and colleagues (1980) pointed out that some extraversion inventories contain questions that assess both sociability and a separate personality trait of impulsivity. Revelle and colleagues argue that how impulsive a person is influences memory performance more than how sociable they are. This makes sense in explaining differences between introverts and extraverts in their frequency of guessing errors, or intrusions. In recalling a word list, for example, less impulsive individuals (who are often, but not always, introverts) make fewer intrusion errors: misrecalling a word that had not been on the list. Impulsive people (who happen to score high on extraversion) are willing to venture a guess when they are not sure if they remember (e.g., Craig et al., 1979). (When it comes to grading essay exams, I prefer the attempts by less impulsive students. Impulsives write lots and lots of stuff, hoping some of it might be right.)

Another hypothesis is that introverts are more sensitive to nonreward and punishment than are extraverts, and, conversely, extraverts are more sensitive to reward (Gray, 1972). Extraverts try to maximize rewards by guessing; introverts try to minimize errors by not guessing. This differential sensitivity was illustrated in a study using Greenspoon's verbal conditioning task (Chapter 4). The participants are asked to make up sentences, choosing from a list of pronouns to use in each. In the reward condition, the experimenter reinforces the subjects for selecting the pronouns I or WE by saying "good" each time one is used, and saying nothing when any of the other pronouns (HE, SHE, IT, THEY) are selected. In this condition, extraverts increased their use of the rewarded pronoun, but the introverts increased only slightly. In the punishment condition, the experimenter says "poor" when either I or WE is used. In this condition, the introverts greatly decreased their use of those words, but the extraverts decreased only a little (Gupta & Shukla, 1989).

Has extraversion been shown to affect learning outside of the laboratory? One study of name learning in elderly adults did not find a difference between extraverts and introverts (Gratzinger et al., 1990) and another study found that personality scores did not correlate with several measures of academic learning such as high school rank in class or university GPA (Goff & Ackerman, 1992). Given the hypotheses presented earlier, one could see how the two traits would balance one another out across a series of learning situations, depending whether more or less arousal was required, whether impulsivity aided of inhibited performance, or reward or punishment was the anticipated outcome.

Anxiety

The debilitating effects of test anxiety are all too familiar to many students. As the exam is distributed, your heart starts to race; as you scan the first few questions, you read but without comprehending; you try to calm yourself, only to realize you have used up valuable exam time. In such cases, the obvious effect of anxiety has been to impair performance.

Anxiety can be described along several dimensions. There are the physical reactions involving heart rate, rapid breathing, and sweating; emotional feelings of distress; and cognitive symptoms of worry and distraction. In addition, anxiety can be situational or it can be relatively constant. State anxiety is a temporary arousal of anxiety provoked by certain situations, such as on the morning of the SAT or GRE exams. We have considered test anxiety, an instance of state anxiety, in several other places in this text. *Trait* anxiety is a relatively stable personality trait. Trait anxiety can be thought of as a continuum, and someone is chronically more or less nervous. How does this trait of anxiousness affect cognition? There is evidence that it affects memory in several ways: by increasing arousal, limiting the available capacity of working memory, and influencing attention.

The discussion of arousal in Chapter 9 suggested that in some cases, additional arousal of the nervous system is beneficial for encoding. Just as with the introverts discussed earlier, the extra arousal coming from being anxious sometimes improves performance. However, a high level of anxiety, combined with a difficult task, most likely will impair new learning or impair retrieval of previously learned material (Eysenck, 1981).

A second hypothesis states that anxiety reduces the capacity of working memory that is available for processing (M. W. Eysenck, 1979; Hasher & Zacks, 1988). Anxiety is accompanied by worry, or self-talk, about how you are doing. These task-irrelevant thoughts coopt some of the capacity of working memory. Working memory, therefore, is divided between the cognitive task and worrying. An anxious individual can compensate for some divided attention if the task is easy enough. However, with a difficult task, there may not be sufficient spare capacity to maintain accurate performance.

The differential effects of anxiety on working memory are demonstrated by comparing performance on an easy and a difficult task (e.g., Sorg & Whitney, 1992). In a *word-span* test, which is comparable to a simple digit span (Chapter 8), the participant simply needs to remember a list of two to seven words. In a *reading-span* task, after listening to lists of two to six sentences, the participant must recall the final words of each sentence, and also be prepared to answer a question about one of the sentences. These two tasks contrast simple maintenance in short-term memory (the word-span task), and maintenance plus comprehension (in the reading span). Individuals who are low or high on trait anxiety did not differ in word span, but the high-anxious did worse on the reading-span task.

A third hypothesis is that anxiety biases how events are perceived and interpreted, and thus remembered. A more anxious individual may remember as much as a less anxious person, but each may remember different things. For example, anxiety predisposes the interpretation of ambiguous stimuli as being potentially threatening. Homophones are two different words that sound alike, and so when spoken can potentially take on either of two meanings. For example, GILT and GUILT sound alike. Mathews, Richards, and Eysenck (1989) gave anxious and nonanxious adults a spelling test in which some of the words were homophones that had an emotional or unpleasant alternate meaning, such as PAIN/PANE, or DISCUSSED/DISGUST. Clinically anxious adults, that is, those who were then being treated for anxiety, were more likely to write the emotional spellings of the homophones than were nonanxious adults.

The bias toward a negative interpretation of information also can be reflected in enhanced recall of negative information. The *self-reference effect* refers to the fact that we remember information that refers to ourselves better than nonpersonal information. Young and Martin (1981) presented anxious and nonanxious subjects with fictitious personality descriptions. They used a very convincing procedure in which the subjects first completed some personality inventories and a little later were read a series of adjectives that were ostensibly the results of the tests. Actually, everyone heard the same list of descriptors, which contained both positive and negative traits. The participants were later asked to recall as many of the trait adjectives as possible. The high-anxious subjects recalled many more negative words (that supposedly applied to themselves) and fewer positive words; the less anxious subjects recalled more positive and fewer negative words. Note that the high- and low- anxious participants recalled the same total number of words. The difference was in what was remembered.

Does anxiety predict everyday memory problems? Several studies have found correlations between scores on an anxiety inventory and on the Cognitive Failures Questionnaire (Martin & Jones, 1984). Anxious people report more instances of forgetting, habit slips of doing the wrong thing, misperceiving stimuli, forgetting what they just read, and so on. In addition, people working in high-stress jobs (i.e., critical care nurses) also had high Cognitive Failures scores.

Learning can be seriously impaired in other psychological disorders. Research on two, post traumatic stress disorder and schizophrenia, are discussed in Box 12.1.

Learning Styles

A topic of continuing interest in the field of education is that of learning styles. The phrase "learning style" is used in many ways. For instance, style may contrast individuals who can generalize across differences versus those who make fine discriminations (so-called lumpers and splitters). Another use is in reference to those whose style is said to be more left brain versus more right brain, roughly corresponding with verbal versus visual-spatial learning. Is it the case that people really differ in their preferred style of learning? Much of the prose on learning styles has generated more heat than light. Although theories and inventories of style have been developed, there is little empirical work to validate that people of different styles learn differently. A few typologies, however, have generated some empirical support.

Field Dependence.   One well-studied style is that of *field dependence* versus *field independence.* People who are strongly influenced by the context surrounding to-be-learned material are said to be field-dependent; they are dependent on that "field" for interpretation and

BOX **12.1**

Learning and Psychopathology

The field of psychopathology, or abnormal psychology, deals with behavioral and psychological disorders. Some researchers in this field seek to determine whether and how cognitive processes such as learning and remembering are impaired in mental illnesses. Learning and memory are directly involved in certain psychological disorders, such as psychogenic amnesias; and indirectly involved in others, possibly as a side effect of brain or biochemical abnormalities.

Schizophrenia is a severe psychological disorder characterized by emotional and social impairments, and in more serious cases, by hallucinations and delusions (false, irrational beliefs). Neurological research has implicated a number of brain regions and chemical processes in this disease. Schizophrenia is believed to involve frontal-lobe dysfunction, as evidenced by increased distractibility. Short-term verbal and spatial memory are both reduced in schizophrenic individuals, consistent with similar impairments found with frontal lobe injuries (Park, Holzman, & Goldman-Rakic, 1995). Those who are researching the genetic basis for schizophrenia have found similar working-memory deficits among close relatives of schizophrenic individuals, relatives who are themselves free of the disorder. The hippocampus has also been found to be smaller in schizophrenics. As you should know by now, the hippocampus is important in both explicit memory recall and in spatial memory.

Posttraumatic stress disorder (PTSD) is a disorder that has altered memory functioning as a central symptom. PTSD, which results from a traumatic experience, is characterized by repetitive and intrusive memories of the initiating event. The memories can be ongoing and ruminative, appear in dreams and nightmares, or be triggered by stimuli in the environment. Does PTSD affect other memory forms of learning? One reaction that is manifested is increased startle reaction to sudden stimuli, and sometimes a failure to habituate to those stimuli when they are repeated. Classical conditioning may also be affected, especially aversive conditioning. In one study, individuals diagnosed with PTSD (war veterans, firefighters, or assault victims) were compared with controls who suffered similar traumas but did not develop PTSD. Classical conditioning consisted of discrimination training between pairings of a colored disk (e.g., yellow) with shock and a different color (e.g., blue) without shock. The PTSD group (1) had higher reaction levels to the stimuli at baseline before conditioning began; (2) showed more fear conditioning to the stimulus paired with shock; and (3) showed more persistence of conditioned responding during extinction, when the non-PTSD subjects had ceased reacting to the stimulus (Orr, et al., 2000). These several findings suggest the PTSD victims had chronically higher levels of emotional arousal, thus inhibiting habituation to neutral stimuli, and enhancing fear to aversive conditioned stimuli. The researchers questioned whether this higher level of fear is an aftereffect of the trauma, or whether the emotionality existed before the trauma and predisposed these individuals to develop PTSD.

PTSD patients also show deficits on standard measures of memory (Bremner et al., 1993). Viet Nam war veterans were impaired at word-list learning, remembering a paragraph of information, and reproducing visual (but nonmeaningful) designs. These materials are not trauma related, so the findings suggest that trauma victims suffer a generalized deficit in new learning and remembering. Traumatic experiences affect numerous functions in the nervous system, from neurotransmitter levels to hormone secretions to cell death and loss. We can only speculate which are most relevant to the learning deficits shown by PTSD victims. One suggestion is that trauma-induced arousal of the amygdala strengthens or consolidates emotional, unconscious, and implicit memories (such as conditioned fear responses); while correspondingly, overarousal of the hippocampus makes it *less able* to preserve the declarative and conscious aspects of memory (van der Kolk, 1994).

structure. Those who can treat an object free of its context are said to be field-independent. Independence–dependence is sometimes measured using a perceptual test, such as the embedded-figures test. Here, the subject must find a target object (say, a triangle) that is embedded within a more complex drawing. Field independents more readily detect the hidden figure, presumably because they are less influenced by the context surrounding the target figure.

Do field independents and dependents learn differently? The early research showed little in the way of differences in overall learning. In free recall of word lists, field-independent subjects cluster words more often during recall, indicating active attempts to organize the lists. Yet the field dependents recall just as much with less clustering (summarized by Goodenough, 1976). More recent research suggests that field independents tend to do better in school, in a variety of subjects ranging from math and science to reading and language (Davis, 1991). This suggests the dimension may simply be an indirect measure of scholastic ability or general intelligence.

The dimension of field independence–dependence may be more meaningful in a broader sense of "learning style," that of one's chosen major. Field-independent students prefer areas involving analytic skills such as mathematics, engineering, and science. Field-dependent students favor areas that draw on interpersonal relations, such as the social sciences, humanities, counseling, or teaching. Within psychology, field independents prefer experimental psychology, which includes the psychology of learning; field dependents prefer clinical psychology (Claxton & Murrell, 1987).

Kolb.   Another conception of learning style is a two-dimensional organization offered by Kolb (1984). One dimension describes a preference for learning from *concrete* experiences (such as hands-on activities) versus a preference for learning in the *abstract* (such as principles taught by lecture or text). The second dimension expresses a preference for deriving knowledge through *reflection* (thinking as a source of generalizations) versus active *experimentation* (trying out newly derived principles). As shown in Figure 12.6, any one individual's learning style depends on his or her location in this two-dimensional space (based on Claxton & Murrell, 1987; Kolb, 1984). A person's location in this grid is determined by answers to an inventory. However, there is little data to show that these individuals indeed learn differently. One impediment to testing hypotheses is that, whereas a given student may have a preferred style of learning, it may be subverted by a teacher who approaches instruction from a different style. One suggestion from educators who write on learning styles is that teachers and students should be matched by style, or instructors could use different styles over the course of a semester to accommodate different student styles (Claxton & Murrell, 1987). Either proposal would be difficult to implement in an educational setting. Alternatively, one could attempt to teach students to adopt different learning styles as appropriate to the learning situation.

Sternberg.   One ambitious attempt to match student and instructional style has been reported by Sternberg and Grigorenko (1997; Grigorenko & Sternberg, 1997). Students taking a summer general psychology course were first tested to determine which of three cognitive styles they possessed: analytical, creative, or practical thinking. As examples, analytic teaching involves asking students to compare and contrast, evaluate, or critique an idea. The creative style asks students to invent or answer "imagine/what if" types of ques-

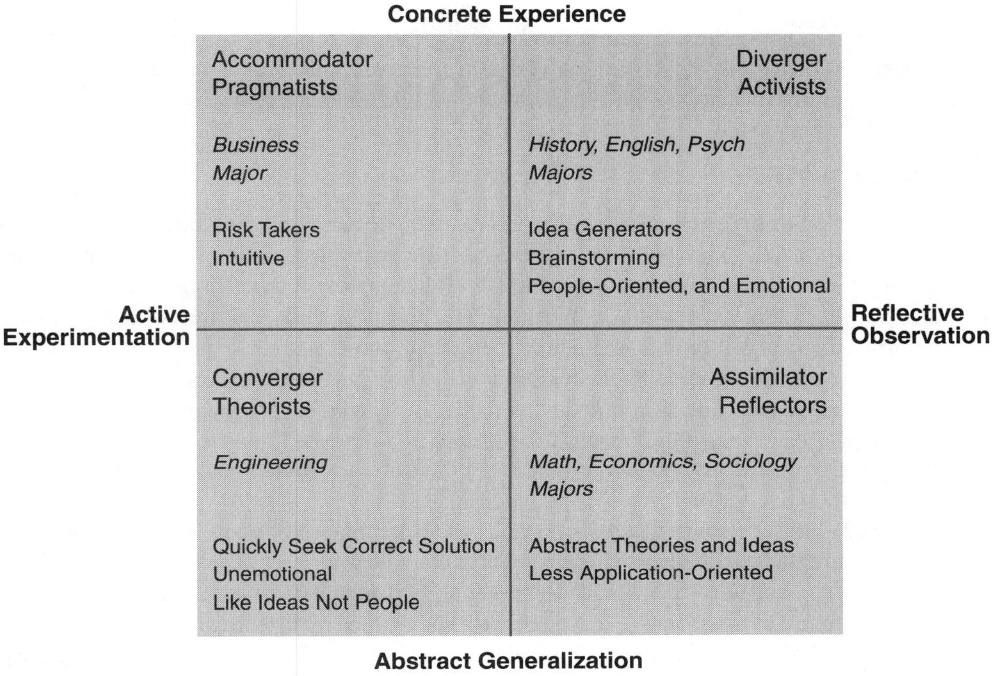

Concrete Experience

Accommodator Pragmatists *Business* *Major* Risk Takers Intuitive	Diverger Activists *History, English, Psych* *Majors* Idea Generators Brainstorming People-Oriented, and Emotional
Converger Theorists *Engineering* Quickly Seek Correct Solution Unemotional Like Ideas Not People	Assimilator Reflectors *Math, Economics, Sociology* *Majors* Abstract Theories and Ideas Less Application-Oriented

Active Experimentation (left)   **Reflective Observation** (right)

Abstract Generalization

FIGURE 12.6   Kolb's Learning Styles.

Source: Kolb, 1984.

tions. Practical thinking is taught by asking students to demonstrate how something could apply in the real world. The students were then assigned to course sections that were taught using analytical, creative, or practical styles. Thus, students could be in a course that matched their preferred mode (e.g., creative students in a section emphasizing creative thinking) or were explicitly mismatched. In addition, some mixed classes were formed of students with each learning style. End-of-course tests indicated that students did well in courses that matched their learning styles and particularly when the tests were of that same style (i.e., creative students were given tests asking for creative answers and applications rather than analysis and practical application). Thus, superior performance required three elements to be matched: student style, instructional style, and testing style. This suggests a practical impediment to implementing of style theories to educational settings, where such matching cannot be accomplished realistically.

Social and Cultural Differences

Do different cultures emphasize different aspects of remembering? It's possible that verbal memory is more important in some societies, whereas spatial learning is more useful to others. Is memory enhanced in societies that value remembering? To what extent do schooling and education change the way we learn and use memory? These are questions that cross-cultural studies of learning and memory can address. By studying other cultures, we may be able to discern certain universal aspects of memory and, conversely, how our own conceptions of memory are shaped by the culture and society we live in.

Epic Memories

We all learned in high school about the Greek poet Homer, who would tell the epic tales the *Iliad* and the *Odyssey*. We were stunned to hear that these stories were repeated from memory, without a written version to consult. How do poets and performers do this?

Earlier in the last century, anthropologists began to study cultures whose literature was primarily oral rather than written. For example, the Gola people of Liberia in Africa remember extensive genealogical histories (D'Azevedo, 1962). These family histories would be repeated at formal ceremonies or to settle disputes, giving the new generation opportunities to learn their family tree. The elders who knew the lineages were respected individuals. But outsiders who studied the Gola did not know the genealogies and so could not verify their accuracy.

Lord (1960) began in the 1930s to study the performance of poets who sang folk tales in areas of Yugoslavia where this oral tradition continued to exist. These songs sometimes ran to thousands of lines and would take hours to perform. Experienced singers claimed to know 30 or more of these epics. New tales had to be learned by listening to other performers, and some singers claimed they could learn a new song after hearing it once. Accepting such claims at face value reinforces a belief that memory can be especially well developed in a nonliterate society. Without written sources to consult, memory had to improve to accommodate. But had these accomplished performers really memorized these poems?

Lord found that the singers had a very different skill than what we are daily exposed to in Western societies. Our singers do indeed memorize the words to relatively short songs. The singers in the oral tradition, however, remembered the outline of the story, the main characters, and some specific facts, but otherwise essentially recomposed the story for each performance. The singers knew formulas, fillers, and different ways of phrasing the same idea. They would then select an appropriate phrase to fit the rhyme or meter. The same story would be related in each performance, yet each performance would be somewhat different. Although the performers claimed to remember "word for word," this phrase has no correspondence in a culture without writing; that is, what is a word? Instead, the performers were referring to the accuracy and veracity of their recall. Performances by these poets are probably analogous to the way many professors lecture: They speak from an outline, but don't give the same lecture verbatim each time. Certain catch phrases and specific terms repeat from semester to semester, but the lecture is, in a sense, reconstructed on the spot.

We can derive several lessons from Lord's study of oral poetry in Yugoslavia. First, this reconstructive aspect of memory is in accord with some current conceptions of memory retrieval. Some theorists argue that remembering is not so much the activation of a static trace stored in memory, but instead is the refabrication of the earlier experience. Second, denying that these folk performers remember the epic tales verbatim in no way diminishes their abilities. Instead, we now perceive that their talent is of a different sort: They create anew each time that they perform. And, third, anecdotal reports of memory should not be accepted uncritically.

Goody (1998) made the paradoxical observation that it is literate cultures that most emphasize the veridical recall of written texts. Homer's epic tales and the Bible have existed in written form for over 2,000 years, and the Quran for over a thousand. The texts are used to guide and correct verbatim memorization, and indeed the texts may be structured and worded to facilitate rote memorization (through the use of rhyming lines, meter, assonance, etc.). A truly oral culture has no concept of how their sacred texts were worded in the distant past.

Experimental Studies

Experimental studies in countries other than the United States, and in cultures other than Western European, may shed important light on universal versus specific factors of learning and memory. Our theories assume there are certain universal features of memory, for example, separate short-term and long-term memory systems. We have also seen variable factors that may be less universal, such as the strategies of rehearsal, organization, or imagery that sometimes need to be taught. We have also noted that memory seems to develop in children. Is this unfolding of memory a maturational or age-related phenomenon, or is it due to the effects of schooling, television, or other constants of Western societies? Comparisons with other cultures may help answer such questions.

A modern classic in cross-cultural research is D. Wagner's "Memories of Morocco" (1978). One of his research goals was to see whether certain memory capacities were universal, such as short-term memory. If so, then children with widely differing life experiences should still be similar. A second goal was to determine whether certain memory capacities were culturally influenced. If so, the use of strategies such as rehearsal might differ among same-aged children as a function of schooling or urbanization.

Wagner tested short-term memory for a sequence of seven cards, each having an animal drawn on it. The cards were shown one at a time for 2 seconds each before being turned upside down and placed in a row before the participant. A test card was then shown, and the child had to indicate where that picture had occurred in the list. Several samples of children ranging in age from 6 to 19 were obtained: children from an urban and a rural area of Morocco, and within each of these areas, children who attended school or were unschooled. The recall of the test card's location improved with age. This is not surprising, given what we reviewed earlier about the development of memory. What was new was the finding that schooled children, particularly adolescents and older, remembered more than did unschooled children. This was especially so when the probe assessed memory for the first cards in the list. Schooling was associated with a primacy effect, which most likely reflects the development of rehearsal. Wagner's results suggest that the use of intentional learning strategies, like rehearsal, are due to experiences in school, such as the demands placed on new learning.

These results are supported by another series of studies, this time done in the Yucatan Peninsula of Mexico (Sharp, Cole, & Lave, 1979). In a free-recall experiment, children and adults were read a list of 20 common nouns divided into several categories (e.g., animals, clothing). Separate subject groups differed in age, education, and ethnic background. Adults and adolescents with schooling recalled more of the words. But more importantly, the educated adults (but not the uneducated ones) categorized the items during recall. Again, earlier in this chapter we noted that older children, but not younger, cluster semantically similar items at output. Sharp and colleagues' study shows that this strategy of organization can be a function of schooling and not just of age.

We should be careful not to overemphasize the benefits of schooling on memory. Schools may teach some types of strategies for organizing material to enhance learning, such as categorically grouping items with similar meanings (e.g., grouping food names, toys, or animals). However, there are other ways of organizing groups of to-be-remembered items that are not enforced in school but nevertheless are useful in the world. For example, items could be organized temporally (by time sequence), by their locations, or by the functions they serve. Rogoff and Waddell (1982) tested children's memory for objects and their location by placing the objects within a realistic model of a town. The panorama contained roads, houses, a mountain, and a lake. The children, both Guatemalan Mayan and American, watched as 20 objects (small cars, people, animals, furniture) were placed within the town layout. Afterwards, the objects were removed and placed among 60 other objects. The children then tried to reconstruct the scene. The Guatemalan children performed slightly better than did the American children. The latter attempted to rehearse the objects, which is a school-learned strategy that works well for lists, but is less effective for remembering objects in context.

What about a popular notion that other cultures may excel at different forms of memory? We earlier reviewed Lord's observations of oral poetry in Yugoslavia. Another study assessed a hypothesis derived from evolutionary psychology, that people living in hunter-gatherer societies have better-developed visual or spatial memories, necessary for survival in the environments they occupy, than people from industrialized societies. Kearins (1981) tested this idea by measuring object location memory in Australian aborigines and in Australians of European descent. The participants were all school children, aged 12 to 16 years. The stimuli were objects placed within a matrix or grid and shown briefly to the subjects. Each array contained between 12 and 20 items, either all man-made (e.g., thimble, eraser) or all natural objects (rock, leaf). In some cases, the objects were all of the same class (all bottles or different rocks). After 30 seconds of viewing the array, the experimenter heaped all the objects in a pile, and the children then had to replace each item back in its original location. Previous research on the aborigines had shown nearly uniformly that they performed poorly on cognitive tests, even after attempts to make the tests culture-fair. However, in this case of location memory, the aboriginal children excelled. In every test (natural and man-made objects, all the same category or all different), the aboriginal children did better than the children of European descent. One striking finding was the number of times that the aboriginal kids had perfect scores: 75 percent were perfect on at least one of four trials and 41 percent on two trials, whereas only 18 percent of the European children were perfect on one trial and none on two.

Contemporary Cultural Psychology.   The initial goals of cross-cultural research were to seek out cognitive universals and specific adaptations, such as the effects of schooling on rehearsal or location memory in aboriginal populations. We now realize that we cannot measure a general, universal memory ability in tasks that are unrelated to everyday experience. How we test memory influences how well memory appears to function. If we ask people to display memory in a way that resembles what they do in school (e.g., remembering lists of items in the sequence the experimenter presented them), then people with schooling do better. The current trend in research is toward investigating cognitive skills as they relate to everyday behavior within a culture, rather than as universal traits that are culture-free. Indeed, this trend is represented by a change from the label "cross-cultural" psychology to simply "cultural" psychology (Rogoff & Chavajay, 1995).

Summary

The experimental approach to learning focuses on those variables that can be manipulated by researchers, in order to determine the effects of such variables on learning. A correlational approach focuses on variables that experimenters cannot control, such as gender, personality, or age, but that nevertheless may be important determinants of memory ability.

The Genetics of Learning Ability

Learning ability is affected by genetic predispositions. Tryon's classic experiments used the method of selective breeding to produce two strains of rats, maze bright and maze dull, that differed in maze-learning ability. Genetic differences in learning have also been demonstrated by inducing mutated genes in fruit flies, and transplanting genes between mice. Environment still plays an important role even where there are genetic differences: The extremes of either deprived or enriched rearing conditions equated the bright and dull rats in maze learning. In human studies, identical twins are more alike in cognitive ability than are fraternal twins.

Age Differences in Learning and Memory

Both learning and memory show developmental trends, from infancy to old age. Prenatal learning of the mother's voice has been shown, and taste-aversion conditioning in prenatal rats. Infants as young as 10 days old show classically conditioned eye-blink responses, and newborns show olfactory conditioning.

Episodic memory appears to develop in children. The phenomenon of childhood amnesia may indicate a true absence of memories for the first years of life, possibly due to neural maturation—or simply an inability for adults to recollect those years. However, the method of elicited imitation shows that infants as young as 11 months old can reproduce specific sequences of activities.

What develops as children age? Children and adults may differ in the capacity of short-term or working memory, and thus also in the ease of forming long-term memories. Young children have a smaller knowledge base that limits new learning. Younger children do not use strategies, such as rehearsal and elaboration, as much as older children. Knowledge about the functioning of memory does develop early in children's lives, but metamemory judgments are neither accurate nor sophisticated.

Similarly, some aspects of memory decline with aging. We can ask what it is that changes. The capacity of working memory is lessened, although this may be due to slowing of mental processing rather than a reduction in the amount that can be retained. Metamemory is unchanged in the elderly, although expectancies and stereotypes may affect the belief that one's memory is less competent. Memory performance may decline because of other factors associated with aging, such as illness, depression, or the side effects of medications.

Intellectual Deficits

Principles of learning have been used in training retarded individuals. Retarded and nonretarded individuals typically classically condition at about the same rate. Mental retardation due to Down syndrome, a genetic abnormality, impairs conditioning to a similar extent as does aging. Down syndrome infants also have poor spatial learning.

Other research has investigated the roles of working-memory capacity, memory strategies such as rehearsal, and metamemory in the retarded. A deficit in memory strategies can contribute to the poor memory performance of retarded individuals. Training in rehearsal increases recall, but there is little tendency to generalize beyond the immediately given task. Cognitive-skills training does not eliminate the difference between the retarded and age-matched control participants.

A learning disability is an impairment of a specific cognitive ability, whereas other abilities are at or near normal. The learning disabled may have both verbal and nonverbal working-memory deficits, which does not correlate with the type of disability (reading, math, language). The learning disabled have difficulty encoding information into memory; they are less likely to rehearse or to use organization or elaboration to facilitate encoding if they do rehearse.

Exceptional Memory

The history of psychology is replete with examples of mnemonists, people with exceptional memories. Luria's friend *S* employed strategies such as imagery, and mnemonics such as the method of locations. His sensory experience was cross-modal, cutting across sensory modalities, a property called synesthesia. Other mnemonists use verbal elaboration. Nonsense syllables or unfamiliar words are mentally translated into meaningful items. Savants, individuals having an exceptional ability but who are otherwise retarded, may excel in memory within a specific content area or domain, but do not have superior general memory ability.

Gender and Cognitive Abilities

Do men and women differ in their memory abilities? Here, some evidence for better verbal memory in women was presented. Even if performance does differ by gender, this does not necessarily indicate that this is due to inherent biological differences between the sexes. Gender differences have been shown to occur when there are differences in knowledge or experience, interest levels, self-handicapping, or gender expectancies or stereotypes about how one should perform.

Personality and Learning

Some personality traits interact with learning and remembering. The dimension defined by extraversion at one end and introversion at the other is one well-studied personality trait.

One hypothesis is that introverts have higher levels of cortical arousal than extraverts and therefore perform better on simple tasks and worse on demanding tasks. Another hypothesis is that introverts are less impulsive and thus less likely to guess if unsure than extraverts. A third hypothesis is that introverts seek to minimize nonreward or punishment, whereas extraverts seek to maximize reward in spite of punishment. Although introverts and extraverts may differ in specific instances, we cannot say whether one personality has a better overall memory.

High levels of anxiety can affect memory by increasing arousal, directing attention to threatening or negative information, and limiting the available capacity of working memory. Worry and irrelevant thoughts may coopt memory capacity. Anxious participants recall more negative information that refers to themselves, whereas the nonanxious recall more positive information. Anxiety does correlate with self-reported everyday memory problems.

Learning Styles

Several theories of learning styles have been developed, but there is little empirical work to validate that, in fact, people of different styles learn differently. Well-developed style theories include the dimension field dependence–field independence; and Kolb's two dimensions of concrete versus abstract learning and reflective versus active application of knowledge. Sternberg is studying analytic, creative, and practical styles, matched to corresponding teaching methods, but the results are still preliminary.

Social and Cultural Differences

Cross-cultural studies of learning and memory can address questions about universal determinants of memory, different demands placed on memory by different environments, or specific effects of social changes such as schooling. Descriptions of memory in nonliterate societies, while impressive, do not often produce verifiable data. Singers in an oral tradition, for example, remember the outline and general features of an epic story, but otherwise recomposed the story during each performance. Experimental studies in other countries, such as Morocco and Mexico, show that recall increases somewhat with age, but that schooling enhances memory even more so through the development of strategies such as rehearsal.

REFERENCES

Aarons, L. (1976). Sleep-assisted instruction. *Psychological Bulletin, 83,* 1–40.

Abramson, L. Y., & Seligman, M. E. P. (1977). Modeling psychopathology in the laboratory: History and rationale. In J. D. Maser & M. E. P. Seligman (Eds.), *Psychopathology: Experimental models* (pp. 1–26). San Francisco: Freeman.

Abramson, L. Y., Seligman, M. E. P., & Teasdale, J. D. (1978). Learned helplessness in humans: Critique and reformulation. *Journal of Abnormal Psychology, 87,* 49–74.

Adam, N. (1979). Disruption of memory functions associated with general anesthetics. In J. F. Kihlstrom & F. J. Evans (Eds.), *Functional disorders of memory* (pp. 219–238). Hillsdale, NJ: Erlbaum.

Adams, C. D. (1982). Variations in the sensitivity of instrumental responding to reinforcer devaluation. *Quarterly Journal of Experimental Psychology, 34B,* 77–98.

Adams, J. A. (1987). Historical review and appraisal of research on the learning, retention, and transfer of human motor skills. *Psychological Bulletin, 101,* 41–74.

Ader, R., & Cohen, N. (1975). Behaviorally conditioned immunosuppression. *Psychosomatic Medicine, 37,* 333–340.

Ader, R., & Cohen, N. (1982). Behaviorally conditioned immunosuppression and murine systemic lupus erythematosus. *Science, 215,* 1534–1536.

Ader, R., & Cohen, N. (1993). Psychoneuroimmunology: Conditioning and stress. *Annual Review of Psychology, 44,* 53–85.

Alba, J. W., & Hasher, L. (1983). Is memory schematic? *Psychological Bulletin, 93,* 203–231.

Alessandri, S. M., Sullivan, M. W., & Lewis, M. (1990). Violation of expectancy and frustration in early infancy. *Developmental Psychology, 26,* 738–744.

Allen, P. A., & Crozier, L. C. (1992). Age and ideal chunk size. *Journal of Gerontology: Psychological Sciences, 47,* P47–P51.

Amsel, A. (1962). Frustrative nonreward in partial reinforcement and discrimination learning: Some recent history and a theoretical extension. *Psychological Review, 69,* 306–328.

Amsel, A. (1994). Precis of Frustration Theory: An Analysis of Dispositional Learning and Memory. *Psychonomic Bulletin and Review, 1,* 280–296.

Anderson, J. R. (1983). *The architecture of cognition.* Cambridge: Harvard University Press.

Anderson, M. C., & Green, C. (2001). Suppressing unwanted memories by executive control. *Nature, 410,* 366–369.

Anderson, N. H., & Clavadetscher, J. (1976). Tests of a conditioning hypothesis with adjective combinations. *Journal of Experimental Psychology: Human Learning and Memory, 2,* 11–20.

Anderson, R. C., & Pichert, J. W. (1978). Recall of previously unrecallable information following a shift in perspective. *Journal of Verbal Learning and Verbal Behavior, 17,* 1–12.

Andrade, J. (1995). Learning during anaesthesia: A review. *British Journal of Psychology, 86,* 479–507.

Anisman, H., deCatanzaro, D., & Remington, G. (1978). Escape performance following exposure to inescapable shock: Deficits in motor response maintenance. *Journal of Experimental Psychology: Animal Behavior Processes, 4,* 197–218.

Arbuckle, T. Y., Gold, D. P., Andres, D., Schwartzman, A., & Chaikelson, J. (1992). The role of psychosocial context, age, and intelligence in memory performance of older men. *Psychology and Aging, 7,* 25–36.

Arkes, H. R., & Harkness, A. R. (1980). Effect of making a diagnosis on subsequent recognition of symptoms. *Journal of Experimental Psychology: Human Learning and Memory, 6,* 568–575.

Arnold, M. E., Petros, T. V., Beckwith, B. E., Coons, G., & Gorman. N. (1987). The effects of caffeine, impulsivity, and sex on memory for word lists. *Physiology and Behavior, 41,* 25–30.

Arrigo, J. M., & Pezdek, K. (1997). Lessons from the study of psychogenic amnesia. *Current Directions in Psychological Science, 6,* 148–152.

Ash, D. W., & Holding, D. H. (1990). Backward versus forward chaining in the acquisition of a keyboard skill. *Human Factors, 32,* 139–146.

Aspinwall, L. G., & Taylor, S. E. (1992). Modeling cognitive adaptation: A longitudinal investigation of the impact of individual differences and coping on college adjustment and performance. *Journal of Personality and Social Psychology, 63,* 989–1003.

Astrachan, J. M. (1991) COMO ESTAS: A mnemonic for the mental status examination. *New England Journal of Medicine, 324*(9), 324–336.

Astur, R. S., Ortiz, M. L., & Sutherland, R. J. (1998). A characterization of performance by men and women in a virtual Morris water task: A large and reliable sex difference. *Behavioural Brain Research, 93,* 185–190.

Atkinson, R. C., & Raugh, M. R. (1975). An application of the mnemonic keywords method to the acquisition of Russian vocabulary. *Journal of Experimental Psychology: Human Learning and Memory, 1,* 126–133.

Atkinson, R. C., & Shiffrin, R. M (1968). Human memory: A proposed system and its control procedures. In K. W. Spence & J. T. Spence (Eds.), *The psychology of learning and motivation* (Vol. 2). New York: Academic Press.

Atkinson, R. C., & Shiffrin, R. M. (1971, August). The control of short-term memory. *Scientific American,* 152–161.

Averill, J. R., & Rosenn, M. (1972). Vigilant and nonvigilant coping strategies and psychophysiological stress reactions during anticipation of electric shock. *Journal of Personality and Social Psychology, 23,* 128–141.

Ayllon, T. (1963). Intensive treatment of psychotic behavior by stimulus satiation and food reinforcement. *Behavior Research and Therapy, 1,* 53–61.

Ayllon, T., & Azrin, N. H. (1964). Reinforcement and instructions with mental patients. *Journal of the Experimental Analysis of Behavior, 7,* 327–331.

Ayllon, T., & Azrin, N. H. (1968). Reinforcer sampling: A technique for increasing the behavior of mental patients. *Journal of Applied Behavior Analysis, 1,* 13–20.

Ayres, T. J., Jonides, J., Reitman, J. S., Egan, J. C., & Howard, D. A. (1979). Differing suffix effects for the same physical suffix. *Journal of Experimental Psychology: Human Learning and Memory, 5,* 315–321.

Baddeley, A. D. (1966). Short-term memory for word sequences as a function of acoustic, semantic, and formal similarity. *Quarterly Journal of Experimental Psychology, 18,* 362–365.

Baddeley, A. D. (1978). The trouble with levels: A reexamination of Craik and Lockhart's framework for memory research. *Psychological Review, 85,* 139–152.

Baddeley, A. D. (1981). The cognitive psychology of everyday life. *British Journal of Psychology, 72,* 257–269.

Baddeley, A. D. (1992a). Working memory. *Science, 255,* 556–559.

Baddeley, A. D. (1992b). Implicit memory and errorless learning. In L. R. Squire & N. Butters (Eds.), *Neuropsychology of memory* (2nd ed., pp. 309–314). New York: Guilford Press.

Baddeley, A. D., & Hitch, G. (1974). Working memory. In G. H. Bower (Ed.), *The psychology of learning and motivation* (Vol. 8, pp. 47–89). New York: Academic Press.

Baddeley, A. D., & Hitch, G. (1977). Recency re-examined. In S. Dornic (Ed.), *Attention and performance VI* (pp. 647–667). Hillsdale, NJ: Erlbaum.

Baddeley. A. D., & Hitch, G. J. (1994). Developments in the concept of working memory. *Neuropsychology, 8,* 485–493.

Baddeley, A. D., & Longman, D. J. A. (1978). The influence of length and frequency of training session on the rate of learning to type. *Ergonomics, 21,* 627–635.

Baddeley, A. D., Thomson, N., & Buchanan, M. (1975). Word length and the structure of short-term memory. *Journal of Verbal Learning and Verbal Behavior, 14,* 575–589.

Baddeley, A. D., & Wilson, B. (1986). Amnesia, autobiographical memory, and confabulation. In D. C. Rubin (Ed.), *Autobiographical memory* (pp. 225–252). New York: Cambridge University Press.

Badia, P. (1990). Memories in sleep: Old and new. In R. R. Bootzin, J. F. Kihlstrom, & D. L. Schacter (Eds.), *Sleep and cognition* (pp. 67–76). Washington, DC: American Psychological Association.

Baeyens, F., Eelen, P., & Crombez, G. (1995). Pavlovian associations are forever: On classical conditioning and extinction. *Journal of Psychophysiology, 9,* 127–141.

Bagozzi, R. P. (1991). The role of psychophysiology in consumer research. In T. S. Robertson & H. K. Kassayjian (Eds.), *Handbook of consumer research* (pp. 124–161). Englewood Cliffs, NJ: Prentice Hall.

Bahrick, H. P. (1969). Measurement of memory by prompted recall. *Journal of Experimental Psychology, 79,* 213–219.

Bahrick, H. P. (1979). Maintenance of knowledge: Questions about memory we forgot to ask. *Journal of Experimental Psychology: General, 108,* 296–308.

Bahrick, H. P. (1984a). Semantic memory content in permastore: Fifty years of memory for Spanish learned in school. *Journal of Experimental Psychology: General, 113,* 1–29.

Bahrick, H. P. (1984b). Memory for people. In J. E. Harris & P. E. Morris (Eds.), *Everyday memory, actions, and absentmindedness* (pp. 19–34). New York: Academic Press.

Bahrick, H. P., Bahrick, P. O., & Wittlinger, R. P. (1975). Fifty years of memory for names and faces: A cross-sectional approach. *Journal of Experimental Psychology: General, 104,* 54–75.

Bahrick, H. P., & Hall, L. K. (1993). Long intervals between tests can yield hypermnesia: Comments on Wheeler and Roediger. *Psychological Science, 4,* 206–208.

Bahrick, H. P., & Phelps, E. (1987). Retention of Spanish vocabulary over 8 years. *Journal of Experimental Psychology: Learning, Memory, and Cognition, 13,* 344–349.

Bahrick, L. E., Parker, J. F., Fivush, R., & Levitt, M. (1998). The effects of stress on young children's memory for a natural disaster. *Journal of Experimental Psychology: Applied, 4,* 308–331.

Ball, G. F., & Hulse, S. H. (1998). Birdsong. *American Psychologist, 53,* 37–58.

Balota, D. A., Duchek, J. M., & Paullin, R. (1989). Age-related differences in the impact of spacing, lag, and retention interval. *Psychology and Aging, 4,* 3–9.

Banaji, M. R., & Crowder, R. G. (1989). The bankruptcy of everyday memory. *American Psychologist, 44,* 1185–1193.

Banaji, M. R., & Hardin, C. D. (1996). Automatic stereotyping. *Psychological Science, 7,* 136–141.

Banbury, S., & Berry, D. C. (1997). Habituation and dishabituation to speech and office noise. *Journal of Experimental Psychology: Applied, 3,* 181–195.

Banbury, S. P., Macken, W. J., Tremblay, S., & Jones, D. M. (2001). Auditory distraction and short-term memory: Phenomena and practical implications. *Human Factors, 43,* 12–29.

Bandura, A. (1965). Influence of models' reinforcement contingencies on the acquisition of imitative responses. *Journal of Social and Personality Psychology, 1,* 589–595.

Bauer, P. J. (1996). What do infants recall of their lives? Memory for specific events by one- to two-year-olds. *American Psychologist, 51,* 29–41.

Bechara A., Tranel, D., Damasio, H., Adolphs, R., Rockland, C., & Damasio, A. R. (1995). Double dissociation of conditioning and declarative knowledge relative to the amygdala and hippocampus in humans. *Science, 269,* 1115–1118.

Beck, S. B. (1963). Eyelid conditioning as a function of CS intensity, UCS intensity, and Manifest Anxiety Scale score. *Journal of Experimental Psychology, 66,* 429–438.

Becker, J. T., Butters, N., Hermann, A., & D'Angelo, N. (1983). Learning to associate names and faces: Impaired acquisition on an ecologically relevant memory task by male alcoholics. *Journal of Nervous and Mental Disease, 171,* 617–623.

Beitz, J. M. (1997). Unleashing the power of memory. *Nurse Educator, 22,* 25–29.

Bekerian, D. A., & Goodrich, S. J. (2000). Recovered and false memories. In G. E. Berrios & J. R. Hodges (Eds.), *Memory disorders in psychiatric practice* (pp. 432–442). Cambridge, UK: Cambridge University Press.

Bellezza, F. S., & Young, D. R. (1989). Chunking of repeated events in memory. *Journal of Experimental Psychology: Learning, Memory, and Cognition, 15,* 990–997.

Bellugi, U., Klima, E. S., & Siple, P. (1974–1975). Remembering in signs. *Cognition, 3,* 93–125.

Bellugi, U., Wang, P. P., & Jernigan, T. L. (1994). Williams Syndrome: An unusual neuropsychological profile. In S. H. Broman & J. Grafman (Eds.), *Atypical cognitive deficits in developmental disorders* (pp. 23–56). Hillsdale, NJ: Erlbaum.

Benjamin, M., McKeachie, W. J., Lin, Y.-G., & Holinger, D. P. (1981). Test anxiety: Deficits in information processing. *Journal of Educational Psychology, 73,* 816–824.

Berkowitz, L. (1983). Aversively stimulated aggression: Some parallels and differences in research with animals and humans. *American Psychologist, 38,* 1135–1144.

Berkun, M. M., Bialek, H. M., Kern, R. P., & Yagi, K. (1962). Experimental studies of psychological stress in man. *Psychological Monographs: General and Applied, 76,* Whole No. 534.

Berlyne, D. E. (1969). The reward value of indifferent stimuli. In T. J. Tapp (Ed.), *Reinforcement and behavior* (pp. 179–214). New York: Academic Press.

Bernstein, I. L. (1991). Aversion conditioning in response to cancer and cancer treatment. *Clinical Psychology Review, 11,* 185–191.

Bernstein, I. L., & Webster, M. M. (1980). Learned taste aversions in humans. *Physiology and Behavior, 25,* 363–366.

Bernstein, J. (1993, October). In many tongues. *The Atlantic Monthly,* 92–102.

Berrios, G. E., Markova, I. S., & Girala, N. (2000). Functional memory complaints: Hypochondria and disorganization. In G. E. Berrios & J. R. Hodges (Eds.), *Memory disorders in psychiatric practice* (pp. 384–399). Cambridge, UK: Cambridge University Press.

Best, M. R. (1975). Conditioned and latent inhibition in taste-aversion learning: Clarifying the role of learned safety. *Journal of Experimental Psychology: Animal Behavior Processes, 1,* 97–113.

Bevan, W., & Steger, J. A. (1971). Free recall and abstractness of stimuli. *Science, 172,* 597–599.

Bever, T. (1992). The logical and extrinsic sources of modularity. In M. R. Gunnar & M. Maratsos (Eds.), *Modularity and constraints in language and cognition: The Minnesota Symposia on Child Psychology* (Vol. 25, pp. 179–212). Hillsdale, NJ: Erlbaum.

Birch, L. L., & Marlin, D. W. (1982). I don't like it, I never tried it: Effects of exposure on a two-year-old children's food preferences. *Appetite, 3,* 353–360.

Birnbaum, I. M., Parker, E. S., Hartley, J. T., & Noble, E. P. (1978). Alcohol and memory: Retrieval processes. *Journal of Verbal Learning and Verbal Behavior, 17,* 325–335.

Bjork, B. J., & Landauer, T. K. (1978). On keeping track of people and things. In M. M. Gruneberg, P. E.

Morris, & R. N. Sykes (Eds.), *Practical aspects of memory* (pp. 52–60). New York: Academic Press.

Blake, M. J. (1967). Time of day effects on performance in a range of tasks. *Psychonomic Science, 9,* 349–350.

Bloom, L. C., & Mudd, S. A. (1991). Depth of processing approach to face recognition: A test of two theories. *Journal of Experimental Psychology: Learning, Memory, and Cognition, 17,* 556–565.

Blum, K., Cull, J. G., Braverman, E. R., & Comings, D. E. (1996). Reward deficiency syndrome. *American Scientist, 84,* 132–145.

Bolles, R. C. (1972). Reinforcement, expectancy, and learning. *Psychological Review, 79,* 394–409.

Bolles, R. C. (1975). *Theory of motivation* (2nd ed.). New York: Harper & Row.

Bolles, R. C., & Fanselow, M. S. (1982). Endorphins and behavior. *Annual Review of Psychology, 33,* 87–102.

Boorstin, D. J. (1983). *The discoverers.* New York: Random House.

Bornstein, M. H., Kessen, W., & Weiskopf, S. (1976). Color vision and hue categorization in young human infants. *Journal of Experimental Psychology: Human Perception and Perfomance, 2,* 112–129.

Bornstein, R. F. (1989). Exposure and affect: Overview and meta-analysis of research, 1968–1987. *Psychological Bulletin, 106,* 265–289.

Borresen, C. R., & Klingsporn, M. J. (1992). Some perceptual and cognitive factors in mirror tracing: Their limits. *Journal of General Psychology, 119,* 365–384.

Bousfield, W. A. (1953). The occurrence of clustering in the recall of randomly arranged associates. *Journal of General Psychology, 49,* 229–240.

Bouton, M. E. (1994). Conditioning, remembering, and forgetting. *Journal of Experimental Psychology: Animal Behavior Processes, 20,* 219–231.

Bovjberg, D. H., Redd, W. H., Maier, L. A., Holland, J. C. et al. (1990). Anticipatory immune suppression in women receiving cyclic chemotherapy for ovarian cancer. *Journal of Consulting and Clinical Psychology, 58,* 153–157.

Bower, G. H. (1970). Analysis of a mnemonic device. *American Scientist, 58,* 496–510.

Bower, G. H. (1981). Mood and memory. *American Psychologist, 36,* 129–148.

Bower, G. H., & Clark, M. C. (1969). Narrative stories as mediators for serial learning. *Psychonomic Science, 14,* 181–182.

Bower, G. H., Clark, M. C., Lesgold, A. M., & Winzenz, D. (1969). Hierarchical retrieval schemes in recall of categorized word lists. *Journal of Verbal Learning and Verbal Behavior, 8,* 323–343.

Bower, G. H., & Hilgard, E. R. (1981). *Theories of learning* (5th ed.). Englewood Cliffs, NJ: Prentice Hall.

Bower, G. H., & Karlin, M. B. (1974). Depth of processing pictures of faces and recognition memory. *Journal of Experimental Psychology, 103,* 751–757.

Bower, G. H., Monteiro, K. P., & Gilligan, S. G. (1978). Emotional mood as a context of learning and recall. *Journal of Verbal Learning and Verbal Behavior, 17,* 573–585.

Bower, G. H., Thompson-Schill, S., & Tulving, E. (1994). Reducing retroactive inteference: An interference analysis. *Journal of Experimental Psychology: Learning, Memory, and Cognition, 20,* 51–66.

Bowers, J. S., & Schacter, D. L. (1990). Implicit memory and test awareness. *Journal of Experimental Psychology: Learning, Memory, and Cognition, 16,* 404–416.

Brady, J. V., Porter, R. W., Conrad, D. G., & Mason, J. W. (1958). Avoidance behavior and the development of gastroduodenal ulcers. *Journal of the Experimental Analysis of Behavior, 1,* 69–72.

Bransford, J. D., & Franks, J. J. (1971). The abstraction of linguistic ideas. *Cognitive Psychology, 2,* 331–350.

Bransford, J. D. & Johnson, M. K. (1973). Considerations of some problems of comprehension. In W. G. Chase (Ed.), *Visual information processing* (pp. 383–438). New York: Academic Press.

Bransford, J. D., Nitsch, K. E., & Franks, J. J. (1977). Schooling and the facilitation of knowing. In R. C. Anderson, R. J. Spiro, & W. E. Montague (Eds.), *Schooling and the acquisition of knowledge* (pp. 31–55). Hillsdale, NJ: Erlbaum.

Breland, K., & Breland, M. (1961). The misbehavior of organisms. *American Psychologist, 61,* 681–684.

Bremner, J. D., Krystal, J. H., Southwick, S. M., & Charney, D. S. (1995). Functional neuroanatomical correlates of the effects of stress on memory. *Journal of Traumatic Stress, 8,* 527–553.

Bremner, J. D., Scott, T. M., Delaney, R. C., Southwick, S. M., Mason, J. W., Johnson, D. R., Innis, R. B., McCarthy, G., & Charney, D. S. (1993). Deficits in short-term memory in postraumatic stress disorder. *American Journal of Psychiatry, 150,* 1015–1019.

Bretz, R. D., & Thompsett, R. E. (1992). Comparing traditional and integrative learning methods in organization training programs. *Journal of Applied Psychology, 77,* 941–951.

Brewer, J. B., Zhao, Z., Desmond, J. E., Glover, G. H., & Gabrieli, J. D. E. (1998). Making memories: Brain activity that predicts how well visual experience will be remembered. *Science, 281,* 1185–1187.

Brewer, W. F., & Treyens, J. C. (1981). Role of schemata in memory for places. *Cognitive Psychology, 13,* 207–230.

Brewin, C. R., & Andrews, B. (1998). Recovered memories of trauma: Phenomenology and cognitive mechanisms. *Clinical Psychology Review, 18,* 949–970.

Broadbent, D. E., Cooper, P. J., & Broadbent, M. H. P. (1978). A comparison of hierarchical and matrix retrieval schemes in recall. *Journal of Experimental Psychology: Human Learning and Memory, 4,* 486–497.

Broadhurst, P. L. (1963). *The science of animal behavior.* Baltimore: Penguin.

Brooks, B. M. (1994). A comparison of serial position effects in implicit and explicit word-stem completion. *Psychonomic Bulletin and Review, 1,* 264–268.

Brooks, J. O., & Watkins, M. J. (1990). Further evidence of the intricity of the memory span. *Journal of Experimental Psychology: Learning, Memory, and Cognition, 16,* 1134–1141.

Brown, A. L., Campione, J. C., Bray, N. W., & Wilcox, B. L. (1973). Keeping track of changing variables: Effects of rehearsal training and rehearsal prevention in normal and retarded adolescents. *Journal of Experimental Psychology, 101,* 123–131.

Brown, A. S., & Murphy, D. R. (1989). Cryptoamnesia: Delineating inadvertant plagiarism. *Journal of Experimental Psychology: Learning, Memory, and Cognition, 15,* 432–442.

Brown, J. (1958). Some tests of the decay theory of immediate memory. *Quarterly Journal of Experimental Psychology, 10,* 12–21.

Brown, J. S. (1969). Factors affecting self-punitive locomotor behavior. In B. A. Campbell & R. M. Church (Eds.), *Punishment and Aversive Behavior* (pp. 467–514). New York: Appleton, Century, Crofts.

Brown, M. F., & Moore, J. A. (1997). In the dark II: Spatial choice when access to extrinsic spatial cues is eliminated. *Animal Learning & Behavior, 25,* 335–346.

Brown, R., & Kulick, J. (1977). Flashbulb memories. *Cognition, 5,* 73–99.

Brown, R., & McNeil, D. (1966) The "tip of the tongue" phenomenon. *Journal of Verbal Learning and Verbal Behavior, 5,* 325–337.

Brown, R. T., & Wagner, A. R. (1965). Resistance to punishment and extinction following training with shock or nonreinforcement. *Journal of Experimental Psychology, 68,* 503–507.

Brown, S., Conover, J., Flores, L., & Goodman, K. (1991). Clustering and recall: Do high clusterers recall more than low clusterers because of clustering? *Journal of Experimental Psychology: Learning, Memory, and Cognition, 17,* 710–721.

Bryant, R. A., & Harvey, A. G. (1995). Avoidant coping style and post-traumatic stress following motor vehicle accidents. *Behaviour Research and Therapy, 33,* 631–635.

Buckner, R. L. (1996). Beyond HERA: Contributions of specific prefrontal brain areas to long-term memory retrieval. *Psychonomic Bulletin & Review, 3,* 149–158.

Burns, D. J. (1990). The generation effect: A test between single- and multifactor theories. *Journal of Experimental Psychology: Learning, Memory, and Cognition, 16,* 1060–1067.

Bushman, B. J., & Baumeister, R. F. (1998). Threatened egotism, narcissism, self-esteem, and direct and displaced aggression: Does self-love or self-hate lead to violence? *Journal of Personality and Social Psychology, 75,* 219–239.

Butters, N., & Cermak, L. S. (1986). A case study of the forgetting of autobiographical knowledge: implications for the study of retrograde amnesia. In D. C. Rubin (Ed.), *Autobiographical memory* (pp. 253–272). New York: Cambridge University Press.

Byrne, R. (1979). Memory for urban geography. *Quarterly Journal of Experimental Psychology, 31,* 147–154.

Cameron, D. E. (1963). The processes of remembering. *British Journal of Psychiatry, 109,* 325–340.

Cammen, T. J., Simpson, J. M., Fraser, R. M., Preker, A. S., & Exton-Smith, A. N. (1987). The memory clinic: A new approach to the detection of dementia. *British Journal of Psychiatry, 150,* 359–364.

Canas, J. J., & Nelson, D. L. (1986). Recognition and environmental context: The effect of testing by phone. *Bulletin of the Psychonomic Society, 24,* 407–409.

Candland, D. K. (1962). *Psychology: The experimental approach.* New York: McGraw-Hill.

Candland, D. K. (1993). *Feral children and clever animals.* New York: Oxford University Press.

Cann, A., & Ross, D. A. (1989). Olfactory stimuli as context cues in human memory. *American Journal of Psychology, 102,* 91–102.

Capaldi, E. J. (1971). Memory and learning: A sequential viewpoint. In W. K. Honig & P. H. R. James (Eds.), *Animal memory* (pp. 112–154). New York: Academic Press.

Capaldi, E. J. (1994). The relation between memory and expectancy as revealed by percentage and sequence of reward investigations. *Psychonomic Bulletin & Review, 1,* 303–310.

Caplan, P. J., MacPherson, G. M., & Tobin, P. (1985). Do sex-related differences in spatial abilities exist? *American Psychologist, 40,* 786–799.

Capretta, P. J., & Berkun, M. M. (1962). Validity and reliability of certain measures of psychological stress. *Psychological Reports, 10,* 875–878.

Caramazza, A., & Hillis, A. E. (1991). Lexical organization of nouns and verbs in the brain. *Nature, 349,* 788–790.

Carey, M. P., & Burish, T. G. (1988). Etiology and treatment of the psychological side effects associated with cancer chemotherapy: A critical review and discussion. *Psychological Bulletin, 104,* 307–325.

Carney, R. N., Levin, J. R., & Morrison, C. R. (1988). Mnemonic learning of artists and their paintings. *American Educational Research Journal, 25*, 107–125.

Cave, C. B. (1997). Very long-lasting priming in picture naming. *Psychological Science, 8*, 322–325.

Ceci, J. S., & Bronfenbrenner, U. (1985). "Don't forget to take the cupcakes out of the oven": Prospective memory, strategic time-monitoring, and context. *Child Development, 56*, 152–164.

Chance, P. (1992, November). The rewards of learning. *Phi Delta Kappan*, 200–207.

Chapman, G. B. (1991). Trial order affects cue interaction in contingency judgement. *Journal of Experimental Psychology: Learning, Memory, and Cognition, 17*, 837–854.

Charness, N. (1987). Component processes in bridge bidding and novel problem-solving tasks. *Canadian Journal of Psychology, 41*, 223–243.

Chase, W. G., & Ericsson, K. A. (1981). Skilled memory. In J. R. Anderson (Ed.) *Cognitive Skills and Their Acquisition* (pp. 141–180). Hillsdale, NJ: Erlbaum.

Chen, S., Swartz, K. B., & Terrace, H. S. (1997). Knowledge of the ordinal position of list items in rhesus monkeys. *Psychological Science, 8*, 80–86.

Chi, M. T. H. (1978). Knowledge structures and memory development. In R. Siegler (Ed.), *Children's thinking: What develops?* (pp. 73–96). Hillsdale, NJ: Erlbaum.

Chorover, S. L., & Schiller, P. H. (1965). Short-term retrograde amnesia in rats. *Journal of Comparative and Physiological Psychology, 59*, 73–78.

Christianson, S.-A., Loftus, E. F., Hoffman, H., & Loftus, G. R. (1991). Eye fixations and memory for emotional events. *Journal of Experimental Psychology: Learning, Memory, and Cognition, 17*, 693–701.

Christianson, S.-A., & Nilsson, L.-G. (1984). Functional amnesia as induced by a psychological trauma. *Memory & Cognition, 12*, 142–155.

Clark, D. M., & Teasdale, J. D. (1982). Diurnal variation in clinical depression and accessibility of positive and negative experiences. *Journal of Abnormal Psychology, 91*, 87–95.

Claxton, C. S., & Murrell, P. H. (1987). *Learning styles: Implications for improving education*. Washington, DC: Association for the Study of Higher Education.

Cofer, C. N. (1979). Human learning and memory. In E. Hearst (Ed.), *The first century of experimental psychology* (pp. 323–269). Hillsdale, NJ: Erlbaum.

Cohen, G. (1989). *Memory in the real world*. Hillsdale, NJ: Erlbaum.

Cohen, G. (1990). Recognition and retrieval of proper names: Age differences in the fan effect. *European Journal of Cognitive Psychology, 2*, 193–204.

Cohen, G. (1996). *Memory in the real world* (2nd ed.). East Sussex, UK: Psychology Press.

Cohen, G., & Faulkner, D. (1986). Memory for proper names: Age differences in retrieval. *British Journal of Developmental Psychology, 4*, 187–197.

Cohen, L. B. (1976). Habituation of infant visual attention. In T. J. Tighe & R. N. Leaton (Eds.), *Habituation: Perspectives from child development, animal behavior, and neurophysiology* (pp. 207–238). Hillsdale, NJ: Erlbaum.

Cohen, R. L. (1983). Effect of encoding variables on free recall of words and action events. *Memory & Cognition, 11*, 575–582.

Cole, C. A., & Houston, M. J. (1987, February). Encoding and media effects on consumer learning deficiences in the elderly. *Journal of Marketing Research, 24*, 55–63.

Coleman, S. R. (1975). Consequences of response-contingent change in US intensity upon the rabbit nictitating membrane response. *Journal of Comparative and Physiological Psychology, 88*, 591–595.

Collins, A, M., & Loftus, E. F. (1975). A spreading activation theory of semantic processing. *Psychological Review, 82*, 407–428.

Collins, A. M., & Quillian, M. R. (1969). Retrieval time from semantic memory. *Journal of Verbal Learning and Verbal Behavior, 8*, 240–247.

Conrad, R. (1958). Accuracy of recall using keyset and telephone dial, and the effect of a prefix digit. *Journal of Applied Psychology, 42*, 285–288.

Conrad, R. (1964). Acoustic confusions in immediate memory. *British Journal of Psychology, 55*, 75–83.

Conrad, R. (1970). Short-term memory processes in the deaf. *British Journal of Psychology, 61*, 179–195.

Constans, J. I., Foa, E. B., Franklin, M. E., & Mathews, A. (1995). Memory for actual and imagined events in OC checkers. *Behaviour Research and Therapy, 33*, 665–671.

Conway, M. A., Cohen, G., & Stanhope, N. (1991). On the very long-term retention of knowledge acquired through formal education: Twelve years of cognitive psychology. *Journal of Experimental Psychology: General, 120*, 395–409.

Cook, M., & Mineka, S. (1990). Selective associations in the observational conditioning of fear in rhesus monkeys. *Journal of Experimental Psychology: Animal Behavior Processes, 16*, 372–389.

Cooney, J. B., & Swanson, H. L. (1990). Individual differences in memory for mathematical story problems: Memory span and problem perception. *Journal of Educational Psychology, 82*, 570–577.

Cooper, R. M. & Zubek, J. P. (1958). Effects of enriched and restricted early environments on the learning ability of bright and dull rats. *Canadian Journal of Psychology, 12*, 159–164.

Coppage, E. W., & Harcum, E. R. (1967). Temporal vs. structural determinants of primacy in strategies of serial learning. *Journal of Verbal Learning and Verbal Behavior, 6,* 487–490.

Coren, S. (1994). *The intelligence of dogs.* New York: The Free Press.

Cornell, E. H., & Heth, C. D. (1979). Response versus place learning by human infants. *Journal of Experimental Psychology: Human Learning and Memory, 5,* 188–196.

Craig, M. J., Humphreys, M. S., Rocklin, T., & Revelle, W. (1979). Impulsivity, neuroticism, and caffeine: Do they have additive effects on arousal? *Journal of Research in Personality, 13,* 404–419.

Craik, F. I. M., & Lockhart, R. S. (1972). Levels of processing: A framework for memory research. *Journal of Verbal Learning and Verbal Behavior, 11,* 671–684.

Craik, F. I. M, & Tulving, E. (1975). Depth of processing and the retention of words in episodic memory. *Journal of Experimental Psychology: General, 104,* 268–294.

Crawford, M., Herrmann, D. J., Randal, E., Holdsworth, M., & Robbins, D. (1989). Self perception of memory performance as a function of gender. *British Journal of Psychology, 80,* 391–401.

Crespi, L. P. (1942). Quantitative variation in incentive and performance in the white rat. *American Journal of Psychology, 55,* 467–517.

Crigger, N., & Forber, W. (1997). Assessing neurologic function in older patients. *American Journal of Nursing, 97,* 37–40.

Cronbach, L. J. (1957). The two disiciplines of scientific psychology. *American Psychologist, 12,* 671–684.

Crook, T. H., & Larabee, G. L. (1990). A self-rating scale for evaluating memory in everyday life. *Psychology and Aging, 5,* 48–57.

Crowder, R. G. (1972). Visual and auditory memory. In J. F. Kavanagh & I. G. Mattingly (Eds.), *Language by ear and by eye* (pp. 251–275). Cambridge, MA: The MIT Press.

Crowder, R. G. (1976). *Principles of learning and memory.* Hillsdale, NJ: Erlbaum.

Crowder, R. G. (1993). Short-term memory: Where do we stand? *Memory & Cognition, 21,* 142–145.

Crutcher, R. J., & Healy, A. F. (1989). Cognitive operations and the generation effect. *Journal of Experimental Psychology: Learning, Memory, and Cognition, 15,* 669–675.

Cuddy, L. J., & Jacoby, L. L. (1982). When forgetting helps memory: An analysis of repetition effects. *Journal of Verbal Learning and Verbal Behavior, 21,* 451–467.

Cutler, S. J., & Grams, A. E. (1988). Correlates of self-reported everyday memory problems. *Journal of Gerontology: Social Sciences, 43,* S82–S90.

Cytowic, R. E., & Wood, F. B. (1982). Synesthesia 1. A review of major theories and their brain basis. *Brain and Cognition, 1,* 23–35.

Dadds, M. R., Bovbjerg, D. H., Redd, W. H., & Cutmore, T. R. H. (1997). Imagery in human classical conditioning. *Psychological Bulletin, 122,* 89–103.

Dallal, N. L., & Meck, W. H. (1990). Hierarchical structures: Chunking by food type facilitates spatial memory. *Journal of Experimental Psychology: Animal Behavior Processes, 16,* 69–84.

Dalton, T. C., & Bergenn, V. W. (Eds.). (1995). *Beyond heredity and environment: Myrtle McGraw and the maturation controversy.* Boulder, CO: Westview Press.

Daneman, M., & Carpenter, P. A. (1980). Individual differences in working memory and reading. *Journal of Verbal Learning and Verbal Behavior, 19,* 450–466.

Daneman, M., & Merikle, P. M. (1996). Working memory and language comprehension: A meta-analysis. *Psychonomic Bulletin & Review, 3,* 422–433.

Dark, V. J., & Benbow, C. P. (1990). Enhanced problem solving translation and short-term memory: Components of mathematical skill. *Journal of Educational Psychology, 82,* 420–429.

Dark, V. J., & Benbow, C. P. (1991). Differential enhancement of working memory with mathematical versus verbal precocity. *Journal of Educational Psychology, 83,* 48–60.

Darwin, C. (1859). *On the origin of species by means of natural selection, or the preservation of favoured races in the struggle for life.* London: John Murray (New York: Modern Library, 1967).

Daum, I., Channon, S., & Canavan, A. G. M. (1989). Classical conditioning in patients with severe memory problems. *Journal of Neurology, Neurosurgery, and Psychiatry, 52,* 47–51.

Daum, I., & Schugens, M. M. (1996). On the cerebellum and classical conditioning. *Current Directions in Psychological Science, 2,* 58–61.

Davey, G. C. L. (1994). Is evaluative conditioning a qualitatively distinct form of classical conditioning? *Behaviour Research and Therapy, 32,* 291–299.

Davey, G. C. L. (1995). Preparedness and phobias: Specific evolved associations or a generalized expectancy bias? *Behavioral and Brain Sciences, 18,* 289–325.

Davey, G. C. L., & Matchett, G. (1994). Unconditioned stimulus rehearsal and the retention and enhancement of differential "fear" conditioning: Effects of trait and state anxiety. *Journal of Abnormal Psychology, 103,* 708–718.

Davies, G., & Robertson, N. (1993). Recognition memory for automobiles: A developmental study. *Bulletin of the Psychonomic Society, 31,* 103–106.

Davis, H. P., & Bernstein, P. A. (1992). Age related changes in explicit and implicit memory. In L. Squire & N. Butters (Eds.), *The neuropsychology of memory* (2nd ed., pp. 249–261). New York: Guilford Press.

Davis, H., & Bradford, S. A. (1991). Numerically restricted food intake in the rate in a free-feeding situation. *Animal Learning & Behavior, 19,* 215–222.

Davis, J. K. (1991). Educational implications of field dependence-independence. In S. Wapner & J. Demick (Eds.), *Field dependence-independence: Cognitive style across the life span* (pp. 149–176). Hillsdale, NJ: Erlbaum.

Davis, M. (1970). Effects of interstimulus interval length and variability on startle-response habituation in the rat. *Journal of Comparative and Physiological Psychology, 72,* 177–192.

Davis, M. (1974). Sensitization of the rat startle response by noise. *Journal of Comparative and Physiological Psychology, 87,* 571–581.

Davis, M., & Heninger, G. R. (1972). Comparison of response plasticity between the eye blink and vertex potential in humans. *Electroencephalography and Clinical Neurophysiology, 33,* 283–293.

Davis, M., & Wagner, A. R. (1969). Habituation of startle response under incremental sequence of stimulus intensities. *Journal of Comparative and Physiological Psychology, 67,* 486–492.

Davison, G. C. (1968). Systematic desensitization as a counterconditioning process. *Journal of Abnormal Psychology, 73,* 91–99.

Dawson, M. E., & Schell, A. M. (1987). Human autonomic and skeletal classical conditioning: The role of conscious cognitive factors. In G. C. L. Davey (Ed.), *Cognitive processes and Pavlovian conditioning in humans* (pp. 27–55). Chichester, UK: Wiley.

Dawson, M. E., Schell, A. M., & Banis, H. T. (1986). Greater resistance to extinction of electrodermal responses conditioned to potentially phobic CSs: A noncognitive process? *Psychophysiology, 23,* 552–561.

D'Azevedo, W. L. (1962). Uses of the past in Gola discourse. *Journal of African History, 3,* 11–34.

DeCasper, A. J., & Fifer, W. P. (1980). Of human bonding: Newborns prefer their mother's voices. *Science, 208,* 1174–1176.

DeCasper, A. J., & Spence, M. J. (1986). Prenatal maternal speech influences newborns' perception of speech sounds. *Infant Behavior and Development, 9,* 133–150.

Deese, J. (1959). On the prediction of occurrence of particular verbal intrusions in immediate memory. *Journal of Experimental Psychology, 58,* 17–22.

DeHaan, E., & Newcombe, F. (1991, February 9). What makes faces familiar? *New Scientist,* 49–52.

deJongh, A., Muris, P., Ter Horst, G., & Duyx, M. P. (1995). Acquisition and maintenance of dental anxiety: The role of conditioning experiences and cognitive factors. *Behavioural Research and Therapy, 33,* 205–210.

Dekker, E., Pelser, H., & Groen, J. (1957). Conditioning as a cause of asthmatic attacks: A laboratory study. *Journal of Psychosomatic Research, 2,* 97–108.

Delis, D., Fleer, J., & Kerr, N. H. (1978). Memory for music. *Perception and Psychophysics, 23,* 215–218.

Delis, D. C., Kramer, J. H., Kaplan, E., & Ober, B. A. (1987). *California verbal learning test* (manual). San Antonio, TX: Psychological Corporation.

DeMarie-Dreblow, D. (1991). Relation between knowledge and memory: A reminder that correlation does not imply causality. *Child-Development, 62,* 484–498.

Dempster, F. N. (1988). The spacing effect: A case study in the failure to apply the results of psychological research. *American Psychologist, 43,* 627–634.

Dempster, F. N. (1996). Distributing and managing the conditions of encoding and practice. In E. L. Bjork & R. A. Bjork (Eds.), *Memory* (pp. 317–344). New York: Academic Press.

DeNike, L. D., & Spielberger, C. D. (1963). Induced mediating states in verbal conditioning. *Journal of Verbal Learning and Verbal Behavior, 1,* 339–345.

deQuervain, D. J., Roozendaal, B., & McGaugh, J. L. (1998). Stress and glucocorticoids impair retrieval of long-term spatial memory. *Nature, 394,* 787–790.

Descartes, R. (1641/1960). *Discourse on methods* and *Meditations.* Indianapolis, IN: Bobbs-Merrill.

Desimone, R. (1996). Neural mechanisms for visual memory and their role in attention. *Proceedings of the National Academy of Sciences, 93,* 13494–13499.

Dess, N. K., & Chapman, C. D. (1998). "Humans and animals"? On saying what we mean. *Psychological Science, 9,* 156–157.

Detterman, D. K. (1975). The von Restorff effect and induced amnesia: Production by manipulation of sound intensity. *Journal of Experimental Psychology: Human Learning and Memory, 1,* 614–628.

Deweer, B., & Sara, S. J. (1984). Background stimuli as a reminder after spontaneous forgetting: Role of duration of cuing and cuing-test interval. *Animal Learning & Behavior, 12,* 238–247.

de Wijk, R. A., Schab, F. R., & Cain, W. S. (1995). Odor identification. In F. R. Schab & R. G. Crowder (Eds.), *Memory for odors* (pp. 21–37). Hillsdale, NJ: Erlbaum.

de Winstanley, P. A. (1995). A generation effect can be found during naturalistic learning. *Psychonmic Bulletin & Review, 2,* 538–541.

Diamond, B. (1969, September). Interview regarding Sirhan Sirhan. *Psychology Today*, 48–55.

DiCara, L. V. (1970). Learning in the autonomic nervous system. *Scientific American, 222*, 30–39.

Dickinson, A. (1980). *Contemporary animal learning theory*. Cambridge: Cambridge University Press.

Dienes, Z., & Berry, D. (1997). Implicit learning: Below the subjective threshold. *Psychonomic Bulletin & Review, 4*, 3–23.

di Nardo, P. A., Guzy, L. T., & Bak, R. M. (1988). Anxiety response patterns and etiological factors in dog-fearful and non-fearful subjects. *Behaviour Research and Therapy, 26*, 245–252.

Dobrzecka, C., Szwejkowska, G., & Konorski, J. (1966). Qualitative versus directional cues in two forms of differentiation. *Science, 153*, 87–89.

Dog roams 840 miles, finds family after move. (1983, March 27). *Charlotte Observer*, p. 12A.

Dollard, J., & Miller, N. E. (1950). *Personality and psychotherapy*. New York: McGraw-Hill.

Domjan, M. (1976). Determinants of the enhancement of flavored-water intake by prior exposure. *Journal of Experimental Psychology: Animal Behavior Processes, 2*, 17–27.

Domjan, M. (1987). Animal learning comes of age. *American Psychologist, 42*, 556–564.

Domjan, M., & Purdy, J. E. (1995). Animal research in psychology: More than meets the eye of the general psychology student. *American Psychologist, 50*, 496–503.

Dulany, D. E. (1968). Awareness, rules, and propositional control: A confrontation with S–R behavior theory. In T. R. Dixon & D. H. Horton (Eds.), *Verbal behavior and general behavior theory* (pp. 340–385). Englewood Cliffs, NJ: Prentice Hall.

Dulany, D. E., Carlson, R. A., & Dewey, G. I. (1984). A case of syntactical learning and judgment: How conscious and how abstract? *Journal of Experimental Psychology: General, 113*, 541–555.

Duncan, C. P. (1949). The retroactive effect of electroconvulsive shock on learning. *Journal of Comparative and Physiological Psychology, 42*, 32–44.

Dweck, C. S. (1975). The role of expectations and attributions in the alleviation of learned helplessness. *Journal of Personality and Social Psychology, 31*, 674–685.

Dweck, C. S., & Reppucci, N. D. (1973). Learned helplessness and reinforcement responsibility in children. *Journal of Personality and Social Psychology, 25*, 109–116.

Dweck, C. S., & Wagner, A. R. (1970). Situational cues and correlation between CS and US as determinants of the conditioned emotional response. *Psychonomic Science, 18*, 145–147.

Eacott, M. J., & Crawley, R. A. (1998). The offset of childhood amnesia: Memory for events that occurred before age 3. *Journal of Experimental Psychology: General, 127*, 22–33.

Ebbinghaus, H. (1964). *Memory: A contribution to experimental psychology* (H. A. Ruger & C. E. Bussenius, Trans.). New York: Dover. (Original work published 1885)

Egger, M. D., & Miller, N. E. (1963). When is a reward reinforcing? An experimental study of the information hypothesis. *Journal of Comparative and Physiological Psychology, 56*, 132–137.

Eich, E. (1985). Context, memory, and integrated item/context imagery. *Journal of Experimental Psychology: Learning, Memory, and Cognition, 11*, 764–770.

Eich, E. (1995). Mood as a mediator of place dependent memory. *Journal of Experimental Psychology: General, 124*, 293–308.

Eich, E., Macaulay, D., Loewenstein, R. J., & Dihle, P. (1997). Memory, amnesia, and dissociative identity disorder. *Psychological Science, 8*, 417–422.

Eich, J. W., Weingartner, H., Stillman, R. C., & Gillin, J. C. (1975). State dependent accessibility of retrieval cues in the retention of a categorized list. *Journal of Verbal Learning and Verbal Behavior, 14*, 408–417.

Eikelboom, R., & Stewart, J. (1982). Conditioning of drug-induced physiologcal responses. *Psychological Review, 89*, 507–528.

Einstein, G. O., & McDaniel, M. A. (1990). Normal aging and prospective memory. *Journal of Experimental Psychology: Learning, Memory, and Cognition, 16*, 717–726.

Einstein, G. O., McDaniel, M. A., & Lackey, S. (1989). Bizarre imagery, inteference, and distinctiveness. *Journal of Experimental Psychology: Learning, Memory, and Cognition, 15*, 137–146.

Einstein, G. O., McDaniel, M. A., Richardson, S. L., Guynn, M. J., & Cunfer, A. R. (1995). Normal aging and prospective memory: Examining the influences of self-initiated retrieval. *Journal of Experimental Psychology: Learning, Memory, and Cognition, 20*, 996–1007.

Eisenberger, R. (1972). Explanation of rewards that do not reduce tissue needs. *Psychological Bulletin, 77*, 319–399.

Eisenberger, R., & Cameron, J. (1996). Detrimental effects of reward: Reality or myth. *American Psychologist, 51*, 1153–1166.

Eisenberger, R., Weier, F., Masterson, F., & Theis, L. Y. (1989). Fixed-ratio schedules increase generalized self-control: Preference for large rewards despite high effort or punishment. *Journal of Experimental Psychology: Animal Behavior Processes, 15*, 383–392.

Elliott, M. H. (1928). The effect of change of reward on the performance of rats. *University of California Publications in Psychology, 4,* 19–30.

Ellis, H. C., & Muller, D. G. (1964). Transfer in perceptual learning following stimulus predifferentiation. *Journal of Experimental Psychology, 68,* 388–395.

Ellis, N. C., & Hennelly, R. A. (1980). A bilingual word-length effect: Implications for intelligence testing and the relative ease of mental calculation in Welsh and English. *British Journal of Psychology, 71,* 43–52.

Ellis, N. R., Detterman, D. K., Runcie, D., McCarver, R. B., & Craig, E. M. (1971). Amnesic effects in short-term memory. *Journal of Experimental Psychology, 89,* 357–361.

Emmons, W. H., & Simon, C. W. (1956). The non-recall of material presented during sleep. *American Journal of Psychology, 69,* 76–81.

Engen, T. (1987). Remembering odors and their names. *American Scientist, 75,* 497–503.

Engen, T., Kuisma, J. E., & Eimas, P. D. (1973). Short-term memory of odors. *Journal of Experimental Psychology, 99,* 222–225.

Engle, R. W., & Marshall, K. (1983). Do developmental changes in digit span result from acquisition strategies? *Journal of Experimental Child Psychology, 36,* 429–436.

Engle, R. W., Nations, J. K., & Cantor, J. (1990). Is "working memory capacity" just another name for word knowledge? *Journal of Educational Psychology, 82,* 799–804.

Erber, J. T., & Rothberg, S. T. (1991). Here's looking at you: The relative effects of age and attractiveness on judgements about memory failure. *Journal of Gerontology, 46,* P116–P123.

Erdelyi, M. H., & Kleinbard, J. (1978). Has Ebbinghaus decayed with time?: The growth of recall (hypermnesia) over days. *Journal of Experimental Psychology: Human Learning and Memory, 4,* 275–289.

Ericsson, K. A., & Charness, N. (1994). Expert performance: Its structure and acquisition. *American Psychologist, 49,* 725–747.

Ericsson, K. A., Chase, W. G., & Faloon, S. (1980). Acquisition of a memory skill. *Science, 208,* 1181–1182.

Ericsson, K. A., Krampe, R. T., & Tesch-Romer, C. (1993). The role of deliberate practice in the acquisition of expert performance. *Psychological Review, 100,* 363–406.

Erikson, G. C., Hager, L. B., Houseworth, C., Dungan, J., Petros, T., & Beckwith, B. E. (1985). The effects of caffeine on memory for word lists. *Physiology and Behavior, 35,* 47–51.

Essman, W. B. (1983). *Clinical pharmacology of learning and memory.* New York: Spectrum Publications.

Estes, W. K. (1944). An experimental study of punishment. *Psychological Monographs, 57* (3, No. 263).

Estes, W. K. (1972). An associative basis for coding and organization in memory. In A. W. Melton & E. Martin (Eds.), *Coding processes in human memory* (pp. 161–190). Washington, DC: V. H. Winston.

Estes, W. K. (1974). Learning theory and intelligence. *American Psychologist, 29,* 740–749.

Estes, W. K. (1997). Processes of memory loss, recovery, and distortion. *Psychological Review, 104,* 148–169.

Evans, G. W., Fellows, J., Zorn, M., & Doty, K. (1980). Cognitive mapping and architecture. *Journal of Applied Psychology, 65,* 474–478.

Evans, G. W., & Johnson, D. (2000). Stress and open-office noise. *Journal of Applied Psychology, 85,* 779–783.

Eysenck, H. J. (1981). *A model for personality.* Berlin: Springer.

Eysenck, M. W. (1979). Anxiety, learning, and memory: A reconceptualization. *Journal of Research in Personality, 13,* 363–385.

Eysenck, M. W. (1983). Individual differences in memory. In A. Mayes (Ed.), *Memory in animals and humans* (pp. 282–311). Wokingham, England: Van Nostrand Reinhold (UK).

Eysenck, M. W. (1987). Cognitive functioning and anxiety. *Psychological Research, 49,* 189–195.

Eysenck, M. W., & Eysenck, M. C. (1979). Processing depth, elaboration of encoding, memory stores, and expended processing capacity. *Journal of Experimental Psychology: Human Learning and Memory, 5,* 472–484.

Fabiani, M., & Donchin, E. (1995). Encoding processes and memory organization: A model of the von Restorff effect. *Journal of Experimental Psychology: Learning, Memory, and Cognition, 21,* 224–240.

Fein, G., Davenport, L., Yingling, C. D., & Galin, D. (1988). Verbal and nonverbal memory deficits in pure dyslexia. *Developmental Neuropsychology, 4,* 181–197.

Feingold, A. (1988). Cognitive gender differences are disappearing. *American Psychologist, 43,* 95–103.

Fendrich, D. W., Healy, A. F., & Bourne, L. E. (1991). Long-term repetition effects for motoric and perceptual procedures. *Journal of Experimental Psychology: Learning, Memory, and Cognition, 17,* 137–151.

Ferster, C, B., & Skinner, B. F. (1957). *Schedules of reinforcement.* New York: Appleton, Century, Crofts.

Finkel, D., & McGue, M. (1993). The origins of individual differences in memory among the elderly: A behavior genetic analysis. *Psychology and Aging, 8,* 527–537.

Fisher, R. P., & Quigley, K. L. (1992). Applying cognitive theory in public health investigations: Enhancing food recall. In J. Tanur (Ed.), *Questions about questions* (pp. 154–169). New York: Sage Press.

Fitzgerald, H. E., & Brackbill, Y. (1976). Classical conditioning in infancy: Development and constraints. *Psychological Bulletin, 83,* 353–376.

Flavel, J. H. (1971). First discussant's comments: What is memory development the development of? *Human Development, 14,* 272–278.

Foa, E. B., Steketee, G., Grayson, J. B., Turner, R. M., & Latimer, P. R. (1984). Deliberate exposure and blocking of obsessive-compulsive rituals: Immediate and long-term effects. *Behavior Therapy, 15,* 450–472.

Fogarty, S. J., & Helmsley, D. R. (1983). Depression and the accessibility of memories—A longitudinal study. *British Journal of Psychiatry, 142,* 232–237.

Folkard, S., & Monk, T. H. (1980). Circadian rhythms in human memory. *British Journal of Psychology, 71,* 295–307.

Folkard, S., & Monk, T. H. (1985). *Hours of work: Temporal factors in work scheduling.* New York: Wiley.

Folkman, S., & Lazarus, R. S. (1985). If it changes it must be a process: Study of emotion and coping during three stages of a college examination. *Journal of Personality and Social Psychology, 48,* 150–170.

Franks, C. M., & Trouton, D. (1958). Effects of amobarbital sodium and dexamphetamine on conditioning of the eyeblink response. *Journal of Comparative and Physiological Psychology, 51,* 220–222.

Fraut, A. G., & Smothergill, D. W. (1978). A two-factor theory of stimulus-repetition effects. *Journal of Experimental Psychology: Human Perception and Performance, 4,* 191–197.

Freedman, D. G. (1958). Constitutional and environmental interactions in rearing of four breeds of dogs. *Science, 127,* 585–586.

Freud, S. (1901/1960). *The psychopathology of everyday life.* New York: Norton.

Friedman, A. (1979). Framing pictures: The role of knowledge in automatized encoding and memory for gist. *Journal of Experimental Psychology: General, 108,* 316–355.

Fuller, J. L., & Thompson, W. R. (1978). *Foundations of behavior genetics.* St. Louis, MO: Mosby.

Furedy, J. J., & Scull, J. (1971). Orienting-reaction theory and an increase in the human GSR following stimulus change which is unpredictable but not contrary to prediction. *Journal of Experimental Psychology, 88,* 292–294.

Gabrieli, J. D. E., Corkin, S., Mickel, S. F., & Growdon, J. H. (1993). Intact acquisition and long-term retention of mirror-tracing skill in Alzheimer's disease and global amnesia. *Behavioral Neuroscience, 107,* 899–910.

Garcia, J., & Koelling, R. A. (1966). Relation of cue to consequence in avoidance learning. *Psychonomic Science, 4,* 123–124.

Gardiner, J. M. (1987). Generation and priming effects in word-fragment completion. *Journal of Experimental Psychology: Learning, Memory, and Cognition, 14,* 495–501.

Gardiner, J. M., Gawlik, B., & Richardson-Klavehn, J. (1994). Maintenance rehearsal affects knowing, not remembering; elaborative rehearsal affects remembering, not knowing. *Psychonomic Bulletin & Review, 1,* 107–110.

Garry, M., Manning, C. G., Loftus, E. F., & Sherman, S. J. (1996). Imagination inflation: Imagining a childhood event inflates confidence that it occurred. *Psychonomic Bulletin & Review, 3,* 208–214.

Gartman, L., & Johnson, N. F. (1972). Massed versus distributed repetition of homographs: A test of the differential-encoding hypothesis. *Journal of Verbal Learning and Verbal Behavior, 11,* 801–808.

Gatchel, R. J. (1975). Effects of interstimulus interval length on short-term and long-term habituation of autonomic components of the orienting response. *Physiological Psychology, 3,* 133–136.

Gathercole, S. E. (1994). The nature and uses of working memory. In P. E. Morris & M. Gruneberg (Eds.), *Theoretical Aspects of Memory* (pp. 50–78). London: Routledge.

Geiselman, R. E., Fisher, R. P., MacKinnon, D. P., & Holland, H. L. (1985). Eyewitness memory enhancement in the police interview: Cognitive retrieval mnemonics versus hypnosis. *Journal of Applied Psychology, 70,* 401–412.

Gesell, A., & Thompson, H. (1929). Learning and growth in identical twins: An experimental study by the method of co-twin control. *Genetic Psychology Monographs, 6,* 1–23.

Gibson, E. J. (1969). *Principles of perceptual learning and development.* New York: Appleton, Century, Crofts.

Gibson, E. J., & Walk, R. D. (1956). The effect of prolonged exposure to visually presented patterns on learning to discriminate them. *Journal of Comparative and Physiological Psychology, 49,* 239–242.

Gilliland, K., & Andress, D. (1981). Ad lib caffeine consumption, symptoms of caffeinism, and academic performance. *American Journal of Psychiatry, 138,* 512–514.

Gilmore, R. F., & Secunda, E. (1993, November–December). Zipped TV commercials boost prior learning. *Journal of Advertising Research,* 28–38.

Glanzer, M. (1972). Storage mechanisms in recall. In G. H. Bower (Ed.), *The psychology of learning and motivation* (Vol. 5, pp. 129–193). New York: Academic Press.

Glanzer, M., & Cunitz, A. R. (1966). Two storage mechanisms in free recall. *Journal of Verbal Learning and Verbal Behavior, 5,* 351–360.

Glass, D. C., & Singer, J. E. (1972). *Urban stress: Experiments in noise and social stressors.* New York: Academic Press.

Glazer, H. I., & Weiss, J. M. (1976a). Long-term and transitory interference effects. *Journal of Experimental Psychology: Animal Behavior Processes, 2,* 191–201.

Glazer, H. I., & Weiss, J. M. (1976b). Long-term interference effect: An alternative to "learned helplessness." *Journal of Experimental Psychology: Animal Behavior Processes, 2,* 202–213.

Glisky, E. L., & Schacter, D. A. (1989). Extending the limits of complex learning in organic amnesia: computer training in a vocational domain. *Neuropsychologia, 27,* 107–120.

Glover, J. A. (1989). The "testing" phenomenon: Not gone but nearly forgotten. *Journal of Educational Psychology, 81,* 392–399.

Gobet, F., & Simon, H. A. (1996). Recall of rapidly presented chess positions is a function of skill. *Psychonomic Bulletin & Review, 3,* 159–163.

Godden, D. R., & Baddeley, A. D. (1975). Context-dependent memory in two natural environments: On land and underwater. *British Journal of Psychology, 66,* 325–331.

Goettl, B. P., Yadrick, R. M., Connolly-Gomez, C., Regian, W., & Shebilske, W. L. (1996). Alternating task modules in isochronal distributed training of complex tasks. *Human Factors, 38,* 330–346.

Goff, L. M., & Roediger, H. L. (1998). Imagination inflation for action events: Repeated imaginings lead to illusory recollections. *Memory & Cognition, 26,* 20–33.

Goff, M., & Ackerman, P. L. (1992). Personality-intelligence relations: Assessment of typical intellectual engagement. *Journal of Educational Psychology, 84,* 537–552.

Gold, P. E. (1987). Sweet memories. *American Scientist, 75,* 151–155.

Gold, P. E. (1992). Modulation of memory processing: Enhancement of memory in rodents and humans. In L. R. Squire & N. Butters (Eds.), *Neuropsychology of memory* (2nd ed., pp. 402–414). New York: Guilford Press.

Goldman, M. S. (1983). Cognitive impairment in chronic alcoholics. *American Psychologist, 38,* 1045–1054.

Goldman-Rakic, P. (1996). Regional and cellular fractionation of working memory. *Proceedings of the National Academy of Sciences, 93,* 13473–13480.

Goldsmith, T. E., Johnson, P. J., & Acton, W. H. (1991). Assessing structural knowledge. *Journal of Educational Psychology, 83,* 88–96.

Goldstone, R. L. (1998). Perceptual learning. *Annual Review of Psychology, 49,* 585–612.

Goodenough, D. R. (1976). The role of individual differences in field dependence as a factor in learning and memory. *Psychological Bulletin, 83,* 675–694.

Goodwin, C. J. (1991). Misportraying Pavlov's apparatus. *American Journal of Psychology, 104,* 135–141.

Goody, J. (1998). Memory in the oral tradition. In P. Fara and K. Patteson (Eds.), *Memory* (pp. 73–94) Cambridge, UK: Cambridge University Press.

Gordon, W. C. (1989). *Learning and memory.* Pacific Grove, CA: Brooks Cole.

Gormezano, I. (1966). Classical conditioning. In J. B. Sidowski (Ed.), *Experimental methods and instrumentation in psychology* (pp. 385–420). New York: McGraw-Hill.

Gormezano, I., & Coleman, S. R. (1973). The law of effect and CR contingent modification of the UCS. *Conditional Reflex, 8,* 41–56.

Gormezano, I., & Kehoe, E. (1975). Classical conditioning: Some methodological-conceptual issues. In W. K. Estes (Ed.), *Handbook of learning and cognitive processes* (Vol. 2, pp. 143–179). Hillsdale, NJ: Erlbaum.

Gormezano, I., & Moore, J. W. (1969). Classical conditioning. In M. H. Marx (Ed.), *Learning: Processes* (pp. 212–203). Toronto, Canada: Macmillan.

Gorn, G. J. (1982, Winter). The effects of music in advertising on choice behavior: A classical conditioning approach. *Journal of Marketing, 46,* 94–101.

Gould, J. L., & Able, K. P. (1981). Human homing: An elusive phenomenon. *Science, 212,* 1061–1063.

Gould, S. J. (1990, August). Muller Bros. Moving & Storage. *Natural History,* 12–16.

Grady, C. L., McIntosh, A. R., Horwits, B., Maisog, J., Ungerleider, L. G., Mentis, M. J., Pietrini, P., Schapiro, M. B., & Haxby, J. V. (1995). Age-related reductions in human recognition memory due to impaired encoding. *Science, 269,* 218–220.

Graf, P., & Schacter, D. L. (1987). Selective effects of interference on implicit and explicit memory for new associations. *Journal of Experimental Psychology: Learning, Memory, and Cognition, 13,* 45–53.

Graf, P., & Schacter, D. L. (1989). Unitization and grouping mediate dissociations in memory for new associations. *Journal of Experimental Psychology: Learning, Memory, and Cognition, 15,* 930–940.

Graf, P., Squire, L., & Mandler, G. (1984). The information that amnesic patients do not forget. *Journal of Experimental Psychology: Learning, Memory, and Cognition, 10,* 164–178.

Grant, D. S. (1982). Stimulus control of information processing in rat short-term memory. *Journal of Experimental Psychology: Animal Behavior Processes, 8,* 154–164.

Grant, L., & Evans, A. (1994). *Principles of behavior analysis.* New York: HarperCollins.

Gratzinger, P., Sheikh, J. I., Friedman, L., & Yesavage, J. A. (1990). Cognitive interventions to improve face-name recall: The role of personality trait differences. *Developmental Psychology, 26,* 889–893.

Gray, J. A. (1972). The psychophysiological basis of introversion-extraversion: Modification of Eysenck's theory. In V. D. Nebylitsyn & J. A. Gray (Eds.), *The biological bases of individual behavior* (pp. 372–399). New York: Academic Press.

Green, R. (1991, August 18). Woods: Shorten shorts days. *Charlotte Observer,* p. 14C.

Greene, R. L. (1986). Sources of recency effects in free recall. *Psychological Bulletin, 99,* 221–228.

Greenough, W. T. (1985). The possible role of experience-dependent synaptogenesis, or synapses on demand, in the memory process. In N. M. Weinberger, J. L. McGaugh, & G. Lynch (Eds.), *Memory Systems of the Brain* (pp. 77–103). New York: Guilford.

Greenspoon, J. (1955). The reinforcing effect of two spoken sounds on the frequency of two responses. *American Journal of Psychology, 68,* 409–416.

Greenwald, A. G., & Banaji, M. R. (1995). Implicit cognition: Attitudes, self-esteem, and stereotypes. *Psychological Review, 102,* 4–27.

Grigorenko, E. L., & Sternberg, R. J. (1997). Styles of thinking, abilities, and academic performance. *Exceptional Children, 63,* 295–312.

Groninger, L. D., Groninger, D. H., & Stiens, J. (1995). Learning the names of people: The role of image mediators. *Memory, 3,* 147–167.

Groves, P. M., & Thompson, R. F. (1970). Habituation: A dual-process theory. *Psychological Review, 77,* 419–450.

Gudjonsson, G. H. (1979). The use of electrodermal response in a case of amnesia. *Medicine, Science and the Law, 19,* 138–140.

Gunter, B., Berry, C., & Clifford, B. R. (1981). Proactive interference effects with television news items: Further evidence. *Journal of Experimental Psychology: Human Learning and Memory, 7,* 480–487.

Gunther, L. M., Miller, R. R., Matute, H. (1997). CSs and USs: What's the difference? *Journal of Experimental Psychology: Animal Behavior Processes, 23,* 15–30.

Gupta, S., & Shukla, A. P. (1989). Verbal operant conditioning as a function of extraversion and reinforcement. *British Journal of Psychology, 80,* 39–44.

Gustavson, C. R. (1977). Comparative and field aspects of learned food aversions. In L. M. Barker, M. R. Best, & M. Domjan (Eds.), *Learning mechanisms in food selection* (pp. 23–44). Waco, TX: Baylor University Press.

Gustavson, C. R., & Garcia, J. (1974, August). Pulling a gag on the wily coyote. *Psychology Today, 8(3),* 68–72.

Guthrie, J. P., Ash, R. A., & Bendapudi, V. (1995). Additional validity evidence for a measure of morningness. *Journal of Applied Psychology, 80,* 186–190.

Haberlandt, K. (1971). Transfer along a continuum in classical conditioning. *Learning and Motivation, 2,* 164–172.

Hagan, J. W., Barclay, C. R., Anderson, B. J., Feeman, D. J., Segal, S. S., Bacon, G., & Goldstein, G. W. (1990). Intellective functioning and strategy use in children with insulin dependent diabetes mellitus. *Child Development, 61,* 1714–1727.

Hall, G. (1994). Pavlovian conditioning: Laws of association. In N. J. Mackintosh (Ed.), *Animal learning and cognition* (pp. 15–43). San Diego, CA: Academic Press.

Hall, G., & Channell, S. (1985). Differential effects of contextual change on latent inhibition and on the habituation of an orienting response. *Journal of Experimental Psychology: Animal Behavior Processes, 11,* 470–481.

Hall, G., & Honey, R. (1989). Perceptual and associative learning. In S. B. Klein & R. R. Mowrer (Eds.), *Contemporary learning theories: Pavlovian conditioning and the status of traditional learning theory* (pp. 117–147). Hillsdale, NJ: Earlbaum.

Hall, G., & Schachtman, T. R. (1987). Differential effects of a retention interval on latent inhibition and the habituation of an orienting response. *Animal Learning & Behavior, 15,* 76–82.

Hall, J. L., Gonder-Frederick, L. A., Chewning, W. W., Silveira, J., & Gold, P. E. (1989). Glucose enhancement of performance on memory tests in young and aged humans. *Neuropsychologia, 27,* 1129–1138.

Hall, S. S. (1998, February 15). Our memories, our selves. *The New York Times Magazine,* 26–33, 49, 56–57.

Hapern, D. (1989). The disappearance of cognitive gender differences: What you see depends on where you look. *American Psychologist, 44,* 1156–1157.

Hamann, S. B., Squire, L. R., & Schacter, D. L. (1995). Perceptual thresholds and priming in amnesia. *Neuropsychology, 9,* 3–15.

Hammerl, M., & Bloch, M., & Silverthorne, C. P. (1997). Effects of US-alone presentations on human evaluative conditioning. *Learning and Motivation, 28,* 491–509.

Hampson, E. & Kimura, D. (1988). Reciprocal effects of hormonal fluctuations of human motor and perceptual-spatial skills. *Behavioral Neuroscience, 102,* 456–459.

Hanley-Dunn, P., & McIntosh, J. L. (1984). Meaningfulness and recall of names by young and old adults. *Journal of Gerontology, 39,* 583–585.

Harlow, H. F. (1959). Love in infant monkeys. *Scientific American, 200(6),* 68–74.

Harrington, D. L., Haaland, K. Y., Yeo, R. A., & Marder, E. (1990). Procedural memory in Parkinson's disease: Impaired motor but not visuoperceptual learning. *Journal of Clinical and Experimental Neuropsychology, 12,* 323–339.

Harris, B. (1979). Whatever happened to Little Albert? *American Psychologist, 34,* 151–160.

Harris, J. E. (1978). External memory aids. In M. M. Gruneberg, P. E. Morris, & R. N. Sykes (Eds.),

Practical aspects of memory (pp. 172–179). London: Academic Press.

Harris, J. E. (1980). Memory aids people use: Two interview studies. *Memory & Cognition, 8,* 31–38.

Harris, J. E. (1984). Remembering to do things: A forgotten topic. In J. E. Harris & P. E. Morris (Eds.), *Everyday memory, actions and absentmindedness* (pp. 71–92). New York: Academic Press.

Harris, J. R. (2000). Context-specific learning, personality, and birth order. *Current Directions in Psychological Science, 9,* 174–177.

Hart, J. T. (1965). Memory and the feeling-of-knowing experience. *Journal of Educational Psychology, 56,* 208–216.

Hasher, L., & Griffin, M. (1978). Reconstructive and reproductive processes in memory. *Journal of Experimental Psychology: Human Learning and Memory, 4,* 318–330.

Hasher, L., & Zacks, R. T. (1988). Working memory, comprehension, and aging: A review and a new view. *The Psychology of Learning and Motivation, 22,* 193–225.

Hastie, R., & Kumar, P. A. (1979). Person memory: Personality traits as organizing principles in memory for behaviors. *Journal of Personality and Social Psychology, 37,* 25–38.

Haut, J. S., Beckwith, B. E., Petros, T. V., & Russell, S. (1989). Gender differences in retrieval for long-term memory following acute intoxication with ethanol. *Physiology & Behavior, 45,* 1161–1165.

Hawkins, R. D., Cohen, T. E., Greene, W., & Kandel, E. R. (1998). Relationships between dishabituation, sensitization, and inhibition of the gill- and siphon-withdrawal reflex in *Aplysia californica:* Effects of response measure, test time, and training stimulus. *Behavioral Neuroscience, 112,* 24–38.

Hayes, B. K., & Delamothe, K. (1997). Cognitive interviewing procedures and suggestibility in children's recall. *Journal of Applied Psychology, 82,* 562–577.

Healy, A. F., & Bourne, L. E. (1995). *Learning and memory of knowledge and skills.* Thousand Oaks, CA: Sage.

Healy, A. F., Clawson, D. M., McNamara, D. S., Marmie, W. R., Schneider, V. I., Rickard, T. C., Crutcher, R. J., King, C. L., Ericsson, K. A., & Bourne, L. E. (1993). The long-term retention of knowledge and skills. *The Psychology of Learning and Motivation, 30,* 135–164.

Healy, A. F., & McNamara, D. S. (1996). Verbal learning and memory: Does the modal model still work? *Annual Review of Psychology, 47,* 143–172.

Heaps, C., & Nash, M. (1999). Individual differences in imagination inflation. *Psychonomic Bulletin & Review, 6,* 313–318.

Hearst, E., & Jenkins, H. M. (1974). *Sign tracking: The stimulus-reinforcer relation and directed action.* Austin, TX: Psychonomic Society.

Hebb, D. O. (1949). *Organization of behavior.* New York: Wiley.

Hebb, D. O. (1955). Drives and the C. N. S. (conceptual nervous system). *Psychological Review, 62,* 243–254.

Heindel, W. C., Butters, N., & Salmon, D. P. (1988). Impaired learning of a motor skill in patients with Huntington's disease. *Behavioral Neuroscience, 102,* 141–147.

Hepper, P. G. (1989). Foetal learning: Implications for psychiatry? *British Journal of Psychiatry, 155,* 289–293.

Herlitz, A., Nilsson, L. G., & Backman, L. (1997). Gender differences in episodic memory. *Memory & Cognition, 25,* 801–811.

Herman, L. M., & Gordon, J. A. (1974). Auditory delayed matching in the bottlenose dolphin. *Journal of the Experimental Analysis of Behavior, 21,* 19–26.

Herrmann, D. J. (1987). Task appropriateness of mnemonic techniques. *Perceptual and Motor Skills, 64,* 171–178.

Herrmann, D. J., Crawford, M., & Holdsworth, M. (1992). Gender-linked differences in everyday memory performance. *British Journal of Psychology, 83,* 221–231.

Heth, C. D. (1976). Simultaneous and backward fear conditioning as a function of number of CS-UCS pairings. *Journal of Experimental Psychology: Animal Behavior Processes, 2,* 117–129.

Heuer, F., & Reisberg, D. (1992). Emotion, arousal, and memory for detail. In S.-A. Christianson (Ed.), *The handbook of emotion and memory* (pp. 151–180). Hillsdale, NJ: Erlbaum.

Higbee, K. L. (1994). More motivational aspects of an imagery mnemonic. *Applied Cognitive Psychology, 8,* 1–12.

Hilgard, E. R., Jones, L. V., & Kaplan, S. J. (1951). Conditioned discrimination as related to anxiety. *Journal of Experimental Psychology, 42,* 94–99.

Hill, W. F. (1978). Effects of mere exposure on preferences in nonhuman animals. *Psychological Bulletin, 85,* 1177–1198.

Hillner, K. P. (1978). *Psychology of learning: A conceptual analysis.* New York: Pergamon Press.

Hilts, P. J. (1995). *Memory's ghost: The strange tale of Mr. M. and the nature of memory.* New York: Simon & Schuster.

Hintzman, D. L. (1967). Articulatory coding in short-term memory. *Journal of Verbal Learning and Verbal behavior, 6,* 312–316.

Hintzman, D. L. (1990). Human learning and memory: Connections and dissociations. *Annual Review of Psychology, 41,* 109–139.

Hintzman, D. L., Block, R. A., & Summers, J. J. (1973). Modality tags and memory for repetitions: Locus of the spacing effect. *Journal of Verbal Learning and Verbal Behavior, 12,* 229–238.

Hiroto, D. S. (1974). Locus of control and learned helplessness. *Journal of Experimental Psychology, 102,* 187–193.

Hirst, W., Spelke, E., Reaves, C. C., Caharack, G., & Neisser, U. (1980). Dividing attention without alternation or automaticity. *Journal of Experimental Psychology: General, 109,* 98–117.

Hogervorst, E., Riedel, W. J., Schmitt, J. A. J., & Jolles, J. (1998). Caffeine improves memory performance during distraction in middle-aged, but not in young or old subjects. *Human Psychopharmacology, 13,* 277–284.

Hollis, K. L. (1997). Contemporary research on Pavlovian conditioning: A new "functional" analysis. *American Psychologist, 52,* 956–965.

Holloway, F. A. (1978). State dependent retrieval based on time of day. In B. Ho, D. Richards, & D. Chute (Eds.), *Drug discrimination and state dependent learning* (pp. 319–344). New York: Academic Press.

Holmes, D. S. (1992). The evidence for repression: An examination of sixty years of research. In J. L. Singer (Ed.), *Repression and dissociation* (pp. 85–102). Chicago: University of Chicago Press.

Holyoak, K. J., & Mah, W. A. (1982). Cognitive reference points in judgements of symbolic magnitude. *Cognitive Psychology, 14,* 328–352.

Homme, L. E., Debaca, P. C., Devine, J. V., Steinhorst, R., & Rickert, E. J. (1963). Use of the Premack principle in controlling the behavior of nursery school children. *Journal of the Experimental Analysis of Behavior, 6,* 544.

Hornbein, T. F., et al. (1989). The cost to the central nervous system of climbing to extremely high altitude. *New England Journal of Medicine, 321,* 1714–1719.

Horowitz, L. M., Lampel, A. K., & Takoniski, R. N. (1969). The child's memory for unitized scenes. *Journal of Experimental Child Psychology, 8,* 355–388.

Horton, D. L., & Mills, C. B. (1984). Human learning and memory. *Annual Review of Psychology, 35,* 361–394.

Hostetler, A. J. (1988, January). If you said it once, you'll say it again. *APA Monitor,* p. 9.

Houston, J. P. (1983). Psychology: A closed system of self-evident information? *Psychological Reports, 52,* 203–208.

Houston, J. P. (1985). Untutored lay knowledge of the principles of psychology: Do we know anything they don't? *Psychological Reports, 57,* 567–570.

Houts, A. C., & Liebert, R. M. (1984). *Bedwetting: A guide for parents and children.* Springfield, IL: C. C. Thomas.

Hovland, C. I. (1951). Human learning and retention. In S. S. Stevens (Ed.), *Handbook of experimental psychology* (pp. 613–688). New York: Wiley.

Howard, D. V., & Howard, J. H. (1992). Adult age differences in the rate of learning serial patterns: Evidence from direct and indirect tests. *Psychology and Aging, 7,* 232–241.

Howarth, E. (1969). Personality differences in serial learning under distraction. *Perceptual and Motor Skills, 28,* 379–382.

Hudson, J. A. (1990). The emergence of autobiographical memory in mother-child conversation. In R. Fivush & J. A. Hudson (Eds.), *Knowing and remembering in young children* (pp. 166–196). New York: Cambridge University Press.

Hudson, J. A., & Nelson, K. (1983). Effect of script structure on children's story recall. *Developmental Psychology, 19,* 625–635.

Hull, C. L. (1943). *Principles of behavior.* New York: Appleton, Century, Crofts.

Hull, C. L. (1948). Reactively heterogeneous compound trial-and-error learning with distributed trials and serial reinforcement. *Journal of Experimental Psychology, 38,* 17–28.

Hull, C. L. (1949). Behavior postulates and corollaries—1949. *Psychological Review, 57,* 173–180.

Hulme, C., & Mackenzie, S. (1992). *Working memory and severe learning difficulties.* Mahwan, NJ: Erlbaum.

Hunt, E., & Love, T. (1982). The second mnemonist. In U. Neisser (Ed.), *Memory observed* (pp. 390–398). San Francisco: Freeman.

Hunt, R. R. (1995). The subtlety of distinctiveness: What von Restorff really did. *Psychonomic Bulletin & Review, 2,* 105–112.

Hunt, R. R., & Elliott, J. M. (1980). The role of nonsemantic information in memory: Orthographic distinctiveness effects on retention. *Journal of Experimental Psychology: General, 109,* 49–74.

Huston, J. P., Mondadori, C., & Waser, P. G, (1974). Facilitation of learning by reward of post-trial memory processes. *Experientia, 30,* 1038–1040.

Hyde, T. S., & Jenkins, J. J. (1969). Differential effects of incidental tasks on the organization of recall of a list of highly associated words. *Journal of Experimental Psychology, 82,* 472–481.

Hydén, H., & Egyhazi, E. (1963). Glial RNA changes during a learning experiment with rats. *Proceedings of the National Academy of Sciences, 49,* 618–624.

Hypnotized witnesses may remember too much. (1978, February). *American Bar Association Journal, 624,* 187.

Ince, L. P., Brucker, B. S., & Alba, A. (1978). Reflex conditioning of a spinal man. *Journal of Comparative and Physiological Psychology, 92,* 796–802.

Inhoff, A. W., & Gordon, A. M. (1997). Eye movements and eye-hand coordination during typing. *Current Directions in Psychological Science, 6,* 153–157.

Intons-Peterson, M. J., & Smyth, M. M. (1987). The anatomy of repertory memory. *Journal of Experimental Psychology: Learning, Memory, and Cognition, 13,* 490–500.

Israel, L., & Schacter, D. L. (1997). Pictorial encoding reduces false recognition of semantic associates. *Psychonomic Bulletin & Review, 4,* 577–581.

Jacoby, L. L., Kelley, C. M., Brown, J., & Jasechko, J. (1989). Becoming famous overnight: Limits on the ability to avoid unconscious influences of the past. *Journal of Personality and Social Psychology, 56,* 326–338.

James, W. (1890). *The principles of psychology* (2 vols.) New York: Henry Holt. (Dover reprint edition, 1950).

Janet, P. (1907). *The major symptoms of hysteria.* New York: Macmillan.

Janis, I. L., & Astrachan, M. (1951). The effects of electroconvulsive treatments on memory efficiency. *Journal of Abnormal and Social Psychology, 46,* 501–511.

Janowsky, J. S., Shimamura, A. P., Kritchevsky, M., & Squire, L. R. (1989). Cognitive impairment following frontal lobe damage and its relevance to human amnesia. *Behavioral Neuroscience, 103,* 548–560.

Jenkins, H. M., & Moore, B. R. (1973). The form of the autoshaped response with food or water reinforcers. *Journal of the Experimental Analysis of Behavior, 20,* 163–181.

Jenkins, J. G., & Dallenbach, K. M. (1924). Obliviscence during sleep and waking. *American Journal of Psychology, 35,* 605–612.

Jenkins, J. J., & Russell, W. A. (1952). Associative clustering during recall. *Journal of Abnormal and Social Psychology, 47,* 818–821.

Jensen, A. R. (1962). Temporal and spatial effects of serial position. *American Journal of Psychology, 75,* 390–400.

Johnson, M. K. (1988). Reality monitoring: An experimental phenomenological approach. *Journal of Experimental Psychology: General, 117,* 390–394.

Johnson, M. K., Foley, M. A., Suengas, A. G., & Raye, C. L. (1988). Phenomenal characteristics of memories for perceived and imagined autobiographical events. *Journal of Experimental Psychology: General, 117,* 371–376.

Johnson, M. K., Kahan, T. L., & Raye, C. L. (1984). Dreams and reality monitoring. *Journal of Experimental Psychology: General, 113,* 329–344.

Johnson, M. K., Nolde, S. F., Mather, M., Kounios, J., Schacter, D. L., & Curran, T. (1997). The similarity of brain activity associated with true and false recognition memory depends on test format. *Psychological Science, 8,* 250–257.

Johnson, M. K., & Raye, C. L. (1981). Reality monitoring. *Psychological Review, 88,* 67–85.

Johnson, W. G. (1974). The effects of cue prominence and obesity on effort to obtain food. In S. Schacter & J. Rodin (Eds.), *Obese humans and rats* (pp. 53–60). Hillsdale, NJ: Erlbaum.

Jones, B. F., & Hall, J. W. (1982). School applications of the mnemonic keyword method as a study strategy by eighth graders. *Journal of Educational Psychology, 74,* 230–237.

Jones, M. C. (1924). The elimination of children's fears. *Journal of Experimental Psychology, 7,* 382–390.

Jones, W. T. (1952). *A history of Western philosophy.* New York: Harcourt, Brace & World.

Kail, R. (1990). *The development of memory in children* (3rd ed.). New York: Freeman.

Kalish, H. I. (1958). The relationship between discriminability and generalization: A re-examination. *Journal of Experimental Psychology, 55,* 637–644.

Kamin, L. J. (1956). The effects of termination of the CS and avoidance of the US on avoidance learning. *Journal of Comparative and Physiological Psychology, 49,* 420–424.

Kamin, L. J. (1969). Predictability, surprise, attention, and conditioning. In B. A. Campbell & R. M. Church (Eds.), *Punishment* (pp. 279–296). New York: Appleton, Century, Crofts.

Kandel, E. R. (2001). The molecular biology of memory storage: A dialogue between genes and synapses. *Science, 294,* 1030–1038.

Karni, A., Tanne, D., Rubenstein, B. S., Askenasy, J. M., & Sage, D. (1994). Dependence on REM sleep of overnight improvement of a perceptual skill. *Science, 265,* 679–682.

Kassin, S. M., Tubb, V. A., Hosch, H. M., & Memon, A. (2001). On the "general acceptance" of eyewitness testimony research. *American Psychologist, 56,* 405–416.

Kausler, D. H., Wiley, J. G., & Lieberwitz, K. J. (1992). Adult age differences in short-term memory and subsequent long-term memory for actions. *Psychology and Aging, 7,* 309–316.

Kazdin, A. E. (1987). *Conduct disorders in childhood and adolescence.* Newbury Park, CA: Sage.

Kazdin, A. E. (1994). *Behavior modification in applied settings* (5th ed.). Pacific Grove, CA: Brooks/Cole.

Kazdin, A. E., & Wilcoxon, L. A. (1976). Systematic desensitization and nonspecific treatment effects: A methodological evaluation. *Psychological Bulletin, 83,* 729–758.

Kearins, J. M. (1981). Visual spatial memory in Australian aboriginal children of desert regions. *Cognitive Psychology, 13,* 434–460.

Keenan, J., McWhinney, B., & Mayhew, D. (1977). Pragmatics in memory: A study of natural conversation. *Journal of Verbal Learning and Verbal Behavior, 17,* 549–560.

Keeney, T. J., Cannizzo, S. R., & Flavell, J. H. (1967). Spontaneous and induced rehearsal in a recall task. *Child Development, 38,* 953–966.

Kempermann, G., Kuhn, H. G., & Gage, F. H. (1997). More hippocampal neurons in adult mice living in an enriched environment. *Nature, 386,* 493–495.

Kendler, H. K. (1987). *Historical foundations of modern psychology.* Chicago: Dorsey.

Kennedy, T. E., Hawkins, R. D., & Kandel, E. R. (1992). Molecular interrelationships between short-term and long-term memory. In L. R. Squire & N. Butters (Eds.), *Neuropsychology of memory* (pp. 557–574). New York: Guilford Press.

Keppel, G. (1964). Facilitation in short- and long-term retention of paired associates following distributed practice in learning. *Journal of Verbal Learning and Verbal Behavior, 3,* 91–111.

Kesner, R. P., Hopkins, R. O., & Chiba, A. A. (1992). Learning and memory in humans, with an emphasis on the role of the hippocampus. In L. R. Squire and N. Butters (Eds.), *Neuropsychology of memory* (pp. 106–121). New York: Guilford Press.

Kientzle, M. J. (1949). Ability patterns under distributed practice. *Journal of Experimental Psychology, 39,* 532–537.

Kiewra, K. A., DuBois, N. F., Christian, D., McShane, A., Meyerhoffer, M., & Roskelley, D. (1991). Notetaking functions and techniques. *Journal of Educational Psychology, 83,* 240–245.

Kihlstrom. J. F. (1987). The cognitive unconscious. *Science, 237,* 1445–1452.

Kihlstrom, J. F., Schacter, D. L., Cork, R. C., Hurt, C. A. & Behr, S. E. (1990). Implicit and explicit memory following surgical anesthesia. *Psychological Science, 1,* 303–306.

Kim, J., Allen, C. T., & Kardes, F. R. (1996). An investigation of the mediational mechanisms underlying attitudinal conditioning. *Journal of Marketing Research, XXXIII,* 318.

Kimble, G. A. (1967). The definition of learning and some useful distinctions. In G. A. Kimble (Ed.), *Foundations of conditioning and learning* (pp. 82–99). New York: Appleton, Century, Crofts.

Kintsch, W. (1970). *Learning, memory, and conceptual processes.* New York: John Wiley and Sons.

Kirby, F. D., & Shields, F. (1972). Modification of arithmetic response rate and attending behavior in a seventh-grade student. *Journal of Applied Behavior Analysis, 5 ,* 79–84.

Klatzky, R. L. (1984). *Memory and awareness: An information-processing perspective.* New York: Freeman.

Klein, D. C., & Seligman, M. E. P. (1976). Reversal of performance deficits and perceptual deficits in learned helplessness and depression. *Journal of Abnormal Psychology, 85,* 11–26.

Knee, K. (1990). Memory of specific learning disabled readers using the California Verbal Learning Test for Children. American Psychological Association Meeting. Eric Document 350792.

Kobre, K. R., & Lipsitt, L. P. (1972). A negative contrast effect in newborns. *Journal of Experimental Child Psychology, 14,* 81–91.

Kohn, A. (1993). *Punished by rewards: The trouble with gold stars, incentive plans, A's, praise, and other bribes.* Boston: Houghton Mifflin.

Kolb, B., & Whishaw, I. Q. (1985). *Fundamentals of human neuropsychology* (2nd ed.). New York: Freeman.

Kolb, D. A. (1984). *Experiential learning: Experience as the source of learning and development.* Englewood Cliffs, NJ: Prentice Hall.

Kolers, P. A. (1975). Memorial consequences of automatized encoding. *Journal of Experimental Psychology: Human Learning and Memory, 1,* 689–701.

Konorski, J. (1967). *Integrative activity of the brain.* Chicago: University of Chicago Press.

Kopelman, M. D. (1987). Amnesia: Organic and psychogenic. *British Journal of Psychiatry, 150,* 428–442.

Kopelman, M. D. (1994). Working memory in the amnesic syndrome and degenerative dementia. *Neuropsychology, 8,* 555–562.

Koriat, A. (1997). Monitoring one's own knowledge during study: A cue-utilization approach to judgments of learning. *Journal of Experimental Psychology: General, 126,* 349–370.

Koulack, D., & Goodenough, D. R. (1976). Dream recall and dream recall failure: An arousal-retrieval model. *Psychological Bulletin, 83,* 975–984.

Kozlowski, L. T., & Bryant, K. J. (1977). Sense of direction, spatial orientation, and cognitive maps. *Journal of Experimental Psychology: Human Perception and Performance, 3,* 590–598.

Kozma, A. (1969). The effects of anxiety, stimulation, and isolation on social reinforcer effectiveness. *Journal of Experimental Child Psychology, 8,* 1–8.

Kraiger, K., Ford, J. K., & Salas, E. (1993). Application of cognitive, skill-based, and affective theories of learning outcomes to new methods of training evaluation. *Journal of Applied Psychology, 78,* 311–328.

Kramer, J. J., Nagle, R. J., & Engle, R. W. (1980). Recent advances in mnemonic strategy training with mentally retarded persons: Implications for educational practice. *American Journal of Mental Deficiency, 85,* 306–314.

Krane, R. V., & Wagner, A. R. (1975). Taste aversion learning with a delayed shock US: Implications for the "generality of the laws of learning." *Journal of Comparative and Physiological Psychology, 88,* 882–889.

Kreutzer, M. A., Leonard, C., & Flavell, J. H. (1975). An interview study about children's knowledge about memory. *Monographs of the Society for Research in Child Development, 40*(1).

Kreutzer, M. A., Leonard, C., & Flavell, J. H. (1982). Prospective remembering in children. In U. Neisser (Ed.), *Memory observed* (pp. 343–348). San Francisco: Freeman.

Krug, D., Davis, T. B., & Glover, J. A. (1990). Massed versus distributed repeated reading: A case of forgetting helping recall? *Journal of Educational Psychology, 82,* 366–371.

Kuhara-Kojima, K., & Hatano, G. (1991). Contribution of content knowledge and learning ability to the learning of facts. *Journal of Educational Psychology, 83,* 253–263.

Kulhavy, R. W., Dyer, H. W., & Silver, L. (1975). The effects of notetaking and test expectancy on the learning of text material. *Journal of Educational Research, 68,* 363–365.

Kulhavy, R. W., Schwartz, N. H., & Peterson, S. (1986). Working memory: The encoding process. In G. D. Phye & T. Andre (Eds.), *Cognitive classroom learning* (pp. 115–140). New York: Academic Press.

Kunovich, S. S., & Rashid, R. G. (1992). Mirror training in three dimensions for dental students. *Perceptual & Motor Skills, 75,* 923–928.

Kunst-Wilson, W. R., & Zajonc, R. B. (1980). Affective discrimination of stimuli that cannot be recognized. *Science, 207,* 557–558.

Kurbat, M. A., Shevell, S. K., Rips, L. J. (1998). A year's memories: The calendar effect in autobiographical memory. *Memory & Cognition, 26,* 532–552.

Kurtz-Costes, B., Schneider, W., & Rupp, S. (1995). Is there evidence for intraindividual consistency in performance across memory tasks? New evidence on an old question. In F. E. Weinert and W. Schneider (Eds.), *Memory performance and competencies: Issues in growth and development* (pp. 245–262). Hillsdale, NJ: Erlbaum.

Kvavilashvili, L. (1992). Remembering intentions: A critical review of existing experimental paradigms. *Applied Cognitive Psychology, 6,* 507–524.

Lamming, M., Brown, P., Carter, K., Eldridge, M., Flynn, M., Louie, G., Robinson, P., & Sellen, A. (1994). The design of a human memory prosthesis. *The Computer Journal, 37,* 153–163.

Landauer, T. K. (1969). Reinforcement as consolidation. *Psychological Review, 76,* 82–96.

Landauer, T. K., & Bjork, B. J. (1978). Optimum rehearsal patterns and name learning. In M. M. Gruneberg, P. E. Morris, & R. N. Sykes (Eds.), *Practical aspects of memory* (pp. 625–632). New York: Academic Press.

Landers, S. (1987, December). Aversive device sparks controversy. *APA Monitor,* p. 15.

Landers, S. (1988, June). Skinner joins aversives debate. *APA Monitor,* p. 22.

Lang, P. J., & Melamed, B. G. (1969). Avoidance conditioning therapy of an infant with chronic ruminative vomiting. *Journal of Abnormal Psychology, 74,* 1–8.

Langer, E. J., Rodin, J., Beck, P., Weinman, C., & Sptizer, L. (1979). Environmental determinants of memory improvement in late adulthood. *Journal of Personality and Social Psychology, 37,* 2003–2013.

Lashley, K. S. (1917). The effect of strychnine and caffeine upon rate of learning. *Psychobiology, 1,* 141–170.

Lashley, K. S. (1929). *Brain mechanisms and intelligence.* Chicago: University of Chicago Press (Dover reprint, 1963).

Lashley, K. S. (1951). The problem of serial order in behavior. In L. A. Jeffress (Ed.), *Cerebral Mechanisms in Behavior* (pp. 112–136). New York: Wiley.

Lazarus, R. S. (1982). Thoughts on the relations between emotion and cognition. *American Psychologist, 37,* 1019–1024.

Lawton, C. A. (1994). Gender differences in way-finding strategies: Relationship to spatial ability and spatial anxiety. *Sex Roles, 30,* 765–779.

Leaton, R. N., & Buck, R. L. (1971). Habituation of the arousal response in rats. *Journal of Comparative and Physiological Psychology, 75,* 430–434.

Leccese, A. P., & Grant, D. S. (1980). Posttrial injections of strynine sulfate: Facilitation of consolidation or retrieval? *Animal Learning & Behavior, 8,* 258–264.

Lechner, H. A., Squire, L. R., & Byrne, J. H. (1999, March/April). 100 years of consolidation: Remembering Muller and Pilzecker. *Learning & Memory, 6,* 77–87.

Lee, C. L., & Estes, W. K. (1977). Order and position in primary memory for letter strings. *Journal of Verbal Learning and Verbal Behavior, 16,* 395–416.

Lehner, G. F. (1941). A study of the extinction of unconditioned reflexes. *Journal of Experimental Psychology, 29,* 435–456.

Lemonick, M. D. (1995, July 24). Einstein strikes again. *Time,* 55.

Lenehan, M. (1986, April). Four ways to walk a dog. *The Atlantic Monthly,* 35–48, 89–99.

Lenneberg, E. H. (1967). *Biological foundations of language.* New York: Wiley.

Lepper, M. R., Greene, D., & Nisbett, R. E. (1973). Undermining children's intrinsic interest with extrinsic rewards: A test of the overjustification hypothesis.

Journal of Personality and Social Psychology, 28, 129–137.

Levin, H. S., Lilly, M. A., Papanicolaou, A., & Eisenberg, H. M. (1992). Posttraumatic and retrograde amnesia after closed head injury. In L. Squire & N. Butters (Eds.), *Neuropsychology of memory* (2nd ed., pp. 290–308). New York: Guilford Press.

Levin, I. P., & Hinrichs, J. V. (1995). *Experimental psychology: Contemporary methods and applications.* Madison, WI: WCB Brown & Benchmark.

Levin, M. E., & Levin, J. R. (1990). Scientific mnemonomoes: Method for maximizing more than memory. *American Educational Research Journal, 27,* 301–321.

Levine, M., Marchon, I., & Hanley, G. L. (1984). The placement and misplacement of you-are-here maps. *Environment and Behavior, 16,* 139–157.

Levinger, G., & Clark, J. (1961). Emotional factors in the forgetting of word associations. *Journal of Abnormal and Social Psychology, 62,* 99–105.

Lewis, D. J. (1979). Psychobiology of active and inactive memory. *Psychological Bulletin, 86,* 1054–1083.

Lewis, D. J., & Duncan, C. P. (1958). Expectation and resistance to extinction of a lever-pulling response as a function of percentage of reinforcment and number of acquisition trials. *Journal of Experimental Psychology, 55,* 121–128.

Ley, P., Bradshaw, P. W., Eaves, D., & Walker, C. M. (1973). A method for increasing patients' recall of information presented by doctors. *Psychological Medicine, 3,* 217–220.

Leyland, M., Robbins, T., & Iverson, S. D. (1976). Locomotor activity and exploration: The use of traditional manipulators to dissociate these two behaviors in the rat. *Animal Learning & Behavior, 4,* 262–265.

Lieberman, D. A., McIntosh, D. C., & Thomas, G. V. (1979). Learning when reward is delayed: A marking hypothesis. *Journal of Experimental Psychology: Animal Behavior Processes, 5,* 224–242.

Light, L. L., & Anderson, P. A. (1985). Working memory capacity, age, and memory for discourse. *Journal of Gerontology, 40,* 737–747.

Linden, W. (1981). Exposure treatments for focal phobias. *Archives of General Psychiatry, 38,* 769–775.

Linscheid, T. R., Iwata, B. A., Ricketts, R. W., Williams, D. E., & Griffin, J. C. (1990). Clinical evaluation of the self-injurious behavior inhibiting system (SIBIS). *Journal of Applied Behavior Analysis, 23,* 53–78.

Linton, M. (1982). Transformations of memory in everyday life. In U. Neisser (Ed.), *Memory Observed* (pp. 77–91). San Francisco: Freeman.

Little, A. H., Lipsitt, L. P., & Rovee-Collier, C. K. (1984). Classical conditioning and retention of the infant's eyelid response: Effects of age and inter-

stimulus interval. *Journal of Experimental Child Psychology, 37,* 512–524.

Littman, R. A., & Manning, H. M. (1954). A methodological study of cigarette brand discrimination. *Journal of Applied Psychology, 38,* 185–190.

Liu, D., et al. (1997). Maternal care, hippocampal glucocorticoid receptors, and hypothalamic-pituitary-adrenal responses to stress. *Science, 277,* 1659–1662.

Lobb, H., & Hardwick, C. (1976). Eyelid conditioning and intellectual level: Effects of repeated acquisition and extinction. *American Journal of Mental Deficiency, 80,* 423–430.

Locke, J. (1690/1956). *An essay concerning human understanding.* Chicago: Geteway Edition, Henry Regnery.

Locke, J. L., & Fehr, F. S. (1971). Young children's use of the speech code in a recall task. *Journal of Experimental Child Psychology, 10,* 367–373.

Lockhead, G. R., & Crist, W. B. (1980). Making letters distinctive. *Journal of Educational Psychology, 72,* 483–493.

Loftus, E. F. (1979). *Eyewitness testimony.* Cambridge: Harvard University Press.

Loftus, E. F. (1991). Made in memory: Distortions of recollection after misleading information. In G. Bower (Ed.), *Psychology of learning and motivation* (Vol. 27, pp. 187–215). New York: Academic Press.

Loftus, E. F., & Burns, T. E. (1982). Mental shock can produce retrograde amnesia. *Memory & Cognition, 10,* 318–323.

Loftus, E. F., & Ketcham, K. (1994). *The myth of repressed memory.* New York: St. Martin's Press.

Loftus, E. F., & Loftus, G. R. (1980). On the permanence of stored information in the brain. *American Psychologist, 35,* 409–420.

Loftus, E. F., Loftus, G., & Messo, J. (1987). Some facts about "weapon focus." *Law and Human Behavior, 11,* 55–62.

Loftus, E. F., Miller, D. G., & Burns, H. J. (1978). Semantic integration of verbal information into a visual memory. *Journal of Experimental Psychology: Human Learning and Memory, 4,* 19–31.

Loftus, E. F., & Palmer, J. C. (1974). Reconstruction of automobile destruction: An example of the interaction between language and memory. *Journal of Verbal Learning and Verbal Behavior, 13,* 585–589.

Loftus, E. F., & Pickrell, J. E. (1995). The formation of false memories. *Psychiatric Annals, 25,* 720–725.

Loftus, E. F., Smith, K. D., Klinger, M. R., & Fiedler, J. (1992). Memory and mismemory for health events. In J. M. Tanur (Ed.), *Questions about questions* (pp. 102–137). New York: Russell Sage Foundation.

Logan, F. A., & Wagner, A. R. (1962). Direction of change in CS in eyelid conditioning. *Journal of Experimental Psychology, 64,* 325–326.

Logigian, E. L., Kaplan, R. F., & Steere, A. C. (1990). Chronic neurologic manifestatons of Lyme disease. *New England Journal of Medicine, 323,* 1438–1444.

Logue, A. W., Forzano, L. B., & Ackerman, K. T. (1996). Self-control in children: Age, preference for reinforcer amount and delay, and language ability. *Learning and Motivation, 27,* 269–277.

Lord, A. B. (1960). *The singer of tales.* Cambridge: Harvard University Press.

Luborsky, L. (1988). Recurrent momentary forgetting: Its content and its context. In M. J. Horowitz (Ed.), *Psychodynamics and cognition* (pp. 223–251). Chicago: University of Chicago Press.

Lubow, R. E. (1973). Latent inhibition. *Psychological Bulletin, 79,* 398–407.

Luh, C. H. (1922). The conditions of retention. *Psychological Monographs, 31* (Whole No. 142).

Lukowiak, K., & Jacklet, J. W. (1972). Habituation and dishabituation: Interactions between peripheral and central nervous systems in Aplysia. *Science, 178,* 1306–1308.

Luria, A. R. (1968). *The mind of a mnemonist.* New York: Basic Books.

Lye, R. H., O'Boyle, D. J., Ramsden, R. T., & Schady, W. (1988). Effects of unilateral cerebellar lesion on the acquisition of eye-blink conditioning in man. *Journal of Physiology, 403,* 58P.

Lynch, G., Larson, J., Staubli, U., Ambros-Ingerson, J., & Granger, R. (1991). Long-term potentiation and memory operations in cortical networks. In R. G. Wister & H. J. Weingartner (Eds.), *Perspectives on cognitive neuroscience* (pp. 110–131). New York: Oxford University Press.

Lynch, S., & Yarnell, P. R. (1973). Retrograde amnesia: Delayed forgetting after concussion. *American Journal of Psychology, 86,* 643–645.

MacFadyen, J. T. (1986, October). Educated monkeys help the disabled to help themselves. *Smithsonian,* 125–132.

MacKinnon, M. M. (1972). Adaptation-level theory, anchor theory, and the peakshift phenomenon. *Journal of Motor Behavior, 4,* 1–12.

Mackintosh, N. J. (1974). *The psychology of animal learning.* New York: Academic Press.

Mackintosh, N. J. (1983). *Conditioning and associative learning.* New York: Oxford University Press.

MacLeod, C. M., & Dunbar, K. (1988). Training and Stroop-like interference: Evidence for a continuum of automaticity. *Journal of Experimental Psychology: Learning, Memory, and Cognition, 14,* 126–135.

Madigan, S., & O'Hara, R. (1992). Short-term memory at the turn of the century: Mary Whiton Calkins's memory research. *American Psychologist, 47,* 170–174.

Maguire, E. A., Gadian, D. G., Johnsrude, I. S., Good, Catronia D., Ashburner, J., Frackowiak, R. S., & Frith, C. D. (2000). Navigation-related structural change in the hippocampi of taxi drivers. *Proceedings of the National Academy of Science, 97* (8), 4398–4403.

Maier, N. R. F., & Schneirla, T. C. (1935). *Principles of animal psychology.* New York: McGraw-Hill.

Maier, S. F., Seligman, M. E. P., & Solomon, R. L. (1969). Pavlovian fear conditioning and learned helplessness: Effects on escape and avoidance behavior of (a) the CS-US contingency and (b) the independence of the US and voluntary responding. In B. A. Campbell & R. M. Church (Eds.), *Punishment and aversive behavior* (pp. 299–342). New York: Appleton, Century, Crofts.

Maier, S. F., Watkins, L. R., & Fleshner, M. (1994). Psychoneuroimmunology: The interface between behavior, brain and immunity. *American Psychologist, 49,* 1004–1017.

Maki, R. H. (1981). Categorization and distance effects with spatial linear orders. *Journal of Experimental Psychology: Learning, Memory, and Cognition, 7,* 15–32.

Mandler, G. (1967). Organization and memory. In G. H. Bower (Ed.), *The psychology of learning and motivation* (Vol. 1, pp. 327–372). New York: Academic Press.

Mandler, G. (1992). Memory, arousal and mood: A theoretical integration. In S.-A. Christianson (Ed.), (pp. 93–110). *The handbook of emotion and memory.* Hillsdale, NJ: Erlbaum.

Mandler, J. M., & Ritchey, G. H. (1977). Long-term memory for pictures. *Journal of Experimental Psychology: Human Learning and Memory, 3,* 386–396.

Manning, C. A., Hall, J. L., & Gold, P. E. (1990). Glucose effects on memory and other neuropsychological tests in elderly humans. *Psychological Science, 1,* 307–311.

Manning, C. A., Parsons, M. W., & Gold, P. E. (1992). Anterograde and retrograde enhancement of 24-h memory by glucose in elderly humans. *Behavioral and Neural Biology, 58,* 125–130.

Manza, L., & Bornstein, R. F. (1995). Affective discrimination and the implicit learning process. *Consciousness and Cognition, 4,* 399–409.

Manza, L., & Reber, A. (1997). Representing artificial grammars: Transfer across stimulus forms and modalities. In D. C. Berry (Ed.), *How implicit is implicit learning?* (pp. 73–106). New York: Oxford University Press.

Manza, L., Zizak, D., & Reber, A. S. (1998). Artificial grammar learning and the mere exposure effect: Emotional preference tasks and the implicit learning process. In M. A. Stadler & P. A. Frensch (Eds.),

Handbook of implicit learning (pp. 201–222). Thousand Oaks, CA: Sage.

Marks, I. (1977). Phobias and obsessions: Clinical phenomena in search of a laboratory model. In J. D. Maser and M. E. P. Seligman (Eds.), *Psychopathology: Experimental models* (pp. 174–213). San Francisco: Freeman.

Marler, P. (1970). A comparative approach to vocal learning: Song development in white-crowned sparrows. *Journal of Comparative and Physiological Psychology, 71,* 1–25.

Marlow, D. R. (1969). *Textbook of pediatric nursing.* Philadelphia: Saunders.

Marquis, D. P. (1941). Learning in the neonate: The modification of behavior under three feeding schedules. *Journal of Experimental Psychology, 29,* 263–282.

Marslen-Wilson, W. D., & Teuber, H. L. (1975). Memory for remote events in anterograde amnesia: Recognition of public figures in news photographs. *Neuropsychologia, 13,* 347–352.

Martin, A., Heyes, M. P., Salazar, A. M., Law, W. A., & Williams, J. (1993). Impaired motor skill learning, slowed reaction time, and elevated cerebrospinal-fluid quinolinic acid in a subgroup of HIV-infected individuals. *Neuropsychology, 7,* 149–157.

Martin, E. (1975). Generation-recognition theory and the encoding specificity principle. *Psychological Review, 82,* 150–153.

Martin, I., & Levey, A. B. (1987). Learning what will happen next: Conditioning, evaluation, and cognitive processes. In G. Davey (Ed.), *Cognitive processes and Pavlovian conditioning in humans* (pp. 57–81). Chichester, UK: Wiley.

Martin, M., & Jones, G. V. (1984). Cognitive failures in everyday life. In J. E. Harris & P. E. Morris (Eds.), *Everyday memory, actions and absentmindedness* (pp. 173–190). New York: Academic Press.

Martin, V. L., & Pressley, M. (1991). Elaborative interrogation effects depend on the nature of the question. *Journal of Educational Psychology, 83,* 113–119.

Martinetti, R. F. (1989). Sex differences in dream recall and components of imaginal life. *Perceptual and Motor Skills, 69,* 643–649.

Maslow, A. H. (1937). The influence of familiarization on preferences. *Journal of Experimental Psychology, 21,* 162–180.

Masserman, J. (1943). *Behavior and neurosis: An experimental psychoanalytic approach to psychobiologic principles.* Chicago: University of Chicago Press.

Mathews, A., Richards, A., & Eysenck, M. (1989). Interpretation of homophones related to threat in anxiety states. *Journal of Abnormal Psychology, 98,* 31–34.

Mathews, R. C., Buss, R. R., Stanley, W. B., Blanchard-Fields, F., Cho, J., & Druhan, B. (1980). Role of implicit and explicit processing in learning from extended examples: A synergistic effect. *Journal of Experimental Psychology: Learning, Memory, and Cognition, 15,* 1083–1100.

Matthews, D. B., Best, P. J., White, A. M., Vandergriff, J. L., & Simpson, P. E. (1996). Ethanol impairs spatial cognitive processing: New behavioral and electrophysiological findings. *Current Directions in Psychological Science, 5,* 111–115.

Maylor, E. A., & Rabbitt, P. M. A. (1993). Alcohol, reaction time, and memory: A meta-analysis. *British Journal of Psychology, 84,* 301–317.

McCarthy, R. A., & Warrington, E. K. (1988). Evidence for modality-specific meaning systems in the brain. *Nature, 334,* 428–430.

McCarthy, R. A., & Warrington, E. K. (1990). *Cognitive neuropsychology: A clinical introduction.* New York: Academic Press.

McClearn, G. E., Johansson, B., Berg, S., Pedersen, N. L., Ahern, F., Petrill, S. A., & Plomin, R. (1997). Substantial genetic influence on cognitive abilities in twins 80 or more years old. *Science, 276,* 1560–1563.

McClosky, M., Wible, C. G., & Cohen, N. J. (1988). Is there a special flashbulb memory mechanism? *Journal of Experimental Psychology: General, 117,* 171–181.

McCrae, R. R., & Costa, P. T. (1986). Clinical assessment can benefit from recent advances in personality psychology. *American Psychologist, 41,* 1001–1003.

McDonald, R. J., & White, N. M. (1993). A triple dissociation of memory systems: Hippocampus, amygdala, and dorsal striatum. *Behavioral Neuroscience, 107,* 3–22.

McGaugh, J. L. (1974). ECS: Effects on learning and memory in animals. In M. Fink, S. Kety, J. McGaugh, & T. Williams, (Eds.), *Psychobiology of convulsive therapy* (pp. 85–97). New York: Wiley.

McGaugh, J. L. (1991). Neuromodulation and the storage of information: Involvement of the amygdaloid complex. In R. G. Wister & H. J. Weingartner (Eds.), *Perspectives on cognitive neuroscience* (pp. 279–299). New York: Oxford University Press.

McGeoch, J. A., & Irion, A. L. (1952). *The psychology of human learning* (2nd ed.). New York: Longmans, Green.

McGuire, W. J. (1961). A multiprocess model for paired associate learning. *Journal of Experimental Psychology, 62,* 335–347.

McKeithan, K. B., Reitman, J. S., Rueter, H. H., & Hirtle, S. C. (1981). Knowledge organization and skill differences in computer programmers. *Cognitive Psychology, 13,* 307–325.

McLaughlin, J. P., Cicala, G. A., & Pierson, D. K. (1968). Von Restorff effect in rat maze learning. *Journal of Comparative and Physiological Psychology, 66,* 427–431.

McNally, R. J. (1987). Preparedness and phobias: A review. *Psychological Bulletin, 101,* 283–303.

McNaughton, B. L., & Smolensky, P. (1991). Connectionist and neural modeling: Converging in the hippocampus. In R. G. Wister & H. J. Weingartner (Eds.), *Perspetives on cognitive neuroscience* (pp. 93–109). New York: Oxford University Press.

McNish, K. A., Betts, S. L., Brandon, S. E., & Wagner, A. R. (1997). Divergence of conditioned eyeblink and conditioned fear in backward Pavlovian conditioning. *Animal Learning & Behavior, 25,* 43–52.

McWeeny, K. H., Young, A. W., Hay, D. C., & Ellis, A. W. (1987). Putting names to faces. *British Journal of Psychology, 78,* 143–149.

Meacham, J. A., & Kushner, S. (1980). Anxiety, prospective remembering, and performance of planned actions. *Journal of General Psychology, 103,* 203–209.

Means, B., & Loftus, E. F. (1991). When personal history repeats itself: Decomposing memories for recurring events. *Applied Cognitive Psychology, 5,* 297–318.

Means, L. W., Lutz, J., Long, T. E., & High, K. (1995). Memory for parking location in large lots. *Psychological Reports, 76,* 775–779.

Medin, D. L. (1974). The comparative study of memory. *Journal of Human Evolution, 3,* 455–463.

Meehl, P. E. (1950). On the circularity of the law of effect. *Psychological Bulletin, 47,* 52–75.

Melcher, J. M., & Schooler, J. W. (1996). The misremembrance of wines past: Verbal and perceptual expertise differentially mediate verbal overshadowing of taste memory. *Journal of Memory and Language, 35,* 231–245.

Melton, A. W. (1963). Implications of short-term memory for a general theory of memory. *Journal of Verbal Learning and Verbal Behavior, 2,* 1–21.

Memon, A., Wark, L., Holley, A., Bull, R., & Koehnken, G. (1997). Context reinstatement in the laboratory: How useful is it? In D. G. Payne & F. G. Conrad (Eds.), *Intersections in basic and applied memory research* (pp. 175–191). Mahwan, NJ: Erlbaum.

Menzel, E. W. (1973). Chimpanzee spatial memory organization. *Science, 182,* 943–945.

Merzenich, M. M., Jenkins, W. M., William, M., Johnston, P., Schreiner, C., Miller, S. L., & Tallal, P. (1996). Temporal processing deficits of language-learning impaired children ameliorated by training. *Science, 271,* 77–81

Messier, C., & White, N. M. (1984). Contingent and noncontingent actions of sucrose and saccharin reinforcers: Effects on taste preference and memory. *Physiology & Behavior, 32,* 195–203.

Midkiff, E. E., & Bernstein, I. L. (1985). Targets of learned food aversions in humans. *Physiology and Behavior, 34,* 839–841.

Milgram, S., & Jodelet, D. (1976). Psychological maps of Paris. In H. M. Proshansky, W. H. Ittelson, & L.G Rivlin (Eds.), *Environmental psychology* (pp. 104–124). New York: Holt, Rinehart & Winston.

Miller, G. A. (1956). The magical number seven plus-or-minus two: Some limits of our capacity for processing information. *Psychological Review, 63,* 81–97.

Miller, L. C., Barrett, C. L., & Hampe, E. (1974). Phobias of childhood in a prescientific era. In A. Davis (Ed.), *Child personality and psychopathology: Current topics* (pp. 89–134). New York: Wiley.

Miller, M. E., Adesso, V. J., Fleming, J. P., Gino, A., & Lauerman, R. (1978). Effects of alcohol on the storage and retrieval processes of heavy social drinkers. *Journal of Experimental Psychology: Human Learning and Memory, 4,* 246–255.

Miller, N. E. (1935). A reply to "sign-gestalt or conditioned reflex?" *Psychological Review, 42,* 280–292.

Miller, N. E. (1948). Theory and experiment relating psychoanalytic displacement to stimulus-response generalization. *Journal of Abnormal and Social Psychology, 43,* 155–178.

Miller, N. E. (1959). Liberalization of basic S-R concepts: Extensions to conflict behavior, motivation, and social learning. In S. Koch (Ed.), *Psychology: A study of a science* (Vol. 2, pp. 196–292). New York: McGraw-Hill.

Miller, N. E. (1969). Learning of visceral and glandular responses. *Science, 163,* 434–445.

Miller, N. E. (1985). The value of behavioral research on animals. *American Psychologist, 40,* 423–440.

Miller, N. E., & Dollard, J. (1941). *Social learning and imitation.* New Haven, CT: Yale University Press.

Miller, R. R., Barnet, R. C., & Grahame, N. J. (1995). Assessment of the Rescorla-Wagner model. *Psychological Bulletin, 117,* 363–386.

Miller, R. R., & Springer, A. D. (1973). Amnesia, consolidation, and retrieval. *Psychological Review, 80,* 69–79.

Mineka, S. (1979). The role of fear in theories of avoidance learning, flooding, and extinction. *Psychological Bulletin, 86,* 985–1010.

Mineka, S. (1992). Evolutionary memories, emotional processing, and the emotional disorders. In D. L. Medin (Ed.), *The psychology of learning and motivation* (Vol. 28, pp. 161–206). San Diego, CA: Academic Press.

Mishkin, M., & Appenzeller, T. (1987, June). The anatomy of memory. *Scientific American, 256 (6),* 80–89.

Modigliani, V., & Hedges, D. G. (1987). Distributed rehearsals and the primacy effect in single-trial free recall. *Journal of Experimental Psychology: Learning, Memory, and Cognition, 13,* 426–436.

Moore, R. B., & Strunkard, S. (1979). Dr. Guthrie and Felis domesticus, or tripping over the cat. *Science, 205,* 1031–1033.

Moore, T. E. (1982). Subliminal advertising: What you see is what you get. *Journal of Marketing, 46,* 38–47.

Morris, C. D., Bransford, J. D., & Franks, J. J. (1977). Levels of processing versus transfer appropriate processing. *Journal of Verbal Learning and Verbal Behavior, 16,* 519–533.

Morris, P. E., & Fritz, C. O. (2000). The name game: Using retrieval practice to improve the learning of names. *Journal of Experimental Psychology: Applied, 6,* 124–129.

Morris, P. E., Tweedy, M., & Gruneberg, M. M. (1985). Interest, knowledge and the memorising of soccer scores. *British Journal of Psychology, 76,* 415–425.

Morris, R. G. M. (1981). Spatial localization does not require the presence of local cues. *Learning and Motivation, 12,* 239–260.

Morton, J. (1967). A singular lack of incidental learning. *Nature, 215,* 203–204.

Mowrer, H. O. (1947). On the dual nature of learning—A reinterpretation of "conditioning" and "problem solving." *Harvard Educational Review, 17,* 102–148.

Muller, G. E., & Pilzecker, A. (1900). Experimentalle Beitrage zur Lehre vom Gedachtnis. *Zeitschrift fur Psychologie, 1,* 1–300.

Murdock, B. B. (1968). Serial order effects in short-term memory. *Journal of Experimental Psychology, 76* (Pt. 2), 1–15. (Monograph.)

Naitoh, P. (1971) Selective impairment of Pavlovian conditional responses by electroconvulsive shock. *Physiology & Behavior, 7,* 291–296.

Nathan, P. E. (1976). Alcoholism. In H. Leitenberg (Ed.), *Handbook of behavior modification and behavior therapy* (pp. 3–44). Englewood Cliffs, NJ: Prentice Hall.

Naus, M. J., Ornstein, P. A., & Aivano, S. (1977). Developmental changes in memory: The effects of processing time and rehearsal instructions. *Journal of Experimental Child Psychology, 23,* 237–251.

Naveh-Benjamin, M. (1987). Coding of spatial location information: An automatic process? *Journal of Experimental Psychology: Learning, Memory, and Cognition, 13,* 595–605.

Naveh-Benjamin, M. (1991). A comparison of training programs intended for different types of test-anxious students: Further support for an information processing model. *Journal of Educational Psychology, 83,* 134–139.

Naveh-Benjamin, M., & Ayres, T. J. (1986). Digit span, reading rate, and linguistic relativity. *Quarterly Journal of Experimental Psychology: Human Experimental Psychology, 38A,* 739–751.

Neath, I. (1998). *Human memory: An introduction to research, data, and theory.* Pacific Grove, CA: Brooks/Cole.

Neath, I., Surprenant, A. M., & Crowder, R. G. (1993). The context-dependent stimulus-suffix effect. *Journal of Experimental Psychology: Learning, Memory, and Cognition, 19,* 698–703.

Neely, J. H. (1989). Experimental dissociations and the episodic/semantic memory distinction. In H. L. Roediger & F. I. M. Craik (Eds.), *Varieties of memory and consciousness: Essays in honor of Endel Tulving* (pp. 229–270). Hillsdale, NJ: Erlbaum.

Neisser, U. (1967). *Cognitive psychology.* New York: Appleton, Century, Crofts.

Neisser, U. (1978). Memory: What are the important questions. In M. M. Gruneberg, P. E. Morris, & R. N. Sykes (Eds.), *Practical aspects of memory* (pp. 3–24). New York: Academic Press. (Reprinted in Neisser, 1982.)

Neisser, U. (1982). Snapshots or benchmarks. In U. Neisser (Ed.), *Memory observed* (pp. 43–48). San Francisco: Freeman.

Nelson, C. A. (1995). The ontogeny of human memory: A cognitive neuroscience approach. *Developmental Psychology, 31,* 723–738.

Nelson, D. L., & Schreiber, T. A. (1992). Word concreteness and word structure as independent determinants of recall. *Journal of Memory and Language, 31,* 237–260.

Nelson, T. O. (1976). Reinforcement and human memory. In W. K. Estes (Ed.), *Handbook of learning and cognitive processes* (Vol. 3, pp. 207–246). Hillsdale, NJ: Erlbaum.

Nelson, T. O. (1978). Detecting small amounts of information in memory: Savings for nonrecognized items. *Journal of Experimental Psychology: Human Learning and Memory, 4,* 453–468.

Nelson, T. O., & Gerler, D. (1984). Accuracy of feeling-of-knowing judgments for predicting perceptual identification and relearning, *Journal of Experimental Psychology: General, 113,* 282–300.

Nelson, T. O., & Leonesio, R. J. (1988). Allocation of self-paced study time and the "labor-in-vain effect." *Journal of Experimental Psychology: Learning, Memory, and Cognition, 14,* 676–686.

Nemiah, J. C. (1979). Dissociative amnesia. In J. H. Kihlstom & F. J. Evans (Eds.), *Functional disorders of memory* (pp. 303–323). Hillsdale, NJ: Erlbaum.

Neumann, D. L., Lipp, O. V., & Siddle, D. A. T. (1997). Conditioned inhibition of autonomic Pavlovian conditioning in humans. *Biological Psychology, 46,* 223–233.

Neuringer, A., Kornell, N., & Olaf, M. (2001). Stability and variability in extinction. *Journal of Experimental Psychology: Animal Behavior Processes, 27,* 79–94.

Newell, A., & Rosenbloom., P. S. (1981). Mechanisms of skill acquisition and the law of practice. In J. R. Anderson (Ed.), *Cognitive skills and their acquisition* (pp. 1–55). Hillsdale, NJ: Erlbaum.

Nickerson, R. S., & Adams, M. J. (1979). Long-term memory for a common object. *Cognitive Psychology, 11,* 287–307.

Nicolson, R. (1981). The relationship between memory span and processing speed. In M. Friedman, J. P. Das, & N. O'Connor (Eds.), *Intelligence and learning* (pp. 179–184). New York: Plenum.

Niederehe, G. (1991). Depression and memory impairment in the aged. In L. Poon (Ed.), *Handbook for clinical memory assessment of older adults* (pp. 226–237). Washington, DC: American Psychological Association.

Nigro, G., & Neisser, U. (1983). Point of view in personal memories. *Cognitive Psychology, 15,* 467–482.

Nilsson, L. (1987). Motivated forgetting: Dissociation between performance data and subjective reports. *Psychological Research, 49,* 183–188.

Nisbett, R. E., & Wilson, T. D. (1977). Telling more than we can know: Verbal reports on mental processes. *Psychological Review, 84,* 231–259.

Nissen, M. J., & Bullemer, P. (1987). Attentional requirements of learning: Evidence from performance measures. *Cognitive Psychology, 19,* 1–32.

Nolan, J. (2001, March). Memento mori. *Esquire, 135*(3), 186.

Norman, D. A. (1981). The categorization of action slips. *Psychological Review, 88,* 1–15.

Norman, G. R., Brooks, L. R., & Allen, S. W. (1989). Recall by expert medical practioners and novices as a record of processing attention. *Journal of Experimental Psychology: Learning, Memory, and Cognition, 15,* 1166–1174.

Nyberg, L., Cabeza, R., & Tulving, E. (1996). PET studies of encoding and retrieval: The HERA model. *Psychonomic Bulletin & Review, 3,* 135–148.

O'Conner, N., & Hermelin, B. (1989). The memory structure of autistic idiot-savant mnemonists. *British Journal of Psychology, 80,* 97–111.

Ogden, J. A. & Corkin, S. (1991). Memories of H. M. In W. C. Abraham, M. C. Corballis, & K. G. White (Eds.), *Memory mechanisms* (pp. 195–215). Hillsdale, NJ: Erlbaum.

Ohman, A., Fredrikson, M., Hugdahl, K., & Rimmo, P. (1976). The premise of equipotentiality in human classical conditioning: Conditioned electrodermal responses to potentially phobic stimuli. *Journal of Experimental Psychology: General, 105,* 313–337.

Ohman, A., & Mineka, S. (2001). Fears, phobias, and preparedness: Toward an evolved module of fear and fear learning. *Psychological Review, 108,* 483–522.

Olds, J., & Milner, P. (1954). Positive reinforcement produced by electrical stimulation of septal area and other regions of rat brain. *Journal of Comparative and Physiological Psychology, 47,* 419–427.

Olson, G. M. (1976). An information-processing analysis of visual memory and habituation in infants. In T. J. Tighe & R. N. Leaton (Eds.), *Habituation: Perspectives from child development, animal behavior, and neurophysiology* (pp. 239–277). Hillsdale, NJ: Erlbaum.

Olton, D. S. (1977, June). Spatial memory. *Scientific American, 236,* 82–98.

Olton, D. S. (1978). Characteristics of spatial memory. In S. H. Hulse, H. Fowler, & W. K. Honig (Eds.), *Cognitive processes in animal behavior* (pp. 341–374). Hilladale, NJ: Erlbaum,

Olton, D. S. (1979). Mazes, maps, and memory. *American Psychologist, 34,* 583–596.

Olton, D. S., Collison, C., & Werz, M. A. (1977). Spatial memory and radial arm maze performance in rats. *Learning and Motivation, 8,* 289–314.

Olton, D. S., & Samuelson, R. J. (1976). Remembrance of places passed: Spatial memory in rats. *Journal of Experimental Psychology: Animal Behavior Processes, 2,* 97–116.

Ornstein, P. A., Naus, M. J., & Liberty, C. (1975). Rehearsal and organizational processes in children's memory. *Child Development, 46,* 818–830.

Ornstein, P. A., Naus, M. J., & Stone, B. P. (1977). Rehearsal training and developmental differences in memory. *Developmental Psychology, 13,* 15–24.

Orr, S. P., Metzger, L. J., Lasko, N. B., Macklin, M. L., Peri, T., & Pitman, R. K. (2000). De novo conditioning in trauma-exposed individuals with and without posttraumatic stress disorder. *Journal of Abnormal Psychology, 109,* 290–298.

Osgood, C. E. (1953). *Method and theory in experimental psychology.* New York: Oxford University Press.

Overman, W. H., Pate, B. J., Moore, K., & Peuster, A. (1996). Ontogeny of place learning in children as measured in the radial arm maze, Morris search task, and the open field task. *Behavioral Neuroscience, 110,* 1205–1228.

Paivio, A. (1969). Mental imagery in associative learning and memory. *Psychological Review, 76,* 241–262.

Papini, M. R., & Bitterman, M. E. (1990). The role of contingency in classical conditioning. *Psychological Review, 97,* 396–403.

Papka, M., Ivy, R. B., & Woodruff-Pak, D. S. (1997). Eyeblink classical conditioning and awareness revisited. *Psychological Science, 8,* 404–408.

Park, D. C., Smith, A. D., & Cavanaugh, J. C. (1990). Metamemories of memory researchers. *Memory and Cognition, 18,* 321–327.

Park, S., Holzman, P. S., & Goldman-Rakic, P. S. (1995). Spatial working memory deficits in the relatives of schizophrenic patients. *Archives of General Psychiatry, 52,* 821–828.

Parkin, A. J., Lewinsohn, J., & Folkard, S. (1982). The influence of emotion on immediate and delayed retention: Levinger & Clark reconsidered. *British Journal of Psychology, 73,* 389–393.

Parkin, A. J., & Streete, S. (1988). Implicit and explicit memory in young children and adults. *British Journal of Psychology, 79,* 361–369.

Paul, G. L. (1967). Insight vs. desensitization in psychotherapy two years after termination. *Journal of Consulting Psychology, 31,* 333–348.

Pavlov, I. P. (1927/1960). *Conditioned reflexes* (G. V. Anrep, Trans.) (Dover reprint, 1960.)

Pavlov, I. P. (1928). *Lectures on conditioned reflexes* (W. H. Gantt, Trans.). New York: International Publishers.

Pearce, J. M. (1997). *Animal learning and cognition: An introduction* (2nd ed.). East Sussex, UK: Psychology Press.

Pearce, S. A., Isherwood, S., Hrouda, D., Richardson, P. H., Erskine, A., & Skinner, J. (1990). Memory and pain: Tests of mood congruity and state dependent learning in experimentally induced and clinical pain. *Pain, 43,* 187–193.

Peckstein, L. A., & Brown, F. D. (1939). An experimental analysis of the alleged criteria of insight learning. *Journal of Educational Psychology, 30,* 38–52.

Penfield, W. (1955). The permanent record of the stream of consciousness. Proceedings of the 14th International Congress of Psychologists. *Acta Psychologica, 11,* 46–69. (Reprinted in T. K. Landauer, *Readings in physiological psychology.* New York: McGraw-Hill, 1967.)

Penfield, W., & Jasper, H. (1954). *Epilepsy and the functional anatomy of the human brain.* Boston: Little, Brown.

Penfield, W., & Rasmussen, T. (1950). *The cerebral cortex of man.* New York: Macmillan.

Perfetti, C. A., & Lesgold, A. M. (1979). Coding and comprehension in skilled reading and implications for reading instruction. In L. B Resnick & P. A. Weaver (Eds.), *Theory and practice of early reading* (pp. 57–84). Hillsdale, NJ: Erlbaum.

Perkins, C. C. (1968). An analysis of the concept of reinforcement. *Psychological Review, 75,* 155–172.

Perlmutter, M. (1978). What is memory aging the aging of? *Developmental Psychology, 14,* 330–345.

Perrig, W., & Kintsch, W. (1985). Propositional and situational representations of text. *Journal of Memory and Language, 24,* 503–518.

Perrot-Sinal, T. S., Kostenuik, M. A., Ossenkopp, K. P., & Kavaliers, M. (1996). Sex differences in performance in the Morris water maze and the effects of initial hidden platform training. *Behavioral Neuroscience, 110,* 1309–1320.

Peterson, L. R. (1966). Short-term verbal memory and learning. *Psychological Review, 73,* 193–207.

Peterson, L. R., Hillner, K., & Saltzman, D. (1962). Time between pairings and short-term retention. *Journal of Experimental Psychology, 64,* 550–551.

Peterson, L. R., & Peterson, M. J. (1959). Short-term retention of individual items. *Journal of Experimental Psychology, 58,* 193–198.

Petri, H. L., & Mishkin, M. (1994). Behaviorism, cognitivism and the neurpsychology of memory. *American Scientist, 82,* 30–37.

Petros, T. V., Beckwith, B. E., & Anderson, M. (1990). Individual differences in the effects of time of day and passage difficulty on prose memory in adults. *British Journal of Psychology, 81,* 63–72.

Pezdek, K., Whetstone, T., Reynolds, K., Askari, N., & Dougherty, T. (1989). Memory for real-world scenes: The role of consistency with schema expectation. *Journal of Experimental Psychology: Learning, Memory, and Cognition, 15,* 587–595.

Pfautz, P. L., Donegan. N. H., & Wagner, A. R. (1978). Sensory preconditioning versus protection from habituation. *Journal of Experimental Psychology: Animal Behavior Processes, 4,* 286–295.

Pieters, R. G. M., & Bijmolt, T. (1997). Consumer memory for television advertising: A field study of duration, serial position, and competition effects. *Journal of Consumer Reseach, 23,* 362–372.

Pillemer, D. B., Goldsmith, L. R., Panter, A. T., & White, S. H. (1988). Very long-term memories of the first year in college. *Journal of Experimental Psychology: Learning, Memory, and Cognition, 14,* 709–715.

Pillsbury, W. B., & Sylvester, A. (1940). Retroactive and proactive inhibition in immediate memory. *Journal of Experimental Psychology, 27,* 532–545.

Pinker, S. (1994). *The language instinct.* New York: Morrow.

Pintrich, P. R., & DeGroot, E. V. (1990). Motivational and self-regulated learning components of classroom academic performance. *Journal of Educational Psychology, 82,* 33–40.

Pliner, O. (1982). The effects of mere exposure on liking for edible substances. *Appetite, 3,* 283–290.

Plomin, R. Nature and nurture of cognitive abilities. In R. Sternberg (Ed.), *Advances in the psychology of human intelligence.* (Vol. 4, pp. 1–34). Hillsdale, NJ: Erlbaum.

Plomin, R., Owen, M. J., & McGuffin, P. (1994). The genetic basis of complex human behaviors. *Science, 264,* 1733–1739.

Plous, S. (1996). Attitudes toward the use of animals in psychological research and education: Results from a national survey of psychology majors. *Psychological Science, 7,* 352–358.

Poucet, B. (1993). Spatial cognitive maps in animals: New hypotheses on their structure and neural mechanisms. *Psychological Review, 100,* 163–182.

Premack, D. (1962) Reversibility of the reinforcement relation. *Science, 136,* 235–237.

Premack, D. (1965). Reinforcement theory. In D. Levine (Ed.), *Nebraska symposium on motivation* (pp. 123–180). Lincoln: University of Nebraska Press.

Pressley, M., Levin, J. R., Hall, J. W., Miller, G. E., & Berry, J. K. (1980). The keyword method and foreign word acquisition. *Journal of Experimental Psychology: Human Learning and Memory, 6,* 163–173.

Pressley, M., & Dennis-Rounds, J. (1980). Transfer of a mnemonic keyword strategy at two age levels. *Journal of Educational Psychology, 72,* 575–582.

Pressley, M., & Ghatala, E. S. (1989). Metacognitive benefits of taking a test for children and young adolescents. *Journal of Experimental Child Psychology, 47,* 430–450.

Pressley, M., Levin, J. R., & Ghatala, E. S. (1988). Strategy comparison opportunities promote long-term strategy use. *Contemporary Educational Psychology, 13,* 157–168.

Pressley, M., McDaniel, M. A., Turnure, J. E., Wood, E., & Ahmad, M. (1987). Generation and precision of elaboration: Effects on intentional and incidental learning. *Journal of Experimental Psychology: Learning, Memory, and Cognition, 13,* 291–300.

Prokasy, W. S., & Whalley, F. L. (1961). Manifest anxiety scale and classical conditioning. *Journal of Experimental Psychology, 62,* 560–564.

Rachman, S., & Lopatka, C. (1988). Return of fear: Underlearning and overlearning. *Behaviour Research and Therapy, 26,* 99–104.

Raichle, M. E. (1994). Images of the mind: Studies with modern imaging techniques. *Annual Review of Psychology, 45,* 333–356.

Rajaram, S., & Roediger, H. L. (1993). Direct comparison of four implicit memory tests. *Journal of Experimental Psychology: Learning, Memory, and Cognition, 19,* 765–776.

Rand, G. & Wapner, S. (1967). Postural states as a factor in memory. *Journal of Verbal Learning and Verbal Behavior, 6,* 268–271.

Raymond, M. J. (1964). The treatment of addiction by aversion conditioning with apomorphine. *Behaviour Research and Therapy, 1,* 287–291.

Rea, C. P., & Modigliani, V. (1985). The effect of expanded versus massed practice on the retention of multiplication facts and spelling lists. *Human Learning, 4,* 11–18.

Reason, J. T. (1984). Absent-mindedness and cognitive control. In J. E. Harris & P. E. Morris (Eds.), *Everyday memory, actions and absent-mindedness* (pp. 113–132). New York: Academic Press.

Reason, J. T. (1990). *Human error.* Cambridge: Cambridge University Press.

Reason, J. T. (1993). Self-report questionnaires in cognitive psychology: Have they delivered the goods? In A. Baddeley & L. Weiskrantz (Eds.), *Attention: Selection, awareness, and control: A tribute to Donald Broadbent* (pp. 406–423). Oxford: Clarendon Press.

Reason, J. T., & Lucas, D. (1984). Using cognitive diaries to investigate naturally occurring memory blocks. In J. E. Harris & P. E. Morris (Eds.), *Everyday memory, actions and absent-mindedness* (pp. 53–70). New York: Academic Press.

Reber, A. S. (1967). Implicit learning of artificial grammar. *Journal of Verbal Learning and Verbal Behavior, 6,* 855–863.

Reber, A. S. (1976). Implicit learning of synthetic languages: The role of instructional set. *Journal of Experimental Psychology: Human Learning and Memory, 2,* 88–94.

Reber, A. S. (1993). *Implicit learning and tacit knowledge: An essay on the cognitive unconscious.* New York: Oxford University Press.

Reber, R., Winkielmanm, P., & Schwartz, N. (1998). Effects of perceptual fluency on affective judgements. *Psychological Science, 9,* 45–48.

Reed, G. (1979). Everyday anomalies of recall and recognition. In J. F. Kihlstrom & F. J. Evans (Eds.), *Functional disorders of memory* (pp. 1–28). Hillsdale, NJ: Erlbaum.

Reed, P. (2001). Human response rates and causality judgments on schedules of reinforcement. *Learning and Motivation, 32,* 332–348.

Reeves, R. R., & Bullen, J. A. (1995). Mnemonics for ten DSM-IV disorders. *Journal of Nervous and Mental Disease, 183,* 550–551.

Reige, W. H., Metter, E. J., Kuhl, D. E., & Phelps, M. E. (1985). Brain glucose metabolism and memory functions: Age decrease in factor scores. *Journal of Gerontology, 40,* 459–467.

Reiser, B. J., Black, J. B., & Kalamarides, P. (1986). Strategic memory search processes. In D. C. Rubin (Ed.), *Autobiographical memory* (pp. 100–121). Cambridge: Cambridge University Press.

Rescorla, R. A. (1967). Pavlovian conditioning and its proper control procedures. *Psychological Review, 74,* 71–80.

Rescorla, R. A. (1980). *Pavlovian second-order conditioning.* Hillsdale, NJ: Erlbaum.

Rescorla, R. A. (1987). A Pavlovian analysis of goal directed behavior. *American Psychologist, 42,* 119–129.

Rescorla, R. A. (1988). Pavlovian conditioning: It's not what you think it is. *American Psychologist, 43,* 151–161.

Rescorla, R. A. (2001). Experimental extinction. In R. R. Mowrer & S. B. Klein (Eds.), *Handbook of contemporary learning theories* (pp. 119–154). Mahwah, NJ: Erlbaum.

Rescorla, R. A., & Solomon, R. L. (1967). Two-process learning theory: Relationships between Pavlovian and instrumental learning. *Psychological Review, 74,* 151–182.

Rescorla, R. A., & Wagner, A. R. (1972). A theory of Pavlovian conditioning: Variations in the effectiveness of reinforcement and nonreinforcement. In A. H. Black & W. F. Prokasy (Eds.), *Classical conditioning II* (pp. 64–99). New York: Appleton, Century, Crofts.

Restle, F. (1957). Discrimination of cues in mazes: A resolution of the "place-vs.-response" question. *Psychological Review, 64,* 217–228.

Revelle, W., Humphreys, M. S., Simon, L., & Gilliland, K. (1980). The interactive effect of personality, time of day, and caffeine: A test of the arousal model. *Journal of Experimental Psychology: General, 109,* 1–31.

Revusky, S., Coombes, S., & Pohl, R. W. (1982). US preexposure: Effects on flavor aversions produced by pairing a poisoned partner with ingestion. *Animal Learning & Behavior, 10,* 83–90.

Reznick, J. S., Fueser, J. J., & Bosquet, M. (1998). Self-corrected reaching in a three-location delayed-response search task. *Psychological Science, 9,* 66–70.

Riahi-Belkaoui, A. (1986). *The learning curve: A management accounting tool.* Westport, CT: Quorum Books.

Riccio, D. C., Rabinowitz, V. C., & Axelrod, S. (1994). Memory: When less is more. *American Psychologist, 49,* 917–926.

Richardson, R., Guanowsky, V., Ahlers, S. T., & Riccio, D. D. (1984). Role of body temperature in the onset of, and recovery from, hypothermia-induced anterograde amnesia. *Physiological Psychology, 12,* 125–132.

Rilling, M. (1996). The mystery of the vanished citations. *American Psychologist, 51,* 589–598.

Risley, T. R. (1968). The effects and side effects of the use of punishment with an autistic child. *Journal of Applied Behavior Analysis, 1,* 21–34.

Roberts, S. (1981). Isolation of an internal clock. *Journal of Experimental Psychology: Animal Behavior Processes, 7,* 242–268.

Robbins, L. C. (1963). The accuracy of parental recall of aspects of child development and of child rearing practices. *Journal of Abnormal and Social Psychology, 66,* 261–270.

Robinson, K. J., & Roediger, H. L. (1997). Associative processes in false recall and false recognition. *Psychological Science, 8,* 231–237.

Rodda, M., & Grove, C. (1987). *Language, cognition and deafness.* Hillsdale, NJ: Erlbaum.

Roediger, H. L. (1973). Inhibition in recall from cueing with recall targets. *Journal of Verbal Learning and Verbal Behavior, 12,* 644–657.

Roediger, H. L. (1980). The effectiveness of four mnemonics in ordering recall. *Journal of Experimental Psychology: Human Learning and Memory, 6,* 558–568.

Roediger, H. L. (1990). Implicit memory: Retention without remembering. *American Psychologist, 45,* 1043–1056.

Roediger, H. L., & Crowder, R. G. (1976). A serial position effect in recall of United States presidents. *Bulletin of the Psychonomic Society, 8,* 275–278.

Roediger, H. L., & McDermott, K. B. (2000). Tricks of memory. *Current Directions in Psychological Science, 9,* 123–127.

Roediger, H. L., & McDermott, K. B. (1995). Creating false memories: Remembering words not presented in lists. *Journal of Experimental Psychology: Learning, Memory, and Cognition, 21,* 803–814.

Roediger, H. L., Stellon, C. C., & Tulving, E. (1977). Inhibition from part-list cues and rate of recall. *Journal of Experimental Psychology: Human Learning and Memory, 3,* 174–188.

Roediger, H. L., & Thorpe, L. A. (1978). The role of recall time in producing hypermnesia. *Memory & Cognition, 6,* 296–305.

Rogers, L. (1989, September). Home, sweet-smelling home. *Natural History,* 61–66.

Rogoff, B., & Chavajay, P. (1995). What's become of research on the cultural basis of cognitive development. *American Psychologist, 50,* 859–877.

Rogoff, B., & Waddell, K. J. (1982). Memory for information organized in a scene by children from two cultures. *Child Development, 53,* 1224–1228.

Roitblat, H. L., Penner, R. H., & Nachtigall, P. E. (1990). Matching-to-sample by an echolocating dolphin.

Journal of Experimental Psychology: Animal Behavior Processes, 16, 85–95.

Rose, S. (1992). *The making of memory.* New York: Doubleday.

Rosenzweig, M. R. (1996). Aspects of the search for neural mechanisms of memory. *Annual Review of Psychology, 47,* 1–32.

Rosenzweig, M. R., et al., (1992). Studying changes of memory formation with chicks. In L. R. Squire & N. Butters (Eds.), *Neuropsychology of memory* (2nd ed., pp. 533–556). New York: Guilford Press.

Roth, S., & Cohen, L. J. (1986). Approach, avoidance, and coping with stress. *American Psychologist, 41,* 813–819.

Rotter, J. B. (1990). Internal versus external control of reinforcement: A case history of a variable. *American Psychologist, 45,* 489–493.

Rovee, C. K., & Rovee, D. T. (1969). Conjugate reinforcement of infant exploratory behavior. *Journal of Experimental Child Psychology, 8,* 33–39.

Rovee-Collier, C. K., Sullivan, M. W., Enright, M., Lucas, D., & Fagan, J. W. (1980). Reactivation of infant memory. *Science, 208,* 1159–1162.

Royer, J. M. (1986). Designing instruction to produce understanding. In G. D. Phye & T. Andre (Eds.), *Cognitive classroom learning* (pp. 83–113). New York: Academic Press.

Rozin, P., & Kalat, J. W. (1971). Specific hungers and poison avoidance as adaptive specializations of learning. *Psychological Review, 78,* 459–486.

Rubin, D. C. (1977). Very long-term memory for prose and verse. *Journal of Verbal Learning and Verbal Behavior, 16,* 611–621.

Rundus, D. (1971). Analysis of rehearsal processes in free recall. *Journal of Experimental Psychology, 89,* 63–77.

Ryan, E. B. (1992). Beliefs about memory changes across the adult life span. *Journal of Gerontology: Psychological Sciences, 47,* 41–46.

Ryan, J. D., Althoff, R. R., Whitlow, S., & Cohen, N. J. (2000). Amnesia is a deficit in relational memory. *Psychological Science, 11,* 454–461.

Sachs, J. S. (1967). Recognition memory for syntactic and semantic aspects of connected discourse. *Perception & Psychophysics, 2,* 437–442.

Sachs, O. (1985). *The man who mistook his wife for a hat.* New York: Summit Books.

Sahley, C., Rudy, J. W., & Gelperin, A. (1981). An analysis of associative learning in a terrestrial mollusc: I. Higher-order conditioning, blocking and a transient US-preexposure effect. *Journal of Comparative Physiology, 144,* 1–8.

Saint-Cyr, J. A., & Taylor, A. E. (1992). The mobilization of procedural learning: The "key signature" of the basal ganglia. In L. R. Squire & N. Butter (Eds.),

Neuropsychology of memory (2nd ed., pp. 188–202). New York: Guilford Press.

Salisbury, S. A. (1991). Cognitive assessment of the older client. In W. C. Chenitz, J. T. Stone, & S. A. Salisbury, (Eds.), *Clinical gerontological nursing* (pp. 91–118). Philadelphia: Saunders.

Salthouse, T. A. (1994). The aging of working memory. *Neuropsychology, 8,* 535–543.

Saufley, W. H., Otaka, S. R., & Bavaresco, J. L. (1985). Context effects: Classroom tests and context independence. *Memory & Cognition, 13,* 522–528.

Saykin, A. J., Gur, R. C., Gur, R. E., Mozley, P. D., Mozley, L. H., Resnick, S. M., Kester, D. B., & Stafiniak, P. (1991). Neuropsychological function in schizophrenia: Selective impairment in memory and learning. *Archives of General Psychiatry, 48,* 618–624.

Schacter, D. L. (1983) Amnesia observed: Remembering and forgetting in a natural environment. *Journal of Abnormal Psychology, 92,* 236–242.

Schacter, D. L. (1995). Implicit memory: A new frontier for cognitive neuroscience. In M. S. Gazzangia (Ed.), *The cognitive neurosciences* (pp. 815–824). Cambridge, MA: The MIT Press.

Schacter, D. L. (1996). *Searching for memory.* New York: Basic Books.

Schacter, D. L. (1999). The seven sins of memory: Insights from psychology and cognitive neuroscience. *American Psychologist, 54,* 182–203.

Schacter, D. L., Chiu, C. Y. P., & Ochsner, K. N. (1993). Implicit memory: A selective review. *Annual Review of Neuroscience, 16,* 159–182.

Schacter, D. L., Cooper, L. A., Delaney, S. M., Peterson, M. A., & Tharan, M. (1991). Implicit memory for possible and impossible objects: Constraints on the construction of structural descriptions. *Journal of Experimental Psychology: Learning, Memory, and Cognition, 17,* 3–19.

Schacter, D. L., & Graf, P. (1986). Effects of elaborative processing on implicit and explicit memory for associations. *Journal of Experimental Psychology: Learning, Memory, and Cognition, 12,* 432–444.

Schacter, D. L., Wang, P. L., Tulving, E., & Freedman, M. (1982). Functional retrograde amnesia: A quantitative case study. *Neuropsychologia, 20,* 523–532.

Scheier, M. F., & Carver, C. S. (1993). On the power of positive thinking: The benefits of being optimistic. *Current Directions in Psychological Science, 2,* 26–30.

Schendel, J. D., & Hagman, J. D. (1982). On sustaining procedural skills over a prolonged retention interval. *Journal of Applied Psychology, 67,* 605–610.

Schilling, R. F., & Weaver, G. E. (1983). Effects of extraneous verbal information on memory for telephone numbers. *Journal of Applied Psychology, 68,* 559–564.

Schmidt, R. A., & Bjork, R. A. (1992). New conceptualizations of practice: Common principles in three paradigms suggest new concepts for training. *Psychological Science, 3,* 207–217.

Schmidt, R. A., Young, D. E., Swinnen, S., & Shapiro, D. C. (1989). Summary knowledge of results for skill acquisition: Support for the guidance hypothesis. *Journal of Experimental Psychology: Learning, Memory, and Cognition, 15,* 352–359.

Schneiderman, N., Fuentes, I., & Gormezano, I. (1962). Acquisition and extinction of the classically conditioned eyelid response in the albino rabbit. *Science, 136,* 650–652.

Schooler, J. W., Ryan, R. S., & Reder, L. (1996). The costs and benefits of verbally rehearsing memory for faces. In D. Herrmann, C. McEvoy, C. Hertzog, P. Hertel, & M. K. Johnson (Eds.), *Basic and applied memory research* (Vol. 2., pp. 51–65). Mahwan, NJ: Erlbaum.

Schramke, C. J., & Bauer, R. M. (1997). State-dependent learning in older and younger adults. *Psychology and Aging, 12,* 255–262.

Schultz, D. P., & Schultz, S. E. (1996). *A history of modern psychology* (6th ed.). Fort Worth, TX: Harcourt Brace & Company.

Schwartz, B. L., & Hashtroudi, S. (1991). Priming is independent of skill learning. *Journal of Experimental Psychology: Learning, Memory, and Cognition, 17,* 1177–1187.

Schwartz, B. N. (1978). *Psychology of learning and behavior.* New York: Norton.

Schwartz, G. E. (1975). Biofeedback, self-regulation, and the patterning of physiological responses. *American Scientist, 63,* 314–324.

Scoville, W. B., & Milner, B. (1957). Loss of recent memory after bilateral hippocampal lesions. *Journal of Neurology, Neurosurgery and Psychiatry, 20,* 11–19.

Scrivener, E., & Safer, M. A. (1988). Eyewitnesses show hyperamnesia for details about a violent event. *Journal of Applied Psychology, 73,* 371–377.

Sehulster, J. R. (1989). Content and temporal structure of autobiographical knowledge: Remembering twenty-five seasons of the Metropolitan Opera. *Memory & Cognition, 17,* 590–606.

Seligman, M. E. P. (1970). On the generality of the laws of learning. *Psychological Review, 77,* 406–418.

Seligman, M. E. P. (1972). Phobias and preparedness. In M. E. P. Seligman & J. L. Hager (Eds.), *Biological boundaries of learning* (pp. 451–462). New York: Appleton, Century, Crofts.

Seligman, M. E. P. (1975). *Helplessness: On depression, development, and death.* San Francisco: Freeman.

Seligman, M. E. P., & Johnson, J. C. (1973). A cognitive theory of avoidance learning. In F. J. McGuigan & D. B. Lumsden (Eds.), *Contemporary approaches to conditioning and learning* (pp. 69–110). Washington, DC: Winston.

Seligman, M. E. P., Maier, S. F., & Geer, J. H. (1968). Alleviation of learned helplessness in the dog. *Journal of Abnormal Psychology, 73,* 256–262.

Semb, G. B., Ellis, J. A., & Araujo, J. (1993). Long-term memory for knowledge learned in school. *Journal of Educational Psychology, 85,* 305–316.

Seymoure, P., Dou, H., & Juraska, J. M. (1996). Sex differences in radial maze performance: Influence of rearing environment and room cues. *Psychobiology, 24,* 33–37.

Shah, P., & Miyake, A. (1996). The separability of working memory resources for spatial thinking and language processing: An individual differences approach. *Journal of Experimental Psychology: General, 125,* 4–27.

Shallice, T. (1988). *From neuropsychology to mental structure.* Cambridge: Cambridge University Press.

Shallice, T. & Burgess, P. (1991). Deficits in strategy application following frontal lobe damage in man. *Brain, 114,* 727–741.

Shallice, T., & Warrington, E. K. (1970). Independent functioning of verbal memory stores: A neuropsychological study. *Quarterly Journal of Experimental Psychology, 22,* 261–273.

Shand, M. A., & Klima, E. S. (1981). Nonauditory suffix effects in congenitally deaf signers of American Sign Language. *Journal of Experimental Psychology: Human Learning and Memory, 6,* 464–474.

Shanks, D. R. (1991). Categorization by a connectionist network. *Journal of Experimental Psychology: Learning, Memory, and Cognition, 17,* 433–443.

Shanks, D. R. (1993). Human instrumental learning: A critical review. *British Journal of Psychology, 84,* 319–354.

Shanks, D. R. (1995). *The psychology of associative learning.* Cambridge: Cambridge University Press.

Shanks, D. R., & Dickinson, A. (1991). Instrumental judgment and performance under variations in action-outcome contingency and contiguity. *Memory & Cognition, 19,* 353, 360.

Sharp, D., Cole, M., & Lave, C. (1979). Education and cognitive development: The evidence from experimental research. *Monographs of the Society for Research in Child Development, 44* (1–2, Serial No. 178).

Sharps, M. J., Welton, A. L., & Price, J. L. (1993). Gender and task in the determination of spatial cognitive performance. *Psychology of Women Quarterly, 17,* 71–83.

Shaughnessy, J. J., Zimmerman, J., & Underwood, B. J. (1972). Further evidence on the MP-DP effect in free-recall learning. *Journal of Verbal Learning and Verbal Behavior, 11,* 1–12.

Shea, V. T. (1982). State-dependent learning in children receiving methylphenidate. *Psychopharmacology, 78,* 266–270.

Sheffield, F. D. (1948). Avoidance training and the contiguity principle. *Journal of Comparative and Physiological Psychology, 41,* 165–177.

Sheffield, F. D., & Roby, T. B. (1950). Reward value of a non-nutritive sweet taste. *Journal of Comparative and Physiological Psychology, 43,* 471–481.

Sheffield, F. D., Wulff, J. J., & Backer, R. (1951). Reward value of copulation without sex drive reduction. *Journal of Comparative and Physiological Psychology, 44,* 3–8.

Sheingold, K., & Tenney, Y. J. (1982). Memory for a salient childhood event. In U. Neisser (Ed.), *Memory observed* (pp. 201–212). San Francisco: Freeman.

Sher, K. J., & Mann, B. (1984). Cognitive dysfunction in compulsive checkers: Further explorations. *Behavioural Research and Therapy, 22,* 493–502.

Sherry, D. F., & Schacter, D. L. (1987). The evolution of multiple memory systems. *Psychological Review, 94,* 439–454.

Sherwin, B. B. (1988). Estrogen and/or androgen replacement therapy and cognitive functioning in surgically menopausal women. *Psychoneuroendocrinology, 10,* 325–335.

Sherwin, B. B. (1994). Estrogenic effects on memory in women. *Annals of the New York Academy of Science, 743,* 213–231.

Shettleworth, S. (1975). Reinforcement and the organization of behavior in golden hamsters: Hunger, environment, and food reinforcement. *Journal of Experimental Psychology: Animal Behavior Processes, 1,* 56–87.

Shiffrin, R. M. (1993). Short-term memory: A brief commentary. *Memory & Cognition, 21,* 193–197.

Shimamura, A. P., Salmon, D. P., Squire, L. R., & Butters, N. (1987). Memory dysfunction and word priming in amnesia. *Behavioral Neuroscience, 101,* 347–351.

Shimamura, A. P., & Squire, L. R. (1986). Memory and metamemory: A study of feeling-of-knowing phenomenon in amnesic patients. *Journal of Experimental Psychology: Learning, Memory, and Cognition, 12,* 452–460.

Shimp, T., Stuart, E. W., & Engle, R. W. (1991). A program of classical conditioning experiments testing variations in the CS and context. *Journal of Consumer Research, 18,* 1–12.

Sholl, M. J. (1987). Cognitive maps as orienting schemata. *Journal of Experimental Psychology: Learning, Memory, and Cognition, 13,* 615–628.

Shore, D. I., Stanford, L., MacInnes, J. W., Klein, R. M., & Brown, R. E. (2001). Of mice and men: Virtual Hebb-Williams mazes permit comparisons across species. *Cognitive, Affective, & Behavioral Neuroscience, 1,* 83–89.

Siddle. D. A. T. (1985). Effects of stimulus omission and stimulus change on dishabituation of the skin conductance response. *Journal of Experimental Psychology: Learning, Memory, and Cognition, 11,* 206–216.

Siddle, D. A. T., Kuiack, M., & Kroese, B. S. (1983). The orienting reflex. In A. Gale & J. A. Edwards (Eds.), *Physiological correlates of human behavior* (pp. 149–170). London: Academic Press.

Siddle, D. A. T., & Lipp, O. V. (1997). Orienting, habituation, and information processing: The effects of omission, the role of expectancy, and the problem of dishabituation. In P. J. Lang, R. F. Simons, & M. T. Balaban (Eds.), *Attention and orienting: Sensory and motivational processes* (pp. 23–40). Mahwah, NJ: Erlbaum.

Siddle, D. A. T., & Remington, B. (1987). Latent inhibition and human Pavlovian conditioning: Research and relevance. In G. C. L. Davey (Ed.), *Cognitive processes and Pavlovian conditioning in humans* (pp. 115–146). Chichester, UK: Wiley.

Sidman, M., & Stoddard, L. T. (1967). The effectiveness of fading in programming a simultaneous form of discrimination for retarded children. *Journal of the Experimental Analysis of Behavior, 10,* 3–15.

Siegel, S. (1974). Flavor preexposure and "learned safety." *Journal of Comparative and Physiological Psychology, 87,* 1073–1082.

Siegel, S. (1982). Pharmacological habituation and learning. In M. L. Commons, R. J. Herrnstein, & A. R. Wagner (Eds.), *Quantitative analyses of behavior* (Vol. 3, pp. 195–217). Cambridge, MA: Ballinger.

Siegel, S. (1984). Pavlovian conditioning and heroin overdose: Reports by overdose victims. *Bulletin of the Psychonomic Society, 22,* 428–430.

Siegel, S. (1991). Feedforward processes in drug tolerance and dependence. In R. G. Lister & H. J. Weingartner (Eds.), *Perspectives on cognitive neuroscience* (pp. 405–416). New York: Oxford University Press.

Siegel, S. & Allan, L. G. (1996). The widespread influence of the Rescorla-Wagner model. *Psychonomic Bulletin & Review, 3,* 314–321.

Siegel, S., Hinson, R. E., Krank, M. D., & McCully, J. (1982). Heroin "overdose" death: Contribution of drug-associated environmental cues. *Science, 216,* 436–437.

Silverman, I., & Eals, M. (1992). Sex differences in spatial abilities: Evolutionary theory and data. In J. H.

Barkow, L. Cosmides, & J. Tooby (Eds.), *The adapted mind: Evolutionary psychology and the generation of culture* (pp. 533–549). New York: Oxford University Press.

Singh, D. (1970). Preference for bar pressing to obtain reward over freeloading in rats and children. *Journal of Comparative and Physiological Psychology, 73,* 320–327.

Singh, S. N., Mishra, S., Bendapudi, N., & Linville, D. (1994). Enhancing memory of television commercials through message spacing. *Journal of Marketing Research, 31,* 384–392.

Skinner, B. F. (1938). *The behavior of organisms.* New York: Appleton, Century, Crofts.

Skinner, B. F. (1953). *Science and human behavior.* New York: Macmillan.

Skinner, B. F. (1956). A case history in scientific method. *American Psychologist, 11,* 221–233. (Reprinted in S. Koch (Ed.), *Psychology: A study of a science* [Vol. 2, pp. 359–379]. New York: McGraw-Hill.)

Skinner, B. F. (1971). *Beyond freedom and dignity.* New York: Knopf.

Skinner, B. F. (1988, June). A statement on punishment. *APA Monitor,* p. 22.

Skinner, N. F. (1985). University grades and time of day of instruction. *Bulletin of the Psychonomic Society, 23,* 67.

Slamecka, N. J., & Graf, P. (1978). The generation effect: Delineation of a phenomenon. *Journal of Experimental Psychology: Human Learning and Memory, 4,* 592–604.

Smith, M. (1983). Hypnotic memory enhancement of witnesses: Does it work? *Psychological Bulletin, 94,* 384–407.

Smith, S. M. (1979). Remembering in and out of context. *Journal of Experimental Psychology: Human Learning and Memory, 5,* 460–471.

Smith, S. M. (1985). Background music and context-dependent memory. *American Journal of Psychology, 98,* 591–603.

Smith, S. M., & Vela, E. (2001). Environmental context-dependent memory: A review and meta-analysis. *Psychonomic Bulletin & Review, 8,* 203–220.

Smotherman, W. P. (1982). Odor aversion learning by the rat fetus. *Physiology and Behavior, 29,* 769–771.

Sno, H. N., & Linszen, D. H. (1990). The déjà vu experience: Remembrance of things past? *American Journal of Psychiatry, 147,* 1587–1595.

Snowman, J. (1986). Learning tactics and strategies. In G. D. Phye & T. Andre (Eds.), *Cognitive classroom learning* (pp. 243–275). New York: Academic Press.

Snyder, J., Schrepferman, L., & St. Peter, C. (1997). Origins of antisocial behavior. *Behavior Modification, 21,* 187–215.

Sokolov, Y. N. (1963a). *Perception and the conditioned reflex.* London: Pergamon Press.

Sokolov, Y. N. (1963b). Higher nervous functions: The orienting reflex. *Annual Review of Physiology,* 545–580.

Solomon, P. R., & Pendlebury, W. W. (1992). Aging and memory: A model systems approach. In L. R. Squire & N. Butters (Eds.), *Neuropsychology of memory* (2nd ed., pp. 262–276). New York: Guilford Press.

Solomon, R. L. (1980). The opponent-process theory of acquired motivation: The costs of pleasure and the benefits of pain. *American Psychologist, 35,* 691–712.

Solomon, R. L., & Turner, L. H. (1962). Discriminative classical conditioning in dogs paralyzed by curare can later control discriminative avoidance responses. *Psychological Review, 69,* 202–219.

Solomon, R. L., Turner, L. H., & Lessac, M. S. (1968). Some effects of delay of punishment on resistance to temptation in dogs. *Journal of Personality and Social Psychology, 8,* 233–238.

Sorg, B. A., & Whitney, P. (1992). The effect of trait anxiety and situational stress on working memory capacity. *Journal of Research in Personality, 26,* 235–241.

Spear, N. E. (1967). Memory for reinforcer magnitude. *Psychological Review, 74,* 216–234.

Spear, N. E. (1973). Retrieval of memory in animals. *Psychological Review, 80,* 163–194.

Spear, N. E., & Riccio, D. C. (1994). *Memory: Phenomenon and principles.* Boston: Allyn & Bacon.

Spear, N. E., Smith, G. J., Bryan, R. G., Gordon, W. C., Timmons, R., & Chiszar, D. A. (1980). Contextual influences on the interaction between conflicting memories in the rat. *Animal Learning & Behavior, 8,* 273–281.

Speidel, G. E. (1978). Forward and backward associations in learning letter sounds. *Psychological Reports, 43,* 159–164.

Spelke, E. S., Breinlinger, K., Macomber, J., & Jacobson, K. (1992) Origins of knowledge. *Psychological Review, 99,* 605–632.

Spence, J. D. (1984). *The memory palace of Matteo Ricci.* New York: Viking.

Spence, K. (1956). *Behavior theory and conditioning.* New Haven, CT: Yale University Press.

Spence, K. W. (1937). The differential response in animals to stimuli varying within a single dimension. *Psychological Review, 44,* 430–434.

Sperling, G. (1960). The information available in brief visual displays. *Psychological Monographs, 74* (Whole Number 11).

Spiegler, M., & Guevremont, D. (1993). *Contemporary behavior therapy* (2nd ed.). Pacific Grove, CA: Brooks/Cole.

Sporer, S. L. (1991). Deep-deeper-deepest? Encoding strategies and the recognition of human faces. *Jour-*

nal of Experimental Psychology: Learning, Memory, and Cognition, 17, 323–333.

Squire, L. R. (1981). Two forms of human amnesia: An analysis of forgetting. *Journal of Neuroscience, 1,* 635–640.

Squire, L. R. (1987). *Memory and brain.* New York: Oxford University Press.

Squire, L. R. (1992). Memory and the hippocampus: A synthesis from findings with rats, monkeys, and humans. *Psychological Review, 99,* 195–231.

Squire, L. R., & Cohen, N. J. (1984). Human memory and amnesia. In J. L. McGaugh, G. Lynch, & N. Weinberger (Eds.), *Neurobiology of learning and memory* (pp. 3–64). New York: Guilford Press.

Squire, L. R., Knowlton, B., & Musen, G. (1993). The structure and organization of memory. *Annual Review of Psychology, 44,* 453–495.

Squire, L. R., & Slater, P. C. (1975). Forgetting in very long-term memory as assessed by an improved questionnaire technique. *Journal of Experimental Psychology: Human Learning and Memory, 1,* 50–54.

Squire, L. R., Slater, P. C., & Miller, P. L. (1981). Retrograde amnesia and bilateral electroconvulsive therapy. *Archives of General Psychiatry, 38,* 89–95.

Staddon, J. (1995, February). On responsibility and punishment. *The Atlantic Monthly,* 88–94.

Standing, L., Conezio, J., & Haber, R. N. (1970). Perception and memory for pictures: Single trial learning of 2560 visual stimuli. *Psychonomic Science, 19,* 73–74.

Staats, A. W., & Staats, C. K. (1958). Attitudes established by classical conditioning. *Journal of Abnormal and Social Psychology, 57,* 37–40.

Ste-Marie, D. M., & Lee, T. D. (1991). Prior processing effects on gymnastic judging. *Journal of Experimental Psychology: Learning, Memory, and Cognition, 17,* 126–136.

Sternberg, R. J., & Grigorenko, E. L. (1997). Are cognitive styles still in style? *American Psychologist, 52,* 700–712.

Stevens, A., & Coups, P. (1978). Distortions in judged spatial relations. *Cognitive Psychology, 13,* 422–437.

Stevenson, H. W., & Zigler, E. F. (1958). Probability learning in children. *Journal of Experimental Psychology, 56,* 185–192.

Stickgold, R., Hobson, J. A., & Fosse, M. (2001). Sleep, learning, and dreams: Off-line memory reprocessing. *Science, 294,* 1052–1057.

Stigler, J. W., Lee, S. Y., & Stevenson, H. W. (1986). Digit memory in Chinese and English: Evidence for a temporally limited store. *Cognition, 23,* 1–20.

Stoltz, S. B., & Lott, D. F. (1964). Establishment in rats of a persistent response producing a net loss of reinforcement. *Journal of Comparative and Physiological Psychology, 57,* 147–149.

Stone, W. S., Rudd, R. J., & Gold, P. E. (1990). Amphetamine, epinephrine, and glucose enhancement of memory retrieval. *Psychobiology, 18,* 227–230.

Storm, T., & Caird, W. K. (1967). Effects of alcohol on serial verbal learning in chronic alcoholics. *Psychonomic Science, 9,* 43–44.

Stronmeyer, C. F., & Psotka, J. (1970). The detailed texture of eidetic images. *Nature, 225,* 346–349.

Sullivan, R. M., Taborsky-Barbar, S., Mendoza, R., Ition, A., & Leon, M. (1991). Olfactory classical conditioning in neonates. *Pediatrics, 87,* 511–518.

Swanson, H. L. (1993). Working memory in learning disability subgroups. *Journal of Experimental Child Psychology, 56,* 87–114.

Swanson, H. L., & Cooney, J. B. (1991). Learning disabilities and memory. In B. Y. L. Wong (Ed.), *Learning about learning disabilities* (pp. 103–127). New York: Academic Press.

Swanson, J., & Kinsbourne, M. (1976). Stimulant-related state-dependent learning in hyperactive children. *Science, 192,* 1354–1357.

Swartz, G. E. (1975). Biofeedback, self-regulation, and the patterning of physiological processes. *American Scientist, 63,* 314–324.

Sweet, R. C. (1969). RNA "memory pills" and memory: A review of clinical and experimental status. *Psychological Record, 19,* 629–644.

Swinnen, S. P. (1990). Interpolated activities during the knowledge-of-results delay and post-knowledge-of-results interval: Effects on performance and learning. *Journal of Experimental Psychology: Learning, Memory, and Cognition, 16,* 692–705.

Swinnen, S. P., Schmidt, R. A., Nicholson, D. E., & Shapiro, D. C. (1990). Information feedback for skill acqisition: Instantaneous knowledge of results degrades learning. *Journal of Experimental Psychology: Learning, Memory, and Cognition, 16,* 706–716.

Taffel, C. (1955). Anxiety and the conditioning of verbal behavior. *Journal of Abnormal and Social Psychology, 51,* 496–501.

Talland, G. A. (1968). *Disorders of memory and learning.* Middlesex, UK: Penguin.

Tang, Y.-P., Shimizu, E., Dube, G., Rampon, C., Kerchner, G., Zhuo, M., Liu, G., & Tsien, J. (1999). Genetic enhancement of learning and memory in mice. *Nature, 401,* 63–69.

Taylor, H. A., & Tversky, B. (1992). Spatial mental models derived from survey and route descriptions. *Journal of Memory and Language, 31,* 261–292.

Taylor, J. (1953). A personality scale of manifest anxiety. *Journal of Abnormal and Social Psychology, 48,* 285–290.

Taylor, S. E., & Thompson, S. C. (1982). Stalking the elusive "vividness" effect. *Psychological Bulletin, 89,* 155–181.

Teitelbaum, J. S., Zatorre, R. J., Carpenter, S., Gendron, D., Evans, A. C., Gjedde, A., & Cashman, N. R. (1990). Neurologic sequelae of domic acid intoxification due to the ingestion of contaminated mussels. *New England Journal of Medicine, 322,* 1781–1786.

Tenenbaum, G., Tehan, G., Stewart G., & Christensen, S. (1999). Recalling a floor routine: The effects of skill and age on memory for order. *Applied Cognitive Psychology, 13,* 101–123.

Terrace, H. S. (1971). Escape from S–. *Learning and Motivation, 2,* 148–163.

Terrace, H. S. (1974). On the nature of non-responding in discrimination with and without errors. *Journal of the Experimental Analysis of Behavior, 22,* 151–159.

Terry, W. S. (1983). Effects of food primes on instrumental acquisition and performance. *Learning and Motivation, 14,* 107–122.

Terry, W. S. (1987). Everyday forgetting: Data from a diary study. *Psychological Reports, 62,* 299–303.

Terry, W. S. (1994). On the relative difficulty in recalling names and occupations. *American Journal of Psychology, 107,* 85–94.

Terry, W. S. (1995). When proper names are not forgotten: Recall of eponymous medical disorders. *Perceptual and Motor Skills, 81,* 923–928.

Terry, W. S. (1996). Retroactive interference effects of surprising reward omission on serial spatial memory. *Journal of Experimental Psychology: Animal Behavior Processes, 22,* 472–479.

Terry, W. S., & Anthony, S. G. (1980). Arousal and short-term memory: Effects of caffeine and trial spacing on delayed alternation performance. *Animal Learning & Behavior, 8,* 368–374.

Terry, W. S., & Bello, J. (1997). *Serial position and memory for commercials.* Washington, DC: Eastern Psychological Association.

Terry, W. S., & Wagner, A. R. (1975). Short-term memory for "surprising" versus "expected" unconditioned stimuli in Pavlovian conditioning. *Journal of Experimental Psychology: Animal Behavior Processes, 1,* 122–133.

Thapar, A., Petrill, S. A., & Thompson, L. A. (1994). The heritability of memory in the Western Reserve Twin Project. *Behavior Genetics, 24,* 155–160.

Thomas, D. R., Windell, B. T., Bakke, I., Kreye, J., Kimose, E., & Aposhyan, H. (1985). I. Long-term memory in pigeons: The role of discrimination problem difficulty assessed by reacquisition measures. II. The role of stimulus modality assessed by generalization slope. *Learning and Motivation, 16,* 464–477.

Thompson, L. A., Detterman, D. K., & Plomin, R. (1991). Associations between cognitive abilities and scholastic achievement: Genetic overlap but environmental differences. *Psychological Science, 2,* 158–165.

Thompson, R. F., & Glanzman, D. L. (1976). Neural and behavioral mechanisms of habituation and sensitization. In T. J. Tighe & R. N. Leaton (Eds.), *Habituation: Perspectives from child development, animal behavior, and neurophysiology* (pp. 49–93). Hillsdale, NJ: Erlbaum.

Thompson, R. F., Donegan, N. H., Clark, G. A., Lavond, D. G., Lincoln, J. A., Madden, J., Mamounas, L. A., Mauk, M. D., & McCormick, D. A. (1987). Neuronal substrates of discrete, defensive conditioned reflexes, conditioned fear states, and their interactions in the rabbit. In I. Gormezano, W. F. Prokasy, & R. F. Thompson (Eds.), *Classical conditioning* (3rd ed., pp. 371–399). Hillsdale, NJ: Erlbaum.

Thompson, R. F., & Gluck, M. A. (1991). Brain substrates of basic associative learning and memory. In R. G. Wister & H. J. Weingartner (Eds.), *Perspetives on cognitive neuroscience* (pp. 24–45). New York: Oxford University Press.

Thompson, R. F., Groves, P. M., Teyler, T. J., & Roemer, R. A. (1973). A dual-process theory of habituation: Theory and behavior. In H. V. S. Peeke & M. J. Herz (Eds.), *Habituation. Vol. 1: Behavioral studies* (pp. 239–271). New York: Academic Press.

Thompson, R. F., & Spencer, W. A. (1966). Habituation: A model phenomenon for the study of neuronal substrates of behavior. *Psychlogical Review, 73,* 16–43.

Thorndike, E. L. (1898). Animal intelligence: An experimental study of the associative processes in animals. *Psychological Review Monograph Supplements, 2* (Whole No. 8).

Thorndike, E. L. (1911). *Animal intelligence: Experimental studies.* New York: Macmillan.

Thorndike, E. L. (1931). *Human learning.* New York: Century. (Cambridge, MA: The MIT Press, 1966.)

Thorndyke, P. W., & Stasz, C. (1980). Individual differences in procedures for knowledge acquisition from maps. *Cognitive Psychology, 12,* 137–175.

Tighe, T. J., & Leaton, R. N. (1976). *Habituation: Perspectives from child development, animal behavior, and neurophysiology.* Hillsdale, NJ: Erlbaum.

Timberlake, W. (1994). Behavior systems, associationism, and Pavlovian conditioning. *Psychonomic Bulletin & Review, 1,* 405–420.

Timberlake, W., & Allison, J. (1974). Response deprivation: An empirical approach to instrumental performance. *Psychological Review, 81,* 146–164.

Tinklepaugh, O. L. (1928). An experimental study of represenative factors in monkeys. *Journal of Comparative Psychology, 8,* 197–236.

Tolman, E. C. (1933). Sign-gestalt or conditioned reflex? *Psychological Review, 40,* 391–411.

Tolman, E. C. (1948). Cognitive maps in rats and men. *Psychological Review, 55,* 189–208.

Tolman, E. C., & Honzik, C. H. (1930). Introduction and removal of reward, and maze performance in rats. *University of California Publications in Psychology, 4,* 257–275.

Tolman, E. C., Ritchie, B. F., & Kalish, D. (1946). Studies in spatial learning: II. Place learning versus response learning. *Journal of Experimental Psychology, 36,* 221–229.

Tolman, E. C., Ritchie, B. F., & Kalish, D. (1947). Studies in spatial learning: IV. The transfer of place learning to other starting points. *Journal of Experimental Psychology, 37,* 39–47.

Tomarken, A. J., Mineka, S., & Cook, M. (1989). Fear-relevant selective associations and covariation bias. *Journal of Abnormal Psychology, 98,* 381–394.

Treffert, D. A. (1989). *Extraordinary people: Understanding "idiot savants."* New York: Harper & Row.

Tryon, R. C. (1940). Genetic differences in maze learning in rats. *Yearbook of the National Society for the Study of Education, 39,* 111–119.

Tuber, D. S., Hothersall, D., & Voith, V. L. (1974). Animal clinical psychology: A modest proposal. *American Psychologist, 29,* 762–766.

Tully, T. (1996). Discovery of genes involved with learning and memory: An experimental synthesis of Hirschian and Benzerian perspectives. *Proceedings of the National Academy of Sciences, 93,* 13460–13467.

Tulving, E. (1962). Subjective organization in free recall of "unrelated" words. *Psychological Review, 69,* 344–354.

Tulving, E. (1969). Retrograde amnesia effect in free recall. *Science, 64,* 88–90.

Tulving, E. (1983). *Elements of episodic memory.* Oxford, UK: Clarendon Press.

Tulving, E. (1985). How many memory systems are there? *American Psychologist, 40,* 385–398.

Tulving, E. (1989). Remembering and knowing the past. *American Scientist, 77,* 361–367.

Tulving, E., & Pearlstone, Z. (1966). Availability versus accessibility of information in memory for words. *Journal of Verbal Learning and Verbal Behavior, 5,* 381–391.

Tulving, E., & Schacter, D. L. (1990). Priming and human memory systems. *Science, 247,* 301–306.

Tulving, E., Schacter, D. L., & Stark, H. A. (1982). Priming effects in word-fragment completion are independent of recognition memory. *Journal of Experimental Psychology: Learning, Memory, and Cognition, 8,* 336–342.

Tulving. E., & Thompson, D. M. (1973). Encoding specificity and retrieval processes in episodic memory. *Psychological Review, 80,* 352–373.

Tulving E., & Watkins, M. J. (1975). Structure of memory traces. *Psychological Review, 82,* 261–275.

Tun, P. A., Nathan, D. M., & Perlmuter, L. C. (1990). Cognitive and affective disorders in elderly diabetics. *Clinics in Geriatric Medicine, 6,* 731–746.

Turkkan, J. S. (1989). Classical conditioning: The new hegemony. *Behavioral and Brain Sciences, 12,* 121–179.

Tversky, B. (1992). Distortions in cognitive maps. *Geoforum, 23,* 131–138.

Uecker, A., Mangan, P. A., Obrzut, J. E., & Nadel, L. (1993). Down syndrome in neurobiological perspective: An emphasis in spatial cognition. *Journal of Clinical Child Psychology, 22,* 266–276.

Underwood, B. J. (1964). The representativeness of rote verbal learning. In A. W. Melton (Ed.), *Categories of human learning* (pp. 47–56). New York: Academic Press.

Underwood, B. J. (1983). *Attributes of memory.* Glenview, IL: Scott, Foresman.

Underwood, B. J., Boruch, R. F., & Malmi, R. A. (1978). Composition of episodic memory. *Journal of Experimental Psychology: General, 107,* 393–419.

van der Kolk, B. A. (1994). The body keeps the score: Memory and the evolving psychobiology of post-traumatic stress. *Harvard Review of Psychiatry, 1,* 253–265.

van der Kolk, B. A., & Fisler, R. (1995). Dissociation and the fragmentary nature of traumatic memories: Overview and exploratory study. *Journal of Traumatic Stress, 8,* 505–525.

Vaughn, W., & Greene, S. L. (1984). Pigeon visual Memory capacity. *Journal of Experimental Psychology: Animal Behavior Processes, 10,* 256–271.

Verhaeghen, P., Marcoen, A., & Goossens, L. (1992). Improving memory performance in the aged through mnemonic training: A metaanalytic study. *Psychology and Aging, 7,* 242–251.

Waddill, P. J., & McDaniel, M. A. (1998). Distinctiveness effects in recall: Differential processing or privileged retrieval? *Memory & Cognition, 26,* 108–120.

Wagner, A. D., Maril, A., & Schacter, D. L. (2000). Interactions between forms of memory: When priming hinders new episodic learning. *Journal of Cognitive Neuroscience, 12: Supplement 2,* 52–60.

Wagner, A. D., Schacter, D. L., Rotte, M., Koutstaal, W., Maril, A., Dale, A. M., Rosen, B. R., & Buckner, R. L. (1998). Building memories: Remembering and forgetting of verbal experiences as predicted by brain activity. *Science, 281,* 1188–1191.

Wagner, A. R. (1969). Frustrative nonreward: A variety of punishment? In B. A. Campbell & R. M. Church (Eds.), *Punishment and aversive behavior* (pp. 157–181). New York: Appleton, Century, Crofts.

Wagner, A. R. (1976). Priming in STM: An information processing mechanism for self-generated or retrieval-generated depression in performance. In T. J. Tighe & R. N. Leaton (Eds.), *Habituation: Perspectives from child development, animal behavior, and neurophysiology* (pp. 95–128). Hillsdale, NJ: Erlbaum.

Wagner, A. R., & Brandon, S. E. (1989). Evolution of a structured connectionist model of Pavlovian conditioning (AESOP). In S. B. Klein & R. B. Mowrer (Eds.), *Contemporary learning theories: Pavlovian conditioning and the status of traditional learning theory* (pp. 149–189). Hillside, NJ: Erlbaum.

Wagner, A. R., Logan, F. A., Haberlandt, K., & Price, T. (1968). Stimulus selection in animal discrimination learning. *Journal of Experimental Psychology, 76,* 171–180.

Wagner, A. R., & Rescorla, R. A. (1972). Inhibition in Pavlovian conditioning: Application of a theory. In R. A. Boakes & M. S. Halliday (Eds.), *Inhibition and learning* (pp. 301–336). London: Academic Press.

Wagner, A. R., Rudy, J. W., & Whitlow, J. W. (1973). Rehearsal in animal conditioning. *Journal of Experimental Psychology, 97,* 407–426. (Monograph.)

Wagner, A. R., Siegel, S., Thomas, E., & Ellison, G. D. (1964). Reinforcement history and the extinction of a conditioned salivary response. *Journal of Comparative and Physiological Psychology, 58,* 354–358.

Wagner, A. R., & Terry, W. S. (1975). Backward conditioning to a CS following an expected vs. a surprising UCS. *Animal Learning & Behavior, 3,* 370–374.

Wagner, A. R., Thomas, E., & Norton, T. (1967). Conditioning with electrical stimulation of motor cortex: Evidence of a possible source of motivation. *Journal of Comparative and Physiological Psychology, 64,* 191–199.

Wagner, D. A. (1978). Memories of Morocco: The influence of age, schooling, and environment on memory. *Cognitive Psychology, 10,* 1–28.

Waites, E. A. (1997). *Memory quest: Trauma and the search for personal history.* New York: Norton.

Walcott, C. (1989, November). Show me the way to go home. *Natural History,* 40–46.

Waldvogel, S. (1948/1982). Childhood memories. In U. Neisser (Ed.), *Memory observed* (pp. 73–76). San Francisco: Freeman.

Walk, R. D., Gibson, E. J., Pick, H. L., & Tighe, T. J. (1958). Further experiments on prolonged exposure to visual forms: The effect of single stimuli and prior reinforcement. *Journal of Comparative and Physiological Psychology, 51,* 483–487.

Walker, S. (1987). *Animal learning: An introduction.* London: Routledge & Kegan Paul.

Walls, R. T., Zane, T., & Ellis, T. (1981). Forward and backward chaining, and whole task methods: Training assembly tasks in vocational rehabilitation. *Behavior Modification, 5,* 61–74.

Wang, A. Y. (1983). Individual differences in learning speed. *Journal of Experimental Psychology: Learning, Memory, and Cognition, 9,* 300–311.

Warrington, E. K., & Weiskrantz, L. (1968a). A new method of testing long-term retention with special reference to amnesic patients. *Nature, 217,* 972–974.

Warrington, E. K., & Weiskrantz, L. (1968b). A study of learning and retention in amnesic patients. *Neuropsychologia, 6,* 283–291.

Wasserman, E. A., Dorner, W. W., & Kao, S. F. (1990). Contributions of specific cell information to judgments of interevent contingency. *Journal of Experimental Psychology: Learning, Memory, and Cognition, 16,* 509–521.

Watson, J. B. (1907). Kinesthetic and organic sensations: Their role in the reactions of the white rat to the maze. *Psychological Review Monograph Supplement,* No. 33.

Watson, J. B. (1936). Autobiography. In C. Murchison (Ed.) *A history of psychology in autobiography* (Vol. 3, pp. 271–281). Worcester, MA: Clark University Press.

Watson, J. B., & Rayner, R. (1920). Conditioned emotional reactions. *Journal of Experimental Psychology, 3,* 1–20.

Waugh, N. C., & Norman, D. A. (1965). Primary memory. *Psychological Review, 72,* 89–104.

Weingartner, H., Adefris, W., Eich, J. E., & Murphy, D. L. (1976). Encoding-imagery specificity in alcohol state-dependent learning. *Journal of Experimental Psychology: Human Learning and Memory, 2,* 83–87.

Weingartner, H., Miller, H., & Murphy, D. L. (1977). Mood-dependent retrieval of verbal associations. *Journal of Abnormal Psychology, 86,* 276–284.

Weinstock, S. (1954). Resistance to extinction of a running response following partial reinforcement under widely spaced trials. *Journal of Comparative and Physiological Psychology, 48,* 318–322.

Weiskrantz, L. (1971). Comparison of amnesic states in monkey and man. In L. E. Jarrard (Ed.), *Cognitive processes of nonhuman primates* (pp. 25–46). New York: Academic Press.

Weiss, J. M. (1977). Psychosomatic disorders. In J. D. Maser & M. E. P. Seligman (Eds.), *Psychopathology: Experimental models* (pp. 232–269). San Francisco: Freeman.

Weldon, M. S., & Roediger, H. L. (1987). Altering retrieval demands reverses the picture superiority effect. *Memory & Cognition, 15,* 269–280.

Wells, G. L., Hoffman, C., & Enzle, M. E. (1984). Self-versus other-referent processing at encoding and retrieval. *Personality and Social Psychology Bulletin, 10,* 574–584.

Werker, J. F. (1989, January–February). Becoming a native listener. *American Scientist, 77,* 54–59.

West, R. L., Crook, T. H., & Barron, K. L. (1992). Everyday memory performance across the life span: Effects of age and noncognitive individual differences. *Psychology and Aging, 7,* 72–82.

Wetherington, C. L. (1982). Is adjunctive behavior a third class of behavior? *Neuroscience & Biobehavioral Reviews, 6,* 329–350.

Wheeler, M. A., & Roediger, H. L. (1992). Disparate effects of repeated testing: Reconciling Ballard's (1914) and Bartlett's (1932) results. *Psychological Science, 3,* 240–245.

White, N. H., & Milner, P. M. (1992). The psychobiology of reinforcers. *Annual Review of Psychology, 43,* 443–471.

Whitlow, J. W. (1975). Short-term memory in habituation and dishabituation. *Journal of Experimental Psychology: Animal Behavior Processes, 1,* 189–206.

Whitlow, J. W., & Wagner, A. R. (1984). Memory and habituation. In H. V. S. Peeke & L. Petrinovich (Eds.), *Habituation, sensitization, and behavior* (pp. 103–153). New York: Academic Press.

Whitten, W. B., & Leonard, J. M. (1981). Directed search through autobiographical memory. *Memory & Cognition, 9,* 566–579.

Wickelgren, I. (1997). Getting a grasp on working memory. *Science, 275,* 1580–1582.

Wickelgren, W. A. (1970). Multitrace strength theory. In D. A. Norman (Ed.), *Models of human memory* (pp. 65–100). New York: Academic Press.

Wickens, D. D. (1972). Characteristics of word encoding. In A. W. Melton & E. Martin (Eds.), *Coding processes in human memory* (pp. 191–216). Washington, DC: Winston/Wiley.

Wiens, A. N., & Menustik, C. E. (1983). Treatment outcome and patient characteristics in an aversion therapy program for alcoholism. *American Psychologist, 38,* 1089–1096.

Wiggs, C. L. (1993). Aging and memory for frequency of occurrence of novel, visual stimuli: Direct and indirect measures. *Psychology and Aging, 8,* 400–410.

Wightman, D. C., & Sistrunk, F. (1987). Part-task training strategies in simulated carrier landing final-approach training. *Human Factors, 29,* 245–254.

Wilcoxon, H. C., Dragoin, W. B., & Kral, P. A. (1971). Illness-induced aversions in rats and quail: Relative salience of visual and gustatory cues. *Science, 171,* 826–828.

Wilkins A. J., & Baddeley, A. D. (1978). Remembering to recall in everyday life: An approach to absent-mindedness. In M. M. Gruneberg, P. E. Morris &

R. N. Sykes (Eds.), *Practical aspects of memory* (pp. 27–34). New York: Academic Press.

Wilkins, S. M., Jones, M. G., Koral, D. L., Gold, P. E., & Manning, C. A. (1997). Age-related differences in an ecologically based study of route learning. *Psychology and Aging, 12,* 372–375.

Williams, B. A. (1994). Conditioned reinforcement: Neglected or outmoded explanatory concept? *Psychonomic Bulletin & Review, 1,* 457–475.

Williams, J. M. G., & Markar, H. R. (1991). Money hidden and rediscovered in subsequent manic phases: A case of action dependent on mood state. *British Journal of Psychiatry, 159,* 579–581.

Williams, L. M. (1994). Recall of childhood trauma: A prospective study of women's memories of childhood sexual abuse. *Journal of Consulting and Clinical Psychology, 62,* 1167–1176.

Willingham, D. B., Nissen, M. J., & Bullemer, P. (1989). On the development of procedural knowledge. *Journal of Experimental Psychology: Learning, Memory, and Cognition, 15,* 1047–1060.

Wilson, B. A. (1984). Memory therapy in practice. In B. A. Wilson & N. Moffat (Eds.), *Clinical management of memory problems* (pp. 89–111). Rockville, MD: Aspen.

Wilson, B. A. (1987). *Rehabilitation of memory.* New York: Guilford Press.

Wilson, B. A. (1992). Rehabilitation and memory disorders. In L. R. Squire & N. Butters (Eds.), *Neuropsychology of memory* (2nd ed., pp. 315–321). New York: Guilford Press.

Wilson, M. A., & McNaughton, B. L. (1994). Reactivation of hippocampal ensemble memories during sleep. *Science, 265,* 676–679.

Wilson, W. R. (1979). Feeling more than we can know: Exposure effects without learning. *Journal of Personality and Social Psychology, 37,* 811–821.

Winograd, E. (1981). Elaboration and distinctiveness in memory for faces. *Journal of Experimental Psychology: Human Learning and Memory, 7,* 181–190.

Winograd, E. & Soloway, R. M. (1986). On forgetting the locations of things stored in special places. *Journal of Experimental Psychology: General, 115,* 366–372.

Wirtz, P. W., & Harrell, A. V. (1987). Effects of postassault exposure to attack-similar stimuli on long-term recovery of victims. *Journal of Consulting and Clinical Psychology, 55,* 10–16.

Witkin, H. A. (1954). *Personality through perception: An experimental and clinical study.* Westport, CT: Greenwood Press.

Witt, E. D., Ryan, C., & Hsu, L. K. G. (1985). Learning deficits in adolescents with anorexia nervosa. *Journal of Nervous and Mental Disease, 173,* 182–184.

Wittman, W. T., & Healy, A. F. (1995). A long-term retention advantage for spatial information learned naturally and in the laboratory. In A. F. Healy & L. E. Bourne, (Eds.), *Learning and memory of knowledge and skills* (pp. 170–205). Thousand Oaks, CA: Sage.

Wixted, J. T. (1991). The conditions and consequences of maintenance rehearsal. *Journal of Experimental Psychology: Learning, Memory, and Cognition, 17,* 963–973.

Wixted, J. T., & McDowell, J. J. (1989). Contributions to the functional analysis of single-trial free recall. *Journal of Experimental Psychology: Learning, Memory, and Cognition, 15,* 685–697.

Wogalter, M. S., & Laughery, K. R. (1996). Warning! Sign and label effectiveness. *Current Directions in Psychological Science, 5,* 33–37.

Wolf, A. S. (1980). Homicide and blackout in Alaskan natives. *Journal of Studies on Alcohol, 41,* 456–462.

Wolf, M. M., Giles, D. K., & Hall, R. V. (1968). Experiments with token reinforcement in a remedial classroom. *Behavior Research and Therapy, 6,* 51–54.

Wolfe, J. B. (1936). Effectiveness of token-rewards for chimpanzees. *Comparative Psychology Monographs, 12* (No. 60).

Woloshyn, V. E., Willoughby, T., Wood, E., & Pressley, M. (1990). Elaborative interrogation facilitates adult learning of factual paragraphs. *Journal of Educational Psychology, 82,* 513–524.

Wolpe, J. (1969). *The practice of behavior therapy.* New York: Pergamon Press.

Woodruff-Pak, D. S., Papka, M., & Simon, E. W. (1994). Eyeblink classical conditioning in Down's syndrome, fragile X syndrome, and normal adults over and under age 35. *Neuropsychology, 8,* 14–24.

Woolfolk, A. E., & Hoy, W. K. (1990). Prospective teachers' sense of efficacy and beliefs about control. *Journal of Educational Psychology, 82,* 81–91.

Wright, A. A., Cook, R. G., Rivera, J. J., Shyan, M. R., Neiworth, J. J., & Jitsumori, M. (1990). Naming, rehearsal, and interstimulus interval effects in memory processing. *Journal of Experimental Psychology: Learning, Memory, and Cognition, 6,* 1043–1059.

Wright, A. A., Santiago, H. C., Sands, S. F., Kendrick, D. F., & Cook, R. G. (1985). Memory processing of serial lists by pigeons, monkeys and people. *Science, 229,* 287–289.

Wulf, G., & Schmidt, R. A. (1989). The learning of generalized motor programs: Reducing the relative frequency of knowledge of results enhances memory. *Journal of Experimental Psychology: Learning, Memory, and Cognition, 15,* 748–757.

Wynn, K. (1992). Addition and subtraction by human infants. *Nature, 358,* 749–750.

Wynn, K. (1995). Infants possess a system of numerical knowledge. *Current Directions in Psychological Science, 4,* 172–177.

Wyrwicka, W. (1972). *The mechanisms of conditioned behavior.* Springfield, IL: C. C. Thomas.

Yates, F. A. (1966). *The art of memory.* Chicago: University of Chicago Press.

Yerkes, R. M., & Dodson, J. D. (1908). The relation of strength of stimulus to rapidity of habit-formation. *Journal of Comparative Neurology of Psychology, 18,* 459–482.

Young, A. W., Hay, D. C., & Ellis, A. W. (1985). The faces that launched a thousand slips: Everyday difficulties and errors in recognising people. *British Journal of Psychology, 76,* 495–523.

Young, G. C. D., & Martin, M. (1981). Processing of information about self by neurotics. *British Journal of Clinical Psychology, 20,* 205–212.

Young, M. E. (1995). On the origin of personal causality theories. *Psychonomic Bulletin & Review, 2,* 83–104.

Zajonc, R. B. (1968). Attitudinal effects of mere exposure. *Journal of Personality and Social Psychology Monograph, 9* (Part 2), 1–28.

Zangwill, O. L. (1937). An investigation of the relation between the processes of reproducing and recognizing simple figures, with special reference to Koffka's trace theory. *British Journal of Psychology, 27,* 250–276.

Zhao, X. (1997, October). Clutter and serial order redefined and retested. *Journal of Advertising Research, 37,*(5), 57–73.

Zola-Morgan, S., & Squire, L. R. (1993). Neuroanatomy of memory. *Annual Review of Neuroscience, 16,* 547–563.

Zoladek, L., & Roberts, W. A. (1978). The sensory bases of spatial memory in the rat. *Animal Learning & Behavior, 6,* 77–81.

NAME INDEX

SUBJECT INDEX